P9-ARZ-965

THE G.I.'s

By the same author

KING CHOLERA
THE WATERDRINKERS
HOW WE LIVED THEN
IF BRITAIN HAD FALLEN
THE WORKHOUSE
THE REAL DAD'S ARMY

In preparation
THE DAY WE WON THE WAR
TARGET 53: COVENTRY

NORMAN LONGMATE

THE G.I.'s
The Americans in Britain
1942-1945

CHARLES SCRIBNER'S SONS
NEW YORK

229225

Copyright © 1975 Norman Longmate

Copyright under the Berne Convention

All rights reserved. No part of this book
may be reproduced in any form without the
permission of Charles Scribner's Sons.

1 3 5 7 9 11 13 15 17 19 V/C 20 18 16 14 12 10 8 6 4 2

Printed in the United States of America
Library of Congress Catalog Card Number 75-38222

ISBN 0-684-14578-2

To

F.E.L.

One of millions who helped to make them welcome

CONTENTS

ILLUSTRATIONS

Acknowledgements for Illustrations

Imperial War Museum: 1, 2, 4, 5, 7, 9, 14, 21, 23, 32, 33, 34, 38, 39, 41, 42, 43
Keystone Press Agency: 3, 6, 16, 17, 20, 22, 24, 29, 30, 45
Hulton Picture Library: 8, 15, 19, 25, 26, 27, 28, 37
Associated Press: 10, 44, 46
Fox Photos Ltd: 11, 12, 13, 31, 47
The Sunday Times Ltd: 18

United States Army (via Nautic): 35, 36
American Battle Monuments Commission: 40

Line-drawings in the text

The *Stars and Stripes*: pages: 108, 111, 212, 259, 283, 347
Punch: pages: 39, 170, 190, 235, 260
Messrs Whitbread Ltd: page: 216

London Express News and Features Services: pages: 321, 362
(with acknowledgement to Paul Webb)

FOREWORD

THIS book had its origins in the period it describes. Before 1941 I had met only one American, an extremely agreeable young man who spent a year in my house at school, but from 1942 onwards GIs were frequent visitors to my home in Berkshire, while in 1944, after joining the army, I found myself in an Anglo-American headquarters, working for American officers and along-side American enlisted men and WACS. As an extremely 'green' eighteen-year-old, fresh from boarding school, the experience made a lasting impression upon me, and, subsequently, while writing my first book about the war, *How We Lived Then*, I discovered that the impact the GIs had made upon an enormous number of other British citizens was equally traumatic. In the memories of British women in particular it was clear that the American invasion rated second only to the bombs as the outstanding feature of war-time life. The single chapter I was able to devote to the subject in *How We Lived Then* was clearly inadequate to do full justice to it. This book is the result.

Apart from consulting the obvious printed authorities, both contemporary and post-war, I inserted appeals in newspapers and magazines throughout the British Isles and the United States for personal recollections of the peaceful confrontation between Yanks and Britons and my first debt is to the editors who carried my letters. The extent of the response will be obvious from the list of contributors and if any American state or British county is unrepresented there the fault almost certainly lies with a local newspaper which ignored my request. My second, and even greater, debt is clearly to all those correspondents who wrote their reminiscences for me. Without them this book could not have been written and it is due to their willing co-operation (even though, as many remarked in their letters, 'This writing business isn't as easy as it looks') that I have been able to lay upon the bare bones of fact, which must form the basis of any serious history, the flesh and blood of authentic individual experience. I am particularly grateful to those, on both sides of the Atlantic, who readily answered my follow-up enquiries and combed their memories for the details of incidents which had occurred thirty years before, and who generously entrusted me with letters, autograph books, programmes of wartime concerts, souvenirs, scrapbooks, Press cuttings and a wealth of other primary source material, which has helped me to recapture the feel of the period even when I have not quoted directly from it in the text. My only complaint about any members of this loyal and long-suffering army of informants is that a few proved to be excessively security minded, and I failed completely, for example, in a long correspondence, to persuade one wartime clerk to reveal the location of her office in Buckinghamshire or the nature of the 'research' in which it was engaged, while the WAAF officer who sat next to General Eisenhower the night before D-Day equally firmly refused to identify the headquarters concerned. (Information from readers who will enable me to fill these and similar gaps in a future edition will be welcomed.)

My third debt is to other informants who answered specific enquiries, especially Mr Ron Olsen of Anglia Television, Norwich, who kindly suggested various sources of information and made available to me a transcript of his 1972 television film, *The Men Who Flew the Liberators*. I am also grateful to Messrs Whitbread and Co. for details of the history of The GI public house; to the Navy, Army and Air Force Institutes; to the Seattle, Washington, Public Library; the City Library, Norwich; the European Office of the American Battle Monuments Commission; Mr Stuart Wyton, then Acting Controller of the BBC in Belfast; and to Mr W. E. Weld, Jr, then of the United States Embassy in London, all of whom helped me in various ways.

I am also grateful to the staff of the various libraries who assisted my researcher or myself, especially the British Museum, the Imperial War Museum, the American section of the University of London Library, and the Public Record Office. Those who helped me personally were Mrs Sue Sabbagh and Mrs Angela Taylor, who collected and processed the original contributions; Miss Idina le Geyt, who undertook much tedious factual research with unflagging enthusiasm; Miss Christine Vincent, who searched for unfamiliar illustrations; and Miss Stephanie Toombs, Miss Gillian Morgan and Miss Sue Pratt, who typed the manuscript. I also employed an assistant in New York.

This book is being published almost simultaneously in both the British Isles and the United States, but, since this comes naturally to me as an Englishman, I have thought it sensible to retain British usage and spelling throughout, irritating though this may occasionally be to American readers. Equally, I hope British readers will be indulgent where I have thought it necessary to include a brief word of explanation of British custom or currency for the benefit of those Americans unfamiliar with them.

Apart from some brief quotations from correspondents in the final chapter I have deliberately tried to avoid judgments based on hindsight or influenced by the post-war history of the two countries. From this point of view — though certainly from no other — it is probably fortunate that I have never visited the United States, nor met more than a few Americans since the war, so that my experience has been similar to that of the vast majority of those whose story I have told here. I have not tried to provide an analysis of international relations, much less a sociological study, but merely to illuminate, through the experience of ordinary people of both nations, one brief but significant episode in Anglo-American history.

N.R.L.

I

GOD AND UNCLE SAM

'I cannot see how the British Empire can defeat Germany without the help of God or Uncle Sam. Perhaps it will take both.'

– Colonel Raymond E. Lee, United States Military Attaché in London,
3 June 1941.

WHEN on Saturday, 26 January 1942, Private First Class Milburn H. Henke of Hutchinson, Minnesota, stepped on to the soil of Northern Ireland at Dufferin Quay, Belfast, he found a distinguished reception committee awaiting him. 'The top brass', as the British were soon to learn to describe senior officers, were there in force: the Duke of Abercorn, Governor of Northern Ireland, representing King George VI; the Prime Minister of Northern Ireland; the Major-General, Air Vice-Marshal and Rear-Admiral commanding British troops in the province; even the Inspector-General of the Royal Ulster Constabulary. The British Government was represented by Sir Archibald Sinclair, Secretary of State for Air, who, *The Times* reported, 'addressed the crowded ships from the quayside. From the prairies and the teeming cities of Iowa and the North-West, he said, these American soldiers had come through thousands of miles, not to sojourn among strangers, but among grateful friends. Their safe arrival marked a new stage in the world war.'

As the speeches continued, the strains of a military band and the muffled noise of the rubber-soled boots of a column of American infantrymen on the march could be heard from a nearby road. Despite the careful plans, a whole contingent of GIs had already come ashore and, with no fuss or welcome at all, had set off smartly for their camp. Pfc Henke, far from being the first American soldier to arrive, was in fact about the 501st. SNAFU, as the American Forces cynically called it – short for 'Situation Normal, All Fouled Up' – had triumphed again. Later it was to achieve another minor victory. A BBC reporter, greeting an arriving soldier with a microphone, ready to record his expression of delight at being in the British Isles, was mistaken for a representative of an American radio network and told by the obliging soldier what he thought his listeners would like to hear: 'Gee, Mom, I sure wish I was back home again.'

This first convoy of GIs had arrived on two transports, the *Straithaird* and the *Château Thierry*, which had anchored off Bangor as they were too large to go up the Victoria Channel into the Belfast docks. The men were ferried ashore on tenders – the *Canterbury*, the *Royal Daffodil*, the *Maid of Orleans*, and the *Princess Maud* – to be confronted by gaily decorated buildings and the band of the Royal Ulster Rifles playing the 'Star-Spangled Banner'.

Over their heads the Stars and Stripes and the Union Jack flew side by side, a symbol of the co-operation to come. By any test, the arrival of the 34th US Division in Great Britain – commemorated by a memorial pillar unveiled near the spot a year later – was a historic moment, a milestone in the history of Anglo-American relations and in the course of the Second World War.

The people of Northern Ireland were delighted by this peaceful invasion; the Government of the Irish Republic, officially at least, took a very different view. Indifferent, in theory, to who won the war – though even the most Anglophobe Irishman can hardly have supposed that Hitler's victory would actually benefit his country – the Prime Minister of Eire felt obliged publicly to protest on the following day. 'The Irish Government', pointed out de Valera, 'had not been consulted either by the British Government or the American Government with regard to the coming of the American troops to the Six Counties', whose very existence was, he declared, contrary to President Wilson's principle of 'national self-determination' and President Lincoln's belief in keeping a nation united, even at the price of Civil War. 'The maintenance of the partition of Ireland is as indefensible as aggressions against small nations elsewhere which it is the avowed purpose of Great Britain and the United States in this way to bring to an end,' declared the Irish Government. 'It is our duty to make it clearly understood that, no matter what troops occupy the Six Counties, the Irish people's claim for the union of the whole of the national territory . . . will remain unabated.' De Valera's fears were, in fact, unfounded. The presence of United States troops in Ireland had no effect whatever upon Eire's political status and individual Americans who crossed the Border were invariably well received.

Looking back, the involvement of the United States in the war in Europe now seems to have been inevitable, but in 1939 the likely pattern of future events had looked very different. Between the United Kingdom and the United States lay a wide gulf of misunderstanding and distrust, as wide and deep as the Atlantic itself, and every attempt to bridge it generated new suspicions among the many millions of Americans who deeply distrusted the country which had once ruled their ancestors. Probably not one Englishman in twenty could have explained the meaning of the Boston Tea Party and not one in fifty could have named any American President before Franklin Delano Roosevelt, except Lincoln. Most British people had long since forgotten, even if they had ever known, that there had ever been any

American colonies and before 1939 American history had not been so much badly taught in British schools as wholly ignored. In the United States, however, every child knew the date of the Declaration of Independence, every American family still celebrated the Fourth of July, if only as a holiday.

The institution of monarchy, which had once united the two countries, now helped to divide them. While most British people accepted its value without question, the idea of a hereditary sovereign was regarded with open hostility by many Americans, in whom republicanism, in the non-party sense, was equally instinctive.

The first-ever visit to the United States by a reigning British monarch had not occurred till shortly before the outbreak of war, in June 1939, and had lasted only four days. The reception given to King George and Queen Elizabeth by the Washington crowds had been rapturous – 'British re-take Washington' ran the tactless headline in one newspaper – but the King had been advised not to take the British Foreign Secretary, Lord Halifax, with him for fear of encouraging the suspicion that the British were trying to draw the United States into 'entangling alliances'.

In fact, British diplomacy at this time was directed rather to the impossible task of trying to placate Hitler and Mussolini by appeasement than to the far more rewarding one of trying to enlist American support for a policy of firmness, difficult though this would have been. Most Americans were disillusioned about using American men or American money to bolster up the 'old world', for when they had done so, in 1917, the result had not been to make the world safe for democracy, but had led instead to the rise of a new tyranny, far worse than the Kaiser's. Equally discouraging, in American eyes, the vast loans made to Great Britain and America's other allies had largely gone unrepaid, and in 1934 the Johnson Act made illegal the granting of any further credits to countries still in America's debt. (Six years later, when the need became desperate, the Act, though never repealed, was, in the words of one American writer, 'merely overlooked'.)

As for men, what had the United States to send? The US Navy, which, like the Royal Navy, had its own air arm, was already a force to be reckoned with, but the entire Army Air Corps, on 1 July 1939, numbered only 17000 men, while the army, excluding these, totalled 113000, in the United States, plus 45000 already serving overseas, mainly in the Far East. By the autumn, with the war in Europe already in progress, the American forces, excluding the navy, amounted to 227000. Even Britain, pitifully weak as she was, had by this time nearly 1600000 men and women under arms.

So determined was the average American not to become drawn into Europe's squabbles that between 1935 and 1937 Congress passed three Neutrality Acts, all designed to keep the United States safely remote from them. The strictest provisions banning the export of arms to any belligerent or the use of American merchantmen to transport them, were repealed in 1939, but any American who volunteered to take part in a foreign war continued to risk the loss of his citizenship. With the exception of a sizable interventionist group that was fervently anti-Hitler, the more the storm clouds darkened on the other side of the Atlantic the greater the determination of most Americans not to become involved. 'Europe was a long way off', one wartime GI recalls. 'What happened there was none of our business.' The British Government's policy of appeasement, totally ineffective in halting Hitler and Mussolini, succeeded in alienating such supporters as Britain had in the United States. When in 1935 Italy invaded Abyssinia some of the sizable minority of Americans of Italian descent may have been pleased, but the vast majority of the population remained indifferent. The start of the Spanish Civil War in 1936, despite the fact that a few American volunteers fought on the Government side, aroused nothing like the popular concern it did in Great Britain. Hitler's seizure of Austria in March 1938, the final proof that he was set on the road of aggression, produced comparatively little reaction in America, except approval among the minority who admired him as a potential barrier to communism, or who actively sought friendship with Nazi Germany.

Hard though it would have been for British people to realize this, the growing danger to France aroused far more sympathy in the United States than the long-term threat to Great Britain, for those same American school-boys who had been taught to remember the misdeeds of George III and General Cornwallis had also been taught to honour the memory of Lafayette, the French marquis who in 1777 had aided the rebel colonists in their fight and, back in France, had preached during the French Revolution the same ideals of liberty already applied in the newly founded United States. When in September 1938 both France and Great Britain caved in before Hitler's threats and handed over to him large areas of Czechoslovakia to which he had no possible claim, it was those Americans who thought most deeply about foreign affairs who were most disgusted. 'We lived in an atmosphere that was friendly to France and looked upon her as a sister republic', one Wall Street banker, who subsequently served in the Royal Navy, later wrote. Had the democracies stood firm over Czechoslovakia, he believed, there would have been an irresistible demand for the repeal of the Neutrality Acts and thousands of Americans, legally or illegally, would have flocked to fight for France. As it was, 'Hitler's cry that the nations of the world were decayed began to look like the black truth.' This man, clearer-sighted than most, nevertheless offered his services to the British Consul in New York only to be told that, with the danger of war averted, the Royal Air Force was no longer interested in foreign recruits.

When in September 1939 Britain and France declared war in support of Poland there was a revival of enthusiasm for their cause, which was quickly dispelled as it was realized that they had no plans to help their new ally. Although very few Americans wanted to become actively involved in the fighting, most undoubtedly hoped that the Allies would win and, late in 1939, the Neutrality Act was revised to enable the Allies to order munitions in the United States, though they still had to transport them in their own ships, on a 'cash-and-carry' basis. The conquest of Denmark and Norway in April 1940, the rapid overrunning of Belgium and Holland in May, and finally the collapse of France, in June, after only six weeks' resistance, all of which stiffened resolve in Great Britain to fight on, had a very different effect in the United States. With France prostrate, aid to Britain seemed to many people pointless. What American mother wanted to see her son's life thrown away in an attempt to save the British, whose defeat seemed both certain and deserved?

Colonel, later General, Raymond E. Lee, a frankly pro-British soldier who had already served for several years as military attaché in London and was soon to return there, was shocked by the 'amount of defeatist talk' he heard in Washington in mid-June. There was, he noted in his diary, an 'almost pathological assumption that it is all over but the shouting . . . that it is too late for the US to do anything and so on. It makes me reflect that when I was a younger man one of the great American bywords was "God hates a quitter".'

Much of the responsibility for the widespread pessimism about Britain's prospects which was felt in the United States must rest with the then American Ambassador Joseph P. Kennedy. Few envoys can have served so disastrously both their own country and that to which they were accredited. In June, Colonel Lee found, Kennedy was taking a frankly defeatist line. The reason, according to a confidant in the State Department, was that 'the war itself will lower the stock market' and 'Kennedy's securities are the only things he thinks about'. Back in London, Kennedy told a visiting delegation of admirals and generals that 'the only chance', for the British, 'was for them to stick it out until the US elections and then get the Americans "to pull them out" '. Lee's own assessment was more realistic. 'What a wonderful thing it will be if these blokes do win the war', he wrote in his journal in June. 'By every test and measure I am able to apply these people are staunch to the bone and won't quit.' Most other Americans in Britain had reached a similar conclusion. American consuls all over the country reported that morale was high, except in the City of London – Britain's Wall Street – where Kennedy's cronies were to be found. When on 22 July Lee asked all the officers on his staff if they believed that Britain would still be in the war at the end of September the answer was a unanimous 'Yes'.

Happily for Britain and the United States, the soldiers were believed where the ambassador was distrusted, and the replacement of the weak and discredited Chamberlain by the resolute and determined Winston Churchill convinced President Roosevelt and his advisers that Hitler was not going to enjoy another bloodless victory. As Roosevelt himself later remarked, 'if today was already late to help Britain, tomorrow would be even later'. In June, half a million old rifles, preserved since World War I, 80000 machine guns and 900 ancient field guns were shipped across the Atlantic, and in September an agreement was signed for an even more valuable reinforcement, the loan of fifty obsolete but serviceable destroyers, 'the fifty ships that saved the world'. The United States drove a hard bargain, obtaining in return the long-term right to various bases in the British West Indies to protect her Atlantic seaboard, but this helped to make the transaction acceptable to American public opinion. Among private citizens Britain's refusal to surrender in the face of overwhelming odds was equally admired. The Wall Street banker already quoted was so impressed by Churchill's famous speech in May 1940 offering only 'blood, sweat, toil and tears' that, having previously qualified as a pilot, he decided to seek refresher training from Speed's Flying Service at Flushing Airport, Long Island (rumoured to be a backdoor into the RAF, for the school's proprietor, of Czech descent, was a fervent anti-Nazi).

A few Americans had already taken up arms in England. In June, soon after the Local Defence Volunteers had been formed of civilians willing to train as soldiers in their spare time, an all-American unit was activated in London, under Brigadier-General Wade Hayes, US Army retired, formerly on General Pershing's staff, who soon became Lieutenant-Colonel Hayes, Home Guard. The 'First American Squadron, Home Guard', or 'Red Eagles', released British soldiers for other assignments by taking over guard duties at night at a British army headquarters, and during the war 128 Americans – mainly businessmen and students – served in the unit, though its maximum strength at any one time was seventy-five. Nearly a quarter went on to become officers in the Allied forces – eleven of them in the British services before the United States entered the war – and the 'Red Eagles' were much envied by other Home Guards because they were fully mobile, with their own cars, and the first in Britain to be equipped with tommy guns, bought from their own pockets.

On the 10 June, a week before France asked for an Armistice, President Roosevelt promised in a broadcast the fullest material aid to Britain, and Winston Churchill, listening at midnight in the Admiralty War Room, cabled his thanks for 'the grand scope of your declaration'. Ordinary citizens were less enthusiastic. Mollie Panter-Downes, the shrewd London correspondent of the *New Yorker*, reported that the 'now universal question was "Will the Americans come in?" People simply cannot believe that the great power whose chief representative spoke to them so nobly on Monday night can continue to contemplate these horrors unmoved.' Unfortunately, if not unmoved, Roosevelt remained unmoving, and as admiration mounted in the United States for British endurance during the Battle of Britain, which began in earnest in August 1940, and the night blitz on British cities, launched in early September, frustation at America's failure to take the plunge into war increased in the United Kingdom. As General Lee observed, the British people were disappointed and puzzled at how little the United States had done to help, rather than grateful for the supplies that had been sent. Very few Englishmen understood the strength of non-interventionist sentiment in the United States, or even suspected the existence of the 'America First' Committee, dedicated to keeping clear of Europe's troubles. Fewer still realized that those Americans who did want their country to become an active ally of Great Britain were prompted less by admiration for her solitary stand against Hitler than by awareness of the fact that ever since the Presidency of Thomas Jefferson, in 1808, it had been a basic axiom of American policy that a strong Europe, under a single aggressive ruler, represented a long-term threat to the United States.

In 1939 few British people questioned the necessity of fighting the war; in June 1940, almost none at all. In the United States, however, a public opinion poll in the spring of 1940 showed 93 per cent of the population opposed to intervention, and the figure was still 85 per cent on the eve of Pearl Harbour.

Pro-British sentiment was always strongest among the highly educated and those already involved in national defence. 'I had a very high regard for England . . . Because I had a speciality in English history . . . and I believed England . . . to be the parent of the United States constitutional, economic, political and social system,' recalls one man who in December 1941 was working for his Ph.D at the University of Illinois. 'Like most New Englanders, we felt a distant kinship to England,' remembers a Harvard graduate then serving with the Ninth Infantry Division at Fort Bragg, North Carolina, 'and as reserve officers we kept abreast of the war events with considerable admiration for the way the English were conducting their war.' Others felt an emotional attachment to Great Britain. 'Big Ben had always meant something to me', one man from Sterling, Massachusetts, later to be drafted in the air force, and to see the famous clock for himself, remembers. 'When still in school I had made an all-wave radio receiver and the first thing I heard was the BBC and the striking of Big Ben.' 'I developed a strong empathy towards England due in some measure to the songs like "The White Cliffs of Dover", the movies, like *Mrs Miniver*, and the pro-British *New York Times*,' admits the then claims manager of a New York trucking company, another future GI.

That so many Americans, even though anxious to avoid embroilment in a war, did admire Britain's achievements was due in large measure to the exceptionally able team of American correspondents based in London at this time. Due to syndication they often reached a vast audience, which accorded their opinion far more respect than the average British columnist received from his readers. They met almost every night at the Savoy Hotel, which became their unofficial headquarters, and formed a powerful pressure group pleading Great Britain's cause. The regular dispatches of resident correspondents such as Ben Robertson of the newspaper *PM* were supplemented by the reports of visiting writers like Quentin Reynolds, who, in August 1941, made a famous broadcast attacking Hitler ('Herr Schicklgruber'), Ernie Pyle, later killed in action, and Ralph Ingersoll, who returned in uniform and fought in France. The most influential of all was probably Edward R. Murrow of the Columbia Broadcasting Corporation, who reported nightly from the heart of the capital from August 1939 until June 1941. His opening announcement, 'This is London', became world-famous, as did the eyewitness accounts of air raids which often followed it.

A favourable picture of Britain and her will to resist was also painted by most of the army and air force officers attached to the American Embassy and the scores of others sent from the United States on short-term attachments to the British Forces. In the US Navy, where professional jealousy provided a ready soil for it, Ambassador Kennedy's defeatism had struck deep, but most other Americans who had witnessed Britain's resistance at first hand were eager to see their country fighting alongside her. When in September 1940 President Roosevelt promised 'all aid short of war', General Lee, a staunch friend of Britain, was not impressed. 'I wonder if it ever occurs to the people in Washington', he confided to his diary, 'that they have no God-given right to declare war. They may wake up one day to find that war has suddenly been declared upon the United States.' Lee's own view was simple, and forthright:

If a pyromaniac starts setting fires all over the town, of course you have to send the fire department to put them out, but you don't stop there, do you? You also get the police department to run the criminal down and lock him up. So if Hitler is responsible for a lot of assorted trouble in South America we ought to stop it mainly by going after him and knocking him on the head.

Lee and his colleagues had no time at all for their ambassador and the day in October 1940 when he finally left London was a joyous one in Grosvenor Square. Once back in Washington, however, Kennedy did his best to make further trouble by giving what Lee described as 'a perfectly damn-fool interview to the *Boston Globe,* making the remark: "Democracy is finished in England" together with a lot of other idiotic statements.' 'The "off the record" observations of Mr Joseph Kennedy have caused much interest here', Mollie Panter-Downes informed the sophisticated readers of the *New Yorker* in December:

He had been so boosted by the Press that the public had become mesmerized into thinking that a man with nine children and such an expansive smile, not to mention an impressive golf handicap, must necessarily be a prince of good fellows and as pro-British as they come. When it was discovered that those much publicized teeth had actually bit the hand that patted him, resentment was general and acute. . . . Just as Mayfair was taken in by Ribbentrop, so those in the vast middle section of the populace now feel mournfully certain that the beaming paterfamilias from Washington has somehow managed to do them dirt.

General Lee, in London, was alarmed at fresh reports from Washington of the former ambassador's trouble-making, recording that 'Kennedy has infected Wall Street with his pessimism and has also succeeded in poisoning the minds of the admirals of the navy'. In fact, though inadvertently, he had rendered the interventionists a signal service, for his support of the Democrats in the presidential election in November convinced many voters that Franklin D. Roosevelt could not, as they had feared, be about to involve America in the war. Both Roosevelt and his Republican rival, Wendell Wilkie, fought their campaign on a platform of aid to Britain, while arguing fiercely about the effects of the New Deal, and both pledged themselves to preserve the technical neutrality of the United States. Most people in both countries had the impression Roosevelt was the more dedicated to helping the Allies and his re-election was interpreted in Britain as a defeat for Hitler. In fact, the immediate results were so disappointing that the British Foreign Secretary, Anthony Eden, wrote to Churchill three weeks after the election: 'The United States administration is pursuing an almost entirely American policy rather than one of all possible aid to Britain.'

But this was unjust, for in December 1940, when both the British and American authorities were beginning to worry about the running out of British credit in America, Congress carried, on the President's initiative, the Lend-Lease Act which authorized the United States Government to build ships, tanks and other war supplies at its own expense and then lease them to any friendly power. No provision was made for repayment – indeed, it is hard to see how one could return a shell that had been fired, or an aircraft that had been shot down – and no formal accounts were kept, but, in Churchill's words, 'it transformed immediately the whole position', providing Great Britain with an almost unlimited, and free, supply of the weapons needed to fight Hitler. The plan, based on an obscure statute of 1892 which empowered the Secretary of War to lend army property for up to five years 'when in his discretion it will be for the public good', was compared by President Roosevelt, in a famous phrase, to lending one's garden hose to a neighbour whose house had caught fire, and he justified it on strictly practical grounds:

The best immediate defence of the United States is the success of Great Britain defending itself; and . . . therefore, quite aside from our historic . . . interest in the survival of democracy in the world as a whole, it is equally important from a selfish point of view and of American defence that we should do everything possible to help the British Empire to defend itself.

Churchill took a nobler view, describing the arrangement as 'the most unsordid act in the history of any nation' and whatever the motives behind it, Lend-Lease became one of the great catch-phrases of the Second World War, used by many who had little idea what it meant. One American, serving in the Royal Navy, recalls himself and an American friend being humorously introduced on mess night at a dinner at the Royal Naval College, Greenwich, as 'Mr Lease' and 'Mr Lend'.

By now the armed forces of the United States and Great Britain were drawing as close together as those of any two nations could which were not in open military alliance. Before the war almost the only contact between them had been that British officers studied the campaigns of the American Civil War at their staff college. (Curiously enough, the syllabus did not include the defence of the British Isles.) At a pre-war naval conference, General Lee observed, there had been such a bitter argument between the British and United States delegates as to whether cruisers should carry six-inch or eight-inch guns that 'one would have thought they were preparing to go to war with each other'. Now, although some lingering distrust remained, British and American officers found themselves discussing such questions as the standardization of rifle calibres, the difference of 0·003 inch between the two nation's basic infantry weapons being sufficient to prevent their using the same cartidges, although both in fact continued to be made. Co-operation was most cordial in the case of the air forces, both anxious to test their theories about victory through air power and less hamstrung by ancient rivalries than the other services. By April 1941 not merely was the US Army Air Corps cheerfully supplying its prized 'Flying Fortress' B–17s to the RAF, which did not like them, but also the newer, longer-range B–24 'Liberators', which British crews greatly preferred. Even more helpfully, the American commander, General Arnold, offered to British airmen a third of the places in United States training courses for pilots.

By now even vote-conscious congressmen and senators realized that if America was not deliberately drawing closer to the war the war was drawing closer to America. During 1940 record appropriations of 18 billion (i.e. 18 000 million) dollars were voted to create a large two-ocean navy, able to challenge any potential rival; to expand the Army and Navy Air Corps – there was as yet no independent Air Force – to 35 000 planes; and to build an army of 1 200 000, six times the size of America's peacetime forces. The National Guard, a force of volunteer reservists corresponding to Britain's Territorial Army, was called out for intensive training, and, most striking of all in freedom-loving America, conscription was introduced with the compulsory registration, under an Act passed in September 1940, of all men aged from twenty one to thirty five. Of these 800,000 were to be selected by lot for a year's military training, although these 'selectees' or 'draftees' could not be sent outside the western hemisphere, a vague expression which tended to be interpreted as it suited the Government. Thoroughgoing interventionists longed, however, to see a more complete commitment. When in November 1940 the Germans refused to allow a United States ship to run the blockade of the British Isles to collect American civilians clamouring to go home, General Lee was delighted. The Germans, he rejoiced, 'are now quite prepared to accept the United States as an additional enemy, which, of course, we are'.

Nineteen-forty-one began with a broadcast by Ed Murrow. 'This is London,' he told listeners in America early on 1 January. 'The New Year is nearly an hour old and we have not been bombed tonight.' That month the first tripartite American, British and Canadian Staff conference, known as ABC-1, assembled in Washington, the American delegates rapidly agreeing that if their country should be 'compelled' to resort to war there should be full co-operation between the three parties and, whatever other countries became involved, Germany should be regarded as the primary enemy. It was agreed, too, to try to keep Japan out of the war, but each country was to be responsible for defending her own possessions in the Far East. By May, the United States was passing on to Great Britain information she had gained from breaking the Japanese military code and General Lee in London was offering to seek information from United States diplomatic representatives in Budapest about the results of British efforts to interfere with traffic on the Danube. In July 1941 United States troops landed in Iceland – conveniently agreed to be within the western hemisphere – to release British troops for service elsewhere, and it was announced that American ships supplying the troops there would be escorted by American warships and that submarines which challenged them would be treated as hostile. A proposal for joint American-British convoys, under United States escort, was dropped as too close an approach to military alliance, but the logic of events clearly pointed to such an alliance. 'I . . . cannot see how the British Empire can defeat Germany without the help of God or Uncle Sam', General Lee confided to his diary in June 1941, three weeks before Hitler's attack on Russia. 'Perhaps it will take both.'

On the last day of the month United States involvement in Europe became a stage deeper with the arrival, in great secrecy, of 400 American civilian technicians in Northern Ireland, followed before October by a further 600. They had been sent under a plan first discussed in March to build American naval and air bases in Ulster, the most westerly part of the British Isles, from which transatlantic convoys could be protected and where American warships could refuel and refit after facing the perils and storms of the North Atlantic. The original contract, signed on 12 June, was for work costing $7500000, paid for by the British Government, and the skilled craftsmen concerned were, in theory, its employees. To avoid upsetting the isolationists rather than to reduce the risk of attracting attention from the Luftwaffe – with the possible loss of American lives – the American presence was kept as quiet as possible. The supervising United States officers wore civilian clothes; the Americans were referred to merely as 'the visitors'; and the workmen concerned were under such strict orders not to talk that they earned a reputation – astonishing for their countrymen – of being aloof and standoffish. But, as the official Northern Ireland historian later wrote, 'Everyone was impressed with their high output and their powers of concentration. When machinery and materials arrived, they settled down to work with "a concentration of effort not familiar to this country".'

If not an outright breach of neutrality, this was certainly stretching it rather far, but unfortunately the British public knew nothing of these preparations which clearly pointed to ultimate American participation in the war. There was therefore widespread and public disappointment when, after a tremendous preliminary build-up, the deputy Prime Minister, the colourless Clement Attlee, announced in mid-August that the President and Prime Minister had met off Newfoundland to issue a joint proclamation – not, as was hoped, a declaration of war, but a vague statement of long-term aims, grandiosely called the Atlantic Charter, unhappily reminiscent of President Wilson's still unrealized 'Fourteen Points'. General Lee heard the broadcast in the United Services Club, crowded with British officers. 'I got the impression they were all very much disappointed,' he admitted, and 'had been hoping for some very tangible movements towards war by the United States.' *The Times* expressed the universal reaction to what it regarded as a time-wasting piece of political window-dressing.

The flood is raging and we are breasting it in an effort to save drowning civilization. America throws out a line to us, and will give us dry clothes if we reach the shore. We understand her attitude, but . . . we think it would be no strain on her resources to wade in, at least up to her waist . . . We are frankly disappointed with the American contribution to the rescue.

The *New Yorker* recorded equal dissatisfaction. 'Many Britons seemed to feel', reported Mollie Panter-Downes, 'that their Premier had gone the dickens of a long way merely to reiterate a stand which, in their simplicity, they thought everyone knew they had been prepared to die for, probably unpleasantly.'

If Munich had been Great Britain's least glorious hour, mid-1941 was surely America's. In August the House of Representatives carried by only a single vote the Bill to extend the period of conscript service from twelve months to two and a half years. In September, General Lee, enquiring about the prospects for the excellent British propaganda film *Target for Tonight,* in the United States, learned that 'Many distributors in America have refused to handle it because they thought it might be taken as British propaganda and an incitement to war.'

At sea, something approaching war was already being waged. In early September the United States destroyer *Greer* was attacked by a U-boat while on passage to Iceland and President Roosevelt broadcast a warning that German or Italian warships entered waters the United States considered vital to her safety at their own peril. American warships now began to escort British convoys over a vast area of the Atlantic, their unfamiliar silhouette causing some confusion at first. One wrongly identified American escort narrowly escaped being sunk by a British destroyer, the American captain mildly remarking that he knew all about 1776 and 1812 but 'was willing to let bygones be bygones'. At the end of October another American destroyer, the *Reuben James,* was torpedoed by a U-boat and sunk with heavy loss of life, the first American casualties in the undeclared war. But the United States' role was still too passive for General Lee. 'America', he confided to his diary, 'visualizes its mission as the preservation of Britain from defeat. Not yet does it see that this can be conclusively done only by the defeat of Germany. Our minds are soaked in defensive thought. They must become offensive if this whole affair is to be wound up.'

This was a conclusion which at least 20000 Americans had already reached for themselves; from September 1939 onwards a growing trickle of young men crossed the Canadian border to enlist in the armed forces or to make their way to England. By mid-1942, when they were given the opportunity to transfer to their own country's forces, the Canadian Army and Royal Canadian Air Force each contained about 10000 Americans, though not all of them had succeeded in getting to Europe. The most publicized American recruits to the Allied cause before Pearl Harbour were, however, the members of the famous Eagle Squadron, who, having volunteered in Canada, arrived at Southampton late in August 1940.

Number 71 (Eagle) Squadron, Royal Air Force, and the two other American squadrons later formed on the same lines, Nos 121 and 133, provided British airmen with their first experience of serving with Americans – and they were not impressed. The squadron's historian, an American Air Force Colonel, admits that: 'In the early days of their fighting the Eagles were not of much value. They were so poor, in fact, that the commanding officer of the station said they should be disbanded. He pointed out that the first Eagle shot down was very probably shot down by the Eagles themselves', while other early casualties occurred in flying accidents caused by recklessness. Although the Eagles laughed derisively at a particularly exaggerated film about their exploits, released in 1941, they constantly behaved like characters in a bad Hollywood movie. So appalling was their discipline that the British commanding officer of the station at which they were based concluded 'They'll never make a team'. These reckless young men, their Medical Officer admitted, 'didn't expect to live out the war and didn't particularly give a damn. They were a wild lot . . . out to get every possible thrill and to them the most thrilling adventure of all was flying.' Commanding the Eagles, a duty entrusted in turn to two Americans and two English officers – the two sister squadrons always had American COs – was a thankless task and one of their British COs no doubt often had cause to remember his own dictum, which became a squadron catchphrase, 'Brave and calm, chaps, brave and calm.' Unhappily his pilots rarely followed this advice, as the American colonel already quoted frankly acknowledges:

Long before they were trained, long before they were ready to go into action against the highly experienced Luftwaffe the Eagles were screaming for action. . . . Despite their being in uniform, when the Eagles first arrived in England they were unmistakably civilians; military courtesy or discipline had almost no meaning at all for them. . . . They forgot to rise when a senior officer came into the room. They forgot to stand at attention when reporting to the CO. Then, too, the soft modulation of the voice, so common in the English officers mess, was not characteristic of some of the Eagles. One Eagle . . . could make more noise, day or night, than thirty Englishmen or ten Australians. And English officers . . . marvelled at the table manners and the methods of drinking of some of the newly arrived Eagles. . . . Some of the boys would reach across a neighbour's platter, spear the margarine with their fork, yell for some goddam water, bust a potato with their fist and gobble it down, skin and all.

When drunk, as they often were, some members of the squadron would run amok with their weapons, shooting at whatever provoked them. One man burst in upon his sleeping commanding officer armed with a loaded gun, shouting, 'Sir, you have got my popsy in your bed,' the Wing Commander concerned replying prudently, with typically British restraint, 'Positively not. You may look for yourself.' Another pilot, furious at being grounded, smashed up the officers' mess, stole a tommy gun, and wandered from room to room, shooting at his reflection in every mirror he saw.

The Eagles ended their riotous, semi-independent, career when they were transferred to the newly arrived US Eighth Air Force. They had by then shot down seventy-three enemy aircraft, plus half a Dornier, shared with a British squadron, a pleasant example of early Anglo-American co-operation.

If the Americans who joined the RAF succeeded to some extent in imposing their own standards upon it, the position of those who volunteered for the Royal Navy – totalling only nine or ten – was very different. Oldest, most traditional, and most respected of the British services, the navy made very plain to would-be recruits that it would only accept them on its own terms, as the Wall Street banker already quoted, whose name was A. H. Cherry, discovered, when in April 1941, after contacting the British consul in New York, he was invited to apply for a commission as a naval officer. (He had flipped a 'penny' to decide whether to join the navy or the RAF and it had turned up with Lincoln's head uppermost.)

Like other early 'joiners' of the British forces, Lieutenant Cherry, Royal Navy Volunteer Reserve, as he became after being interviewed by the Rear-Admiral commanding the British Third Battle Squadron at Halifax, Nova Scotia, had little sympathy with his less far-sighted fellow countrymen. 'These fatuous sleepwalkers on the shores of Time . . . ' he later wrote, 'wanted . . . to sit pretty while the British navy made their shores safe for them.' But taking action was not as easy as it seemed. In joining the forces of a belligerent power, he was he found, liable to a fine of 20000 dollars, ten years in jail and – the unkindest cut of all – the loss of his citizenship, and he was greatly relieved when the Customs Officer at Boston, from which he sailed to Newfoundland to join his ship, accepted his explanation that he was going 'for some shooting'.

Once safely on board his new ship he scandalized his shipmates by writing a letter to Franklin D. Roosevelt: 'Dear President, I'm backing your foreign policy to the nth degree. I've done what you really wanted. I've joined Nelson's navy.' The reaction of the White House is not on record, but that 'former naval person' Winston Churchill would surely have approved.

Cherry's later experiences were probably not very different from those of many Americans in the British forces at this time. He found a general friendliness but many misconceptions, not least on the part of the captain of one destroyer, who was, ironically, in command of one of the fifty American vessels handed over in the winter of 1940–1. This Englishman believed that all Americans were 'people who wore big broad cowboy hats, toted a couple of guns, were quick on the draw and ready to shoot from the hip', and he made no attempt to conceal his distaste at his new officer's ignorance of British naval procedure. 'It's the custom of the navy that matters,' he told Cherry severely. 'When I speak to you it's not "Very good, sir", it's "Aye, aye, sir", and when a rating addresses you it's not "Right" or "Right-ho", it's "Very good". . . . What's the use of fighting a war only to have you sabotage everything we've ever prized?' Other British officers proved more congenial. Impressed by American films, showing his native country as a land of peace and plenty, their response to his sacrifice was one of amazement. As they stumbled out into the cold and dark of a windswept Scottish winter night, while attending an anti-submarine course near Glasgow, they asked him incredulously: 'What made you give it all up and come over and join up with us, Yank?'

Churchill's next call was to the Foreign Office to put in hand a formal declaration of war on Japan, which had not yet attacked the British colony of Malaya, though it did so a day later. His great fear was that the United States might remain at peace with Germany and concentrate her whole attention on the Pacific, while, perhaps, cutting off the flow of munitions to Britain to equip her own expanding forces. Happily the Germans settled the matter, for on the morning of 8 December Hitler issued orders to his navy to attack American ships wherever they were encountered, though it was not until three days later, on Thursday 11 December 1941, that Germany and Italy formally declared war on the United States.

Just as in England the attack on Poland had finally convinced even the last-ditch appeasers that Britain must stand and fight, so the suddenness and perfidy of the Japanese attack – and the damaging blow its astonishing success delivered to American pride – forced even the most blinkered isolationists to rally behind the flag. At 12.30 p.m. on Monday, 8 December, as the President entered the House of Representatives to deliver his famous 'day which will live in infamy' speech, Republicans and Democrats alike rose to applaud him. In six minutes he had called on Congress to declare war, within sixty it had responded.

As Franklin Roosevelt's words rang out over the radio loudspeakers, Washington was briefly silent. A Staff Sergeant from Baltimore, whose unit was on its way back from the Carolina manoeuvres to its base camp, at Fort Meade, Maryland, remembers how the column of vehicles 'was stopped dead in the streets of Washington, DC, with loudspeakers placed up and down our column so that we could hear the President's message'. Much sobered, they then resumed their journey, reflecting 'that we were soon going to put our training to use'.

That Monday night at the Savoy the American correspondents, noted Mollie Panter-Downes, 'had everybody worked up to slapping backs and singing "O say, can you see?",' the opening words of the American National Anthem. Three days later the formal declaration of war on Germany by the United States, of far more immediate importance to most British citizens, was 'received quietly. There was little outward jubilation over an event which every intelligent Briton has been quite frankly praying for since it became evident that, for all the fine phrases, something more than the tools was going to be necessary before there could be a possibility of finishing the job.'

On 15 December 1941, a week after Pearl Harbour, President Roosevelt signed Orders, approved by both Houses of Congress, extending the period of service for National Guardsmen and men drafted into the services from two and a half years to a date six months after the end of hostilities. He authorized, too, the employment of American forces anywhere in the world. Neither item of news made for a cheerful Christmas for American servicemen. While Winston Churchill and a high-powered delegation of generals and officials were preparing to cross the Atlantic to establish 'the grand alliance', the first of several million GIs were preparing to make the journey, in a good deal less comfort, in the reverse direction.

2

AN ISLAND OFF THE COAST OF FRANCE

'The only thing I knew about England was that it was an island off the coast of France.'

– Army Private from Roslindale, Massachusetts, recalling 1942.

IN December 1941 the average American's ignorance of Great Britain and the British was equalled only by the ordinary British citizen's lack of knowledge about the United States. Until the first GIs arrived, most people in the British Isles and the United States had never met, or even seen, a citizen of the other country. A transatlantic flight was such a hazardous adventure that airmen who made the journey became members of a special, unofficial club whose membership card was a dollar-bill, signed by co-passengers and known as a 'short-snorter'. (The club's solitary rule was that this had to be produced to a fellow member on demand under penalty of paying for drinks all round.) Radio broadcasts between the two countries were a novelty, television was a toy; in the whole United Kingdom only 20000 sets were in use. There existed only one popular source of information about life on the far side of the Atlantic, the 'movies', or 'the pictures', which were misleading rather than informative. It is hard today for an Englishman to look without embarrassment at most productions of the pre-war British film industry while the output of Hollywood, if glossier and more professional, was even more remote from real life.

The impression one Plymouth, Massachusetts, young man, eighteen at the time of Pearl Harbour, had acquired of the British in his regular visits to the cinema was, he recalls, 'that the wealthy were snobs or idiots and that the poor were all dishonest and conniving slobs, living in squalor'. A twenty-five-year-old postal clerk from Bridgeport, Connecticut, 'pictured the English as cold, haughty, proud, having no sense of humour . . . and not having sense enough to drive on the right side of the street'. A seventeen-year-old, living in Troy, New York, had never met an Englishman but had concluded the country was peopled by 'butlers and Scotland Yard types'. 'I expected to find stiff, reserved "old school tie" people,' confesses a then twenty-year-old bakery worker from Kansas. Such impressions were not uncommon even among educated people. 'My feelings about the English,' admits a physician and surgeon from Oakdale, California, then in his thirties, 'were that they were a bit stodgy, slow on the pick up, stiff and formal, and a bunch of tea-drinkers – and would use anyone to gain their end.'

Even harder for the British to accept, however, would have been the realization that many Americans actively disliked them. Most emigrants from the British Isles who had sailed to America had left because their native country had ill-treated them. The Pilgrims, in the seventeenth century, had gone in search of religious freedom; the Southern Irish, in the 1840s, had fled from the great famine. While the descendants of immigrants from other European countries still felt some loyalty to their parents' or grandparents' homeland, and perhaps still spoke its language or preserved its customs, many of those who had come from the British Isles rejoiced in the British Government's difficulties at least as fervently as their fellow countrymen of German or Italian origin. The attitude of one wartime GI from Long Island was typical. His father was 'a fervent Irish Catholic from Cork' and his son's earliest childhood recollection was of 'cranking the victrola to play the old Irish ballads, mostly about the Irish martyrs and the atrocities of the Black and Tans'. In this household the term 'English' was never used, only the contemptuous 'Limey', the Scots and Welsh being dismissed with equal scorn as 'some kind of Limeys. I was so bigoted and prejudiced about the British at that time', this man admits, 'that I'm positive that no educator, theologian or political historian (no matter how eloquent) could have convinced me that the average British farmer or worker or working man was not really much different from the American worker or farmer.'[1] 'My grand-uncle had been executed in the 1917 rising,' remembers a then Corporal of similar background in the 102nd Engineer Combat Regiment, from New York City. 'I was raised in an . . . environment in which the English were not spoken of kindly.' Such extreme cases apart, however, most American servicemen destined for service in Britain were remarkably ignorant about that country. His total knowledge of the United Kingdom, confesses a then twenty-one-year-old truck driver from Roslindale, Massachusetts, came from 'a geography book. The only thing I knew about England was that it was an island off the coast of France.'

In the early days exaggerated fears about security led to little effort being made to fill the gaps in the GIs' knowledge of Britain before they crossed the Atlantic. The men of one unit, according to the civilians to whom they later talked in the Midlands town of Derby (pronounced 'Darby') were given only this pithy and pertinent, if hardly comprehensive, advice from one officer who had visited England in peacetime: 'If they had

1. The name 'Limey' derived from the sensible practice of English sailors of drinking lime-juice to ward off scurvy. This man, incidentally, returned to America in 1945 with a Scottish bride and plans when retired to live permanently in the British Isles.

to choose between running over an Englishman or his dog, they should choose the man – as they'd never be forgiven for killing the dog.'

Later units were better prepared. One B–17 gunner who arrived in Scotland in 1944 recalls a special film starring Burgess Meredith, which helpfully explained the differing meanings that some innocent-sounding American words possessed to English ears, and some enterprising commanding officers arranged lectures for their men from soldiers already familiar with Britain. The chief means, however, of informing incoming Americans about what lay in wait for them was a thirty-eight page handbook produced jointly by the War and Navy departments, under the title *A Short Guide to Great Britain*, published anonymously, although its principal author was Eric Knight, whose novel *This Above All*, had caused a minor sensation and proved an immediate best-seller on its first appearance in 1941. (Sadly, its author, by now a Major, had no chance to fulfil his early promise, being killed in an air crash in 1942.)

Many of the GIs who received the booklet are still grateful for the excellent combination of simple, factual information and crisp common sense it provided, though one, rather cynically, recalls that his reaction was 'that I did not think the army was smart enough to get one out and hence was pleasantly surprised.'[1] Much of the document's value lay in its refusal to avoid potentially embarrassing topics:

If you come from an Irish-American family, you may think of the English as persecutors of the Irish, or you may think of them as enemy Redcoats who fought against us in the American Revolution and the War of 1812. But there is no time today to fight old wars over again or bring up old grievances. We don't worry about which side our grandfathers fought on in the Civil War, because it doesn't mean anything now. . . . The first and major duty Hitler has given his propaganda chiefs is to separate Britain and America and spread distrust betwen them. . . . We can defeat Hitler's propaganda with . . . plain, common horse sense. . . . The most evident truth of all is that in their major ways of life the British and American people are much alike. They speak the same language. They both believe in representative government, in freedom of worship, in freedom of speech. But each country has minor national characteristics which differ. . . . You defeat enemy propaganda not by denying that these differences exist, but by admitting them openly and then trying to understand them.

True to this policy, the *Guide* stressed something that most British people found hard to accept, that by American standards the whole British Isles were remarkably small:

You will find out right away that England is a small country, smaller than North Carolina or Iowa. The whole of Great Britain – that is England and Scotland

---

1. There was some excuse for this view. I recall my Anglo-American unit being issued with a booklet about France although we were, we knew, destined for Denmark.

and Wales together – is hardly bigger than Minnesota. England's largest river, the Thames (pronounced Tems) is not even as big as the Mississippi when it leaves Minnesota.

All this led up to some sensible practical advice.

You are coming to Britain from a country where your home is still safe, food is still plentiful and lights are still burning. . . . So stop and think before you sound off about lukewarm beer, or cold boiled potatoes, or the way English cigarettes taste. If British civilians look dowdy and badly dressed, it is not because they do not like good clothes or know how to wear them. All clothing is rationed and the British know that they help war production by wearing an old suit or dress until it cannot be patched any longer. Old clothes are 'good form'. If they need to be... the British . . . can be plenty tough. The English language didn't spread across the oceans and over the mountains and jungles and swamps of the world because people were panty-waists.'[1]

After some practical information on currency and language differences, to be mentioned later, the authors of *A Short Guide* concluded their homily with

SOME IMPORTANT DO'S AND DONT'S

Be FRIENDLY – but don't intrude anywhere it seems you are not wanted. . . .

Don't show off or brag or bluster – 'swank' as the British say. If somebody looks in your direction and says, 'He's chucking his weight about', you can be pretty sure you're off base. . . . That's the time to pull in your ears. . . .

Don't make fun of British speech or accents. You sound just as funny to them but they will be too polite to show it . . .

Don't . . . make wisecracks about the war debts or about British defeats in this war.

NEVER criticize the King or Queen . . .

The British counterpart to *A Short Guide to Great Britain* was *Meet the Americans*, a fourteen-page leaflet produced in July 1942 by the Army Bureau of Current Affairs, an organization suspected by Winston Churchill, with some reason, of encouraging Britain's four million servicemen to challenge the pre-war social order. *Meet the Americans* was intended for the use of officers leading discussion groups and its author was a somewhat little known British professor who had lived in the United States. Where the American *Guide* was crisp and forthright, the British publication was restrained and somewhat dull, but it led, one wartime officer recalls, to one of the best 'ABCA sessions' he ever conducted, no doubt because, as the professor warned, 'all of us are only too ready to air our views about "foreigners".'

We had better dismiss from our minds many of the ideas we may have picked

1. A 'panty-waist' is defined by a standard dictionary as someone who is 'cowardly, effeminate or cissy'.

up from the cinema. . . . They will have the same trouble, for just as we have a kind of stage Irishman and stage American in the national gallery of literary mythology, so the Americans have a stage and cinema Englishman. Don't be offended if you are measured up against certain characters in Dickens, or more likely against Bertie Wooster and Jeeves. It is poetic justice, and you will live down the comparison, and be taken as a 'regular guy' when your friends and guests get to know you. . . .

The similarity of the two languages may easily lead us into thinking that our two countries and our two peoples are practically the same, but we should expect Americans to be different from us. After all, their forefathers and predecessors in the American continent fought desperately to be independent of us. . . . America is 'abroad' and if Americans are not exactly foreigners, they are certainly not a kind of Englishmen. . . . The American soldier's mind is still in 'civvies' even when his body is in uniform. The Americans are naturally individualists, easy and friendly, who run their own affairs in a democratic way.

Finally, the author attempted a detailed analysis of the American attitude to life:

Americans do business as they play games, with great attack and vigour, zest and enjoyment. . . . The money is not sought for its own sake particularly and Americans are not more avaricious than other people in business. But the dollar is a scalp, the symbol of achievement and success and is pursued as such. . . . England is a country where men of leisure often take to business, while America is a country where men of business take to leisure only occasionally and reluctantly. . . . Americans do not value a man according to his income. That is one of the most persistent misconceptions of the European peoples who exploit them. Americans are more interested in what a man is and where he is going than in what he has and where his people came from. He likes making money and he likes spending. Extreme refinement of speech is not admired in most American male circles, nor is a reserved manner. Among themselves they delight in tall tales, wordy battles full of cross-talk, wisecracks and jeering remarks which sound, and are meant to *sound* (but not to be) fantastically offensive. Sometimes, where there is not much wit, this becomes mechanical and boring to our rather different taste and humour, but at its best this humour of exaggeration is grand fun.

The author was also informative on the two nations' differing attitudes towards the law. The GI, warned the professor, 'will seem rather lawless to us . . . a bit inclined to dodge the rules or break them, or interpret them away. No doubt we shall seem rather a tame lot to him in that respect.' Nor, British troops were reminded, was the average American likely to be impressed by the national tendency – at its worst during the war when the phrase 'Don't you know there's a war on?' was often used to justify avoidable inefficiency – to make excuses for inactivity: 'He will firmly believe that something can be done about anything and will try to do it, whereas we know that nothing much can be done about anything – just yet.'

(This last was, incidentally, exactly the attitude which had already

infuriated many American observers with the British forces. The American
Military Attaché in London, handling their reports had, been shocked at the
accounts of badly maintained equipment, needlessly uncomfortable camps,
'scruffy' troops and a universal readiness to find excuses for poor conditions
instead of trying to rectify them. 'I have never heard the word "can't" used
so often', one officer told that pro-British American General Raymond E.
Lee after a tour of the Middle East. 'The British simply do not know how to
try.')

Although, unlike British troops, British children were to need no per-
suasion to welcome the GIs, the Board of Education distributed to schools
in 1943 an official pamphlet, *Meet the US Army* designed 'to enable teachers
to give such information to their pupils as will make easier the meetings
between them and members of the AEF.' It had only been issued after much
high-level discussion within the British Government and the result – although
the author was the poet Louis Macneice – was distinctly unexciting.
('You will get a good mark if you have heard of Babe Ruth (the W. G.
Grace of baseball).')

The best of the guides to mutual understanding which appeared in
Britain at this time was written by an American, the anthropologist Margaret
Mead. Her threepenny pamphlet, *The American Troops and the British
Community*, intended for civilian readers, also appeared, in March 1944,
under the imprint of the Army Bureau of Current Affairs, as *The Yank in
Britain*. By April', predicted its editor optimistically, 'all parties concerned
should have a much clearer understanding than they had in February of the
apparently "mysterious" differences between American and British ways of
talking, thinking and behaving.' The Army Bureau of Current Affairs
listed some questions on which officers were to invite their men's opinions:

What is the main contrast between an American bar and an English pub?
Why do Americans 'talk big' and why do British people habitually understate?
What attitude on the part of British girls is most calculated to keep Americans
at their best level of social behaviour?

Margaret Mead's pamphlet made one valuable point, that while to an
Englishman age generally implied worth to an American the reverse was true.

Most of the American soldiers over here view the past as something to go beyond
and forget. . . . They have learned to value nothing that is old, only something
that is this year's model, or better still, next year's. In America . . . thoughts
about the past lead inevitably to unfortunate comparisons, between the man
whose grandfather was a cobbler in France and the man whose grandfather was a
landowner in Hungary. . . . On the whole American men are not prepared to
like anything because it is old or historic, an attitude that is a shock to many
British people, especially if they have met the . . . American tourist of the past.

Apart perhaps from the last-named, none of the publications quoted above really faced up to the two problems which were to cause more ill-feeling between the GIs and the British public than any others, sex and colour. 'Swiping his girl,' *A Short Guide to Britain* remarked with almost English understatement, was likely to 'slow up the friendship' expected to develop between the American and the British soldier. *Meet the Americans* ignored the subject, merely referring to the need for 'goodwill, respect and patience' between the two races. *A Short Guide* assured its readers that England was 'still one of the great democracies' despite the survival of ' "lords" and "sirs" ', but not that it treated its few coloured inhabitants as equal citizens. *Meet the Americans* approached no nearer the subject than to mention the existence of 'coloured people in the south'; the attitude of many whites towards them was ignored. Louis Macneice's teachers' guide was little braver:

It must be remembered . . . that while the Negroes form a very large section (one in twelve) of the American nation, they are in the unique position of being descended from slaves; the memory of slavery, being still fresh, retains a psychological hold both on the Negroes themselves and on many of their white fellow citizens. . . . From this they will only gradually break free. Any American Negro who comes to Britain must be treated by us on a basis of absolute equality. And remember never to call a Negro a 'nigger'.

This was all sound enough – and it was something perhaps that it had survived before publication the anxious scrutiny of the Foreign Office, but the truth was, as every British citizen was soon to realize, that such remarks needed to be addressed rather to American troops than to British school-children.

Easy though it is to smile at them (and many Britons found the *Short Guide* highly entertaining reading), these well-meaning publications probably did *some* good, even if they left their readers apprehensive about meeting their new Allies. One Dorset woman remembers two GIs who 'crept round to the back door' from their nearby billet, and asked, 'Please could they come in and talk to us. They were', she discovered, 'not allowed to go out and mix with the English until they had had all the lectures about our "odd ways" ', but could not wait to inspect these strange natives for themselves.

If the major source of American misconceptions about the British was sheer ignorance, resulting from pre-war indifference to Europe, many British people suffered from an even more dangerous condition, a wholly distorted view of the United States, created by the Hollywood 'dream factory' which pictured the country as a paradise of wealth and luxury, peopled by wise-cracking he-men and alluring blondes. One eighteen-year-old woman clerk, living in London, who had never met a single American in the flesh, believed that 'they must live in a world of big houses with gardens', apart from a few flat-dwellers, who were, of course, housed in enormously tall and luxurious blocks, and a tiny and under-privileged minority, living in shacks. The Americans, a secretary at Falmouth was convinced, 'were usually a jump ahead of us, with streamlined cars, sky-scrapers, fashions'. At a time when car-ownership was still in Britain a sign of affluence, in America, she assumed, 'only a few poor people did not own a car'; even the young teenager Andy Hardy, hero of many a pre-war family film, possessed one. A seventeen-year-old boarding-school pupil from Bury St Edmunds, Suffolk, pictured the United States as a land of 'gracious living, servants, and money no object'. 'They had lovely homes, all were rich,' believed a fourteen-year-old London girl, who was greatly 'in love with Bing Crosby'. A fifteen-year-old girl living in Cornwall also knew what to expect: 'gold teeth, large trilby hats, and dual-toned men's shoes'. A young civil servant, working at the Air Ministry, was aware that the United States consisted of 'a mixture of slaves in the South, gangsters in Chicago and musicals with Fred Astaire'. A landgirl, twenty-three in 1941 and living by the time the first GIs arrived there in a hostel near Evesham, had never met an American, but she did know something of the American Civil War, which 'I associated with *Gone with the Wind*, damn Yankees marching through Georgia, Southern gentlemen, and a poem learnt in my childhood in which Barbara Frietchie put her old grey head out of a window, looked down on the cornfields of Maryland and defied the Yankees by flying the Confederate flag.' Hardly less misleading were her other impressions:

I . . . had a mental picture of covered wagons, cowboys and Indians in the Wild West; Texas, a land of open country where men wore ten-gallon hats and spoke with a drawl; Chicago, full of gangsters, all resembling James Cagney, wearing trilby hats and speaking with a strong nasal accent; and Boston and New England, highly respectable places, where people walked to church along tree-lined roads and dwelt in Georgian-type houses. Of course, too, there was New York, which conjured up pictures of skyscrapers. The coloured Americans consisted of pickanninies and mammies in cotton fields by day and singing spirituals by night; the men were all like Uncle Remus or Uncle Tom. There was the glittering world of Hollywood, where film stars thought nothing of divorce and I rated Clark Gable and Gary Cooper ('Coop') among my cardboard heroes.

Another impression soon to be corrected was of an eleven-year-old Belfast schoolboy who believed, on the basis of his weekly trip to 'the pictures', that the Americans 'were all gangsters' and agreed with his father's comment on Pearl Harbour, that 'They ought to win easily as they are all so used to guns.' But the prize for ignorance about the United States must surely go to a girl then aged seven, evacuated to a castle at Tarporley, in Cheshire, where the visits of GIs were soon to be eagerly looked forward to. In 1941, she confesses, 'I had never even heard of an American!'

A few British people still had memories of that earlier American Expeditionary Force which had passed through the British Isles after 1917. One Edinburgh woman whose mother had welcomed American sailors from the naval hospital at nearby Leith now found herself entertaining the sons of those same veterans, given her address by their fathers. The reaction to the news of America's entry into the war by one forty-four-year-old soldier of the First World War, now serving as a clerk at an RAF aircraft repair depot in Lancashire, was 'Thank God for that'. More than twenty years before he had been a patient in an American hospital when badly wounded in France:

'After the almost prison-like life in British hospitals in war areas, the treatment and kindliness I received from the American doctors, nurses and orderlies left me grateful to them for life,' he remembers. Nor was his optimism untypical. 'Morale on the airfield and in the workshops got a tremendous uplift,' he observed, 'and the feelings of despondency at once changed to "Now we can't lose."'

3

A DATE WITH VON RUNDSTEDT

'The mission of the Commanding General, European Theatre, will be to prepare for and carry on military operations . . . against the Axis Powers and their Allies.'

– US War Department Directive, June 1942.

THE decision to send American troops to the British Isles was taken at the series of conferences held in Washington over Christmas 1941. The Prime Minister, although spending the holiday far from home, was in a cheerful mood. In a short speech to crowds gathered outside the White House, where the traditional Christmas tree stood on the lawn, he recalled the 'ties of blood' which linked him to the United States and 'the commanding sentiment of comradeship in the common cause of great peoples who speak the same language, who kneel at the same altars and . . . pursue the same ideals'. Behind the scenes, too, there was cause for rejoicing; the President and his advisers had already accepted the 'Europe first' strategy which Churchill considered vital to winning the war, and a few days later, having formally founded the alliance known as the United Nations, the two great powers agreed to move the first American formations across the Atlantic at the earliest possible date. Both sides were pleased at the prospect, as Churchill recorded:

I felt that the arrival of sixty or seventy thousand American troops in Ulster would be an assertion of the United States' resolve to intervene directly in Europe. . . . The War Secretary, and his professional advisers also found this move to Ireland in harmony with their inclination to invade Europe at the earliest moment. . . . We hoped also that this would detain German troops in the West and thus be not unhelpful to the Russian struggle. . . . The Germans would certainly consider the move as an additional deterrent against the invasion of the British Isles.

The few surviving isolationists no doubt regarded the news, released late in January, that combat troops had already been sent to Great Britain as another triumph for English guile over American simple-mindedness. The truth was very different. In March and April the newly formed Operations Division of the General Staff in Washington, under an equally newly promoted, so far strictly temporary, Major-General, Dwight D. Eisenhower, had studied exhaustively all the possibilities for defeating Germany, including a landing in North Africa, and had concluded in his own words that 'the difficulty of attacking Germany through the mountainous areas on her southern and south-western flanks', and the fact that 'the full might of Great Britain and the United States could not possibly be concentrated in the Mediterranean', both pointed to 'an operation which used England as a base'. There was one other factor which Eisenhower did not mention. It was a basic axiom of American military thinking (even though one pessimistic planner had advised starting the liberation of Europe in Liberia in West Africa) that the shortest way was also the quickest way, a principle which was to emerge again, with equal importance, when the debate began as to where the Allies should land on the Continent.

In May General Eisenhower flew to London, with a fellow Major-General also destined for higher rank, Mark W. Clark, to inspect the country selected by the American Government as 'the greatest operating military base of all time'. The journey gave him his first experience of British weather; heavy fog kept the party of VIPs waiting impatiently at Prestwick for two days, a delay etched in the memory of the British civilian driver assigned to meet him in London, for it involved her being up needlessly at 5.30 on two successive mornings, and when, on the third day, the visitors did at last arrive her vigil proved to have been wasted for they all piled into Ambassador John Winant's car. Later General Eisenhower met the woman, Kay Summersby, who soon afterwards became his trusted driver and secretary for the rest of the war. She introduced him to his first English 'pub' in Beaconsfield and took him on a tour of the badly bombed areas of Lambeth, where she had driven an ambulance during the blitz. The damage deeply impressed him. She in her turn warmed to her passenger, who 'both took time to treat me as a human being' a welcome change 'from the chill dignity of British staff officers, the dirty wisecracks, wandering hands, and childish chatter of many American and Canadian officers'. A month later Eisenhower was back, bearing a gift of 'oranges, lemons and grapefruit'; amid all the cares of high command he had remembered a promise to bring her some fruit if he ever returned to London. In fact, back in Washington, Eisenhower had submitted a proposal for 'unified command of all American forces allocated to the European area' which had not merely been accepted but had led to his being appointed to the post of Commanding General of the European Theatre of Operations, US Army, which included operational control over US naval forces in Britain. The air force, contrary to British practice, was already an integral, if largely autonomous, part of the army. The formal directive from the War Department, which the General had himself drafted, set out his formidable task: 'The mission of the Commanding General, European Theatre, will be to prepare for and carry on military operations in the European Theatre against the Axis powers and their allies.'

ETOUSA, as it was immediately and universally known, began work at 20 Grosvenor Square, a modern block of flats occupied for the past year by the 'Special Observers' who had previously represented the United States forces in England. Its formerly luxurious fittings were soon replaced by the functional look of a high-level headquarters, though Eisenhower disliked having to 'establish an operating headquarters in a great city' and only stayed there because nowhere else was available.[1] In the whole United Kingdom there were no more than 35 000 American servicemen, mainly with V Corps in Northern Ireland. The air force accounted for 2000 of these, almost all busy taking over airfields in or around Huntingdonshire and in setting up what was to become the giant repair base and supply depot at Burtonwood, near Warrington in Lancashire. In the whole London area there were only 1000 and even they tended to behave as though they would not be there long. The *New Yorker* correspondent Mollie Panter-Downes remarked, rather tartly, that August, on 'the impatience of the American troops now in London, most of whom talk as though they were somewhat doubtful of being able to give the town a quick once-over before leaving to keep a date with von Rundstedt, which they seem to imagine will be around Thursday week at the latest'.

Some of this sense of urgency was no doubt due to their commanding General who had already begun to impress his personality upon all those working around him. His British woman driver, Kay Summersby, found that Eisenhower's arrival had produced a 'sharp change in American army discipline'.

The motor pool had once been rather a social centre; we went to work around ten in the morning, took an hour and a half for lunch, knocking off about teatime in the afternoon. Now it was run on strictly military lines. Headquarters had been reorganized. Instead of the easy-going group of 'observers' whose schedules included long liquid lunches and early cocktail hours, 20 Grosvenor Square was peopled by army men . . . on a seven-day week. General Eisenhower had come over to do a job; he was wasting no time. Within a few weeks numerous men-who-had-been-in-London-too-long were on their way back to the States . . . General Eisenhower often remarked, when irritated by some too-social officer: 'I'd like to send him back on a slow boat, without destroyer escort.'

1. Eisenhower was always distrustful of over-luxurious headquarters accommodation. When his 'Communications Zone' staff 'jumped direct from Grosvenor Square to the George V and the Majestic hotels in Paris in 1944', according to one officer, 'its arrival . . . was accompanied by such a soft, squashy sound of sinking into plush that Eisenhower ordered [General] Lee to take his headquarters out of Paris immediately,' although due to lack of communications elsewhere, they remained. Eisenhower himself refused to live in the city: his Supreme Headquarters stayed at Versailles.

Eisenhower himself worked a long day with only 'candy or peanuts' for lunch and though he moved from Claridges to the slightly less fashionable Dorchester in Park Lane, his dislike of big-city life, perhaps stemming from his small-town boyhood in Texas, led him to move again in August to a small house 'as picturesque as an English Christmas card', standing in ten acres of grounds off Kingston Hill, about ten miles from his office. Despite its name the only telephone at Telegraph Cottage was a private line to Grosvenor Square and the accommodation was modest: living-room, dining-room, three bedrooms and – to the horror of visiting American VIPs – only one bathroom. 'I don't want to worry when we get out here', Eisenhower told his entourage, and he did his best to relax over bridge, at threepence a hundred points, 'western' stories, and an occasional hole of golf, though never a complete round, on the adjoining course. At 'home' he 'lounged around the living-room in GI slacks, old shirt, a half-suède, half-leather jacket and a shabby pair of straw slippers which dated back to duty in Manila'. Those who worked closely for him soon fell victim to the famous Eisenhower charm, the basis of which his British driver decided was his 'unassuming curiosity'. There was no pretence at the godlike knowledge many Generals seem to believe their rank demands. 'If he didn't know something he asked questions as a friendly, curious man. Later, I was to see that blessed gift directed at chiefs of state . . . with phenomenal . . . success.'

It was owing to the excellent foundations laid in these few months that what was often called 'the American occupation' of Britain was to be accomplished with so little ill-feeling. Eisenhower appreciated from the first, as he later wrote, that, beside the usual 'preliminary organizational tasks' which every commander faced, 'another task for which we had to organize very specifically was almost unique in character. It involved the fitting of our training, building and organizational activities into British life.' He was under no illusions about the problems this involved:

The plan to bring large fighting forces to Great Britain required these highly populated islands to ready themselves for the absorption of 2 000 000 Americans and to provide for them necessary facilities, including training grounds, in which to prepare for the great invasion. England's insufficiency in food supplies had already led to a programme of placing even sub-marginal ground under intensive cultivation, while to save fuel and power, any unnecessary transportation and power facilities had been eliminated. Our friendly invasion would vastly increase the strain on the population. . . . If the United Kingdom had possessed great open spaces in which to concentrate the American forces, the problem would have been less acute, but because of the density of population every soldier arriving in England made living conditions just that much more difficult. Every American truck on the streets, and every piece of ground withdrawn from cultivation, added to the irritations.

But the greatest source of annoyance, he realized, was psychological:

Except during World War 1, the United States public has habitually looked upon Europe's quarrels as belonging to Europe alone. For this reason every American soldier coming to Britain was almost certain to consider himself a privileged crusader, sent there to help Britain out of a hole. He would expect to be treated as such. On the other hand, the British public looked upon itself as one of the saviours of democracy, particularly because, for an entire year, it had stood alone as the unbreakable opponent of Nazism. . . . Failure to understand this attitude would . . . have unfortunate results.

The British Government was meanwhile suffering even greater anxieties, for, though the landing of the first GIs in Northern Ireland in January had been widely publicized, no one had yet revealed that many had now also arrived in England and Scotland and far more were to follow. The main reason seems to have been the fear of raising hopes among the British public that victory was already in sight. But, in a paper dated 16 June, the Chiefs of Staff Committee pointed out that 'the work of preparing for the reception and maintenance of the American forces is being hindered by the strict secrecy at present enforced . . . that the news is leaking out and cannot be withheld . . . much longer', and that editors could be privately reminded of 'the importance of damping down further speculation on the possible opening of a second front in Europe this year'. Strangely enough, like General Eisenhower, Sir Alan Brooke and his colleagues were doubtful about the ability of the GIs and British civilians to mix without friction. 'Untold harm may result,' warned the Chiefs of Staff, 'if relations between the American soldiers and the local inhabitants go awry. If relations are to be maintained on a friendly basis after the first novelty has worn off, the attitude of the public must be controlled from the start by carefully designed publicity.' Such fears were, in fact, groundless, but the Cabinet agreed on 18 June 1942 that news of the impending arrival of large numbers of GIs should now be released, though 'the locations and strengths of United States formations must be kept strictly secret'.

Even this, however, was to prove none too easy, for the preparations for the invasion of Europe involved the British Government in providing the Americans on a vast scale with three essentials: accommodation for men and equipment; storage space and handling facilities for the mountains of supplies needed; and training grounds where they could prepare for the great offensive. Even land was scarce. 'The whole of the British Isles,' as Eisenhower commented, 'is only slightly larger than Colorado.' He was therefore delighted to be offered 'Salisbury Plain, the best training ground in the United Kingdom', and the traditional home of the British Army Here at Tidworth, an 'army town' even in peacetime, General Mark Clark set up the headquarters of the US II Corps, though he had at first few men to command.

Eisenhower's stay in England was brief. By mid-July 'it was clear to the Chiefs of Staff', directing the war from Washington, DC, 'that no significant invasion of Western Europe was possible in 1942' and 'it became increasingly doubtful to the American headquarters that a full-out attack could be launched in the early spring of 1943. . . . We began to realize that a large-scale invasion might not be possible before the spring of 1944.' The desire to attack the Axis with American land forces somewhere in 1942 led, on 24 July, to the decision to invade North Africa, under the code-name 'Operation GYMNAST', later to become 'Operation TORCH' and Eisenhower was appointed Commander-in-Chief of the expedition. He left London on 5 November, three days before the landings began. He was not to return, this time to command a far greater enterprise, until 14 January 1944.

After 'Ike' had gone, the most important American left in England in 1942, although his name never became well known, was Major-General John C. H. Lee who had arrived in May 1942, even before ETOUSA had been set up, to take charge of the Services of Supply (SOS) organization in the British Isles, and remained until August 1944. Upon him, wrote General Eisenhower, fell 'the appalling task of preparing ports and building warehouses, camps, airfields and repair facilities, all of which would be needed before we could start an offensive from the British base. The work accomplished under his direction was vital to success.' Lee was not the man to attract popular acclaim, much less affection. 'He was', wrote his commander:

an engineer officer of long experience, with a reputation for getting things done, but because of his mannerisms and his stern insistence upon the outward forms of discipline . . . was considered a martinet by most of his acquaintants. He was determined, correct and devoted to duty . . . a man of the highest character and religious fervour. I sometimes felt that he was a modern Cromwell.

One British secretary who worked at his headquarters can recall the service 'in an improvised chapel' each Sunday, at which 'everybody in the congregation would stand when General Lee walked up the aisle to take his front pew' often to listen to a coloured preacher delivering a sermon 'of the real "hell-fire" variety'. He was also punctilious about receiving the military respect due to him. The wife of one of his closest friends in Cheltenham, a Presbyterian minister, remembers that Lee insisted on being accompanied by a two-man escort, 'who had to stand outside on the doorstep until he went'.

The code word which dominated the working hours of all those, British and American, responsible for accommodating and supplying the American forces in Britain was BOLERO chosen, it was said, because, like Ravel's masterpiece, it built up gradually towards a climax. A joint BOLERO

Committee in Washington, second in importance only to the Combined Chiefs of Staff, advised what units were to be expected and what accommodation and services they would need, while requirements for roads, runways, warehouses and huts were worked out in detail by the BOLERO Combined Committee in London, meeting at Norfolk House, St James Square. To this committee seven others, covering such subjects as medical services, transport and accommodation, reported, and a special committee of the British Cabinet, under the Lord President of the Council, Sir John Anderson, arbitrated between the conflicting claims of various Government departments. No one was in any doubt about the ultimate purpose of their work. As the BOLERO Committee's terms of reference reminded them, their task was to co-ordinate plans 'for the reception, accommodation and maintenance of United States forces in the United Kingdom . . . in accordance with the requirements of the plans for the invasion of Europe'.

The great invasion of the United Kingdom began slowly but news soon leaked out in Whitehall that this was only the beginning and on 24 April 1942 the Director General of the Office of Works, the Government department responsible for public building and for allocating building labour and materials, wrote anxiously to the Engineer-in-Chief at the War Office:

I am alarmed by a report that you are contemplating accommodation for one million American troops in this country in the next six months, partly in billets or requisitioned houses and partly in camps. Even if only a small part is to go into hutted camps, of however rough a description, the demand for labour and materials would be enormous and I know no means of meeting it from civilian labour. Can you let me know what truth there is in the story?

He learned soon enough. The first BOLERO Key Plan – there were scores of other minor plans covering the various details – was issued on 31 May 1942 and warned that accommodation would be needed for 1 049 000 men, of whom 240 000 were from the air forces. (Providing them with accommodation and airfields was the responsibility of the British Air Ministry and its work will be described in a later chapter); 294 000 of the men arriving in the British Isles would be supporting troops, 235 000 fighting troops, 277 000 would join the Services of Supply and the rest would be assigned to ETOUSA and other headquarters. On 25 July the second Key Plan raised the total to 1 147 000, and though a third plan, issued in mid-August, showed a reduction in the numbers needing accommodation in the near future, due to the outflow of troops for the North African invasion in November, this was soon to be more than made up by the build-up for the cross-Channel invasion. The fourth, and supposedly last, Key Plan, issued in 12 July 1943, required room to be found for 1 340 000 men by 30 April 1944, but even this total was exceeded and at the end of May 1944 American strength in Britain reached an all-time peak of 1 526 965. It was as though the British Government had been asked to squeeze into its already overcrowded country, with 50 000 000 people packed into an area about the size of New Mexico and half the size of Texas, the whole population of the State of Washington, or Arkansas, Maryland or Connecticut. And this was, of course, only the maximum number of Americans in Britain *at one time*. The number who passed through the country *en route* for North Africa or France was far larger, probably totalling two million.

Unlike civilians, however, this vast influx would need, not merely accommodation, but training-grounds and firing-ranges, storage space for bombs, ammunition, explosives, roads and hard-standing heavy enough to take tanks and artillery, and airfields able to accommodate thousands of bombers and fighters. The growing demand all these needs made upon the already stretched resources of Great Britain is clear from the records of the British War Cabinet, to which BOLERO soon began to cause concern. On 11 August 1942, the Minister of Labour, Ernest Bevin, reported that 'contracts worth £26 000 000 had been cleared by the United States authorities, which meant that the general location had been agreed,' and that 'considerable enthusiasm had been aroused and success achieved, in the organization of the building labour required.' He was, however, alarmed that 'only 14 per cent of the total contracts' – excluding the airfield building programme – had so far been placed, due to delays in the choice of actual sites involved. Another memorandum from Bevin four months later, in mid-December 1942, pointed out that he could not, as ordered, cut the labour force in the building industry by 225 000 by the end of 1943, unless the airfield building programme were reduced. The Minister of Health, responsible for housing, complained that 'work had been proceeding satisfactorily' on the repair of bomb-damaged houses 'which could still be made habitable with a relatively small expenditure of labour and materials . . . until the labour had been diverted for the . . . BOLERO programme. There were now some 97 000 houses . . . waiting repair.' The Minister of Agriculture had a similar problem . . . 'Without a small number of new cottages for agricultural workers,' he warned, he would find it difficult to carry through the expanded programme of food production. Recruitment for the Women's Land Army had had to be suspended largely because of difficulty in finding living accommodation.

By May 1943 it was not only the civilian Ministries which were feeling the effects of BOLERO. On the nineteenth all three service ministers protested that if a new scheme proposed by the Minister of Production 'for reducing their departments' allocations of building labour went ahead' urgent works needed by the army, navy and RAF would be held up. Sir James Grigg pointed out that if his building programme was halted he would have to reduce 'the rate of call-up for the army' and hence 'could not discharge his responsibility for producing the forces required for service overseas'. 'The proposed reduction in the labour force allocated to the Ministry of War Transport', another minister told his colleagues, 'might involve a serious deterioration in road surfaces. This would not only involve increased consumption of rubber and petrol, but might even lead to some loss of efficiency in transportation.'

The War Cabinet finally decided that the Americans would have to be told that Britain simply could not achieve unaided all that had been asked of her. As its secretary recorded:

The Minister of Production, in consultation with the . . . other Ministers concerned, would prepare a statement showing the urgent importance of relieving the strain on our building resources by securing the agreement of the United States authorities (i) to accept lower standards of accommodation for United States troops, and (ii) to undertake, by United States military labour, a larger proportion of this building work. This statement should be prepared in a form suitable for communication to the United States Government but before it was so communicated the Chiefs of Staff should be consulted.

But BOLERO continued to intrude, ghost-like, into one meeting after another of the War Cabinet that summer. On 3 June the Cabinet agreed, to use Bevin's own phrase, that 'men in the building industry . . . due to be called up in the latter half of June should be put "at the back of the pack" ', and that those already in the RAF would have to make a small sacrifice to free more labour for helping the Americans. Hitherto they had slept only fifteen to a Nissen hut. Now the Air Ministry was to accept 'the same standard of austerity as the War office . . . in the sleeping of other ranks', namely eighteen per hut. Some Americans, however, were to be asked – or rather told – to endure far greater hardship. The Cabinet agreed that if the expected numbers 'of United States troops . . . reached this country in December, January and February, it would be necessary to put them under canvas on arrival'.

Even all these measures were not enough. On 23 June the Minister of Production informed his colleagues that the bottom of the construction industry barrel had finally been reached. 'The labour left for maintenance work is certainly in some places at or below the safety level', he pointed out in a memorandum. 'I am unable to recommend any further cuts in . . . the Government building programme, either service or civilian.' There were, however, two encouraging signs. The US Army had 'agreed that their forces shall, if necessary, accept British standards of accommodation' and 'to provide the labour for any additional works which they may require'. The Cabinet decided on 29 June 'to press the Americans to send over more construction units, at the cost of the movement of operational troops, rather than to disturb the call-up in this country'. Ten days later matters came to a head. On 8 July 1943, with the target date for completing BOLERO now eleven months off, the Minister of Production had to report that: 'The United States authorities are pressing me for the necessary labour to complete various projects. They state very strongly that, unless we can find the labour, the military plans decided upon at the Washington Conference cannot be fulfilled.' Only by postponing the call-up of building workers, and a general lowering of construction standards, was BOLERO saved so that the build-up of the American forces could go ahead as planned.

Winston Churchill had described the development of war production as leading 'in the first year to a trickle, in the second to a river, in the third to a flood', and this is how the Americans reached the British Isles. About 4000 arrived by sea in January 1942 and, though in February and April none landed at all, 25 000 came in May, 26000 in July and – as the *Queen Mary* and *Queen Elizabeth* joined the Atlantic run, as described in the next chapter – 74000 in August.[1] The numbers fell during the winter, and there was actually a decline in the number of GIs in the British Isles as most of the early arrivals moved on to North Africa, so that in February 1943 only 105 000 remained, but during the summer of 1943 the build-up began in earnest, with 50 000 men landing in June, 76 000 in September and 175 000 in October, the flow continuing at a high level until in April 1944 a peak number of reinforcements – 217000 – flooded in, mainly through the ports of the Western Approaches, from the Mersey to the Clyde. That was the peak, though in May 108000 more landed. Then the island was, unofficially at least, declared full, and the great crusade was ready to set forth.

As the number of arrivals rose the American forces spread through the British Isles. Eventually they occupied 100000 buildings, ranging from single thatched cottages to vast warehouses, scattered over 1100 locations, from tiny hamlets to the West End of London. Wherever possible, existing buildings were used, but often these needed extensive conversion. This work was planned, and largely carried out, by the British, who drew both on civilian labour and on the Royal Engineers and Pioneer Corps. The whole programme (excluding all work for the air forces) cost about £50000000 ($200000000), of which about a third was spent respectively on accommodation, hospitals and storage depots.

Eventually about 60 per cent of all GIs were housed in former British camps or requisitioned buildings and 40 per cent in specially built huts or tents. Just before D-Day (excluding the air force) about 650000 men were living in existing camps, vacated by the British forces, 162000 in new huts, specially built for American use, and 112000 in billets of various kinds. The

1. This, and the succeeding figures, relate only to landings by sea, but the totals of servicemen in the United Kingdom include those who arrived by air, amounting to about 5 per cent of the total.

remainder were accommodated under canvas, 90000 in reasonably weather proof 'winter camps' and 193000 in tents suitable only for summer use. With 500 men on the job a hutted camp for 1000 men could be built in just over two months, and, to save effort, most camps were built in one of six standard sizes – accommodating from 250 to 1500 men. With fewer, but larger camps, the construction rate could have been speeded up, but to ensure racial segregation the Americans demanded a considerable number of small camps, where black troops could be kept well away from white units. Even a small camp, however, took up a good deal of land. To house 1000 men under canvas required about 200 tents, spread over thirty-four acres. A hutted camp for 1000 men needed forty acres and, including sick bays, mess halls, bath houses, 'guardhouse' and the rest called for 123 separate buildings.

" They won't let on who the camp is for."

Different building methods caused many problems. The Americans were amazed to find British workmen still painfully clearing sites, digging holes for posts and laying concrete by hand. The British were shocked at the lavish American use of timber. The GIs simply threw away wood not of the right length. Even American rations presented a problem; the fat in army tinned food soon blocked up the grease traps and filter beds of British drains.

In the end the camp-building programme was carried out mainly by British labour to British designs. The standards adopted for all kinds of quarters were British and far lower than those prevailing in the US Army, though senior American officers were full of praise for the British construction industry, commending both the high craftsmanship and the low cost.

The second group of buildings needed were hospitals and here British labour worked to American designs. 'The construction, though hutted' wrote an official British historian, 'was essentially of a semi-permanent type and hardly that of a theatre of war. . . . The staff accommodation was on a generous scale. Covered ways with smooth paving without steps connected the surgical wards with the operating block and the theatre appointments were of the costliest and most modern types.' These comments applied to the thirty-three new 'station' hospitals built, intended for about 800 patients each, and the seventeen 1100-bed 'general' hospitals, which cost £250000 ($1000000) each. Between them these hospitals were expected to provide nearly 48000 beds, while 45000 more were to be found from taking over, and extending existing hospitals handed over by the British Army, and by the use of 'dual-purpose' or 'conversion' camps which could become hospitals. In fact, due to shortage of labour, only 62000 beds were ready by 30 April 1944, 31000 short of the target, the gap being filled by tented annexes – which to the horror of their staff – had no water in the wards and only bucket sanitation. The third, and most demanding, of all the BOLERO projects was the provision of storage depots, of which ninety-four were constructed or extended. The largest were the 'G', for 'general', depots and the first to be built, at Sudbury-Egginton, near Burton on Trent, cost £1650000 to produce a million square feet of covered storage and 9500000 square feet of open storage. In December 1942 work began at Wem, in Shropshire, on a 'model' depot, substantially smaller, which was finished in six months and became the prototype for several more, costing rather over £500000 ($2000000) each, Eventually twenty 'G' depots were built, some of them, as at Lockerly, between Salisbury and Winchester, by all-American labour, but most by Americans working under British supervision, and alongside British civilians, and army engineers. Each depot was a far more visible sign of the American presence than the average military camp. The largest G–38, set up at Bristol in July 1942, eventually embraced fourteen separate installations in 200 separate buildings, spread over an area thirty-five miles across. G–24, at Honeybourne near Evesham in Worcestershire – the great fruit-growing area of Britain – now offered a wider variety of produce, with a staff of 3000 supplying American units all over the Midlands from thirty-six large warehouses, each surrounded by specially built hard standing. G–23, at Histon, near Cambridge, had at its peak 3500 on its strength, supplying the rapacious demands of air force units throughout East Anglia. Over the country as a whole the depot building programme involved constructing 6000000 square feet of covered storage areas, 35000000 square feet of open areas, 210 miles of road, 176 miles of railway and a whole range of associated works, from Red Cross huts to dispensaries. The work was finished on time, in the early spring of 1944.

The network of camps and hospitals, supply depots and workshops, was manned and controlled through five headquarters known as 'base sections' covering the same area as one or more British Army commands: Northern Ireland Base section; Western Base, which stretched from the River Severn right up the middle of the country, and included the whole of Wales and Scotland; the Eastern Base from the Scottish Border to the edges of London and the Southern Base, covering the whole of the rest of the country, apart from the area immediately around London which was at first known as the London Base Command and then as the Central Base section. After the invasion of North Africa, Northern Ireland receded in importance; Eastern Base section was, from first to last, largely the preserve of the air force. Western Base contained all the great ports on the Bristol Channel, the Mersey and the Clyde, through which the vast majority of American troops entered Britain. The Southern Base was the great troop-quartering and training area and was soon to assume even more importance as, to quote an American historian, 'the springboard for the cross-Channel operation', to which all this costly effort was directed.

4

THAT GREAT AMERICAN SHIP,
THE *QUEEN MARY*

'They said they came over on the Queen Mary, *which was built in the United States.'*

— *A woman living in Armagh, recalling 1942.*

FEW GIs knew they were being sent to Britain. 'At no time were we told what our overseas destination was to be', one Army Air Corps mechanic – in peacetime a construction surveyor – from Denver, Colorado, recalls. 'We could only guess by the absence of any tropical clothing issue that we were headed for the European theatre', though the cynics deduced that this meant they must be earmarked for Africa or the Pacific. When, as often happened, units were warned to prepare for a cold climate, this was usually assumed to be Iceland. One WAC[1] Sergeant (the Women's Army Corps was America's equivalent to Britain's Auxiliary Territorial Service), who had made her home in Orlando, Florida, and received such orders recalls that at her training camp at Oglethorpe, Georgia, the chief attempt to prepare the girls for the ordeals ahead was a reminder from their commanding officer, 'On the night before we sailed, "Men don't make passes at girls who wear glasses",' and even this she soon found 'didn't hold true overseas'.[2]

No country in the world cared for its soldiers as well as the United States, but no amount of forethought and concern could make a voyage on an overcrowded troopship an agreeable experience. Happily, no troopship on the Atlantic run was sunk by enemy action, but cramped quarters and seasickness were by themselves sufficient to make those few days on board ship the most wretched of many men's whole service career and the constant changes of course at full speed which the largest liners made as they zig-zagged their way across the Atlantic unescorted added to their passengers' discomfort. The immediate plan, agreed during the Washington discussions after Pearl Harbour, had been to send only two divisions – about 30000

1. The Women's Army Corps was originally known as the Women's Auxiliary Army Corps. See footnote on page 104.
2. The correct quotation, from the journalist Dorothy Parker, is 'Men seldom make passes. . . .'

men – to Northern Ireland, but Churchill, eager to consolidate the new Alliance, then offered as troopships the two greatest liners in the world, the *Queen Mary* and the *Queen Elizabeth*. Both these great vessels held a special place in British affections. The launching of the *Queen Mary* in 1934 had been a visible symbol that Britain was emerging from the Depression, and the whole nation had followed eagerly her maiden voyage in 1936 when she captured the Blue Riband for the fastest Atlantic crossing. No publicity had attended the first voyage of the *Queen Elizabeth*, displacing 83700 tons against the *Queen Mary*'s 81200, but her safe arrival in New York in March 1940 had been hailed as a major victory. Churchill's offer of the ships was a generous one, for it would have been a heavy blow to British morale had either been sunk, but the decision to cram into them every man they could carry was taken by the American Chiefs of Staff. 'General Marshall', Churchill wrote later, 'asked me how many men we ought to put on board, observing that boats [and] rafts could only be provided for about 8000. If this were disregarded they could carry 16000 men. I gave the following answer: "I can only tell you what we should do. You must judge for yourself the risks you will run." ' Having weighed the dangers, Marshall decided, after a few voyages with only the 'safe' load of soldiers aboard, that the ships should, in Churchill's words, be 'filled to the brim'.

Many servicemen who sailed on the Queens, despite a warning on this very point in the *Guide* previously quoted, found it hard to believe that any country but their own could have built them. 'How come,' one asked a woman manning an enquiry desk at an American camp in Kew, 'you don't build ships like that in your country?' A British seaman who served on board the *Queen Mary* found all his passengers genuinely convinced that 'all the big troopships', including both Queens and the *Mauretania* were American, and got great satisfaction at their bewilderment when the Red Ensign, flag of the British merchant service, was hoisted at the start of each voyage.

The use of the Queens from August 1942 onwards transformed the American military presence in Europe. By the end of the year thirty-eight convoys – many in fact 'single-ship' convoys consisting of a solitary fast vessel – had ferried 227000 men into British ports. During 1943 the build-up was even more rapid. In one month alone, October, 175000 reached the British Isles, and during the whole year sixty-six convoys arrived safely, with 681000 men on board. A smaller, but still significant number arrived by other routes – from the Middle East and North Africa, and Italy – while the United States Air Force was by 1943 flying crews and aircraft into Britain almost every day.

The *Queen Mary* had been designed to carry 2000 passengers, and on her first journeys accommodated 6000 GIs, but this figure was soon raised to 10500 and then to 15000. The one consolation for their discomfort was that the voyage lasted only five or six days from the time the ship was escorted out of Halifax or New York by American or Canadian destroyers until it picked up an escort of destroyers as it approached the Clyde. The belief that the Queens' remarkable speed, 28½ knots, would enable them to outrun any U-boat proved justified and the only tragedy to mar the whole operation occurred in October 1942, when the *Queen Mary*, zigzagging at speed, rammed an escort vessel, the *Curacoa*, and sliced her in two with the loss of 338 lives. One young soldier from Norfolk, Virginia, who witnessed the collision, from 'the portside bow' still remembers how 'both sides sank in a few minutes' and on their arrival in port, a day later, he found himself landing without possessions for 'my baggage, along with that of many others, was in the bow of the *Queen Mary* and was lost'. The disaster was hushed-up at the time and never mentioned by the crew, as one Army Air Corps officer, who sailed on the *Queen Mary*'s next crossing, after her bows had been repaired in Boston, recalls. There were, however, still ample grounds for anxiety because 'the ship came close to capsizing, being top heavy with anti-aircraft guns' and the Captain's major worry, it was whispered aboard, was 'fear of the German pocket battleships'. All on board had to wear a life-jacket at all times and there were 'daily abandon-ship drills'.

Some sailors seem to have delighted in making the flesh of their passengers creep. One army Captain, who had reached Pier II, on Staten Island, New York, by way of Camp Lee, Virginia, Shenango, Pennsylvania, and Camp Kilmer, New Jersey, vividly remembers the gloomy tale which greeted him and 600 other officers and men when they boarded the *North King*, a small ship built in Kiel before the First World War. This unlucky vessel had, he was told, been scuttled during World War I and only raised again after two years on the bottom, since when it had rammed an iceberg. The crew, it soon transpired, had an equally unlucky history, the first steward, a Dane, having witnessed repeated attacks on his ship on a run to Murmansk, while the third mate, an Englishman, had been torpedoed off Liverpool. To raise spirits still further, a cat which had 'brought her kittens on board one by one by the nape of the neck from a ship alongside, attempted, just before the ship sailed, to take her kittens down the gang plank. The crew said that was a bad sign.' But to the relief of both passengers and crew the cautious mother finally 'changed her mind' and cat, kittens, and GIs all sailed together. A Sergeant aircraft mechanic from Patchogue, Long Island, remembers an equally dismal start to his journey to Europe. His outfit embarked from Pier 13, Staten Island, an unlucky number in any language, and they soon found their ship, in a large convoy, had been given 'the lead front corner position' known as 'Coffin Corner', though, after a fourteen-day crossing, they also arrived safely.

Beside the two Queens, many other famous liners also carried GIs, among them the 45 000-ton *Aquitania,* formerly the pride of her line, but now dismissed by one reluctant traveller as 'an ancient converted four-stacker', and the *Mauretania* (36 000 tons), both of which could accommodate about 8000 men. Other ships called into service were the *Île de France* (43 000 tons) and *Pasteur* (29 000), (which had belonged to France,) the Dutch *Nieuw Amsterdam* (36 000), the *Andes,* the *Empress of Australia,* the *Empress of Scotland* (known in earlier days as the *Empress of Japan*), the *Monarch of Bermuda,* the *Dominion Monarch, Cape Town Castle,* the *Britannic,* and the American-owned *Brazil, Uruguay,* and *Argentina.*

Although a few men embarked at Boston the vast majority of GIs sailed from New York. Because of the need for secrecy they rarely enjoyed any formal send-off, so that there were none of the cheers and flag-waving made familiar by films about earlier wars. The men of the 24th Station Complement Squadron, another Pfc remembers, 'boarded the *Aquitania* on 2 August 1943, with much confusion, most of it created by us. Some idiot started mooing as we herded aboard and the rest of us picked it up.' The men had, perhaps, some reason for feeling disgruntled for they had come from Camp Shanks, New York, where 'we were told that we were going to Africa and issued all the appropriate equipment and given all the necessary shots' and 'we sailed on 4 August thinking the first Englishmen we had met, the crew, were crazy. They kept telling us, "You may be going to Africa . . . mates, but this bloody tub don't go to any place but England," ' – a prediction soon proved correct.

A few GIs found that the novelty and interest of a transatlantic crossing swamped all other reactions. One member of the 95th Bomb Group remembers on moving 'from Camp Kilmer to New York harbour' in May 1943 being 'greeted by an awe-inspiring sight – the *Queen Elizabeth.* To a farm boy from Colorado this seemed very adequate transportation.'

The reactions of one twenty-eight-year-old Technical Sergeant in the Corps of Engineers, from the small, 1000-population, town of Grafton Illinois, were similar. After leaving Fort Dix, New Jersey, he had boarded a ship which had sailed at night. The following morning, going on deck, he found they were 'in a huge convoy, which was an amazing sight to behold. I was suddenly being educated, as I had never seen the ocean before that time and could hardly believe there were that many ships in the world.'

While the Queens crossed unescorted, in four or five days, a convoy, though heavily protected, might take as long as seventeen, especially if there was a wait off Halifax, Nova Scotia, while the whole force was assembled. The experiences of a Staff Sergeant from Louisiana, who crossed on the *Duchess of Atholl* after embarking at New York on 21 February

1942, were probably typical of most of those who made the slower journey. 'After stopping at Halifax, the crew informed us we would be attacked by subs as soon as we got to "bomb alley" off Greenland,' and the men were not encouraged when 'off Iceland our escort of nineteen destroyers, a battleship and cruiser left us,' *en route* for Murmansk. Few pilgrims to the New World can have been as relieved to see land as these travellers were to sight Belfast on 3 March 'after thirteen stormy days'.

Those travelling on fast ships avoided such protracted discomfort, but were far more vulnerable if, as sometimes happened, the vessel broke down in mid-Atlantic. One twenty-three-year-old GI in the 654th Engineers, in peacetime a student at Rollins College, Winter Park, Florida, who embarked on the *Aquitania* late in 1942, remembers how, despite being assured the vessel had 'a complete set of engines which would propel her at nearly twenty-five knots – fast enough to outrun the wolf pack of Nazi subs then lurking in the Atlantic sea lanes' the troops aboard 'were somewhat apprehensive . . . as we realized that we were on our own for the trip'. They soon had even greater reason for their anxiety.

The voyage was rough, but the ship had made many winter crossings like it before. The British crew seemed unperturbed through it all – until one engine quit in mid-Atlantic. There was then much scurrying about, completely uncharacteristic of British unflappability. . . . From my quarters directly above the engine room, I could hear goings on below that sounded exactly like someone trying to start a balky car on a cold winter's day. Efforts were rewarded finally, the engine came to life, and the old bucket leaned her four stacks four or five degrees to starboard and sped off into the foam again, to everyone's immense relief. It was what the deck officer referred to later as 'quite a sticky wicket there for a bit'.

Not all Americans, many now admit, appreciated at the time the hazards of the Battle of the Atlantic, for, naturally enough, few details of the disastrously heavy losses of 1941 and early 1942 had been published, but, even so, an unwontedly devout air prevailed in some troop decks. A Jewish air force chaplain, from Sioux City, Iowa, making the seven-day trip from New York to the Firth of Forth on the *Queen Mary* in 1944, found that 'the chapels were jammed day and night with pious (read "frightened") GIs of every religious denomination. Coming back in a slow Liberty ship twenty months later, in twelve days I couldn't get one quorum of ten men for a Sabbath or any other Jewish service. . . . There were no German U-boats in the Atlantic then.'

What most GIs now remember best about their voyage to Britain, however, is not the danger, but the grim conditions. To accommodate every possible man bunks had been jammed into the staterooms and lounges until there was barely room to climb into them. One engineer officer, who had volunteered for the army 'to get his year in', i.e. complete his military service, in June 1941, and had trained at Fort Knox, Kentucky, and with the Fifth Armoured Division, recalls his four-day crossing on the *Queen Elizabeth* in June 1943. 'The officers were assigned to the old cabins with bunks hastily constructed to put about twenty men in what was formerly a four berth cabin. The enlisted men were "double-bunked". Half of them spent twenty-four hours on deck while the other half spent the same period down in the bunks. For the next twenty-four-hour period the roles were reversed.' One nineteen-year-old from Portland, Maine, who had volunteered for the US Air Force while a senior at Derring High School and by mid-1942 was a Pfc in an Ordnance Unit of the 91st Bomb Group, responsible for servicing bombs and ammunition for Flying Fortresses, experienced 'double-bunking' for himself on the *Queen Mary*. 'Sixteen men slept in one stateroom every other night and the alternate night slept in the passage way with a couple of blankets, so that sixteen others could have the stateroom that night. There were four bunk-bed units consisting of four beds each.' On the same ship, a year later, conditions were no better. One Eighth Air Force NCO remembers that 'some nights on that trip we slept on the forward deck and George K. and I actually slept on a tiny sloping area of deck that is next to the forward cabin, but above the cross-wise rail. That way we didn't roll with the ship which changed course every fifteen minutes. It was the only real rest we got until we landed.'

Conditions on the *Mauretania*, on a voyage which began on 8 October 1943, were, one officer remembers, even worse. 'It was necessary for about 140 of my men to sleep on the tables from which meals were eaten during the day. I spent many hours each night going among the men making sure they were able to get some rest.'

The memories of a manufacturers' sales agent in Hartford, Connecticut, who had been scheduled to return to civilian life one week after Pearl Harbour, and found himself instead, on 5 December 1942, boarding the *Queen Mary*, are similar. 'The gossip was that Cunard was getting $70 per passenger' (about £17) but 'the overcrowding in the quarters assigned to the enlisted men was such that a good percentage chose to sleep on the promenade deck, catch-as-catch-can. This was not uncomfortable temperature-wise as after the second day at sea, we were in the warm waters of the Gulf Stream. Nevertheless, crossing the North Atlantic in the cold season is rugged.' For this Captain's three companies of soldiers there was an additional source of discomfort for they 'had been detached for processing through a Pennsylvania army post and through some mix-up . . . arrived wearing anti-gas garments; the odour was horrible and the men terribly uncomfortable but it was too late to correct the situation and they had to wear these garments until reaching their permanent station in the United Kingdom'.

way. Some enterprising males fastened messages to tent pegs and swung them overboard on long lines to tap against the girls' portholes. 'I come from Des Moines. I am a Sergeant. Who are you and what do you look like?', ran one such dispatch, concentrating on essentials. Eventually the authorities relented sufficiently to allow the WACs to invite their 'dates' to special parties, though admission was strictly by printed invitation only, documents which commanded a high value in the crap games with which many GIs whiled away the long days at sea.

Gambling, although it could lead to fights, was always a popular way of passing the time. One NCO of the 392nd Bomb Group, travelling in July 1943, remembers that 'by the time we got to England one man had thousands of dollars and two hired body-guards'.

For all its unpleasantness, many of the millions who crossed the Atlantic between 1942 and 1944 remember the voyage as a peaceful interlude in their military lives, a brief time out of war. One young man from New Hampshire, already quoted, sailing on 'the Duchess of something-or-other' – probably the *Duchess of Atholl* – remembers how he 'spent much of the time at the bow', during the long summer days of July 1942, watching 'the dolphins dip and glide across our path. I still regard the dolphin as the most beautiful and desirable animal in the world. I wondered if they were the same dolphins that so often came up to wish us good day when as children we rowed across Penobscot Bay in the morning.' One nineteen-year-old GI, formerly a senior at Deering High School in Portland, Maine, found life on the *Queen Mary* in mid-1942 had its compensations: 'There was plenty of leisure time for letter writing, reading, card and dice games, though occasionally someone would catch you to sweep the deck or polish a rail.' Another GI destined to serve at Supreme Headquarters in Bushy Park, Teddington, filled in the time learning hairdressing from a fellow soldier who had followed this trade in civilian life, and arrived in Britain a fully fledged barber, 'happy with a well-paid easy number' that enabled him 'to dodge drills and general routine'.

'The weather was good', one Pfc from Providence, Rhode Island, headed for a replacement depot in England as a message centre clerk, recalls. 'A group of us spent most of our time playing cards in the forward hold that held the anchor chain.' He had time, too, to reflect wryly, that his ship, the *George Washington*, had twenty-five years earlier carried President Wilson to the conference to 'end all wars'.

An Australian seaman who served on the Atlantic run, mainly in the small 'Alcoa' ships owned by the Aluminium Company of America, which carried about 200 troops in addition to their usual cargo, remembers being equally struck by the diversity of accents and tastes among their passengers. The first request from those from the South was whether the diet included their accustomed cornmeal bread and 'blackeyed Susans', the seeds of the cowpea, which were white with black spots, though men from Northern states would not touch either. All, however, displayed remarkable ignorance, and men embarked in New York given the opportunity of going ashore in Florida would ask if they needed a different currency. They knew even less of the British Empire. A favourite question to this man was whether he came from 'the capital of Australia, New Zealand?' Two queries, common to every shipload, covered the whole extent of their curiosity about England: 'Are the girls willing?'; and 'Are there red lights outside the whorehouses so you can find one when you want one?'

Probably the most contented men aboard ship were the small number of quiet, intellectual GIs, who had their own reasons for being eager to see England. Typical of this group was a future Harvard Ph.D and head of a Los Angeles college, who had enlisted with reluctance and was now a Master Sergeant in the Military Police. 'All my life I had wanted to visit England', he later wrote. . . . 'Although far away in a geographical sense, England, to any American who reads a great deal, always seems very near, a land just beyond the horizon.' His particular passion was for the Brontës, whom he had admired since discovering *Jane Eyre*, and, while his comrades were rowdily celebrating their last few days in New York, he had haunted the city library, discovering, to his delight, that it contained a book about the family he had not yet read. The news of the ship's destination, revealed in mid-Atlantic, delighted him, and he never forgot 'the last evening on board our transport just outside of an English port', standing on deck chatting with another Brontë enthusiast he had discovered.

In 1939 a transatlantic flight was still an adventure and most Americans assigned to duty in Britain at that time made the journey in two stages, changing aircraft at Lisbon. This remained the usual civilian route, but as early as November 1940 the first bomber, a Hudson, was delivered direct, taking off from Montreal at midnight and touching down at Prestwick, on the west coast of Scotland, the following noon. Although an experiment in towing gliders across the Atlantic proved unsuccessful, by mid-1942 heavy bombers and transports were regularly making the journey, refuelling at Prestwick before resuming their journey south. The airport was popular with the crews who landed there, not merely because it was dry land, after what seemed endless sea, but because the transit hotel was one of the few places in the British Isles where eggs were regularly on the breakfast menu. Longer acquaintance with the town was less satisfactory, if these disillusioned lines by an unknown GI give an accurate picture:

> No bloody games,
> No bloody dames,
> Here in bloody Prestwick
> They won't even tell you their bloody names,
> Here in bloody Prestwick.

An apprentice tool-maker from Bridgport, Connecticut, who had joined the Army Air Corps in September 1942, remembers an exciting journey in the spring of 1944. The B–17 in which he was an aerial gunner flew first from Kearney, Nebraska to Manchester, New Hampshire, and then to Goose Bay, Labrador, where, after a few hours' rest, they took off again, a nerve-racking experience 'because the plane ahead of us crashed on take-off and all the cre w members were lost'. Hardly, however, had their own machine 'got out over the Atlantic, on our way to Iceland, when we had a runaway prop. We had to turn off our engine and feather our prop and return to Goose Bay. . . . We landed . . . just as a snowstorm started up.' The combination of a damaged engine and unfavourable weather kept the crew holed up for two weeks in this remote spot, where 'we spent our time snow shoeing and ice fishing' and 'in the evening we played cards or listened to records or went to the movies', which included 'the world première of *Going my Way*'.

Bombers were rarely attacked while making the crossing but unarmed transport aircraft were more vulnerable. One Lieutenant-Colonel, ordered to England as a replacement in February 1945, remembers boarding a C–54 transport at Washington National Airport with no prior warning of his destination, which was only revealed when he broke open his sealed orders an hour after take-off over New York City. Their plane managed to land at Gander despite a six-inch snowfall, but next morning only reached Prestwick 'after dodging two Focke-Wulfes in a cloud bank over Northern Ireland. The pilot told us they lay in wait for these slow-moving transports regularly.'

The overwhelming reaction of GI's on discovering their destination was one of relief, if not of delight. At Camp McCoy, in the middle of the Western plains, the news that one unit was headed for England was enthusiastically received on the grounds that 'it couldn't be colder than Wisconsin'. And as one wartime airman candidly admits, at least 'Britain seemed more civilized than some South Pacific island'.

5

THE YANKS IN IRELAND

'We soon realized that the Yanks were no ordinary soldiers.'

– Belfast man, then aged twelve, recalling 1942.

NORTHERN IRELAND in early 1942 was, as it still is, the least typical part of the United Kingdom. Although the majority of its citizens was passionately loyal to the British Crown, old animosities, long since forgotten elsewhere, still flourished and many Irish villages were still virtually untouched by the war. Londonderry, where British warships on convoy duty were based, and Belfast, which had been heavily bombed in 1941, had both felt the impact of the war, but the province as a whole had been comparatively little affected by it. Nowhere in the British Isles was by American standards so 'backward' or, on the face of it, less likely to absorb uncomplainingly many tens of thousands of brash young GIs.

Both sides had already had a foretaste of the satisfactions – and problems – ahead with the arrival during 1941 of the 1000 American civilians mentioned in an earlier chapter. The original intention was for them to build berths and refuelling facilities for American warships in Lough Foyle, the four-mile-long stretch of water connecting Londonderry with the sea, plus a temporary submarine base – until a permanent one was ready at the Gareloch in Scotland – close to the city docks. A flying-boat base, to shelter four squadrons of Catalinas, was to be constructed at Lough Erne, near Enniskillen in County Fermanagh, with an ammunition depot in Kiltierney deer park, eleven miles from Enniskillen, and a 200-bed all-American hospital at Necarne Castle. The Americans built a large, underground headquarters at Talbot House, Londonderry, where they also established what was to remain throughout the war their main naval radio station in the European Theatre. By December 1941, most of the work was already finished, but America's entry into the war led to a whole new constructional programme being launched. The need for secrecy had now gone and soon, around Londonderry, American camps were going up at Holcomb, Lisahally, Beech Hill and Springtown, with radio installations at Clooney Park and Rossdowney and a 200-bed hospital at Creevagh. By autumn 1942 most of this constructional work for the army and navy was finished, although the

Lough Erne base was never used by the US Navy, being handed over in June 1942 to the US Army, and later to the British forces.

The heart of the American naval presence in Europe at this stage of the war was Londonderry, which soon became as familiar to many sailors as Boston or New York, and, to everyone's surprise, it proved a popular port of call. As an American historian observed, 'Londonderry, a stronghold of strict Irish Presbyterians, offered bluejackets slight recreation on the Sabbath, but seemed like Coney Island after Reykjavik, and the green Irish countryside was heaven compared with the barren waste of Iceland.' It was to make the same impression upon many soldiers, though, as many admit, any land would have 'looked fine' to them after the miseries of the Atlantic crossing in mid-winter. 'As our convoy got nearer and nearer to the coast,' one GI from Maryland recalls, 'the thick and beautiful mist climbed luxuriously upward, as if the greenness was a wall that it was trying to scale.' After the constant noise on shipboard he was struck by 'the utter stillness except for a gull or two'.

The first American servicemen to arrive in Ireland after Pearl Harbour were not the much-publicized soldiers who came ashore at Duffering Quay, Belfast on 26 January 1942, but the crews of the US trawler *Albatross*, which had limped into Londonderry for repairs eight days before, followed on 21 January by four destroyers, *Wilkes, Roper, Madison* and *Sturtevant*, which were given an official welcome by the Royal Navy, after escorting convoy HX169 into British waters. The soldiers followed, and the initial disembarkation, already described, was a great success, with everyone concerned safely in camp or temporary billets by nightfall. Some were 'tickled to death to have come all the way from the Middle West of America to arrive at Bally-go-Backwards in Northern Ireland five minutes before schedule'.

Although the US Navy remained in Ulster for most of the war – the Londonderry base, commissioned on 5 February 1942, was not formally disbanded until 15 July 1944 – the American Army's occupation fell into two distinct stages, from January to October 1942, and autumn 1943 to June 1944, with relatively few troops in the country during the intervening year. The original intention had been to send 167000 GIs to Northern Ireland, but the worsening situation in the Far East caused the numbers to be cut, and by the end of May 1941, four convoys had brought in only about 38000 men, among them the 1st US Armoured Division, whose tanks, ferried ashore through Larne, were the first to be seen in Ulster. It was stationed in South Down, with headquarters at Castlewellan. The 34th Infantry Division, the first to arrive, was based around Omagh, with some troops in County Tyrone and Fermanagh, while the headquarters of V Corps, with which came some Corps troops, was at Brownlow House, Lurgan.

During the summer of 1942 these troops engaged in large-scale manoeuvres with the British Army, though, tactfully, each side fielded an Allied force: it was not, officially at least, Yanks versus British. In September and October 1942 almost all the first arrivals moved on to North Africa, and it was not until the second week of October 1943 that the American Army returned to Ulster in strength. Then it arrived in a flood. Within two months a Corps Headquarters, with supporting troops, four divisions – three infantry and one airborne – and a large US Air Force contingent, poured into Ulster, to disappear almost as suddenly between February and June 1944. In between, wrote a local historian, 'to the people of Northern Ireland the Americans appeared to be everywhere. . . . Every inch of accommodation in camps, barracks and hotels was taken up by them.'

During 'the wet and dismal winter of 1943', to quote the same observer, the GIs spread over most of Ulster. The 2nd Infantry Division, arriving at Belfast in October, was soon established in Armagh and Newry, the Divisional Headquarters being at Armagh. They were followed by the 5th Division, absorbed by camps in County Down, with headquarters at Newcastle, by the 82nd Airborne, which made the Cookstown and Castledown areas its own, by the 8th Infantry Division, which settled into County Fermanagh around Omagh, and by the headquarters of XV Corps, at Lurgan. At the end of February 1944 US strength in Northern Ireland reached its peak: around 120000 of whom about one in ten were working for the Services of Supply, 20000 were airmen and a few hundred were WACs. Then, almost as suddenly as they appeared, the GIs were gone. 'The citizens were astonished at the speed and secrecy of the moves', wrote one observer. 'To them the departure of so many thousands of American troops appeared almost magical.'

Northern Ireland was never an operational base for the US Air Force, but without its seven airfields, already under construction for the RAF in December 1941, the American air offensive against Germany could hardly have been carried on, for they provided the great staging post, aircraft assembly depot, testing ground and aircrew replacement depot for the whole Eighth Air Force. The first squadrons, from the 52nd Pursuit Group, arrived in July 1942, but later went to North Africa, and in September the Eighth Air Force Composite Command moved into Kircassock House, near Lurgan. Under its direction, gunners who were soon to be in action over the Continent practised their craft over the peaceful Irish coastline, at Dumdrum Bay, near Ballymartin, and at Cushendall in County Antrim, and there was a large assembly area near Belfast where fighters sent as deck cargo on tankers, or boxed on cargo ships, were hastily reassembed – at peak at a rate of twenty-four a day – and flown to Langford Lodge for testing. Between July 1943 and April 1944 nearly 1000 arrived in this way, while many bombers were flown direct into Ireland for final examination before being passed fit for combat, or were sent back from the battle front in England for repair or modification. It was at Greencastle in Northern Ireland, too, that the members of many aircrews met for the first time, as newly arrived pilots, navigators and bombadiers were formed into crews before being sent on to take the place of those lost in action.

The centre of all this activity, which many Army Air Force men will remember – even though few spent more than a few days or weeks in Ireland – was Langford Lodge, a large estate in County Antrim, near the then village of Crumlin. It was decided in February 1942 to give the construction of this aerodrome and its vast workshops absolute priority and to make it the main American aircraft repair and servicing base in the European Theatre, a role it later shared with Burtonwood in England. To finish Langford Lodge on time became a matter of national prestige, involving several thousand Irish workmen, the building of a special railway line to transport them and the expenditure by the British Government of £1 000 000 ($4 000 000). 'The work of support, maintenance and experimen at Langford Lodge', wrote a Northern Ireland historian, 'was indispensable to the success of the bomber effort of the Eighth US Army Air Force.' It was finished, in August, ahead of schedule, and the US Air Force did not finally leave Ulster until May 1945.

By then the war in Europe was won. But when, nearly three and a half years earlier, the first GIs arrived the outlook had been very different. 'The war,' remembers one woman then serving as driver of a mobile canteen in Belfast, 'was in its third dreary year, the fall of Singapore seemed imminent' – it actually capitulated on 15 February – the 'butter ration was down to two ounces a week and it was the coldest winter I ever remember'. The girls were delighted when they were warned to be ready to meet the first shipload of Americans, and one night 'when the phone rang we girls pulled on slacks and jumpers, tore the curlers from our hair and ran to action, but after a long, cold wait, we returned to our warm beds', for it proved to be a false alarm. The real summons came on another bitterly cold morning, 26 January, when at Pollack Docks, Belfast, 3900 GIs came ashore to the tune of 'The Star Spangled Banner' played by the band of the Royal Ulster Rifles, to be welcomed with the classic symbol of British hospitality – cups of tea and cakes.

An NCO in the signal platoon of the 4th Battalion of the East Lancashire Regiment, then stationed near Bangor, County Down, had a similar experience. The special duties to which they had been allocated were never explained, until roused unwillingly from sleep they were ordered to collect rations from the cookhouse, and, equipped with a small 'walkie-talkie' wireless set, to march to the quayside. Here, half suspecting that they were about to be flung into a sudden commando raid against enemy territory – their job was in fact to maintain ship to shore communications – they were ordered to embark on a small tug.

It was a pitch-black night and as soon as we left the harbour we pitched about all over. After some time a large boat loomed out of the darkness and we bobbed up and down like a cork at the side of it. A hatch opened in the side of the boat and a rope ladder was thrown out. We were then instructed to climb aboard: a horrible experience I can remember to this day. One minute we were level with the hole, the next, yards below it. I remember jumping, catching the ladder and being dragged in by a couple of burly sailors. As soon as we gained our feet we observed blokes in strange-looking uniforms. We thought at first they were French or Belgian troops and that we had joined some sort of invasion force. One or two of these men spoke to us in queer-sounding English and after a while we realized they were Yanks.

One Staff Sergeant remembers his unit's unimpressive arrival at Belfast in February 1942, with their possessions 'jammed into two blue barrack bags, tied together so that our necks would support them. As our names were called we rolled and staggered off the ship and on to rough cobblestones. After twelve days at sea our land feet were gone and we appeared drunk.' As they were led to a nearby hall for refreshments 'crowds lined both sides of the street and they sympathetically enjoyed our sea-leg shambling'.

The arrival of the first Americans had been a well-kept secret and the first most of the population knew of their coming was the sight of them in the streets. Many people remarked at this time on a phenomenon which seemed strange to those accustomed to the noisy clatter of British Army boots, the silent rubber soles of the GIs which meant, in town after town, that the inhabitants found their streets full of young men in strange uniforms, who had materialized like a regiment of ghosts. 'The locals had expected to see them arriving or at least to hear them,' remarks a Londonderry woman. Instead they appeared 'quietly in the night'.

Before long, however, silence was the last quality most people associated with GIs and their cheerful approaches to anyone in sight, especially if female, were soon shattering the age-old peace of many quiet main streets. In Ballymena, County Antrim, so the story ran, the first exchange between an American Sergeant and an attractive passer-by foundered in a linguistic misunderstanding. 'Say, honey, what do you do about sex over here?' he asked hopefully. 'Oh,' she replied, 'we do be having our tea about that time.'

The arrival of the GIs inevitably brought new problems to the province. A woman living in the small seaside town of Newcastle, forty miles away, remembers how its residents first learned that the Yanks were coming from the erection of a large notice reading 'Early Treatment Station' outside 'two little white cottages' in the centre of the old town. The early treatment was, of course, for VD and the establishment was soon well patronized, for the arrival of jeeps bearing names like *Dagwood, Baby Sugar, Honey Child, Pancake* and *Breezy*, was closely followed by train-loads of prostitutes from Belfast.

Many of the first Americans to arrive in Ireland were puzzled, after being warned that they were entering a war zone, to find themselves in a country where the fighting seemed as far away as in the United States. A woman living in one seaside village, quiet even by local standards and a favoured spot for retirement, remembers a typical GI wisecrack: 'Gee, Rostrevor's a swell little place but why the hell don't they bury their dead?' One wartime soldier, who arrived in Ireland from Staten Island, New York, still remembers his outstanding impressions: 'Dirty floors' and 'a late-night snack of "chips" hot from the fat, enjoyed in front of smouldering peat in a shallow fireplace'.

In fact, many of the men in the first party to arrive, the 34th Infantry Division, 'came from the mountains', the NAAFI girl already quoted remembers, 'and had never been in a town before or seen a tram', but they rapidly showed a marked disinclination to walk anywhere and, with cars scarce due to the petrol shortage, were soon doing their sightseeing in a typically Irish form of transport, the horse-drawn 'jaunting car'.

The frequent absence of electricity also caused astonishment. One woman staying at a hotel in Bangor in County Down, remembers returning to her hotel to find two Americans 'vainly trying to light the incandescent gaslight in their room, which was quite beyond their comprehension. I obliged with a match and was asked to stay for a drink.' Although she declined, 'Next morning when I went down to breakfast I found them seated at the next table. A ginger-beer bottle was extended to me. Not being addicted to ginger pop for breakfast, I again declined, saying that my coffee was just coming; to which the very charming GI replied, "Believe me, sister, this ain't ginger beer: it's good Scotch!" '

For the benefit of American civilian audiences the Crown Film Unit produced a thirty-five minute documentary *A Letter from Ulster*, released in the United States in November 1942 and in London in January 1943. A popular song, 'Johnny Doughboy found a Rose in Ireland', was the outstanding hit of June 1942 in the United States, while in Ireland it led to a beauty contest to find the perfect 'Irish rose'. By July one T–5 from Detroit had already written 'The Yanks in Ireland' for which an army dance-band, The Ambassadors of Swing, arranged a setting.

> We're the Yanks in Ireland
> And we're glad to be here too . . .
> It's a long long way from home,
> But we're not the type to groan,
> 'Cause the Irish are swell,
> And we're happy as well,
> We're the Yanks in Ireland.

Reports on the GIs in Ulster stressed, naturally enough, the links between

the two countries rather than the points of difference, and none prepared
in any way for the climate, poor even by British standards. The peculiarly
persistent and penetrating Irish rain led many sodden, dispirited soldiers
to remark that 'Ireland would be OK if only it had an umbrella over it', a
comment later applied to the whole British Isles. One cartoon in the official
US Army newspaper, the *Stars and Stripes*, showed a GI standing on guard
with rifle in one hand and upraised umbrella in the other, and rarely was
any soldier depicted at this time except in mud-soaked leggings and boots,
standing miserably on guard in a downpour, or glumly watching the rain
dripping through the roof of his hut. 'Believe it or not', ran the caption to
one such drawing in 1944, showing an incredulous GI staring at an old man,
'Patrick O'Shamrock of Ballybaloney distinctly remembers a day without
rain, recorded in 1898.' The remarkably fine and healthy complexion of
British girls was generally attributed to the rain which beat constantly
upon their skin, although one infantryman, from an anti-British Irish family
in Loudonville, New York, remembers the prevailing opinion in his hut
was that their 'rosy cheeks were chapped from the damp'. As for the
islanders' Empire they had clearly been driven to find warmer territories
overseas by the 'penetrating damp weather and lack of central heating'.

Many GIs were stationed in villages miles from the nearest cinema,
and were forced to set up their own, but even those in more civilized
areas found a visit to a 'movie-house' a memorable experience, as *Stars and
Stripes* warned newcomers in July 1942:

Going to the movies in Northern Ireland is like reaching into the grab bag at
a church social. You think you're ready for anything but you're always surprised.
The first step is selecting the picture you want to see the second time. It's bound
to be the second time. There will be no pictures showing that you haven't already
seen at home. . . . Maybe you'd like to see *The Perils of Pauline* (Chapter 6:
Flaming Death) or . . . a late Harold Lloyd comedy (late in the 1890s). The best
seats are located as far away from the screen as possible. The extra de luxe seats
are placed about 200 yards back of the projection machine. . . . It's too far to see
the action on the screen so you settle yourself to sleep this one out. You can't.
No one but an acrobat could get comfortable. . . . There are some good points.
You can smoke all you want. Fact is you have to smoke in self-defence. Sometimes
it's best to wear your gas-mask. You can't see the picture anyway and if you
could it would be for the second time.

One aspect of the relationship between the Americans and the local
population which was soon to be repeated everywhere was the warm
rapport which developed between the GIs and the local child population.
One man who was then a twelve-year-old Belfast boy remembers how he
and his friends turned out early in 1942 'to welcome one of the early shiploads with musical honours. As the first soldier came down the plank we
regaled him with "The Minstrel Boy", "Land of Hope and Glory" and

"God save the King".' Another man, of the same age, born and brought up
in the small village of Mountfield in County Tyrone, slap in the middle of
one of the army field training areas, vividly remembers the delighted
realization that the GIs were 'no ordinary soldiers':

The 'Yanks', as they were always known locally, arrived without warning.
One evening there had been empty fields and clearings in the surrounding wood-
land; the next morning there were mushroom towns of bell-tents, lorry parks,
jeep lines and field kitchens. It was a day or so before actual contact was established
between 'local' and 'Yank'. It was the village youngsters who broke through the
reserve of the gate guards and picket patrols to receive the first of what was to
become the Yanks' passport to fame, 'the candy hand-out'. . . . Surprise was our
first reaction. . . . Here were real live soldiers giving away by the handful, out of
apparently bottomless pockets, candy, chocolate, chewing gum and, to the older
ones, cigarettes. . . . The first time we received those long sugar-coated multi-
coloured candy sticks such was our ignorance that the GIs had to show us by
example that they were really for eating. Needless to say once this new revelation
had been savoured and enjoyed any poor GI who ventured far from his compound
was assured of an ever present and growing following of local kids.

But this was not the only reason why the local children regarded the
newcomers as benefactors:

Next to candy the delight of all the kids was the mobile cinema. You can imagine
what a mystery and delight a cinema show was to youngsters who up till then
were not even accustomed to normal electric house lighting and to very many
even hearing a radio programme was a luxury. Now here with the GIs was real
magic; to use the new Yankee term, 'the movies' had arrived. The movies were
shown to the troops weekly in an old disused barn loft. With usual GI benevolence
the local kids squeezed in at most of these showings. I can vividly remember the
occasion of my first visit. . . . I think it was with apprehension that my mother
allowed me to attend. . . . I can remember my excitement when she eventually
agreed. . . . At the show I was squeezed in on a hard wooden form between two
young GIs and in the best traditions they kept me amply supplied with candy.
What the movie was called I don't know, I only remember it was a comedy. . . .
The projector, to rousing cheers, broke down at least twice. From where I was
sitting it was quite near, and its clicking, flashing and buzzing was of such great
interest to me that I can remember a bemused GI trying to instruct me that I should
be watching the screen and not the projector. . . . He must have thought Irish
kids dense. . . . We knew nothing of the outside world, but thanks to the help of
the Yanks, we were learning fast.

The Americans in Ulster displayed in microcosm many of the characteristics which were soon to provide a talking point throughout the British
Isles. Among them was a notable ignorance of recent history. One man
then working as a tea-boy at an American camp when 'The walls of Belfast
were plastered with the slogan "Remember Dunkirk" ' was amazed to hear

an American Sergeant remark 'that he [Dunkirk] must have been one hell of a guy'. The existence of shortages and rationing also puzzled these new allies. One serviceman's wife, living with her parents in Ulster while awaiting the arrival of her baby, found that 'they thought money could buy everything and couldn't understand why they couldn't buy clothes without coupons'. She, and other women, forgave them, however, because of their equally conspicuous courtesy. One American, who enjoyed going shopping with her, 'used to carry the basket, an unheard of thing for a Northern Irishman to do'.

Although many Americans were proud of their Irish ancestry, and had even retained some trace of an Irish brogue, the appearance in Lurgan of black GIs with such names as 'O'Mahoney' and 'Concannon' came as a surprise, until the locals discovered they were common in black communities in Tennessee or Kentucky. Equally astonishing to Americans not of Irish ancestry was the extent to which the local population managed to keep old hatreds alive. A cartoon in the *Stars and Stripes* showed one bewildered GI asking another of an angry-looking old man sitting outside his tumble-down cottage, 'Who's he mad at? Hitler?' and being told, 'No, Cromwell.' One US Army Lieutenant narrowly escaped becoming involved in the violent sectarian warfare which periodically rages in Northern Ireland between Protestants and Roman Catholics, after being asked to collaborate with the local constabulary, whom he greatly admired.

The town of Lurgan at its centre had a formation of a large Y made by the streets passing through the town. Sitting on the apex of this was a large Catholic church; down the one street was considered Catholic territory and down the other Protestant territory. It seemed this particular night a group of one faction was coming back home from a visit to another town and due to arrive some time around midnight. By ten o'clock the area was filling with people and the Chief already expecting trouble. . . . After he explained the situation I said I would be behind him and his men. I failed to mention I had already fully decided I would be far behind. I would be far behind. I notified all my men to stay close and be ready to depart at a second's notice. . . . The crowd got bigger and more boisterous and the local constables took it in their stride. . . . Finally the train arrived and the local group got off, formed a marching line and with a full band going full blast started off down the street, the milling crowd swarming beside them on both sides shouting, catcalling and so forth, till during a short intermission someone was heard to shout in a loud, strong voice 'Down with the bloody king!', followed with an equally loud and strong 'Down with the bloody Pope!', with which fists and clubs started flying. I quickly gathered my men together and we watched for a few minutes then quietly got into our vehicles and departed. Somehow I couldn't see myself travelling all those miles to indulge in a local brawl and I admired the local police for not ever mentioning our deserting them.

Later, as Acting Provost Marshal for Northern Ireland, he faced an even more serious situation, when 'the local constabulary were most conspicuous by their absence'. A GI had (wrongly, he claimed) been suspected of cheating at cards and was now the centre of an angry mob outside a local park, who were proposing to hang him – no idle threat, it seemed, for 'several men were seen with ropes in their hands'.

We looked over the scene for a minute or two, then my First Sergeant drove the jeep through the crowd to the GI, I got out and forced him into the jeep and told the Sergeant to take off. I never realized I would be in any danger, but found myself in turn surrounded and words flying to the effect that I would be as good a rope candidate as the man I had rushed off. I drew my forty-five and advised, after making sure a round was in the chamber, that if I had to go there were going to be a few go with me. Fortunately my Sergeant looked back and he had the man we rescued get out and again drove the jeep into the crowd and I jumped in and we took off.

Although incidents of this kind did not get into the British papers, being in Ulster an almost everyday matter, there was intense curiosity among people in other parts of the British Isles about the American bridgehead in Northern Ireland. Even *The Times*, whose readers were better informed than most, faithfully recorded every detail of the appearance of the first detachment, as observed by its reporter in January 1942. Unlike British troops, with their ugly battledress jacket, buttoned to the neck, and in wet weather a shapeless groundsheet slung round their shoulders to protect them from the rain, GIs, he noted, 'wear an open-neck tunic with black tie' and 'a light raincoat'. A route march was casually described by the Americans as 'a hike' and 'it may be that a more intimate and easy-going relationship exists between officers and men than . . . in the British Army'.

Far from envying them, however, British troops in Ireland formed from the first a low opinion of their new Allies. A twenty-three-year-old NCO in the East Lancashire Regiment, stationed at Ballykinler Camp, near Downpatrick in County Down, remembers being 'appalled at the apparent lack of discipline' of the Americans on guard outside a local range. 'Where we mounted a ceremonial guard each night they leaned on their rifles, chewed gum, smoked cigarettes and generally adopted a most unsoldierly-like attitude. The general opinion was "God help us if we have to rely on this lot".' The great aim of British troops involved in exercises against American units was, this man remembers, 'to get captured, then you were taken to Ballykinler Camp and fed on American grub until being returned to your own mob'. The Americans, for their part, were often disgusted by what seemed to them the tame acceptance by British troops of poor conditions, made worse by low standards of hygiene. The gulf of mis-understanding and dislike which soon developed between the British and American forces first began to show itself in Northern Ireland. A classic example of how not to endear yourself to your allies was witnessed by one officer, a New Yorker serving in the Royal Navy, when, with another American in British uniform, he visited a Londonderry pub early in 1942:

'How's the war going?' a perky carrot-haired GI inquired, smoking a big cigar. 'Still losing. . . ?'

The Sergeant surveyed us with the air of a conqueror. 'Cheer up. The American Army's here.'

'No need to worry, sailors,' resumed the perky GI, drawing on his cigar and blowing a cloud of smoke. 'We won the last war for you, didn't we?'

'Before my time, I should say,' I said.

The perky GI . . . gave me a twisted smile. 'Don't you have history books? Don't they tell you we win your wars? Hear that, fellows? It's top secret here. . . . We'll win this war for you, too. . . . When the Krauts hear we're coming they'll head for Berlin.'

This particular incident ended amicably when it dawned on the loud-mouthed new arrivals that they were addressing fellow Americans, and one produced a 'useful' address in Paris, thoughtfully given him by his father, a veteran of World War I, which he expected to need shortly.

In Ulster, too, the first shadow was cast by a problem that was later to become far more serious. One soldier from Roxbury, Massachusetts, recalls that his unit had hardly arrived in Belfast when its commanding officer warned 'that he was tired of hearing that the men were getting into fights with the black soldiers who were stationed in town, because they were squiring white girls. We had a large number of lads from the South who simply could not understand why anyone should allow a black man to go around with a white woman.' No hint of such incidents appeared in the reports about the Yanks which frequently appeared in the British Press in the early months of 1942 and which caused the British public for the first time to realize that the United States was not merely a larger British Isles on the other side of the ocean. The famous Pfc Henke, the first GI to land at Belfast, turned out, rather embarrassingly, to be of German descent, and most of his comrades, recruited from the farmlands of the Middle West, to be of Scandinavian origin. It was big news when, in March, another large detachment arrived, mainly from Iowa, South Dakota, Minnesota, Nebraska and Illinois, strange names which now began to become familiar to English ears. In April the American Chief of Staff, General Marshall, paid a ceremonial visit to his men, and British banks announced that GIs could open accounts with them – something very few British soldiers were able to afford. In May the first US tanks, guns and Army nurses arrived. In June a V-mail service was opened between Great Britain and the United States, enabling the exchange of short letters, written on a printed form, which were then photographed and reduced in size, like the 'Airgraphs' used by British servicemen. But even this innocent difference in name would cause misunderstanding. One woman remembers a staid older colleague at the 'Information' desk of a Red Cross Club recoiling in horror from a request for a V-mail: she had, it transpired, thought her GI customer had asked for 'a female'.

6

SO GREEN IT HURTS THE EYES

'The countryside was so green that it hurt our eyes.'
  – WAC Staff Sergeant recalling her arrival in Scotland, 16 May 1944.

WHETHER they came ashore at Belfast, as the first arrivals did, at Greenock, in Scotland, the main port of entry, or, as many did later, in Liverpool, Avonmouth, Plymouth or one of a variety of smaller ports, the dominant emotion of all GIs was one of relief. 'Scotland was beautiful,' one Air Corps Technical Sergeant from Detroit recalls. 'It was solid ground after so much water.' Another unenthusiastic sailor, a twenty-four-year-old Second Lieutenant from Alexandria, Virginia, was so glad to hear the anchor go down from the troopship *General Simmonds* on arrival in the Firth of Clyde that he noted the precise moment in his diary, 1026 hours on 20 March 1944. The journey from New York had taken almost a month – the ship had had to turn back to Newfoundland due to engine trouble – and two days earlier another ship in the convoy, close to his, a tanker, had suddenly and frighteningly burst into flames on being torpedoed. But Scotland made up for these delays and adventures. 'The town of Greenock', he wrote, 'nestled at the foot of a barren ridge on the south side of the bay. Everything about the town appeared neat and clean. . . . The black, narrow streets glistened in the rain like straight rivers of water.'

Looking eagerly for signs of life – the streets were empty due to the rain – this engineer officer, destined, though he did not know it, for a Technical Intelligence unit in France, observed two: 'A large sign on a low, low building near the water's edge read "Street Shelter" and a sign over a large green building read "Dancing".'

Most GIs felt an equal curiosity, among them Robert S. Arbib, a camouflage technician in an airfield construction unit. His 'outfit', the 820th Engineers, had speculated about being sent to Iceland or Russia when issued with winter equipment, or to North Africa, on receiving mosquito nets and yellow-fever injections. Arbib, knowing the current construction programme for building 150 airfields, had expected to end up in the British Isles and was proved right when the first Spitfires – the only British aircraft the GIs could identify – flew welcomingly above their convoy in August 1942.

These men, too, were delighted at their first glimpse of the 'incredibly green and fine landscape of Scotland', though chastened by the sight of 'our first barrage balloons moored to barges in the river' and of 'a freighter with a gaping torpedo hole at the waterline'. They puzzled over the open spaces in the streets on shore, wondering if they were bombed sites – as they were – while the riverside scene as a whole seemed 'camouflaged, old and neglected'. They were struck by the absence of cars on the roads, by the bright red tramcars and by the 'little trains' which 'whizzed up and down the tracks along the river, their engines hitched on backwards'. 'Just like the British,' remarked one man, 'always doing everything hind-end to.'

Their first exchanges with the local inhabitants idling on the quay introduced them to the local dialect. They were, they learned, in 'Glazzga':

'How are the women?' someone shouted tentatively.. . . .
'Yew'll soon find oot'. . . .
'When does the next boat sail for America?'
'Canna tell ye thot. Bu' ah can teel ye thus . . . yew'll no' be on ut.'

'I was overwhelmed by the beauty of the British Isles', confessed one twenty-two-year-old from Ullens, West Virginia, where he had been a departmental manager for a food company, who had now joined a unit stationed at Roseneath, on the Firth of Clyde, in August 1943.

It was the late afternoon as we made our way up the Firth. The sun was shining and . . . as we looked at the countryside everyone was taken by its beauty. It was a picturesque scene – the thatched roofs on the homes dotted [about] the hillside and the beautiful green of the grass. At that moment it seemed as though every-where in the world there should be nothing but peace. It certainly didn't seem to be a locality that was so close to a world of strife and killing. . . .

Some GIs, expecting to find universal devastation, were surprised at how peaceful the Scottish countryside looked. One battalion commander in an Air Corps Service Group who arrived in December 1942 recalls that 'from the impression created by newsreels and radio broadcasts from England we had expected to debark in bombed-out ruins. Instead . . . we were impressed with the neatness and the permanency of the stone and brick buildings.' One of his men, even more ignorant about Britain than most, 'when he heard a civilian at the quayside talking immediately yelled back to his companions on the gang plank, "Jeez, these god-damned foreigners speak English." ' Equally tactless was one member of a unit which arrived on the *Aquitania* in August 1943 to be 'met on the deck by a bagpipe band playing stirring music and all decked out in their kilts and such. Most of us were very impressed but one loudmouth had to pass a crack about someone's slip showing.' Women provided a more appreciative audience. 'The impression made on the young WACs by the "kilty band",' one from

California who arrived at Glasgow in March 1943 remembers, 'was: "Oh, what beautiful knees".' The 578th Squadron Eighth Air Force was, one member of it recalls, also played ashore by a pipe band when the men disembarked from the *Queen Mary* at Clydebank in July 1943. He was personally more intrigued by glimpsing a few hours later 'a young couple making love on a hillside not too far from the railroad tracks', which he regarded as a hopeful omen for the future.

The reception given to each contingent of GIs varied enormously. Some were not even told where they had landed; others received a full-scale formal welcome, complete with speeches. One GI who arrived on the *Aquitania* remembers that before the men disembarked a British General broadcast a message of greeting. On their subsequent train journey, to Tetbury in Gloucestershire, after 'chuffing along the lush countryside completely bereft of billboards, neon and gas stations' the GIs were delighted when they suddenly came upon 'endless rows of red brick factories with Scottish girls waving to us out the windows'. Often the *Short Guide* already quoted was handed out on the voyage and the men were also given on landing a four-page leaflet prepared by the *Stars and Stripes*, containing the latest war news and a message from Winston Churchill:

To each American soldier who has left home to join the great forces now gathering in this island, I send a message of greeting and welcome. Wherever you may go in our country you will be among friends. Our fighting men look upon you as comrades and brothers in arms. Welcome to you while you are with us: and when the time comes we will all go forward together and carry the good cause to final victory.

The diarist Lieutenant already mentioned, who arrived in the spring of 1944, has preserved a detailed account of his experiences:

At 1830 hours we left our ship and boarded a small boat which took us to the dock and the terminal of the London Midland and Scottish Railway, where we boarded a train for Bristol, England. Before the train pulled out, American Red Cross girls plied us with coffee and doughnuts. We closed the blackout curtains at dark and pulled away from the station at 2045.

21 March 1944. After a rough, cold night, trying to sleep in a sitting position on the little train we stopped at Derby and got on the platform for a stretch. Here uniformed women volunteer workers . . . gave each of us hot coffee and a bag of pastries – meat pies, cakes and cookies – a very rich and unusual food for break-fast. . . . The countryside from Derby to Bristol resembles that around Chester and Montgomery Counties in SE Pennsylvania. However, one significant and notable difference is that every single plot of ground is used in some way in England – either as a pasture for cattle or ploughed for crops or planted with rows of vegetables. . . . The green and brown fields were bordered with neatly clipped hedges and, here and there, a patch of trees with their bare, feathery tipped, twisted and gnarled limbs broke the monotony of barren fields.

We changed trains at Cheltenham and got the 1115 for Bristol, a ride of about
1 hour and 10 minutes. At Bristol, we transferred to GI 2½ ton trucks which
drove us to US Army Depot No. 2 headquarters . . . where casual officers are
sorted out and sent to permanent stations. Our quarters were in a huge, grey
stone building with high ceilings, long, dank and gloomy corridors and stone
floors on the ground floor, like a medieval castle. This building used to be an
orphanage and if that is what an orphan lives in in the UK, thank God I was
never born one.

This vast Victorian institution is still remembered by many who stayed
there, but once away from its dismal atmosphere, this officer was soon
enjoying himself. The following day he 'went into the city of Bristol in the
evening and visited the Grand Hotel for a cocktail and then went to a dance
at the Victoria Rooms'. Two days after his arrival he joined a group of
officers on an eight-mile hike along a main highway in the suburbs of
Bristol. 'We passed one . . . barrage balloon station which was manned
by uniformed women. Friendly, ribald exchanges were passed back and
forth until we hiked past.' On the 24th, only four days after docking at
Greenock, this officer received his assignment, to G–2 (Intelligence) in
London and by evening was safely installed in a comfortable requisitioned
hotel in the West End, and had discovered 'the girls were friendly' and
experienced his first air-raid warning: another American was safely settled
in wartime Britain.

Apart from the difference in accommodation – and some enlisted men
also found themselves in luxurious quarters – the experiences of most non-
commissioned GIs were probably not very different, though each tends to
remember what interested him most. Unlike his comrades, one Staff
Sergeant from Iowa, a farmer in civilian life, who landed in Belfast had
eyes principally for the island's four-legged inhabitants. 'The farms were
neat and well kept,' he observed, 'and the cattle and horses the finest breed
I had ever seen.' One man from Argyle, New York, was intrigued to find
himself in August 1942 in Argyle, Scotland, amid 'beautiful and picturesque
surroundings', including 'heather on the hills and stone houses with
chimney pots'. Having gone ashore 'by ferry to a railroad station, where a
kilty band greeted us', they boarded 'a funny miniature train . . . rode all
day and part of the night, stumbled out in pitch black carrying everything
we owned, got into "carriers" and marvelled how the driver could see in
the dark'. Finally, exhausted, they found themselves tumbling out into a
field, and groping their way to a vacant spot in one of the small round tents
erected there, each designed to hold eight men. The nightmare quality of the
whole journey was increased by the fact that, with a strict black-out in
force and no sign-boards on the roads or stations, they had no idea where
they were; it was in fact a field at Lopcombe Corner, Wiltshire, a large
camp, half hutted, half in tents, on the road between Andover and Salisbury.

The principal port of entry in England itself was Liverpool. One GI arriving there in the *Mauretania* in 1944 experienced a 'tremendous thrill', for his own 'ancestor came to America about 1779' from that same city. This shipload of GIs had a particularly warm reception 'as German radio had announced that we had been sunk' and as the great liner came into view 'shouts went up from the dock'. Equally cordial was the welcome given to other arrivals by some of the young people of Liverpool, as one woman, then aged eighteen and living only minutes from the pierhead, from whose floating bridge thousands of Americans disembarked on British soil, recalls. Her friends and herself, keen film-goers, greeted one detachment with cries of 'How are the Brooklyn Dodgers?' The chap that was leading the platoon stopped dead in his tracks and shouted, 'Hey, fellars, did yar hear that?', doubly impressed, they later discovered, because he came from Brooklyn.

A Captain in an infantry unit, arriving in August 1943, also remembers the sobering approach to Liverpool, for in the Mersey he 'counted seven ships sunk in the harbour' and could see 'many buildings . . . bombed and gutted by fire'. But some shiploads of GIs seemed to be surprised to find any buildings standing. One infantry officer found that his men had hardly started to march through the streets when they began to declare that 'all they had heard of the war and the bombing was not true because they didn't see bomb damage right away and possibly dead bodies laying around'. Before long, however, they were confronted with more than enough to satisfy them, and he 'constantly had to keep them moving as they would slow down' to peer at every wrecked building they passed. Finally, 'about halfway to our destination . . . German planes came over and started dropping bombs. None came too close to us but at least it shook them up and the men quickly lost their interest in the local scenes.'

Sometimes the Germans obligingly laid on an air raid on a unit's first night ashore. A Second Lieutenant in a field artillery battalion which had arrived in the Mersey on aboard the *Britannic* on 18 December 1943 remembers how that day ended:

It was nearly midnight on a dark drizzly night when we got off the train in a dark empty station that had no signs to tell us where we were. We were met by a small number of American soldiers assigned to us as a quartering party. They put us into trucks and hauled us off into the night. After what seemed to be a very long ride, the trucks stopped and began to unload us. Suddenly, right in the middle of all this confusion, came the scary up and down wail of a nearby air-raid siren. We were in a muddle. What should we do? Soon we heard airplane engines overhead, but they passed over without any action. We didn't know it then, but this was to be almost a nightly experience as the German bombers flew by on their way to bomb London.

GIs arriving at Avonmouth, in South-West England, received an equally

striking reminder of the dangers ahead. One, whose wretched experiences
during the twenty-eight-day voyage of the *Sythia* have already been
described, recalls his feelings as this unhappy ship, in port at last, was
manoeuvred into its berth:

Then we saw it, our first look at bomb damage – all round the area, huge
craters, *fresh*! The fear ran through the ship like a shot. What in hell would
happen if a raid came in now? We were land-locked and crowded in an impossible
jumble. In what seemed like an eternity the day passed; we were to debark after
sunset. We left the *Sythia* in the blackest night I can ever remember. . . . Only
the sound of shuffling feet and a few shouted orders led us to the train. We were
scared, dirty, sick and starved, besides being wet and cold. All I could think of
was: if we were fresh American troops arriving at the front, God help us.

These Americans, as mentioned earlier, had formed a poor opinion of
Englishmen. They now decided as they waited on the station platform
that English women were a very different matter:

From out of the blackness came the sweetest sound we could imagine. Women's
voices, chatting, tinkling voices with accents most of us heard only rarely. In the
station a faint light lit a small wagon with hot tea and cakes and these lovely women
were there to dispense this manna to us. Our sworn limey enemy also came in
women sizes, – but these were angels. How nice it was just to talk to them. . . .
We pulled out of Avonmouth full of hot tea and cakes and pleasant thoughts.

Hours later the men were roused to board trucks for a five-mile ride through
the countryside to a dimly seen barracks where they found themselves 'in a
large mess hall' in the early hours of the morning:

Stacked on trays were hundreds of sandwiches. They looked like ham on rye.
I grabbed a dozen plus a quart of hot coffee, and commenced a feast. The ham
was spam, the rye was wartime black bread . . . but that was the best meal I can
remember. We were given one horse blanket and a folding cot and pointed to the
sleeping quarters. After assembling the cot I rolled up in the horse blanket and
died for twelve hours. I awoke sometime in November 1943 at 6 p.m. in Raglan
Barracks, Devonport, a suburb of Plymouth, England.

Another man who landed at Greenock in October 1942 recalls that 'the
biggest shock', in the meal they were given in a local hall, 'was the bread
made of potato flour, which was greying in colour and not too pleasant to
the palate'. This was the notorious National Loaf, made from wholemeal
flour, and highly unpopular even among British people hardened to wartime
shortages.

An officer who arrived at Liverpool has equally vivid recollections of
his first encounter with an even more notorious wartime dish at the transit
camp in Wales where he stopped *en route* for Northern Ireland:

The meat course was large hot dogs, or frankfurter-like sausages. Having always liked our own sausage, and being hungry, I looked forward to eating with some enjoyment. Well, the first bite of those sausages and I was no longer hungry. I do not know what was in those things but sawdust would have been most palatable by comparison. . . . I don't remember ever coming in contact with this particular item of English tablefare again, but that was perfectly all right with me.

An American Army nurse, who made an even longer journey, from Scotland to London, remembers that after a night in the train they stopped at a station 'and a little paper bag was handed through the window. We found a cold pork pie for our breakfast. That was all.' Later arrivals received more familiar food. One man in a Quartermaster Supply Company, who arrived in Liverpool on the *Princess of Australia* on a 'cold rainy night', was cheered to be greeted by ARC girls 'with their big smiles, hot coffee and doughnuts. I ate six doughnuts, drank three cups of coffee. I've been partial to plain doughnuts ever since.' As the war went on a growing number of Americans arrived by air, and few crews can have made so dramatic an appearance as one whose arrival was witnessed by a Wren – a member of the Women's Royal Naval Service, British equivalent of America's WAVES – at Warrington in late 1943. As it was a Sunday morning the airfield was 'swarming with local ATC [Air Training Corps] cadets', boys aged fourteen to seventeen doing part-time training, as well as with the Wrens, most of whom were little older.

We were cycling to a dispersal site when a large aircraft appeared out of the mist and landed half on the perimeter track, brakes shrieking, bursting a tyre and narrowly missing Commander Flying, in a small van. Our job as Wrens was to check any aircraft newly in, so we raced after it on our cycles, followed by the ATC boys. The hatch of the Liberator opened and down came several airmen in flying suits, bristling with daggers, and pistols at the ready. They asked where they had landed, and were very relieved when they heard they were in England. They had apparently just flown the Atlantic and were afraid they were in Southern Ireland and might be interned for the rest of the war They must have thought that our country was scraping the barrel, to be met by Wrens and ATC schoolboys.

It is the greenness of England that most Americans now remember best. 'How green England is in May!' remembers one former member of the Eighth Air Force, then, as a nineteen-year-old from Pittsburg, seeing the country for the first time. 'Our landfall was the coast of Cornwall, destination Mawgan. I have flown into England several times since this first trip but I have never had the same impression of beautiful green that I got that day. The small neat fields were lovely as we viewed them for the first time. It was as if England put on a show to welcome us.' The girls of a WAC unit from Florida were equally impressed by Maytime in Scotland as they looked curiously from windows of the train bearing them south a few weeks before D-Day. 'The countryside,' remembers one, 'was so green it hurt our eyes.' A GI from Colorado recalls how in May 1943 his 'first impressions of England were "green". Field after field of green crops and trees bisected by innumerable hedges and good curved but narrow roads.' One British citizen, then living at Hessle in Yorkshire, largest of the English counties, remembers how 'The GIs were quite taken by surprise by the extent of our countryside. Travelling from Liverpool to Hull they imagined it would be a continuous stretch of town after town. The beautiful green lush of the fields, the buttercups, and daisies they saw for the first time, the trees and country lanes, made them exclaim, "England is one vast park!"'

But the realization that Britain was different in many ways from their own country had begun to dawn on many GIs even before they left the ship. The British practice of driving on what was, in American eyes, the wrong side of the road was one of the first peculiarities to attract their attention. One demolition specialist in the 245th Engineering Combat Battalion remembers that he watched, fascinated, while their ship drew into the Avonmouth docks to see a ''37 Chevrolet driving along a narrow dirt road paralleling the dock. Another car approached from the opposite direction. The Chev. veered to the *left*! I gasped. But the other car also veered to the left and they passed safely.' Another GI marching from Cuddington station to Delamere Park Camp in Northwich, in Cheshire, remembers his regiment 'looking twice at our first British motor car coming down the road with its steering wheel on the "wrong" side'. Soon they were staring even harder, for a dog appeared to be driving it – until they realized the steering wheel as this was a British car was on the right and the animal was in fact occupying the passenger seat.

7

DOESN'T IT EVER STOP RAINING?

'Soldiers in the European Theatre of Operations are entitled to one more pair of woollen socks.'

— US Army order, 1 December 1942.

As they woke on their first morning in England, often to the sound of rain pattering upon the tent canvas or hut roof, the first thought of most GIs was, in their own phrase, to 'get washed up', i.e. clean. The sailor already quoted from the *Sythia*, where water had been strictly rationed, remembers on his first morning in Plymouth being determined to find a shower:

It was across a court yard behind the barracks – an open-air affair in full view of the three upper floors of the tenements surrounding the walls. The women would cheer us on as we showered. . . . The air was cold, the water hot – as long as you stood in the water it was good. Step out and you froze solid. . . . After shower and shave . . . I dressed in my 'blues' and ate a decent meal . . . I still hadn't seen where we were and there was no way to get out – we were confined. No one had any money anyway. . . . A couple of guys had been outside with a work party to bring our gear in from the station, and the hairy things that they had seen in town were hard to believe. We all had seen newsreels of war-torn towns but this town had really been pounded. I discovered this a few days later.

In being housed in a permanent building this man, though he certainly did not realize it, was fortunate. Many GIs spent their first few nights in England literally on British soil, lying in a tent separated from the ground only by a groundsheet, and, if they were lucky, a straw palliasse. This was particularly true of the construction units which arrived in 1942. The 820th Engineers, to which Staff Sergeant Robert Arbib belonged, was typical. After a long train journey in August from Scotland to the village of Debach – known as 'Debich' – in the heart of rural Suffolk, the GIs found themselves sleeping under canvas in a small wood. Then, and nightly thereafter until they moved into huts a few weeks later, through the black-out resounded anguished cries of 'Where the hell am I?', 'Somebody come and pull me out of these bushes!' and 'there were vague, indefinite sounds as lost souls struggled to free themselves from some web, or found themselves ploughing lengthwise through a dense hedge'. A few alarmists, not yet hardened to life in Britain, reminded everyone in earshot that the Germans were barely a hundred miles away. 'I wouldn't be surprised if they came around tonight and dropped cards saying "Welcome 820th Engineers. Hope you get your airdrome built soon. We'll wait until it's completed before we bomb it",' predicted one man encouragingly.

Even 'headquarters types', as the British called them, suffered their share of discomfort. One radio operator in the advanced echelon of the head-quarters squadron of the Fighter Command of the Eighth Air Force remembers arriving as one of a party of about 400 at High Wycombe, already the home of the RAF's Bomber Command. 'After a two- or three-mile hike up Wycombe Abbey Hill we were welcomed by a plate of mutton stew and tents under the bushes, all prepared by the RAF. By the time we had eaten and found a tent, it was dark. All of the mattresses were in one of the tents, no lights were allowed, so I spent my first night in England using my overcoat as a mattress. Then the rains came. The tent leaked every place the bush touched it, so [I had] very little sleep that first night.'

Often the new arrivals had no idea where they were. One artillery Lieutenant who, as mentioned earlier, had arrived at an unknown spot, in a dark December night in the middle of an air raid, found to his surprise as the grey winter dawn broke that the camp overlooked the sea, but had little idea whether it was the Atlantic, the Irish Sea, or the North Sea. Enquiry, and a map, eventually revealed that his men were occupying the Aldwick Bay Estate at Bognor Regis, in Sussex, and that the grey waters they could glimpse through the unending drizzle were the English Channel. One Private from Rhode Island in an infantry unit who had arrived at Haverfordwest in the middle of one October night in 1943, woke to noises like the sound track of a British film, Welsh voices, horses' hooves, and the sound of 'hob-nailed shoes on cobbled streets'. He set out eager to inspect this peaceful backwater and confidently entered the first shop he saw advertising it to ask for ice-cream. 'Sorry,' he was told politely, 'we haven't had ice-cream since 1939.'

A few GIs found themselves plunged at once into contact with the natives. A driver in a transport unit learned that first morning a new variant on the traditional military saying 'Never volunteer' – 'Never get up early.' He had collapsed exhausted into bed the previous night after a long journey from Scotland to Lopcombe Corner in Wiltshire, but was up at daylight, and wandered out into the camp with his room-mates 'to see what England looked like'. Unfortunately, just at that moment the camp's commanding officer received an urgent demand for drivers and the inquisitive early birds found themselves ordered, while their comrades still slept, to set off for Ash Church and Cheltenham, names that meant nothing to them, 'to pick up trucks and equipment'. From there they were sent on to Liverpool, where they spent their second night in England 'on a stable floor at Aintree

Race Track', and, no rations having been provided, 'had to find a fish-and-chip shop to get anything to eat'. The journey back, driving their new vehicles on the 'wrong' side of the road through a signpost-less landscape, was equally bewildering, and left the party scattered 'all over Southern England and two in London'. The journey did, however, provide an opportunity to get to know the English. One young woman obligingly signed her name beneath the inscription chalked on one truck, 'All blondes register here,' and later 'two ancient gentlemen on a bike' stopped to puzzle over it.

Warned of British reserve, most GIs were agreeably surprised at the friendly reception they received. Many – even those from the South – were gratified to be greeted with cries of 'Hello, Yank!' as they walked down their first English street, and one remembers in Eastbourne, one of the staidest of English towns, an elderly woman crossing the road to 'shake hands with and talk to an American'. 'My estimation of the British people made an abrupt about face after one trip out of camp,' recalls a member of the 635th Postal Unit, stationed at Bushy Park in August 1942. 'I have never been treated more cordially any place.' Before long he had even been 'invited to play cricket with some English kids, and after the game spent about two hours answering questions about the USA. While the kids, about twenty of them, were grouped around me, a "bobby" joined us, and asked if the children were bothering me. When I told him that they weren't, he hung around for a while, and asked a few questions himself.'

Hardly had the first GIs reached Northern Ireland when dismal reports of the almost continuous rain to be expected in the British Isles reached those in the United States still waiting to cross the Atlantic. Many, especially those from the 'sunshine states' where even a cloud was a rarity, must have wondered if the British climate could possibly be as unpleasant as legend had it – and speedily discovered for themselves that it could. The outstanding impression of one American army nurse, who arrived in Scotland in August 1943 fresh from the 'dry hot heat of the South-West US', was of 'a damp penetrating chill that soaked right into one's bones. . . . The whole first winter seemed miserably cold and damp.' 'Cold and dreary' was the immediate verdict of an aircraft mechanic from New Jersey who reached Liverpool three months later. 'Everything looked rather dingy.' 'It was cold and foggy. . . . The buildings were dirty from coal dust', observed another airman, fresh from training in the very different surroundings of Hamilton Field, California. 'England was no place for a boy from Miami, Florida,' concluded another GI who disembarked in the late autumn. 'I looked at the dark, grey day, with no grass, no leaves on the trees – cold, damp, dreary – and wondered to myself, "What did Germany want with this place?"'

Some GIs had arrived in England believing that they were already hardened to the cold. They were rapidly disillusioned. One was a Technical Sergeant, from Manhattan, serving in East Anglia, whose unit had formerly been in Salt Lake City, where the temperature was twenty degrees below zero. 'We did not expect to feel the cold in England,' he admits, 'but soon found that the damp climate was awful. We just turned around and around by the coke heater like fowls on a spit.' Such sufferers were not at all surprised to read the official announcement that appeared in the *Stars and Stripes* on the first day of December 1942: 'Soldiers in the European Theatre of Operations are entitled to one more pair of woollen socks.'

Almost every type of building was pressed into service to shelter the GIs, from country mansions to disused factories, and from race-course stands and offices to estates of small houses left unfinished at the outbreak of war – the occupants slept four or five to a small room and took their meals in a local church hall or similar place. The commonest type of 'home', however, for most GIs in the British Isles was a 'Quonset' hut or 'Nissen' hut. Under the BOLERO programme these were erected in tens of thousands all over East Anglia and Southern England – usually clustering together on an airfield or round a supply depot, but sometimes scattered in threes or fours on a hill-top or in an isolated field. The Nissen hut, a British invention – the American Quonset with straight sides and a flat roof was slightly superior in appearance, but little more comfortable – consisted of a series of curved corrugated iron plates, buckled together to form a half-cylinder housing twenty or thirty men. There were a few windows in the sides, a brick wall at either end, a concrete floor, and, in the centre, a coke-burning stove. That was all. Washing and toilet facilities were usually provided communally in a separate building, known to the British Army as 'the ablutions', a term readily adopted by the GIs, and one can remember a hut mate announcing that he was off to ablute himself.

The Nissen hut's chill and cheerless interior seemed the natural habitat for 'the Sad Sack', the most famous cartoon character of the period, a lugubrious soul whose service career consisted of one minor disaster after another. The unofficial history of one Eighth Air Force unit, the 332nd Service Squadron, defined a Nissen hut as 'an ice-box open at both ends.' When there was some form of central heating in a billet it was rarely efficient. 'Keep going, bud, maybe we'll get it warm by morning', one GI was shown saying to another, as they sat wrapped in overcoats on a radiator, in a cartoon which appeared in the *Stars and Stripes* in November 1942. The Nissen hut relied for warmth on a small stove, described by one infantry officer as 'characteristic British. Cast-iron, smoke-pipes too small, would barely prevent freezing.' 'The roof leaked in many places, the mice and a few rats always with us. We couldn't keep the fire alive in the little iron stoves' – these are the recollections of one army nurse of the 121st General Hospital at Yeovil in Wiltshire. The PX here, as in many places, experienced a mysterious run on one commodity rarely in much demand, for 'we threw lighter fuel on the coal and flames shot up the chimney'. The GIs at the Great Ashfield bomber base would have despised such half-measures, however, for after the girls who worked in the Red Cross club had complained to two airmen who had 'adopted' them that they could not get the 'tortoise stove' in their barracks to burn the men 'went in and poured a tin of aviation spirit on it and then threw in a match. Much to their amazement not only did the stove blow to bits, the chimney pipe as well, also a great piece of roof went out, there was soot all over our beds and clothes. It took an army of GIs to repair the damage so that we could sleep there.'

The Midlands had been described by one British poet as 'sodden and unkind' and this was a description to which many GIs would heartily have assented. One man stationed on an airfield in Nottinghamshire shivers still at the memory of 'mud, biting cold winds, rain, sleeping in clothes, cold water . . . stealing coke from comrades to keep rigid Quonset huts warm'. A Technical Sergeant serving with the 392nd Bomb Group, which had previously suffered from 'the taste of sand in our food' and the oppressive heat in the middle of the Alamagorodo Desert in New Mexico, recalls how the living quarters on his Liberator base near King's Lynn:

were heated with little coke heaters about a foot in diameter and three feet high. Each week we were given a shipment of coke for each barracks and a little coal to start it with. The trick was to see if you could take a bit more than you should have so you just might stay warm. . . . In each barracks the men who slept on each side of the stove always had a cold for it was too hot when they went to bed, but in the night it went out like it had been turned off, and then they got too cold. I slept in a corner where the wind blew snow into my shoes. . . . The coke and coal pile was actually in a fenced area with a twenty-four hour guard.

There was, however, one consolation for these discomforts: stoves in the central buildings were attended by girls who 'made the rounds several times each day' and who were willing to engage in 'a little bedhopping at night if anyone was interested'.

The occupants of this base, as of many others, believed that Lord Haw Haw, the renegade Englishman broadcasting for German radio, was well informed about every move they made. It was rumoured that he had welcomed this unit by name to its new home and shortly before its first squadron of planes arrived had revealed that they were the first Liberators to be fitted with an extra turret in the nose. Whether such stories were true seems highly doubtful and if Lord Haw Haw had really wished to lower American morale he might have done better to stress how their Allies had failed to cope with one of the oldest of military problems: mud. Sometimes the fault was the Americans' own. One man working for a construction company with a contract to supply all the raw materials needed for building US aerodromes and buildings in Northamptonshire remembers how, used to their own climate, the Engineer Battalion he worked with from August 1942 refused to believe that 'they would get some rain during our summer, which was likely to turn the clay soil into sticky mud. They learned from experience,' he admits. The heavy, sodden fields of East Anglia, their rich soil suddenly ravaged by roads and runways, took their revenge on their despoilers, like the meadows of Flanders a generation before. The heavy equipment and vehicles churned up the unmacadamized sections of the new airfields and camps into a morass and some GIs stationed on them never felt either dry or clean. 'The mud really was awful,' remembers one Suffolk woman who worked on the base at Great Ashfield near Stowmarket. 'It was very heavy clay land and with all the heavy lorries running over it it soon churned up into stuff like thick soup.' She remembers a bizarre incident involving a GI who 'had one front false tooth with which he used to greet us, by pushing it out over his bottom lip, until one day he pushed it too far and the darn thing dropped out in this sea of mud. We were all hauled out to rake through this mess until it was found.'

Mud features large in the cartoons of the time and in the regimental histories published at the end of the war. In the *Stars and Stripes*, in February 1943 that famous veteran of World War I, 'Old Bill', swathed in overcoat and muffler, was seen consoling a shivering GI. 'I know mud pretty good, mate, but this sort's new to me.' At Debach, near Ipswich in Suffolk, that first winter the damp and bedraggled gangs of GIs joked that they were building an underwater aerodrome for seaplanes and that a periscope had been sighted on number two runway. The story spread that in fact this was not meant as a real airfield at all, but was merely a decoy designed to 'fool Hitler' and have the Luftwaffe dropping its bombs harmlessly into a sea of mud. A year later conditions on new aerodromes had improved little. The history of the 452nd Bombardment Group, for example, which arrived in Deopham Green, near Wymondham in Norfolk, in January 1944 has two typical examples. In one drawing an officer in mud almost to his thighs is reproving two melancholy-looking GIs in a similar plight: 'You men need boots!' In another, recalling the unit's early days in England, an endless 'chow line' is seen weaving back and forth between pools of water towards a large Nissen hut labelled: 'Mess Site: Eat All You Get When And If You Get It.'

'Roads of mud, rivers of mud . . . lakes of mud', were almost lovingly described in the official history of that first year:

Fortresses, if they stray from the runways, bog down in it hub-deep, trucks sink to their axles, small Pfcs go down to their hip pockets. English mud is infinite in its variety and ranges from watery slop to a gelatinous mass with all the properties of quick-setting cement. Grizzled veterans swear they have never seen anything like it – since the last war. One infamous station had a living site known as Mudville – its Nissen huts rose like lonely islands from a two-acre lake of watery mud . . . eight inches deep.

Living conditions were 'rugged' to use the favourite airdrome adjective. . . . The interminable distances on a bomber station that had to be traversed on foot with passing vehicles plastering you with freezing mud . . . the apparently permanent absence of sunlight – these things were subjects of universal lamentation and complaint. . . . Men actually came to take a melancholy pride in the duration of their particular cold in the head and boasted hoarsely about it to the boredom of their fellows.

Many Americans had arrived in England convinced that it was a country of enormous class distinctions, its landscape dotted with magnificent mansions from which an ancient squirearchy condescendingly directed the labours of the servile surrounding peasantry, but few can have foreseen that they would find themselves actually living in such houses. One artillery officer formerly stationed at Fort Lewis, Washington, found his battalion headquarters 'located in one wing of Arundel Castle, the ancestral home of the Duke of Norfolk. . . . The Duke was very hospitable and took us on guided tours through the rest of the Castle and permitted us to use the Great Hall for dances and other parties.' Where, as here, the owner was still in residence, his property was respected, but if he was absent some GIs seem to have protested at the evidence of aristocratic privilege all round them by doing all the damage they could. One infantryman from New Jersey remembers what happened to one large house, near Swindon in Wiltshire, when his unit moved in. He was impressed by 'the great square staircase and the opposite door with the family crest above, with a little white hart's head with dainty golden horns', but such reactions did not save this stately home.

Under American occupation it quickly became a ruin. . . . Before long it was not necessary to open the glass French doors in the drawing-room to go out into the garden. The French doors had disappeared. I walked out into the garden. It was mostly weeds with here and there a hardy perennial. There was a scummy fish pond full of goldfish which had also turned green. The fish seemed very hungry and I always saved some of the 'national' bread to feed them with. Behind the house were great trees the like of which I had never seen before. I have never seen any field-grown trees in America or anywhere else as big as those English trees. Perhaps they flourish in the everlasting dampness.

Most occupants of such houses soon realized that life in them was more uncomfortable than luxurious. One member of a Signal Service company, stationed on an aristocratic estate near Bournemouth, remembers how 'The chow line ran along a large hallway leading to the kitchen . . . and there was a bathroom located directly above the hallway. Invariably someone would flush the "john" just before mealtime and invariably water would come pouring down on us through the ceiling. There was a trout pond on the estate from which one of my buddies extracted a rather respectable brown trout.' The men of a chemical warfare unit housed in the grounds of another estate near Bristol to reach their mess hall had to cross a park where 750 hungry deer still roamed at will and after dark they always gave the great gate 'a good shake . . . to scare off the deer eating out of the garbage cans', to avoid bumping into them in the black-out.

The most luxurious accommodation was acquired by higher echelons of the Air Corps, which, arriving first and staying longest, could take its pick of the property available. Some senior commanders worked in pleasantly panelled libraries or drawing-rooms in country houses, later relaxing with their staff officers in a baronial-size hall with an open fireplace, though the enlisted men were less lavishly housed. The most famous premises of all were those occupied by the Commanding General of the Eighth Air Force, who set up his headquarters at Daws Hill Lodge in Buckinghamshire, formerly occupied by an exclusive girls' school, Wycombe Abbey. The chief reminder of its former occupants was said to be a bell by each bed labelled 'If you need a mistress in the night, ring twice.'

Incredible though it seemed to them one of the hardships some GIs had to endure was a shortage of water. One man who, in August 1943, was sent to Braunton in Devon to build assault training camps, recalls that as 'troops began to arrive in the sleepy village and we had kerb-to-kerb GIs the town's water supply dropped to nil and bathing became a criminal offence'. But coping with such emergencies was just the type of challenge at which the Americans excelled. 'We immediately went to work to build the town a completely new water system for which the villagers never ceased to thank us.' A British civilian engineer, working for His Majesty's Office of Works, responsible for wartime building, discovered that the standard American requirement for water was seventy-five gallons per person per day, three times the British figure. After being sent, in 1942, to Salisbury Plain to take charge of the mechanical and electrical installation side of a 1000-bed BOLERO hospital he had his first encounter with his American opposite number while supervising the drilling of a large borehole:

I had a very good driller and mate on the job and was making good progress when, one lovely summer morning whilst I was in the wood talking to the driller, a very American voice started to shout at us about what we were doing. I took no notice but let the shouting continue until it got a wee bit objectionable. On my enquiring what [the person responsible] wanted I was informed that he was looking for a guy from the Ministry of something. When informed that I was the guy he came across complaining that he had been talking to himself, which I informed him he would be doing for a long time unless he altered his method of approach. He saw the point and apologized, then started asking questions as to why we wanted a 40 feet steel derrick to bore the hole and how long it had taken to erect it. When told 'ten days' he responded by saying that in his country

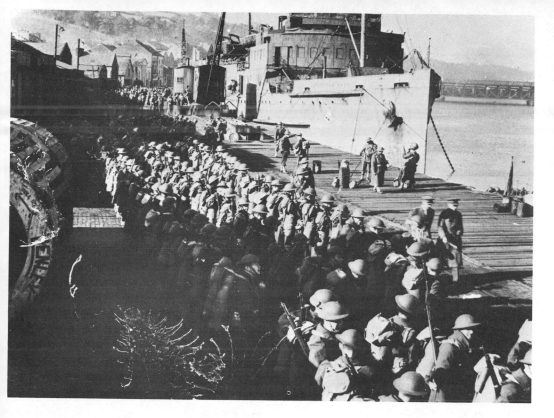

1 & 2. Arrival. Newly arrived GIs in Belfast, 1942.

3. The 'chow line'. These troops had only recently landed and did not yet have permanent quarters.

4. Under canvas. The GI invasion could not have been accommodated without the extensive use of tented camps, but few men stayed in them long.

5. In Southern England US tanks became a familiar sight during 1943 and early 1944.

6. On the march in England. Note the missing signposts, removed to confuse German invaders.

7. Morning service. The high proportion of church-goers among GIs surprised most British people. This chapel on a permanent US base is housed in a superior form of Nissen hut, similar to those in which many GIs lived.

8. Coloured troops enjoyed 'hot-gospelling' services, complete with harmonium, like this one. The huts in the background are typical of the commonest type of accommodation on American camps.

9. American fighters on their way to a US airfield. Note the trolley-bus, a type of vehicle that has now disappeared from British streets.

10. A B—17 Flying Fortress on an English airfield. The gardeners are GIs cultivating a forty-acre site as part of Britain's 'Dig for Victory' campaign. Gardening was also encouraged as a means of helping men to relax off duty.

11. Mobile Machine Shop in action. This B−17 had crash-landed after just making it home across the Channel, and the aim was to repair it on site so it could leave under its own power.

12. Arming and overhauling a Mustang. This long-range fighter transformed the air battle over Germany.

13. Uncovering the bombs. Under direction of a Major, these GIs are removing the camouflage netting from a bomb dump on a US airfield in England in October 1943.

14. The waiting guns. These artillery pieces, still protected against the sea air and the weather, were photographed in a gun-park in Southern England shortly before D-Day.

15. US armoured car on manoeuvres. The supply trucks, fording this English stream, were used to bring up supplies of petrol and ammunition in action.

16. Combat engineers during an exercise, 1944. Coloured troops were employed extensively on jobs like airfield construction and the clearing of minefields but were not used as ordinary infantry until almost the end of the war.

they would come along with their tackle and within a matter of hours would be well on their way down. On my suggestion that he was not now in Texas boring for oil but on Salisbury Plain in England and that we were having to go down 675 feet with a fourteen inch hole which had to be steel lined after we passed through approximately 200 feet of block chalk . . . he was keen to know how I had depicted him as a Texan oil man which he was, and introduced himself as Major H., American Corps of Engineers, who had been detailed to link up with me.

From this beginning mutual respect soon blossomed. The Texan having confidently predicted that, when the borehole was finished, it would prove to be at least two feet from the vertical, the Briton patriotically bet him £5 that the error would be no more than five inches. It was in fact only four and a half. The Texan paid up readily, and 'it was quite a time before he ceased to comment on the achievement'.

Cleanliness came high up every American's list of priorities. A twenty-one-year-old Chief Petty Officer in the Wrens stationed in the ancient Dorset town of Lyme Regis in autumn 1943 and engaged to a British soldier serving in Malta, remembers how at first 'talk of high living standards among GIs only reinforced our feelings of superiority'. The girls, serving in a small wireless telegraphy establishment and living in the clubhouse on the golf-course were, she acknowledges, 'proud of our toughness', but when she visited the American camp for the first time in temporary huts 'halfway down the cliffs below us' she 'was impressed by its cleanliness' and by 'their fitting pipes for hot water, then punching holes in them to get makeshift showers. The GIs were appalled that British troops there before had no hot-water system, baths or showers, except for a handful of officers.'

An even harder trial for many Americans was the primitive sanitation in the earliest camps, quaintly known to the GIs as 'honey-buckets' and disposing of their contents presented commanding officers with a disagreeable problem. 'The honey-buckets were put over a fire and cooked until only an ash remained,' one member of the 346th Engineers, used to the civilized 'comfort-stations' of Wichita, Kansas, but in 1943 stationed at Borton-on-Lugg near Hereford, remembers. 'This was within about 400 feet of the mess tent where mutton was usually cooking. The combination of odours caused many a Yank to pass up his meal.' A Captain from Virginia, serving as quartermaster at General Depot G–24, five miles from Evesham, where a British-built sanitary system, designed for 1200 users, proved inadequate to meet the needs of 3000 men, was forced to set up temporary latrines outside each warehouse, but a call for volunteers to man the 'honey-bucket' special, a truck which daily collected their contents, met with no response until 'I told the men that they could have every other day off'. The resulting volunteers 'tied handkerchiefs round their faces' and removed the full buckets to a distant field where the contents were disposed of on British 'Riley Stoves', a relic, this officer was told, of the Crimean War, which had finished in 1856. They consisted of 'large pots suspended over an open grate' and though 'scrap wood was burned in the grates, in the rainy weather that prevailed in England most of the time the wood became wet, and at one time there were about seventy buckets awaiting boiling to ash'. This led to what could have been a serious inter-Allied incident, for a British Lieutenant-Colonel 'inspected the procedure one day and found dissatisfaction with the way things were going'. The GI in charge retorted that 'he came over to fight a war not to be boiling this stuff' and was promptly reported to the Depot Executive Officer for insolence. The American Colonel in charge wisely let the matter drop: it is only too easy to imagine what the British and American popular Press – let alone Lord Haw Haw – might have made of the case.

The Americans were astounded at the low standard of domestic comfort accepted by the British, and more than one GI announced his intention of returning to Britain after the war to sell central heating and modern sanitary appliances. The practice of placing pipes vulnerable to freezing-up on outside walls caused particular astonishment, prompting one humorist, a US Naval Reserve Lieutenant, to offer an explanation: the system had 'no doubt [been] developed by some jealous Briton who didn't trust the plumber in the house with his wife'. GIs billeted on British families were also amazed at the inadequacy of the hot-water supply, for even in homes which had bathrooms – and little more than half did – a bath was usually a major event indulged in only once a week. Many GIs were delighted to discover public baths, and one Pfc, from Bridgeport, Connecticut, billeted on a Bristol family, remembers how he 'wouldn't use up their water but would go down to the centre of town' to take advantage of this useful amenity. An NCO from New York, stationed at Rugby in the Midlands while working as a Railway Transport Officer, recalls that there was 'no heat in the cottage', where he found lodgings, 'except for a small gas heater in the dining-room', though he has nothing but praise for his landlady, who 'always woke me with a huge cup of hot tea, which was so welcome on those cold damp mornings'. Her goodwill, however, and the absence of an indoor toilet, led to an embarrassing struggle:

'Mom' Taylor provided me with a chamber pot and constantly reminded me that I should use it, but I was too embarrassed at the prospect and always went outside on those rare occasions when, after too many pints at the pub, I found myself having to go in the middle of the night. But on one occasion, at two or so in the morning with a cold drizzle falling, I finally used the chamber pot. Next morning, I planned to tiptoe out to the toilet and empty the pot, but as I was descending from my bedroom, Mrs Taylor was coming up and, spotting the chamber pot, started a tug-of-war, I holding on, insisting I wanted to empty it, she equally insistent that it was her job. . . . Needless to add, I lost, but I never used the pot after that.

The unreliability of British lavatory cisterns was also a constant source of ribaldry wherever GIs met and from well-flushed Detroit in 1946 one naval Lieutenant published an 'Ode written in a country hotel to a WC', composed by a 'fellow-sufferer, in wartime England':

It's built with the greatest simplicity,
Say those who know it best,
Just one little pull on the chain will do –
The whatsit does the rest.
So after off-handedly yanking it –
One single yank – no more,
With confidence born in the USA
I started for the door . . .
NOTHING HAPPENED.

I sat on the edge of the bathtub
And considered carefully
This Anglo-Saxon denial of
The law of gravity.
Now all that there was was a hanging box,
A box which sounded full
And all I could think of was – grab the chain
And pull another pull . . .
NOTHING HAPPENED.

I pulled the thing like a sexton
With an old and rusty bell.
I pumped up and down like a farmer,
With a temperamental well.
I pulled on the chain like a madman
'Til both my palms were sore.
I jiggled and jiggled and jiggled
And cursed and fumed and swore . . .
NOTHING HAPPENED.

I'm a veteran now of the hanging chain
That grows in the ETO.
I sneer at the neophytes who swear
That they can't make it go.
For never again will I pull and pull
And pray unheard for rain
And waken the house with the rhythmic clank
Of a wretched piece of chain.

(WHEN NOTHING HAPPENS ON THE FIRST
TRY I GET A BUCKET OF WATER FROM
THE KITCHEN.)

Most houses in rural areas were not yet linked to main sewers and the young Suffolk woman mentioned earlier remembers how the GIs were intrigued by the Elsan chemical closet in a neighbour's 'olde worlde cottage with beams and open fireplaces' where they were frequent guests. 'During the nights they had been drinking they had no difficulty in filling it. The highlight of the evening came when one would return to the room and state, "Well, I guess she won't take it", then off they would go up the garden with the bucket to empty it, armed with blacked-out torches. Two would do the emptying, while the others sang "Dan, Dan the Sanitary Man".'

8

MEN FROM MARS WITH AMERICAN ACCENTS

'Suddenly the GIs were there. . . . If they'd have dropped from Mars we couldn't have been more surprised.'

– A Derby woman, recalling 1942.

WHEN, in 1942 and 1943, the GIs suddenly descended in force upon one British town and village after another it represented the biggest influx of foreigners in most places since the coming of the Normans. For nine centuries no hostile army had landed on British soil while the British Isles had also escaped the mass immigration which, from the mid-1850s, had transformed the racial background of the United States. Outside London and a few ports there had been before the war no sizeable groups of foreigners anywhere in the country. Now, overnight it seemed, there were friendly invaders everywhere, strange of speech and appearance, eager to get acquainted and unused, in any of the affairs of life, to taking 'No' for an answer. In village after village the locals listened, looked and pondered, finally declaring sagely that nothing would ever be the same again.

One curious feature of the Americans' arrival was that they were often, if only briefly, mistaken for Germans, for years of war films had conditioned invasion-minded civilians to regard a close-fitting 'coal-scuttle'-type steel helmet as the distinctive trademark of the enemy. One man from Wisconsin, serving near Northampton with the 815th Engineers, employed on airfield construction, remembers how on their arrival in June 1942 'to accustom the English citizenry to the American soldier we would go on marches through the British countryside, wearing our helmets and field uniforms'. He personally believed that confusion was unlikely for 'our marching, loose and easy, was in contrast with the exaggerated arm movement and foot stomping that characterized the British and was sharply different from the goosestepping Nazi trooper'. Several people now confess, however, to having reacted to the first sight of their new Allies with alarm. One girl working for the evacuated Bank of England at Whitchurch, watching 'this enormous motorcade surging down the main street', concluded 'for a frightful moment' that it was part of some victorious Panzer force, roaring deep into Hampshire. When this girl and her colleagues discovered that the convoy was part of the 2nd US Armoured Division, *en route* to Tidworth, they were merely contemptuous. 'We realized with curling lips that they were Americans. We were all disgusted that they had sat on the fence for so long and were determined to have nothing whatsoever to do with them' – a resolve which lasted in most cases only to the first telephone call, for the Americans had also noticed the watching girls.

A family at Headington, on the outskirts of Oxford, had even better reason for supposing that the Nazis had arrived for 'one evening when we had just got all the children to bed . . . we heard a tremendous noise of low flying aircraft,' followed by 'large black shadows going past'. On rushing out they discovered that one parachute 'had landed and caught on the roof of our house but the man was hanging on the end'. The family assumed him to be a German and were highly relieved when he 'shouted back at us in a very American voice', revealing that he had been the victim of a navigational error during a practice drop.

A fifteen-year-old Plymouth girl made a somewhat similar mistake:

One morning I saw sitting on a little grassy mound on the . . . side of the road a most oddly-dressed young man. . . . He was blond, curly-headed with a little knitted brown hat perched on the back of his head. He wore pale green overalls. . . . The thought, 'German prisoner!', shot through my mind and I hurriedly crossed over . . . when a paper boy on a bike, cycled past and called out to the young man, 'Good morning, my Yankee Boy.' 'Good morning,' replied the odd man, then to me, 'Good morning.' I answered, amazed. THAT was an American! Could I be one of the first girls in Plymouth to speak to one?

Indeed she could – though certainly not the last.

An even younger girl, then aged ten and living in a Norfolk village, dutifully reported to her foster mother that she had met a man in a strange green uniform who had asked her where he could buy a bicycle, rewarding her with chewing gum. Even this clue proved insufficient. The newcomer, the grown-ups decided, was clearly one of that most harmless of breeds, an Italian prisoner of war. One man, then an accounts clerk at the RAF depot at Burtonwood, a veteran of World War I, recalls being asked, one day in early March 1942, by a security policeman to give his opinion on a man he had detained. 'I entered the office to meet a sodden, weary but cheerful young chap in an olive-drab raincoat, with two silver bars on the epaulettes and a golden eagle cap badge. . . . I thrust out my hand to him: "Hiya, Lootenant, what can we do for you?"' The response was heartfelt, in an unmistakable accent. 'Christ, so there *is* somebody alive round here!', and the first US officer had reached Burtonwood.

If Burtonwood, in Lancashire, was soon to become automatically associated with the US Air Force, Tidmouth, in Hampshire, was before long familiar to thousands of US soldiers. Although they had already seen more than their share of British troops, there was nothing half-hearted about the welcome given by the local people to these latest arrivals. The executive officer of one infantry regiment, who himself came from Sarasota, Florida, remembers their arrival at Kandahar Barracks: 'I hadn't been there more than twenty-four hours when I received a visitition from the local mayors desiring to assure that every man in the regiment was invited to a home for tea the first weekend they could get off.'

The counties of Hampshire, Berkshire and Wiltshire formed the US Army's heartland in Great Britain, followed, as will be described, by the area further west: but few parts of the British Isles totally escaped some American settlement, if only of two or three men manning a Railway Transport Office. At its peak the number of American establishments, sometimes detachments of a dozen or so men, known by name in the local pubs and perhaps 'shacked up' with British women, sometimes vast camps containing whole armies of 'faceless' foreigners, must have run into thousands. Many areas with few combat or supply troops contained large general hospitals, in country houses or peacetime sanatoria loaned by the British, or specially-built huts, while from mid-1942 onwards large supply depots were, as already described, opened in one part of England after another. The whole vast machinery was directed from Cheltenham, a peaceful, elegant, town famous for its therapeutic waters and the high proportion of retired officers among its population. Now the former Colonels and naval Captains were outnumbered by the Pfcs and Top Sergeants of the US Army, for here, in June 1942, Major-General (later Lieutenant-General) John C. Lee set up his Services of Supply headquarters in requisitioned hotels and houses and in temporary single-storey office blocks. From here orders went out to District SOS Headquarters at Wilton, Taunton, Oxford and Tidworth.

Apart from London, locally based GI's were a common sight in Liverpool and Manchester, Cardiff and Glasgow, in East Anglia, and over much of the Midlands. There were many American establishments in Oxfordshire and Buckinghamshire, and Oxford itself seemed full of young men in doughboy caps and army-issue jackets, many of them merely indulging the American passion for sightseeing. Comparatively few Americans were stationed permanently in Scotland – 'permanently' in wartime meaning for at least several months – apart from Glasgow, but many passed through the Battle Training School at Inveraray in the Western Highlands. In Wales there were a considerable number around Cardiff and such ports as Swansea and Barry, with a large staging camp near Bridgend for those travelling on to Northern Ireland. North Wales, the haunt of Welsh-speaking hill farmers, who rarely saw anyone from the next village let alone another continent, was one of the few areas where it would have been possible to get through the war without seeing an American, the others being the more rural parts of Cumberland and Westmorland, in the far north of England, and some isolated areas in the Highlands and Islands of Scotland. By the end of the war there can have been few male Britons who had not exchanged at least a few words with an American, and few female Britons under sixty who had not been whistled at, smiled at, or been politely addressed as 'Ma'am' by some amorous or gallant GI.

This was probably the best way to discover that the 'Yanks' had arrived; when first encountered *en masse* they rarely created a very favourable impression. One eighteen-year-old serving in 1942 at Burtonwood was scandalized by her sight of American airmen.

The motley crew that descended had to be seen to be believed. They had all manner of clothes on, mainly the camouflaged variety, topped with all sorts of hats, caps and comforters (even in midsummer) and what shocked us as we stood at the windows watching was the array of sports gear they had brought with them. There were golf clubs, baseball bats, fishing tackle, footballs, and all manner of things guaranteed to make any sportsman blissfully happy. One couldn't help wondering, in our fun-starved island, which they had come to do, help with a war or compete in a World Sports Competition?

Another girl in the same locality, 'directed' by the Ministry of Labour to a job on the same vast camp, was equally struck by the 'startling attire' of her new employers 'off duty':

It was like a scene from a wild-west film. All shapes and sizes, pastel-coloured shantung-type suits, gaudy shirts and ties, but the boots and shoes on all these figures who rolled along – the Americans never did seem to walk well – took my attention. There were white-leather boots, suède boots, some ankle-hugging and others calf-length, zipped, with stiletto heels. I remember thinking my own stiletto heels on my court shoes seemed to belong to the boots of those men.

The impact of American men on British women was to be one of the great talking points of the war and among the first places where the tongues were soon wagging on this agreeable theme was Prestwick. The experiences of this Scotswoman, then a teenager, were soon to be paralleled in many other towns:

My first actual encounter with an American was when, in the spring of 1942, I was walking along the main street with my friend, a rolled-up umbrella tucked under my arm, when I realized that the umbrella was slowly being slid away from behind me. I spun round, to be greeted by a cheeky, grinning GI who, when I asked for it back, replied, 'What will you give me for it?' I was too green at that time to know what to say or do, so I just threatened to call a policeman. He said 'Okay, okay' and gave it back to me, asked my name, which I told him, and asked him his. . . . Up popped another Yank and asked my friend what she had in the oil can she was carrying. We were getting highly fed up with the situation by now, so she said, 'Rat poison, help yourself!', and off we ran, hotly pursued by Chester and pal. In desperation, we jumped on to a bus which was standing at the nearby traffic lights and which, mercifully, was just about to start, thus escaping from heaven knows what and collapsing into hoots of laughter in the safety of the friendly bus.

A young schoolgirl, living at home in Preston, Lancashire found *her* first meeting with the GIs disturbing.

It was Sunday . . . I had been sent on an errand to my aunt's house on the other side of town. The main street, Fishergate, was almost deserted. . . . It was around ten o'clock in the morning. Coming towards me was a group of GIs. Their voices were very loud and they were laughing!

I was a very shy girl . . . just about to enter my teens. I decided it would be too much of an ordeal to pass them, so I started to cross the road. Just as I was about to do this, one of the Americans called out, 'Hey there, honey!' I remember blushing to the roots of my hair and feeling helplessly trapped. Having grown up in a garrison town the servicemen I was used to seeing around were terribly stiff, reserved and very smart in appearance. I turned round and was quickly surrounded by a group of smiling faces. 'Gee, you've got lovely eyes,' one of them remarked. I blushed even more. 'She's just like a baby Betty Grable!' I stood smiling and feeling rather silly. Then one of them said, 'Could you tell us the way to the railroad station?' I managed to tumble out directions . . . ending with a 'You can't miss it!' This they made me repeat two or three times. 'You can't miss it! You can't miss it!' – they were delighted with this saying. I couldn't help but notice that they didn't seem to relish the fact that they had a quarter of a mile to walk to get to the station . . . and was amazed when one of the GIs said, 'Can we get a cab?' . . .

On reaching my aunt's, I couldn't wait to tell my cousin, who was the same age as me, all about my first Americans. When my aunt called out . . . 'What are you two laughing at in there?' I didn't tell her. It was 'a secret'.

In the village of Appleshaw near Andover, the then seventeen-year-old daughter of the village shopkeeper remembers how the roads were suddenly full of 'leisurely, relaxed, strolling US soldiers. One charming but excited GI gave me a quick hug and kiss.' Happily he did not see the sequel: 'I thought I would catch a disease if a foreigner kissed me and promptly rushed home and gargled with disinfectant.' Before long, however, the GIs were constant visitors at her parents' home; their own son had recently been killed in North Africa.

Another seventeen-year-old girl on leave from her job with the Women's Land Army had an equally startling introduction to the men who were soon to become not merely her friends but her employers. The family had been turned out of their comfortable old home at Elmswell, Bury St Edmunds, to make way for a US airfield, and an only child, the product of a middle-class home and a fee-paying boarding school, she had, she admits 'led a rather sheltered life' and 'had a lot to learn'. The lessons were now about to begin, for as she was cycling peacefully along a Suffolk lane one afternoon 'There seemed to be dozens and dozens of huge lorries, jeeps, command cars, etc., tearing along the road in both directions, full of Americans, wearing what seemed to me awful uniforms, sloppy and untidy. . . . They all yelled, shouted and whistled and drove at the most hair-raising speed. . . . All this shattered me. I thought them extremely coarse.' Soon afterwards her father was dismayed at *his* first contacts with the American Air Force; having called on the CO of one newly arrived unit 'with the idea of inviting him to dinner', he found this officer so drunk that the invitation remained unuttered.

A group of girls, working at Ulverston, a quiet market town in North Lancashire, had an equally classic introduction to the GIs as one describes:

One evening I went into town with several other young nurses. The open space around the Coronation Hall was packed with GIs. As we crossed the public footpath adjacent to the Hall, there were shouts of 'Girls!' and they surged forward and surrounded us. They all seemed to be handsome six-footers with friendly grins and toothpaste advert teeth. The impression was of frustrated vitality. They were obviously pleased to see us. . . . They told us they had just arrived in England by sea from the States and would be confined to the Hall for a week. which accounted for the air of frustration. We must have been among the first English girls they had seen. Several GIs begged us to get them some beer [as] they were completely mystified by the English money which had just been issued to them and trustingly held out handfuls of half-crowns, florins and shillings for us to take what we needed. When we returned with the beer I watched with fascination as they removed the caps with those super teeth.

Some women – it was usually women because most young Englishmen were away at war – met their first Americans under even more memorable circumstances. A nineteen-year-old Cambridge resident's first sight of a GI was nearly her last. Approaching the family car as she drove along the Newmarket Road in the spring sunshine of 1942 came 'the biggest truck, driven by the biggest black man' she had even seen, roaring straight towards her on the wrong side of the road. Since he had obviously not learned the English rule of the road, she prudently forgot it herself and 'nipped to the other side'.

The daughter, then aged sixteen, of a Hereford couple, who ran a golf club just outside the town, remembers how, one peaceful evening in February 1944 while the family were listening to *Saturday Night Theatre* on the wireless, 'suddenly the door of the living-room was flung open and three strange men in khaki uniform walked in . . . shouting and arguing with each other . . . one of them . . . obviously in pain'. The excited intruders turned out to be Americans, from a truck which had run off the road a hundred yards away and was now lying upside down after a ten-foot drop. Once the injured man's wounds had been bathed he refused to let his rescuers call a doctor and insisted on setting off with his friends on the three-mile walk back to camp. The explanation became clear next day, when the police telephoned to enquire about a missing American lorry, stolen the previous night.

To many British observers the Americans seemed to come less from another country than another world. A Derby woman, then aged eighteen, remembers when she and her friends stopped for a drink after a long day's work at their war factory. 'We went into our local pub, the Green Man, and there they all were. If they'd dropped from Mars we couldn't have been more surprised. They were different all right . . . we couldn't understand their accents or idiom a lot of the time – but we soon made friends.'

Few women awaited the arrival of the GIs with more interest, often mingled with apprehension, than those who worked for the British NAAFI, equivalent of the American Red Cross, on camps taken over by the American Army. One girl, then aged seventeen, working at Tidworth, remembers how the staff were given so many warnings about how to behave when these dangerous Allies arrived that 'in the end we really thought that the men were coming from outer space, and were not very clean ones at that'.

The manageress of another NAAFI canteen at a former RAF station in Lincolnshire, also remembers how eagerly she and her staff watched from their kitchen window one hot June day in 1942 for their first sight of Britain's tough new Allies. They proved to be 'a large number of khaki-clad men ambling along the road' and looked far from frightening, for 'they kept breaking ranks to gather poppies on the roadside to put in their hats or tunics'.

The Americans' infectious gaiety was always hard to resist. 'As good as a tonic', was the verdict of one man at Tidworth. 'For a while the people forgot about the war.' 'A refreshing change,' felt one young Liverpool girl. 'The arrival of the GIs was certainly something our drab, dreary old town needed.' 'They brought new life to a very old-fashioned part of the country,' decided one young wife in Anglesey, North Wales. At Christmas 1942, when they arrived in force, recalls a resident of Grimsby, 'the town came alive. . . . You could hear their friendly "chatting-up" of elderly ladies in the shops' – the younger shop assistants had now been directed into war work – 'see them playing with children in the park and on the beach. They talked to you with respect, they made you realize you were still female and young enough to laugh.' Before they arrived in force, any woman seen with one ran the risk of 'being mentally tarred and feathered. Within a year they were well and truly at home pushing prams round the market, charming the most Victorian mamas of their girl friends, being accepted by their families. For me and my friends they shortened the long days in carefree laughter and fun. The Yanks had brought a ray of sunshine.' Rivalling the GIs' gaiety was their generosity, all the more welcome in rationed, austerity

Britain. A Government construction engineer, already quoted, experienced a typical example while having breakfast in the Prince of Wales hotel at Ludgershall near Tidworth. 'Three young American officers came through the dining-room door having great fun juggling two large grapefruit each, something that I had not seen for many a long day. You can imagine my delight when one of them said "Catch!" and threw one to me. What a difference it made to my meagre breakfast of scrambled powdered egg and dry toast.' A woman then serving in the WAAF remembers how she and her room-mates at Swanage, in Dorset, learned of the GIs' coming. One girl 'staggered in with a large boxful of food, sweets, cakes, biscuits, etc., plus cigarettes, soap and the inevitable gum. She had gone out to post a letter and had been accosted by an American wandering up the road with this box of food looking for someone to whom he could give it.' Not everyone succumbed to American charm. 'The teenagers of Dereham were just crazy about the Americans,' one woman, then in her thirties and living near Beeston in Norfolk remembers, but 'some older people called them "b. (for 'bloody') Yanks" and had no time for them.' The father of a thirteen-year-old Norwich girl delivered himself, after seeing his first GIs, of a disparaging verdict she still recalls: 'They never clean their boots . . . most of them have big backsides but will stuff things in their back pockets making themselves look even worse.' 'Loud-mouthed show-offs, slovenly soldiers and sex crazy,' was the equally candid summing-up of one worldly-wise divorcee in her thirties after meeting her first GIs at a dance hall at Cricklewood in North-West London. 'One of them told me he would follow for miles a girl who wobbled as she walked.'

'Not really grown up,' was the terse, disapproving verdict of one Northampton woman. 'All over everywhere' like 'one great traffic jam', felt an RAF flight mechanic, returning on leave to his native Reading. And many towns were scandalized, not perhaps disagreably, at the GIs' cheerful defiance of local conventions. One Norwich woman did not approve of the airmen from Horsham St Faith who 'ate food in the street, lounged about, propped themselves against walls. I was very shocked once to see two or three actually sitting on the pavement.' The solid citizens of Edinburgh suffered an equal sense of outrage, when, as one recalls, they saw 'the hallowed window-ledges of Jenners, the local Harrods, actually being sat upon by khaki-clad American soldiers'.

As the American invasion engulfed one locality after another alarming rumours spread of the havoc to be expected when the first detachment arrived. The rumour was heard on all sides that many units consisted of paroled criminals, the usual American crew-cut being widely identified as a 'prison hair-cut'. Other GIs, it was believed in Andover, had come straight from Iceland, and as they had not seen a 'white woman' for years (Icelanders being supposed to be some form of Eskimo) no British female would be safe when they arrived. The local people, one Plymouth woman remembers, were 'frankly dismayed' when they learned that two barracks in the Crownhill district had been earmarked for American sailors. 'My father, on naval service, wrote to my mother telling her to lock me up in the evenings.'

Children always had an appeal for the tender-hearted GI and a pretty girl wheeling a pram was irresistible. To the carload of Americans driving along the road from Kelvedon to Coggeshall in Essex one day in 1942 the sight of a sixteen-year-old girl and 'another young nurse taking some twenty-four children for a walk' proved impossible to ignore. 'We had two prams with four children in each and sixteen children walking,' one of the nurses employed by the famous Dr Barnardo's Children's Home, then evacuated from London, remembers. 'An astonished crew of Americans pulled up and asked to whom the children belonged. Thinking of our Homes as a universal household word we said, "Dr Barnardo". A look of sheer disbelief came over their faces and one of the men said, "Gee, your local doctor must be some man!"'

9
WORKING FOR THE YANKEE DOLLAR

'The work was being done with typical American hustle.'

– The Times, *June 1942.*

BECAUSE they usually saw them off-duty, most British civilians found it hard to believe that the GIs worked at all. Their casual discipline, their vast capacity to enjoy themselves, treating life as a permanent party, made them at first appear more as licensed entertainers, sent to relieve the grey tedium of wartime life in a besieged island, than as serious soldiers. The British never really understood that the average American tackled whatever he was doing – earning a living, pursuing a girl, relaxing – in top gear, but that he drew a sharp line between work and pleasure, visibly reflected in his change of clothes. While the British soldier had to 'walk out' in the unbecoming battledress and weighty boots in which he spent the day the GI changed once work was done into a totally different outfit, leaving behind with his discarded 'fatigues' or combat overalls all thoughts of the day's labours. Of the hundreds of civilians who entertained GIs, or even had them billeted in their homes, very few ever discovered exactly how their guests spent the working day. Reluctance to talk about their military duties was wrongly ascribed to the GIs being 'security-minded'; the truth was that to an American, work and leisure belonged to two different worlds.

One Hampshire woman who found herself, in her early thirties, working as a driver at Tidworth realized that 'The GIs seemed obsessed with SPEED. They would drive up to my HQ at full steam only to brake at the entrance in a cloud of dust and scream of tyres, and before the engine's fly wheel had ceased revolving the dispatch rider would be halfway up the steps of the building, to deliver what would, as likely as not, be of minor consequence and seldom urgent.' The chief result of this frenzied and unnecessary activity was to waste precious petrol, which in the US Army 'flowed on all sides', but, she realized, 'Every man must be seen to be "right on the ball".'

If a vehicle had pulled up carelessly or blocked oncoming traffic the GI behind would not hesitate to overtake, even if it meant bumping up on a grass bank or knocking down anything in the way . . . [The Americans] made a shambles of Tidworth in their first winter: with the garrison roads a sea of slush and the one-time neat grass edges rutted by the wheels of the enthusiastic GIs. In contrast, Bulford, the next army establishment, run by the British, was immaculate.

A Richmond, Surrey, woman – whose own days were fully filled with a job, serving as part-time Air Raid Warden, caring for her young son, and helping at the Milestone Club in Kensington – remembers an all-too-typical encounter:

During intervals of quiet I was busy knitting socks for my elder son, then in the Italian campaign. A young American watched for some time and then he approached my desk and said, 'Say, are those for anyone special?' I explained. His surprise was great. 'You got a son? In Italy? Gee, I didn't know you had an army there.' I . . . pointed out that nearly every woman in the Club – indeed in the country – had someone in the Forces. He scratched his head. 'But I ain't seen no stars in no windows,' he remarked, puzzled. . . . I then learned of the habit that would seem so sentimental and unnecessary to us . . . of displaying in the window of an American home, one paper star for each member of the family serving in the Forces. This lad – and how many like him, I wonder? – had completely discounted Britain's war effort because instead of paper stars our windows were stuck with protective netting. He was mightily impressed, and said he would sure pass the word on.

The British were impressed from the first by the dedicated energy with which the GIs tackled any job. 'The work of unloading', *The Times* reported enthusiastically, when the first freighter loaded solely with supplies for the American forces arrived in June 1942, 'was being done with typical American hustle' and the result 'seemed likely to break recent records in the turn-round of ships in this port.' The reporter was particularly impressed that as each brand-new lorry was lifted ashore it was filled with petrol and oil, stacked with the cargo which had arrived with it, and sent rolling on its way with no more formality than having 'OK' chalked on its side. Before long at Hull it took only two minutes twenty-eight seconds from the time a truck touched down on British soil for it to be driving off under its own power.

One example of the efficiency which made the American Army so much more formidable than its critics supposed was witnessed by a then schoolboy at Wimbourne, in Dorset, in the pre D-Day period:

Because of a mistake a large convoy of DUKWs [amphibious landing craft] turned up in Wimborne. The streets were very narrow and winding. A Dodge one-tonner arrived at a corner in one of these streets and an American officer got out with three men. They looked about them and went into a shoe shop on the bend. The men helped the ladies in the shop clear it out. They then went across the road and repeated the same thing in a stationers. The Dodge then backed up and went away. A few minutes later a DUKW came round the corner and, without even slowing, went straight into the front of the shoe shop; it then backed into the stationers and pulled round the corner. This DUKW was followed by a large number of others. Each one repeated the operation – inch perfect – all controlled by a GI casually waving a lethargic paw. At the end came two lorries full of Negro troops. The trucks stopped and the men jumped out. They were all over the two shops, under command of a shouting Master Sergeant. . . . The shops were refitted completely, even down to painting and the whole job was done in a couple of hours by about twenty men on each shop.

GIs who had to work alongside, and sometimes direct, British workmen often found the experience disillusioning. One US Captain, involved in building the 'G' depot at Honeybourne near Evesham, was shocked that the British labour force 'had tea breaks twice a day and worked each week to Saturday noon'. It hardly surprised him that, on his being ordered to build a camp to hold 800 PoWs, the British proved unable to supply the poles required. American resourcefulness speedily found a way, for he constructed 'a fine stockade . . . with a double fence interlaced with barbed wire,' from '300 poles that were to be used as football goal posts'. One Ordnance Sergeant, in charge of a mixed British civilian and American army team carrying out wiring work in air force barracks in East Anglia, was 'amazed at the outdated equipment and material that was used. Back home in Philadelphia we had stopped using two wire systems long ago.' But he was even more shocked at the slow pace of his civilian craftsmen. 'The general reaction of many Americans to the British people was,' he admits, 'If they'd forget the damn tea and crumpets in the middle of the afternoon, wake up and get moving, we wouldn't have to fight their war for them.'[1] A woman working at a US Army documentation centre at Duke Street in the West End remembers equal amazement being caused one afternoon soon after D-Day when she 'went twice for a cup of tea. . . . The Sergeant opposite remarked in sarcastic reprimand, "You folks over here sure do like that stuff",' while 'one chap at the desk said that San Francisco was the biggest trade union city in the world but that no union would stand for staff who went out twice in one afternoon for tea'. 'Our workday opened my eyes to British workmen,' admits one Eighth Air Force Technical Sergeant, employed on sorting maps at High Wycombe for dispatch to American airfields. 'I started at 9 a.m. and at 10 to 1030 we had tea. They furnished the tea, so I felt I should do something . . . so I went to a little nearby bakery and bought cakes . . . I took off to lunch at 12, where they usually left at 1, but they didn't want to upset my normal schedule so they

---

1. 'Crumpets', so often linked with tea in GI's memories, were in fact only eaten in the summer and at home or in a teashop. They would certainly have seemed out of place on a construction site.

told me to go ahead at 12, but to stay gone till 2, when they got back. Then at 3 to 3.30 we had tea again. At 4.30 we got the place cleaned up and we left shortly before 5. It wasn't a hard day.'

But some British workers found themselves forced to adapt instead to the American work tempo. 'Can't we go any faster?' the Colonel in charge of railway transport would demand of the British driver of one of the engines which chugged about the supply base at Tidworth. 'I'd say we were going full out,' this man remembers, and he would say, 'Hell, we shall never win the war like this.' 'If he thought we were doing well he would give men and the fireman a cigar each.'

The British fireman (i.e. driver's mate who stoked the boilers) of an American-operated hospital train found similar encouragement from the Major in command, whose leadership 'made us really do our best even when things got rough'. He 'donned overalls on one trip, took a share of the firing and finished up saying "Now I know who does the work",' remarking that the driver handled the brake handle ' "like a surgeon's knife". Could you wonder why we liked the guy? And could you picture an English commanding officer doing this?'

'Great fun but kept at it,' was the verdict of one forty-two-year-old housewife who went to work in the American army post office at Sutton Coldfield in the Midlands. Notices and loudspeaker announcements constantly urged on the clerks to greater efforts in readdressing GIs' mail, with reminders of the greatest number of letters so far handled in a day. As the soldiers in charge threw new bundles down the long trestle tables 'they kept shouting, "Beat the record, girls" '. The only light relief came when a letter bearing some particularly odd American name appeared, for 'one of the girls collected same, so we would shout out, "Ann, take this down!" '

A twenty-one-year-old shorthand typist working near Beer in Devonshire who volunteered for the WRNS, found herself offered instead the choice of joining the ATS as a fourteen shillings a week cook or the Americans as a £5 a week secretary. 'Without a moment's hesitation I said, "I'll take that",' she remembers, 'and on the 14 November 1942, armed only with a railway warrant and no other information, I travelled up to Cheltenham wondering whatever I had let myself in for.' Her arrival 'about 8 p.m. on a cold and murky evening on a deserted station', did nothing to raise her spirits but she was rescued by a lone GI, who turned out to be General Lee's driver, and found her transport to 'The Garth' a beautiful private house in Eldorado Road, Cheltenham . . . commandeered by the US Army'. Here she was 'warmly welcomed by the Warden, introduced to a number of girls who had arrived earlier that day . . . given a delicious meal and was soon sitting chatting', a reception she would assuredly not have received in the ATS.

The following day at 8 a.m. we were transported to the Services of Supply, at Benhall Farms, [a] complex of one-storey buildings formerly part of the British War Office. After a short form-filling session at the Personnel Office, another inmate of The Garth and myself were told to go into a room where we would be interviewed by a Captain who required two stenographers . . . and looked at us . . . as if he were at a horse sale. He then said to me 'How do you spell "aluminium"?' (pronounced by him of course, as 'aloominum'). My reply apparently satisfied him that I was a competent stenographer as he said, 'OK, you'll do,' and then, pointing to my new friend, Joyce, he remarked, 'and you'll be the other.' By mid-morning we were in a car being taken to the other US army headquarters in Cheltenham, Oakley Farms.

This girl, who was to stay with the Americans for three years, in Cheltenham and London, began work at the Post Quartermaster's office, responsible for issuing and delivering rations to local hotels taken over as officers' billets, and soon found that 'a happy atmosphere prevailed in this office. There was rejoicing when a GI got an extra stripe, and we would feel honoured to sew it on his tunic. We saw countless photos of their wives and girl friends in the States, and quickly we became "one happy family". I think,' sums up this observer, 'the GIs stationed in Cheltenham from 1942 to 1944 were as content as any serving soldiers could be on foreign soil – and they appreciated it. The people of Cheltenham liked them, the town was beautiful in all seasons of the year, and before we left it seemed as if we'd all been there for a very long time.'

One quality valued by all who worked for the Americans was the lack of 'stuffiness' and rank-consciousness of even senior officers. A woman telephone engineer, sent with a man who was teaching her the trade to fit an extension telephone in a large house in Birmingham taken over by the American Army, remembers a typical encounter:

I had been grubbing along a long passage on my knees all morning fixing wiring and was not feeling at my best, when word was sent to us that the American Colonel had invited us to have dinner with him . . . I felt very mixed about this in my grubby overall and slacks! However, when the time came an officer was sent to escort us across the road to another large house. The Colonel was waiting in the drive entrance for us and a very charming and courteous man he was too. When we entered the large dining-room to my horror there were about a dozen officers sitting at the table. They all stood up and the Colonel introduced them one by one. So there I sat, one slightly grubby female and certainly not looking my best for such an occasion. I cannot imagine . . . an English Colonel making a gesture such as that, just for two telephone engineers.

The British woman driver at Tidworth, quoted earlier, remembers the end of her first day's work for another US Colonel, which was, she knew (her father was an Admiral), very different from the way in which a British senior officer would have behaved:

I stood alongside my staff car with a smart salute as he got out. He stared at me and in a gruff voice that shook me to the core he said, 'I'm afraid we are not going to get along.' I stammered my apologies and realised where I'd blundered. Then he gave a broad grin, tapped me on the shoulder and departed with 'See you tomorrow . . . and don't you fail me – I'm counting on it. Good night.'

10

A LITTLE PRIVATE WAR

'We had our own little World War II going on.'

– American sailor, recalling Plymouth, 1942.

RELATIONS between the GI and the civil population were cordial from the first, but when the first GIs arrived, in early 1942, they were as yet 'unblooded' by combat, and many barely troubled to conceal their opinion that the British Army's long run of defeats had been due to incompetence, or worse. The story of the GI said to have asked for a pint of beer 'as quickly as the British got out of Dunkirk' was widely quoted, though not the riposte 'Is that how the Yanks swam at Pearl Harbour?' – shouted by British soldiers as they hurled the offenders into the nearest river. No doubt such insults were exchanged on occasion. There *were* Americans who made remarks like 'The English always have to have Yanks to win their wars,' though one who said this in a pub in Chelmsford was, as an eye-witness remembers, 'silenced by an RAF man who asked, "I say, old boy, did you win the Battle of Britain?"' This famous victory was invoked so often that even well-disposed Americans became irritated at being reminded of it, and among US airmen 'the Battle of Britain' meant their own campaign against British girls. When 'There'll Always Be An England' was played over the radio in the mail forwarding centre near Sutton Coldfield, the GIs would remark to the British women clerks, 'Sure, so long as we're there to keep it for you,' until this became a jocular catch-phrase. While an atmosphere of goodwill soon surrounded the GIs in their dealings with British civilians the hostility between the servicemen of the two countries, especially at the lower levels, was soon both obvious and notorious.

Eventually an attempt was made to reduce misunderstandings between the two armies by arranging exchange visits between British and American soldiers, but these seem to have strengthened existing prejudices rather than removed them. 'Cases occurred,' noted one scandalized British observer, 'of enlisted men addressing NCOs by their surnames only. . . . There was an amazing lack of discipline in the British Army sense.' This eyewitness was impressed by the 'hotwater supply and scrupulously clean huts', and one potent cause of trouble was helpfully examined: the GIs acknowledged that their rates of pay were high, but pointed out that 'they sent a lot home',[1] and that the scales were geared to the much higher cost of living in the United States.

Although it did not appear in any official report, the type of incident which made Americans despair of the British Army was this telephone-answering ritual, observed in Northern Ireland by one American Captain from Maryland.

One day I visited the British Fire Fighting Unit to make arrangements to have my men trained in handling British fire-fighting equipment. . . . I entered a small room and walked up to a very small counter-like affair behind which were crowded a British Sergeant-Major, a Sergeant and a Corporal. . . . Several pads of paper, pencils and a telephone were sitting on the counter at one end which happened to be occupied by the Sergeant-Major. Salutes were exchanged and I introduced myself and we were warming up to our subject when the phone rang. An immediate pushing and struggling with sucking-in of breath began so that the Corporal, who was at the opposite end of the counter, could squeeze past and answer. . . . He put the phone down, again struggled back to his original place behind the counter, and then, and only then, did he say to the Sergeant, 'A phone call for the Sergeant-Major.' The Sergeant in turn advised the Sergeant-Major of this fact. I don't suppose I shall forget that struggling back and forth by these three men till the day I die.

Much of the hostility of the British forces to the Yanks was undoubtedly based on mere envy. There was, though this was rarely admitted, a sour, disgruntled spirit among most British servicemen, many of whom had been left to rot in unemployment before the war and knew very well that few politicians now cared much about their well-being. Until the GIs began to arrive in 1942 British soldiers had regarded squalid conditions, petty tyranny, coarse clothes, poverty-stricken dependants and an insultingly low rate of pay as the inevitable consequence of being unlucky enough to be called up. The arrival of the Americans proved that none of this was necessary, and though the real culprits were the British Government, it was easier to blame the Americans for being better off. The GI in turn, not realizing his own good fortune, tended to despise, rather than sympathize with, the British soldier for putting up with conditions and, above all, pay which would have had the average American unit in a state of mutiny and every senator from Maine to California in full voice.

The ill-feeling between the two armies was remarked on by many observers. A Wren serving near Glasgow discovered that 'while the GIs would do anything for us girls, they had no time for British servicemen'. Another Wren, at Warrington, discovered that 'in the Western Approaches

---

1. This was true. In April 1942 US troops in the United Kingdom drew 26 per cent of their pay, remitted 49 per cent to their families, and allotted 25 per cent to buy War Bonds or other savings.

area, many of our sailors were bitter about the Americans. They had been in the Mediterranean and North Africa in the thick of the war. Returning home they found their girl friends and some wives had gone over to the Americans. One matelot was so sour about this happening, we could hardly get a civil word out of him for months.'

Further west, at Plymouth, a newly arrived American sailor, who already detested the Limeys, as mentioned in an earlier chapter, for the way British merchant seamen had exploited their passengers on the voyage to Britain, found that his unit was confined to camp for several days on their arrival in 1943. 'They only let us loose with orders to avoid certain sections of town because of friction between Allied personnel. Americans, Brazilians, New Zealanders were all based here and we had our own little World War II going on.'

British sailors, who tended like those of every nation to drink too much after coming ashore, frequently started the trouble. A GI stationed at Bristol recalls how one inoffensive man came back to barracks one night badly beaten up, after a totally unprovoked assault by two English sailors. Retaliation was swift, if wrongly directed. 'My buddy . . . a pretty tough guy from Brooklyn . . . went into town the next night and came back with nine English sailor hats and threw them on John's bunk and said that should even the score.'

One Flight Engineer serving with the 333rd Bomb Squadron of the 94th Bombardment Group, at Rougham, near Bury St Edmunds, Suffolk, found that the RAF 'were jealous of our daylight bombing raids' and called the American airmen 'big show-offs, etc.', a particularly unjust accusation in his case since he had already been wounded in action.

On one occasion four men from my crew and I were having a pint in a pub and were outnumbered by RAF blue uniforms. They tried to pick a fight by bumping me whenever I tried to take a drink, made snide remarks, etc., but we wouldn't bite. One fellow who stood behind me at the bar (also in RAF blue) told me to stand fast and not let them egg me into anything. Since I would not give the bloke (who was trying to provoke me) the satisfaction of starting some-thing, he announced, for all to hear, that he and his pals would wait for us outside and do us in proper. At this the chap behind me took one step away from the bar and called his Flight to attention. More than half of the men in blue snapped to. The Flight-Sergeant told the bully to take his 'Limey crew' and head back to their billets before he and his 'Cannucks' (the Canadians) splattered the cobble-stones with them. They fled into the night and were no more to be seen.

The GIs' protectors then 'told us they were discriminated against almost as bad as the Yanks. . . . They told of some merchants, NAAFIs, etc., that refused them service because they didn't wear British uniforms. Some expressed the hope that when the war was over the US would give England all her conquered lands and let Canada join the United States.'

A Suffolk woman living at Elmswell, near Bury St Edmunds, remembers an unpleasant incident at a village dance attended by GIs from Great Ashfield who went to see what they could pick up in the way of girls' Instead, they acquired a crop of bruises; 'what they didn't know was that the Black Watch were billeted in a large house and park in the village'. The resulting fight only ended when 'a fleet of ambulances were sent over' to collect the badly beaten-up GIs. One Second Lieutenant from Rhode Island remembers a similar incident that ended less peacefully, at Little-hampton, a decorous, minor seaside resort in Sussex, in 1944. His men had organized a dance and

made arrangements for the required number of English girls to be in attendance. It was by intention an all-American affair so far as the hosts were concerned, but during the evening, some men from a British commando unit stationed nearby tried to gain admission. When they were restrained from entering, they upset some of our trucks, slashed some tyres and put sand in the carburettors. The next day there were rumours of reprisals from both sides. However, nothing came of it other than we had to obtain replacement trucks in an unusually short time to be ready to go in the invasion.

Although the Allied failure at Arnhem in September 1944 was, as we now know, due to a combination of bad luck and command errors, the British airborne forces blamed the Americans, quite unjustly, because some of the supplies dropped to them by Dakotas had fallen short. One post woman remembers the arrival of some of these embittered men in Newbury, the nearest town to the airfield at Greenham Common from which many of the paratroopers had come.

One day I went into the post office and saw some Red Beret paratroopers. I flew down to the sorting office. 'Girls, girls!' I shouted. 'British men!' We rushed up to the public counters only to recoil in a puzzled daze. The eyes of these men were the eyes of those returned from hell. They had come to that air base with the express intention of killing one American for every one of their mates lost at Arnhem. That night the feeling in the dark streets was one of absolute quiet and fear. Knots of men stalked about. They didn't even see the women. They were crazed to kill. American military police combed the pubs and cinemas and every GI was hustled back to base. The British MPs came and hustled the Red Berets off. I heard of only one – not fatal – knifing in a pub.

The American dislike of British troops, however, did not extend to servicewomen – though one wartime ATS girl has never forgiven the 'full-blooded Indian boy' she danced with in Taunton, who 'much to my disgust thought me a bus-conductor'. They also had a particular admiration for the Women's Land Army. 'My WLA red and rough hands,' remembers one woman from Cornwall, 'evoked as much sympathy as though I had lost an arm in battle.' Another landgirl recalls how 'One miserably cold wet night, as I was crossing Worcester, and standing for a moment by the kerb, I had a flower pinned to my lapel and a big kiss off a tall American who told me it represented his country's thanks for my war efforts.' One other reason for the popularity of British women was no doubt the lack of the home-grown variety. It was not until May 1943 that the first members of the Women's Army Corps arrived. 'Eleven American girls', reported the *Stars and Stripes*, 'looked out of their sleeping-car windows on the grey morning landscape. One of them said: "Isn't England cute?" and fell to lipstick and powder drill.' This first tiny contingent of six officers and five enlisted women was expected to be the advance guard of a far larger force – but the reporter revealed, 'they wear cotton stockings so as not to make English girls anxious' and their 'jersey slips and panties are olive drab so that . . . if a WAC slips all you see is one colour.'[1]

Like the 'first' GI to land in Ireland, the first WACs to reach England had been preceded by others, five WAAC officers having arrived in December 1942 to serve as senior secretaries, though they had barely disembarked before being sent on to North Africa. Although both the Eighth Air Force and the army asked for WACs to be sent to Britain, they were given such a low priority that it was not until 16 July 1943 that the first battalion of 555 enlisted women and 194 officers – volunteers like all WACs – landed in England and were assigned to various air force stations.

Although General Eaker had originally expressed surprise that 'military secrets were going to have to be kept by women', he soon admitted that they were equally trustworthy and 'in emergencies keep more calm than men'. A War Department memo put it more precisely: 'One WAC typist could replace two men while eating only half as much.'

Most WAC officers were employed on administrative duties, or as photographic interpreters, censors and cryptographers, while, despite express orders to the contrary from Washington, nearly one in eight became a 'personal assistant' or chauffeur to a senior officer. The most famous was General Eisenhower's chauffeur-secretary Kay Summersby, a British civilian who later became an American citizen, although it required the intervention of both her boss and General Marshall to overcome the opposition of the

1. In the British women's forces, more voluminous dark knickers were worn, being nicknamed 'black-outs' or 'passion-killers'.

Until President Roosevelt on 1 July 1943 signed the Bill setting up the Women's Army Corps, as part of the United States Army, the organization lacked full military status and was known as the Women's Auxiliary Army Corps. Even after July 1943 it was often referred to by the old name, or as the WAAC. As very few women reached England before July 1943, I have used the term WAC throughout.

WAC authorities.[1] But clothing the small contingent of WACs did prove troublesome. For several months the WACs suffered from 'bulky and unbecoming' uniform trousers and jackets which 'shrank and faded' when laundered in the field. 'A smart three-piece wool uniform', records the Corp's historian, 'was therefore designed for the European theatre – slacks, skirt and battle jacket – which was found to be durable, warm, lightweight and becoming for wear either under field conditions or in the city', but 'the War Department refused to authorize it'; it was eventually made and issued in England. Warm underclothing, for women used to American sunshine and central heating, proved essential for WACs working on the night shifts in underground operation centres and 'the issue of enlisted men's long-sleeved undershirts and long drawers was authorized', but WACs were found to be catching cold because of a certain reluctance to wear these ill-fitting garments. Eventually, a special issue was made of 'wool underwear, wool shirts, a field jacket and wool liner, with matching trousers and trouser liner, combat boots and long wool hose', which were practical if not very glamorous.

Perhaps because of their very virtues the WACs made very little impact on the civilian population. 'WACs', acknowledged their own commanders, 'were in a rather different position from that of the American men. . . . Though a large majority . . . were entertained in British homes, few of them visited these homes more than once or twice.'

'It has always been a rare sight in London', an American historian noted, 'to see a WAC with a member of any foreign service or with a civilian from any country other than her own. Almost any man from the States seemed to think it was a crime for any WAC to cast more than a pleasant glance at a foreigner, when there were so many Americans in Europe.' The basic reason, however, why the WACs left no mark on British life, despite the considerable publicity given to the first arrivals in June 1943, is that they were never very numerous. By September there were only just over 1000 in the United Kingdom, by December 1943 only 1200, and only in 1944 was there a rapid increase to a peak strength of 4715 in June. Few of these women stayed in England long, for they began from mid-July to move to the Continent with the forward echelon of the communications zone, and by VE-Day, of a total WAC strength in Europe of 7530, only a handful remained in England.

The British public did see rather more of American army nurses, who

1. Miss Summersby, by now married and divorced, was briefly in the news again in 1973 when an American writer suggested that General Eisenhower had wished to give her a further promotion and make her Mrs Eisenhower, only to be dissuaded by General Marshall from leaving his wife, Mamie. Although acknowledging that she was on friendly terms with 'Ike' and greatly admired him, Miss Summersby vigorously denied the reports. She died in early 1975 with the full facts still unrevealed.

were often billeted out. They ranked as officers, however, and their numbers – 4600 at the peak in late 1943 – were also too small for them to be a prominent feature of the wartime scene.

The Home Guard, Britain's part-time army of unpaid soldiers who trained in the evenings and at weekends, was a constant source of amusement, only 'saved from being the butt of every other joke by the GIs' coming', as one naval lieutenant put on record. A *Stars and Stripes* cartoon interpreted the organization's title in a novel way, showing a clearly suspicious father in Home Guard uniform, with finger twitching on the trigger keeping a close eye on his daughter, seated beside an amorous GI. 'Poppa's in the Home Guard, aren't you, Poppa?' she is explaining.

In view of the great achievements of the two armies in alliance it is sad that the British comment about the GIs still best remembered on both sides of the Atlantic is that they were 'overpaid, overfed, oversexed and over here'. (The American retort that British servicemen were 'underpaid, underfed, undersexed and under Eisenhower' is usually forgotten.)

Comparison between the two armies' pay scales is difficult, since conditions varied enormously. NCOs, for example, seemed far more plentiful in the US Army than in the British; while all US troops received an allowance merely for being overseas. There were, too, many items which the US soldier received free or almost free for which his British comrade in arms had to pay. The detailed tables are given in an appendix, but here it may be said that the lowest-ranking American earned about five times as much as the British Private, and an American Sergeant nearly four times as much as a Briton of the same rank. The gap narrowed as one went higher up the military hierarchy, so that a US Major, not receiving command pay, was only about one and a half times better off than his British counterpart. The gulf in earnings which existed between the earnings of US enlisted men and British other ranks seemed even greater because the British Army had a weekly pay parade while the Americans were paid monthly. When the GI had empty pockets he tended to stay in camp; when, briefly, he had a bulging wallet, he liked to go out and empty it.

One woman who ran a pub in Norfolk, for example, remembers how her RAF customers began to stay away when the GIs arrived, one explaining that the Americans' superior pay made them feel uncomfortable. She pressed him to return that evening, knowing that it was pay-night for the Americans and, 'as the boys came down they said, "Take what I owe, Daisy, it's in there";' their lavish rounds had only been financed by drinking on 'tick'. 'I'm afraid we were not always very thoughtful,' admits one former artilleryman from Greenwich, New York, recalling the day his unit was first paid in British currency. 'We made a big show of ourselves [asking each other] "Where the hell do they get this over-sized wallpaper for money?" [and] throwing it on the ground.' A Staff Sergeant from Louisiana has **not** forgotten the sad reply of a British soldier in a fish-and-chip shop whom he urged to ignore two drunken GIs who were abusing him, 'They're lucky to be able to afford to *get* drunk!' Civilians, too, were often unfavourably impressed by the GIs' astonishing extravagance. A woman living in Woodstock, in Oxfordshire was shocked that 'they thought nothing of hiring taxis to London', sixty-four miles away, and even more when a local telephone operator told her that 'they would often put shillings in the call-box when only pennies were required'.

In addition to envy over the American servicemen's superior pay the British soldier was understandably jealous of the GIs' light, smart and well-tailored uniform, a striking contrast to his own heavy battledress, thick woollen shirt and army boots, with only a shapeless groundsheet hung round his neck to protect him from the rain and, worst of all, his coarse khaki jacket buttoned on the neck. The importance of the smart uniform worn by Americans can hardly be overestimated. They made even the humblest Private resemble a British officer and hence, by definition, a 'gentleman', even though this was a concept the GIs themselves would have rejected with scorn.[1]

As early as April 1942 one journalist was noting in his diary that British troops in Northern Ireland were 'fed up because the American soldiers, owing to their wearing a collar and tie, get the best girls'. The former seemed, he noted, to have the same inferior position in relation to the GIs that the French *poilus* had had to the British Tommies in the First World War.

The GIs also enjoyed other advantages in the competition for British women. 'One of the main attractions,' admits a landgirl living in a hostel near Evesham, 'was that they sent a truck to fetch us, and we were delivered home again, right to the door. That was a luxury indeed in the days when going to a dance generally meant walking or cycling miles in a state of deep freeze.' 'It was food,' confesses one physiotherapist at Bury St Edmunds, which really tipped the scales in her Nurses' Home, between a dance in the nearest British Army canteen and the local USAAF base. . . . 'You didn't get good coffee, ice-cream, hot dogs, etc., in the army canteen, it was more likely to be bottled Camp coffee, luncheon-meat sandwiches and NAAFI beer.'

Many were the jokes that circulated about the American tendency to 'talk big'. A typical story concerned a GI overheard boasting of the size of their cabbages, only to be told by an Englishman that the gasometers to be seen in every town were what the British used for cooking *theirs*. A Berkhamsted, Hertfordshire, housewife claims to have dealt with an American who remarked, 'Hitler couldn't be bothered to take this potty

1. During 1944 collar-attached shirts and ties began to be issued to British other ranks in the army, though British soldiers never did receive shoes or raincoats.

little island,' by telling him the navy shipped American sailors overseas in packing cases – all that was needed for 'Yanks with the wind taken out of them.'

Army Cartoons

"Der I wus, with six redskins ridin' at me, and me with both guns empty."

The lavish displays of ribbons on almost every American chest provided a constant source of amusement to their allies. 'Heard of the three Yanks who went to a war film?' ran a typical story. 'One immediately fainted and the other two got a medal for carrying him out.'

The 'European-African Theatre ribbon' was known by GIs themselves as the 'Spam medal', and in March 1944, the US authorities issued figures to show that combat medals, at least, were not 'handed out with the rations'. It was pointed out that the European Theatre 'was the toughest in the world for fliers' and that Air Medals and Distinguished Flying Crosses accounted for eight out of nine of the 126 526 medals so far issued. Even these required high-level approval, while recommendations for the highest decorations, the Congressional Medal of Honour and the Distinguished Service Medal, had to be approved by Washington. As for the navy, far from being over-decorated, its 2 800 000 men could so far muster only 7307 medals between them.

The Americans' description of Britain as a war zone also amused civilians who had been living there since 1939 and had, by 1942, long forgotten a time when the siren sent them scurrying for cover. A woman working in a Cheltenham gown shop remembers how, to general amusement, the first GIs to reach the town enquired about the location of the nearest shelters, and as luck would have it, the air-raid warning – rarely heard in the district – sounded just as the first GIs were walking through the town. Instantly, the soldiers were

galvanized into action. They started to run to the right, left and ahead and, to my amusement, they began to take off their greatcoats which I had been admiring so much and which they just threw on the pavement and ran like mad in the direction of the American Red Cross Club at the top of the Promenade. Before they had even reached it, however, the All Clear sounded and rather sheepishly they came back to retrieve their discarded coats.

The female staff of a NAAFI at Tidworth were equally amused when on the warning sounding 'the whole garrison took to the hills. My Cockney friend and I,' one of them remembers, 'stared with open mouths the first time it happened, because, both having lived in London through the blitz, we had never actually seen anyone run away before.' While their brave male defenders scurried for shelter, all these girls did 'was stand and laugh, which did not endear us to any of the men in our barracks. . . . They went right of Minnie and me for a bit!' A similar incident at Weston-super-Mare prompted a famous local catchphrase after the GIs 'ran and threw themselves in the ditches' without bothering to dress. Thereafter any reference to any American activity prompted unkind listeners to ask 'if they had their trousers on.'

The Americans by contrast vastly admired what one Kentucky man, in an infantry unit, considered 'the imperturbability of the average Englishman under stress.' An army nurse from Tranquil, Oklahoma, remembers her first leave in London with a colleague in early 1944 during the 'Little Blitz'.

We got up and dressed and went downstairs. It felt like the whole building was shaking, with all the racket, and I was shaking right along with it. Then I saw the English lady who lived there and ran the billet, sitting quietly knitting and talking with some people. This had a calming effect on me. Air raids never frightened me as much any more.

The real test, both for war-weary civilians and Americans still new to living under fire, came in mid-June 1944, with the start of the flying-bomb offensive which until the end of August poured down a deluge of up to seventy V–1s a day on the capital. A housewife living in 'Flying-Bomb Alley' at Deptford in Kent, was astonished to see some locally billeted GIs 'throwing all their tins of food into the river. . . . Their idea was if they got bombed out they would have some food.' Their house remained undamaged and next morning, rather sheepishly, they were 'diving into the river' to retrieve their breakfast stores. The GIs by contrast had nothing but praise for the reaction of British civilians to this new weapon. One chaplain from Iowa recalls as he was going down into the Underground to shelter during one alert finding beside him a man who 'had obviously been badly wounded very recently. He was bandaged almost everywhere and some of his wounds were leaking blood. The sight of him affected me so that I felt faint and swayed. At that he reached out a bandaged arm to steady me, smiled, and said, "There, there, old chap; we can't have it all *our* way, can we now?".'

One sailor from Los Angeles has not forgotten his first night at the British barracks at HMS *Portland* at Portland Bill near Weymouth. 'The V–1s came puttering over from France,' he remembers. 'I dove under my bunk, only to emerge, sheepishly, when it was all over to discover that not a British serviceman had left his bed.' A young tomato grower at Deopham remembers an evening in the local pub when 'a Yank came running in . . . saying a flying bomb had just gone over heading towards Watton. There was absolute panic. "We're getting to goddamed hell out of here," was the cry, beer was left; the place was empty of Yanks in one minute flat. They were not seen any more that night.'

Not merely British servicemen, but civilians were shocked – or amused – at what seemed to them the casual attitude of the average GI towards his military duties. One Northern Ireland woman remembers how her father 'was appalled at . . . the fact their Sergeant would often smoke while drilling the men'. A Birkenhead shipyard worker decided that 'the lessons of Pearl Harbour had not been fully learned' when he saw 'a sentry-box bigger than a normal-sized garage full of female camp followers, being chatted up by a lackadaisical sentry'. This was the reaction of one old soldier, living in Birkenhead, just across the river from Liverpool, to his first sight of 'a contingent of American troops foot-slogging along the main Chester road. Their lines were ragged, their uniforms were not uniform, sporting every shade from green to grey and six different types of hats. Quite a few "Old Contemptibles" were almost apoplectic over their appearance and convinced that England would stand a better chance if the GIs were on Adolf's side.' One Manchester woman recalls how it 'excited some contempt from the sturdy hob-nailed Tommies and their wives' who sarcastically referred to the Americans' style of marching as 'the soft-shoe shuffle'. A young girl in Staffordshire was equally unimpressed. To her the first column of GIs she saw, in March 1942, in their 'pale green rough clothes seemed to sway like wheat blown by a wind in a field'. This was how the entrance of the US Army into the Berkshire village of Long-worth, ten miles from Oxford, was recalled thirty years later by one local shopkeeper's wife:

Their arrival was different altogether from that of the British soldiers. The Yanks only slouched, never marched as we understood it. The little crowd of expectant village people were amazed when they saw them coming down the village street, looking rather like a large class of senior schoolboys being shown rapidly round the zoo, out of step, with their hands doing nothing in particular. They turned into the farm entrance and were followed by an avalanche of self-propelled road making (and breaking) machinery and then by a long procession of lorries. There was a large field in front of the farmhouse and this was used as the Transport Depot. They disturbed our nights with their constant revving up. A guard was always on the entrance to this field and he would lounge about smoking, often with a crowd of kids round him during the day. When an officer approached we were amused to see that these Yanks were not the sort to salute their superiors – no Sir! – not even to stiffen to attention!

A local government officer, living at Swindon in Wiltshire, remembers the unusual scene which greeted his eyes when, in pouring rain, he passed the stone gateway of a local estate. While British troops 'would have stood guard phlegmatically, our two US friends . . . had drawn from the coach-house a carriage with one of those folding hoods and there they sat in style, carbines across their knees, with the inevitable cigars in their mouths'. In this district the sight of GIs sitting on the kerbside outside the post office, waiting for the Sergeant to call, 'Fall in, you guys!' was a signal to the locals to assemble for their morning's entertainment.

Copr. 1942, King Features Syndicate, Inc., World rights reserved Britain

"I wish you wouldn't call me 'Butch' when other Generals are present!"

More creditable to the American army, but almost as startling to the class-conscious British, was the freedom with which officers, NCOs and enlisted men mixed both off-duty and on. A WAAF Flight Officer in County Londonderry remembers visiting the newly arrived Americans at Limavady with the Station Administration Officer. The American CO welcomed them cordially, but, noticing the upright figure of her companion, 'waved his hand and remarked, "Relax, buddy, relax!" We strolled outside and a soldier carrying a dustbin passed by and called to Squadron Leader/ Admin., "Say, buddy, where do you dump the garbage round here?"' A civilian working alongside Americans in the Glasgow docks was equally startled when, on a high-ranking British visitor enquiring for a certain American officer, 'the Sergeant in charge never saluted, but turned and whistled for the Captain who was further up the shed'. NCOs were held in no greater awe, as a housewife attending a party given for residents of her village in Sussex discovered. 'Whilst at this dinner, I noticed a Sergeant stop a GI walking through the mess and point to a discarded match on the floor. The GI shrugged his shoulders, walked on, saying, "That's not mine, I don't smoke."'

A girl living at Broadwindsor, near Beaminster in Dorset, was struck by the fact that 'they were all "buddies". It didn't matter what rank they were, they were always friends. A Private would just go up and say, "Hey, Bud, can I borrow your Cadillac?" to any officer and was rarely refused, the "Cadillac" being a jeep.'

The Americans found it hard to appreciate that their own easy-going attitude did not prevail in the British Isles, as one typically democratic-minded Corporal from Norfolk, Virginia, discovered when he encountered a real 'old style British Sergeant-Major.'

There was a pub about a half-mile from the Post.... My buddy and I went there one night. The place was quite full – mostly British soldiers. I walked up to the bar, tapped a soldier on his arm and said, 'How about moving over, Bud?' 'Bud' turned around and I can still see the fury that was in his face. I was taught real fast and in no uncertain terms that a Corporal in the United States Army, did not tap a Sergeant-Major and tell him to move over.

One Wren officer, stationed in Norfolk with the highly class-conscious Royal Navy, observed that the 'US officers did not belong to any sort of "upper class". They were merely the men who were best at their job.' Equally, no GI considered that lowly military rank debarred him from enjoying himself wherever he could afford to. 'The Americans used London more than we did ourselves,' acknowledges one woman, then an impression-able sixteen-year-old working with fifty GIs in an office of the Army Fiscal Division in Cavendish Square. 'They invaded the "toffs" areas, which the general working-class public would not have dared to do, even if they could have afforded to.' A thirty-two year old WAC from Vermont, working in the Civil Affairs Division of SHAEF, in Victoria Street recalls what happened after she had stayed at the Paisley home of an ATS girl.

I invited my Scottish friend to have dinner one night at the Dorchester. . . . She shied away from the very thought of going in *there*. I told her in the United States, we felt we could go any place we wanted to as long as we had the money to pay for it. I also remember sitting in the highest-priced seats in the theatre in London along with a lot of other Privates, Corporals, Sergeants, etc., and hearing British Majors, Captains etc., in the lower-priced seats in back of us muttering about 'those bloody Americans'.

An NCO from New York, stationed at Army Depot G–24 at Honeybourne in Worcestershire, was equally surprised on arriving at an hotel in Stratford upon Avon to be told by the proprietor that 'while not "off-limits" to EMs (enlisted men) most of the guests were officers'. This might well have been enough to discourage a British other rank, but this GI recalls, 'I told the manager that I wasn't at all embarrassed or frightened at the prospect of having officers around.'

In theory the American army retained saluting but it was often only in theory. Issue after issue of the *Stars and Stripes* reminded enlisted men that it was a military offence not to salute an officer. 'As representatives of the United States Army,' ordered the Adjutant General's Office for the European Theatre of Operations in November 1942, 'soldiers were to conduct themselves with a smart soldierly bearing that will help maintain the prestige of and respect for Americans.'

Many GIs, though still reluctant to salute their own officers, tried to avoid offending their Allies and obligingly saluted everyone who might conceivably hold the King's Commission. 'We had been warned that we were to show proper respect,' remembers a Technical Sergeant from Illinois, serving with the Corps of Engineers at Greenham Common, and 'as a result we were saluting everyone in uniform, including ATS Privates and, I suspect, even hotel doormen for a while.' (Cinema commissionaries, elderly figures in peaked caps and heavily gold-braided uniforms, were often mistaken for Allied Generals and frequently returned undeserved salutes with military precision.)

What to the British people seemed a natural respect for authority often appeared to Americans to be mere timidity or servility and even the Briton's readiness to wait his turn in a queue was alien to many GIs' whole approach to life. The manageress of the NAAFI canteen serving the 66oth Engineers at Kew Gardens near London, accustomed to dealing with the rigidly disciplined men of the Coldstream Guards, remembers how the crowds round the counter clamouring for coffee and biscuits, meant that

the girls could not serve the men at the back, so I asked them if they would line up during the busy breaks. They said they were not Limeys so I pulled down the

shutters and said I would open them again when they did what I asked. They booed
and catcalled, then all of a sudden there was silence. I looked, thinking the canteen
was empty. Instead they were all in line and we never had any more trouble.

Reared though they were on Westerns and gangster films, it still came
as a surprise to many civilians to find that Americans felt it necessary to
carry arms in peaceful England, even when off-duty. One Liverpool,
Lancashire, gunsmith remembers his amazement when his first-ever GI
customer, a Military Policeman, entered the shop 'complete with his Colt .45
automatic pistol slung low down . . . with the hammer drawn back ready
for firing', explaining that 'it was no use going about armed without one
was ready to draw and shoot instantly'. Before long, wherever the Americans
were stationed, it became a popular amusement to see them collect the
monthly payroll from a local bank. The inhabitants of the small, East
Anglian town of Halesworth, where there was rarely any crime more
serious than riding a bicycle without a lamp, were highly diverted at the
arrival of a jeep in the sleepy market place, followed by 'a couple of MPs
jumping out and standing guard with revolvers at the ready while two
more went in to draw the money'.

One army truck driver from Fort Warren, Wyoming, 'detailed to ride
shotgun' along with 'a big tall Texan' when 'picking up the payroll in the
small, dinky village of Frome' – in fact, before the GIs arrived, an exceedingly
sleepy market town in Somerset – admitted 'I liked this job. I felt secure
with a loaded MI (machine-carbine) and a big, tall Gary Cooper-type of
cowboy riding with me.' A British Detective-Sergeant recollects a similar
scene at Carfax in the centre of peaceful, academic Oxford, where he came
upon four burly Military Policemen stationed around a bank entrance with
their jeep parked outside, covering the inoffensive but intrigued population
with sub-machine guns. 'On enquiring what they were doing,' he recalls,
'I was told they were collecting the payroll.'

This same police officer had previously discovered the American belief
that even in England armed desperadoes might descend upon any large
consignment of cash. While on duty at the police station a Top Sergeant
had arrived and casually asked for 'a couple of armed G-men' to attend on
the following day at the American-occupied Churchill Hospital, when two
months' pay was to be issued to his newly arrived unit. They could muster,
he explained shamefacedly, not a single firearm between them, the arms
having been on a ship which had been lost. Application to the local British
forces – the obvious source of firearms – was ruled out on the grounds of
national pride, but happily, the Oxford police rose to the challenge, for
though unable to muster any G-men, the British Sergeant did discover
'a rather rusty old revolver', which he carried conspicuously as the pay
was issued. (Fortunately, no pay-snatch was attempted; he had no ammunition for the gun.)

Another difference between the British and American forces was the latter's marked trigger-happiness. One RAF armourer, servicing American bombs and weapons at Aldermaston in Berkshire, observed two examples. One GI, on his way back from enjoying a drink in the hated black-out, 'startled by a horse in the field opposite the public house . . . in true cowboy fashion whipped out his revolver and shot the horse dead'. Although the offender was court-martialled, this did not discourage another GI amusing himself by tilting back his chair while drinking, 'drawing his revolver and taking potshots at the patterns around the ceiling'. Thereafter, the publican insisted that in future no weapons would be allowed on the premises and 'one could see outside each pub, a pile of arms with a GI on guard'. Another airman, stationed at Steeple Morden fighter station, a satellite of Bassingbourn in Hertfordshire, remembers how on the GIs' 'arrival, it was obvious they thought they were in a hostile country. The first night after the planes came in I was on guard duty at the main gate when the guards on the planes started firing their guns in all directions. I was glad my sentry-box was sandbagged.'

A Top Sergeant from Detroit, serving as a Flight Engineer in B-17s with the 91st Bomb Group in East Anglia, witnessed just such a panic, from the firing end, during a refresher course in gunnery at a camp near the Wash:

We were camped around the edge of an open field next to the hedges. One night all hell broke loose. Flares, gunfire, mortar fire, machine-gun fire, the whole works. Being tent commander I posted a couple of men at the front of the tent facing the open area. With the flares we could see if even a mouse tried to cross the field. With all the small-arms fire we were sure we were right in the middle of a landing of Jerries. However, we didn't see anything move and there were no bullets or mortar shells in our direction. Came the dawn, we found out that the Home Guard had an exercise the night before and had not notified us. One of the men guarding the gun emplacement on the beach panicked and was found some twenty miles away in a dazed condition. Didn't even know his name.[1]

But despite the frequent misunderstandings, and worse, which occurred between British and American servicemen, those who worked closely together often developed a deep mutual respect. I saw myself at SHAEF how closely American and British troops could work together in an integrated unit. The head of my division was a British Brigadier, his deputy an American Colonel, while I shared an office with another American Colonel, a British Major and an American Captain. British and Americans united in grumbling about a pompous senior officer (who was, as it happened,

1. It is only fair to record that British troops had been involved in a similar panic in the same area in September 1940 and that the British Home Guard were also notorious for reckless firing as described in my *If Britain had Fallen* (Hutchinson, 1972 and Arrow Books, 1975) and *The Real Dad's Army* (Arrow Books, London, 1974).

an American) and a hard-driving 'go-getter' of a Lieutenant-Colonel, who was, equally by chance, British.

The British other ranks at SHAEF, who in my experience never expressed a word of admiration for any British commander – certainly not for the boastful Montgomery or the deeply distrusted Churchill – regarded 'Ike' as a hero. He was believed to be genuinely concerned with the welfare of everyone working at headquarters, as his insistence that British soldiers should enjoy PX privileges seemed to prove. I would wholeheartedly agree with the verdict of a GI, two years older than me and working in G–2 (Intelligence) off Oxford Street, a former sophomore at the University of Miami. General Dwight D. Eisenhower, he believed,

was loved and respected by almost everyone. It was generally known that he wanted all red tape cut for better relationships between the British and the Americans. When an English co-worker, a Corporal from Manchester, asked me to visit his home I was overwhelmed by the happiness of both American and British officers. You would have thought Corporal W. and I were both doing them a favour.

Eisenhower, in this American's view, was 'the man of the century, a man of men, who could blend these forces into one happy and united team, where national rivalry was not so much ignored as unthinkable.'

This GI recalls an example of the happy atmosphere prevailing at SHAEF, which had its origins in a tragedy, when twenty-four of his comrades were killed by a V–1.

That night about a dozen GIs and WACs decided to go together to a bar and try to erase the horror of the morning from their minds. The British Major-General Strong, head of G–2, heard of the gathering and thought it proper to send a chaperone with this mixed group. He picked a young shy Lieutenant S. (British) to accompany us. Lt. S. was then the target of the fun-loving Americans. They saw to it that he had a few too many drinks and then proceeded to teach him an American game called 'Prunes'. This game is played by a boy and a girl holding their lips close and saying 'Prunes'. Lt. S. was the champion player that night and when he arrived at his desk the next morning, he found a dried prune occupying a very conspicuous place on it. I think that was Lt. S's last chaperone job.

11

BLACKS TUESDAY, WHITES WEDNESDAY

'It appears that . . . difficulties may be caused by the presence among the population of coloured troops.'

– Letter from the Home Office to Chief Constables, 4 September 1942.

WHEN the first GIs arrived in the British Isles even the phrase 'colour problem' was unknown here. The vast majority of towns and villages did not contain a single coloured resident and most children, and many adults, had never seen a non-white person. Thirty years later, the reaction of the British people to the influx of coloured GIs would certainly have been very different, for Britain itself by then included a large immigrant community. In 1942, however, 'black' or 'darkie' was a term of affection, and the word 'nigger' was used without intention to offend; discrimination on racial grounds was not so much rejected as never even considered.

Although they were 'drafted' just like white men, the American army did not employ Negroes as fighting troops, and only the Ardennes crisis of December 1944 brought about a reversal of this policy. Then fifty-three platoons of coloured infantrymen – all of whom volunteered to make the transfer – were formed within Twelfth Army Group, though they fought at first under a white Lieutenant and platoon Sergeant, forming a fifth platoon in a four-fifths white rifle company. The Sixth Army Group was braver. It formed all-black units and treated them as, in all respects, equal to white ones. The first coloured platoon entered the fighting late in March 1945 and, according to an official army historian, 'earned the appreciation and respect of their white associates, presaging a more rational use of Negro manpower in the years to come'.

In 1942, however, the US Army wished to bring coloured troops to Europe only to serve in their traditional role since the Civil War – road-building, camp-construction and maintenance, stores-handling and transport. Even this was enough to cause the British Government alarm. As General Eisenhower shrewdly remarked, the wealthy classes were the only ones in Britain to feel colour prejudice and – as Ike did not say – most fiercely reactionary of all was the Prime Minister.[1]

1. Churchill had served in India in his formative years as a young subaltern in the 1880s. His bitter opposition to any move towards self-government for India was largely responsible for keeping him out of pre-war Conservative Governments.

But colour in 1942 was a sensitive subject on both sides of the Atlantic. In the Atlantic Charter, so proudly proclaimed in 1941, advancement of coloured peoples' status had not been mentioned among the two nation's war aims but in the United States both the National Association for the Advancement of Coloured Peoples, and forward-looking politicians like Wendell Wilkie, the defeated Republican candidate in 1940, were pointing out that after the war the race issue in the United States could no longer be dealt with in the traditional way, by ignoring it.

British ministers faced a difficult decision. If they refused to allow discrimination against American coloured troops in Britain it meant public conflict between white and black GIs. If the Government did follow American practice it would offend colonial opinion and cause an outcry by the British public, especially when the colour bar also began to be lowered against Commonwealth troops. In April, when four US marines attacked a West Indian in the famous Lyons Corner House restaurant at Marble Arch – he was rescued by a British policeman – the United States Embassy was given a strong hint to prevent such incidents in future. By June, when General Eisenhower reached London, similar incidents involving coloured US troops had become common. 'Ike' himself born in Texas was no liberal reformer, but his attitude to colour as a military problem was within its limits, sensible and honourable.

Prior to his arrival in England in June 1942:

... censorship had been established by American headquarters on stories involving minor difficulties between Negro troops and other soldiers, or civilians. These incidents frequently involved social contacts between our Negro soldiers and British girls. . . . The small-town British girl would go to a movie or dance with a Negro quite as readily as she would with anyone else, a practice that our white soldiers could not understand. Brawls often resulted and our white soldiers were further bewildered when they found that the British Press took a firm stand on the side of the Negro. When I learned at the Press conference that stories of this kind were on the censored list, I at once revoked the order and told the pressmen to write as they pleased. . . . To my astonishment, several reporters spoke up to ask me to retain the ban. . . . They said that trouble-makers would exaggerate the importance of the incidents and that the reports, taken up at home, would cause domestic dissension. I thanked them but stuck to my point, with the result that little real excitement was ever caused by ensuing stories.

'Ike's' judgment was confirmed by the *Stars and Stripes* in July. 'In England', it reported, 'the Negroes have found the people ready and willing to make them feel at home.' And a British publican was quoted as having stalwartly declared: 'My pub is open to everyone who behaves himself. The Negroes could teach some of our boys some manners.' As more coloured men arrived and the system of discrimination became ever clearer, the British public took refuge in anti-white GI stories. One, current in

September, told of a racially conscious hostess who asked a local American CO to send her six non-Jewish men to tea. When six huge Negroes arrived instead, their leader replied to her protest that there must have been some mistake: 'No, ma'am, Colonel Cohen, he selected us himself personally.' 'I don't mind the Yanks,' ran another much-heard witticism, 'but I can't say I care for those white chaps they've brought with them.'

Meanwhile, however, a few Britons felt it their duty to try to rouse their countrymen to the dangers confronting them with a fervour that no southerner could have bettered, like the wife of the then vicar of Worle in Somerset whose advice to her husband's female parishioners was recorded that autumn both in the sensational *Sunday Pictorial*, which vigorously repudiated it, and subsequently in a 'Most Secret' Cabinet paper:

1. If a local woman keeps a shop and a coloured soldier enters she must serve him, but she must indicate that she does not desire him to come there again.
2. If she is in a cinema and notices a coloured soldier next to her, she moves to another seat immediately.
3. If she is walking on the pavement and a coloured soldier is coming towards her, she crosses to the other pavement.
4. If she is in a shop and a coloured soldier enters, she leaves as soon as she has made her purchases or before that if she is in a queue.
5. White women, of course, must have no relationship with coloured troops.
6. On no account must coloured troops be invited into the homes of white women.

Two weekends later, the Public Relations Division of ETOUSA found more disagreeable reading in Lord Beaverbrook's usually Conservative *Sunday Express*. 'The colour bar must go', proclaimed the headline over an article by Churchill's old crony Brendan Bracken, now Minister of Information, although he had in fact written it several months before, about coloured British troops. In October there was more trouble. The manager of an Oxford snack-bar wrote to *The Times*, the classic way for an Englishman to protest against injustice, to record his disgust at the contents of a letter presented to him by a Negro customer. 'Private ———', it read, 'is a soldier in the US Army. . . . It is necessary that he sometimes has a meal, which he has, on occasions, found it difficult to obtain. I would be grateful if you would look after him.'

Even more effective in stirring ministers to action was a question in the House of Commons at the end of September from a recently elected MP who had beaten the official Conservative candidate in a by-election. Would the Prime Minister, he asked, 'make friendly representations to the American military authorities asking them to instruct their men that the colour bar is not the custom in this country?'

The Prime Minister's answer was, not surprisingly, evasive, but in private the Government consoled themselves with an assurance from the Americans that the proportion of coloured men sent to Britain would not be allowed to exceed 10 per cent of the total. On 31 August 1942 they accepted a recommendation from the Foreign Secretary, Anthony Eden, the very epitome of a conventional upper-class Englishmen, that 'having regard to the various difficulties to which this policy was likely to give rise . . . we were justified in pressing the United States to reduce as far as possible the number of coloured troops . . . sent to this country.' Hypo-critically, it was suggested that their 'health would be likely to suffer during the English winter'.

On 4 September 1942 the Home Office made the official policy clear in a confidential letter to all Chief Constables:

It is not the policy of His Majesty's Government that any discrimination as regards the treatment of coloured troops should be made by the British authorities. The Secretary of State, therefore, would be glad if you would be good enough to take steps to ensure that the police do not make any approach to the proprietors of public houses, restaurants, cinemas or other places of entertainment with a view to discriminating against coloured troops. If the American Service authorities decide to put certain places out of bounds for their coloured troops, such pro-hibition can be effected only by means of an Order issued by the appropriate American army and naval authorities. The police should not make themselves in any way responsible for the enforcement of such orders.

In the following month the *Stars and Stripes* reported that the senior Negro officer in the US Army, after touring the whole country, had on leaving 'expressed his gratitude to the British people for the way they have received coloured troops and expressed the hope that this was part of "the new social order" which is certain to follow the end of the war'. It is fortunate that he was not present at a Cabinet meeting that month when, on hearing that a coloured official of the Colonial Office had been turned away from his usual West End restaurant Churchill commented jocularly: 'That's all right. If he takes a banjo with him they'll think he's one of the band.'

This uncomprehending attitude was shared by many Old Guard senior officers, like the Major-General in charge of Administration in Southern Command, who had issued in August to his subordinate commanders some remarkable *Notes on Relations with Coloured Troops*. They began with the singular assertion that in the Southern States the Negroes 'have equal rights with white citizens and there is no discrimination between the two'.

They have their own churches, schools and social gatherings. They have their own areas in towns and villages to live in. In cars and buses they have seats allocated and have their own reservations in cinemas.

They are sympathetically treated by the white man, and in their relationship with each other there is a bond of mutual esteem. The white man feels his moral duty to them as it were to a child. . . .

While there are many coloured men of high mentality and cultural distinction the generality are of a simple mental outlook. They work hard when they have no money and when they have money prefer to do nothing until it is gone. In short they have not the white man's ability to think and act to a plan. Their spiritual outlook is well known and their songs give the clue to their nature. They respond to sympathetic treatment. . . . Too much freedom, too wide associations with white men tend to make them lose their heads. . . . This occurred after the last war due to too free treatment . . . which they had experienced in France.

The way to keep the Negro his usual carefree self was clear:

White women should not associate with coloured men. They should not walk out, dance or drink with them.

Soldiers should not make intimate friends with them, taking them to cinemas or bars. Your wish to be friendly . . . may be an unkind act in the end. Try and find out from American troops how they treat them and avoid such action as would tend to antagonize the white American soldier.

Although he deplored that the 'Notes' had been put in writing, the Secretary of State for War, Sir James Grigg, an unimaginative reactionary detested by ordinary soldiers, circulated them approvingly as part of a Cabinet paper on 3 October 1942, commenting that they had been 'generally welcomed' and that 'relations between British and American troops have since improved considerably'.

The population of this country . . . are naturally inclined to make no distinction between the treatment of white and coloured troops and are apt to regard such distinctions as undemocratic. The average white American soldier does not understand the . . . British attitude . . . and his respect for this country may suffer if he sees British troops and British Women's Services drawing no distinction between white and coloured. There have already been instances of American white troops walking out of canteens and public houses on seeing coloured American soldiers being served. . . . The War Office finds itself on a razor's edge and its attitude has been to maintain a nice balance between these two conflicting views.

This was the policy for which he now sought Cabinet approval:

(a) To make full use of the American administrative arrangements for the segregation of coloured troops, but where those fail to make no official discrimination against them;

(b) To give the Army through ABCA a knowledge of the facts and history of the colour question in the USA;

(c) To allow Army officers . . . to interpret these facts to the personnel of the Army . . . and so educate them to adopt towards the USA coloured troops the attitude of the USA Army authorities.

The idea of using the Army Bureau of Current Affairs, strongly distrusted by Churchill as spreading progressive ideas, to stamp out the spread of racial equality has a certain wry appeal, though surely destined to fail. In any case, however, Grigg faced tough opposition from other ministers, like the Home Secretary, who circulated his views on the following day. Reports received by the Home Office from Chief Officers of Police show that on the whole the American coloured troops in this 'country have behaved well', noted Herbert Morrison. 'Apart from isolated incidents, there have been no difficulties created by . . . the association . . . with the civil population.' But according to some Regional Commissioners, there was an exception:

Some British women appear to find a peculiar fascination in associating with men of colour and . . . the morale of British troops is likely to be upset by rumours that their wives and daughters are being debauched by American coloured troops. . . . A difficult social problem – might be created if there were a substantial number of cases of sex relations between white women and coloured troops and the procreation of half-caste children. There is also . . . a risk that respectable English girls may not realize that if they show to coloured men from the United States the same friendliness as they commonly show to our own servicemen the coloured man from America is likely to misunderstand their intentions. . . .

I can therefore see a case for giving some warning to the members of the ATS and the other women's Services on this subject. [But] segregation is not really feasible. . . . Separate canteens, public houses, cinemas or places of entertainment are not available. . . . There would be a large body of opinion in this country which would strongly resent [such] a policy.

Finally, on 12 October, the Minister of Information, Brendan Bracken, who was responsible for co-ordinating hospitality to American troops, circulated to the War Cabinet a letter he had sent to the War Office a month before. It was sensible and forthright:

The Americans have exported to us a local problem which is not of our own making. . . . The American policy of segregation is the best practical contribution to the avoidance of trouble. Let us second it in every way. But I cannot feel that we ought by any process, visible or invisible, to try to lead our own people to adopt as their own the American social attitude to the American Negro. . . . The Service Departments can fairly tackle this subject among their own personnel . . . specially in the Women's Services . . . I do not think the mass of the civilian population ought to be approached at all. . . . A wrong step would be disastrous and there is not sufficient prospect of any real success, however wise one's attitude.

On 13 October, armed with this formidable array of conflicting advice, the War Cabinet finally faced up to making a historic decision. Should Britain turn her back on her tradition by introducing a colour ba The result was a victory for liberty. Although the Cabinet agreed th 'it was desirable that the people of this country should avoid becoming to friendly with coloured American troops', they ruled firmly that th Americans 'must not expect our authorities civil or military to assist the in enforcing a policy of segregation. . . . So far as concerned admission t canteens, public houses, theatres, cinemas and so forth, there would, and must, be no restriction of the facilities hitherto extended, to coloured persons.' Sir James Grigg was even induced to agree that 'some amendment of his paper was called for' the task being entrusted to the Lord Privy Seal, Sir Stafford Cripps, in consultation with Morrison and Grigg himself. They finally agreed on a policy which 'after a short discussion' was accepted by the War Cabinet on 20 October 1942. A totally new edition of *Notes on Relations with Coloured Troops* would be sent to Lieutenant-Colonels and upwards, but the Press would be asked not to mention it, being consoled by being shown privately the ABCA pamphlet being issued to all units. This, the Cripps committee agreed, offered 'the best chance of avoiding bad publicity and indeed all publicity, which is what we wished'.

And here the Government succeeded. The revised *Notes* remained secret but were vastly more truthful and liberal than the old. 'No discrimination' became 'no legal discrimination', while the authors admitted that 'In the South the white population still tend to regard Negroes as children. . . . They are not considered "equal" to white men and women any more than children are considered "equal" to adults.' There was, however, 'no reason why British soldiers should adopt the American attitude', though one should try 'to avoid unpleasantness, by not inviting white and coloured guests together'. The ABCA article, issued on 5 December as *The Colour Problem as the Americans See It*, was even more innocuous, stressing the attempts being made to improve the coloured man's position, and daringly for the time, admitting that 'the present struggle to preserve freedom' may 'have an even deeper meaning . . . to the coloured people than it has to us'.

The Government's earlier fears about the public attitude to Negro troops soon proved unfounded, as extracts from letters opened by the censor and passed on to the Foreign Office revealed. Wrote one canteen helper in Hull in February 1943:

We find the coloured troops are much nicer to deal with; in canteen life and such we like serving them, they're always so courteous and have a very natural charm that most of the whites miss. Candidly, I'd far rather serve a regiment of the dusky lads than a couple of the whites. . . . It's marvellous the spirit these lads have. All my friends – most of them . . . colour-conscious before - who serve in canteens feel the same.

Another tribute, in its way, to the success of the British Government's policy came in this cry from the heart of a white GI in another letter opened a year later by the British censor and duly passed to the Foriegn Office:

There is no colour bar here at all and the girls go with the blacks as readily as the whites, and we boys don't like it. Naturally the b—s[1] take advantage of it and have the time of their life, and if we even start an argument with them it's

1. These blanks appear in the Foreign Office original.

court martial for us! There are no Negroes here as natives and no coloured women, so they go to our dances and get 'em some 'white stuff' and it's usually the blondest blonde they can find.

Sad confirmation of this jaundiced view came in the following month from a coloured soldier:

There is no racial discrimination here but our boys are messing things by their number. . . . In parts of the city you can notice a distinct chilly attitude towards us. I can't say I blame them, as our boys are a — when they get started. A little money, a few drinks, the opportunity to be around and mix with women of another race and they are gone. Too bad . . . as the English liked the American Negro to start with.

This last comment was certainly true, although there was sometimes a hint of patronage about the white attitude as in the song 'Choc'late Soldier from the USA', released in London in 1944:

> Choc'late drop, always fast asleep
> Dozin' in his cosy bed,
> Choc'late drop has got no time for sleep
> He's riding in a jeep instead.
>
> They used to call him Lazybones in Harlem,
> Lazy good for nothing all the day,
> But now they're mighty proud of him in Harlem,
> Choc'late soldier from the USA.

Not vastly different was the treatment given by the *Stars and Stripes* to 'Negro Week' that February. In a public quiz on distinguished Negroes, it reported, the two 'most asked about personalities' were Paul Robeson the singer and 'Dr George Washington Carver, famous Negro scientist who discovered many industrial uses for the peanut'.

Almost everyone in Britain at this time regarded a coloured GI as an interesting novelty, and they made a particularly deep impression on children. One seven-year-old girl, evacuated to the village of Beckford in Gloucestershire, was thrilled when an American Negro Sergeant asked if he and two friends could attend the village church. 'I can remember vividly how I thought I would burst with pride when I walked into that church, my hand in the large hand of my American GI friend, with two of his friends coming up behind us.' The impact on a thirteen-year-old schoolgirl in Dorchester of the coloured GIs who arrived in the nearby village of Martinstown below Maiden Castle, the ancient earthworks immortalized in Hardy's *Tess of the Durbervilles*, was even greater:

Huge vehicles dominated the lanes and quickly all of us children were off to investigate. The only dark Americans I had seen were on films or in history books, so it was shattering and fascinating to see not one darkie soldier but hundreds. . . . The thing which stood out most were the palms of their hands . . . almost pink, the sparkling white teeth and glinting eyes against the dark skin, the gentleness and big stature. My sisters and I being very fair-skinned, [with] blonde hair, and petite, the contrast was enormous. They quickly made friends and we were happy to sit and listen. We didn't need story books, here were people of a strange land, speaking a different kind of English, a different colour; this was a storybook come to life. They loved to talk of their homeland. Just a spot on a map became real [with] family snapshots in everyone's wallets. . . . Every available daylight hour off on our bikes we would go to Maiden Castle. . . . Colour prejudice just didn't happen. We learnt they were just like us underneath, same joys, fears, love and feelings. . . .

Even children, however, soon realized that some mystery surrounded these new playmates. Close to Supreme Headquarters itself some were puzzled that the dark-skinned soldiers, by tacit agreement, crossed Kingston Bridge on one pavement, while white GIs kept to the other. A grammar-school boy at Launceston was horrified that while 'the coloured GIs seemed just the same as the white ones . . . they were in their own camp down the road and obviously inferior. It seemed wrong to us.' A long-awaited trip to the Manchester Zoo was spoiled for one ten-year-old girl from Norwich when she joined a crowd peering through some wire netting and found herself peering into 'an encampment of coloured soldiers, washing out tin mugs, peeling potatoes and other chores and trying to ignore the gaping crowd. I looked for an explanation at the grown ups but . . . they said nothing. I turned away, my feelings in a ferment of shame and confusion and wanted nothing but to go home.' One sixteen-year-old trainee children's nurse, working at a Dr Barnardo's Home, near Coggeshall in Essex, remembers what happened when in 1943 she filled-in time in the Abbey Gardens at Bury St Edmunds.

It was February and there were few people about, but . . . I noticed a coloured American soldier, walking alone. He eventually sat down beside me and I was immediately anxious. . . . Remembrance of my mother's warning of never speaking to strangers, coupled with the fact that I had never seen, let alone spoken to, a very black man before in my life frightened me to death. He asked me where I was going and I replied that I was going home on leave. He thought that my suitcase was too small to hold enough clothes for a holiday, obviously not appreciating the fact that clothes were rationed and most of a nurse's coupons seemed to vanish on uniform. He then suggested that he took me to the shops and bought me some clothes. This suggestion really frightened me and I thought of a fate worse than death and immediately said it was time to catch my bus. He insisted on giving me an enormous bar of chocolate, which in my dramatic way I thought must be drugged and with wild thoughts of white slave traffic I beat a hasty and ignominious retreat and waited for my bus elsewhere.

Those women who overcame such fears soon realized there had been no reason for them. One bus conductress working in Hampshire and Wiltshire found her coloured passengers 'extremely well mannered and friendly and very grateful for any help we could give them'. 'The Negroes appeared to have an in-built dignity of which the white Americans were completely devoid,' considers a WAAF who saw both in Bedfordshire. A Launceston woman, who had confided to her diary that the first white GIs she had seen in a 'Wings for Victory' parade in June 1942 were 'a fat swarthy lot', later attended a 'mixed' dance in the Town Hall and danced impartially with one white and one coloured GI. 'The coloured boy was jolly and friendly,' she recorded, 'the white lad I thought a bit slovenly in his dress and I didn't like his swaggering walk.' A young landgirl, working near Chelmsford, met her first black man on a lonely country lane when the milk-van she was driving was stopped by twelve of them linking arms to prevent her passing. 'Say, babe, how about selling us some milk?' they cried cheerfully as she pulled up and began opening the back of the van to help themselves. Indignation at this affront to the rationing regulations overcame her fear. 'How dare you?' she upbraided them. 'Put that back! Do you realize that one person on his own gets half a pint every other day, and you want to take their rations?' The confrontation ended with one small girl ('I was five feet two inches and weighed eight stone' (112 lb)) routing twelve large GIs. 'The lecture I gave them made them see sense and with smiles all round they waved me on.'

Many were the stories that circulated concerning the difficulty of seeing coloured GIs in the black-out. Another landgirl working near Evesham remembers how the local coloured troops provided a curious landmark for her as she walked home in the black-out, as 'they had a watch-tower from which they surveyed the main Evesham–Worcester road, situated near the Fladbury crossroads . . . . I could see the whites of their eyes gleaming in the dark, and . . . knew I was nearing my destination.' A woman staying in Crewe recalls turning round in a cinema, 'and seeing nothing but a sea of eyes reflected in the light of the projector'. A then eighteen-year-old in Liverpool was regularly scared, she confesses, at the sight of two apparently disembodied 'white eyes' and a mouthful of 'white teeth' coming towards her after dark. A former student nurse from Salford never forgot the literally 'blind date' she made with an American voice at a bus-stop. A week later the owner duly kept it, and on coming downstairs she found 'standing in the hall, the biggest, blackest Negro' she had ever seen.

As in every country with a coloured minority stories were heard on all sides of the men's legendary sexual prowess. Recalls a wartime policeman, then stationed at Banbury, a little cynically: 'They were very popular with the local prostitutes and ran close rivals to the Italian prisoners of war on the farms in the area for top position as lovers.' Despite the alarmist tales spread by white GIs from the South, sexual assaults on women by black

GIs were extremely rare. None of my informants – even the handful of anonymous letter-writers – recall any such experiences, while many admit to a struggle to escape from over-amorous white American hands. One young WAAF, given a lift by a coloured driver from Andover back to her camp at Middle Wallop, found him 'exceedingly courteous . . . whereas a white GI might have made a pass'. Another young woman, who worked as driver for SHAEF, found herself in a situation which would have horrified any Southern belle, being required to 'stay overnight at an all-male coloured camp. The only "bed" available being the operating table in the hospital. I was locked in for the night with a guard assigned, who even had to accompany me to the "loo".' But she suffered nothing worse than 'a few wolf whistles, made purely in fun'.

At least one coloured GI owed his life to British public opinion – a Negro driver sentenced to death in May 1944 for raping a white housewife at a village near Bath. According to *her* story, which the court martial believed, the accused man had knocked on her door late at night to ask the way to Bristol, and on her going outside, in nightdress and coat, to direct him, she had been pushed over a wall into a field and raped. According to *his* account, she had had intercourse with him twice before in the same field, charging £1 a time, but on this occasion, when he refused to pay £2 she had threatened to get him into trouble. The case was taken up by the *Daily Mirror* and other newspapers, 30 000 signatures to a petition pleading for clemency were collected, and on 18 June General Eisenhower set aside the conviction on grounds of 'insufficient evidence', a verdict with which anyone now studying the facts must surely agree.[1]

Incidents of this kind were extremely rare, but there were many occasions when black and white GIs came to blows, and to try to prevent this the American Army made extensive use of 'zoning', under which certain towns or villages, or individual public houses, were reserved for the use of one racial group or the other. One white B-17 crew member from Connecticut, an essentially non-discriminatory state, stationed near Bury St Edmunds, remembers the nearest village, Rougham, was 'off-limits', while the then licensee of the Duke of York, at Ditchingham, near Bungay, recalls readily accepting the suggestion of the local Provost Marshal that his pub, serving two airfields, Seething and Flexton, and a bomb dump at Earlsham, should be earmarked for the use of black troops. They were, he soon found, 'very popular with my local customers and joined in all their games. . . . We had many jolly evenings, and there was always one who would play the piano,' notably 'Daffodil', who always wore this flower in his lapel. Some licensees applied unofficial 'zoning' with coloured drinkers tacitly or openly confined to one bar. A Wolverhampton man recalls that one landlord who adopted

1. This case may have been the origin of a similar incident described in Nevil Shute's novel, *The Chequer Board*, published in 1947.

this solution, following complaints from white GIs, then faced a revolt by his indignant civilian customers. Although they wished publicly to champion the black men's cause, he finally persuaded them to accept the compromise for his sake. At Marlborough, the dances were open to white GIs one week and black the next. 'Often the whites would ask girls if they had been to the dance the previous week,' another WAAF remembers, 'and if so, would refuse to dance with them.' One regular at the village pub at Hollins in Lancashire remembers that the locals found the blacks' stories of discrimination in the United States hard to credit – until, to universal embarrassment, one Saturday night 'one darkie got carried away, shouted out, "Oh why was we born black?", and broke down crying'.

One woman who attended 'a rather nice roadhouse' in Crewe at the height of the coloured occupation of the town witnessed a scene with an equally revealing ending.

After a while we noticed a Negro soldier going the rounds of the tables . . . to ask if we would mind their having a sing-song; nobody objected and in a few minutes silence settled on the gathering as we listened . . . to a folk concert . . . patriotic songs, Negro spirituals, hymns, etc., interspersed with real jazz tunes, played on the piano by someone with undoubted talent. As the barman called 'Time', the senior Sergeant got up on the bar and thanked us all for giving them such a good time; he said that they had had an evening, blacks and whites together, such as would have been impossible back home.

Where there was only one town or village to provide recreation a common arrangement was to apply some such rule as 'Blacks Tuesday, Whites Wednesday'. A landgirl stationed at Newton Abbot in Devon confesses that 'we got really scared they had so many fights' until the town became 'one night white, the second night black'. A woman civil servant, then aged nineteen, recalls an identical arrangement, for the same reason, in the formerly tranquil cathedral city of Hereford. A then eighteen-year-old office worker in the Midlands can 'vividly remember going one summer night to meet a cousin off a train and as I walked across the town alone I was warned by white "Snowballs" to get off the streets, as it was BLACK night in Derby'. At these times, another local resident remembers, white GIs were expected to seek recreation instead in Burton-on-Trent, ten miles away. She recalls losing a white boy friend who, because she lived in Derby, asked her accusingly if she associated with blacks during their weekly visits, to which she hotly retorted that it was no concern of his.

The contrast between the white GI's normal good nature and his contempt for his black comrades still bewilders many civilians. The Hampshire bus conductress previously quoted was puzzled that 'even the great bunch we knew wouldn't drink in a pub if there was a coloured American in the bar. I've actually seen white GIs walk out of a pub when a coloured man was served. On the bus they would rather stand than sit alongside a coloured man.' A WAAF telephonist stationed at Warminster witnessed similar scenes in cafés. 'I've seen white Americans walk out rather than stay in the same place . . . In the cinema there was a whole row of empty seats except for one coloured airman.' One helper from the Red Cross Club in Exeter, enjoying a drink in a small country hotel, was equally astounded when 'a GI went up to an officer having a drink with an attractive girl and said, "Did you know she was out with a black last night?" Neither looked at the girl or said anything to her. The officer just got up and left.'

A woman who helped her husband keep a village store at Longworth, about ten miles from Oxford, still remembers the reaction of her regular GI customers after half a dozen blacks, delivering stores in the village, had called in to do some shopping. 'When the white Americans returned a number of them burst into the shop. Sam F., almost angry with us, commented, "You actually served niggers in your store." "Yes," we replied, "black or white, wearing the American Army uniform or not, so long as they behave themselves of course we treat them as human beings." They were very argumentative and kept asking, "Would you like your daughter to marry a nigger?" ' This couple's stand against discrimination did not prevent them incurring the wrath of their nephew, a young scientist, recently down from Cambridge, then working at the radar research establishment at Great Malvern, who in October 1944 wrote them a reproving letter which accurately reflects the contemporary attitude of most Englishmen:

In her letter Mother says that there are some Negro soldiers in Longworth, but you have not invited any in to supper . . . for fear that Jo [another GI friend of the family] may come. . . . Have you really been shunning Negroes for fear of incurring Jo's displeasure. . . ? Would you humour him in his foul and despicable attitude towards his fellow men. . . ? Should Jo arrive one evening when you have Negro guests, introduce them to each other and if he objects or misbehaves in any way, ask him to leave. Such a man is not fit to be your friend.

Whatever efforts were made to keep them apart white and black GIs inevitably came in contact at times, with results that astounded every Briton. 'I have personally seen the American troops literally kick, and I mean kick, the coloured soldiers off the pavement,' recalls a Blackpool aircraft worker, and, on being questioned . . . the answer was always more or less the same. "Stinking black pigs", "black trash" or "uppity nigger".' People in many places – Watford, Cambridge, Grimsby and elsewhere – remember seeing a white GI pointedly smash a glass recently used in a pub by a black customer, a shilling or half a crown being flung down to pay for it. Two little Herefordshire girls now learned for the first time the meaning of racialism. When one proudly showed her black doll to some white GIs loading a lorry outside their home, 'They said they hadn't seen a black doll before . . . placed it on a post and snowballed it.'

Within their own camps white GIs made even less pretence of regarding black men as human beings. One NAAFI girl at Tidworth was shocked at 'the way the Negro soldiers were treated. They had every dirty job there was . . . latrine cleaning, road sweeping.' A British girl secretary, working for the Services of Supply at Cheltenham, was amazed at the reaction to the news that a Negro detachment would soon be arriving. 'I don't think the despondency could have been greater if they had been told the Germans were moving in. When a coloured soldier had to call at our office he unfailingly appeared polite and almost servile, but it was easy to detect an atmosphere build up in those few minutes such as never occurred in the ordinary routine.' This woman remembers an incident which occurred while she was dining at a Chinese restaurant in London with one officer she greatly respected, 'an advocate and a deeply religious man, from Water Valley, Mississippi. . . . Two coloured GIs came and sat at the next table to us, and, although halfway through our meal, Lt. K. said, "Do you mind if we move across to that other table? I just can't eat with those niggers so close." '

Train journeys, so often an occasion for British people to learn about the United States, provided, less happily, an object-lesson in race relations there. One Trowbridge woman still remembers two white GIs who, after one horrified glance inside, refused to share the compartment containing herself, several British soldiers – and one black American. 'The coloured American,' she remembers, 'looked most uncomfortable,' until a British sailor pointedly offered him a cigarette and engaged him in conversation, in which the whole compartment soon joined, leaving the two segregationists standing uncomfortably in the corridor.

Civilians could, of course, do as they pleased, but many British servicemen and women were disgusted at the way in which their own army meekly adopted the American attitude. One wartime ATS girl, then aged twenty-five, remembers how in the summer of 1943 in Birmingham 'the Senior Commander came over and told us that she had been requested by the Americans to ask us not to dance with the coloured soldiers at the Casino Dance Hall'. A WAAF who had met a black soldier at a dance at Covent Garden and had invited him to join her at another near her station at Beaulieu 'was told by her CO to cease seeing him', even though 'the padre knew and vouched for him'.

It is sad to have to record that in the American forces there were clearly a sizeable number of men who would have been more at home in Hitler's SS as the young Suffolk girl, quoted in earlier chapters, who worked in the canteen at Great Ashfield observed:

When the GIs on our base had nothing better to do, they got together in bands of twelve or even twenty, armed themselves to the teeth with razors, cut-throats, and knives and would then go off on what they called nigger-hunting. They would

sit in the canteen sharpening these things and telling us what they were going
to do. We were appalled at it and said so but to them it was a sort of a joke. It
happened all the time at home, so they didn't see why it shouldn't happen here,
they could see nothing wrong in it, it was their way of life; the 'nigger' was a
form of animal, to be beaten up whenever they felt like it. They would come back
boasting of their victories and if they could actually kill one they walked ten
feet tall. . . . Even those from the more Northern states who didn't go in for that
sort of thing still looked upon it with an air of tolerance. The white American
authorities turned a completely blind eye to it, in fact when we talked to the CO
we were told to mind our goddam business. . . . We felt powerless to do anything
to stop this dreadful thing happening in our country. It made them completely
alien to us.

A Liverpool gunsmith witnessed a horrifying example of racial hatred,
when an archetypal Southerner 'with a cigar and a southern accent' asked to
'inspect a large calibre Winchester Repeating Rifle' in his shop, and after
commenting that it was 'one of the finest rifles ever made, remarked in all
seriousness, "Hit a nigger in the back of the head with one of those bullets
and you'd blast the front of his face away."' He was painfully surprised to
be ordered out of the shop. One Chippenham woman, who later married an
American officer, recalls 'a Southern boy' from the 11th Armoured Division,
'who was appalled at my grandmother's "Black Mama" knitting bag.
"Ma'am," he commented politely, "we shoot niggers where we come
from."'

And yet, however reluctantly, British civilians sometimes found themselves
forced to adopt American standards. One woman who ran a YMCA hostel
at Winchester remembers that when they did allow a party of blacks to
stay there, the result was that the white troops who had previously used it
were withdrawn, until the 'blacks' had been assigned a different leave
centre. A member of the WVS who helped to run their hostel at Weston-
super-Mare recalls rather shamefacedly, 'a cold, pouring wet night, when a
coloured . . . driver who had driven a long distance throughout the day
came in and asked if we could accommodate him overnight'. Remembering
a ban on black residents 'the one in charge was in a dilemma' until the
black said, 'It's all right, ma'am, I quite understand. Perhaps you would
kindly direct me to another which accommodates coloured troops' – which
meant him driving twenty-five miles on to Taunton. 'We all felt *dreadful*
about it,' this woman acknowledges.

Racial discrimination was contrary to the whole tradition of the Red
Cross and when the first black men arrived in Britain they were, in theory,
allowed to use white ARC clubs though a British woman observed in the
club in Southampton how 'some of the whites would get up and go out . . . if
a coloured man came in'. As more blacks arrived, a black Director was
sent from the United States to set up a separate club, staff being attracted

by the offer of higher pay. This was the usual pattern and before long almost every club was exclusively 'white' or 'coloured', although not openly labelled as such. A Manchester woman who volunteered to teach French to the 'largely uneducated' blacks who used the Manchester club was disgusted by the attitude of an American General who carried out an official inspection of the Club, his only comment at the end of his tour being 'Not bad for nigras.'[1]

Other British women who worked in coloured clubs also have nothing but praise for the men they met. One Liverpool girl was 'most impressed with the remarkable friendliness of the GIs she met there and – despite the alarmist tales of the whites – found that their favourite recreation was Chinese Checkers. 'She used to play for hours with them,' her sister remembers, 'and she always had a group of men behind her to give good advice. They treated my sister with a mixture of old-established friendship and old-world courtesy.' Once they picked her up and carried her across a huge puddle outside the station to prevent her wetting her feet and, after being invited to this family's home, insisted on keeping the grass cut, regarding it as unthinkable that she should do such a menial job herself. This woman observed how a white American driver would regularly pull up to give a lift back to camp to a fellow soldier, until 'having seen his face and found it to be black he would drive on and let him walk'.

In justice to the Americans it must be said that even in 1942-5 by no means all British people regarded the black GIs as their equals. Some still admit frankly that the sight of a black man 'gave them the creeps' and a Norwich girl remembers a disastrous dance to which she was taken with other girls only to find that their hosts were black. 'No one had the courage to say, "We don't dance with blacks," ' she remembers, 'but we filtered away one by one back to the cloakroom and walked half a mile up the dark country road to another 'drome,' which 'sent us home in their truck.'

Mere prejudice may not have been to blame here, however, for most girls soon realized that to dance with black men was to run the risk of becoming a permanent 'wall-flower' at white dances. One woman then working for the Admiralty in Bath remembers 'asking a GI why a group of pleasant girls were sitting alone, ignored, when so many men had no partners'. They came, he explained 'from a village where the blacks went'. A fifteen-year-old factory worker, attending her first dances in a local hall at Pollock near Glasgow, found that 'if you danced with the coloured Americans you were blacklisted by the white ones. They kept a list at the camp of these girls and passed it on to the new troops coming in.'

Even girls who would willingly have danced with coloured GIs were often afraid to do so for fear of the bloodshed that might follow. A wartime ATS girl remembers a typical incident at a dance in Burton dance hall,

1. This woman later married a white American officer and settled in New York.

when she was circling the floor with a white American. 'Suddenly he stopped dancing and stared towards the door . . . A tall Negro soldier had entered the hall, he stood inside and looked around, took another step forward . . . gave another glance round, turned and walked out.' Her partner brushed the incident aside: 'I was just looking at that guy. If he had attempted to come in . . . I'd have slung him out' but she retorted, 'If he is good enough to come over here to fight he is good enough to mix with us all,' and walked off the floor. Another teenage girl remembers a similar incident at a dance near Warrington. 'Two black Americans came in, the band stopped, the dance stopped, and two white Americans walked across the floor, and took hold of the blacks by their collars and threw them out of the front door; then the dance went on. I asked one of the Americans why. It was an awful thing to do. . . . He said . . . they were not going to breathe the same air as a black American.' A Wren Petty Officer, who danced with two Americans one evening in Lyme Regis, on learning that 'this would antagonize the whites I had previously danced with' bravely 'offered to escort' her black partners 'back to camp'. They refused, perhaps fearing her presence might make things worse, and she 'later heard that one of them was knifed walking home'.

Such attacks soon became all too common. In Manchester the sight of a black sailor kissing a white girl at the railway station set off a series of race riots which led to all GIs being banned from places of entertainment in the city for a fortnight and one woman reporter then living in Weymouth remembers two horrifying incidents within a week. One night, 'staying with a friend in some isolated coastguard cottages, after attending a US Army camp dance, I heard the most dreadful screaming. . . . We found next day that a black soldier had been castrated by his white comrades for dancing with a white girl all the evening. This was an almost all-Southern outfit, the 1st Division, and offending GIs were merely transferred round to different outfits, the officer being "a Southern gentleman" himself.' A few days later, climbing down from the pier for a swim, she found herself treading 'on a dead black man with a knife in his back'. He had, it appeared, been guilty of a similar 'crime'.

The idea that perfectly respectable women could willingly associate with coloured GIs is one that some white Americans can still not accept. Several believe that some blacks successfully convinced British citizens that they had been selected as 'night fighters and [would] get an injection, upon returning to the States, which would turn them white again'. Others were said to have convinced equally gullible listeners that they were 'the real American Indians', a story, British people soon learned, which infuriated men of genuine Red Indian descent.

Prejudice, it became clear, was many-sided. A Glasgow housewife remembers one GI who 'despised the Negro and saw nothing illogical in his attitude' although himself a Jew 'filled with great bitterness against his persecutors'. A WAAF stationed near Andover remembers a dark-skinned GI from Costa Rica who was bitterly upset when described as 'a Puerto Rican'.

Even when an uneasy truce existed between whites and blacks violence lurked only just below the surface. A Leicester aircraft worker recalls that near one 'black-zoned' pub, 'the American MPs would rope-off the ends of the street and let them fight it out. . . . Any passing GI could slip over the ropes and join in after being frisked for knives, etc., by the MPs.' A Wrexham woman recalls 'The Battle of Mount Street', where British commandos arrived to reinforce the blacks against the hated Yanks, withdrawing only when the MPs arrived.

Brawls between men who had been drinking were nothing new in industrial cities, but many peaceful market towns containing black troops now echoed for the first time to the noise of shouts and blows. A then teenager at Bridgwater in Somerset remembers 'fierce fighting both inside the pubs and in the street', while in the remote village of Nanpean, in mid-Cornwall, the dance held in the church hall in celebration of 'Wings for Victory' week in 1943 was to prove the most memorable in its history, as one of the organizing committee, then a fifteen-year-old commercial college student, remembers:

The evening began well with a contingent of coloured men partnering the local girls, when about ten o'clock a party of white Americans came straight from the local public house with bottles bulging their pockets to swell the party. The inevitable happened: because the local girls were already dancing with the coloureds the whites were unable to find partners. . . . A somewhat ugly scene ensued when bottles crashed and knives flashed and someone got hurt. . . . The girls, who were unused to such behaviour and had never seen an incident of this kind anywhere excepting at the cinema, panicked and ran to the back stage of the hall to try and make their getaway through a back door. Unfortunately it was locked and so we had to climb through windows to gain access to the yard. . . . The Military Police were luckily on the prowl and with guns at the ready they herded their flock to waiting lorries and back to camp.

With guns plentiful, there were shooting affrays at many places, including Bamber Bridge near Preston in Lancashire, Bristol, where a machine gun was brought into action, and Kingsclere, near Newbury, in December 1944, where blacks driven from a local pub by white GIs fetched their weapons and bombarded it with rifle-fire, killing the licensee's wife. The most notorious such affair, though no one was killed in it, was the 'Battle of Launceston' when, allegedly after drinking, a group of black men agreed to teach the local whites a lesson, fetched rifles, and returned, armed, to the square in the centre of this small Cornish town. Their response to a call from the Military Police to disperse was 'rude remarks', and eventually they opened fire, wounding two MPs. The sequel came a month later, in October 1943, at Paignton, where fourteen blacks faced a court martial of ten white officers on charges of mutiny and attempted murder. The British Press widely reported the affair – though *The Times*, absurdly, omitted the essential fact of the defendants' colour – but the verdict was never published. Until recently, however, residents in Launceston still pointed to 'the bullet holes in a shop window' as a lasting reminder of one little-remembered battle of World War II.

12

WHO'S AFRAID OF THE FOCKE-WULF?

'We won't do much talking until we've done more fighting.'
— Speech by Brigadier-General Ira Eaker, Commanding Eighth Air Force
Bomber Command, 1942.

MOST Americans had come to Britain to *prepare* to fight. The airmen began their battle at once. Their base was the great central plain of England, stretching from the high ground on the western borders of the Midlands to the great curve of East Anglia, where Norfolk and Suffolk reach out into the North Sea, towards Germany. From this flat, lush landscape, with its wide horizons, where the chief enemy had for centuries been the encroaching sea, the American aircrews flew to face the flak and fighters; to its quiet villages, with their tall churches, and its small towns (famous for their profusion of pubs), they returned at night, those who were lucky.

There were many reasons why, in early 1942, the American effort in Europe was concentrated on the air force. Only the air offered at that time the means of striking an immediate blow against Germany, only the air provided the opportunity to establish beyond doubt the United States' total commitment to the war in Europe. The air force had, too, other motives for desiring a rapid build-up in England. They were anxious to demonstrate that their service, then part of the army, could operate independently, and many senior officers dreamed of achieving victory through air power alone, and bringing Germany to her knees without a single doughboy having to get his feet wet. These strategists longed, understandably and honourably, to try out their belief in unescorted precision daylight bombing, a doctrine widely distrusted since the costly failure of the earliest RAF daylight raids on German targets and the defeat of the Luftwaffe in the Battle of Britain. Great Britain was to serve not merely as a giant aircraft carrier moored close to the Continent but as a laboratory where a vital experiment in the art of war could be carried out.

In 1939 the total strength of the American Air Force had been under 20 000 men; only in 1941 did it top the 100 000 mark; by early 1944 it numbered 2 383 000, of whom the Eighth Air Force, based in England for the strategic air offensive against Germany, accounted for about 185 000 officers and enlisted men. 'The mighty Eighth', as one historian described it, had formally come into existence in January 1942 in Georgia, and a small party of staff officers arrived in London in the following month, but the earliest ground units did not land – at Liverpool and Newport, Monmouthshire – until May, and the first B–17s of the 97th Group only touched down in July, at Polebrook in Northamptonshire and Grafton Underwood, its nearby satellite. Some units, including the 97th, left in the autumn to serve in the Twelfth Air Force in North Africa, while others destined for the Mediterranean also trained briefly in Britain during 1942. In 1944 a whole new air force, the Ninth, known to the veterans of the Eighth as 'Junior', was created to provide tactical support for the coming invasion but soon after D-Day its bases were moved across the Channel. It was the Eighth which came first and stayed longest, the Eighth to which, for three long and crowded years, England was 'home'.

It was, of course, the combat wings which made the deepest impression. In other parts of the country, one woman living in Northamptonshire remembers, 'the Americans were spoken of derisively. To us, among whom they lived – and died – it seemed incomprehensible.' In fact, however, fewer than one man in ten flew against the enemy, for along with the combat wings went a whole range of supporting services. A list compiled by the British Air Ministry in June 1942 showed no fewer than sixty-one separate US Air Force units already established, or shortly expected, in the area of Eastern Command, ranging from the 817th and 818th Engineering Battalions, Air, at Stansted Mountfitchet and Great Dunmow, to the 688th MP Company (Aviation), at Polebrook. They varied enormously in size. The 1st platoon of the QM Company (Mobile Shoe and Textile Repair) detachment at Wellingborough mustered no more than fifty; an anti-aircraft regiment, based on Rattlesden, more than 1200. But the heart and purpose of the whole scattered array, was of course, the bomber groups, supported by interceptor, photographic and transport squadrons, largely at first based at Chelveston.

The original plan was for the Eighth Air Force to grow to some 3500 aircraft by April 1943, spread over some seventy-five airfields, but in the event it required 122, stretching from the Wash to High Wycombe. Near this latter town Brigadier-General Ira C. Eaker, appointed in June with the reputation of being a tough commander, set up his Eighth Air Force Bomber Command, close to his British opposite number, Sir Arthur Harris. The American Air Staff Officers worked and slept in a luxurious country house, Daws Hill Lodge, formerly occupied by the exclusive Wycombe Abbey Girls' School. Bomber Command transmitted its orders to its squadrons via a number – usually three or four – of Bombardment Wings, which in September 1943 were renamed Air Divisions, although the terms 'Wing' and 'Combat Wing' remained in use for various purposes. Each

Wing consisted of three groups, which formed the basic tactical unit, and it was to these that most airmen felt their first loyalty, and whose titles – or rather numbers – became most familiar to British civilians: the 97th, which came first but moved on in October 1942 to North Africa, the 'Bloody Hundredth', so-called because of its appalling losses, especially in the early days, the 303rd, the 'Hell's Angels', the 492nd, stationed at 'North Pick' – North Pickenham, in Norfolk – remembered by one air gunner from Middleboro, Massachusetts, as consisting of 'a small common with a horse-watering trough, a mailbox and a bright red telephone booth'. (There was no group between 101 and 300, these numbers being traditionally reserved for the National Guard.) Each group consisted of four squadrons, based on one or two airfields, a squadron containing in theory twelve aircraft, though in practice, due to losses and the claims of maintenance, the actual number which took the air was usually nine or ten. Their crews lived on or near the airfields, which each covered about 500 acres and accommodated about 460 officers and 2700 men, a major addition to the population of this thinly populated area.

The 250 stations erected by the British Government for the United States, of which the Eighth Air Force occupied about half, had cost the British taxpayer more than £600 million, a major example of 'reverse Lend-Lease', for only eight aerodromes contained any permanent pre-war buildings. Away from the operational airfields there were many other Eighth Air Force establishments: gunnery schools, quartermasters' depots, combat crew replacement centres, and three maintenance and repair depots, at Warton, near Liverpool, Burtonwood, in Lancashire – destined to revert to US occupation after the war – and, as already mentioned, Langford Lodge in Northern Ireland. Of more immediate importance to the combat crews were Wing (or later Divisional) Headquarters, mainly set up in ancient and imposing stately homes: Brampton Grange, near Alconbury in Huntingdonshire, Elveden Hall in West Suffolk, not far from Thetford, and Ketteringham Hall, near Norwich, comfortable, often panelled mansions in spacious grounds, offering a sharp contrast to the bleak, windswept airfields.[1] These were named as distinctively as possible, to avoid confusion, so were not always called after the nearest village, but even so they read like a roll-call of the ancient hamlets of rural England: Attlebridge and Alconbury, Bungay and Bassingbourn, Deenethorpe and Deopham Green, Seething and Snetterton Heath, Wendling and Wattisham. Many of the bomber airfields were some way inland. The supporting fighters tended to be further forward, to give them extra range. Fighter Command Head-quarters was at Bushey Hall in Hertfordshire, close to RAF Fighter Command, with Wing Headquarters at Walcot Hall, near Stamford, in Lincolnshire, Saffron Walden, in Cambridgeshire, and Sawston Hall, near

1. The 1949 film *Twelve O'Clock High* accurately portrays both types of establishment.

Cambridge, an enchanting Elizabethan country house, complete with priest's hole and ghost, which is still occupied by the descendants of the original owners.

From its sprawling hutted headquarters in Bushy Park near London, known as 'Widewing', Major-General Carl Spaatz, in command of the Eighth Air Force, supervised the activities of his Fighter Command, Bomber Command, Ground–Air Support Command and Air-Service Command. These last were responsible for supply on the ground, and for the fleets of transport aircraft, especially the sturdy C–47 Dakotas, which soon became so familiar in the English sky. All their efforts were directed, however, to maintaining in the air the combat groups of Bomber Command. Although there were in the Eighth photo-reconnaissance, air–sea rescue and other specialized squadrons, and for a period during 1943 several groups of twin-engined B–26 Marauders, used in low-level and medium-level attacks, it was the four-engined 'heavies' on which the American commanders pinned their hopes and whose crews, ten to a plane, as against a fighter's single pilot and a Marauder's five fliers, became best known to the civilian population.

The Americans' favoured weapon was the B–17 or 'Flying Fortress', described by one historian as 'a battleship of the air', and intended, when it first flew, in 1935, to further the claims of the Army Air Corps to a share in the defence of American shores against attacking fleets. The first B–17Cs, incorporating many improvements, were delivered for British use, on a small scale, in early 1942, but the version with which the Eighth Bomber Command began operations a year later was the even more advanced B–17E, which now included – since German fighters had learned to attack from astern – a machine gun in the tail. The B–17F was better still, with twelve .50 calibre machine guns and a superior performance all round. The prototype of what was really a different aircraft, the B–29 Superfortress, first flew in December 1942, but production did not get under way until December 1944, too late to have much effect on the war in Europe. It was the B–17E's and F's which bore the brunt of the fighting and their shapely silhouette, as they took off or landed, with their narrow wings, slim fuselage and high single tail, became familiar to millions of British civilians.

If not the greatest aircraft of the Second World War the B–17 had many virtues, not least, as one RAF air-gunner observed, when he took part in an exchange visit between neighbouring (Allied) squadrons at Mildenhall, that its 'American crew loved it' and felt far safer in it than in any other type. They had good reason for their faith, for the Fortress soon revealed a capacity to take an enormous amount of punishment. Photographs of B–17s with door-sized holes in the fuselage, badly damaged tail-planes, and whole wing-tips blown off frequently appeared in the British newspapers, while at least one battle-damaged B–17 actually managed to 'make it' back to England on one engine. On the debit side, the airman just quoted recalls the Americans' amazement at the sight of the Lancaster's bomb-bays, containing seventeen thousand-pounders; their own aircraft would carry, even on a short raid, no more than four. The Fortress proved happily free, however, of those unforeseen faults, only revealed in operations, which bedevilled so many other types, like the much-maligned Marauder, which had been 'ordered off the drawing board' and arrived in England with a reputation as a crew-killer. It was nicknamed the 'Baltimore Whore' or 'Flying Prostitute' because, it was said, it had no visible means of support.

The Germans greatly admired the B–17. 'It united every possible advantage in one bomber', wrote the then Colonel Galland, the German fighter chief, after a shot-down Fortress had been reassembled in October 1942. 'Firstly, heavy armour; secondly, enormous altitude; thirdly, colossal defensive armament; and, fourthly, great speed.' At first the Germans feared that, provided they held formation, the B–17s would be impregnable, just as the American commanders claimed. The RAF, by contrast, were always sceptical of the aircraft's invulnerability and considered its bomb-load absurdly small, ceasing to use it on unescorted daylight raids after a few unhappy experiences. 'The first Flying Fortresses were . . . badly mishandled by RAF Bomber Command,' considered General Arnold, Head of the American Air Force, and he was only too happy to keep for American use all those that began to pour from the plants of Detroit from 1942 onwards and to supply the British instead with his other four-engined bomber, the B–24 or Liberator, which they 'seemed to like much better'.

The Liberator carried fewer guns than the Fortress but twice the bomb-load, and was faster at the medium altitude the RAF favoured, though slower at the great heights at which the US Air Force so often flew. (It was the caustic, and unjust, comment of some British airmen that 'the only wounds the Yanks got were from frost bite'.) Although many British-manned Liberators went into service with Coastal Command, the Eighth Air Force eventually also had several Groups equipped with them. The first B–24s arrived in October 1942 and there was soon a good deal of rivalry between their crews and those of the B–17s. The Liberator men were proud of their aircraft's superior speed and spaciousness; the Fortress crews mocked its deep fuselage and ungainly, rather square appearance, declaring that it was the crate in which the B–17s were shipped to England, and that it had been intended as a flying boat and only been converted into a bomber because 'they couldn't stop the leaks'. In this criticism there was at least a grain of truth. One man who flew home *en route* to Manhattan, Kansas, in one in 1945 remembers 'a cold windy trip . . . like flying in a tin barn. Wind came in all over the thing and the wings flapped like a duck.'

In the opinion of the Commanding General of US Army Air Forces, General Arnold, 'The main job of the air force is bombardment. . . . The best defence is attack,' and this was the philosophy that inspired the Eighth Air Force from its earliest days in England and to which the Bombers' commander General Eaker was personally dedicated. Many American-made aircraft had taken part in British attacks before Pearl Harbour, and the first American crews, manning DB–7 Bostons, previously supplied to the RAF, flew against the Luftwaffe on 4 July 1942, attacking airfields in Holland. America really entered the European air war, however, on 17 August, when General Eaker personally led fourteen B–17s in an attack on railway marshalling yards in France, an occasion commemorated by a famous, if somewhat glamorized official picture *Return from Rouen*. In the early months such raids were on so small a scale that the total of bombs dropped was announced in pounds, not tons, but the American commanders remained supremely confident that, once sufficient bombers arrived, they would have a war-winning weapon in their hands. The air seemed to many America's natural element, as the sea was Britain's or the land Germany's. 'Our commercial airlines were flying more miles than all the rest of the world's airlines put together', recalled the Commanding General of the Army Air Forces, in an official *Report* recalling conditions before the war. 'We had the best aircrew material in the world. Our youth were accustomed to teamwork, competition and mechanical processes. The mechanical knowledge and experience gained from rebuilding a $10 used car has doubtless saved the life of many an American by enabling him to "nurse" a damaged plane home.'

But what the American airmen lacked was experience and this carried a much higher price tag than $10, though the first arrivals seemed blithely unaware of the fact. One British scientist from the radar research establishment at Great Malvern, who flew with many such crews while testing equipment, found them 'all very raw and young and . . . rather cocky. They had come to make mincemeat of the Huns. . . . They did not want advice. Their Fortresses were invincible.' An RAF NCO assigned to teaching US crews British signal procedures at Polebrooke found them 'sadly undertrained by British standards' and he had to work hard to 'bring their morse speed . . . up to a working rate'. Yet many were inclined to 'shoot their mouths off' – 'shooting a line', the RAF called it. One example was recorded by an American historian: an air-gunner, back from his first-ever mission, referring excitedly to 'the worst flak I've ever seen'.

But there was one important exception to the prevailing over-confidence. Ira Eaker was under no illusions about the task he faced and when called on to speak at a dinner at High Wycombe soon after his arrival made a short but classic reply: 'We won't do much talking until we've done more fighting. When we leave, I hope you'll be glad we came.'

The Eighth suffered their first battle casualties on 21 August during an attack on the docks at Rotterdam, from which some aircraft returned with dead and wounded aboard, but the myth of the 'invincible' Fortress was not finally destroyed until 6 September when two B–17s of thirty sent to Rouen were shot down. The first major landmark in the offensive came, however, on 9 October, with a raid on a steel-works at Lille, the maiden mission of the Liberators, which had flown the Atlantic in formation to join the 93rd Group at Alconbury. A hundred and eight aircraft took part, a total not to be surpassed for six months, and the returning gunners claimed a great victory over the enemy fighters. Fifty-six it was at first believed, had definitely been shot down, twenty-six probably shot down, and twenty damaged, though these figures were reduced after checking to twenty-one certain 'kills', twenty-one 'probables' and fifteen needing repair. The true facts were different. Not merely had the bombing been inaccurate, killing many friendly civilians, but against the Eighth Air Force's four bombers the Germans had lost only two fighters, with none damaged.[1] The optimists proclaimed, on this false evidence, that the heavy bombers would always be able to fight their way to the target and back. General Arnold later denied ever sharing this view. 'We always knew that we would have to have long-range fighter escort', he wrote, 'to carry the campaign to a conclusion but we also knew that we couldn't wait for it.'

The consequences of not waiting began to be clear as the B–17s and B–24s ranged further afield, with steadily mounting losses, considered acceptable at the time due to the supposed destruction of the Luftwaffe's fighters. The German losses were, we now know, invariably overestimated by a factor of five or even ten, while a cheap single-seater fighter, whose pilot was probably saved, was in any case a poor exchange for a costly bomber and its ten-man crew. There was certainly nothing imaginary about the American losses, which by the end of 1942 had reached thirty-three bombers and nine US fighters in twenty-six raids. Little damage had been borne by the German war machine, but the Eighth's sacrifice had not been wasted, for already many Luftwaffe units had been withdrawn from other points to protect the Reich.

That first winter, runways and crews alike were still raw and untried, but apart from the weather and the living conditions, already described, what threatened morale most seriously was the lack of replacements – of spare parts for damaged planes, of new aircraft for those 'written off', of new crews to replace those killed or wounded. Morale was affected even more by missions called-off at the last moment, sometimes after the crews were actually on their way to the target. Such cancellations left many men as exhausted as an actual mission, but did not count towards the twenty-five needed to complete a tour and return to the United States. Later the total needed was raised to thirty and one woman, then a young girl at Wymond-

1. In the confusion of battle such overestimates were, of course, understandable. Similarly exaggerated claims had been made by both sides during the Battle of Britain.

ham in Norfolk, where the local hospital contained many Eighth Air Force casualties, remembers the appalling shock this gave to men who had already completed twenty-three or twenty-four operations.

The principal cause of the frequent last-minute cancellations was the weather. In November 1942, because of poor visibility there were only eight missions, in December only four. By now suggestions were being made in high places that the whole daylight offensive was not so much a failure as a non-starter and that its aircraft should be used to strengthen the RAF's night offensive. The American commanders fought a desperate, and successful, battle to preserve their independent role, and at the Casablanca Conference in January 1943, attended by General Eaker, the decision was taken to extend day bombing farther afield, into Germany. This was 'the big one', for which (so it was said) the Eighth's bomber crews had been eagerly waiting and on 27 January 1943 fifty-three bombers attacked Wilhelmshaven, of which fifty got safely home. Thereafter, as the number involved grew and the bombers penetrated deeper into the Reich, the proportion of losses began to mount. In April, when 107 B–17s attacked an aircraft factory at Bremen and sixteen were shot down, it rose well above 10 per cent, the level normally considered prohibitive, though the average on all operations, including attacks on 'softer' targets nearer home, was still only 3 per cent. But worse was to come. On 17 August 1943 thirty-six wrecked B–17s were left littering the fields of southern Germany of 200 sent out, during an attack on the Messerschmitt factory at Regensburg and a ball-bearing plant at Schweinfurt, one of those 'panacea' targets whose destruction, the experts were always predicting, would shorten, or even end, the war. On 6 September came another 'maximum effort' strike at an instrument factory at Stuttgart by 338 Fortresses. General Arnold, on a visit to England, was assured that the raid had been a great success. He only discovered later that, in the words of one historian, it had been 'the biggest fiasco of the year', for not one of the aircraft involved had even seen the target and the forty-eight that had attacked it had bombed 'blind' through the cloud. The price of the negligible results achieved was forty-five aircraft, and one squadron, the 563rd from Knettishall in Norfolk, was wiped out. It had occupied 'Purple Heart Corner', in the bottom rear corner of the formation 'box', the favourite target for enemy fighters, and hence the likeliest place to earn a Purple Heart for being wounded in action.

The Stuttgart affair caused even the staunchest devotees of precision bombing to begin to wonder if it were practicable in Europe's overcast skies. Until now the boast had been that a Fortress, with its Norden bomb-sight, could land a bomb in a pickle-barrel from 20 000 feet, for in the sunny skies of California, under perfect conditions, picked crews flying at that height had often managed to hit a circle only a hundred feet across. But as two American authors wrote in 1944, 'What good was a bomb-sight that permitted you to drop a stick of bombs in a barrel, if prevailing hazy weather . . . blanked out a view of the barrel?' And even if it *were* visible, it was most unlikely to be hit. By 1944, except by the propagandists, the early, exaggerated claims had been abandoned, and, as the official Eighth Air Force historian admitted in that year: 'Under combat conditions in the Western European theatre our bombers have had a good day when, operating from 25000 feet, they managed to concentrate their destructive load in a factory area the size of a city block.'[1] This realization followed 'Black Week', when in a series of deep-penetration raids the attacking bombers suffered appalling losses, reaching their climax on 'Black Thursday', 14 October 1943, in the air battle labelled 'second Schweinfurt'. Of 291 B–17s which took off from England, only thirty came back undamaged. Sixty-two were shot down and many of the rest were so badly crippled that, when they finally staggered in to land laden with dead and dying, they were past repair. The Germans had lost about thirty-five fighters – the figure believed at the time was 186 – and, though heavy damage had been done to the target, production was resumed elsewhere within a few days. What did suffer irreparable injury was the doctrine of the self-defending bomber, for almost all the American losses had occurred after the escorting fighters had had to turn back.

For the rest of the winter the Eighth Air Force attacked targets nearer home, acquired new aircraft – now flooding from the American factories at the barely credible rate of 8000 a month – tried to rebuild its badly dented morale and waited for the arrival of a long-distance fighter which could clear the skies ahead of the bombers and protect them every mile of the long flight there and back.

The Eighth Air Force had contained fighters since its formation, the first being the 4th Group formed from three former RAF Eagle Squadrons in September 1942, at Debden, near Saffron Walden, described by German radio as 'the Debden gangsters'. Like the earlier groups to arrive from the United States, it was equipped with British Spitfires, but a trickle of American fighters had begun to arrive in July, shooting down their first enemy aircraft, encountered by chance during a training exercise, in August. By June 1943 almost all the pilots were flying American machines and British aircraft spotters – and every boy in those years 'collected' new types with all the zeal of a peacetime bird-watcher – had added a new name to their lists of sightings, the Thunderbolt, or P–47, an ungainly-looking blunt-nosed single-seater with an exceptionally noisy engine. The P–47 weighed twice as much as most comparable types of aircraft and was unpopular from the first with pilots used to the daintier Spitfire. They nick-

1. British night bombing was, of course, even more inaccurate. Bomber Command by 1942 placed its faith in 'area bombing' of whole cities, although the public pretence was kept up that only military objectives were being attacked.

named it 'the flying milkbottle' or 'the jug' – short for 'Juggernaut'. It was followed a few months later by the P–38, or Lightning, then a novelty with its small central cabin and twin booms, a distinctive appearance which protected it from all but the wildest B–17 gunners. The Thunderbolt, by contrast, closely resembled the Germans' fast and deadly new fighter, the Focke-Wulf 190, produced to reinforce their faithful Messerschmitt 109. It was a sign of growing maturity, in contrast to the over-confidence of the early days, that when one airman pinned to a mess hall notice-board a magazine photograph of a smiling bomber-pilot asking cockily, 'Who's afraid of the new Focke-Wulf?' every combat officer on the station signed his name below, headed by the Group Commander.

The first Thunderbolts had flown from British bases on operations in April 1943 but the Lightning made its début as a cross-Channel escort in October, earlier squadrons having been sent on to North Africa. Although effective at lower altitudes, neither aircraft could match the German fighters, flying over their home territory, at heights of 25 000 feet or more, and the Lightning in particular proved sadly liable to mechanical trouble in the damp and cold of Europe. More serious, however, was that, even with extra drop-tanks, it had a range of only 600 miles – the Thunderbolt's was considerably less – so that constantly the American fighters had to turn back, as on the way to Schweinfurt, just as the real attacks began. What was needed was a high-performance long-range machine which could fly all the way to the target, engage in fuel-consuming combat on equal terms with the German fighters, and still have petrol enough to get home. At last, in early 1944, the aircraft factories began to produce just such an aircraft. I can well remember my own first sight of this war-winning machine while visiting an RAF base in Sussex, as a schoolboy cadet in the Air Training Corps, in 1943. The lines of this single-engined fighter, even on the ground, suggested speed, and as keen aircraft-spotters, we instantly identified it as the P–51 or Mustang, a happy example of Allied co-operation, with a Rolls-Royce engine mounted in an American airframe. This version of the Mustang earlier ones had been under-powered – proved immediately popular with American pilots, especially those used to the Spitfire. When its dazzling performance on its first appearance, over Hanover, was described to Reichsmarschall Göring he told his staff that they must have been 'seeing things'; when he witnessed it in action for himself he exclaimed, 'We have lost the war!' With extra 'drop' tanks in its wings, the Mustang could reach Berlin and still achieve a speed of 440 miles an hour at the extreme heights at which the air battle was now being fought.

The air offensive against the German homeland, muted after Schweinfurt in October 1943, was resumed in full force in February 1944, the month the famous 4th Group were re-equipped with Mustangs. The Eighth Bomber Command had its revenge for 'Black Week' in 'Big Week' when, in the first spell of good weather for more than a month, a force of nearly 1000 bombers, escorted by fighters, attacked German aircraft factories. Claimed the official Report of the Commanding General; 'The week of 20 to 27 February 1944 may well be classed by future historians as marking a decisive battle of history: one as decisive [as] Gettysburg,' and though this prophecy has not so far been fulfilled it is true that thereafter the Germans were tactically as well as strategically on the defensive, and always sought local superiority before opening fire.

The next great landmark came on 4 March 1944 with the first, modest attack on 'big B', Berlin. A major raid, with 660 bombers, followed two days later, of which sixty-nine were shot down, plus eleven fighters, figures which six months before would have seemed insupportable. Now the aircraft factories and aircrew training schools were pouring into Europe a flood of reinforcements which, logistically at least, made such losses endurable. The raids on Berlin continued until almost the end of the war, but far more important was the systematic destruction of enemy transport and, above all, of German oil dumps and refineries which at last began to achieve that paralysis of the enemy war effort which the advocates of strategic bombing had so long, and hitherto so fallaciously, predicted. Now no part of Germany was safe from attack by the Eighth, at its peak strength of 2000 bombers and 1000 fighters, while other squadrons flew in from North Africa and Italy, on 'exchange' trips, by which aircraft based in England flew on to bases in the Mediterranean, while bombers from there landed in East Anglia. In North-West Europe the Reich was under attack, too, from the Ninth Air Force, which arrived early in 1944 to provide tactical support for the coming invasion and between 1 May and D-Day on 6 June flew more than 1000 sorties a day against the railways, bridges and defence works of 'Fortress Europe', before moving on into France, en route for Germany. But for the Eighth Air Force D-Day was not quite the climax of their efforts. That came on 24 December 1944, when, in their greatest-ever strike against the enemy, 2034 bombers attacked airfields along the Rhine and other targets in support of the troops hard-pressed by von Rundstedt's Ardennes offensive. Only four were shot down and another five made crash landings – losses which would have seemed unbelievably light only a few months before and which showed the Eighth's success in achieving air superiority since 1942. As the tonnage of bombs dropped increased – it was to reach 700 000 tons by the end of the war, the heaviest total delivered by any United States Air Force – so losses declined even more sharply, though not sufficiently to prevent the Eighth from suffering by far the largest number of casualties. General Eaker himself was on record as saying 'that this was the toughest theatre in the world for fliers'. How tough the figures show only too clearly. The worst-hit Group, the 91st from Bassingbourn, had reported by the end of the war 197 Fortresses 'Missing in Action', plus others that crashed on landing, and many other Groups had lost more than 150, all their forty to fifty aircraft having been replaced three or four times over. By early 1944 the average operational life of a B–17, including periods for maintenance and modification, was down to 231 days, during which it would fly twenty-one missions. One aircraft, near-miraculously, had scored 125 by the end of the war, with several others over the hundred mark and one crew member, a Master Sergeant of the 569th Squadron at Framlingham in Suffolk, also reached his 'century'. His final total of missions flown was 104 and several others completed two tours and reached fifty to sixty. But these were the lucky exceptions. With an average life of twenty-one missions, the ordinary pilot, bombardier or air-gunner was, statistically speaking, already dead before he reached the end of his tour.

During 1945 the previously appalling losses dropped steadily. Crew members began to realize, almost incredulously, that perhaps, after all, they might live to see the end of the war. And at last, on 16 April, General Spaatz was able officially to inform General James M. Doolittle, commander of all American air forces in Britain, that the Strategic Air Offensive was over; there were no worth-while targets left to destroy. Henceforward the Eighth Air Force could concentrate on giving tactical support to the advancing armies. On 19 April the bombers fought their last battle, when six B–17s were shot down near Prague by three Me 262s, the new German jet fighter, two of which immediately fell to the escorting Mustangs; and later that day another flight of Mustangs had their final, triumphant, dog-fight against their old adversaries the Me 109 and the FW 190. The last bombs to be dropped by the Eighth went down on the Skoda works near Pilsen on 25 April 1945, from the B–17s of the 384th Group flying from Grafton Underwood in Northampton, the same airfield from which the Americans had flown their first heavy-bomber mission nearly three long and blood-stained years before.

13

AIR FORCE COUNTRY

'When we used to call in at the pub and enquire "Where's Tex?" or "Where's Pennsylvania?" they would just say they hadn't made it back.'

– British servicewoman then stationed at Bedford, recalling 1943.

'THE sky was never still.' This is the dominant impression that has remained with one Norfolk man, aged fourteen in 1942, of the three years that followed.[1] 'My life revolved round missions, listening to the planes going off early morning and for the telephone call in the afternoon which told me he was safe.' Such was the wartime experience of a Cambridge office worker, aged twenty-three when she met her first American airman. Another woman remembers the piles of bombs stacked by the roadside around the village of Bowden near Market Harborough in Leicestershire and how, as they took corners at speed, the trucks carrying them to the airfields would often fling the heavy objects out on to the verges of the country lanes. A wartime housewife recalls how the brief after-dark peace of the village of Wilby near Horsham Saint Faith in Norfolk was often shattered by the sudden arrival of an unproariously cheerful aircrew, celebrating the unexpected 'scrubbing' of the next day's operations and come to take out her husband, who worked on the base, for a late-night drink. For her the characteristic sound of those years was 'the ringing of bicycle bells' and loud American voices directed at the bedroom window, calling 'Put yer pants on, Stan, you old bastard, and come on down!'

The impact of the Eighth Air Force on East Anglia began with the devastation of whole stretches of countryside by the airfield construction gangs. Among them was Robert Arbib at Debach in Suffolk, where concrete was poured and levelled round the clock, and meals were eaten at the work-face as the new runways were pushed forward. Arbib's own job, as a camouflage specialist, had in that summer of 1942 an idyllic quality:

I enjoyed that first week. . . . Every day I walked alone across the fields and along the lanes with a map. On this map I noted in minute detail the aspect of each field. Here the hedgerow was ten feet wide with a deep ditch on the north side lined

---

1. The experience made such an impression that thirty years later he wrote a history of the Eighth Air Force. See: 'Note on Sources'.

by scattered trees. Here were three haystacks, there a farm shed. Through another field wound a footpath; I drew it on the map. I wandered through fields of wheat and oats, barley and clover, mustard and cabbages. I flushed rabbits and pheasants along the hedgerows and coveys of partridges in the grain. I had numbered each field systematically and took copious notes on the appearance, texture and tone of each. I made little sketches of special points of identification that we would later paint across runways and perimeter tracks. With my notes, drawings and special ideas, I felt that we could perfectly simulate the terrain as it had been before we moved into Debach.

All this effort proved to be wasted, however, for it was soon decided that no disguise, however elaborate, could conceal the aerodrome while under construction, and Arbib found himself assigned to other duties, keeping records of the work done and making a forty-mile drive every day to collect the mail from Sudbury. This welcome daily chore increased his love of the English countryside, which at Debach, he sadly realized, had, within a week of the Americans starting work 'been scarred and marred beyond repair'.

With the departure of the building units and the arrival of the first bombers, even the sky ceased to be peaceful. The tumult began at dawn, or even earlier, as the great machines roared down the runway, for the B–17 was notoriously reluctant to leave the ground when heavily laden. A Suffolk woman, then an eighteen-year-old helper in the Red Cross canteen at Great Ashfield, remembers still 'the deafening noise' of Fortress engines struggling to drag their aircraft off the ground at 'the nerve-racking moment' as they reached the end of the runway. 'A few couldn't get up and that sent the fire engines and ambulances racing out.' On one man, then a fourteen-year-old schoolboy near Seething, the whole experience made a deep impression.

I used to cycle with my friends to the airfields in North Suffolk and South Norfolk and stand at the end of the runways and watch these things taking off, fascinated. There was something about these aircraft, they had a something that no jet aircraft has, they clawed at the air to be liberated from the ground. . . . The noise was fantastic, the old farmhouses used to shake, it went on, it was incessant. . . . We looked up at the spectacle and, if it was a clear day, you could see aircraft for miles, little silver specks and contrails, it was just fascinating, it was something that we just couldn't get over.

For the men in the sky this was, of couse, only the beginning. 'A normal mission', remembers one B–24 pilot, 'would be eight to ten hours. You would take off and climb up to an assembly altitude and that might take an hour or an hour and a half.' Getting the great aircraft into their proper position by use of a garishly coloured 'Assembly Ship' was an art in itself, as this man remembers. 'We had a formation aeroplane called "Little Cookie" . . . polkadot yellow all over. It would shoot off various coloured flares, and we'd all look for that aeroplane when we got to our assembly

altitude and all the other groups in the area were doing the same thing . . .
and then we'd fly down to our target.'

For those left behind their next reminder of the war being fought from
their midst came in late afternoon, often as the short winter daylight was
fading, when a faint droning in the sky set everyone peering into the distance.
The club helper at Great Ashfield, previously quoted, can still picture the
scene.

It was a wonderful feeling to hear them coming back. We would find ourselves
listening for them at about four, several lots would go over in formation to other
bases, but we knew when they were ours when the runway lights were switched on,
in winter, and the aircraft put their lights on and one by one they peeled off,
turned in, and landed. Some had been damaged and ran off the runway, some
couldn't get their wheels down and bellylanded in a shower of sparks, some
crew were injured and were put into the ambulances before the aircraft taxied on to
the hard-stands. We always counted them down to see how many and who was
missing, as we knew each aircraft; each one had a painting or a pin-up of some
kind on the nose and a name, such as *Pregnant Portia* and a row of bombs painted
under her to show how many raids they had been on. There were very few raids
when they all came back, sometimes one missing, sometimes as many as ten.

Few people can have known as much about the progress of the US bombing
offensive as the publicans of East Anglia. 'We used to see the boys sitting
around waiting to go on a mission,' remembers the former licensee of the
King George at Harlow Bridge, near Hethel. 'Some returned and a lot
didn't. The boys would come to the pub and say, "Hank didn't return
last night," but they and we soon forgot.'

A Norwich woman, seventeen when the Americans took over the city,
remembers how: 'Many times, on going to a dance, I have said, "Where's
Jim, Buck, Harry?". . . . Most times all that was needed was a shake of the
head, then never mention him again.' A member of the ATS stationed at
Bedford recalls how 'when we used to call in at the pub and enquire "Where's
Tex?" or "Where's Pennsylvania?" they would just say they hadn't made
it back.' While serving at Norwich, her circle favoured an inn called
the World's End and, as it did not open until 8 p.m., due to the beer
shortage, she could see at a glance which of her GI friends were missing
from the queue waiting outside. A Sudbury woman who helped in the
American Red Cross assessed the scale of losses from the number of raincoats left in the club cloakroom, for the crews to collect on their next visit.
As 'the number of unclaimed raincoats grew one realized that their owners
had been shot down'.

Many airmen developed private rituals to protect them, just as British
civilians had done during the blitz. One Cambridge woman remembers
her boy friend remarking one night ' "You haven't said it tonight. Please
do." Puzzled, I asked what he meant. Apparently I had a habit of saying

"Take care!" as we parted and it had become an important omen to him.'
The charm worked: one Sunday lunchtime 'he came to my home about
2 p.m. a little unsteady on his feet and his coat covered with candlegrease'.
He had been celebrating the completion of his final mission at the local pub,
where 'it was a custom for aircrew to write their names on the ceiling of
this public house with a candle'.[1] A then five-year-old girl who spent much
of her time in just such a pub, near the Shipdham base in Norfolk, where her
grandmother was the licensee, remembers how 'We had to say prayers in
school for the safety of the aircrews who were stationed on our airfield.
My grandmother grieved for those in the bombers who did not come back.'
She still owns a crucifix left with her grandmother, 'by a young American
airman every time he went on a mission. When he returned each time he
collected his crucifix and had a drink to celebrate his survival. One night
he did not come back.'

Although a few Americans adopted a truly British reserve about their
feelings, and even RAF phraseology – 'Red bought it,' some would say – most
saw no virtue in concealing their emotions. 'They were extrovert about
these things,' remembers one woman, then aged twenty and living near
Reading. 'They *talked* of homesickness. They *admitted* fear.' The then
eighteen-year-old Red Cross worker at Great Ashfield, previously quoted,
reached the same conclusion about the B–17 crews based there:

They were far more uninhibited than the British. . . . There was no stiff upper lip.
If it had been a good raid with few lost there was a happy atmosphere, but if it
was a bad one a terrible air of depression hung over the whole place. It was always
so quiet, no piano, no whistling, no radio, they talked quietly together if at all. . . .
Sometimes they would talk to us about it, about the flak, or the altitude they flew
at – they suffered badly from sinus if they were too high for too long. . . . They
were really upset over losing aircraft; some would even break down and cry. . . .
We had to get them away into the sick bay. An upset like that could spread so
very quickly.

Outside the airfields more than one British woman found herself unexpectedly acting as 'mom' to a frightened young man never away from
home before and now in daily peril. A former landgirl, then aged nineteen
and working on a farm at Roxwell near Chelmsford in Essex, whose
landlady brought home two GIs and, unasked, left one with her with the
simple introduction 'Meet Pickles!' remembers how her initial annoyance
rapidly gave way to compassion.

I found he stuttered very badly. I made him a cup of tea and found he couldn't
hold the cup steady. His hand was shaking, his eyes blinked every few seconds. . . .
He was a rear gunner in one of those big planes and . . . before the night was out
he was crying with his head in my lap. I stroked his head and felt like his mother. . . .
He cried for his mom, and I cried with him. I gently laid him on the couch,

1. On some bases the names of targets bombed were recorded in the same way.

covered him with a blanket and sang to him. He slept and I went to bed. Next morning I got up and Pickles was gone. I never saw him again. He was killed on the next mission.

'I could tell by certain signs when a man was on flying duty,' remembers a woman who worked in the Services Club at Mardon Hall, Exeter, 'a quietness, a sort of tenseness and, so often, bitten fingernails. We knew, when their own folks didn't.' She remembers one airman deeply despondent, who revealed that he and one other man were the only two survivors in a hut which had not yet been filled up.

To many British people the GIs' lack of reserve often seemed shocking. 'Americans who crashed were easily picked out, kissing the ground, running around drawing attention to themselves,' remembers one British member of the Royal Ulster Constabulary disapprovingly. The housekeeper in a block of flats in Paddington was astonished, on being invited by some airmen tenants to hear their newly acquired Glenn Miller record 'Don't Fence Me In', 'to see that the boys were tearful. I found these airmen who had been blasting hell out of the Nazis the night before breaking down over a song on a record'.

A few people deduced from such experiences that the American airmen were lacking in courage, but those who worked most closely with them knew better. 'In the beginning they took their casualties extremely hard,' admits one former wireless operator with the RAF. 'Morale was at rock bottom. But once they had ironed out their difficulties their acceptance of casualties and losses was no different from other arms of any other service.' An RAF fighter controller observed how bravely American pilots who 'reached their point of no return' while escorting bombers 'cracked jokes or calmly went on chatting-up the ground staff until they crashed.' Always on an operational station tragedy lurked not far away. One Rabbi from Sioux City, Iowa, responsible for the Jewish crews on the fifty-three airfields of the 2nd Air Division, whose headquarters were at Ketteringham, near Norwich, recalls a typical casualty.

One very morose fellow I'll never forget. He was a Jewish tail gunner on a B–24. I saw him smiling, positively gleeful, just once . . . as he got into his 'flying box-car' one early a.m. before take off for the Ruhr.
'What's with you today, Joe?' I shouted, over the roar of the engines.
'It's my last mission, Chaplain,' he yelled back.
It was. His very last. He never got back to Brooklyn. . . . He and his crew went down in the Channel.

After an aircraft was listed MiA – Missing in Action – hope that the crew might have survived dwindled slowly. For the first few hours there was always the chance they might have landed at another aerodrome; for several days, if they had come down in the sea, there was the chance of their being picked up. The Americans had no air–sea rescue vessels of their own, this service being provided for them by the RAF. The first 'downed' US fliers to be plucked from the sea had an exceptionally warm welcome; all the rescue-launch crews based on a local port had contributed to a 'pool' to go to the first to bring in an American crew. A few aircrews given up for dead turned up again months later. The Red Cross worker at Great Ashfield, previously quoted, remembers one who 'led a charmed life'.

Time and again they were picked up at sea and would all stroll into the canteen grinning from ear to ear. They all had holes and pieces torn out of their sheepskin flying jackets and boots, by either shrapnel or machine-gun bullets, but they themselves were always unscathed. . . . Then came the day when after a raid the other crews saw them crash in France on the way home. . . . None had baled out. The whole base and ourselves was really badly upset; we felt they had come through so much they had a right to live. At least a month later a most extraordinary bunch of civilians came into the canteen. . . . They were wearing the most incredible clothes and, even worse, shoes, very yellow and shiny with pointed toes. It was this crew. They had been picked up in France by the French underground, taken over into Spain . . . walking and climbing through the most appalling conditions and very rough country. What a welcome they got; the party went on all night.

Inevitably there were occasions when crashing aircraft endangered, or claimed, the lives of British civilians, though more than once a pilot sacrificed his chance of baling out to safety to stay with his aircraft to avoid the houses below. The most famous such incident was at Walthamstow in North-East London, where in April 1943 a plaque was unveiled in an official ceremony in honour of a young fighter-pilot, engaged to a British girl, who scraped the roof-tops of a densely packed street to crash on a playing field, killing only himself. Some places had near-miraculous escapes, like the tiny village of Deenethorpe in Northamptonshire, where, one December morning in 1943, a heavily laden Fortress failed to get off the ground and, careering over farmland, crashed into a cottage on the edge of the village. The surviving members of the crew clambered from the wreckage shouting, 'Everybody get out, the bombs are about to go up!' and the hundred villagers took cover, some of them behind a 'mangold clamp' of piled-up mangelwurzels – 'better than sandbags that was', one villager remembers. When, ten minutes later, the bombs exploded, demolishing or damaging every house in the village, and rattling windows in Kettering, twelve miles away, the only British casualty was a calf, killed by a flying propeller, though a dozen pullets 'went missing' and were never seen again. There was no such happy ending for the Lancashire village of Freckleton where a heavy bomber crashed on the village school killing seventy children, as well as many adults, the worst such disaster of the entire war. One woman, who had just started her first job in a Preston dress

shop, vividly remembers how she and a friend had arranged to cycle to
Lytham St Anne, calling on the way at the Sad Sack café in Freckleton,
opened by a couple she knew to attract the booming American trade.
Because the weather turned grey the excursion was called off; that night the
would-be visitors read that the Sad Sack lay in ruins and its owners and
their children were all dead.

To the British families who befriended their crews the names of many
Eighth Air Force machines soon became almost as familiar as those of the
men themselves. 'Their aeroplanes were much more flamboyant than
RAF aircraft,' felt one Norfolk schoolboy. 'The drawings on the nose
usually featuring gorgeous girls . . . made them much more exciting.'
Some crews favoured excruciating puns like *E-rat-icator*, *Dinah Might*,
or *Quitcherbitchin*, or double meanings like *You Can't Miss It*. Some
testified to local pride like *Oklahoma Okie*, *Spirit of Atlantic City*, or,
even more parochial, *Howlett-Woodmere, Long Island*. A few names
seemed designed to tempt providence like *Journey's End*, *Flak Happy* and
Flak Bait, a Marauder which belied its name by completing more combat
missions than any other Eighth Air Force machine and is now in the
Smithsonian Museum in Washington.

Naming the aircraft was always the pilot's prerogative – indeed, as this
airman points out, the picture given by war films of a crew being inseparable
'buddies' is false and 'close as we were when in a plane we did not go about
together in off-duty hours'. The favourite source of inspiration lay in sex
and many were the *Impatient Virgins*, *Piccadilly Lillies* and *Fancy Nancies*
that thundered over Germany. Painting the accompanying figures became
almost an art-form in itself, like carving ship's figureheads during the age of
sail. Several showed a girl undressing, but on the whole the GIs preferred
their women already stripped, like *Virgin on the Verge* (in her underclothes),
Iza Vailable and *Any Time Annie*, both stark naked. The work was often
of a high standard and one Sergeant of the 487th Bomb Group at Lavenham
became famous for his achievements in this specialized field, but probably the
best known aircraft of all was *Eight Ball*, which after part of the nose had
been carried away by a breakaway propellor, was renamed *No Balls at All*.

For war-weary crews the American authorites organized two rest-homes.
One, opened in 1943, was in 'a Thames-side manor-house, surrounded by
wide lawns and flower gardens,' according to the *Stars and Stripes*, with
breakfast served by a butler, and a staff to make the beds. The crews wore
civilian clothes and the only reminder of their normal life was being served
an egg for breakfast, a luxury normally reserved for crews on operations.
This centre could accommodate only forty guests but in the following year,
the Palace Hotel at Southport, an exclusive resort on the North-West
coast, was taken over to house 400 men for a seven-day stay, who were
said to find 'the un-GI atmosphere . . . highly therapeutic'.

Although their sad eyes, looking hopefully for a master who would never return, could have a lowering effect on morale, pets were a favourite aid to relaxation on many bases. The most famous members of one B–17 Group were two cocker-spaniels, Windy, a true democrat, who ate with the enlisted men, and Skipper, who sought her diet, mainly Spam scraps, in the Officers' Mess. The *Stars and Stripes* reporter was concerned that they were being deprived of every GI's birthright. 'The rub is that there are no good-looking WAAF cocker-spaniels on the field, and not once have they had leave to see the shady lights of the lamp-posts in Piccadilly.'

In parts of Suffolk the number of animals running wild after their owners had been shot down eventually became a real problem. 'My father had over 200 young pullets killed by them and several neighbours lost sheep as well as poultry,' remembers one woman then living near Ipswich, 'but we couldn't get any compensation unless we could prove that it was their dogs that had done the damage. One farmer managed to shoot three dogs while they worried his sheep and in the end the GIs were forbidden to keep any dogs at all.'

A few aircrew favoured more exotic pets and smuggled in parrots, monkeys, and even, in the case of the 390th Group stationed at Framlingham in Suffolk, a small 'honey bear', which astonished the local inhabitants when it escaped into the surrounding countryside. The start of 'exchange' flights between American bases in Britain and North Africa also added to the local animal population. 'They brought all sorts of animals back with them, including a donkey,' the Suffolk woman just quoted remembers, but the animal pined for a warmer climate and though 'we made it a coat out of a blanket, which it promptly ate . . . it soon died'.

One wartime Corporal, from Providence, Rhode Island, recalls his even stranger pet, 'a small piglet bought from a farmer! . . . I raised it as a dog and she responded to her name. She roamed loose during the day and returned to the air-raid shelter,' her usual quarters, 'at night.' This intelligent animal also proved a good investment. Her owner having 'paid fifteen shillings for her . . . sold her for six pounds' when ordered home.

Many airmen in East Anglia also tried to forget the war by helping the local farmers. The Great Ashfield girl previously quoted found that all the volunteers, without exception, disliked pulling sugar-beet 'and hated the whole crop from start to finish. Harvest was what they enjoyed most, but we noticed that none of them had the stamina to work really hard for hours on end. They would pitch one load of corn and flop down for a rest. . . . We used to cart and stack wheat by moonlight whenever possible and that to them was the greatest thing – they had never done it before.'

The men on operations certainly had need of something to take their minds off the dangers they faced. Their ordeal began about 7.30 in the evening, with a warning message over the loudspeakers, cutting into the cheerful chatter of the canteen or mess hall, so that the crews named could 'hit the sack' early. One Pittsburg man, then a twenty-two-year-old Second Lieutenant flying a B–24 from Eye, remembers still 'the tossing half-asleep until Sergeant Ramsey came in at 4 a.m. to tell us that breakfast would be at 4.30, briefing at 5.30 and take off at 6.30'. When, on completing thirty-five missions, he was ordered home he decided that 'most of all I wouldn't miss' this grim start to the day. Often what followed was an anticlimax. 'Half our scheduled missions were scrubbed, sometimes on the ground, and sometimes while in the air forming up, due to unceasing mist, fog and clouds,' remembers one member of a B–26, Marauder, crew in the 344th Medium Bomb Group, accustomed in his home town of Conway, New Hampshire, to more cheerful weather than prevailed at Stansted in Essex. The few English children in the area appreciated scrubbed missions, as we gave them our ration of hard candy, issued to sustain us while in the air.'

The sense of let-down when a mission was cancelled affected everyone on an airfield, including the ground crew, who, unlike the fliers, were never 'stood down' due to bad weather and could see no end to their 'tour', except the end of the war.

But even on operational stations there were peaceful periods. In the hard-pressed darkrooms at East Dereham, when no operations were in progress, the Sergeant-in-Charge did 'a lot of extra work in the photo lab on what was called "The Battle of Britain" – pornographic pictures that turned up with each new crew coming in'. These 'were reproduced and enlarged and reprinted at night on surplus print paper. They included work done with professional cameras among the whores of London and pictures from as far away as Africa and the South Pacific.' On this base, too, was one Lieutenant-Colonel whose 'only hobby was porno pictures. Every time a new one came into the photo lab they had to blow him one up to about 14 by 24 and he papered his quarters with them.' This officer 'made one flight . . . and the motors quit and he had to bail out. He never went up again'.

What the presence of several thousand Americans really meant to a quiet English community can be seen by looking in detail at Polebrook, two miles from Oundle in Northamptonshire. Polebrook – station 110 in the Eighth Air Force's Official List – was one of eight airfields occupied by the 1st Bombardment Wing, whose headquarters was at Brampton Grange in Huntingdonshire.

Oundle in 1942 had a population of only 1400, swollen during the school terms by half as much again, with the return of the 600 boys of the famous public school nearby. 'Hitherto the war had been fairly remote,' remembers one woman who was then an impressionable sixteen-year-old. Now the town was about 'to be surrounded by a ring of USAAF bases flying daylight missions with B–17s: Molesworth, Deenethorpe, Apethorpe, Luffenham,

Grafton-Underwood. . . . But it was Polebrook, two miles up the country road, that was to affect . . . our young lives.'

Its first occupants duly arrived that June and flew on their first mission two months later, but in October, after losing four B–17s in action, plus others in accidents – they left for North Africa. Then in April 1943 the four squadrons of the 351st Bombardment Group, formed at Salt Lake City in October 1942, flew in. Here they remained until, two hard-fought years and 124 MiA later, the survivors set sail for home on the *Queen Elizabeth* in June 1945.

What happened to Oundle in between the then sixteen-year-old girl previously quoted still vividly remembers:

By 1943 the GIs were part of our community. We knew the names of their planes. There were the *Dotty J*, *Betty Grable*, *Hell's Angels* and *Attagirl* among them. . . . We knew the crews who flew them and the ground crews who serviced them. . . . Every morning about 5 a.m. we would be awakened by the 'pre-flight' – the warming up of the engines of squadrons of giant B–17s across the fields at Polebrooke. By breakfast they would be taking off, low over our roofs, climbing in threes to gather in vast formations, high in the sky. . . . In the afternoons they would return, we'd hear the thunder of their engines and pause in our games or our work as they limped back, now in two's and threes, low over the Northamptonshire fields, some dropping flares to indicate dead or injured aboard. . . . It was the 508 Bomber Squadron of the 351st Bomb Group we really knew best. On summer evenings they would all come in, on the olive-green GI bikes or an occasional illicit jeep if the MPs weren't around, through the country lanes smelling of beanfields, the great elm trees hiding the shapes of the B–17s back on the base after the day's missions.

There were now weekly dances in the Victoria Hall (proceeds for the war effort). At sixteen we were considered too young to attend, but as Rangers [Senior Girl Guides] we were roped in to serve refreshments. Soon the uniforms of the Yanks became familiar. Already their reputation for being wild, promiscuous and a threat to every female under seventy was well established. Nice girls should never be seen with one. But inevitably Johnny, Hank, Elmer, Chic and the rest became the only boys near our own age that we ever met. We served them steaming tea and wartime cakes and for the life of us we could not understand the terrible menace that our parents saw in them. We were incredibly naive, brought up on sentimental Hollywood films and romantic fiction, but then so were these boys. Many of them had never been away from home before and were often as wary of us as we were of them. There *were* a hard core of drinkers and womanizers who kept the rumours flying but in fact they tended to go off to the bigger towns. . . . Eventually our parents must have relaxed their vigilance because we were allowed to go to the dances at the 'Vic'. Not the correct ballroom dancing we had learned at school! It was a slow cheek-to-cheek shuffle or an exciting jitterbug. These boys knew how to talk to girls, too. . . . It was thrilling to be told 'You look cute in that dress, honey' or 'Gee, you smell sweet!' A picked group of girls was chosen to help at the American Red Cross canteen, the Aero-Club.

It was our first experience of American food. . . . By now we were used to their free ways with gums and cigarettes . . . but the food! *Pails* of ice-cream . . . steaks, hamburgers, hot-dogs, Boston-Cream pie, Pumpkin pie, disappeared as fast as we could serve them – all apparently accompanied by a strange beverage called 'Coke'. . . . And we knew more about the war now. Over at Lilford they had turned the great Hall into an American military hospital. Ambulances sped down the scented country lanes. 'Meat-wagons', they called them. The injured were taken from the returning planes to the hospital. The dead were taken to the American military cemetery at Cambridge. By now the strain of the missions was showing. A straightforward mission was a 'milk-run'. Emden, Stuttgart and deep into Germany were 'rugged missions' (and there were a lot of familiar faces missing from the dances after one of these). An air-gunner – particularly the vulnerable ball-turret gunner – was lucky to last twelve missions. Their thirteenth mission was always surrounded by superstition. 'Section 8' was added to our vocabulary. To go 'Section 8' was to break down psychologically.

Most clearly, and poignantly, of all this woman remembers 'one member of the Eighth, a twenty-year-old GI named Freddie . . . with his pale blond crewcut and his enormous grin, all freshly showered and shaved . . . his Lieutenant's uniform (olive tunic and pink pants) immaculate', who took her to a Glenn Miller concert at Polebrook with 'strict instructions from my parents to take care of me. . . . I had to sit on a girder way high up . . . and poor Freddie was so nervous that I'd fall he never saw a thing. . . . Nobody took care of Freddie. He lies under the grey Cambridge sky, never to see his beloved Indiana again.

> I'm thinking about the Wabash,
> My muddy old buddy, the Wabash,

he would sing. He had a girl in Birdseye, Indiana. He was going to be a farmer after the war.'

14

MORE TROUBLE THAN THE GERMANS

'I sometimes think we caused the British more trouble than the Germans.'

– Airman from Aurora, Nebraska, recalling 1943.

HOWEVER much they were accepted by the British people, Britain remained for most GIs, a foreign country. 'I still can't understand the goddam money,' was a common boast, and many GIs invariably tendered a handful of assorted coins for every purchase. One fifteen-year-old Cheshire girl, accompanying her boy friend to the 'pictures', became used to his cheerful remark at the box office, 'I got all kinds of money. Help yourself.'

Most GIs eventually grasped that a pound note was worth four dollars, though they grumbled about its size and that of the even larger £5 and £10 notes. The more acute eventually appreciated, too, that twenty shillings made a pound, twelve pence went to a shilling (or 'bob'), two halfpence to a penny and two farthings to a halfpenny (pronounced 'haypknee'). The values of florins (worth two shillings), half-crowns (worth two shillings and sixpence), and sixpences or 'tanners', worth six pennies though only a fraction of the size, usually eluded, however, all but the most sophisticated. To confuse foreigners still further, some silver threepenny pieces, closely resembling sixpences, and known as 'joeys', were still in circulation, but the usual threepenny piece was a twelve-sided copper coin, twice as thick as a sixpence but only half the value. One B–17 crewman remembers his bewilderment at receiving one after buying his first meal at Prestwick and asking 'the girl at the cash register what that odd-shaped coin was called. . . . I went back to my table and told my crew mates that it was a "fliptby bit" ' – the Scottish cashier's rendering of 'threepenny bit'. Another airman remembers how, after receiving their pay, his comrades sorted out the threepenny pieces and began 'throwing the "bastard coins" over a hedge. The party that found them got quite a bit.' Pennies, because of their size, weight and low value – although they could still in 1942 purchase a bus ride, or admission to a public lavatory – were also disliked. One seventeen-year-old girl recalls her 'American friend emptying his pockets of our large English pennies and after giving me some, handed the rest to a beggar at the kerb outside the Empire, Leicester Square.'

The tiny, and almost valueless, farthing, on the other hand, was treasured as a curiosity. One airman stationed in East Anglia recalls the long search for this relatively rare coin. Finally 'we found that a store in a small village nearby sold flashlight batteries and in our change you would get a farthing' so there was a sudden run on such purchases.

Their ignorance of British money made it easy for the dishonest minority to take advantage of the GIs, and publicans, taxi drivers and shopkeepers were all widely accused of doing so. One then teenager in Beeston in Nottinghamshire recalls how she 'used to feel very angry when I saw café waitresses who had just served a Yank with coffee, which cost threepence in those days, give about five shillings in small money for his change from a £1 note. The Yank would put it straight into his pocket without knowing he had been deliberately robbed.'

Almost as outrageous was the practice of some café proprietors of having a separate tariff for GIs. One RAF airman, from Manchester, witnessed a typical example when, after an evening spent drinking with six GIs at their expense, he 'insisted on paying for the meat pies and teas in a café. The woman said, "It's twopence a cup of tea for you and threepence the pie. For the Yanks, it's fourpence a cup of tea and sixpence each the pies." I refused to pay and the Yanks wrecked the café,' which never re-opened, for though the proprietress called the police, they took no action.

No doubt their failure to understand English money encouraged the reckless gambling in which many GIs indulged. 'We had no idea of the value of the various coins,' admits one farmer's son from Illinois. 'All we could do was put one coin or two as a bet and then we'd match them, coin for coin, as to size.' This was also the solution adopted, with happy results, by one B–17 Flight Engineer, attending a gunnery course on the Wash, who whiled away the tedium of nights under canvas by starting a game of blackjack with his tent-mates. 'As they doubled on pairs, etc., he confidently 'got to playing with some of these smaller bills, with the ten on them,' i.e. ten-shilling notes. 'All went well and the last hand was played by flashlight. One of the instructors there [knew me] so I went to him for advice in counting up my winnings. . . . When he explained that each one of the bills with the one on was worth $4.03 in American greenbacks, I almost fainted. I had around £200 ($800), not counting my pay envelope. . . . I figured that was my day at blackjack and I haven't played it since. . . .'

Before the Americans arrived the British Government had devoted considerable thought to their legal status in Britain. The question had been studied as early as November 1941 when one member of the American Mission in London had advised that 'he feared that public opinion in the United States . . . would not take kindly to the idea that all offences against the law of the United Kingdom committed by United States troops were liable to be tried by the British Civil Courts. . . . The attitude in the United

States of America would be that as they were helping this country by sending troops here it would be up to His Majesty's Government to give the United States' authorities exclusive control over these troops.' The real problem, commented the British Civil Servant involved, was that 'as Colonel Dalhquist himself observed . . . we have had to legislate for a bunch of Allies which include some whose ideas and standards of justice are very far from being as advanced as our own' – an oblique reference to such unlikely champions of democracy as the Ethiopians, who punished theft by chopping off the offender's hand.

In April 1942, with the problem now 'urgent', the British Foreign Secretary and Home Secretary reported in a long memorandum to the War Cabinet that 'the Americans objected to any proposal to assimilate their forces to those of the small "refugee" Allied Governments', demanding instead full jurisdiction over their own troops. 'The American soldier, they argued, is conscripted and sent overseas against, or at least without, his will. The American public will look with jealousy on the treatment which he receives while outside his native country and particularly at any sentence passed upon him by a foreign court. . . . Apart from the political agitation and misrepresention which would certainly arise . . . if American soldiers were tried by a British court and subsequently detained in a British prison, they feared that a British court would . . . tend to show undue leniency to American offenders' and 'that the United States Government . . . would be bound to assume responsibility for the man's defence.' These arguments, the British officials involved admitted, 'made a great impression' upon them.

The Cabinet finally decided to introduce 'legislation requiring all American service offenders to be handed over to the American authorites'. Even the usually leisurely House of Lords was forced to sit late to enable the United States (Visiting Forces) Bill, 1942, to be hurried into law on 6 August 1942, despite complaints in the Press at such indecent haste. In fact the anticipated difficulties never arose, because of good sense by both sides. Where only Americans were involved, the American court martial dealt with offenders. If a British civilian was the victim, the offender was often handed over for trial in a British court. The British police as always, tried to avoid arresting GIs causing trouble, giving the average 'bobby' a reputation among GIs for leniency and good-nature. 'The English bobby seemed to be held in a different light from his counterpart in my country,' admits a Staff Sergeant from Louisiana. 'Whenever they had to speak to one they were listened to very politely, they carried no weapons, only their authority, and that apparently was enough.'

Robert Arbib also formed a high opinion of the village policeman in his part of Suffolk, 'Sheriff' Moody, who toured the 'badlands' of the American airbases on a bicycle. This 'quiet, soft-spoken, pink-cheeked' man, wrote

Arbib, 'more than anyone else represented England to us. . . . If you wanted
to buy a bicycle, just ask Mr Moody.' PC Moody, for his part, accepted
with the traditional constable's calm the sudden addition to his responsibilities
of a 'roaring pioneer community of 700 young, hardworking and hard-
playing soldiers'. When the construction gangs' work was done he referred
with proprietary pride to 'our little old aerodrome'.

If the British police force had a high reputation with GIs the Americans
in their turn were at first admired for dealing fairly, and, almost more
important, promptly, with any claims made against them. Under arrangements made in 1942 training and manoeuvre claims, such as damage to
growing crops, were settled on their behalf from British Government
funds under 'reverse Lend-Lease', and others, whether caused by troops
off-duty or on, by a United States Claims Commission, which could
disburse up to $5000 (£1250); larger payments required Congressional
approval. In September 1943, however, to the British Government's
consternation, the Americans decided that the existing procedure was
contrary to United States law and called on the British Government to
'pay under reverse Lend-Lease all non-combat claims of third parties . . .
arising out of acts of personnel of the Armed Forces of the United States
in line of duty'. The most important, and most common, were traffic
accidents, claims involving which were being handled so slowly that,
following complaints in Parliament, in February 1944 the matter reached
the War Cabinet. By then a backlog of 8000 to 10 000 claims had piled up
and 1000 new ones were being submitted every week. Extraordinary though
it seemed, the Americans were gaining a reputation as 'tightwads', reluctant
to pay up when in the wrong, and the British Government acted promptly
to speed things up. From 19 March 1944, the Foreign Secretary told the
House of Commons, it would foot the bill for all claims under $5000
arising from incidents on duty, though the Americans would still have to
negotiate the actual amount. The British authorities would also deal with
'off-duty' claims over $5000, which were far fewer. Claims for minor loss
or damage caused by GIs off-duty – as during a fight in a public house –
would still be investigated and settled by the Americans, but any dissatisfied
claimant could sue for compensation in a British court. This solution proved
fair and workable; the problem caused no more trouble between the two
countries.

If the Americans admired the British police force they never had anything
but criticism for another public service, the telephone system; they had yet
to learn that, whatever its wartime defects, it was far more efficient than
any on the Continent. British telephones became the butt of every GIs' wit.
Using one, commented the *Stars and Stripes* as early as July 1942, was
'Like lifting the receiver at home and asking for "Wrong number please".'
Of the careful operating instructions posted in every telephone booth it

remarked: 'OK. Only it doesn't work.' Even that most pro-English of
GIs, Robert Arbib, felt obliged to confess that 'The telephone system is a
constant bafflement. Not merely for the complexity of "Button A" and "Button
B" but for the unpredictable results obtained from manipulating these
gadgets.' Constantly, when connected, or 'through' as the British put it,
they would press 'Button B', which cut them off and returned their twopence,
instead of 'Button A', which completed the connection. One woman then
aged fifteen and living in the Cornish village of Nanpean recalls often
having to come to the rescue of a 'would-be caller in a public telephone
kiosk' – though, seeing a pretty girl approaching, some GIs no doubt made
the most of their helplessness.

A few hopeful callers attempted to 'date' the telephone operator, though
this was hazardous. One Watford man remembers his GI lodger being 'very
excited' that one GPO girl was to be 'waiting outside the telephone exchange
at 8 p.m. wearing a red coat. Later I asked him how he got on. "Boy," he
replied, "you should have seen her! She could not have got through that
door ... I told Bill not to stop but to drive on like hell".' As for the system
itself, it could do nothing right and the *Stars and Stripes* delivered itself in
January 1944 of one final insult. A cartoon showed British girl telephone
operators filing aboard a troop-carrying aircraft, while their escort explained:
'We're dropping them over enemy territory to disrupt communications.'

The British Broadcasting Corporation, which many Britons (and certainly
the BBC itself) secretly considered the best in the world, was also a regular
target for American criticism. Between 1942 and 1945 it offered to listeners
in Britain two programmes, the Home Service, aimed at the 'middle-brow'
domestic audience, and the Forces Programme, consisting largely of comedy
programmes and light music designed for listening in canteens, factories
and barrack rooms. As its audience of American listeners increased, the
BBC did its somewhat earnest best to meet their needs, with international
exchange programmes, in which selected GIs spoke of the 'folks' back home,
and with well-meaning, if faintly embarrassing, programmes like *Let's Get
Acquainted*. An early edition, in June 1942, displayed some typical British
humour – comedian Robb Wilton doing his famous 'Home Guard' sketch –
and included an American and a British Private in a carefully scripted
conversation which revealed that one man in civil life was a 'carpenter' and
the other a 'joiner', and the former had been 'called up' and the latter
'drafted'. 'Most of us thought the BBC radio programming was rather
ludicrous,' remembers one man from Providence, Rhode Island, stationed
at Tetbury in the Cotswolds. 'Largely it was appallingly colourless and dull.
Their newscasters had a way of making the most dramatic war event ...
sound about as exciting as an account of a Sunday afternoon at grandma's.'
Sensitive to such criticisms, the BBC was already, by November 1942,
trying to cater for its critical new audience with an *American Sports Bulletin*,

read by a Master Sergeant from the *Stars and Stripes*, and that month its Assistant Director of Variety promised 'to inject more zip and zing' into comedy programmes, with three a week featuring American stars. The American authorities, meanwhile, arranged morale-boosting short-wave broadcasts from the United States like *News from the Home Front*, heard daily at 7.15 a.m., 8 p.m., and 10 p.m. The real need, however, was for an all-American service based in Britain and this was finally launched on Sunday, 4 July 1943, although at first it could only be heard in a few parts of the country. The American Forces Network, or AFN, carried the BBC news, but its programmes were otherwise all 'home-grown', consisting largely of recordings of shows currently successful in the United States, featuring such stars as Red Skelton, Jack Benny, Bing Crosby, Bob Hope and Dinah Shore, and the presentation was strictly American. AFN was on the air from early morning until 10.30 p.m. (11 on Saturday) on 211·2 or 213·9 metres and, somewhat to the BBC's annoyance, it soon attracted a large 'eavesdropping' audience, whom it helped to familiarize with American language and attitudes. After AFN's appearance American attacks on the BBC ceased; the GIs simply stopped listening to it.

Although GIs had the reputation among British civilians of being far more ready than themselves to call a spade a spade, many Americans discovered that the reverse was true of the communication media. 'I was often astonished by the language I heard in movies and on the wireless,' recollects one veteran of five years of barrack-room life, stationed near Swindon. 'We looked disparagingly at the occasional use of "hell" in the British movies,' remembers a Detroit man disapprovingly. Here was one area where Great Britain enjoyed far more freedom than the United States, as many Americans suddenly realized when the all-powerful Hays Office, responsible for excluding any unwelcome breath of coarseness, or even realism, from Hollywood productions, announced that it had barred the famous Noël Coward film *In Which We Serve* on account of its 'offensive language'. To most GIs this seemed absurdly prudish, especially as the offending expression, 'bastards', had been directed by a sailor at the Germans who had sunk his ship. The *Stars and Stripes*, in a leading article in December 1942, vigorously denounced the mealy-minded stay-at-homes responsible, suggesting that they visit a village school recently bombed by the Germans. 'They would never again question any swear word used to describe a German,' declared the writer.

The explicitness of British advertising also amazed American observers. Many GIs concluded from the frequent advertisements for 'Bile Beans' that constipation must be a universal affliction in Britain, while Robert Arbib was intrigued by another mysterious medicine, widely publicized in Suffolk, called 'Constitution Balls'. To him, as to others, it seemed puzzling that this frankness was combined with an apologetic approach to selling. 'British advertising on posters and in magazines and newspapers,' he commented frankly, 'strikes you as a masterpiece of negation. "Thank you for mentioning it," the ads seem to say, "but we think you'll like our product. We don't want to influence you in any way of course, but we make beer, too".'

Arbib also thought it typical of British journalism that 'the nation's most-respected newspaper [i.e. *The Times*] covers its front page with personal notices and classified advertising', although more to the taste of most GIs was the *Daily Mirror*, whose famous strip cartoon character, Jane, was for ever losing her clothes in embarrassing circumstances. One middle-aged woman, living in Norwich, who had never gone out to work before, but now drove a Church Army canteen around the airfields, 'cut out "Jane" and stuck it up behind the glass door of the van. From then on there were two queues, one of customers . . . another round the back to read "Jane".' The GIs also marvelled over the Sunday *News of the World*, which reported the seamier court cases in lurid detail. Among them, early in 1945 was the 'cleft-chin murder case', so called after the appearance of the victim, a London taxi driver murdered by a GI deserter and a London 'good-time girl'. It perhaps says something for Allied unity that, as the paper reported, British public opinion clamoured for the woman, who was reprieved and sent to prison, to share the same fate as her accomplice, who was hanged. The *News of the World* was also famous for its personal messages. One GI now back in Troy, New Hampshire, still remembers reading a desperate heart-cry on the page in which his fish-and-chips were wrapped – a common source of GI knowledge of the British press: 'Malcolm, come back. I can't go to sleep without you know what. Edith.'

As with broadcasting, the GIs' needs were finally met by a production of their own the *Stars and Stripes*, which provided a notable example of Allied – and newspaper – co-operation. It was written by American journalists and drew on material from the American Press and news agencies, but was produced on the presses of *The Times*, while its 400 000 copies were distributed by the *News of the World*. The British printers nobly forgot all they had learned about 'correct' spelling and became notorious for their eagerness to get 'their' paper 'to bed', while *The Times* took second place. This 'Newspaper of the United States Armed Forces in the British Isles', began weekly publication on Saturday, 18 April 1942 with No. 1 of Volume II; Volume I – last issue June 1919 – had appeared in World War I.

The *Stars and Stripes*, though catering for all services and ranks, was angled in the direction of the ordinary 'GI Joe', whose trials and problems it admirably reflected and whose cause it vigorously championed. The format, slightly above tabloid size, resembling the London *Evening Standard*, and the style both made for easy reading, and the layout skilfully fitted together general war news, items from home, stories about ETOUSA, cartoons and jokes. It was a well-informed, good-humoured newspaper, avoiding the twin weaknesses of American journalism, screaming sensationalism and turgid verbosity, and though its editor was an army Major, and open attacks on the authorities were ruled out, shortages were frankly admitted and grievances openly expressed in its pages.

In mid-June 1942 the *Stars and Stripes* was joined by *Yank*, a specifically army publication, claimed to be 'by and for EMs' and consisting largely of feature material in a magazine-type format. Eventually a place was found for both. *Yank*, costing threepence, was published each Sunday, while from 2 November 1942 the *Stars and Stripes* became a daily, costing a penny, and appearing, like British newspapers, on Monday through to Saturday. It was, an editorial claimed with pride, the first US daily to be printed in Europe since the Paris edition of the *Chicago Herald Tribune* had closed down. By D-Day, when it suffered an exodus of readers such as no circulation manager in history had ever faced before, the paper was selling 600 000 copies. It made its last appearance on Monday, 15 October 1945, after which the few GIs left in the British Isles were served by the edition being produced in Paris.

Although many attempts were made to bridge the linguistic gulf between the two countries, none of these glossaries (perhaps overcome by delicacy) warned against using the few words, harmless in America, which did cause raised eyebrows in Britain. One British woman, then a teenager working in a US Army supply office in London, can still recall her sense of outrage when one officer 'referred to all the crap on his desk' and another 'asked if he could warm his fanny against the radiator'. An engineer from New York City, assigned to St Austell in Cornwall in 1943, 'to acquire real estate' for pre D-Day training, still remembers the Sunday afternoon when he slipped on the path outside his billet. 'I entered the dining-room where tea was in session with the local vicar in attendance and announced I had fallen on my fanny. A stunned silence followed.' A British term which caused equal surprise among GIs was the verb 'knock-up', which to them meant making a girl pregnant. Many were the barely suppressed sniggers when some unsuspecting landlady or girl friend promised to knock them up – i.e. wake them – in the morning – and common variants such as 'Shall I knock you up with a cup of tea?' made the joke even richer. One Plymouth, Massachussetts man, a Pfc in a chemical warfare company, remembers being taken aback at the injunction 'Keep your pecker up' – meaning 'Stay cheerful'. One Second Lieutenant in the Nurse Corps in Northern Ireland picked up another ambiguous expression. 'Things that were particularly nice . . . were said to be "sticking out". If anyone wanted a little more emphasis they were "Sticking out about a fortnight".'

Coining slang expressions was one area, British listeners decided, where American supremacy could not be contested. One Wren working alongside

Americans remembers enlivening family life when on leave with such colourful importations as 'Let's go sidewalk slapping' (i.e. for a walk) or – when offering a woman a cigarette – 'Wanna fag, hag?' 'Grab a wing?' a teenager in Leeds decided, meant 'Hold my arm?' One British accounts clerk at Burtonwood still wonders if a waiter in a cheap American restaurant was really described as a 'bum hash-slinger in a two-bit gut-filling station'. One woman who worked alongside the GIs at a Suffolk airbase still replies to any complaint from her husband she considers unreasonable with an expression acquired then: 'Oh, you want egg in your beer!'

Less innocently, 'Holy cow!', 'Jeeze!' and 'goddam', never heard in American films due to the Hays Office, soon became familiar in British ears, but some British swearwords remained unknown to Americans. One then teenager from Plymouth can still blush at the memory of the afternoon when her first GI boy friend came to tea with her 'very religious and rather strict parents'. 'Suddenly Roy looked up and said, "Say, what does 'bugger' mean?" There was a sort of electric silence and my father fumbled for words, until the guest helpfully remarked, making matters worse, "Well, I guess it's the same as when we say "bastard".' Other British hosts remember similar contretemps, as when one GI explained that his friend was 'piddling in the garden'; the British equivalent was 'pottering'. The expression 'wash-up' was another common cause of misunderstanding. One Oxfordshire village storekeeper remembers hurrying after a GI guest who announced he was going to 'wash up' to point out that this was the family's job, only to find him making for the bathroom. 'Wash up' in America they found, meant to wash oneself not the dishes, though – to add a new and confusing element – to 'wash one's hands' meant in England to go to the lavatory, known to GIs as 'the john' or 'the can'. A similar expression, mainly used by women, 'to spend a penny', regularly amused Americans. One Plymouth woman remembers a visiting GI who placed sixpence or a shilling on the mantelpiece on arrival and when he had 'used it up' by the appropriate number of visits to the lavatory 'would then put out some more'.

Curiously enough, since this was such a major meeting point between the two countries, differences of usage proved most marked in the area of sex. Every British typist working among GIs soon learned that in US Army jargon a 'rubber' was not used to remove errors, though, rather strangely, one official glossary insisted that in the plural it meant galoshes. A woman clerk then working in the Air Transport Command at Cumberland House, Marble Arch, recalls asking the Corporal at the next desk to pass her a rubber. 'The whole office stopped dead as if struck by lightning, then fell about laughing. . . . One of the woman GIs came over and whispered in my ear that surely I meant an eraser?' A secretary in Shrewsbury remembers a splendidly unproductive exchange between a British and American officer discussing shooting game. 'Do you have ptarmigan?' the latter, a

Southerner, was asked, and finally, after looking puzzled, replied, 'Sure but we shoot with them', thinking the Briton had said 'Tommy gun'! One wartime shop assistant in Preston remembers how 'a giant of a Sergeant' with 'a strong Southern accent' came into the shop and 'the senior serving him couldn't understand what he was asking for'. Finally, with great presence of mind, 'she said: "You'll probably get some in the Arcade".'

Before long the GIs became resigned to being called 'Yanks'. Only one word, 'bloke', was constantly misinterpreted. Many GIs wrongly assumed that it had a derogatory ring and either used it as an alternative to Limey or to describe an objectionable Englishman. One then teenager in Northampton remembers her boy friend pleading with her to tell him its 'real' meaning. 'Is it,' he asked, 'as terrible as it sounds?'

More puzzling on the whole than the English language were English place-names. Apart from such obvious pitfalls as Cirencester (pronounced Sissister), Gloucester (pronounced Gloster) and Derby (pronounced Darby), the Americans probably grumbled most about two names which every Briton took for granted. One woman working in an aircraft factory in Oxford recalls being constantly asked: 'Why is the River Thames pronounced that funny way?' (i.e. 'Tems') and 'Why is Reading not Redding?', a mystery even to Englishmen. One wartime telephonist at Truro, then aged seventeen, recalls American voices asking for 'St AusTELL, and 'LarnCESton' – St AUSTell and LAWNston (spelt Launceston) to British callers. At Welsh place-names, unpronounceable even by Englishmen, the GIs wisely gave up. One then schoolboy at Carmarthen remembers how Llanelly became known to all Americans as 'Slash', a name which 'stuck for many years after the war'.

After they had mastered the traumatic shock of realizing, on asking directions to the nearest one, that the nearest drugstore was 3000 miles away, and that even the few goods to be seen in the shops were often 'on coupons', the GIs became popular customers in British shops, particularly those selling antiques, whose supplies had not been affected by the war.

One Buckinghamshire woman remembers with embarrassment a tour of the antique shops in Princes Risborough with a US naval officer determined to find one of 'those lil ole English christening cups', for every shopkeeper looked pointedly at her left hand in search of a wedding ring. Her escort's quest failed, but he was amply consoled by discovering an ancient blunderbuss on a market stall, which he 'sloped' on his shoulder, before leading her into 'the best hotel in the town for dinner'. He cheerfully handed this ancient weapon to the astonished receptionist with the polite request: 'Honey, will yer just put that up your jumper while we have our dinner, please, and yell at me if I forget it?' Rarely was disapproval of American eagerness voiced to their faces but one former GI from Aurora, Nebraska, remembers how, when running for the 'liberty bus' late one night 'a Britisher came round the corner and I knocked him to the street. As I continued on I could hear him repeating over and over: "You bloody, damn Yanks!" I didn't blame him. I sometimes think we caused the British more trouble than the Germans.'

To the British the average American seemed shockingly indifferent to the past. One family at Hessle, East Yorkshire, remember a Sergeant from a part detachment whose reaction to Scarborough Castle, an imposing pile overlooking the sea, was that 'They ought to pull the ruins down. It was a waste of a marvellous site for a hotel.' To the Americans, by contrast, the British often seemed unbelievably backward. 'The British seemed to have some special dispensation from the laws of physics,' recalls one veteran. 'Most of them felt they had stepped back in time,' remembers a British housewife of the GIs she knew. 'They were appalled at the lack of modern living. No fridges, washing machines or any modern conveniences. They considered a woman's life one long round of housework, cooking and drudgery.' British families soon became accustomed to listening indulgently, or in fascination, to travellers' tales of the wonders America afforded: tea in little bags, beer in cans – soon littering many an English roadside – even, as one impressed wartime teenager from the village of Dunham Massey in Cheshire remembers being told – cafés where one could 'put money in a slot, open up a flap and out came the meal of one's choice'. To many Britons American ignorance seemed equally astonishing. The then housekeeper in a block of flats in Paddington remembers dozing off after lighting a fire in an American-occupied flat to be woken by a great commotion. The first GI to come back to it had never seen an open hearth before and thought the flat was alight. One British airman remembers a GI arriving back, after being shot down in France, with an RAF officer's shirt, unfastened at the neck. He had hitherto known only collar-attached shirts and, his 'tutor' remembers, 'I had quite a job teaching him to use collar studs.'

The feeling that the British Isles were merely a large-scale animated museum was widely held among GIs. 'Your great little island has everything,' an enthusiastic American told a Biggin Hill housewife, adding, as the final compliment, 'and one can get around it in a day'. No one *did* get around it in a day, though some came close to doing so, like the two GIs the verger of Winchester Cathedral found in the Cathedral Close. On offering to show them round, 'one replied, "We have only got five minutes", whereupon his companion said, "You do the inside and I'll do the outside".'

Some GIs spent all their leaves visiting towns that took their fancy. Tewkesbury, well-known for its Abbey but off the usual tourist track, was particularly admired by one naval Lieutenant. 'Everything', he wrote, 'was old except the GIs.' Other places remembered with special pleasure are Edinburgh (despite it raining incessantly for the ten days one man spent there), Oxford, and Cambridge, where an academic said to resemble Mr Chips of the famous Greer Garson film, was much valued as a guide.

Both universities were probably seen at their best by the GIs who attended the special six-day academic courses. The lecturers included such internationally known academics as Sir Gilbert Murray and Sir William Beveridge. One Engineer Lieutenant from Maryland, who attended one of the earliest courses, at Emmanuel College, Cambridge, in June 1943 was even more impressed by the 'meticulous service' and 'beer in sterling silver mugs'.

"Wal, Lootenant, it sure has been swell having you here."

Another ancient town much visited by GIs was Winchester though one woman who worked at the Information Desk in the American Club soon discovered that '99 per cent of the questions asked were: (1) What's on at the "flicks"? (2) Where is there a dance? (3) Which pub is open?' Only once did an enquirer betray a more serious interest, asking '"Had we any girls' schools in Winchester?" Thinking he had an educational interest,' she recollects, 'I asked for details. Sheepishly he replied, "Just thought I could get a date."'

Some GIs had private pilgrimages to perform in search of their ancestors, or of the places after which their own home towns had been named, while for literary-minded GIs England proved a delight. The archetypal 'serious American' of this kind was surely a Harvard Ph.D, later head of a Los

Angeles college, but in 1943, most improbably, a Military Policeman stationed at Hull, whose delight at being assigned to the native land of his private passion, the Brontës, has been mentioned earlier. At last, on his first pass, after a journey of 5000 miles from his native Gothenburg, Nebraska, to Haworth in Yorkshire, he found himself 'at the bottom of the hill' in the centre of the ancient village of 'weatherbeaten, plain buildings . . . strangely moved'. Thereafter one pleasent experience followed another. After a tour of the Brontës' house, remarkably unchanged by the passage of time, and lunch at the Black Bull, where the scapegrace son Branwell had done his drinking, until he made a solitary excursion across the moors through sleet and snow, in search of the original 'Wuthering Heights'. 'The day seemed to grow darker and the wind howled and moaned plaintively. . . . The sheep looked at me with their blank, apathetic eyes as if to say, "Well, Yank, what are you doing way up here?" '

15

ONE OF THE FAMILY

'They only liked to come if they could be one of the family.'

– A Winchester woman, recalling 1943.

UNTIL the 1840s, when the railways began to cover the British Isles, the chief excitement in many British towns had been the departure of the mail coach. A century later the same peaceful places witnessed a noisier version of a similar scene: the embarkation of GIs on the 'liberty buses' carrying them back to their bases. For a few minutes the central streets seemed full of shouting and jostling men in American uniforms. One resident of Northampton remembers how the market square was so completely taken over at these times that it was nicknamed 'Texas', while Ipswich in Suffolk, increasingly surrounded by American airfields from mid-1942, was regularly swamped by GIs, even though only 15 per cent of the personnel were allowed off base at a time. Robert Arbib described what this weekly outing meant to the men of his construction battalion, building the runways at Debach, seven miles away.

The evening liberty truck left camp promptly at seven o'clock, overflowing with soldiers dressed up in their only suits of clean, pressed clothes. The truck was designed to carry fourteen men, but usually there were more than twice that number crowded into the dark interior, squatting on the floor, sitting three-deep on each other's lap, hanging over the tail-gate and standing stooped under the low tarpaulin hood. . . . We bounced and careened over the winding road to Ipswich, a trip that often took forty minutes in the unfamiliar black-out. The truck parked in Princes Street and the human cargo spewed forth into the street breaking up into little groups of two, three or four.

Some made for the nearest cinema, although 'often the films were old ones that we had earlier seen in America' and 'the evening performances had already begun'. Almost as popular was any public dance and there was one 'almost every night . . . either at the Co-Operative Hall or St Lawrence's Church Hall,' though tough GIs 'were frankly terrified at the prospect of a "Ladies Invitation Slow Fox-Trot"'. A third contingent of GIs were content to saunter the streets where the girls 'walked along the pavement in pairs, smiling, swinging their supple hips in short skirts, looking after the soldiers' . . . The biggest attraction of all was in the pubs. Ipswich boasted 200, 'family pubs, workers' pubs, railway pubs, seaport pubs, large and small ones, clean and dirty ones', plus several respectable hotels, like Arbib's particular delight, the Great White Horse, scene of the 'curl papers' incident in *The Pickwick Papers*.

In Cambridge, the departure point for the liberty buses was close to the Bus Station in Drummer Street. At eleven o'clock, remembers one Lieutenant on the headquarters staff of the 66th Fighter Wing, stationed at Duxford, 'this was a madhouse, with several hundreds of GIs trying to find their transport back to base from the seemingly hundreds of trucks'. This officer, having gained the entrée to a club-like pub where it was possible, though illegal, to drink after hours, often found himself left high, but not, as he remarks, dry, in Cambridge, ten miles from his base, long after the Duxford bus had left. Later, after the Wing Headquarters had moved to Sawston Hall, several miles nearer, he found the real answer to his transport problem, a bicycle and an obliging landlady who kept a spare room free for him. When the weather was fine he would ride back to Sawston, but his landlady agreed that 'If the steeple of All Saints Church, in the backyard around the corner in Jesus Lane, was hidden in the fog I was to accept her hospitality for the night.'

What most GIs longed for was an invitation to a British home. The American Red Cross alone, between November 1943 and the end of the war, arranged one and a quarter million such visits, usually for a single meal but sometimes for a whole furlough. Hosts and guests were put in touch through local Anglo-American Hospitality Committees, but these were not always very successful. One Reading man, who agreed to organize one in March 1943, acknowledges that it 'never really got off the ground'. Invitations were 'passed on to the chaplain of a unit, who would do his best to find takers for a blind date for afternoon tea on Sunday', but due to a unit moving at short notice or sheer lack of consideration, the result was all too often 'a disgruntled hostess' who had wasted her 'meagre rations'. The complaint that such GI guests failed to turn up was often made and on the whole most successful 'adoptions' of a GI by a British family resulted from a personal invitation. Church was a common meeting place, and seemed to offer some guarantee of respectability on both sides, though a Cheshire housewife remembers one GI fellow worshipper recoiling in alarm when she asked him home after the service, only accepting on being reassured that they would be safely chaperoned by her husband and children.

A single GI guest was often the forerunner of many more. A woman living in Leicester remembers how 'there would be a knock on the door and one, two or three Americans would stand there saying: "Tex told us to look you up".' One regular visitor, she remembers, insisted on being photographed with the baby next door and sending a print to his fiancée, which must have given her a shock. The men arriving in one barrack room at another camp, the wife of a British officer living in Northern Ireland remembers, would find awaiting them 'a note: "Go to No. 106 for coffee"'. A Belfast man and his wife recall being asked for directions to their own house by three GIs; unknown to their parents, the family's three teenage daughters had invited the young men to call.

When invitations were slow in arriving, the GIs, in their cheerful and enterprising way, took the initiative. A Salisbury housewife remembers 'one summer night in 1943. We were sitting in our little kitchen . . . and had our front door . . . ajar because of the heat. . . . Suddenly our passage was invaded by half a dozen huge GIs. My husband stood up and said, "Whatever are you doing in here?" and they said, "Sorry, Pop, saw the light and thought it was a pub! Never mind, have a cigar", and they went off laughing.'

Despite their hair-raising reputation many GIs liked nothing better than to join in familiar domestic rituals. The favourite recreation of one GI who visited a Peterborough family was to scrape out the saucepan after his hostess had been mashing potatoes because 'it reminded him so much of home'. Another housewife, at Great Barr, Birmingham, found that their GIs loved to sit and watch her knitting, having 'never seen anyone do that in the USA'. What symbolized England for her, confessed a WAC to a woman living near Altrincham, was 'a knitted tea-cosy', though American visitors also delighted in the oil lamps which still lit their seventeenth-century house. The GI who stayed with the family who ran the post office and village store at Longworth in Berkshire was equally thrilled to be escorted to his 'funny little bedroom' with a candle. At Stone, in Stafford-shire, one woman engraver with an engineering firm remembers, the gas lighting in homes (still then the rule in many houses, including my own), the 'black ranges for cooking' and the 'slate slab floors' were also lovingly noted.

Sometimes a British home became almost a club in miniature. A former village shopkeeper from Stradbroke, near the Horsham St Faith airbase still treasures the large map of America which then hung in his kitchen, for 'the boys used to write their names in the sea and then dot a line through to the State they lived in'. 'I spent half my time scribbling to relatives of the boys,' remembers one woman, aged seventeen when the first GIs reached her native Appleshaw. 'That way their family could tell what part of England their sons were stationed. As GIs went . . . they would leave at my home their treasured possessions for safe keeping. Bit by bit, as they reached safe zones . . . I would forward their belongings.' She remembers still the items one Pfc, from Bakersfield, California, valued most: 'his best-dress peaked cap, some long leather boots, watch and graduation ring'. The mementoes sent for storage by another GI before dispatch to his home in

Wayne County, Pennsylvania, reflected the progress of the Allied armies: 'SS armbands, badges and German radios'. Equally typical was the friendship which developed between one young and newly-married couple living in Paisley in a modest tenement house with no bathroom and only a shared outside toilet, who went out in search of a GI to entertain and duly discovered 'Pete' from Allentown, Pennsylvania 'standing alone in a shop doorway', one evening; he was training with the First Army at Bellahouston Park, Glasgow. 'Pete' became a frequent guest, at first refusing to accept more than 'a cup of tea and a piece of apple pie' but later spending two leaves with the family, 'sharing our double bed with my husband while I "dossed down" on a camp bed in the kitchen. . . . When I came home in the afternoon,' his hostess remembers, 'I'd find that he had made the bed and washed up his breakfast dishes, leaving everything immaculate. . . . He accepted without comment a breakfast of a scrap of bacon and some reconstituted dried egg.' After serving in North Africa and Italy and returning to Dorset to train for the invasion with, literally, only a scratch caused by barbed wire, Pete, visiting his friends in Scotland, made his first and only complaint: that the family had moved 'an old brass candlestick from the mantelpiece where it had stood during the months when he had been stationed in Glasgow, and begged me to replace it, saying he had so often pictured it in his mind while he was in the desert: "It ain't home without it".'

This proved his last visit. Pete had privately told her husband 'that he knew he wasn't going to survive' and had left with his hosts, for return to his fiancée, a nurse in the Johns Hopkins Hospital in Baltimore, the 'gold ring with large red stone in it' he had worn right through earlier campaigns. Four days after being wounded in Normandy he died in hospital, the news only reaching his friends when a letter to him was returned stamped 'Deceased'. 'When I came home from work that black day', his hostess remembers, 'a little bit of my heart broke. . . . It was like losing a dearly loved young brother.'

When they first entered a British home most GIs behaved, by British standards, with almost exaggerated politeness. Their habit of calling older men 'sir' delighted their hosts, and middle-aged women were captivated by similar courtesies. One man then working in an aircraft factory in Blackpool enjoyed seeing his wife 'escorted by "Johnny Reb" as if she were some great plantation lady of the South, and with that deep Southern accent addressing her as "ma-am", just like Rhett Butler in *Gone with the Wind*'. Such formality often gave way to 'mom' and 'pop' or some private nickname. The steward of a Hereford golf club found himself dubbed 'the reverend', a title which, during a game of poker, caused consternation among those players not in the secret 'when one GI who was having more than his share of bad luck let loose a few swear words'. The daughter of a Suffolk farmer, whose rank of Corporal in the Home Guard the GIs considered 'the funniest thing', regularly addressed him as 'the Brigadier'. But the happiest invention of this kind was the name 'Valholst' applied to a very plump pig belonging to a Goxhill family. It puzzled the pig's owners until one day a very fat NCO arrived at their front door, introduced himself as 'Sergeant Valholst', and explained he had overheard his men laughing about his namesake and had come to inspect it.

Before long an initial hostility to accepting GIs as lodgers had largely disappeared and most hosts would echo the conclusion of 'Pop the cop', a War Reserve constable in Gloucester on whom two US Army nurses were billeted: 'We all settled down together and were very happy.' The then eight-year-old daughter of an Aberdare family recalls how her parents' relief when the billeting officer decided that their 'facilities were not good enough' for American soldiers since 'We had no bathroom and no hot water', later changed to regret on learning of the 'gentlemanly boys' quartered on other residents.

The billeting of Americans on civilian families helped to bring home to the British hosts the varied racial mix which made up the American nation. A Cheltenham minister's wife was astonished to discover that one of her two American lodgers 'was a German'. The two nurses accommodated by 'Pop the Cop' were respectively of Spanish and Swedish stock, from Los Angeles and Wisconsin. The owner of a requisitioned holiday home in Cornwall copied down this revealing list of its recent occupants left pinned to a bedroom door:

> Pfc Don Zwicke
> Pfc Pat Toriello
> Pvt Mart Berman
> Pvt Fred Shaw
> Pvt Arnold Stefferud

Billetting also finally made clear that, contrary to the impression given by Hollywood, the American nation did not consist exclusively of cowboys, gangsters, or wealthy sophisticates. A former Manchester schoolboy, thirteen when 'our first American arrived in March 1944' and a self-confessed 'addict' to American films, was so impressed by the genuine article that he still recalls each man's name and personality. The first resident was 'a real mother's boy', Sanders S., from Columbo, Mississippi, who spoke in a real Southern drawl, then came Charles M., from San Antonio, Texas, 'more of a rugged type. He annoyed Mother by sticking his wife's photograph on his bedroom wall with black insulating tape. When he was overdue in receiving a letter from her, he would have black moods and rip the picture down, only for it to reappear on the wall again as soon as he received a letter. The wall got badly marked. . . . However, he was very likable and . . . whenever he was on canteen duty he used to bring back enormous canisters of ice-cream. . . . Our third and last paying guest was Dorwyn S.

17 & 18. At the pub. 'All Americans were agreed', wrote one GI, 'that the pub was a good thing', but usually white and coloured soldiers kept strictly apart, often using different public houses.

19. Thanksgiving Day party, 1942. The Americans' liking for children and the lavishness of the food provided at their parties, became a legend.

20. The 'candy hand-out' was a popular feature of US parties for sweets-starved British children and often GIs were besieged in the street by young Britions clamourng for 'candy'.

21. A Yank for Christmas. Many GIs became 'one of the family' in British homes and an invitation at Christmas was often the start of a lifelong friendship.

22. Here comes Santa Claus. At this Christmas party for British war orphans in December 1942 Father Christmas arrived by tank. On air force stations he often descended in a Flying Fortress.

23. The sailor on the train. Although the GIs tended to smile at the alleged smallness and backwardness of British trains they were much prized as places to make new acquaintances, especially female.

24. The fancy-dress party. GIs and British friends enjoying a breather during a typically riotous party in London in 1942.

25. Rainbow Corner, close to Piccadilly Circus, the Mecca of every homesick GI on leave.

26. The doughnut-dunkers. These GIs, enjoying an all-American snack inside Rainbow Corner, were indulging in the traditional ritual of dunking their doughnuts in their coffee.

27. Entertainer in action inside Rainbow Corner. Like most US clubs it provided a constant supply of high-quality entertainment, including many top show-business names.

28. A dance at Rainbow Corner. 'Jive' was banned in some public dance halls, not very effectively, but was permissible in this American environment.

29. Eros, boarded-up. Having heard of the delights of Piccadilly Circus, GIs were disappointed to find its centre-piece, a statue of the God of Love, boarded-up to protect it from bomb-damage.

30. The sightseers. The attraction for these camera-carrying GIs was the arrival of Members of Parliament at the House of Commons on 1 August 1945.

31. 'You can't miss it.' A GI on a bicycle became one of the most familiar sights in wartime Britain. These two are being given directions by Cheltenham's oldest inhabitant, aged 100.

32. Helping with the harvest festival. Especially in East Anglia, where many airmen served for long periods, GIs often became active members of their local community.

(Don), from Oregon, who was a religious "nut" who rarely left his bedroom in his leisure hours. He just pored over his Bible and exchanged copious letters with a colleague of a similar bent, discovering new Biblical texts to quote to one another.' Of these three the second is still immortalized by the card game he taught the children for 'he did not know its name so I told him I would call it after him and it is known as "Monty" to this day.'

A Blackpool man whose family ran a boarding house has equally vivid recollections of several of the GIs it accommodated at various times. Among them were:

'Smitty', an ex-hobo who used to enthrall us with tales of the American railroads and . . . who admitted to not having had a pair of decent boots in his life until being drafted into the American Army, 'Sheriff', whose father was a sheriff in Texas, handlebar moustache and all, 'Freddy Flick', because we never could pronounce his Italian name, a veteran of Panama, Lightfoot, a Cheyenne Indian, who used to charm the children with savage war whoops, and 'Dark' . . . the 'dead spit' of gigolo George Raft. . . .

Apart from fringe benefits like extra rations, it was not unprofitable to have a GI billeted in one's home. A woman at Churchtown, near Southport in Lancashire, recalls discovering the very different value the American and British authorities put on their soldiers' comfort. 'On 3 September 1939,' the day the war broke out, she recalls, 'we received a knock at the door and someone roared "Two militia lads – sleep 'em on the floor if you've no beds,"' and that was that, for which we received 3s. 6d. (17½p or 75 cents) per week.' Later came the GIs. '*Their* billets had to be inspected and we were paid £1.1s.' ($4.20). Feared before they came, reluctantly accepted when they arrived, the GIs billeted in private homes were sadly missed when they left. 'We were', admits a Solihull housewife with two such enforced guests, 'sorry to see them go' – and the men themselves were equally sad. On their last night they tried to drown their sorrows and then, as a sociable English gesture, 'made a pot of tea, but were too blotto to get it into the cups'.

A few fortunate Americans were allowed to 'live out' in their own flats and the housekeeper of a block of flats in Paddington, where four young air force officers shared two apartments, found them agreeable, if occasionally troublesome, tenants, who, whenever they threw a party, which was often, never failed to send her down a drink. On one occasion she was astonished to witness the slow progess up the stairs of a 'most peculiar musical instrument, a cross between a concertina, an accordion, and a small organ.' This was in fact a 'one-man band' operated by a busker whom 'the boys' had found entertaining a theatre queue and had 'asked to play for them in their flat. . . . The party went on until the morning.'

16

A YANK FOR CHRISTMAS

'I believed that Santa Claus . . . spoke with an American accent . . . and called all little girls "honey".'

— Norfolk woman, then aged five, recalling 1942.

To most Britons it came as a great surprise to find that so many Americans were ardent churchgoers. One Andover family was amazed that whenever a food parcel from his 'folks' arrived for 'their' GI it also 'had a Testament inside'. An Ulster woman who often received letters from the mothers and sisters of her GI boy friends was 'surprised at the way they quoted the Bible. . . . These people who wrote to us bore no resemblance to the rootin' tootin' guys we knew.' American units often provided a welcome reinforcement to the congregation of many half-empty British churches. One eight-year-old girl living in the 'small prim coastal town of Burry Port', near Llanelly, where a contingent of black soldiers appeared one Sunday at the local Baptist chapel, can still remember 'the volume of joyous sound which arose as we began the first hymn, quite drowning the thin piping which was our usual offering'. It led to 'smiles of pleased surprise . . . on the usual Sunday faces. That anyone could actually enjoy their religion was a new idea to me.' Probably Roman Catholic churches benefited most. A pupil at Carmarthen Grammar School remembers how when the GIs 'first arrived in the neighbourhood the local Catholic church was completely packed out. . . . There was no room for the parishioners. A special Mass was arranged for the GIs on subsequent Sundays until services could be held by their own padre at the camp.' At the Roman Catholic church at Bamber Bridge, near Preston, one British worshipper observed, 'The collection plates were constantly topped with the GI ten-shilling notes.' A Plymouth woman recalls how 'the little church beside the sea outside the dockyard wall was full to the brim with Americans every Sunday. Four tall Sergeants took the collection and during their stay the pastor paid off over £1000 of the church debt.'

Even in peacetime most British families tended to ignore such occasions as St Valentine's Day; not so the GIs. 'They were horrified at the casual way we treated birthdays and anniversaries,' one woman who was then a young schoolmistress in Wales, remembers. 'The GIs soon made up for this and helped to celebrate every trivial anniversary. Their Valentines had to be seen to be believed.' American emotionalism found its fullest expression on Mother's Day, unknown in Britain at that time, although the fourth Sunday in Lent was traditionally named Mothering Sunday. In the United States, Mother's Day ranked second only to Christmas as a family festival, following its establishment in 1914, and amid all his other cares President Roosevelt found time to approve a proclamation calling upon 'the people of the United States to express', on the second Sunday in May, 'the love and reverence which we feel for the mothers of our country' and 'to display the flag on all Government buildings'.

With 'Mom' far away, GI goodwill was directed towards British mothers. A Glasgow mother was astonished when a GI whom her son had brought home for a meal not merely handed her a splendid bouquet but arranged for one to be delivered to the mothers of all her son's friends. A Norfolk licensee, known as 'our English mom' by scores of Eighth Air Force men, recalls the Mother's Day she was laid up in bed, made up in her sitting-room with GIs 'sitting on the floor and the settee . . . and on the bed, when the doctor arrived. He says,' she remembers, '"What are all these men doing here?" I said: "You're more privileged than them, Doctor, you can look at my leg, they can't." I said, "Clear off, boys," and . . . when they went my bed was covered with chocolates and flowers.' It was also the custom on Mother's Day to attend special services and many British civilians remember seeing an ancient church packed out with ranks of unaccustomedly solemn young men, each carrying a carnation – red, for those whose mother was alive, white if she were dead.

In many places arrangements were made for a British mother to 'adopt' a lonely GI, perhaps lunching with him as his guest in a Red Cross Club and then taking him home for tea. At Dereham in Norfolk one woman then in her late thirties remembers finding herself 'mother for the day to a nineteen-year-old airman from Wendling'; only two weeks earlier her own son of the same age had been shot down over Germany. Before long the young man was bringing his laundry to be washed and socks to be mended, and delighting the younger members of the family by cooking popcorn. By the time the 'guest for a day' left to return home, he had become a friend for life.[1]

Another American occasion previously unknown in Britain was Thanksgiving, first celebrated by the Pilgrim Fathers in gratitude for the harvest and since 1863 regularly observed in the US as a public holiday on the last Thursday in November. In the American calendar, Thanksgiving also ranks

1. Twenty-five years later he returned to Norfolk for 'a grand reunion' with his hosts and later his 'second mother', now a widowed pensioner, spent the holiday of a lifetime with his family in Des Moines, Iowa.

close to Christmas and in 1942 it provided an excuse to give British children some overdue instruction in American customs. One Congregational minister living at Long Stratton, Norfolk, used to arrange for a senior American officer to visit each school in the district for this purpose, a popular event as 'invariably sweets were on tap'. He recalls what happened when once he 'overlooked a school':

Two grubby little boys appeared at the base asking to see the Colonel. He saw them and they explained they had been forgotten and so the Colonel not only sent an officer to the school but invited the two boys to Thanksgiving Dinner. . . . He had all his senior officers at a long table, mountains of turkey and pumpkin pie and all vieing to make the boys eat. To round it off every table was cleared of sweets and the boys sent back to school in a jeep laden with goodies.

Christmas 1942 was the first that any GIs spent in England, and for most of them it was also their first away from home. One Peterborough housewife remembers attending a midnight Mass that Christmas Eve at which she and her husband saw one American 'so distressed during the service' that they asked him to visit them. He had, he confessed, been 'crying because we sang the same carols as they did "back home"'. The British wife – then fiancée – of an airman stationed in Sudbury remembers what happened when the chaplain at his base 'asked the GIs to see if they could find some flowers, etc., to decorate the chapel for Christmas. They turned up with some really lovely flowers, wreaths, etc., and on Christmas day it was really lovely. It wasn't until a day later "Father Red" found out that he had preached all his Christmas Masses with the wreaths . . . that the GIs had "borrowed" from Gainsborough's . . . statue that stood in the square in town.'

Not every invitation that Christmas was equally successful. One woman then farming in the village of Bunwell, fourteen miles from Norwich, with her husband, invalided from the navy, remembers arranging through the Forces Club in Norwich for two GIs to join them for Christmas dinner. 'We met the train, at Wymondham station as arranged, also two or more later ones, but no Americans arrived. After contacting the club we were told they had left, supposedly coming to visit us. . . . Later we had an apology from their commanding officer'; the missing pair had gone 'on a drinking spree' instead. But such backsliders were rare. One former student, from Carbondale, Illinois, only just married and never away from home for more than a few days before, remembers as symbolic of the welcome he received from a family who had befriended him at Bridgend, Glamorganshire, 'the steamed plum pudding with the lucky sixpence carefully hidden in the portion that I was to be served'. A woman then aged twenty-one living with her family near Norwich recalls that Christmas 1943 was 'the most gorgeously sentimental time' due to their 'household of Yanks. They taught us all sorts of Christmas "extras", the Advent candle, the Advent calendar, "The Night before Christmas" . . . hanging ginger biscuits on the Christmas tree. . . . One thing *they* had never seen were Christmas crackers, and they loved them.'

Also revealing the true spirit of Christmas were the experiences of a woman working for the Postal Censorship in Liverpool who remembers that an appeal was made over the loudspeaker system, on 23 December, for members of the staff to entertain GIs who had arrived on a recently docked troopship.

After a quick mental calculation of rations I offered to have three. . . . Prompt at one o'clock on Christmas Day there was a knock on the door heralding the arrival of Jim, Claud and Larry, the three youngest-looking GIs I had ever seen, all looking as though they had just stepped out of a bandbox and with the most impeccable manners. Later . . . I learned that they had been briefed in no uncertain terms that they must be punctual, well turned out and courteous and respectful to their hosts . . . and that they were not to accept large portions or second helpings. At 3 p.m. the King's Speech was broadcast on the radio and as one man they all jumped to their feet and stood to attention until the end. Rather shamefacedly my husband and I stood during the playing of the National Anthem the second time around. As the day wore on, they did become a little more relaxed, but when they stood up to leave at 10 p.m. (as per instructions not to outstay their welcome) we felt that the day had not been an overwhelming success.

How wrong they were! Next day the trio telephoned to say thank you and were invited to come again and 'this time the stilted conversation of yesterday became a non-stop buzz of chatter and when they piled into a taxi in the early hours of the following morning we all felt that we had known each other for years'. From then on the three GIs were frequent visitors until the fortunes of war carried them to their different destinations, North Africa, Italy and the Far East. Only thirty years later, when a prosperous-looking businessman with an American accent arrived on his former hosts' doorstep – an older version of one of the shy, 'thin and pathetic-looking' young men they had entertained that Christmas – did they discover how much the invitation had meant to him. 'He said he was just eighteen and had buried his father whilst on embarkation leave, leaving his mother alone. He had never been away from home before and had landed in Liverpool only to be billeted in a stable on the racecourse in the middle of winter', leaving him 'so cold, miserable and downright unhappy that first night that he cried'.

With its combination of good fellowship, sentiment and generosity Christmas was an occasion made for the GIs and many British people still remember the lavish presents they received. One woman, then in her teens and living near Aintree, recalls a Christmas visitor who 'came with a gift for each member of the family. . . . He gave my father a box of fifty cigars . . .

something beyond his wildest dreams,' and 'whilst with us . . . sat down
and wrote to his "mom"', with the result that 'Mom wrote to us expressing
her gratitude and sent three enormous food parcels and continued to send
them right through until the end of rationing'. An air force Sergeant radio
operator from Optima, Oklahoma, remembers a typical invitation for
Christmas 1942 to spend the holiday with his 'buddy' at the Alperton home
of the latter's girl friend. 'We got a forty-eight-hour pass and . . . ten
pounds of sugar and three large cans of peaches from our Mess Sergeant,'
he remembers. Their hosts seemed 'well pleased' with these gifts, as well
as they might be: the sugar ration at this time was eight ounces a week and
tinned fruit was unobtainable.

A woman then living with her parents in Stilton, Huntingdonshire,
recalls the similar bounty which descended upon them, even more unexpectedly, one Christmas Eve. 'We heard a knock on our front door and
when we went to answer it there was no one there, but a huge kitbag full of
presents on the step, which the GIs had left us in appreciation of my mother
doing their washing. There was butter and cheese in tins, chocolate and rich
cakes and games and toys. My young brother asked if Father Christmas
had been and my mother said, "Yes, in GI clothing".' 'Right up to the
time when I finally decided that there was no Father Christmas', remembers
the granddaughter of a Norfolk publican – four when the GIs arrived and
seven when they left – 'I believed that he chewed gum, spoke with an
American accent . . . and called all little girls "honey".'

The event I remember above all was the Christmas Party. It was December
1942. Every child in the school was invited – including all the evacuees from
London – and we were collected from the village green in a fleet of army lorries –
quite a thrill for children more used to horses and carts. The party was held in the
large dining hall. The hall was decorated with tall Christmas trees hung all over
with silver streamers. The food was all set out on little tables – sandwiches, biscuits,
and cakes with fruit juice to drink. The sandwiches were rather disappointing
as they all seemed to be made with peanut butter. I hated peanut butter. There
was also meat spread with what I took to be strawberry jam, but must have been
cranberry sauce. Father Christmas duly arrived, in a Spitfire and no one mentioned
reindeer – and handed out parcels of sweets and biscuits to each child. . . . To
end off we all had a filmshow; mostly Donald Duck and Mickey Mouse, and then
home again in the lorries. It was the only party I went to for a long time and I
have never forgotten it.

A Spitfire was not the only unfamiliar form of transport which Father
Christmas adopted between 1942 and 1944. *The Stars and Stripes* recorded
one party where, rather curiously, the old gentleman having crowned his
traditional red robes and beard with a steel helmet, had arrived by B–17,
but his favourite vehicle was a jeep. One landgirl working near Faringdon
in Berkshire, remembers a draw among the NCOs of a local cavalry

regiment for the right to play Santa Claus and the winner came back proud of his Cockney charm, the guests had been evacuees from London. Even braver were twelve Sergeants from the air force station at Honington in West Suffolk, who distributed 'candy' at the local Dr Barnardo's Home by piling twelve large dishes with sweets, standing 'in the middle of the boys in the large dining hall and shouting "Come and get it!" ' The episode proved a great success. 'The Sergeants disappeared on to the floor under the onslaught' but 'eventually emerged triumphant, although somewhat dishevelled.'

A party was rarely a failure when the GIs were the hosts, but one member of the staff of a Dr Barnardo's Home at Kelvedon in Essex, recalls one in 1944 where disaster was only narrowly averted. The children arrived wildly excited, to be greeted by an apologetic officer – the men had been out on manoeuvres and had only returned ten minutes ago.

Poor dears, everything was against them. They were still in battle-stained clothes, unwashed and unshaven and frightening to behold. . . . We sat on the floor in a draughty Nissen hut too close to the screen and were scared out of our wits by the noisiest films I have ever seen and which the children did not like, and which frightened the two-year-olds to screaming fits. . . . Long trestle tables and high forms were set up and candies and bowls of ice-cream were plied to the children . . . the youngest children could not really see over the tops of the tables and when they leant back they fell off the forms on to the hard concrete floor to the accompaniment of more loud screams. . . . The men did not know what to do with us next. . . . Luckily our matron was made of very stern material and was determined for the men's sake to bring pleasure out of the chaos and took charge with great aplomb. There was a piano of sorts in the hut to which she relegated one of the more talented nurses and then asked the men to sit around the hut with the children and set about entertaining them. The children danced and sang to them, recited poetry and did all the things nursery school children enjoy doing. . . . As the men responded to the children's natural gaiety, they seemed to shed their tiredness and disappointment and gradually from their exhausted ranks, men stood up, remembered they were alive and sang and clowned for and with the children, making the day memorable for the children and, I hope, for themselves.

A Plymouth girl, then in her mid-teens, remembers Christmas 1944 for another reason. Her sister and friends 'arrived at the church', St Michael and St Joseph, known affectionately as 'Mutton Cove', from a local landmark, with 'three Catholic sailors, one Baptist, two Protestants, one Lutheran, one Jew and one Methodist,' for midnight Mass, followed by a modest party at which she was 'grabbed by "Red" who tried to kiss me under the mistletoe. I sat on the floor and covered my face with my hands. Finally I was persuaded to let him kiss me. My first "real" kiss . . . Red was six feet four inches tall, the double of Van Johnson and – for the second time in my life I fell in love . . . I didn't go to sleep for ages thinking about Red's kiss.'

This was the Christmas which everyone had expected to be the first of peacetime. It proved instead the last, and grimmest, of the war. In the Ardennes von Rundstedt's offensive had revealed that the Germans were not beaten yet and an icy belt of snow and fog lay over much of Western Europe, although above England the skies were, for once, clear. The blackout, with the capture of the German airfields in France, had given way to a 'dim-out' and the daughter of one Suffolk rector remembers, as a sign of things to come, seeing the B–17s that Christmas Eve climbing into the darkness in their hundreds with their lights on, no doubt to carry supplies to hungry, shivering Europe. 'I was walking through a white frosted park when they were going out,' she remembers, recalling 'the incredible beauty of the sky, lighting up the trees which were heavy with frost, and the snow, was a sight that became a great comfort to me.' A little later that evening another young woman who helped her parents to run the village shop at Mulfords Hill, within the perimeter of the great American camp at Aldermaston, near Reading, went to the door to see off a group of GIs who had come for supper. 'There had been a fall of snow,' she remembers, 'which had frozen on the trees making icicles. . . . The air was crisp and the hoar frost glistened in the moonlight.' The family had asked their guests to return for Christmas dinner next day, and the GIs had promised: 'You'll be hearing from us soon.' The family learned what they meant when awakened at midnight by the sound of music coming over the tannoy. It was 'Christians Awake', followed by 'Silent Night' sung as a solo by one of their recent guests, a unique and public Christmas greeting.

17

A PEANUT-SIZED WHISTLE

'The passenger trains were a joke with us.'

— Airman from Massachusetts, recalling 1943

'I SUPPOSE my first shock in the ETO was when I stepped off the lighter and saw the train that was to carry the 123rd General Hospital to its destination in Hereford.' Thus the officer appointed troop train commander recalls his arrival at Greenock. 'Imagine my surprise when I saw this motley army of little cars. . . . The train commander's section reminded me of half a dozen stagecoach bodies set end to end.' Such reactions to British trains were frequent. 'The freight cars appear ridiculously small, like little cracker boxes on wheels,' wrote one Engineer officer in his diary in March 1944. 'The engine was small, with only two big drive-wheels and an open cab.' Epitomizing for Americans the fundamental difference, not merely between the two countries' transport systems but between their whole approach to life, was the contrast between the noisy klaxons, constantly sounded, with which American trains announced their approach, and the modest, sparingly used 'peep-peep' of British engines, described by one regimental history as 'pocket-sized Southern Pacific specials with a Lend-Lease peanut whistle mounted on the front end'.

The sound of an American locomotive produced in many GIs a feeling of acute nostalgia. Some had been supplied to British railways as part of Lend-Lease, and the *Stars and Stripes* described how the first eight, in December 1942, 'puffed into London's Paddington Station . . . with double-barrelled whoo-whoos . . . forthright blasts that came right from the USA'. 'One evening one [such engine] came slowly by the platform,' remembers one homesick eighteen-year-old GI from Plymouth, Massachusetts, stationed at Debden. 'We all yelled, asking the engineer to blow the whistle. It sure felt great to hear that "Whoo, whoo, whoo" instead of the then familiar "Peep, peep".'

For a twenty-two-year-old from New York, assigned to a Transportation Corps unit, 'the Lilliputian-sized goods wagons' of British railways also seemed to sum up the modest scale of everything in Britain, though on their first journey south, his men were impressed to be welcomed at Rugby by the stationmaster in his official top hat. A Technical Sergeant from

Manhattan, Kansas, was puzzled, as well he might be, by the fact that 'It was always first class or third class. No one seemed to know whatever happened to second class.'[1] Many Americans never did get over the feeling that British trains were merely 'props' in some Hollywood movie. 'The passenger trains were a joke with us,' admits one Massachusetts man, stationed near Cambridge. 'To get to London we travelled on the LNER. We called it the Late, Never Early, Railroad.'[2]

Despite such gibes, GIs got on well with railway employees. One airman from Fort Hamilton, New York, travelling from Glasgow to join a Medium Bombardment Group at Stansted, never forgot the ticket collector who helped the long journey to pass by teaching him cribbage, for after being shot down he 'played hundreds of games and taught scores of other PoWs the game during our captivity.'

The outstanding memory that former GIs have of British trains is of the 'private carriages', or small separate compartments, common at that time on all but long-distance trains. Whether the advantages outweighed the drawbacks was a much debated subject. If one was with a girl and found one empty, they appeared a splendid invention, but, as more than one GI recalls, 'they should never be used by anyone who has been drinking British beer'. One former employee of the Air Ministry Directorate of Works, still remembers an incident he observed on a non-corridor train between King's Cross and Cambridge, where he shared a compartment with three GIs and a British Sergeant. . . . 'After a few minutes one American said, "Hey, Mac, where's the toilet?" I answered that there wasn't one but that we could hop out at Welwyn and ask the guard to hold the train for five minutes. He said he could not wait and, slightly opening the door, tried to do the necessary through the crack, with disastrous results. There followed a discussion about the wonderful trains in the US and the rotten son-of-a-bitch British railways. The British Army Sergeant then said, "You boys have never been trained properly," produced from his pocket a brown paper bag,' and demonstrated how to solve the problem discreetly, earning the heartfelt tribute, ' "Gee, Sergeant, you British certainly know how to improvise in an emergency." ' Further praise came at Welwyn when, as promised, the train prolonged its scheduled stop for the GI's benefit, which 'they admitted could never happen in the US'.

The absence of name-boards on the stations, removed in 1940 to puzzle parachutists, made many a GI's first solitary cross-country journey a memorable adventure. Even the anglophile Robert Arbib fell victim to it, after being told to change at 'Swumley'. 'The first station had a large sign

1. It had in fact been gradually dropped from Victorian times onwards but 'third' did not become 'second' until 1956.

2. Actually London and North Eastern Railway; now part of the nationalized British Rail.

that said "Hovis". That was obviously not Swumley. The second station was marked "Virol" in equally prominent letters. Funny name for a town.' Having passed his destination, he faced a three-hour wait for the next train back – time to discover that Hovis was a type of loaf, Virol a malt extract, and 'Swumley' was Swamberleigh, being one of those irritating English towns pronounced and written in different ways.

During his journeys Arbib met a rich cross-section of the population of wartime Britain including an 'awfully nice' girl from Harpenden who had never talked to an American before, because her mother didn't think it was proper. . . . 'When we parted at Euston Station she was on the very point of giving me her name and she did say, "I wonder what my mother would say if you should come for dinner Sunday sometimes?" and then she thought it over and shook her head a little sadly.'

Most dining-cars had been removed from British trains in May 1942 and the few survivors, on long-distance routes, vanished in April 1944, after which you either carried your own food or went hungry. The appalled reactions of well-fed GIs to this discovery in mid-journey provided many British travellers with some innocent, though concealed, amusement. An Essex woman, travelling from London to Ross-on-Wye in July 1943 to enjoy a rare, long-overdue holiday, remembers just such a scene:

A young American soldier began by complaining in rather strident tones to anyone who cared to listen . . . of the slowness of the train; the absence of a dining or refreshment car, the somewhat grubby windows and so on. . . . No one appeared to be listening to him, but when he continued with 'Say, over in the States we wouldn't tolerate this,' etc., a rather inoffensive little man suddenly put down his paper and said clearly and quietly, 'Young man, I wonder if you're aware of the fact you are in a country at war? Nowadays every day we, as civilians, are primarily grateful for spared *life*.' There was a momentary hush, and then the young American replied, 'I guess you must all be thinking me a pretty lousy guy, as I see myself right now, and I'm sorry I said what I did.' A very short time afterwards passengers began to bring out wartime packets of sandwiches . . . and the first to offer his small packet to the American was the little man who had shamed him.

Many GIs regarded a railway compartment as an ideal recruiting ground for new girl friends, and especially for 'getting fixed up' for their coming leave. A very 'correct' civil servant, travelling from his Edinburgh office to Whitehall, was very surprised 'when my American drew me into the corridor. . . . "You are a man of the world," he said, "and I want a good time. What about it? Have you any addresses?" I was shocked. What my minister would have replied to such an unparliamentary question I do not know. I certainly could not help. . . . I had no addresses except the WVS (Women's Voluntary Services) or Citizens' Advice Bureau. Somehow I didn't think they would help very much for this occasion.'

One student nursery nurse travelling by train from Birmingham to

Colchester has not forgotten sharing a compartment with a young American 'decidedly "the worse for wear" ' who 'tried to make a pass at me, but I resisted. He then proposed marriage to me and I said, "Not in the state you are in at present." He then gave up and fell fast asleep.' But not all approaches were as unproductive. One Technical Sergeant from Kansas, travelling down to London for his furlough from East Dereham, still remembers 'the pretty 38–24–35 blonde nurse' with a flat in London, 'who made it a habit to pick up a GI non-com on her way to London when she was on leave. I already had a date the day I rode with her so I had to tell her "some other time",' but they parted reluctantly, each recognizing a kindred spirit.

Americans were popular travelling companions. Not merely did they while away many a journey by volunteering their life-story but many were the bottles of whisky passed round among the passengers. Another woman, on her way back to the West Country from Waterloo who had boarded the train without a ticket, and discovered she had too little money to pay the fare, was challenged by the ticket collector, whereupon the GIs in the carriage held a whip-round for her benefit. Railway employees, too, also benefited from the GI's open-handedness. One who worked as a porter at Thatcham Station, close to Greenham Common, was given her first nylons by an American passenger, while at the sight of her struggling with mail bags and luggage, 'Both white and coloured were ever ready to lend a hand, with a "Come on, baby, another push and we'll be there!" '

To GIs who had half-expected to find stagecoaches still rattling along the roads of Britain the double-decker buses, often overcrowded due to the petrol shortage, appeared as the next best thing, and they were delighted by the small burners towed behind some vehicles to generate producer gas. One farmer's son from rural Illinois stationed near Tidworth, remembers trips into town on the local double-decker buses. 'When they stalled, the conductor chased us off, and we ran along behind, perhaps pushing a little. At the top of the hill everyone piled back in at the rear platform and away we all went.'

The relationship between 'Yanks' and the – usually female – conductors was equally cordial. 'I was always overjoyed at the pretty sight of the bus conductors', remembers one Sergeant from Minnesota. 'Their conduct and politeness were always above reproach. This admiration was wholeheartedly reciprocated. One Southampton woman forced to 'go on the buses in Hampshire and Wiltshire' to keep herself and her small child while her husband was overseas in the army remembers being impressed by her GI passengers' 'immaculate cleanliness and plump well-fed look'. The GIs were always generous to the clippies, and she remembers how 'all our girls used to come off the road and gloat over our "loot", "candy", chocolate and gum, and whole packets of cigarettes'. She still remembers the night she 'picked up a crowd of six in Salisbury', the largest place for miles around, 'wanting to go to Whiteparish, which was the sleepiest little country village you ever saw. Someone had kidded them that if they wanted to see a real bit of gay night life Whiteparish was the place to go.'

Trams, which still survived in a few cities, seemed to many a GI to have been preserved for their amusement. A sixteen-year-old Plymouth girl found that they were 'just tickled pink' (i.e. highly amused) about them, and 'could be seen crowding on the upstairs, singing away, especially on a Saturday night'. Horse-drawn vehicles earned even louder cries of 'Gee, ain't that quaint?' One Norwich schoolgirl recalls that 'some enterprising citizen with an eye for a main chance found and brought out some old open landau cabs each with a pair of horses in harness, and charged the GIs so much a ride round the sights of Norwich. They thoroughly enjoyed this, but the sight of well-fed Americans lolling about in an open coach smoking cigars and surveying the scene as though they were the lords of all creation, incensed the townspeople.'

Most GIs were not impressed by British roads. One Supply and Maintenance Officer with the 123rd General Hospital at Hereford remembers many a trying hour 'travelling on their quaint, high-crowned, improperly banked roads that seemed to wind all over the countryside through fields of Brussels sprouts lined with hedges'. When passers-by gave directions, he decided, 'If they finished with "You can't miss it", you knew you were lost.' Before long this famous phrase – often mimicked by GIs – was greeted with a sceptical murmur of 'Like hell you can't!' One artillery Sergeant, stationed at Boxstead in Essex, remembers the infuriating last stages of the 125-mile journey of one convoy of which he was in charge after he sought directions from a pedestrian. 'He told us go down the road, take next left and then right by the big oak tree, "You can't miss it." After driving fifteen miles the road seemed familiar and there we saw the old man again, still walking. We had driven round in a circle.' But never was the absence of signposts cursed more fervently than by a lorry-load of GIs in the West Country who, one of them remembers, had set out to find again a 'Home for Wayward Girls', discovered by chance a few days earlier. The earlier visitors had been rapturously welcomed and urged to return with all the friends they could bring, but the vaguely remembered entrance proved elusive, and eventually the amorous lorry-load were stopped by MPs, who asked why they were driving round and round the same stretch of countryside.

No one was surprised to find that the GIs drove, as they did everything else, at top speed. One artillery officer from Rhode Island acknowledges that 'One American habit, I am sure, caused much concern for English drivers. Our drivers, like they do at home, would maintain speed much closer to an intersection than an English driver and then apply the brakes.

Consequently, many times English drivers would stop and let us go through even though they had the right of way.' This officer remembers how *en route* to the West Downs Firing Range on Salisbury Plain: 'One of our drivers learned to his surprise and sorrow that an American 2½-ton army truck could come out second best in an accident with an English bus. The bus drove away under its own power while our truck had to be towed back to the motor pool.' But, due to the almost empty roads, accidents were rare. One Supply Officer stationed near Hereford, with personal experience of 'driving with black-out lights in fog on long winters nights', is proud of the drivers in his motor pool, who 'averaging 200 000 miles a month for over a year . . . had only four accidents, none of them major.'

One young mother, who had evacuated herself to Newbury with her baby while her husband was serving in Burma, remembers a narrow escape,

" Dear Momma, in England they drive on the left side of the road . . ."

however, while pushing her baby along the main road to Boxford, where she was billeted, 'Having heard of the death of a night worker coming home along that road', she had just reflected that the American ammunition lorries and jeeps rumbling past were going far too fast for the narrow road when suddenly she passed out.

I came to hearing someone screaming and screaming. Then I knew it was me. There was blood on my heels. I passed out again, more screams and the commanding officer of the convoy was shaking and slapping me.
'My baby!' I shrieked.
'He is all right!' he said, and went on shaking me.
'I don't want to see him,' I yelled. I imagined I saw a mangled baby.
'He is all right!' shouted the officer.
The lorry had overturned on top of the pram, but by a miracle the baby had been safe because a bank had kept the lorry off him. . . . The pram was a heap of ruin. When I came out of the hysterical state a cold anger came over me. In a state of shock I started swearing. I went through the entire American history as far as I could remember and swore at each person and historical fact. . . . The commanding officer detailed a young GI to take me to the nearest doctor in Newbury. I saw fear in his eyes. I am sure he would rather have gone into battle. . . . I suddenly saw a gap in the hedge. 'Stop,' I bellowed in his ear. Through that gap I knew I could reach a footpath to the farm and a cup of tea. . . . I leapt through the gap in the hedge, with the baby in my arms, and ran to pour it all out to my landlady. She quickly gave me tea and carefully inspected the baby, but could find no injury. The poor young GI went back and reported that I had disappeared. He got a terrific ticking off. . . . The commanding officer then contacted the police and by intensive enquiries he traced me and found me at twelve that midnight.[1]

The smallness of British cars always amused Americans though it had its advantages, as one woman then in her teens discovered after taking a corner too fast on a snowy road *en route* to a dance in Tidworth, and landing her car on its side. A telephone call to her boy friend's base soon brought five burly GIs, and, after one amused glance at her little 1938 Morris Minor, they simply lifted it back on to the road.[2]

Of all the thousands of American vehicles soon filling the hitherto almost empty roads of Britain the type which first fascinated and then captivated the civilian population was the jeep. One Birkenhead man can vividly remember the amazement with which the first jeep ever to arrive through the Mersey tunnel was greeted:

Somewhere around January or February 1942 two strange vehicles came out of the mouth of the almost deserted tunnel. Used as we were to graceful, coach-

1. The incident ended happily, with the payment of £12 compensation for the ruined pram.
2. This woman kept her date and has now been happily married for many years to the GI she was hurrying to meet.

built cars, the sight of these ungainly, strictly utilitarian vehicles, hung about with
shovels, spares and petrol cans, caused many heads to turn, but what really held
the interest was the marvellous acceleration. It almost seemed as though the
occupants' necks were in danger of dislocation in the sudden leap forward of
these chasses on wheels. Greater manoeuvrability meant tighter turns and the
drivers, conscious of an audience of shipyard workers returning from lunch, put
the strange vehicles through their paces around Queens Square.

The jeep, despite its size, was a remarkably tough vehicle. I can recall
one charging round the corner on which our house stood and crashing head-
on through the front wall of the house next-but-one in the terrace, showering
the room inside with glass and bricks. The occupants, unlike us, had already
gone to bed or would certainly have been killed, for the front of the house
was wrecked, but the jeep backed out unharmed. One British teenager's
chief impression of the jeep was of the 'gaily painted ridiculous names',
it so often bore, 'such as *The Flying Banana* and *The Reckless Virgin*',
while another wartime teenager, working at a brewery in Aberbeeg,
Monmouthshire, regularly visited by GIs in jeeps, observed a typical
example of American boasting. On noticing that the jeep had a handle at
each corner he remarked in astonishment, 'What, four men can lift that?'
and was told, 'Sure, four Americans can, but I guess it would take eight
Englishmen.'

Before they arrived in England most GIs had never ridden, and some had
barely seen, a bicycle, regarding them as mere toys, but before long,
especially in East Anglia, the roads were full of precariously-balanced
crewcut, gum-chewing figures wobbling about. 'I kept meeting them
coming at me on the wrong side of the road,' one wartime schoolboy
remembers, 'shouting, "Gee, sorry, I forgot".' Although even the British
Army did not require a cyclist to salute – the official instructions required,
in 1944, that if he saw an officer he should 'sit to attention' – this was a
problem new to the American forces. One airman recalls an order that
salutes were to be given whatever the circumstances, hastily rescinded
after a group of GIs had each saluted a cycling Major in turn, until, in
trying to return their salutes, he lost control and ran into some barbed wire,
being badly scratched. A Halesworth, Suffolk, schoolboy, aged twelve in
early 1942, whose family ran a local chemist's shop, discovered from the
films the Americans brought in for developing that at first 'They quite
often took back views of lady cyclists (often fat ones) . . . carrying a small
child on the seat fixed over the back wheel,' regarding this as 'a . . . quaint
peasant custom'. Once, however, they realized that 'in wartime Britain
there was no way of getting about unless one had . . . a "wheel" as they
called it' there was a sudden demand for second-hand machines, often given
a new appearance by 'turning the handlebars up on end and then sitting
their new girl friends in the middle of them'. This man remembers how

ancient bicycles brought out of retirement, 'which would have changed hands at between £2 and £3 in 1940' were soon 'fetching £10 to £20'. Another soldier serving in a Signals unit, remembers thinking when he first landed in Scotland, 'their bicycles looked funny with their narrow tyres and high seats. After I got my own I knew why they were built that way.' Before long he had become a cycling enthusiast, even cycling back to London from a leave in Dolgelly in North Wales, via Shrewsbury, Stratford and Oxford, a 300-mile journey. By the time he finally left England he had, he estimated, ridden 3000–4000 miles, almost all on British saddles. The 'GI bike' was considered by this cyclist to be a poor example of American mechanical know-how. To one twenty-year-old airman in the Midlands, already engulfed 'in a strange loneliness, a horrible feeling of being submerged in a weird, permanent war' of mud, rain and biting winds, having to ride such a clumsy and uncomfortable machine seemed the last straw, and making a distinctly English joke he decided that the US Army bicycle must be 'Hitler's secret weapon'. Another GI, based at Debden in Essex, also found British cycles 'much better than our American bikes. . . . It amazed us to see real old dowager-type ladies pedalling along, uphill and down, as unconcerned as if they were sitting on a rocking chair.'

In their good-natured way, the GIs took the interest they aroused in good part and one wartime schoolboy, at Mountfield in County Tyrone, remembers an unofficial trick-cycling team who 'on warm evenings would show off their powers before the village. . . . Bicycles would be ridden on one wheel, or backwards, or perhaps the rider would sit on the handlebars. One GI was very good at doing a handstand on the handlebars while another pedalled the bike. Their finale was always a grand pyramid display with five GIs all on the one bike.'

18

SPROUTS WITH EVERYTHING

'Frankly, chum, I take a dim view of the chow situation.'

— *GI quoted in cartoon in the* Stars and Stripes, *25 April 1944*

'IF you must make a forced landing, do it in a Brussels sprouts patch.' This notice, in the office of one group commander of the 1st Bombardment Wing, stationed at Polebrook, epitomizes the attitude of every GI towards one venerable British institution, 'greens'. The reaction of the same wing to the news that an anti-aircraft shell laid waste an area of fifty square yards of the hated vegetable in the garden of Buckingham Palace would certainly have been widely echoed: 'Hooray! Cabbage next!'

Green vegetables, it must be admitted, *were* often on the menu in wartime England, because they were easily home-grown and provided a valuable source of the vitamins supplied in peacetime by fresh fruit. But, whatever the reasons for their constant appearance, the GIs detested them.

'The little cabbages' often inculcated a dislike of all English food. 'Our ration at our camp after we arrived,' remembers one Medical Corps Captain from Oakdale, California, stationed at Shepton Mallet, Somerset, in January 1943, 'consisted mainly of dried eggs, dried milk, Spam, black English bread – and Brussels sprouts. We had them for breakfast, lunch and dinner. How we got to hate the sight of them.' 'At first,' remembers a Technical Sergeant from Manhattan, Kansas, who arrived at Wendling, Norfolk in August 1943, 'we had Spam and Brussels sprouts three times a day, and I do mean three times a day. Later we got in Australian mutton and it was just as bad as it sounds.' 'I haven't eaten mutton since,' confesses a former Lieutenant-Colonel from Spartanburg, South Carolina. 'I did not like Brussels sprouts, boiled kidneys and a Scottish dish called Haggish,' decided one eighteen-year-old soldier from Longmont, Colorado.[1] One artillery officer, with the 34th Division, from Powhatan, Virginia, who landed in May 1942, and served in various camps staffed by ATS cooks,

1. 'Haggish' (haggis) seems to belong to the same gastronomic family as a dish remembered by another American, 'fish and sticks' (fish and chips). Haggis is in fact a traditional Scottish dish made of offal such as hearts and liver mixed with suet and oatmeal and cooked in a sheep's stomach. It is said to taste as revolting as it sounds.

admits, 'I can't say much for British cooking,' though he generously concluded that 'one could only admire a people able to remain so cheerful despite it.' The verdict of a chief radioman from San Diego, California, stationed in Grosvenor Square, is less polite: 'British food was awful.'

After the war the Brussels sprout was commemorated in a book by a naval Lieutenant who was shown in the frontispiece:

making a special commemorative vegetable bowl from English clay . . . dedicated to the Brussels sprout for valiant and heroic wartime duty. Boiled and beaten to a tasteless mess by English cooks, cursed and cannibalized by GIs, this courageous little vegetable, although drained of its vitamin vigour, managed to fight its way back into so many English menus that it justly deserved its citation of Order of the British Empire.

British sausages, notorious at that time even among British consumers, ran mutton and Brussels sprouts a close third as a source of GI wit. They contained 'at least 80 per cent cereal and 20 per cent meat', decided one Flight Engineer in Suffolk, 'which wasn't so bad because I heard the Germans were using sawdust in theirs'. 'I never could figure whether they were filled with sawdust or cornmeal,' admits an officer who experienced them in Northern Ireland. 'Sawdust in battledress,' was the verdict of a Norfolk, Virginia, man in the 29th Division. 'After availing myself of quite a few meals in the local service canteens,' remembers another GI stationed at Braunton in Devon, 'I resolved that I would never again look a baked bean or an English sausage in the eye.'

The American authorities had already realized that British rations were threatening morale and even efficiency. A former professor of biochemistry, recruited as catering adviser by the Eighth Air Force, obligingly warned that the excessive starch being served to the aircrews could generate gas in the intestines which might make itself painfully felt at 40 000 feet, and recommended instead such solid American dishes as meatloaf and hamburger, with spinach instead of sprouts. Before long, precious shipping space was being devoted to bringing the Americans in England the food to which they were accustomed, including such bulk-consuming luxuries as canned fruit, now only a memory in British homes. To criticisms that British lives were being risked for such items, the American authorities replied that 68 per cent of all their men's food was purchased locally, mainly in the shape of bread and vegetables. But it was the remaining 32 per cent that was most valued, and the arrival of the first truck-loads of American rations was greeted like a relief column reaching a beleaguered garrison. Testifies one former Technical Sergeant, then at Wendling: 'I think the first shipment of peanut butter saved our lives.'

During the war luxury items like grapefruit, bananas, grapes and melons were not imported into the United Kingdom at all, and commoner fruits, like apples and pears, were only available for brief periods. GIs who arrived in summer in the most fertile parts of England found it hard to realize that the bounty around them was short-lived and seasonal. One airman from Kansas remembers being amazed in East Dereham by 'huge onions and . . . strawberries and gooseberries the size of golf balls'. Less misleading was the experience of a medical officer from California at Shepton Mallet; visiting a local family, he found the dessert consisted of one large strawberry on each plate.

Almost unknown in wartime Britain were lemons, as one embarrassed member of the 7th Division discovered. Recalling from an orientation lecture that sugar was rationed, on being offered tea by a British hostess, 'I asked instead for lemon. I was mortified when the hostess came into the room with the most shrivelled-up lemon you had ever seen. She had been keeping it for months for a special occasion and I was it.'

The fruit most missed by GIs was probably the humble orange, only on sale in British shops for brief periods and then restricted, in strictly rationed amounts, to children and expectant mothers. To these favoured beings were now added – and no one begrudged them the privilege – American aircrew, although before long oranges were so plentiful on American bases that many reached GIs whose most hazardous journey was to the nearest pub. One Red Cross worker at Great Ashfield remembers her customers being shocked at radio hints on using orange peel to flavour currantless cakes and Christmas puddings, and GIs were often astounded when their guests at parties begged the peel to take home. One army officer, going on leave from Manchester so heavily laden with oranges that one rolled off the platform, remembers his amazement that the porter 'had the train shunted back so that he could have the orange for his child'.

What the average GI missed most was fresh milk, which was strictly rationed to civilians – often to as little as two pints a week, though Americans were in any case forbidden to drink it, because not all British cows were tuberculin tested. Many men were, however, quite willing to accept the risk, like those stationed at RAF Boxhill. 'If they could sneak to the back door when the milkman was delivering milk for the staff and buy a pint,' remembers the canteen manageress, 'that was an achievement.' Here, however, there were other attractions, for although the kitchen was out of bounds, 'they liked nothing better than to sneak in among the warmth, smell of cooking and the girls, until they were chased out'. A young woman working on a farm near Chippenham found GIs in search of milk frequent visitors, gladly drinking it still warm from the cow if they got the chance.

Most British people were highly indignant to find that in American eyes Britain was a 'dirty' country, just as the British regarded France. British visitors tended to be amused as well as dazzled by the glittering cleanliness of army and air force kitchens, provoking such sour comments as that of one Oxford mother to her daughter: 'If they were less fussy about their food and more fussy about their women they'd be better off.'

For most of the war the ration of fresh eggs for British civilians averaged at most about one a fortnight, and few shortages provoked so much envy of those more fortunate. A woman then helping in the Red Cross Club at Exeter can still recall her sense of outrage on hearing 'one greedy GI' boast that 'he'd had six eggs for breakfast that morning'. A Bury St Edmunds housewife found it equally traumatic to have four eggs fried for her when a cook on one base she visited with her 'tea-wagon', learned that she had not seen one for a month. The source of such riches was the supply allocated to operational airfields for aircrew were allowed an egg before or after every mission, like condemned men enjoying a last breakfast. The GIs on many other camps rarely saw fresh eggs and longed for them as fervently as the surrounding population. To be given an egg was a sign of monumental hospitality. The historian of the Eighth Air Force Bomber Command felt worth recording in 1944 the boast overheard in one mess hall: 'What's more, she gave me a real egg for breakfast, with a shell on it.' A Flight Engineer from Detroit, stationed at Bassingbourn, managed to secure himself a regular supply of eggs from a local farmer, in return for shotgun cartridges from the PX. This arrangement led to another; he 'would give me one fresh shot hare for two shotgun shells and he was a dead shot. . . . We would hear two shots while waiting for the pub to open and in a few minutes he would arrive with his gun strapped to the bike and two hares on the handlebars.'

At first the ban on buying fresh milk deprived the GIs of another favourite dish, ice-cream, of which civilian manufacture was forbidden for most of the war, but before long American ingenuity found a way. One airman from Osawatomie, Kansas, stationed at Wendling, remembers how 'we started mixing ice-cream in twenty-gallon GI cans and putting one in each plane. Coming back from a trip at 22 000 feet they were frozen just right.' Other GIs, according to the *Stars and Stripes* in 1943, devised a home-made freezer operated by a chain drive connected to the wheel of a jeep, and soon ice-cream was mysteriously on offer on most American camps, although the difficulty of transporting it made it a relatively rare gift outside. A Manchester man, then aged thirteen, remembers eagerly awaiting the nightly arrival of their GI lodger, who often came bearing 'enormous canisters' of ice-cream, 'never common-or-garden vanilla but filled with chopped peaches or cherries', riches unknown in England even in peacetime.

If eggs, ice-cream and – according to the *Stars and Stripes* – 'chocolate malted', a form of milk shake, were what the GIs missed most in England, the American dish they least wished to see again in peacetime was Spam. This useful invention was introduced to the British housewife at about the

same time as it appeared on army and air force mess tables and though at
first regarded with suspicion soon became the universal standby for everything from a main meal to a quick snack, its popularity being demonstrated
by its heavy 'points' rating on the ration scales.[1] I remember it with pleasure
as being invaluable when I turned up at home for unexpected weekend
leaves, but many people professed to despise it. 'You guys must have been
awful mad at us when you sent us that stuff,' a British waiter was alleged
to have said to one American customer, while one Cheshire girl remembers
a small boy shouting 'Spam' after her as she walked down the street with
an American, clearly regarding this as a supreme insult. 'And we could
lower their morale by dropping Spam instead of leaflets and bombs, ja?',
a cartoon showed one German suggesting to another. A new variant on the
notorious 'Any gum, chum?' was 'Any Spam, Sam?', while, according to
one Bombardment Wing history, one airman, tucking heartily into his
steak and eggs – reserved for aircrews – had been heard to explain: 'The
only reason I fly is to get away from Spam.' Another was reported to
have gone berserk on eagerly unpacking a parcel from home to find it
contained only yet more tins of the hated product.

The *Stars and Stripes*, never slow to exploit a good story, interviewed
Mr Jay C. Hormel, of Austin, Minnesota, head of the company which had
launched Spam on the world. After admitting good-humouredly that 'I
understand there is one soldier who is saving his last three bullets for me'
and proving 'somewhat vague about the times Spam crops up at the
Hormel household', Mr Hormel made a vigorous defence of his famous
product. It was, he insisted, a unique combination of pork and ham, which
had only appeared on the American market in 1938, the name being thought
up during a competition at a New Year's Eve Party. Spam's reputation,
insisted Mr Hormel, was due to its name being wrongly attached to various
inferior varieties of luncheon meat. The genuine article, by contrast, had
done much to link the Grand Alliance together, vast quantities having been
sold overseas under Lend-Lease, not merely to Great Britain but to the
Russians, whose taste ran to a strongly spiced version, 'Tushanka', flavoured
with bayleaf and black pepper.

Another gastronomic innovation of the Second World War, also appreciated more by British civilians than GIs, was the 'K' – for combat – ration,
which crammed into three slim boxes, labelled 'C', 'D', and 'K', sufficient
nourishment to keep a fighting man in action for a day. Although together
they occupied less than the space of a single pair of shoes, the rations
provided 3700 calories of energy, more than the average American civilian
received. A British woman clerk, working for the Services of Supply at
Cheltenham, remembers living 'on "K" rations for several weeks as an

1. See 'Note on Sources' for details of a book offering an explanation of the British
rationing system.

experiment' at the end of which she and other 'guinea-pigs' agreed they were not merely adequate in amount but 'most delectable' in taste. The GIs, however, did not appreciate when they were well off. 'The only way to achieve variety,' wrote one Lieutenant, 'was to eat the box instead of the contents,' and thousands of 'K' rations ended up in civilian kitchens. Apart from meat and vegetable hash for breakfast, meat and vegetable stew for dinner and pork and vegetables for supper, each ration contained five pieces of 'hard candy', a tube of bouillon, five vitaminized biscuits, sugar, powdered coffee soluble in cold water, and – the final imaginative touch – both chewing gum and toilet paper.

British bread presented the GIs with an interesting test of their adaptability. It was agreed on all sides to be superior in flavour and texture, despite its unpromising grey colour, to their native product, generally compared by British visitors to cotton wool, although the GIs regarded the British habit of selling their loaves uncut as unhygienic and a challenge to American know-how. 'It didn't take long,' remembers one airman stationed at Wendling, 'before each mess hall had a home-made bread slicer made from hacksaw blades.' One woman living near Great Ashfield found that the GIs loved to watch her mother 'spreading butter on to the loaf before cutting the slice off', something outside their experience, while a then six-year-old girl in Beaminster remembers watching open-mouthed as GIs, bewildered at finding loaves unsliced, struggled to tear them apart with their hands.

Many British families had to conceal their amusement at the average GI's ignorance of the British rationing system. The *Guide* issued to every new arrival had stressed the overall scarcity of food, but had failed to bring home to most readers what this really meant. 'They had no idea at all about food shortages,' remembers the Great Ashfield woman just quoted. 'They were amazed that we didn't riot and some even said that we were stupid not to, the Government would have to give us more food if we did. It was beyond their understanding that there just wasn't any more.' A woman then working in a Lyons teashop in London could always identify newly arrived Americans. To the delight of the staff they would 'ask for coffee with cream and six lumps of sugar. . . . You can imagine the answers they used to get from some of the girls.'

Restaurant meals were not on coupons, though supplies to them and the amount they could serve in one meal were strictly controlled, and the portions tiny by American standards. 'I used to go to a restaurant, have the dinner, then go out and find another restaurant and have a second meal,' admits one signals officer from Charleston, South Carolina. A doctor from Oakdale, California, 'will never forget the meals' served during his first leave in London in 1943. 'They were terrible. Breakfast: no fruit, sausage filled with potato and very little meat, potato pancakes (potato and cabbage mixture) and coffee which tasted like mud.' A Sergeant in a light infantry company from Washington DC remembers the unkindest cut of all: 'American cutlet', in a London restaurant, 'turned out to be Spam cooked in batter.' One GI from Troy, New Hampshire, remembers accepting an invitation home from a British airman in Swindon, to sample 'a spiceless English meal of some kind of fish. . . . Weeks later I discovered that Mrs A had stood in line for three hours at the market to get that tasteless fish.' One Pittsburgh, Pennsylvania, man working as a B–24 bomb-loader remembers his first leave at the home of his future wife. 'I had . . . two weeks' leave and gave my girl my ration coupons. The following morning I had what would amount to a normal American breakfast and next morning the fare was not up to the standard of the first morning. I asked where the rest of the food was since I had given her all my coupons and she replied that I had eaten them all up the first morning.' A Detective-Sergeant in the Oxford City Police recalls a similar experience: 'When Bill came to supper we used to put the cheese ration for our whole family of four on the table and he would eat the lot without a second thought' – not too difficult when it was only two ounces a week.

Before long the American authorities, realizing the strain their men's appetites were placing on British pantries, began to issue official 'hospitality rations', in addition to the tins of fruit and bags of sugar that enterprising GIs often begged or 'borrowed' from their cookhouses. One officer who later married a British girl learned from her that 'they could hardly wait for us to go so that they could divide the spoils'. A woman who often gave parties for her American colleagues in her Grosvenor Square office found that 'they always brought so much food and drink that my flatmate once said that if we gave an American party on Monday we could give a British one with the left-overs on Tuesday'. A Weymouth woman recalls sewing on one Sergeant's stripes so he could impress his girl – he had in fact been 'busted' to Private and was no longer entitled to wear them. 'Next day he appeared with a bulky-looking bag and tipped out two ready-for-the-oven chickens. I nearly had a fit, and told him to take them back,' but his reply was unanswerable: 'I've risked my neck getting them out and I'm sure not going to risk it taking them back.' A young woman at Watton, Norfolk, remembers being intrigued at church one Sunday evening by the appearance of 'a very odd-shaped American'. When, after the service, she invited him home, 'the reason for his peculiar shape was revealed when from his pockets he produced a large piece of meat and two large tins of peaches'. A then teenage girl at Clacton remembers how for similar reasons her future husband, a master baker, would often come 'looking a rather fat tall GI and go home a tall, thin one'. One day, as they were going to a dance, she 'couldn't understand why he was holding his waist and looked in pain'. On her asking if he were ill, he explained 'No, . . . but I've six frozen beef steaks in my jacket and they're starting to defrost.' American gifts of food, as of everything else, tended to be on the grand scale. A Dorchester antique dealer, who had invited some GI customers home for a meal recalls two of them turning up with a whole side of beef, hidden beneath a sack in their jeep. A Poynton housewife remembers another visitor, a cook in a Chemical Warfare Company, who arrived to spend the weekend at one in the morning having walked two and a half miles from the station 'draped with rucksacks'. They contained 'ninety-seven tins of food, including fruit, butter, peanuts, sugar, chocolates, frankfurters, Spam, tea-bags, fruit juice and a large tin of chocolates'. Another British girl from Leicestershire, who married an army cook in 1944 – they seem, for obvious reasons, to have been much in demand as husbands – remembers how 'it was quite a regular thing to get up on Sunday morning and find the kitchen table laden with chickens, loins of pork, butter, cheese, tinned fruit. When I went to work in a local factory my mother used to pack up sandwiches for me and more often than not they were chicken. I got so fed up with these I asked anyone if they would like them and before I knew it had a queue of girls round me.' A Wren stationed at Portland Bill remembers receiving a large Christmas cake from the mother of her GI boy friend, though it proved so rich and highly spiced that neither she nor her room-mates could eat it, although, 'the box came in handy for my stiff white collars'.

If any British families felt any sense of guilt at accepting such presents, it was speedily dispelled by the well-documented rumours which were soon circulating of the fantastic waste on American camps. At a time when the combined bacon and ham ration was four ounces a week one Berkhamsted housewife remembers finding a whole ham in an American dustbin, thrown away because it was slightly under-cooked. 'As it was wrapped in paper I took it home. We cooked it again and we had ham for three weeks.' General Lee, responsible for feeding all the GIs in Britain, constantly campaigned against waste, both by notices urging, 'If you don't want it, Don't take it!', and by personal example. One officer stationed near Taunton still remembers the General's visit to his unit. He 'went to a mess hall, took off his coat, rolled up the right sleeve of his shirt, reached to the bottom of a full garbage can, took out a piece of bread and ate it before the eyes of the mess officer, mess Sergeant and the inspecting party'. An order followed 'that all officers and enlisted men would eat everything on their trays and dishes', but in most places ingrained habits proved too powerful. An ATS girl, serving alongside Americans on an AA battery at Beaulieu Heath in Hampshire, was disgusted to discover that if only one teaspoonful of a seven-pound tin of jam had been used 'it had to go into the disposal bin at the end of the day'. The final shock for a seventeen-year-old girl living in a hostel at Flackwell Heath, near High Wycombe, came when she attended an American party, at which six GIs thought it a great joke to 'tie half a pound of butter to each foot and skate across the floor'.

Despite the innate conservatism of both races over food each made valiant efforts to acquire a taste for the other's native dishes, often unsuccessfully. One WAAF at Pinetrees, the Eighth Air Force Bomber Headquarters at High Wycombe, recalls bluntly: 'We hated their food. Imagine coming off night-duty and longing for a cuppa, [i.e. cup of tea], only to find the urns filled with grape juice, cocoa, etc., and to be served waffles and maple syrup and terrible mixtures all sweet and gooey.' Equally unappreciated by an RAF accounts clerk working at Burtonwood was sauerkraut, reminiscent in his view 'of a gas attack in the First World War'. To a meat-starved Briton, serving with the Eighth Air Force at Bassingbourn, the meal which stands out in his memory is the 'sandwich' offered him when he arrived too late for supper: 'a huge lump of fried steak, about an inch thick, between two doorsteps' of bread. A Flight Mechanic was equally staggered on his first day at the former RAF base at Bottesford in Northamptonshire 'to find such things as tablecloths, sugar, cream, etc., already laid out on individual tables. I went to the servery and was given three of the largest pork chops I had ever seen. . . . I commented to an American who sat beside me, "They don't half feed you a dinner here, don't they?" He replied: "Dinner, bud? Dinner's tonight." '

Civilians, on smaller rations than servicemen, were even more amazed at the plenty to be found in American mess halls. One Lancashire woman, then a very shy fifteen-year-old, remembers being 'so overwhelmed by the sight of all the food laid out on trays . . . salami, potato salad, sliced tinned peaches, doughnuts' when taken to the mess hall after helping to entertain the 'boys' at Walton-le-dale outside Preston, that she blurted out, 'I'm not really hungry. I had a big lunch.' She had in fact made herself a portion of dried egg which 'now . . . laid heavy in my inside. . . . Every now and then when my stomach rumbled I coughed slightly to cover up the noise.' Luckily the GIs would not take 'No' for an answer and 'as I daintily filled my mess tin I became suddenly aware that all eyes were watching me. . . . It was a strain trying to look casual . . . averting my eyes from the self-service counter. . . . No matter how much I tried, my eyes seemed to be riveted to the good things', and only pride prevented her loading her tray to overflowing.

Hard though the GIs found it to believe, American soft drinks were in 1942 familiar to British people only as names in films. One teenage girl from Wymondham remembers that the first time she saw someone enjoying a glass of Coca-Cola 'I thought they were drinking vinegar and it took quite a lot of convincing before I would even try it'. A Weston-super-Mare housewife, who proudly laid a steaming cup of cocoa before a GI on her first day in a local canteen, still recalls his incredulous protest: 'I asked for Coke!'; she had never heard of it before. A Bury St Edmunds woman tried, her daughter remembers, to provide corn on the cob to cheer up one homesick GI from Ohio.

We'd never cooked them before and we had to look up instructions etc., and it was to be a great surprise . . . for Sunday supper. The cobs were still pale green and only about five inches long, but my mother served them up in style in a silver-lidded entrée dish. She picked up the lid with the air of a master chef. Rev took one look, and started to laugh. In between spasms, he said, 'Mom, you *can't* eat that, it hasn't even been born yet!'

Equally un-American was the 'Boston Cream Pie' which, one naval Lieutenant wrote caustically, 'was clearly a stranger to both cream and Boston. Either the name had to be dropped or all pies would be confiscated for use in the sandbags which provided protection against air raids.' A Peterborough housewife remembers a strange lesson in spaghetti-making from a real expert, an Italian from Brooklyn: 'Every now and then he would nip off a piece of spaghetti and throw it against the wall. When it failed to fall off, the meal was ready.'

A British dish new to GIs, and widely appreciated, was Yorkshire pudding, served at Sunday lunchtime with roast beef and gravy but happily submerged by GI visitors when they got the chance in jam or syrup. Steam puddings were another general favourite, while a Cambridge office worker found that 'home-made things' such as open 'jam tarts, mince pies and small currant buns' were always well received. Rhubarb was an intriguing novelty. One Liverpool woman remembers two GIs stopping her in the street to ask the identity of the mysterious sticks she was carrying. But the most popular 'native' food was undoubtedly fish-and-chips, and the GIs took with relish to the British custom of eating it straight out of the newspaper in which it was served. British 'chips', solid quarter-inch oblongs four or five inches long, were one of the few products compared favourably to the American alternative, which resembled British crisps. One man from Holrege, Nebraska, regarded fish-and-chips as 'the British substitute for the US hamburger' and an officer from Minneapolis remembers willingly queuing an hour to reach the fish shop counter. One soldier from New York City, wishing to take a treat to the family with whom he was billeted in St Austell, Cornwall, remembers going 'to the local fish-and-chip shop and ordering ten bobs' worth. . . . I had enough fish-and-chips to feed the whole town.' A cartoon in the *Stars and Stripes* showed a GI in a similar situation surrounded by a crowd of expectant-looking cats – feline equivalents of the usual gum-seeking children. One wartime schoolboy at Tidworth found himself waiting 'with mingled astonishment and impatience' while half a dozen Americans with 'truly prodigious appetites' bought up almost all the fish-and-chips in one shop. In Dorchester in the spring of 1944 'small boys were running to the fish-and-chip shops with pound notes' and buying up the whole stock, until a discreet appeal was made to the American authorities to ask their men to spend less.

To the GIs tea was almost synonymous with England and one Pittsburg man, stationed in Suffolk, realized he was becoming truly acclimatized when with a friend 'I would walk to Eye and stop at the inn there for a cup of tea and some delicious home-made bread, toasted'. American acceptance of tea was linked to their discovery of the poor quality of British coffee, variously recalled as 'lousy', 'awful' and 'distressing'. 'When we first arrived in England we soon developed the tea-drinking habit,' explained a leader-writer in the *Stars and Stripes*, 'that is, after having first tried British coffee.'

One Newbury woman remembers how a friend, constantly asked by GI customers for coffee, 'invested some savings in a coffee-making machine' in her café in the centre of the town. She was infuriated when the next American to enter politely asked: 'Cup of tea, please, ma'am.' 'My friend pointed to her new machine. "That cost me the earth, mate," she said. "You have coffee and like it!" ' One GI told an Edinburgh woman 'I always pour my tea into the saucer or else I get the spoon in my eye.' 'My greatest impression of Britain is that the whole land is soaked in tea,' acknowledges one wartime officer, now living there. He still recalls the teatime when he took his fiancée to tea in a small hotel at Knutsford, setting for Mrs Gaskell's tranquil novel, *Cranford*. 'We dutifully lined up around 3.45 p.m. At 4 p.m. the doors were opened. [Then] she was gone and among this country gentry I was against the wall, bruised and battered' while she 'was sitting on two chairs and boldly guarding two afternoon teas'.

Even GIs who developed a taste for tea rarely learned to eat in the British fashion and small children often stared open-mouthed as an American guest cut his food into small fragments, and then discarded his knife and moved his fork to his right hand. GIs often remarked admiringly on the skill that enabled their hosts to handle knife and fork simultaneously, and one Kent housewife remembers one, anxious not to disgrace her, remarking, 'You lead, ma'am, we follow.' A schoolboy at Charterhouse witnessed the sad plight of two Americans entertained there for a fortnight as part of a well-meaning plan to familiarize them with public-school life. Not merely did the two visitors almost starve, faced with 'revolting dishes such as mock duck and bread and marge pudding', but their insistence on slicing up their food before starting to eat, covertly watched by the whole house, 'meant that they were invariably a course behind and usually had to stand for final grace when halfway through their meal. This they probably welcomed as a means of avoiding eating it.'

Among the lesser-known contributions to Anglo-American understanding during the war was a duplicated guide to *British Technique at the Dinner Table*, widely circulated in London.

The British . . . don't eat the way we do at all. Viewed from a distance, an Englishman eating looks very much like a . . . drummer in one of our jazz bands hitting a one-piece swing. He keeps his fork in his left hand and never transfers it to his right as we do, which enables him to maintain a ceaseless beat between his plate and his mouth. . . . Throughout the British Isles . . . American soldiers are trying to master this complicated manoeuvre. It is not easy, it calls for the development of a completely new set of muscles in the left hand as well as a new sense of timing and co-ordination between the shoulder, elbow, wrist, fingers and mouth. It is amazing how easy it is to miss your mouth when you first start, it is also amazing how miserable a fork full of Brussels sprouts feels in the ear when the hand has missed its target. But in the cause of Anglo-American unity the GI Joes all over these islands are doing it. In an effort to do my bit towards co-operation I have been eating that way myself of late and have reached such a point of dexterity that Londoners sitting near me in a restaurant move to another table for fear of being hit by food fragments when my stomach tells my mouth the zero hour is at hand.

On the rare occasions when an egg was offered to American guests they often rewarded their hosts with an equally unexpected performance. 'Boiled eggs was a star turn of theirs,' remembers one housewife living near Weston-super-Mare. 'They would take their penknives out and slash the tops off, which would land anywhere.' A then teenage girl from Appleshaw near Andover recalls staring in amazement as Mike from Chicago broke a boiled egg in his fingers and tipped its contents into the eggcup.

But these eccentricities were as nothing to the American characteristic still recalled with horror in thousands of British homes, that of eating sweet and savoury foods simultaneously. 'Fried bacon and eggs smothered with strawberry jam and Cornish cream,' at Saltash, pork pie spread with apricot jam in Southport, golden syrup on bacon at Broadway in Worcester-shire, jelly, cream and hamburger at Stone in Staffordshire, sardines and bread and butter and jam, eaten in alternate mouthfuls, at Caston, Norfolk – these are some of the mixtures witnessed, whose mere memory can still produce a reminiscent shudder. The warden of a YMCA hostel in Winchester recalls what happened after cooking steaks for a party of Americans for breakfast. 'They shouted, "Where's the porridge, ma'am?" and immediately poured it over the steak . . . cut it all up and stirred it well.' This experience prepared her for what happened the following morning when the fishcakes were spread with marmalade. But the victor in the competition to produce the most repellent combination must be the GI observed by a Portsmouth girl eating beetroot with condensed milk. Yet once at least such exploits had a happy result. A sixteen-year-old at New Malden found herself intrigued by the GI who 'on his first visit to our house . . . spread butter on his chocolate cake'; she later became his wife.

19

POUR IT BACK IN THE HORSE!

'I couldn't get over how different the pub was from the taverns at home.'

– GI from Bridgeport, Connecticut

'WE passed a building with a funny sign out front. It sounded like a party going on inside. I asked a passer-by what the celebration was about and promptly got introduced to a pub.' This is how a Flight Engineer, based at Bassingbourn in Hertfordshire, discovered one British institution for which, there was, he admitted, positively no equivalent back home in Detroit. Despite their rapid disillusionment with British beer, most GIs became firm admirers of the British 'local', which the official *Guide* described as 'the poor man's club'.

This was how Robert Arbib discovered The Dog at Grundisburgh, 'a compact village of brick cottages, with a church, a general store-post office and a public house . . . all surrounding a triangular green, through which flowed the brook'. The men of the 820th Engineers reached it after a peaceful 'walk through the soft Suffolk countryside . . . between high hawthorn hedgerows lined with ancient trees, between fields that were ripe with grain . . . ready for harvest' one late August evening in 1942:

When we entered the little pub, it was almost empty. We found three or four small, plain rooms with wooden benches and bare wooden tables. Each room connected somehow with a central bar – either across a counter or through a tiny window. One of the rooms had a dartboard, and another had an antique upright piano. We went into the room with the dartboard and ordered beer. 'What kind of beer?' asked the man behind the counter, a ruddy, pleasant man whose name was Mr Watson. 'Oh, just beer,' we said. We tried the mild beer. It was weak, watery, and warm. 'Haven't you anything stronger?' we asked. 'They're all about the same now,' he answered. 'Wartime quality, you know. Pretty weak.' We tried the bitter. It was weak, sweet and warm. We tried the brown ale. We tried the stout. We tasted the Guinness. We ended by drinking the light ale, which was the only variety that seemed strong enough to put a foam on the glass. Later, we came to like, or at least became accustomed to, the other types of English brew, and would sit like the natives and talk over our pints of mild, or bitter, or 'arf and 'arf.

Someone must have seen us go into The Dog, for soon the villagers began to arrive. By ones and twos they came, and sat themselves down in their accustomed seats. The front room with the dartboard filled with the younger men – the farm workers in their rough clothes, talking with their musical dialect that puzzled us. The back room filled with the old gaffers, and their evil-smelling pipes filled the room with blue smoke and the smell of burning seaweed. Here the conversation was slower – in fact it bordered on paralysis in social intercourse. . . . Here was contentment, companionship, a time for thinking, and for the slow exchange of ideas. For years they had occupied the same chairs, drank the same pint of bitter from the same silver mugs, talked about the crops, the weather, the latest village gossip, and now another war. Mr Watson could set his old clock by their entrances. He handed them their brimming mugs of 'the usual' with the expected and customary greeting, took their coppers with a nod. These were his 'regulars'. The other two rooms – the front room or 'saloon bar' and the back room with the piano – were for family groups, for casuals, for young couples, and for the women. There was plenty of high-pitched chatter here; there was music, and the beer disappeared faster, with less philosophy.

But this Saturday evening there was excitement and a high tempo in every room in The Dog. 'The Yanks have arrived! There are seven of them in The Dog right now!' People came in from all the farms and cottages and they filled the old public house with a carnival spirit. By eight o'clock there was standing room only, and by nine o'clock even the dark narrow hall between the rooms was full, and you could hardly turn around. The smoke was thick, and the conversation excited. . . . We sat in the little back room with the piano and bought a round of drinks for everyone who joined the group. First there were seven of us, and then ten, and then twenty-one drinks to the round, and then twenty-eight. The last round we bought from the harassed Mr Watson was for forty-seven drinks. There had never been anything like it before in the long history of The Dog. Everyone was shouting, everyone was singing and milling about, holding hands full of glasses over their heads as they pushed through the crowd. The word Yanks was on everyone's lips, and if you turned away from someone it was to answer someone else shouting in the other ear. . . . Just before closing time Mr Watson raised his closing-time chant, and a powerful call it was to cut through the din that rocked the rollicking old Dog that night. 'Time, please, gentlemen!' rang through the house like a brass gong. . . . That was our first welcome to England. We said good night to our new friends many times inside the pub, and many times outside, and how we got home up the pitch-black country lanes to our tents. . . . I cannot quite recall . . . that was Saturday night . . . that welcome at The Dog. On Tuesday night The Dog went dry – stone dry, and Mr Watson hung out a sad little sign on his door – 'No beer' – and closed his inn for the evening – the first time in 450 years of The Dog's history.

The famous phrase 'Time, gentlemen, please!' is as evocative for most GIs as 'You can't miss it' and still reminds them of the transformation scene witnessed in every pub as the clock struck ten when the genial mine-host became in an instant the most unsmiling and inhospitable of men. Many GIs never did master the mystery of licensing hours. 'We found it a bit hard to understand,' admits a topographic draughtsman in the 654th Engineers, stationed at Tetbury in Gloucestershire, 'why the pub was

closed at such odd hours during the day and promptly snapped shut each
evening at ten by the on-duty constable. Many of us got the impression
that as a throwback to medieval times, the British were still a trifle afraid of
their Government, despite centuries of so-called "democracy" in England.'
The caption to one cartoon in the *Stars and Stripes* in October 1942 voiced
a widely held sentiment. 'Say,' one paratrooper was remarking to another,
'I just hope I come down near a pub that's open.'

The afternoon break in hours, designed in 1915 to drive workers back to
their factory, pressed particularly heavily on GIs. It was, remembers the
woman who ran the village inn at Bighton in Hampshire, 'something they
could never get used to' and one Easter Sunday her American customers,
when 'Time' was called, 'brought a fifty-two-gallon cask of beer and rolled
it to the seat in the centre of the village, tapped it, and the whole village sat
around helping them drink it' – a perfectly legal activity so long as no
charge was made. On another occasion 'We closed the pub as they had
bought all the stock . . . and it was some party.'

Although fluctuations in wartime beer supply sometimes caused the
regulars at one pub to desert it *en masse* and descend upon another, better-
supplied, like a flock of thirsty starlings, it was the usual British practice to
stick to one particular pub. One radio operator/gunner, nineteen when he
arrived and never away from home before, found his, near Horsham St
Faith, a great comfort, 'You'd go in there and it would be crowded, but
there was always a piano, someone had a pair of drumsticks and we'd all
gather round and sing the songs of that year, so it was a lot of fun.' A
typical evening out, remembers one 95th Bomb Group mechanic from
Denver, Colorado, then working on bomber maintenance at 'Station 19'
near Diss in Norfolk, consisted of five or six GIs drinking in a 'beer-house'
which was barely a pub at all 'but merely a farmer's dining-room. . . .
The drinking took place around a large dining-room table, and sometimes
with oil-burning lamps for lighting. An added feature might be a piano
played by the neighbour's daughter, and whose talent improved in direct
proportion to the number of "pints" consumed.'[1]

One young infantryman from Connecticut, stationed with part of the 4th
Motorized Division in Devon, remembers how he and his friends would tour
the little town of Seaton each evening, where 'the pub owners used to let us
have a drink or two each night of Scotch, gin, beer and "rough" cider in that
order. Sometimes there would be so many GIs in a certain pub they would
run out of beer mugs. We would go on down the street to another pub, buy
a beer and run back to where the action was, with a pint mug. We used to
wonder if one pub owner ever came up short on mugs and if the popular pub
ever noticed his supply had grown.'

1. 'Beer-houses', not allowed to serve wines or spirits, mainly dated from the 1830s.
(See my book *The Waterdrinkers*). Very few survive now.

Many GIs did their pub-crawling by bicycle though as one unit history warned, if bikes stand outside a pub too long 'they get drunk and are apt to run a man into a ditch or a pole'. This was perhaps the thought that prompted one incident witnessed by the landlord's wife at the Bull at Cavendish near Sudbury. 'One lad . . . the worse for wear . . . ordered a pint of beer . . . went outside and poured it over his cycle, saying "I'm drunk, so are you." ' But this was almost rational behaviour compared to another closing-time scene when a group of GIs 'were trying to roll up the white lines in the centre of the road, watched by the village policeman'.

To obtain a drink after hours was always a rare triumph, and one air force officer stationed at Duxford still marvels at the 'great good luck' which led him on his first evening in Cambridge to a basement pub kept by an 'old dragon of many years . . . who had a motherly fondness for these nephews from across the seas'. His evenings there helped to make this 'one of the most interesting, exciting and productive eras in my whole life' and was to have a lasting influence on it, for there he met his future wife. Initially, however, the 'landlord' made more impression:

Mrs T. was a character of the old-school, sitting perched upon her own high stool. Her sole responsibility for the operation of the pub was to ring up the cash and see that none of the GIs cheated her out of a single penny. . . . In all fairness, however, . . . there was never a GI who found himself shorted in his change because he could not sort out the correct currency. . . . The regulars were a clan unto themselves. . . . Mother T. was the acknowledged matriarch. . . . After ten o'clock closing, when the casuals had been ousted, she would produce an odd bottle of whisky (Scotch) from the back room and the festivities of the inner circle would then begin. Of course this was highly irregular but . . . the constable on the beat would turn a sympathetic eye the other way as long as the piano was silent and no lights showed through the basement windows. . . . To get in after hours one had to know the correct knock on the door at the bottom of the stairs.

One GI stationed at Honeybourne managed to guarantee supplies from the local publican during the winter of 1943-4 'I used to present him with a few cigars and a package of tobacco and in return he always had a bottle of Scotch under the table for me.' At Polebrooke the 'boys' often went down to the local at lunchtime to eat, much less well than on the base, merely to establish themselves as 'regulars' with a claim on that evening's supply of whisky. 'If you were lucky, or were well known, you got a drink or two of Scotch before it ran out,' remembers a platoon Sergeant from a light tank company of his months in Kew Gardens. 'Then you switched to gin, or something exotic, like a bottle of arrack I ran into in a little country pub. When all else failed you ended . . . the evening on beer.'

The GIs' affection, and capacity, for hard liquor became famous. 'Many is the time I killed a bottle of Scotch without even getting high,' remembers one army engineer from New York City, apparently seeing nothing unusual in the feat, and British civilians were regularly shocked to see GIs drinking whisky from the bottle in trains, cinemas and parks. A Nottingham woman remembers an unprecedented sight in an open space in the city centre: 'A drinking party of GIs lying on the grass in the Forest which had lost its iron railings to the war effort, waving bottles of whisky at passers-by to persuade them to join in.' A former Wiltshire landgirl found that her refusal to enter a pub did not deter her 'date' from celebrating his promotion to Staff Sergeant: 'He brought a bottle with him. . . . It was funny going into shop doorways to have a swig.' A Bristol woman whose pilot son was in an RAF hospital at Wroughton discovered that the wire 'cage' protecting his broken leg also concealed several bottles of whisky, smuggled in to an American Sergeant in the same ward. 'Many a toothbrush mugful of whisky passed between the two beds,' she remembers – the start of a friendship that still survives.

Demand, as every good free-enterprise-championing American knew, created supply. The story was heard on all sides of the GI offered a bottle of whisky by an honest publican for the proper price, about £1 ($4), who refused it as he wanted the 'real stuff' worth £5. Where the genuine article was not available, at any price, substitutes were sometimes forthcoming. The GI friend of one Paisley family 'paid a ridiculous sum' for a bottle of 'Scotch' to a 'shady customer in a pub somewhere . . . £4 I think – and it was no more like Scotch whisky than Scottish coffee was like the American variety. Rotgut would have been a more apt description – it was cloudy and dark, and burnt one's throat on the way down.' A former Detective-Inspector with the Glasgow City Police recalls an even more blatant fraud, by petty criminals, then known as 'spivs', who hung about the Central Station, and sold £5 bottles of 'whisky' bearing famous labels to GIs boarding trains. Only when both train and vendor had departed did the GI find he had paid £5 for a pint of cold, milkless tea. One civilian who worked for the Americans at Sudbury remembers a similar and even more ingenious fraud, perpetrated on a cook who had parted with £4 for a bottle which mysteriously ran dry after the first glass. Examination showed 'that the bottle had been filled with weak tea to the neck, a layer of wax poured on and the neck filled with whisky. I broke this with a pencil and out came the tea.'

Sometimes even supposedly reputable establishments were guilty of similar frauds. Another civilian recalls seeing a notice in the bar of a Kensington hotel 'Whisky Only', a sufficiently unusual sight to arouse his interest, as well as that of two GIs standing by the counter, with a civilian. 'I gave a friendly nod to the civilians, who said, "Real nectar of the gods, guv, genuine bourbon." Having tasted the liquid being served,' he decided that far from being of divine origin, it had 'oozed through a bathtub tap from somewhere around London', a diagnosis confirmed when one GI suddenly cried '"My God! My eyes, I can't see"' – blindness, usually temporary, being the consequence of drinking illicitly made 'hooch'. Many GIs, to whom spirits made no appeal, decided that the most enjoyable drink to be found in these uncivilized islands was cider. A Jewish chaplain, from Sioux City, Iowa, also 'loved the apple cider, and especially the carbonated variety. I had visions of making a fortune . . . brewing the stuff in the United States.' One man from South Pasadena, California, who, after 'a two bottle lesson' in Northern Ireland began to enjoy Guinness, later, in the West Country, with the rest of his friends, 'found out the difference between bottled cider and "rough" cider', the cheaper, far more potent draught version. But even 'rough' cider was not sufficiently intoxicating for some hard drinkers. A landgirl working at Lyme Regis, just over the county border in Dorset, remembers how 'The GIs invented a drink which they said made them "higher" than plain cider . . . beer and cider mixed half-and-half. They called it "block-buster".' Even more ferocious was the mixture favoured by coloured GIs at Pewsey: 'a noggin of rum in a pint of cider. . . . It did not take many of these to put them on their backs,' so that the men's first evening-out ended with 'a patrol of their MPs sorting them out and dumping them in a large GI wagon bound for camp'.

When short of funds, or in an area which they had already drunk dry, some units resorted to home-made concoctions. Appleshaw, near Andover, was the birthplace of 'Kickaboo joy joice', based on anti-freeze, which, one eyewitness recalls, 'made them go berserk, climbing trees and butting walls with their heads'. For those of more sophisticated tastes there was 'Italian Moonshine', first produced by local PoWs, and made of half-rotten oranges, collected from the refuse tips. 'When there was nothing else available they would drink the spirit used for cleaning guns,' remembers the wife of a Dorchester antique dealer, while another housewife in the same town was offered a 'cocktail' made of pineapple juice laced with surgical spirit, a popular drink at hospital parties. Barmaids everywhere became accustomed to suppressing their stares or sniggers when asked for 'Scotch on the rocks', while a woman then living in the tiny Cornish village of Nanpean remembers GIs confidently 'ordering "Pink Highballs" or whatever it was, queer-sounding names [which] meant nothing to the local landlord'. One woman sent by the Ministry of Labour to work at US Army Headquarters in Grosvenor Square discovered like many other Britons a new taste sensation: rum and Coco-Cola, a combination which became famous when a song with this title was banned by the BBC because its second line referred ambiguously to 'mother and daughter both working for the Yankee dollar'.

But mostly, like everyone else in wartime Britain, the GIs, although unenthusiastically, drank beer. 'The less said about wartime British beer the better,' considers an infantry Captain from Spartanburg, South Carolina, who frequently sampled it near Salisbury; 'warm, thin, no body, little

taste – I never cared for it.' 'Flat and tasteless,' agrees a wartime airman from
Pittsburgh, Pennsylvania, then a thirsty nineteen-year-old. One Eighth
Air Force man, stationed at Debden, judicially sampled all the varieties of
beer not available back home in Plymouth, Massachusetts. 'In Scotland,'
he remembers, 'we tried "Black and Tans" and "Happy Days" – a mixture
of a dark and light beer,' followed in Essex by ' "light" [i.e. bottled Light
Ale], mild, mild and bitter, stout and Guinness. I finally settled on lager as
my favourite.' To lend flavour to their beer many GIs, to the great scandal
of British drinkers, added salt to it, and a salt cellar on the bar, remembers a
Leicester woman, became the sign of a pub frequented by Americans. A
Bury, Lancashire, publican remembers others scattering cigarette ash in
their drink, to increase its narcotic effect. About the temperature at which
beer was served, however, they could do little and the story was widely
told of a GI who claimed to have heard a woman calling to her husband:
'Come on in, dear, your beer's getting cold!'

A few Americans did eventually acquire a taste for British beer. 'When the
GIs descended upon the metropolis of British brewing, Burton-on-Trent,'
remembers one British soldier stationed there in 1942, 'flat, warm booze,'
they called it. . . . When they discovered its potency their assessment of its
quality underwent a radical change, though they still described 'old and
mild' as 'old and filthy'. The commonest American description of British
beer was even more pointed. One man who had just started work as a
fourteen-year-old at a brewery at Aberbeeg in Wales remembers how four
times a week the big American trucks arrived to pick up supplies, the
drivers announcing simply, 'We've come for the piss.' An artillery officer
from Powhatan, Virginia, serving with the 34th Division in Northern
Ireland, consisting largely of Swedes from Iowa, Minnesota and Wisconsin
accustomed to Scandinavian beer, recalls that their reaction was: 'You can
pour it back in the horse.'

British beer also gained an evil reputation among GIs for its diuretic properties. One former member of a mortar company from Connecticut, who trained near Bristol, remembers its nickname of ' "airplane beer": Drink one and P38' – the P38 being the Lockheed Lightning fighter. 'We soon discovered British beer had one unexpected effect,' remembers a topographic draughtsman from Winter Park, Florida, stationed near Tetbury in Gloucestershire. 'After one or two pints, one had the very uncomfortable feeling that one must dash off to the john at once, not ten minutes from now, but right now! Public rest rooms thereabouts being practically non-existent one had to seek immediate refuge outside near the most convenient hedge where one found oneself accompanied in the dark by several of one's compatriots in similar straits.' This constant need made it doubly puzzling to American drinkers that the sanitary facilities in many pubs, especially in the country, were almost non-existent, usually consisting – as they often still do – of an unlighted lean-to shack containing only a hole in the ground. One Pfc, a demolition expert in the 245th Engineer Combat Battalion, remembers looking round in bewilderment in one such establishment near Bristol for the normal facilities and being instructed by a more experienced comrade: 'Pee on the wall.'

Although the American authorities could hardly forbid their men to drink British beer they always treated it with some suspicion. One Englishman employed in 1943 by the Air Ministry Directorate of Works in Birmingham discovered that the principal task of the US Army medical unit stationed nearby was to analyse British food and drink to decide if it was pure enough for American consumption, a duty which involved many an official pub crawl. The Captain in charge eventually reported 'that the mild beer was excellent for consumption by the GIs, the bitter not so good, although quite intoxicating in quantity, and the bottled beer would have done credit to the Borgias'.

During this useful, and unusual, venture in Anglo-American co-operation his civilian drinking companion also stumbled upon one top-secret piece of research of which up to now no hint has ever been revealed, the epic struggle to make ersatz beer. The proposed ingredients were the humble potato, combined with the excellent Birmingham water, piped from the Welsh mountains. The research, entrusted to a Birmingham University professor, was 'classified' because premature publicity combined with the 'British aversion to new innovations and gastronomical snobbery' would, it was believed, kill all hope of this substitute being accepted. 'The idea was to try the new utility beer out in Birmingham' and, if successful there, 'to extend it to all the British Isles', but, due to supplies of the conventional brew improving, the project never got beyond the experimental stage.

The addition of two million sociable and thirsty young men to the population of Britain made an immediate impact upon the scarce supplies available to native drinkers. One Technical Sergeant from Manhattan, Kansas, remembers the first time he heard 'grumbles about "the bloody Yanks"', when, after a walk with a friend, he found his first pub near their base at Wendling. 'A lot of other men found it too so we drank it dry and when the workmen of the area came home and stopped for the usual pint of mild and bitter there was none.' A Connecticut man, stationed just outside Bristol, remembers how at one local pub 'the GIs would drink up the monthly quota of beer in two weeks'. Eventually the landlord began 'to ration the GIs so the pub could stay open all month'.

GI pub-goers revealed a great desire to join in any activity that was going. Darts, which most GIs had never played before, is the classic pub game and many 'houses' had a darts team, formed from the regulars, which challenged those from other 'locals'. Some Americans discovered a marked aptitude for it. One Philadelphia man, then serving as an Ordnance Corps electrician, still regards as the peak of his wartime career the month when he was darts champion of a Birmingham pub, a valuable accomplishment, as it earned him priority in the allocation of Scotch. A housewife living in the Sussex village of Singleton, midway between Chichester and Midhurst, remembers the knowing looks among the locals on challenging the first GIs to visit the pub to a game of darts, 'losers to pay for the beer'. But the smiles were speedily wiped from the rustics' faces; the GIs won. A former signaller from Des Moines, Iowa, stationed in London, has often 'used the expertise' acquired in England and 'can still win prizes at carnivals where it is necessary to explode balloons by throwing darts at them'.

The other great pub recreation should, literally at least, have helped to promote harmony – singing. 'This was one of the nice reasons for going into a pub,' remembers one GI stationed at Bristol, quoted earlier. 'To hear nice respectable people sing things like "Roll me over" seemed a bit rough for a mixed group by mid-West beliefs,' admits one Technical Sergeant from Osawatomie, Kansas, then at Wendling. One B–17 crew-member from Connecticut, with the 94th Bomb Group at Rougham in Suffolk, recalls that the first time he heard this famous song 'It was being sung and played on the piano by a toothless old lady of eighty.' A Flight Engineer from Detroit, stationed on the same base, joined in another song, even less respectable in its military version, 'When There Isn't a Girl About', as well as 'Knees Up Mother Brown', 'Old King Cole', 'One Man Went to Mow' and 'I've Got Sixpence'.

With the usual few exceptions, the GIs were popular customers with licensees, good-natured, open-handed and paying promptly for any damage.

But from the British customer's point of view, they had two irritating habits, causing much ill-feeling at the time. The first was that of spreading their loose change over the table in front of them, a common practice in the United States. 'The average British habitué of the "local" considered this . . . a flaunting of American affluence,' believes an air force officer who served at Duxford. 'This seemed boastful,' agrees a former Liverpool barmaid. 'We often heard remarks like "You'd think they owned the bloody place".' The second American offence was to monopolize any heating that was going. One young widow, who helped her parents to run the pub at Tortworth in Gloucestershire, patronized by the staff of the nearby American hospital, remembers a typical incident:

Our bar had an open coal fire and hanging on the wall opposite it an old engraving which read:

> All who stand before the fire,
> I pray sit down, 'tis my desire,
> So that others may, as well as you,
> See the fire and feel it too.

One bitterly cold night a GI . . . stood with his back to the fire blocking its warmth from the room. I saw one rustic nudge another and say. 'Tell 'e to read th' notice.' The reply came: 'What 'ud be the use? Thee knows 'e be a Yank. They can't read English.'

Just as in peacetime, closing time was often a rather noisy affair. One woman who lived in a flat in the centre of Banstead in Surrey remembers departing GIs 'making "Yippee" noises like the cowboys' and once witnessed from her window a scene straight from the Keystone Cops. First two GIs, having helped a third, who could not stand, out of the nearby dance hall, 'managed to get him to the stone mason's next door, then carried him to one of the large stone kerbs and laid him on it . . . pulled off some of the hedge . . . and threw it on him, then . . . took off their hats and looked as if they were praying over him.' The 'funeral' over, the 'mourners' sat on a low, adjoining wall and shared a bottle of whisky, then decided to carry the 'corpse' home. They had hardly picked him up when the National Anthem was played in an adjoining dance hall and they respectfully dropped their burden and sprang to attention. By the time it was over they had forgotten the 'corpse' and wandered off in search of the whisky they had left nearby; eventually more GIs appeared and helped all three drunks to stagger home.

A housewife living on the fringe of Woolaton Park, Nottingham, where the 82nd US Paratroop Regiment was in camp, suffered a far more alarming experience one 'black and moonless night'.

Nearing midnight she was shocked by a crash of glass and a heavy thud from the conservatory outside the lounge . . . she jumped out of bed and hurried downstairs. On the hard tiled floor was a crumpled figure in GI rig . . . 'Where on earth,' demanded the startled woman, 'have you come from?' The figure on the floor gingerly fingered his pate, which was somewhat the worse for wear, and blinked drunkenly at his interrogator. Then in a sepulchral voice he replied: 'Ohio, ma'am!'

Some pubs became the unofficial headquarters of a particular unit and bore the marks for long afterwards, in the shape of signed photographs, shoulder flashes and regimental coats of arms. The Cricketers Arms at Beeston in Nottingham, constantly used by the 508th Paratroop Squadron, one woman remembers who worked in a local factory, had almost its own museum, containing 'parts of their uniforms, parachute silk and cords from some of those who came back, badges, buttons. In the yard there was a big oak table, on which every GI was expected to carve his name. Some of them with long names used to complete it over several visits.'

The final proof that the pub, that most distinctively English of institutions, had truly taken the American serviceman to its heart came at the end of the war, when the Central Hotel at Hastings was formally renamed The GI. The Mayor made a speech, remembering, very appositely, that Hastings, having survived another, less friendly invasion, had easily absorbed the GIs, the sun, most untypically for a November day in England, shone

brightly down and a Lieutenant from Texas solemnly unveiled the new sign, before, no doubt, leading his men in drinking a baptismal pint. It is sad to record that The GI sign swings no more in the bitter wind of which so many GIs complained; on the house changing hands in 1962 it became the New Central.

If, like the British, the GIs occasionally suffered from the drink shortage, they never, unlike them, ran out of tobacco. The normal PX ration provided up to four cartons of 200 cigarettes a week, costing fourpence (eight cents) per packet of twenty, plus a tin of tobacco – usually Prince Albert – and four cigars, priced at a penny each. The memory of 'half-smoked cigarettes being thrown in the fire at a time when we were queuing up each day for perhaps five cigarettes if we were lucky' still rankles with one Southport housewife, and a wartime British soldier recalls finding 'one or two cigarettes in the packets they had discarded'. The casually smoked cigar, with its aura of affluence – few British people ever bought one except at Christmas – also became a symbol of American affluence. One infantry Captain, from Spartanburg, South Carolina, remembers being invited to dinner in the Officers' Mess at the Tower of London, after which, while the British officers began to fill their pipes, he took out a cigar.

Six pairs of eyes followed my every movement as I stripped off the cellophane wrapper, lit it and began to puff. I was suddenly conscious of their gaze. . . . Fortunately I always stuffed four or five cigars in each blouse pocket when I went out. I immediately apologised . . . and asked if any of them would care for a cigar. To a man they replied, politely, 'Indeed, if I had another to spare.' I gave each one, and they stowed their pipes quickly. I found that not a man of them had smoked a cigar since late 1939.

GIs rarely sampled British tobacco and when they did thought little of it. A 'chalky powder' taste, considered an army electrician from Philadelphia. 'British cigarettes tasted like burning hay,' decided one GI from Hoffman, Illinois. And a Technical Sergeant from Osawatomie, Kansas, delivers the final insult: 'They were so mild I couldn't tell I was smoking them in the dark.'

With British cigarettes so scarce, and GIs so generous, many young people acquired the tobacco habit from American brands. 'My first cigarette,' one fourteen-year-old boy wonders still, 'was it Camel or a Lucky Strike?' On the whole, however, American cigarettes were regarded by British smokers with little enthusiasm. 'Very loosely rolled and rather strong,' thought a Spalding housewife, though she grudgingly concedes that 'after all, it was a smoke and one tended to accept uncritically in those days'. 'Often burned my lips,' remembers a then teenage girl from Rednal, Birmingham. 'By the end of the evening my chest was raw and my husband said they had burnt off all the hairs on his chest,' recalls a Weston-super-Mare woman. Finally it is comforting to British patriotism to find that British smokers replied to American allegations about the equine origins of British beer with a very similar pleasantry about American cigarettes. The manufacturers of Camels, it was said, were the only ones honest enough to have the picture of their factory, a camel, on every packet.

20

'ARE THEY REAL, MUMMY?'

'I thought all Americans were very rich and either singing or shouting all the time.'

– Norfolk woman, then aged four, recalling 1942.

'WHILE British soldiers were going to fight against Hitler the whole reason for a GI's existence was to dish out candy and chewing gum.' This conclusion, reached by one twelve-year-old schoolboy in Northern Ireland, was soon accepted as self-evident by children all over the British Isles. Sometimes the excitement began before the Americans even arrived. One woman then living at Sprowston, a suburb of Norwich, remembers a 'War Weapons Week' concert in 1942 which ended 'with everyone on the stage and in the audience singing "The Yanks are Coming" at the tops of their voices. I . . . waited for them to come with impatience and curiosity' only to find two weeks later, when the Yanks duly came, 'the predominant feeling in the adults around me was one of acute disapproval. I latched on to this attitude of moral outrage and echoed it amongst my school friends.' But two years later, by now aged twelve, she was forced to reverse her opinion:

One day I went to the pictures with my school friend from the country. Nearly half the audience were Americans and one sat next to me. For some reason this incensed me and I began a long monologue on the iniquities of GIs: the money they had, the way they monopolized the girls, their behaviour in the streets, all the prejudices I had ever heard I reiterated, rather to my friend's discomfort. She kept telling me to hush and pointed to the GI sitting next to me who was shifting uneasily in his seat and sighing now and again. But I took no notice. . . . The cinema lights lowered and the GI rustled something in his pocket. Out came a truly dazzling sight: the most gorgeous bag of sweets I had ever seen, each one lavishly wrapped in a medley of coloured papers, all crackling deliciously as he began to unwrap them with the slow deliberation of grown-ups. I ceased in mid-sentence, eyes riveted on him, relentlessly watching his every movement in utter fascination. Suddenly he turned to me, grinned, and tossed the whole bag into my lap. . . . Such generosity had me quite overwhelmed as I shamefacedly stammered some thanks. From then on I looked at GIs in a new light.

Such generosity was typical of the GIs and, the same informant remembers, 'It was a common sight to see them surrounded by a tight knot of children clamouring for gum and sweets.' 'Any gum, chum?' became a national catch phrase, and there was a solemn correspondence in the Press as to whether the chewing habit harmed children's teeth. Adults became resigned to finding discarded gum stuck to the underside of tables and to seeing American jaws silently moving in public. One Weston-super-Mare woman remembers a show at the Winter Gardens where, due to this ceaseless facial activity, 'as one looked around' she had 'the impression that the whole place was revolving'. The headmaster of one London preparatory school, evacuated to Wales, having issued a stern edict against soliciting 'candy' discovered that his pupils had suspended a fishing net from their dormitory window and were collecting a rich 'catch' from American convoys. One Warwickshire mother remembers becoming worried about her seven-year-old son, for 'whenever I took him from our quiet country home to the county town, he needed urgently and often to go to the loo'. Only after the war was her anxiety resolved: she learned that 'He went there in hopes of meeting a GI, making friendly remarks, and coming out with gum.' Among the Americans at Goxhill, a British canteen manageress remembers, the reminder British mothers addressed to their offspring, 'Say "ta" to the gentleman' had become a catch-phrase, which lent itself to ribald use.

On older children living in isolated areas the effect of the GIs' arrival was often profound. One then twelve-year-old schoolboy living on the remote Lizard peninsula, in Cornwall, and 'born and bred on a farm' with 'no water, except a hand-pump from the garden wall, no electricity, no gas, no drains' and regarded even at his boarding school at Launceston as 'an uncouth backwoodsman' remembers what happened when two American camps suddenly appeared close to the school. The GIs – of the 29th Division – had hardly arrived, when, without asking, they swarmed over the hedge on to the school playing field and on the long summer evenings of Double Summer Time, adapted it to baseball, creating 'sand-bag bases' and 'a pit in the middle of the square where the pitcher's heel turned. For . . . one long summer term . . . we all watched baseball instead of playing cricket . . . American accents calling, "Ball one, strike one" or whatever.'

Another discovery was of American affluence: 'Someone discovered where the GI rubbish dump was. . . . It was a revelation, the debris of a throwaway society as seen by the wartime eyes of children who had lived even in peacetime in the rural semi-poverty of the thirties. . . . One was left with an impression of incredible riches just tossed aside, clothes and boots not worn out, cartons of . . . goods only half-used. . . . We browsed through the material with all the interest of an archaeologist studying ancient potsherds.' Their 'treasure of treasures', easily smuggled in beneath a jacket, was 'the GI magazine with . . . all those pin-ups'.

This boy and his schoolmates were 'fascinated by the whole thing of Americanness', especially the GIs' attitude to sex:

On one side of the playing fields was their camp, on the other the local park, which was liberally strewn with the sheaths left from the night before. Previously their existence had been a matter of conjecture. I doubt whether they existed in the villages and they were not talked about, let alone left lying around. Yet here they were everywhere. And they even had them over the rifle barrels when marching in the rain. All most upsetting for boys from the puritan Methodist backwoods.

One of the endearing qualities of the GIs was that they seldom did anything by halves as children struggling, unsuccessfully, to stretch their miserable ration of two ounces of sweets or chocolate to cover a whole week discovered. On the true American scale were the instructions given to the pupils at one Andover school to bring a pillow case to school the next day, when the jeeps would be calling, and 'they returned home' one beneficiary remembers, 'with it stuffed to the brim with chocolates and candy'. A schoolboy at Bude was introduced to peanut butter by being given a four-pound tin, while a sixteen-year-old secretarial college student at New Malden found 'it quite fantastic to be presented with a carton of twenty-four candy bars'.

Another engaging aspect of American generosity was its spontaneity. A then teenager from Gravesend remembers when a friend and herself were being entertained by two GIs in a London restaurant when the waitress happened to remark that she would shortly be visiting her evacuated children. Next day the GIs returned laden with chocolate and canned fruit: 'Give these to the kids, ma'am.' A schoolboy from the village of Southstoke recalls looking longingly at a shop window full of military badges. 'Suddenly to our surprise an American voice behind us said, "Here, sonny, have these," whereupon he removed his own badges from his uniform and gave them to me.'

The feeling that the GIs hardly belonged to the ordinary mundane world was a common one in those rationed 'utility' years. One woman remembers listening spellbound, as a nine-year-old in the Wiltshire village of Sherston, to tales of life in the New World, as her ancestors might have done four hundred years earlier. 'To us in war-starved England their country seemed like some sort of paradise.' An Aylesbury woman remembers hearing a puzzled small boy, hearing American accents used for the first time outside the cinema, staring hard at these uniformed apparitions and asking loudly: 'Are they real, Mummy?'

Even the wrappings of American goods seemed light-years away from those of drab, wartime Britain. A Liverpool man recalls how his 'two young daughters aged four and six fought over the lovely piece of red ribbon', surrounding a box of chocolates brought by a GI visitor.

Although the relationship between GIs and British children was often one of donor and recipient – with each side eager to play the appropriate role – there were other reasons for the warmth of the bond which soon developed between them. 'Americans never patronized children,' remembers a then teenage girl at Princes Risborough. 'They treated them as *people* and held long conversations with them instead of adopting irritating childish attitudes towards them.' 'Their easy-going nature established a rapport which I had never experienced with adults before,' remembers one man then a schoolboy at Tidworth.

Their liking for candy, comics and the minimum of discipline made ready identification with them very easy, since these were three of my favourite pursuits. Since most children identify one another by nicknames or shortened versions of Christian or surnames it was only logical that these new friends, although adults, should also be afforded this style of address. Hence my memory is filled with the names of Tex, Red, Darky, Porky, Uncle Sam and many other examples of childish invention.... All were quite happy with this situation except Porky, who took rather unkindly to our allusions regarding his figure and how he had come by it. Honour was seen to be done, however, when a ready-filled steel helmet of cold water greeted any child unwary enough to mention the hated name in front of him.

The Norwich girl previously quoted, who began by viewing all GIs with hostility, still vividly remembers Vince, 'tall, broad-shouldered and blond ... like an enormous teddy bear', who was a regular guest at a friend's home. 'He would let us do anything, romp all over him, ride on his back, chase about the garden. We used to go fishing with him and another GI riding on the cross-bar of their bicycles. We thought it very thrilling and daring. They wobbled about precariously and deliberately rode through puddles and over bumps at high speed till we were helpless with laughter. They spread their uniforms on the damp grass for us to sit on, they let us dress up in their smart jackets and their hats. We thought that was marvellous. . . . Something no other grown-up had ever allowed.' Here, surely, was the whole crux of the GI–child relationship: the GIs did not merely *allow* things; they actively joined in and visibly enjoyed them. This attitude was epitomized for one woman then living at Whitchurch and acting as Tawny Owl, or organizer, to the local Brownies by the way in which GIs clustered outside the door of the hall where the pack met, before eagerly accepting an invitation inside. The meeting ended 'with sixteen little girls interspersed with a dozen or so husky soldiers' dancing round the Brownie 'toadstool'.

To the GIs themselves, British children, so manifestly pleased to see them, filled a real need. That shrewd observer, Robert Arbib, decided that as so many Americans were barely in their twenties, 'children figured somewhere in their present lives or in their dreams'. At the same time, British children were, he decided – and other former GIs would agree – easy to like. 'These children were well behaved and modest, they were friendly and yet respectful. . . . They were good fun and good company.'

Children too small to remember a time before the Americans arrived grew up believing them to be a permanent feature of everyday life, like the ration books on the dresser, or the black-out curtains on the windows. The granddaughter of a couple who kept a village pub near the Shipdham airbase in Norfolk, just four years old when the first GIs arrived, remembers how she could not recollect a time when the village and the bars were not full of soldiers speaking in many and varied accents. 'I thought all Americans were very rich and either singing or shouting all the time.'

To this private misconception the GIs themselves were not slow to add others, and she found no difficulty in believing the airman who assured her, after a 'fat and elderly dachshund' belonging to another American had disappeared, 'that it had been made into German sausages'. When she heard that the man said to be responsible was to be 'godfather to my baby cousin, I felt sure the church would fall in on him when he stood at the font'. Although it did not, the offender was guilty of a spectacular solecism, for he 'horrified the entire congregation at the christening by slapping the rector, a *very* reverend gentleman, on the back and asking jovially, "How's the missus?" (The "missus" was a very icy old lady.)'

Many were the other strange beliefs about Americans acquired by British children. One Dorset schoolgirl concluded that all Texans could wiggle their ears, like the only one she had ever met, 'Texas Johnny'. The small children in one London nursery, evacuated to Wales, looked after exclusively by British women, concluded that all men were American, for their GI visitors, the teacher in charge remembers, 'provided the masculine influence so sadly lacking in our little women-dominated community. They acted the father role of throwing the toddlers up in the air and letting them feel in their uniform pockets for "candy".' Slightly older children dreaded the day when the Americans would leave. An Exeter woman remembers a seven-year-old anxiously asking if the GIs would still be there when she grew up, 'because then I could go out with Bob'.

By 1942 toy manufacture in Britain had ceased and every birthday or Christmas meant for parents a desperate search for second-hand dolls' prams or model trains at sky-high prices. Only for children befriended by the GIs was there no shortage. One High Wycombe boy, seven when he attended his first GI-sponsored party, acquired over the next two years an impressive array of presents: 'a toy gun, a flying suit (coveralls in a brown cotton with gold badges) various packs of cards, some showing American states, some showing various war planes, a horse-racing game, dominoes, draughts (they called it checkers)', while his sister received 'a party dress, jigsaw puzzles, solitaire etc.' But unfamiliarity could lead to embarrassment: one Birmingham mother still blushes at the memory of her elder son politely but firmly handing back some curious-tasting 'hard candy' with the explanation: 'My mummy doesn't allow me to eat mothballs.' Undeterred, the generous donor next presented this boy's mother with her first pair of nylons, but on going in put them on she discovered the feet were missing. They made 'smashing fishing nets', explained her son.

The Americans were also only too ready to pay for any service they received. 'Half a crown, then a fortune,' was, one man who was then a schoolboy in Lurgan, Northern Ireland, remembers, the standard reward 'for everything from the loan of our bicycles to an introduction to our sisters.'

To underprivileged children the arrival of the GIs meant even more than to those in ordinary families. A woman then aged seven, evacuated with 250 others, all disabled, to a castle at Tarporley in Cheshire, has warm recollections of the GIs, although when they arrived there she had not 'even heard of an American'. This gap in her education was now joyously remedied. The name 'castle' was enough to attract a flood of a hundred or more camera-hung GIs every Sunday, but soon it was not the architecture which was the attraction but the children, who now eagerly awaited the hitherto dreaded weekend.

My first impression was one of awe. I remember thinking how very rich they must be because they always came laden with such things as ice-cream in huge aluminium crates, doughnuts, bananas, 'candies' and of course chewing gum, which was rather reluctantly forfeited on the following morning at assembly. What we looked forward to most each Sunday were the rides in the jeeps. There would be a mad scramble to get the front seat beside the driver and then as many as was humanly possible would squeeze themselves into the back and in a long convoy we would go round and round the very large circular lawn in front of the castle, until we all felt quite dizzy with delight. . . . Nearly all the men had a camera slung round the neck and appeared to be very interested in photographing everything in sight. We soon learned to become very camera-conscious and a great competition would ensue to get in the front of the picture.

But the GIs' most famous effort among underprivileged children was the *Stars and Stripes* War Orphans Fund, launched in September 1942, following a World War I precedent. The 1942 target was modest, to provide £20 worth of 'extras' a year, for five years, for 500 children who had lost one or both parents during the war, but before long £1000 a week was flowing in, literally by the sackful; some enthusiasts invited their comrades to dispose in this way of bulky British coins. By March 1944 the Fund had reached £50 000 aided by a special song 'A Bob for a Baby', written by 'The Jive Bombers', the band on one bomber station:

> Do you rate with your date?
> Is she colder than ice?
> Give a bob for a baby
> And she's bound to be nice . . .

Posters on some airfields urged, more pessimistically, 'give while ya got it' – and units which raised £100 could specify the age and sex of the child they wished to befriend. Little girls were most in demand, but one combat regiment asked for the toughest little boy to be found. The most famous 'orphan' to be adopted – her mother, a war widow, was in fact still alive – was three-year-old 'Sweet Pea', 'chubby-faced with golden curls and very blue eyes', who became the adored mascot of the First Bombardment Wing and was hoisted on a box to 'christen' a B–17 named after her by painting the propeller. *Sweet Pea* later had a distinguished career on action, while Maureen earned immortality as perhaps the youngest, but not the last, English female to declare: 'I like the nice soldiers!'

AT RAINBOW CORNER

'Travelling singly in Piccadilly was virtually suicide for an unwary GI.'
— William A. Bostick, *England under GI's Reign*, 1946

FOR Americans who visited Europe before the war the one city not to be missed had been Paris. Now, with France occupied by the enemy, it became every GI's ambition to visit, or better still be stationed in, London. The first servicemen to arrive there, before Pearl Harbour, had been marines employed as Fire Guards at the US Embassy, though they had orders to wear civilian clothes off-duty to avoid attracting attention, and the Special Observers had established themselves in Grosvenor Square. With the United States' entry into the war the American presence in London became more obvious. The first enlisted men's billet – at a luxurious sounding address, the Hotel Splendide, 100 Piccadilly – was opened in March 1942, though all stores reaching London still had to be handled in a single room on the fourth floor of No. 20 Grosvenor Square, until a former motor showroom in Oxford Street was taken over as a supply depot. The American forces now began to move into the capital in force with the creation of the Central Base Section of the US Army, covering about 700 square miles, and its strength climbed from about 1000 officers and men in May 1942 to 30 000 two years later, of whom nearly 1000 worked for ETOUSA headquarters, so that by D-Day, the Americans had taken over 300 buildings for EM, thirty-three for officers, including twenty-four hotels.

This was a reminder of the second purpose served by London, that of the ETO's main leave centre. As early as May 1942 the *Stars and Stripes* was doing its best to help. 'The longest street in London is about three blocks and it's a dead-ender', GIs were informed. Trafalgar Square, the Houses of Parliament and Westminster Abbey were also, according to the author, worth a visit, and he added vaguely that 'Big Ben is down that direction somewhere too'. Other 'musts' were 'The Tower of London, the original guardhouse . . . at EC3, if that helps you any'.

A more reliable guide was perhaps the booklet issued by the American Red Cross *For US armed forces in UK – London* around 1943 which, curiously enough, devoted only three lines to the sight which attracted

GIs most, and which they now remember best. 'It was not Piccadilly or Buckingham Palace that was the Mecca of every "boy" on his first visit to London,' remembers one helper at a Red Cross club, 'but Madame Tussaud's', though the only explanation for its popularity she ever received was 'OK – so it's different' or 'My buddy said don't miss it'. Finally, she decided that 'in the heart of the average GI there was a boyish simplicity and naive curiosity that drew him irresistibly to the Wax Museum, as he called it'. By 1944 the exhibition showed many signs of American influence. The 342 exhibits one saw for 1s. 9d. (35 cents) (ordinary civilians had to pay 2s. 3d. (45 cents)) included fourteen US Presidents and a twenty-strong United Nations Group which included General Eisenhower and Admiral Stark.

On the whole, however, what the Yanks enjoyed most were the traditional sights. So long did the queues become at some famous institutions, that admission to them – like so much else – had to be rationed. One man visiting London from Liverpool remembers taking his two children to the Tower of London only to be told that civilians would only be admitted with someone in uniform and this British family had to be 'taken in' by an American Sergeant. (They learned later that – in the lavish fashion of his kind – he had hired a taxi in Southampton to take him to see the Tower during twelve hours' 'stopping off' in England.) Royal residences were also a constant attraction. A cartoon in the *Stars and Stripes* in December 1944 showed a taxi driver pointing into the surrounding fog while assuring his passengers: 'Take my word for it, lads, that's Buckingham Palace!' One army nurse, then with the 121st General Hospital near Yeovil in Somerset, remembers how she arrived for the first time in London with several colleagues determined 'to eat a lot and to see a lot' during their forty-eight-hour pass. Neither objective proved easy to achieve. At Scotts, their chosen restaurant, the girls' hearty appetites attracted so much attention that they finally asked the waiter why everyone was staring at them, while the meal, she remembers,

came to $12 and was not very tasty. When we eased our way out of the restaurant and into a taxicab [and] asked the driver to show us around London for an hour or two he said he could not do this due to the shortage of petrol. My friend Sally . . . pretty peeved by now, said . . . 'Then take us to petrol.' I came to the rescue and said, 'To Buckingham Palace.' The driver wanted to know if we were expected. So we laughed, he laughed and he said for two pounds he would drive us around, first by the Palace.

An equally determined sightseer was Pfc Hogan, winner of a competition in the *Strand* magazine for the best essay on England by a GI, reprinted in the *Stars and Stripes* in December 1942. 'Suddenly you find yourself in the world's most famous street', he wrote, 'trying to look unconcerned. Later you find yourself in the Mall and down there . . . behind the impressive grille, is the enormity [sic] of Buckingham Palace with the King's colours flying up there and in your throat you feel a twinge. . . . Maybe it's history, or simple dignity, or an overpowering sense of permanence.' Such creditable sentiments were, alas, not universal as the British MP and author Harold Nicolson noted in his diary when he took a party of GIs round the Palace of Westminster in January 1943. 'In they slouched, chewing gum . . . determined in no circumstances to be either interested or impressed.' When offered the chance to see the Great Seal of England, 'through the corridors they slouched apathetically expecting to be shown a large wet animal such as they had seen so often at the Aquarium in San Francisco'.

More receptive GIs were often impressed by Speakers' Corner near Marble Arch, where any Englishman, or indeed foreigner, could exercise his right of free speech. One wartime airman still remembers it as 'one of the most amazing places I had seen', unlike anything he had experienced in Torrington, Connecticut, and he was delighted to observe 'people from all walks of life, groups gathered round different individuals, discussing any-thing and everything', including 'one man . . . saying, "I am John the Baptist, and if you do not believe me try to get out of this island" ', a curious piece of logic. Most GIs reacted to London with equal enthusiasm. To one airman serving with the 95th Bomb Group in East Anglia it seemed 'the liveliest, most exciting place in the world' more so even than Denver, Colorado, his home town. 'I always felt that I was standing at the crossroads of the uni-verse when in London.'

Never abashed by famous names, the GIs sauntered as casually into expensive restaurants as any Victorian nobleman. One Second Lieutenant from Pittsburgh, Pennsylvania, where he was a technician in a steel mill, and Eye, Suffolk, from where he flew a B–24, found that he enjoyed fish-and-chips more than dinner in Claridges, 'recommended by Les's aunt, who . . . had read somewhere that it was the best restaurant in Europe'. The meal here was not a success, for one of the party, 'a small-town Ohio boy . . . got discouraged with the French menu and growled to the waiter, "Just bring me some meat and potatoes," ' while they thought the wine 'expensive but too dry'.

One Master Sergeant, an architect in peacetime, stationed at Kew with the 660th Engineers, a highly sophisticated unit consisting largely of 'artists, musicians and scene-painters in Hollywood studios', had a happier exper-ience, as a British acquaintance remembers. 'He got his family to send him all manner of tinned delicacies [which] he persuaded the chef to garnish and serve in the best Claridges tradition with silver and glass, etc., to match. They entered into the spirit of the thing. The architect enjoyed a first-class meal. The chef and waiters ended the richer by generous tips.'

Within a few months of the first GIs appearing in the West End, Ameri-can camps and officers ringed the capital, or were scattered across its central

districts, from the airfields of Essex in the east, to the huts of Eighth Air
Force Headquarters in Bushy Park in the south-west. In London itself the
D-Day planners occupied Norfolk House in St James's Square in the West
End, with G–2 Intelligence housed in offices over a large department store in
Oxford Street and G–5 Civil Affairs in requisitioned houses in Princes
Gardens, South Kensington. Soon everywhere the Stars and Stripes flew
from iron balconies outside once-elegant first-floor drawing-rooms, now
filled with Government-issue 'cots' or trestle tables.

One woman author who returned to her flat in Shepherd Market off
Curzon Street in the autumn of 1942 after an absence of six months observed
the changes which had occurred:

More and more Americans were to be seen in the streets. They called to each
other with strange Red Indian war cries and organized baseball games in the Green
Park. . . . The first uniformed groups were housed in two Piccadilly buildings –
the former Hotel Splendide and the Badminton Club. . . . Then began a pincer
movement converging on our market. South Audley Street became a miniature
Fifth Avenue, the palatial mansion facing Stanhope Gate became a senior US
Officers' Club, and the Washington Hotel in Curzon Street blossomed out as the
American Red Cross Washington Club for doughboys. Meanwhile, Half Moon
Street and Clarges Street, famous in the old days for aristocratic bachelor lodgings
became an American dormitory. There was not a tailor, a shoemaker or a French
[i.e., dry] cleaner . . . that did not start working overtime to cope with this invasion. . . . They hammered and sewed, they ironed and they washed, all day and
far into the night.

By January 1943 there were enough GIs in the West End to justify
opening a PX in South Audley Street. Watching its customers stagger
away, laden with luxuries unobtainable elsewhere in England, became one
of the minor sights of the capital and a year later, when I gained PX privileges myself, I was astounded at the range of goods, from cigarette lighters
to fountain pens, on offer. Even the basic weekly entitlement was impressive:
three razor blades, two candy bars, two candy rolls, seven packs of cigarettes,
four cigars, one box of all brands of 'cookies' [i.e. biscuits] on sale, one
package of gum, one pack of tobacco, plus three bars of soap per month.
Tobacco-starved and sweet-toothed British citizens were not slow in
discovering the location of their nearest PX. One girl admits hanging about
outside hers with a hungry expression and empty bicycle baskets – invariably soon filled. A cartoon in the *Stars and Stripes* showed an ATS Recruiting Sergeant posting herself outside one, while explaining: 'We've
discovered these places are best to find large gatherings of British girls.'

By the spring of 1943 London was full of unfamiliar sights. 'Green
Park,' observed the Shepherd Market resident previously quoted, 'had
become American territory' filled with GIs 'doing physical jerks' watched
impassively by the sheep grazing there as part of the 'grow more food'

drive. These sometimes wandered into the middle of Piccadilly and lay down in front of the GIs' jeeps, their drivers professing to regard this strictly wartime phenomenon as an everyday feature of 'sleepy old' London life.

The smartest GIs in town were the 'Snowdrops' of the 787th Military Police, with headquarters in the bomb-damaged Junior Constitutional Club in Piccadilly, and Green Park for their parade ground. The Mayfair flat-dweller quoted earlier describes the Central London scene one spring morning in 1944:

I turned into Piccadilly . . . to find two lines of white-helmeted Americans drawn up in the Green Park . . . The Stars and Stripes floated impressively in the breeze. The band started to play . . . 'The Star-Spangled Banner' . . . Big Ben struck ten . . . The sun glittered on the brass and the grass was fresh and tender. In the distance a clump of cherry trees made a splash of white blossom. . . . A small crowd stood under a leafy chestnut watching the proceedings; their expressions denoted that content of mind . . . associated with the happy watchers of a cricket match on the village green.

The two great centres of American influence in London, though for very different reasons, were Piccadilly Circus and Grosvenor Square. Although few GIs probably knew much of the history of either, the latter had, by 1941, many links with the United States. The square had been built in 1725, when a contemporary newspaper declared that its houses 'for largeness and beauty . . . far exceed any yet made in or about London', and it was still new when Lord North, generally blamed for the loss of the American colonies, occupied No. 50. Soon afterwards the first American Minister to Great Britain made his home at No. 9, while in 1914 Ambassador Walter Hines Page[1] took over No. 6, becoming, as a commemorative plaque in Westminster Abbey testified, 'the friend of Britain in her sorest need'. Ambassador Joseph Kennedy – of whom no one could have made any such claim – in 1937 established the combined Embassy and Consulate at No. 1 Grosvenor Square, from which they gradually spread into the adjoining buildings. In 1941 Kennedy's admirable successor, John G. Winant, came to 'live over the shop', in a flat at No. 3, and thereafter Grosvenor Square rapidly became more American territory than British. The Special Observers were based on Nos. 19 to 20, and in the latter, a former luxury block of flats, General Eisenhower, in June 1942, set up his ETOUSA headquarters, his Central London home, when he returned in 1944 – though he retired to his Kingston cottage whenever he could – being 'an attractive and nicely furnished town house' called Hays Lodge in nearby Chesterfield Hill. Admiral Stark's mission moved in next door to ETOUSA and it rapidly became a matter of prestige for every American organization, from the OSS to the

1. The first American ambassador was appointed in 1893.

Red Cross, to have at least a foothold there. A 'Consolidated Officers' Mess', better known as 'Willow Run' after the mass-production aircraft factory, was opened in December 1943 in the giant ballroom of Grosvenor House in Park Lane. Here for a modest 2s. 6d. (50 cents) twenty-six servings a minute were dispensed cafeteria-style to 1000 officers at a sitting. According to an American historian, the 500 earlier employees were originally directed by a French chef, but his 'services were . . . dispensed with when it was found that his spirit was crushed by the prospect of serving the contents of the C-Ration can'.

If Grosvenor Square was the heart of the United States in Europe,[1] Piccadilly represented another, hardly less vital, organ. One GI earned himself immortality in the *Stars and Stripes* by being overheard asking: 'Is Piccadilly Circus open to visitors all day?' It is in fact, despite its name, merely a road junction encircling a statue of Eros, god of love, though during the war this was boarded up. His presence, however, still brooded over the area, which soon became notorious as London's 'Red Light District', although – to the surprise of GIs who regarded the British Isles as merely an annexe to the accommodating Continent – both brothel-keeping and soliciting were illegal in Britain. Not every GI, however, had learned of its reputation, as one twenty-three-year-old Lieutenant, fresh from the sheltered life of a senior at Siena College, Loundonville, New York, discovered:

We heard that Piccadilly was the Times Square of London and the heart of the city, so we decided to start our tour from that spot. We somehow managed to get aboard a bus going in that direction and asked the driver to tell us when we arrived. . . . He gave us a wide and knowing grin and there was a titter among some of the passengers who could overhear. We took our seats, a little nonplussed at the . . . smiles and suppressed laughter. When we arrived, the driver pulled up with a flourish and called out 'Here we are, Yanks, Piccadilly! 'Ave a good time!' The other passengers laughed and cheered and the driver waved as he pulled away again. A minute later we found the reason for all the levity when a newspaper vendor tried to sell us condoms . . . In the next few minutes we were propositioned several times.

Similar experiences led a young naval Lieutenant, then working in London while preparing plans of the invasion beaches, to caption a sketch of two US sailors in a West End Street: 'A GI patrol on reconnaissance duty.'

This was extremely hazardous work as the commandos attacked patrols on the sidewalks and taxis rushed in for the kill when the GIs fled into the streets. . . . An American naval task force [i.e., a stronger party of sailors] stands by to attack or

1. The square is still 'little America' in London, with the vast new US Embassy occupying the whole west side, and a statue of President Franklin D. Roosevelt in the centre. It is, however, no longer known as 'Eisenhower Plazt,' and the civilians no longer joke 'I heard an Englishman in Grosvenor Square'.

repel same. The fleet units usually stayed in close formation using wolf-pack tactics and keeping an eye on the lone raider who went ahead to investigate whistle contacts. Travelling singly in Piccadilly was virtual suicide for an unwary GI. The black-out made night operations especially dangerous, since it was difficult for a GI to know what he was getting. GIs were known to have made the fatal error of trying to pick up their own Top Sergeants.

The 'commandos' were, of course, not the military variety but 'Piccadilly commandos' or prowling harlots. (Their sisters-in-arms, willing to sell their favours in the open air, were known as 'Hyde Park Rangers'.)[1] It was the 'commando' label which became famous, however, and one London woman in a US club remembers the onlookers becoming hysterical with laughter when a visiting British officer, knowing no better, gallantly took off one of his Commando shoulder flashes and pinned it on the sleeve of one of the British women helpers.

Another GI, then a twenty-five-year-old technician, from Brooklyn, recalls disputing the £5 he was asked, but 'when I tried to bargain . . . she replied that her favours were for all night'. The 'stock answer' on such occasions, he recalls, was 'Honey, I don't want to buy it . . . just to rent it.'

Often, practising the principles of free enterprise, the women would charge what they thought the market would bear. One officer remembers how 'The "Piccadilly" girls sidled up to men in the pitch dark black-out and felt for their insignia of rank,' before announcing their charge. 'A "trick" standing up in a doorway, dark, of course, or a more lengthy "liaison" in a room some place, was priced according to rank, ten shillings ($2 then) or up.' It was fortunate that he never felt the need of their services; as a Lieutenant-Colonel it would have come expensive.

Staff Sergeant Robert Arbib, who had earlier seen wartime Ipswich during the frenzied airfield-building months of 1942 now recorded his impressions of the capital during the more relaxed era of June 1943:

The centre of London on a Saturday night was Piccadilly Circus. Here was a microcosm of the whole – a combination of crossroads, entertainment centre, restaurant centre and meeting-place. . . . The Americans surged in a never-ending tide around the Rainbow Corner – milling their way in and out of that mammoth beehive, in search of friends, food, dancing, of an hour's sleep before a train left, or of a bed for the night. From the Rainbow Corner the Americans flowed out and around the Circus. Some were in search of restaurants and theatres. Some were in search of bars and beer. Some were looking for girls.

The girls were there – everywhere. They walked along Shaftesbury Avenue and past the Rainbow Corner, pausing only when there was no policeman watching. Down at the Lyons' Corner House on Coventry Street they came up to soldiers waiting in doorways and whispered the age-old questions. At the Underground entrance they were thickest, and as the evening grew dark they shone torches on

1. The 'Rangers' were the US Army's commandos.

their ankles as they walked, and bumped into the soldiers, murmuring, 'Hello, Yank', 'Hello, soldier', 'Hello, dearie!' Around the darker estuaries of the Circus the more elegantly clad of them would stand quietly and wait – expensive and aloof. No Privates or Corporals for these haughty demoiselles. They had furs and silks to pay for.

Down in the Circus, standing on the kerb, were the men who pretended to sell newspapers. 'Poybeeb! Poybeeb!' they shouted. '*News . . . Standard . . . Star!*' But – if you asked them for a newspaper, they turned and growled, 'G'wan beat it!' There were other salesmen, too. There was always a man who came up to you and offered to sell you a bottle of whisky, for £4 or more. There was the man who could take you to a 'bottle-party'. And there was the man who would buy your fountain pen. . . .

Down below the ground, too, the activity is intense. On the first level of the Underground there are swarms of people moving in all directions, people waiting by the telephone booths and pondering the ticket machines. This is where you kiss your girl good night and where the sailors burst into song and where the Military Police stop soldiers and ask to see their passes. As you take the long escalator down to the second level there is always someone sitting on the moving steps, and always a Canadian soldier who is lost. And then the third level where the wind blows dust in your face, and more steps to run down, and then the fourth level, hundreds of feet underground, where the trains run to Watford. Here is Pat in her grey smock, with her back to the tracks, running the show. 'Stanmore Line! All stations to Stanmore! No, this is not the Watford train! Last train to Watford is 11.37. Mind the doors!'

Rainbow Corner, mentioned here, was the most famous of all American wartime institutions in London. There had been a club for Americans in London ever since December 1940, the Eagle, in Charing Cross Road, which in April 1942 was taken over by the American Red Cross to cater for GIs. It was followed two months later by the Washington, in the former Washington Hotel, in Curzon Street, though its charges now were a good deal more modest: 2s. 6d. (50 cents) for bed-and-breakfast, and 1s. 0d. (20 cents) for dinner. But it was Rainbow Corner which became almost synonymous with the term 'GI' in London. This famous club in Shaftesbury Avenue opened its doors for the first time in December 1942 in the former Café Monico, which had been blitzed. The building was extensively restored to provide a café with daily entertainments, an International Room, accommodating 300 couples for dancing, a games room, a writing-room, a library, two lounges, and all the amenities, for which the homesick GI pined, from juke-boxes to a 'home-town' barber shop. Almost every British canteen closed down, like the pubs, around 10 p.m., but Rainbow Corner, which employed 450 professional and volunteer staff, offered hamburgers or American sandwiches all night. Here the GI could obtain an introduction to a British family, join an organized taxi tour with a guaranteed Cockney driver, or, if he had sampled too recklessly the delights of nearby Piccadilly receive immediate treatment at a prophylactic station.

Above the information desk hung an arrow pointing west, inscribed 'New York – 3271 miles' and this was a favourite subject of GI jokes. A British visitor who helped there in November 1943 recalls a hopeful enquiry from one Corporal about trains to Ohio.

Second only to Rainbow Corner in popularity was the Milestone Club opened in a former hotel in Kensington, where, one catering superintendent remembers, the slogan was 'Nothing too good for the boys'. A British helper who for two years dealt with enquiries from GIs on leave in London has not yet forgotten the very first question she was asked: 'Say, where do I get me a blonde?' Later enquiries proved easier: 'Where was the inn where Christopher Marlowe was assassinated?' 'Where did Samuel Pepys live?' and 'Say, could you direct me to where that guy Winston Churchill lives?' Many were thrilled to be in London, and equally flattering in its way was the amazement of the small-town GI, who having asked for a bus to 'London Station' learned that the capital had twelve main-line terminuses.

Apart from Rainbow Corner, The Milestone and The Eagle clubs, enlisted men could visit the Interstate in Dover Street, the Mostyn in Portman Street and the Washington in Curzon Street, all in the heart of the West End. There were two clubs close to Marble Arch, the Columbia and the Victory, both in Seymour Street, and in Kensington the Hans Crescent Club. Officers were catered for at the Duchess Club in Duchess Street, near Oxford Circus, later transferred to coloured troops, the Princes Gardens and Vandyke Club in Kensington, the Jules Club in Jermyn Street, and the Reindeer Club in Clifford Street, both in the West End. WACs visiting London turned towards Charles Street in Mayfair, and its two women-only clubs, one of which was for officers.

Too late on the scene to benefit many GIs – it was opened only in the spring of 1944 – was the Stage Door Canteen at 201 Piccadilly – where film and stage stars were photographed giving their services. One teenage girl from Swinton in Lancashire remembers being duly impressed to be 'served waffles by Bing Crosby'.

For many GIs what a furlough in London – or indeed anywhere else – meant was, above all, girls. A guide issued by the Provost Marshal in April 1943 on *How to Stay Out of Trouble* warned against 'females of questionable character', but these were, of course, the very type which many GIs were seeking. Hyde Park was a favourite picking-up place and one airman from Coral Gables, Florida, sitting there in the sun one day with a friend, remembers witnessing a typical encounter, after two young women had passed them talking loudly.

One said, 'I hate those bloody Yanks.' The other said 'I wish those damned Yanks would go back to America, I hate them.' They walked on out of sight, cursing all Americans. . . . Fifteen minutes later wc heard silly giggling and sugary sweet talk coming near us. We looked up and saw the same two girls walking arm in arm with two American soldiers, kissing and loving so sweetly.

'Being right in London,' one Bostonian, an Engineer officer remembers, 'was an ideal situation for a young bachelor. There was a wide variety of parties and clubs to go to every night and historical places to visit on the weekends. The British people I met were delightful and friendly' – and none more so than a 'pretty blonde "Wren" (forget her name)' met at a dance who introduced the diarist to a very different part of London, a working-class district south of the river.

One night after a dance . . . we took the Tube to Elephant and Castle and then had to walk nearly two miles through an utterly devastated area of the city which had been bombed by the Germans a year or more earlier. My date lived with her mother and younger sister in the bottom floor and cellar of their ruined row house.[1] The father was in the army. There were many other families in the area living in remnants of houses. Despite these horrible conditions these people amazed me by their remarkably cheerful and uncomplaining attitude. When I got back to the Underground station an air-raid siren began sounding off and people began coming into the station. Some were already sleeping or lying on the platform; apparently these people spend every night down there.[2]

This officer's favourite Londoner proved to be 'a lovely brunette girl named Patty, who lived with her parents and maternal grandmother in a row house in Clapham', a little further out than the Elephant.

Her mother and grandmother were charming and very friendly to me but . . . Mrs B. explained that her husband had a dislike for Yanks stemming from an incident occurring in World War I. I finally won his friendship by taking him out to his favourite local pub, buying 'shandies' for a couple of hours and playing darts. I made sure he won most of the time.

Although in love, as in war, life was usually more pleasant for an officer, an enlisted man could also have an enjoyable time in London, as one airman then stationed at Wendling in Norfolk and later at High Wycombe, remembers, in rather different terms: 'Wow! You don't have that much time and space. I sorta felt like I was on a last fling before settling down, so there were always girls.' His favourite was 'Mary':

She was my steady date for over a year. With her I went to the finest cafés and shows and to the zoo and pubs. We ate in the places where they bring the dusty bottle of wine for a taste test and the waiters dress in white tie and tails and the string music was all real 'long hair'. . . . One night we had the front balcony seats at the Haymarket Theatre for a showing of a new movie. The night before the

1. A 'row' house was one in a terrace.
2. This was a common sight in many Underground stations. 'It was,' one GI remembers, 'disconcerting to find oneself stepping off the train into someone's bedroom.'

Queen had had the same seats, so we did attract attention. And since Mary was a nanny I took her and her little charges fishing along the Hampstead Heath lakes. She found me a place to stay up in Hampstead when I was in London. Mary lived across from Keats House, so it was just down Shepherd's Walk to her house. We spent leaves and weekends together and we were really something to each other, but never quite got around to marriage.[1]

Though their behaviour was not always appreciated at the time, the GIs enlivened the life of the capital in many ways, like engaging complete strangers in conversation in the Underground; and 'patting the bald heads' of complete strangers in the street 'and wishing the baldie, "Good luck, bud" '. Many had never attended a theatre before, and one man recalls a memorable evening at the Duke of York's when a foursome of GIs and their girl friends discovered that *Arms and the Man* was not the light-hearted revue they had expected. 'Disappointed in the play the foursome "got cracking" – the LOT PLUS. The stalls watched the play, the circle watched the box. The noise was terrific, the show was stopped, the foursome hustled out.'

With taxis already scarce due to petrol rationing, the arrival of the free-spending Yanks soon made the sight of a vehicle flying a 'For Hire' flag a rare event, and foot-sore Londoners constantly complained that GIs pressed ten-shilling or even pound notes upon none-too-reluctant drivers for two- or three-shilling journeys. The drivers themselves, however, grumbled that GIs did not realize that a tip was obligatory. One protested in the *Stars and Stripes* in December 1942 at being given only sixpenny or

"Hey—taxi!"

ninepenny tips (perfectly reasonable, in fact, for a short ride), and an investigation by the London *Star* three months later found six drivers who had received tips of a penny to threepence (sixpence was the normal minimum), several others who said that they had never been tipped at all by a GI, and only three who grudgingly conceded that 'the Yanks' were 'all right'. This

1. This romance finally ended when Mary married an Irishman and her GI admirer stopped writing as her husband 'was the jealous type'.

evidence must, however, be viewed with suspicion, and one Londoner remembers a taxi driver admitting that 'American servicemen would pay over to him £10 for a ten-shilling fare without turning a hair on realizing the mistake'.

Other London residents who knew at once when a new detachment of GIs had arrived were the pigeons in Trafalgar Square, for every American wanted to be photographed feeding them, and so much discarded gum was soon littering the area that one comedian declared in May 1944 that the birds were now laying rubber eggs, while according to the *Stars and Stripes* sophisticated pigeons could be heard whispering 'Any crumbs, chum?'

The Underground, one of the few British institutions that almost all GIs were prepared to agree was superior to anything in their own country, was a favourite pick-up place. 'It was in Piccadilly Underground station that I spoke to my first GI,' remembers one sixteen-year-old schoolgirl from Waltham Cross who visited London with two girl friends 'one half-term holiday on the pretence of looking around the big shops' but in reality to inspect these already legendary young men. 'I wore a little fur hat and a deep red coat and across the escalator he smiled broadly at me, then ran down the other side and told me I reminded him of his local preacher's wife back home' in Massachusetts, the beginning of an 'unromantic brother and sister friendship that has lasted until the present day'.

The nearest to every man's ideal of the perfect leave in London was probably achieved by a combat engineer in an amphibious unit, from Enterprise, Alabama, who arrived in Britain on D-Day and during the three months he spent with his Harbour Craft Company at Dartmouth before moving to Le Havre managed just one four-day furlough in London.

I found some kind of YMCA-type accommodation, left my satchel and went out in dusk, blacked-out city, walked a long way, drinking it in. On a street corner that night, a man spoke to me. He was a flier with the RCAF and offered to share a bottle of good Scotch in his hotel room. I went along and found he really wanted to talk to someone, which he did for hours. I was then an amateur drinker and sometime that night I vomited all over his bathroom floor. 'It's all right,' he said and mopped it up with a towel, while I lay miserably drunk.

Next morning I told him I was so damned sorry, but he wouldn't hear of that. Bid me a pleasant farewell. A very damned good fellow. Got my satchel and checked it somewhere in a station. Walked along Piccadilly Circus to check out the rumour about Piccadilly Commandos. Found rumour was true.

Went to a London burlesque; good show, first time I ever saw girls stand completely nude on a stage in the dim light, not moving because that was the law.

On street, encountered a crowd. Walked up to look. A London bobby was beating the hell out of a man down on sidewalk with his nightstick. . . . In front of me, a slim, dark-haired girl turned around, covering her face in revulsion. She bumped into me and I put my hands on her shoulders. 'Look, miss, could I buy you a drink?' I said. She looked up and placed me as a Yank. We walked away from there and walked and walked and talked and talked, spending a while on a bench in a nice green peaceful park. It was like being back home, a freshman in college, on a nice date. Don't remember anything we said, but it all seemed so homespun and normal and natural.

When it was night, we were together in a little basement room that had a bed and a bathroom. We made love, in a wonderful way. In the night, the V–1 rockets came in – the ones with the ragged motor noise carrying a ton of explosive. We lay beside each other listening to the motors die, then the silence, followed by the tremendous explosion in London's city streets. I could hear bricks and glass falling into the streets. She was terrified and clung to me very hard. 'This is worse than the blitz,' she said.

We spent the rest of my leave together, and this is still a glorious and holy experience to me. I was brought up in a Puritan, Southern Baptist Christian home and this time with her will always be one of the loveliest and cleanest experiences of my life.

The next day she took me around London and showed me Big Ben and some of the parks and the glories of the city. She asked me nothing, but when she saw me off on the train for Dartmouth I gave her a bed-sheet-sized five-pound note, which was then most of my fortune. By most people's standards we were immoral, I suppose. But we were young and lonely and could die tomorrow.

22

IN DOUGHNUT DUGOUT

'The doughnut was not just diet . . . It was ammunition for the heart and spirit.'

– George Korson, *The Story of the American Red Cross Overseas in World War II*, 1945.

ONE of the oldest international jokes was of the Englishman, miles from civilization, dressing for dinner in the jungle, but many GIs soon showed themselves equally to be slaves of habit and custom. Uprooted from his native Wisconsin or Vermont, the average Yank was ill-at-ease until 'normalcy', in the shape of the American way of life, had been restored and before long it would have been possible for him to spend almost his whole time in Britain without ever being exposed to British ways, or even to any British voice, except that of an occasional telephone operator or civilian helper.

Before the American authorities had set up their own, characteristically lavish, network of clubs and canteens, recreational facilities were provided by NAAFI (short for Navy, Army and Air Force Institutes), the British equivalent of the American Red Cross, and in December 1942, the organization produced for its counter-staff a cautionary pamphlet *When You Meet the Americans* on the lines of those written for the general public and quoted in an earlier chapter. 'Try not to appear shocked at some of their expressions,' urged the broad-minded author. 'Miss Naafi' was also cautioned not to 'make fun of the American's accent or vocabulary' even if he did say he was 'up the pole', which meant not that he was insane, as in British idiom, but 'on the wagon', i.e., teetotal.

Although canteens inside camps were usually run by NAAFI those outside, in towns and villages, were set up and operated by a whole range of voluntary bodies, such as the YMCA, the Church Army, local churches, or groups of public-spirited private citizens. Welfare services in military hospitals were mainly provided by the British Red Cross and private volunteers, while the care of servicemen's dependants was the responsibility of the semi-official but volunteer-run Soldiers', Sailors' and Airmen's Families' Association, or SSAFA. The American system was different. All

these varied services were provided by the American Red Cross, supported
and partly financed by the Government. The ARC had extended its services
to Europe in the week of Pearl Harbour, for the benefit of servicemen stationed at the US Embassy, and in January 1942 handled its first case in
Ulster, that of a Sergeant from Pittsburgh who was anxious for news of his
pregnant wife. Full-time paid ARC personnel began to arrive in March 1942,
and thereafter the spreading pattern of American occupation was reflected
in the new clubs opened, Londonderry being followed by Edinburgh,
Glasgow and, in October 1942, Belfast until in December 1943 a major landmark was reached with the opening of the hundredth club, at Taunton in the
West of England. By D-Day the ARC effort in Britain had reached its
peak, with some 2000 American personnel on its strength plus 500 more in
the hospital service, directing the efforts of 10 000 paid British employees,
mainly domestic staff, and a further 13 000 civilian volunteers. By now there
were 265 clubs of varying size in operation. The largest, like Rainbow
Corner, were designed largely to cater for men on leave but these were
supplemented by others providing recreation on or near a man's base. In
the 'two-star' category were a hundred 'aeroclubs', run by a Director and
two Red Cross girls, with British help, and catering for airfields where 500
or more men were stationed. The first was opened in February 1943 and
those which followed mainly followed the same pattern, with a games room,
library, lounge and snack bar, with, where better furniture was not available,
army cots and mattresses covered with cretonne for use as couches. The
smallest establishments of all were the single-room 'Doughnut Dugouts', in
requisitioned village halls or disused shops in areas thinly populated with
GIs. 'One of the first to be opened', wrote the Red Cross historian, 'was
situated in a quaint little market town surrounded by miles of lonely moors.
. . . The villagers stared curiously as the procession arrived. First rolled a
giant clubmobile, equipped with a machine capable of turning out 5000
doughnuts daily, and large coffee urns. Then came the smaller cars, loaded
with the crew's personal baggage, a phonograph, a pile of records . . . cases
of cigarettes, gum, soft drink.'

The first forty clubmobiles had begun life as Green Line coaches belonging to London Transport, until converted in 1939 into emergency ambulances, and in January 1943 for their new purpose, though later they were
replaced by custom-built American vehicles. Beside helping to set up the
'dugouts' the clubmobiles toured the more remote camps which lacked any
permanent canteen, serving coffee and doughnuts – 250 men, it was said,
could be coped with in twenty minutes – and providing a tiny clubroom,
complete with American newspapers. Squeezed in somehow were bunks for
the three female members of the crew, a corps d'élite, with their own journal,
The Sinker – American slang for 'doughnut'.

An even tougher job was faced by the 'Clubmobile Rangers', who by the end of 1943 had largely taken over from NAAFI and other British agencies the job of providing refreshments for newly arrived GIs at the ports and the main-line railway stations. It meant, one observer remembers, working till one was exhausted in 'heavy GI underwear, battledress, boots, sweaters, coats and, inevitably, raincoats (it always rained) through the drizzle of a fogbound dawn'.

The 'real American doughnut', as the GIs often called it, to distinguish it from its British namesake, almost deserves a history of its own. The American Red Cross's Commissioner in Europe, Harvey D. Gibson, who had worked with the Expeditionary Force in World War I, 'envisioned', wrote the ARC historian, 'the role to be played in World War Two by this humble brown object of succulent dough. The doughnut was not just diet. . . . It was ammunition for the heart and spirit.' Sadly, it proved ammunition that British cooks were unable to forge. One army cook who tried to teach the art to some local housewives eventually gave up in despair, the result, he admits, being 'absolute greaseballs'. The GIs, meanwhile, agreed that British doughnuts had at least one virtue: they were, rumour had it, a sovereign remedy for constipation.

Although many American Red Cross workers, like those manning the clubmobiles, endured both discomfort and fatigue, some seem to have joined up in the expectation that the men they were supposed to serve would look after *them*, and they were not always popular. 'The most rank-conscious lot of females I ever met,' is how one GI sourly remembers them. A British civilian, then in her thirties, who worked at an ARC Club in the West, remembers the British staff being told to expect some 'real lovely girls'. But the six American Red Cross hostesses who arrived instead displayed only:

Hard faces, plain faces, faces with spots and skins like orange peel, loud strident voices and bulky figures. They called the GI 'soldier'. 'Hi, soldier, where you from?' 'Hi, soldier, move over and I'll share your table,' 'Hi, soldier, get me some more coffee.' I never saw that canteen empty so swiftly; they just melted away. . . .

The presence of salaried American staff in so many clubs led to many misunderstandings. One part-time helper in the ARC club at Exeter recalls how gradually it dawned on her that there was not 'the same tradition of voluntary service in the States. . . . I used to feel quite hurt when, if I couldn't answer a question about the food, or do something immediately to be told . . . that I should be able to as "After all you're paid for it," which I wasn't.' Later, when they discovered she gave her services free, 'I was told that I *ought* to be paid for it.' One woman serving in her spare time in the canteen at Weston-super-Mare was surprised, after serving a cup of tea costing 2d. (1½ cents) to find under the saucer a tip for 2s. 6d. (50 cents). A Richmond mother who had sewn on the stripes of a newly promoted soldier while helping at the Milestone Club in Kensington, was infuriated when he 'took a half-crown from his pocket and flung it at me', answering her protests with the surly reply, 'I don't have nothin' I don't pay for.' Only when she had explained that almost all the staff were unpaid volunteers did he stammer, 'I sure didn't know. I'm sorry, ma'am,' and, as she suggested, put his half-crown in the collection box for the British Red Cross, which he then 'rattled under the nose of every GI in the club until it was filled to overflowing'. Other British women discovered, to their surprise, that the GIs, so generous outside, were far more suspicious on 'American' territory. One twenty-five-year-old widow helping in the club at Salisbury used to be infuriated when GIs complained of being given short change. 'When accused of this,' she admits, 'I would let rip. It was funny to see their startled expressions and hear comments like "Gee, wadda dame! Wouldn't care to upset her too much." '

The helper at the Cheltenham club previously mentioned remembers the hot July evening when, having just come off duty, she was 'standing at the corner talking, when a large white lump fell from a window at the side of the club on to the thick bushes below. Curious, we went to have a look and there, still sleeping peacefully and quite unhurt, was a stark naked GI' who had put himself to bed after drinking too much, 'rolled over on the top bunk' and fallen out of both bunk and window. 'We got one of the MPs on duty outside the club, he got another one, and they carried this nude un-conscious boy into the club through the hall stiff with GIs and Reception girls as if they were taking a sack of potatoes. Everyone was too surprised to say a word, but after they got out of sight they just fell on each other, weak with laughing.' Almost as memorable was an evening at the Red Cross club in Taunton when one of the American staff who had been a make-up girl with a film company made up 'a naval Petty Officer to look like Abraham Lincoln. The likeness was uncanny. We took him for a walk all over the building to see what reaction we got. As we came into the main lounge a party of GIs who were somewhat merry staggered in. One of them took one look and fled, swearing to sign the pledge.'

There were other, pre-planned, entertainments. One eighteen-year-old from East Finchley, recruited as a hostess at Rainbow Corner, especially remembers 'a hayride in army trucks filled with straw', which led to 'a picnic of hot-dogs and coke' on Hampstead Heath. 'Another time we had a fancy-dress dance and my friend and I went as two hill-billies which caused a cheer when we went in. She wore her old school summer dress with patches and a sunbonnet with pigtails attached. I wore an old collarless shirt, a pair of ancient overalls with only one strap and a frayed straw hat. We regretted it a bit when we saw all the other girls looking as pretty as possible but we had a lot of fun.'

Conscious that the Red Cross clubs would provide a magnet for precisely the sort of girls that no American mother wanted her son to meet, the authorities went to enormous pains to 'vet' every female who crossed their thresholds. 'British girls who had an American boy friend could apply for a special guest card,' remembers a then seventeen-year-old telegraphist with the Post Office at Gloucester, where the Red Cross had converted the Bon Marché, 'a large departmental store . . . into a club. A form had to be completed and a recent photograph supplied, complete with the signatures of both the sponsoring GI and his girl.' Even when the precious passport had been issued 'you could only enter the club when escorted by your boy friend' – and if you fell out with him it was withdrawn.

One woman, then aged sixteen, who became a part-time 'hostess' to the ARC canteen at Polebrooke, recalls that officially there was 'no sitting down with a GI – but you were allowed to help him with his spelling if he was writing a letter. It was amazing how many of them suddenly needed a lot of help.'

To join the paid staff demanded the credentials of a saint. One highly respectable Suffolk girl, the only child of a local farmer, discovered that despite her impeccable background 'the security was fantastic. They wouldn't take either my word or my parents' that I had never done or said anything to harm the great USA. I was "screened", then I had to produce references from various friends of the family, it was really quite a performance.'

Those who survived this scrutiny were in a unique position to study the off-duty GI at close quarters. 'The British who worked in ARC clubs gained a better impression of the GI than did the average civilian,' believes one Reading housewife. 'Though we saw them with their hair down they were on their own territory and had less occasion to show off or become defensive, to impress the natives or because they felt shy or awkward.' 'We were treated with the greatest respect,' remembers an Isle of Wight woman who worked in an American seamen's canteen at Ryde. 'I was called "the Duchess", "Girlie" and "Blondie".' A young Preston sales girl, invited with others from the gown shop where they worked to become part-time 'hostesses' at the local Red Cross club, found these visits an agreeable oasis in the drab desert of wartime life. 'It was like stepping into another world. The war, rationing and coupons were all forgotten. I would step out into the black-out back to reality, leaving behind the warmth and friendship of America, feeling a little like Anne of Green Gables.'

Only rarely did friction occur between helpers and customers. The commonest reason was dislike of the food provided. One woman who worked in the Red Cross club at Cheltenham, where the cooks, like every British housewife, were usually forced to make scrambled eggs with dried egg, recalls that 'there was a lot of muttering and grumbling going on and we had to take quite a lot of insults. . . . I got so fed up, I said to one belligerent GI: "It's dried egg. You invented it, so shut up!" We heard no more about dried egg after that.' A GI from Osawatomie, Kansas, observed how the 'nice little old British ladies' whose tea wagons brought 'hot tea and sandwiches and rolls' to the construction crews at Wendling while 'shocked at anyone using the word "bloody" took to using GI profanity for slang . . . I remember the Red Cross lady telling my buddy one morning that all she had was Spam for the sandwiches . . . "You Yanks brought the stuff over here, so you have to help eat it. It's all we have, so take it and piss off!" '

A few helpers still look back on their experiences with distaste. One young widow decided after a few days in the club at Salisbury that she 'did not fit in', her reserved response to 'their free and easy manner' leading to references to her as 'Sour Puss' and loudly-asked rhetorical questions whether she ever smiled. 'After a few brushes,' she realized, 'I found I had to go along with them or leave.'

Many women never did become accustomed to the American habit of treating every female aged under fifty as a potential bedmate. One eighteen-year-old who worked as a paid waitress in the American canteen at Bedford between leaving the local girls' high school and going up to Cambridge in 1943 found that she seemed to have no point of contact with the men she served. American films, ruthlessly 'doctored' by the Hays Office, having left her with the impression that moral standards in the United States were even stricter than in Britain, she was horrified to find that every GI assumed she was eager to go out with him, and when rebuffed they complained to the American manageress. Like a delinquent schoolgirl, she was ordered to report to the male Red Cross inspector responsible for disciplining staff guilty of such 'un-American' behaviour, and he explained that in the United States such overtures were merely a routine preliminary to a normal friendship. But soon afterwards, tired of being told by complete strangers 'You've got great big, beautiful bedroom eyes', she resigned. (Her 'attitude', criticized by her recent customers, was not improved by a subsequent encounter on the London Underground where she shared a lift with a GI who was kicking the sides and tearing down the advertising posters and when reproved, replied resignedly: 'Typical Limey. No sense of humour.')

With the clubs and canteens came the entertainers, affording British civilians, as well as US servicemen, the chance to see in the flesh film stars and other celebrities who had hitherto only been names on a record label or cinema cast list. On every major camp there were frequent film shows, but the army authorities also believed that regular 'live' shows were important to morale, and a long procession of top 'names' in the entertainment business crossed the Atlantic from November 1942 onwards, the first performances, at six selected camps, being launched on Thanksgiving Day, 1942 by, among others, Carole Landis, Martha Raye and Kay Francis. Responsibility for organizing such entertainments rested on the USO, or United Services Organization, which corresponded to the British ENSA – Entertainments National Service Association – although the USO shows had a higher reputation than most ENSA productions, and were given a far higher priority than on British camps.

The official aim was to provide every major camp with some kind of live entertainment once a fortnight and at first this also meant drawing on local talent. By March 1943 thousands of GIs who had never before seen a 'straight' play had been given the chance – not always greatly appreciated – to watch British actors in *Private Lives*, *Just Married* and – perhaps more to their taste – *Petticoat Fever*. Then American companies – as distinct from individual artistes – began to arrive in strength. By July, ten were already resident in the UK and were touring on regular circuits of the main American-occupied areas. That summer in Wellingborough in the Midlands one could see *Hollywood Time*, in Bristol *Broadway Time*, in Newbury, and later in Bedford, *Fun Marches On*, in Bury St Edmunds, *Jive Time*, in Bournemouth *Bally Laffs*, in Salisbury *High Lights and Hilarity*, in Derby *Band Waggon*. By October Preston and Plymouth had been added to the areas being covered and *At Ease*, *Full Speed Ahead*, *Yanks Abroad* to the list of available shows, no doubt as undemanding as their names suggested. The *Stars and Stripes* admitted that the most popular number in any show was the *Strip Polka*, in which a dancer discarded her garments in response to a refrain chanted by the audience 'Take it off!'

The way in which GIs took for granted the efforts made to entertain them never ceased to amaze British servicemen and civilians. One woman then in her twenties remembers staring in astonishment at James Cagney, the 'tough guy' hero of many Hollywood films, at the aircraft repair base at Burtonwood. He was, she discovered, 'quite a small man, but a very good tap dancer' and good-naturedly 'gave us a demonstration of this out in the open'. A Wren from the same camp recalls attending a Bob Hope concert, an occasion fixed in her mind by a conversation she overheard on the way out; one GI remarked to another, 'Bob Hope was OK, but I didn't think much of the dame,' while his friend replied, 'I wouldn't mind sleeping with her.' 'We were,' this observer admits, 'quite shocked at this new frankness.' A keen film-goer in Bedford, where there were many 'sightings' of famous faces, could hardly trust the evidence of his eyes when he saw Bing Crosby and Bob Hope walking together through its streets. 'In relation to the wonderful unreality of the *Road to* . . . films' their appearance in the flesh in his native town seemed 'quite unbelievable'.

A few celebrities joined the forces and could frequently be seen in the areas where they were stationed. Probably the most admired was James Stewart, who abandoned an immensely successful career in Hollywood to become a B–24 pilot. Everyone, British and American, who met him in his

air force uniform agreed that he was 'a real nice guy', as modest and unassuming as any man so famous could be. One woman remembers how
impressed her husband, then in the RAF, was when a Liberator landed and
the familiar figure 'got out of the aircraft and in his nonchalant fashion
raised a hand: "Hi, fellahs, I'm Jim Stoort." ' Stewart, a Captain, landed in
England in December 1943 and was a familiar sight around Polebrook, but
even more shattering to the young women of the district was the presence of
Clark Gable, the darkly handsome hero of *Gone with the Wind*. Although,
like Stewart, a Captain in the US Air Force, Gable was not engaged in
routine operational flying but starring in a training film for air gunners.
'He looked like a very decent guy with no angle to his being whom he was,'
decided the *Stars and Stripes*, although 'His moustache has acquired a
slightly RAF look.' American newspapers 'back home', however, could not
resist running frequent stories about the famous star's exploits in Britain,
provoking a good deal of resentment. 'A few 100 000 relatives of Privates in
the Infantry who have been fighting in North Africa want to know why
Gable isn't a Private in the Infantry fighting in North Africa,' noted the
Stars and Stripes. But whatever envious Americans might say, British girls
were delighted that their idol was in Britain. 'We often saw him on a small
motor-bike around town,' remembers a then teenage resident of Oundle.
'I remember a seventeen-year-old girl friend breathed ecstatically to me:
"Clark Gable SPOKE to me!" ' Another wartime teenager has an even more
intimate memory, for she 'took him his breakfast in bed once', at the Bell
Inn at Stilton in Huntingdonshire where he often took a short leave. This
meant far more to her, at fifteen, she recalls, than the fact that Queen Elizabeth had slept there. A Nottingham housewife recalls that he 'made himself
very agreeable at . . . the Palaise de Danse', so that her young sister was ever
afterwards able to boast that she had actually danced with him.

Rather surprisingly, little use was made of the cinema to improve understanding between the GIs and the civilian community. Hollywood war
films tended to ignore the existence of America's Allies and it was not till
just after the end of the war in Europe that any British film showed a recognizable picture of the GIs in Britain, in *The Way to the Stars*, and not till
several years later that the American film industry produced in *Twelve O'
Clock High*, a portrait of the Eighth Air Force with authentic-looking
settings and atmosphere. More avowedly propagandist works proved less
successful, such as *The Canterbury Tale*, released in March 1944, which
recorded the adventures of four people, one of them a GI – in real life a
Sergeant Clerk in a London office – who came together in Canterbury and
learned about Britain's past through a series of flashbacks. The *Stars and
Stripes* observed that 'It is an idea that Hollywood probably wouldn't
touch with a ten-foot camera crane' – and Hollywood, in this instance, may
perhaps have been right.

More enduring has proved the musical *This is the Army*, which, after a previous run on Broadway, opened at the London Palladium in November 1943. One number, 'My British Buddy', was said to have been written after its composer, Irving Berlin, had seen British and American troops enjoying themselves together in the West End – a rare occurrence in real life – and its hit song, 'This is the Army, Mr Jones', can still sometimes be heard today. During an eleven-week run *This is the Army* was seen by 250000 people, among them General Eisenhower – the wartime equivalent of a Royal visit – and raised £80000 ($320000) for British war charities. A film version opened in London six months before D-Day and later went on release throughout the country.

With so much professional entertainment on offer, amateur groups visiting American camps tended to face unenthusiastic audiences, but once 'on pass' the GIs joined heartily in whatever amusement was to be had. A then Cornish schoolgirl can still 'recall a square-dancing session that brought down the ceiling in the Sunday School hall and the crack of benches giving in under the combined weight of four or five GIs during film shows'. Broadway in Worcestershire was the scene of the ultimate in Anglo-American musical co-operation. A local man, entertaining a party of GIs, decided he would like to sing 'Come into the garden, Maud' but 'just couldn't make the high notes', so one of his guests obligingly 'filled in where he couldn't reach'.

23

TALL, DARK AND HANDSOME

'Auntie, surely you never went out with Americans?'

– Question asked of Buckinghamshire woman by 'small nieces and nephews', 1972.

OF all the images of the GIs that survive in British folk memory one is still dominant, that of a cheerful young man with a young girl, usually a blonde, on his arm, listening avidly as he pays her some outrageous compliment or relates improbable tales of his wealth and status back home. Of the fourteen headings under which I sought information for this book it was 'The GIs and women' which attracted by far the largest response, especially from British readers, though one American veteran responded succinctly and revealingly: 'Wow!'

For many young girls everywhere in the British Isles the GIs' coming made daily life not merely tolerable but enjoyable. 'Their bombastic cheek made us automatically retreat whenever the Yanks were on the prowl, and that was most of the time,' recalls one then teenager in Prestwick, 'but how we loved it all.'

Although the Americans' reputation for pursuing any female who looked remotely available was well deserved, there was often at least an equal determination to 'get off' on the part of British women. The outlook, and experiences, of a former nurse, who lived at Goldthorpe, twenty miles from Sheffield, and whose father was so strict that he had even forbidden her elder sister to go to the cinema with a highly respectable school-teacher she had met at church as he did not want 'her name bandied about the village', are probably not untypical. At eighteen, having been released from nursing after deciding she had no vocation for it, she was 'directed' by the Ministry of Labour to a factory at Leicester, manufacturing Merlin engines for Spitfires. At last her big chance to meet one of those fabled beings, an American, had come.

When I got off the train at Leicester the billeting officer was waiting with a girl who had travelled on the same train. . . . 'Marge' had never seen a GI before and as we walked out of the station she clutched my arm and whispered, 'Look at all those Yanks! Boy, aren't we going to have fun?' I agreed with her fervently.

On the night shift at the factory we began work at 7.30 p.m. with an hour break for a meal at 11.30 p.m. and then a short break between 3.30 a.m. to 4 a.m. . . . and it was during these breaks that we (the younger girls) would hasten out into the street to meet the Yanks. We became very adept at spotting a jeep or GI truck from a long distance and knew to an inch almost the distance between the headlamps of British lorries and American trucks. . . . The weekends were our best time. Because we worked on nights, Edna, our landlady, never minded how long we stayed out on Saturday or Sunday nights, so Marge and I would go to the cinema about 7 p.m. after sleeping all day and come out about 11 p.m. Most of the 'competition' would have had to go back home by then and we had hundreds of GIs to choose from. . . . We would cheerfully climb into any jeep for a lift and be driven miles out to a GI camp, say good night to those boys and then start walking back to the city again. We would only have walked a few hundred yards when another jeep would pull up alongside and a voice would shout 'Hop in girls' and in we hopped. We could hardly see their faces but they would invariably say 'Give me five' and grab a hand, then 'Gimme ten' and grab the other. We usually used to start singing and I can remember entertaining a whole bus load of GIs because I knew the words of the song 'You can win, Winsocki, buckle down'.

After 'losing count of the GIs that we went out with for odd dates or perhaps for a couple of weeks', both girls became engaged, Marge to Carl from New Jersey, later killed in Belgium, and this girl to Danny – 'Different Dan the girls at the factory called him because of my habit of defending him with the words, "Yes, but Danny's different". . . . He was with the 325th Infantry Division . . . came from Boston . . . and was fabulous. He had sung with a band back in the States and had a beautiful voice. He would insist on singing at me, though, and I never knew where to look. I always feel sorry for film actresses when the leading man suddenly burst into song gazing at them tenderly – one gets cross-eyed gazing back into the singer's eyes and it never seemed polite to look away.' After a sad farewell in April 1945 'in a little waiting-room on Leicester station' Dan reported that he was helping to greet the Russians on the Elbe – did he sing to them, too, one wonders? – but proved less 'different' than his fiancée had claimed, for not another word was ever heard from him.

One twenty-one-year-old civil servant, then living in Buckinghamshire, had in 1942 never met an American when she and her 'very naive' seventeen-year-old sister decided to spend their first-ever holiday away from their parents, who urged them to 'be careful'. It proved to be very necessary advice.

Little did any of us guess that the Yanks were all over Ilfracombe. . . . As we left the station . . . they were everywhere. . . . We decided not to mention them on Mum's postcard to say we had arrived as it would 'worry' her . . . I felt a terrible weight of responsibility for my sister [although] she later proved to be perfectly capable of coping. . . .
The first evening we tottered into the only dance hall, a rickety little hall on the

pier, through the floorboards of which you could see the sea. . . . I had a wild feeling that all the Yanks in the hall were just that bit more dangerous with nothing but water below and around us. We spent some time in the cloakroom trying to look terribly confident as if we'd been bosom friends with Yanks all our lives, both dreading our first approach from one. Worse still, dreading that we'd be totally ignored. . . . However, from the moment we took a deep breath and walked in the hall we were besieged by successions of Yanks. . . . We had a hilarious time after narrowing the impressively large field to two nice officers . . . Paul and Mac. Then to my horror I missed my sister . . . I imagined everything to the last detail, even to going right back home to my mother to say I'd failed her, my sister had fought to the end, but a Yank had got the better of her and then chucked her over a cliff to feed the seagulls. After half an hour of hell my sister sailed into the hall, all smiles. . . . I dragged her off to the cloakroom and she serenely told me they'd been for a walk to the ruined chapel up the cliff path, and it was so romantic and why was I worried . . . ?

That week in Ilfracombe proved very successful. Paul and Mac stuck to us each evening, 'tried it on', were consistently rebuffed but returned to the charge as if it were all a good game. . . . They had a jeep and a driver and. . . . on our last night it was pouring with rain when we returned to the jeep. I was in the back with Paul (having established my seniority over my sister with the best position) so Paul said to the driver 'Get in, buddy!', which he did beside us. Nobody was embarrassed at all. We (Paul and I) continued our important business. I must admit I felt safer than ever with a gooseberry present on my last night. . . . With my arms firmly clasped round Paul's neck, to my astonishment I found his driver holding both my hands and grinning at me behind Paul's back. . . . When my sister and I left Mac and Paul for the very last time, I very naughtily said, 'Paul, can we kiss the driver goodbye for old time's sake?' Paul just said, 'He's all yours, girls.' In the darkness the driver made up for lost time . . . and breathed in my ear, 'God, honey, what's a feller bin missing?'

A year later this girl found herself working among Americans when they were attached to the secret Government research establishment where she was employed. Her social life now blossomed once again, with the GIs billeted in a large country house a few miles away, across the Oxfordshire border.

The mansion was so remote that a branch-line train ran once in the morning and once in the evening . . . so we couldn't get home after a party. One of the favourite arrangements was for us all to catch the evening commuter train straight from work to the mansion, have supper, get started on the party, play fascinating games like 'Sardines' or 'Murder' in the dark corners . . . inspect the darkroom (where the Yanks got their photos ready to send home to 'mom'), foregather back in the great hall, and fall asleep in the huge chairs after suitably pairing off. . . . The warden and his wife used to make up umpteen camp beds, dormitory fashion, in the large bedrooms, but these were never even ruffled. . . . It was nice and matey in the great hall and certainly warmer by the huge fire clasped perfectly respectably asleep in some Yank's arms. [We would] get woken up at 7 a.m. by the warden, have breakfast, totter off to the little railway halt, fall asleep on the train and totter half a mile from the other end to our job. The Yanks would . . . tell us 'Get your heads down for half an hour, girls, and we'll wake you up and expect some work from you.' And they did.

Occasionally the Americans stayed overnight at the homes of British families near their offices and patronized instead the village dance.

I remember distinctly two post-dance episodes. Once about two dozen of us formed up outside the hall, led by an English part-time fireman who'd been to the dance in his uniform. We sang 'Fireman, Fireman, Save my Child' all the way down the village street, which was a mile long, . . . and nobody even opened a window, at 1.30 a.m. The other episode was when I was staying with my friend and her husband for the night. . . . The procession to her place that night was for the purpose of a birthday celebration after the dance. We got inside her garden gate when somebody happened to mention that there were sometimes glow-worms in the area. Every single Yank produced a torch as one man and . . . I shall never forget the sight of about a dozen officers, NCOs and other ranks crawling round her lawn on hands and knees in pitch blackness and total silence looking for glow-worms, moving so slowly, occasionally 'shushing' us as we giggled help-lessly from the path.[1]

Although a woman had to be plain indeed not to get a second glance from a GI what really appealed to them were well-shaped legs or 'gams'. 'I never knew how important legs were until the GIs came,' confesses a woman then managing a NAAFI canteen in Lincolnshire. 'Nice legs meant feminine women and . . . also represented "SA" . . . Sex Appeal. The Americans . . . were quick to pick out anyone who had "It"!' The American preference for blondes (owing to their mysterious reputation for being 'easier') was well known and 'as a blonde was supposed to look like Betty Grable', remembers a Birmingham woman, then a seventeen-year-old sales girl, 'we tried to look like her, right down to her sheerest dark-seamed nylons'. A good complexion was also much prized, though due to the climate, Americans rarely got the chance to take out girls with another attribute popularized by Hollywood, a deep tan. A WAAF from Atcham in Shropshire remembers a colleague in the cookhouse who was 'beautifully bronzed through sun-bathing and very popular with the GIs' but 'caused a deal of grumbling because she used some of our butter ration to do this'.

The GIs were also greatly disappointed in British women's teeth. 'An intelligent girl but there were cavities in her teeth,' is the damning verdict of one former artillery officer from South Pasadena, California, of a girl he

1. Like several of my informants, this contributor is still unwilling to disclose the exact location of the two places mentioned, or the nature of her work. She does, how-ever, record how 'When my small nieces and nephews hear their mother and I talking of old times . . . they look wide-eyed and say 'Auntie, surely *you* never went out with Americans?'

knew at Dungannon in Northern Ireland. A fine set of molars, by contrast, always came in for admiration. One thin perhaps was worker from Barking near London remembers a compliment paid her at the Hammersmith Palais, most famous of London dance halls, 'Say, peaches, you got teeth like poils?' – rather spoiled by the suspicious afterthought: 'Say, them your own teeth?' Her reply, 'No, they're my mother's. I borrow 'em some nights,' proved a great success. 'He collapsed with laughter in the middle of the dance floor: "Say, babe, you slay me . . . You should be in the movies!"'

Among the many contradictions which British civilians discovered in the American character was that their old-fashioned gallantry was combined with an uninhibited directness about making new acquaintance. In American eyes, British girls discovered, 'Hi there, honey' or 'Let's go, baby' counted as formal introductions, and even words were sometimes considered unnecessary. The first encounter one ATS girl had with a GI was when, on a crowded bus from Worcester to Birmingham, he 'sat down beside me and without a word put his arm round me', leaving her 'astonished and embarrassed'. That evening in camp another girl recounted an identical experience, probably involving the same man. A Caston, Norfolk, girl remembers that when going shopping she invariably had to 'go through the barriers guarded by GIs at RAF, Watton. . . . It was always "Halt – Who goes there?" and a rifle pointed at you. Then . . . "How about me taking you out tonight, honey?" There was one GI who was always so sure he could fix a date that it took at least twenty minutes to get through when he was on duty.' Even more direct was the approach of a GI billeted on an Ayrshire family whose daughter had, she admits, 'seen him get out of the truck and thought "Wow!". . . . We bumped into each other on the stairs between sitting-room and kitchen. What transpired was pure Hollywood. He swept me into his arms and began kissing me. . . . Fortunately someone opened the sitting-room door and saved my life.' A WAAF stationed at Nuneham Courtney found herself having to resist a six-man onslaught while waiting outside a telephone box to telephone her mother:

A GI came out of the pub and started chatting me up. I tried to give him the cold shoulder, but by that time five of his mates joined him. When I went to make my call they followed me . . . I wanted to get rid of them but they just would not go. The operator must have heard the din they were making because he said: 'Is everything all right there, miss?' I had to be quite rude before they decided to go . . . but my mother would have worried if she had heard six men's voices in the telephone box with me.

By American standards any approach to a woman that was not an outright request for a date counted as exceedingly subtle. 'The usual, "Which way is the railroad, ma'm?", or "Where is the drugstore?",' a Warrington girl discovered, 'were always leading up to the GI getting acquainted.' Nor did the universal GI respect for the British Police Force override their simple conviction that a dame was a dame whatever her uniform. 'Some would come up and date me while I was on duty on my own,' an Oxfordshire policewoman remembers.

A seventeen-year-old Cornish girl remembers that an American who sat down beside her on a park bench and began asking personal questions seemed put out that I was cool towards him and said, 'Let your hair down, honey.' I don't think I had heard the expression before . . . so I remember saying, 'My hair is down, thank you.'

For young girls who had only just left school – and sometimes for those still attending it – the Americans provided their first contact with the opposite sex, adding a confusing new element to the normal uncertainties of adolescence. 'We girls had never known what it was to have an English boy friend,' remembers one Plymouth woman, then aged fifteen. 'Most of us were growing up more American than English.' This teenager used to run the gauntlet every morning of the Military Police on duty at the barracks where she worked. She was, she now recalls, 'awakened by the friendliness and teasing by these lads', and by that of a 'fuzzy-headed little GI. His head would pop out from a tank with uncanny timing and a voice would call "Hiya, chicken"!' She was at first too shy to reveal her name, but until they discovered it the Americans solved the problem by addressing her as 'Bashful'.

Many were the methods that the Americans used to secure an introduction. One, constantly refused her name and address by a girl, in desperation made out his will and asked her to witness it, which involved her providing those particulars. But even the Americans failed sometimes. A Watford man, walking in a local park with his two officer lodgers, was deeply embarrassed when, after 'a smart, attractive, young lady passed with a Borzoi dog on a lead . . . one of the officers immediately walked up to her and said, "Can I wheel your dog for you, miss?"' The would-be dog-wheeler was much put out when ignored, commenting loudly, 'A bit snooty, wasn't she?'

Any out-of-the-ordinary garment or uniform gave the GI, at least in his own eyes, a right to accost its wearer. One landgirl visiting Swindon with a friend remembers two GIs following them and calling out 'What kind of uniform is that you're wearing, cow-girls?' Another landgirl, in Peterborough, suffered an even more embarrassing overture from an American officer puzzled by her masculine outfit: 'Excuse me,' he asked, 'but are you a boy or a girl?' Even rebuffs were often turned into excuse for a compliment. One WAAF working at the highly secret photographic interpretation unit at Medmenham remembers parrying so successfully the questions put to her by a GI she met at a shilling 'hop' at the village hall, that he finally said admiringly, if ambiguously, 'I think you WAAFs are wonderful, you just give nothing away.' Women who protested at particularly blatant attempts to 'pick them up' became used to being told, in aggrieved tones, 'But, baby, I'm picking *you out*!'

Even on duty the GIs missed no chance of making a new acquaintance. An ATS teleprinter operator, working in Liverpool, recalls that an official signal from a local American headquarters would be followed by a more personal message: 'WHAT R.U. DOING 2 NITE, CAN I.C.U.?' Even more enterprising was the airman who, to the astonishment of four Wiltshire boys from the village of Collingbourne Ducis, landed his light aircraft, a Piper Cub, in the field where they were walking, 'got out, came across to us and asked if one of us would take a note to a "dame" he had seen walking along the road. . . . The note was a request for a date. Whilst waiting for an answer he took off and flew around, practising low swoops over us. . . . With the return of the messenger, he landed, and his answer being affirmative, took off again.'

Some girls took advantage of the GIs' ignorance of British life to protect themselves from unwelcome attentions. One Glasgow teenager, pressed for her telephone number by a GI on a bus, replied, 'Whitehall 1212.' A redhead who worked at the great air force base at Burtonwood produced in self-defence 'a signed photograph of Arthur Askey (complete with Tyrolean hat with a feather in it) and said that Arthur was the man whom I always wanted to marry. This photo was passed round to crowds of the Americans – unknown to myself – and "This Limey Arthur and Red in HQ" provided a source of conversation and pity which Barbara never anticipated.'[1]

Nurses' homes, landgirls' hostels and similar establishments were often besieged by GIs. Remarks one girl candidly, of her hostel, at Flackwell Heath, near High Wycombe, which accommodated 300 young female munition workers, 'It was like us being the honey pot and them the bees.' Dorchester, by late 1943, contained so many Americans that girls, like other scarce commodities, had to be queued for. 'Every evening at 7.20 the GIs started to line up outside the hospital . . . wet or dry, ready to take out the nurses off-duty at 7.30,' remembers an eyewitness. 'Some of the bolder soldiers tried to storm the nurses' quarters, but were firmly repulsed by the Home sister. Even bribery – tins of fruit and cigarettes – failed to secure entry.'

If, which rarely happened, the Yanks' own efforts to find women failed few had qualms about appealing for outside help. One airman in Chester, having scoured the streets of that ancient city in vain, asked a local resident 'how one met girls in this burgh'. Helpfully, recalling the regular parade round the ancient Roman fortifications, the local man suggested, ' "Have you tried the walls?" "Say, Bud," the would-be swain replied, "Do you think I'm a goddam tomcat?" ' A Rustington, Sussex, man remembers being

1. Arthur Askey was – and is – a famous British comedian, of diminutive stature.

stopped one evening by a group of newly arrived GIs with a far more difficult request: could he tell them where they could 'find some girls and see some bombs drop'. He replied, a little unsympathetically, that he 'couldn't help them in their search for girls and, as for the bombs, they were likely to see plenty where they were going'.

One East London girl, then working for an electrical manufacturer, re-members arriving home one evening to find an American, claiming to be her boy friend, whom she had never seen before. 'My father was making a cup of tea with a grin on his face and Johnny was on a chair perspiring somewhat.' It appeared that a girl friend, asked for her address on a bus and knowing her family would not approve, had handed over her friend's. The family long remembered this visit for 'Johnny was the fattest sailor ever' and, having asked to inspect the family air-raid shelter, 'got in the shelter with Dad's help but couldn't get out.' One Plymouth girl, allowed by her mother to begin 'dating' on her sixteenth birthday, had no immediate problem with father, who 'being in the Royal Navy and away on Russian convoys didn't get to know of my associations. In case he came home unexpectedly, my brother, two years older than I was, was ready to admit that they were friends of his. Hence my handing over regularly a carton of Lucky Strikes to him.'

The curious relationship, at once flirtatious and distrustful, which devel-oped between American men and British women is immortalized in a much-circulated contemporary poem, 'Lament of a Limey Lass':

> They swarm in every tram and bus,
> There isn't room for most of us.
> We walk to let them have our seats,
> Then get run over by their jeeps.
>
> They moan about our lukewarm beer,
> Say beer's like water over here,
> And after drinking three or four
> You'll find them lying on the floor.
>
> Yanks say they've come to shoot and fight,
> It's true they fight . . . yes – when they're tight.
> I must admit their shooting's fine,
> They shoot a damn good Yankee line.
>
> They tell us we have teeth like pearls,
> They love our hair, the way it curls,
> Our eyes would dim the brightest stars,
> Our figures beat Hedy Lamarr's.
>
> And then he leaves you broken-hearted,
> The camp has moved – your love departed.
> You wait for mail that doesn't come,
> Then realize you're awfully dumb.

In a different town – a different place,
To a different girl – a different face,
'I love you darling, please be mine,'
It's the same old Yank – the same old line.

To this famous indictment, which exists in various versions, an unknown GI penned an equally cynical reply. The British public, he complained, critized everything the Americans did:

The way we dance, the way we sing,
The way we do 'most everything.
The only thing that we do right
Is spend our money left and right.

As for British women, they had no reason to feel complacent:

With Yankee girls you can't compare,
The difference is, You're here, They're there.

A more serious contribution to Anglo-American relations in this sensitive field was made by the American anthropologist, Margaret Mead, whose pamphlet *The American Troops and the British Community*, based on long residence in England, has already been quoted on other subjects:

American men and boys enjoy the company of girls and women more than the British do. British boys don't go out with girls unless they have what one British boy described to me as 'an ulterior purpose, good or bad'. If they just want to spend a pleasant evening, more often they spend it with other boys. Even when boys and girls do go to the same school in Britain, they act as if they were still going to separate schools. To an American eye, the absence of flirting and back-chat among secondary-school boys and girls is astonishing. American boys and girls start having dates with each other in the early teens, long before they are emotionally mature enough to be interested in each other for anything really connected with sex. A 'date' is quite a different sort of thing from an evening spent with someone whom one hopes to marry. It exists for itself, just an evening in time, in which two people dance or go to the cinema, [or enjoy] soft-drinks together while they talk to each other in a gay, wise-cracking style, the metaphors and similes changing almost every week.

A good part of any date is spent in proving to each other that the date was a good idea, that each one, the boy and the girl, is really popular. They prove this, however, by exactly opposite behaviour, the boy by boldly demanding innumerable favours, the girl by refusing them. A really successful 'date' is one in which the boy asks for everything and gets nothing but a lot of words; skilful, gay, witty words.

Of course, this is very confusing to British girls who haven't had any practice in wise-cracking. Some of them are insulted by the speed and assurance of the American's approach and turn chilly, making him feel that Britain is a cold – and then he will add – little country. Some of them take his words which sound like wooing for wooing, and give a kiss with real warmth, which surprises him very much.

One custom which Margaret Mead did not describe was what might be called, in the jargon of her profession, 'the involvement of younger siblings in courtship rituals'. A Cornish girl remembers a classic example, when her small brother arrived home with a guilty expression and pockets full of sweets, to tell her that someone was waiting outside to see her. Instantly suspicious she asked, ' "Have you been asking the Americans for sweets?" "Well," he said, "they came over to a gang of us and said 'Have you kids got any big sisters?' And we said 'Have you got any gum?' And then I told them that I had got one of seventeen and they said 'Go get her, kid.' " My reply,' this girl remembers, 'was to the effect that he had better take back his bribe and tell the Yanks I was busy.' In time such transactions were pared down to essentials, the critical enquiry 'Any gum, chum?' being accompanied by the sly promise 'Gotta sister, mister!', though one wartime schoolboy from Northern Ireland admits that to fulfil the strict letter of the contract 'many a three-, four-, five-, six- and seven-year-old was trotted out under false pretences.'

Undoubtedly in many relationships with GIs there was a mercenary element. A then eighteen-year-old office worker from Norwich admits that she 'only went for the dinners', when invited to the Castle Hotel by a Lieutenant, but even the food could not compensate for the fact that 'he was rather dull' and she soon dropped him. Another teenage girl, 'always hungry' while attending a college in Torquay, found herself 'trudging uphill to Babbacombe one night when a drawling voice asked me if I knew someone who could use a pound of butter and a bag of sugar. I fell for the bait immediately and for a couple of weeks went around with Jimmy, until he "fell for" another student.' She sought consolation with another GI, with 'brilliant blue eyes, rose-flushed cheeks and dark wavy hair [but] after about a month I became deadly bored with Richard whose main idea of entertainment was necking on a park bench. . . . He had no watch and I resorted to keeping mine ten minutes fast in order to cut short our meetings.'

Another wartime teenager living in Devon had a series of less conventional romances. Her first GI also, like so many, disappeared after failing to keep a date just before D-Day, but is enshrined in her memory as the donor of 'the only orchids I have ever received – two green ones, which I kept for years pressed in a book. . . . My second encounter was with a dental surgeon – a Russian Jew . . . somewhere outside Exeter. After dinner he showed me his dental surgery. . . . I am sure there aren't many English girls who finished an evening out by actually having a gold plug put in a tooth.' Her third GI, whom she met in a bus queue in Dorchester, took her on a visit to London. 'He was twenty-one and intended taking up medicine after the war, so we visited the Royal College of Surgeons and tried to get into their museum.'

One reason, many women agreed, why they so readily accepted invitations from GIs was the compliment which sprang so naturally to American
lips. 'It was a novelty to have a handsome young American ... breathe into
your receptive ear ... that you had hair "like sun-kissed corn which reminds
me of home" "eyes like amethysts (or sapphire, or pools he could swim in)",'
acknowledges one woman who was then an impressionable nineteen-year-
old in Essex. 'Even now after all these years I can still remember the things
he said to me,' remembers one middle-aged housewife, who in 1944 was a
teenager in Gravesend and much in love with a GI. ' "I love your hair,
Rusty," he'd say. "It's a mixture of autumn leaves and a beautiful sunset." '
The autograph book of a girl then living in a Cotswold manor house contains a typically graceful tribute:

> To Sweet and Lovely Sylvia,
> The girl who has every heart in Combat Command A
> beating just a little bit faster.

On paper, however, the GIs were usually less effective. A teenager at
Appleshaw was uncertain whether to be touched or amused by a letter
describing her as 'my perty browne-eied angle'.

Apart from their eloquence, the Yanks, all these, and many other, observers agree, had a remarkable facility to make their partners feel important.
'We felt like queens,' remembers an Exmouth woman. 'We were thrilled
because they slid our chairs underneath us as we sat down and stood when
we left to go to the powder room.' 'As soon as you sat down in a cinema your
coat was helped off your shoulders as if it were a mink,' agrees a then teenager
from Cheshire. 'They treated me as though I were a Grand Duchess at
least,' recalls a slightly older woman, then living in North Wales. British
soldiers soon suspected, with good reason, that they were being compared
unfavourably with these glamorous newcomers. 'A British soldier would
take a girl for a drink, bore her to death talking about cars or sport, etc. If
he saw any "mates" he abandoned the girl except to buy her a drink now and
then until it was time to go home,' remembers another wartime teenager,
then working in an aircraft factory in Leicester. 'With the GIs it was very
different. The GI would buy me a drink and entertain me as though I were
the only person in the room. I knew that if my back was turned he would
probably be making a date with another girl but this did not seem to matter
as long as he turned to me when I got back.' One Oxford woman, who later
married a GI, recalls a revealing incident when, while working at a servicemen's canteen, she replied to a British airman and a GI who both asked her
for a date for the following day, a Sunday. She explained that she was
expecting her mother to visit her from London for the day whereupon the
Briton said 'Too bad' and dropped the matter. The Yank said ' "That's
OK, we'll take her along with us. I'll get some picnic stuff from the Red

Cross, rent a boat and we'll all go out on the river," which we did, Mother and all.'[1]

But, with all their virtues, the Americans as escorts, it was generally agreed in the offices and factory canteens where such matters were constantly debated, had some noteworthy defects. First, perhaps, was the barely concealed conceit of many GIs. 'They tended to take things for granted,' remembers one woman who was then a twenty-two-year-old WAAF waitress at Martlesham Heath near Ipswich. 'It took them a little while to get used to the fact that you didn't just drop everything if they asked you out.' A sixteen-year-old Donegal girl was not flattered, as intended, when her American marine described her as his 'Sunday girl', implying, she felt, a variety of others on weekdays. A Cambridge office worker, after many 'enjoyable outings' with one 'quietly spoken, shy and very reserved' American, was hurt and indignant 'when he arranged for a girl to ring me and say that he had been taking her out also and could not meet me any more.... He did try to resume the acquaintance at a later date, but found me otherwise engaged.'

If, as they clearly did, some GIs behaved badly to British women there were certainly faults on the other side. A frequent complaint by GIs was of girls who agreed to be seen home and then turned out to live a long distance away, a practice which had become notorious in rural Ireland. But there were also offenders in England, like one who lived in a village eight miles from Derby, as her friend then a thoughtless eighteen remembers:

> She'd meet us in the pub at night – and walk home about 10.30, as the last bus had long since gone. She was engaged to an English boy and intended to marry him. So we'd pick a 'victim' from the GIs and make sure he was paired off with her at going-home time. . . . We always told the poor GI she just lived a little walk down the road. . . . We could hardly wait to hear next day at work how she'd got along. . . . The GIs weren't noted for enjoying long hikes. It said a lot for her charm – and their gallantry, and good nature – that not one ever gave up. They all saw her right to her door, and would enjoy the ribbing they got from us the next time we all met.

A GI from Fort Warren, Wyoming, also discovered the penalty of taking out 'a typical English country maid', who worked at a farm milking cows near Andover. 'Many times Emmy and I would visit the famous white horse [cut in the chalk] overlooking the little valley. This was the last time I have ever chased a female up a mountain.' Later, this young man suffered an even more frustrating experience due to his poor condition, when, by mistake, he drove into the courtyard of a 'home for wayward girls. Ten thousand chicks

---

1. Perhaps one should in fairness add her final comment: 'But I never did tell mother about the hectic wrestling match I had with him later.' How the outing might have ended with the Englishman one can only speculate.

started yelling and asking me to come up. I feebly tried to climb up the window. Some fat dame with a broom beat me and told me to get the hell out or she would scream for the MPs.'

Equally frustrating was the experience of a twenty-year-old Pfc from Plymouth, Massachusetts, who, in the spring of 1944, while stationed at

" Aye, Yank," she says, " I just live a wee bit down the road."

Debden, went with a friend to a village dance at Radwinter where they soon paired off with two girls. Seeing them home meant a five-mile cycle ride each way, but, one of the pair later reported, it had been well worth it:

The first night, and thereafter, my buddy made out like a bandit. I didn't do so well. As I left the young lady at her front door she gave me a half dozen eggs, real fresh eggs. All the way back to the base I sang inside, anticipating the great feed. The next night my buddy decided he'd like to have another go at his newly con-quered English lass and talked me into another try. . . . The second date went the same as the first. This kept up for about four nights. Shep got laid and all I got was eggs. Finally I put my foot down and refused to date the egg donor again. You see, I wasn't even getting the eggs. Every night after we left our three remaining buddies would have an egg orgy, leaving me only the shells. . . . They were very upset when I broke it off. Shep? He just went out and made another conquest.[1]

What, by contrast, were the qualities about British women that particularly attracted the GIs? Sums up one man from Troy, New Hampshire, stationed in Swindon: 'England had remarkably pretty girls who seemed quite free from the American conviction that any relationships between men and women must be a "kill or be killed" proposition. I was astonished to find that it is actually possible to feel relaxed in the presence of a female.' Felt a Captain from Camp Lee, Virginia, 'the girls' around 'had lovely complexions. Their eyes sparkled and they smiled easily and could carry on intelligent conversations on news and topics of the times.' 'I frankly preferred the English girls to the American girls I had known,' admits a Charleston,

"Don't forget, Beryl—the response is 'Hiya, fellers!' and a sort of nonchalant wave of the hand."

1. The eggs episode did not put this informant off English women. He is still happily married to a landgirl he met soon afterwards.

South Carolina, man who grew to know many around Tidworth. 'I was impressed by their lack of demands on me. They were just as happy to go for a long walk as out to dinner and to the cinema. . . . They went out of their way to make a man feel comfortable and wanted.' Reliability was another much-prized quality, as a GI from Gary, South Dakota, remembers. 'I made a date with a WAC when they first came to London and she stood me up. I never had an English girl fail to show up on a date.' The Americans also liked being appreciated. 'We sensed that British women were not used to the deference shown by American men,' acknowledges a former army officer, from Hartford, Connecticut. 'This is part of our tradition, dating back to the days when women in the Wild West were scarce.'

The success of the GIs with British women is now part of English folklore. A Launceston landgirl who 'had heard before they arrived that the Americans were "mazed about women" ' soon found the rumour 'proved correct'. Many GIs were quite candid about their interest as a Winchester schoolboy discovered when, asking a family guest 'what his hobbies were the only thing he could think of saying was "Girls" '. 'Their generosity was as big as their appetite for dames, without whom they did not seem able to live,' is the back-handed compliment paid by a Local Government officer from Liverpool, a member of a concert party which often visited their bases. He was, however, moved by the sight of one soldier met in hospital who, with one leg shot off below the knee, was 'happily chasing girls in his wheelchair just to get them to sit on his good knee, saying "Who says this guy is helpless?" '

24

CUT A RUG, BABY?

'When they had a "Ladies' Excuse-me" dance it was chaos.'

— Airman from Plymouth, Massachusetts, recalling 1943.

DANCES, with their combination of music, gaiety and girls, were occasions made for the GIs. Here the warm Gulf Stream of American spontaneity and innovation and the iceberg of British traditionalism and reserve came most conspicuously into contrast and – inevitably – the Gulf Stream won. For older women during the war, dances, even before the Americans arrived, were oases of pleasure in a wilderness of work and worry; for younger women, after the GIs poured on to the dance floors, they became sheer fairyland. One Plymouth woman who was, in her own words, 'a very-young-for-my-age sixteen-year-old', and whose 'little group centred round our Catholic Church of St Joseph's in Devonport', remembers her life between 1942 and 1945 as being 'full of religion and Yanks', for attached to the church was a hall where weekly parish dances were held. It is those which stand out best in her memory and make this, 'coming as it did after the dreadful blitzes on Plymouth, amongst the rationing and restrictions, black-out, etc . . . one of the happiest periods of my life'.

The way in which the Yanks who attended this church also became involved in its social life is typical of the American readiness to help:

Two of our regular American parishioners sent up to the barracks for a 'scratch band' and their whole band turned up! It was fantastic and every Thursday . . . they used to come and play at our dances. Need I say how much of a success they were? Was ever music more wonderful, men so handsome, was the summer really that hot, were the jokes funnier, laughter more merry than at any other time during the world's history? . . . I recall one summer night, so hot that the GIs took off their coats and were in their shirt-sleeves, the doors were wide open and many people were dancing in the children's playground. The band was playing 'You'll Never Know, Dear'. I danced with a good friend . . . a quiet slim unassuming married man probably thirty – I always danced with him once or twice and we talked of many things. He asked if I would like to dance outside and when I rather too quickly refused he looked very slightly hurt and said, 'I only thought it would be cooler.' I felt instantly ashamed and when I hesitated he squeezed my hand and said 'No matter' with such an understanding smile and we danced quietly very close but not cheek to cheek, it wasn't like that, with a kind of perfect understanding and drowsy companionship through the quiet beat of that song. That remains to this day one of those moments of my life that could have gone on for ever and ever.

This idyllic period came to an end when the church hall was suddenly burnt down, a fate which the parish priest considered 'a judgment from heaven because a rather low element of girls . . . were turning up at the dances . . . wearing skin-tight, very low dresses', though his flock ascribed it, more mundanely, to someone who smoked like a chimney and was usually half sloshed'. The congregation rallied round, however, and simply moved to 'the school hall', but this 'was bumpy and never the same'.

It was what the Americans called SOP (Standard Operational Procedure) for invitations to dances on their own camps to be sent to local hostels, and a landgirl working in Berkshire remembers how highly organized finding partners became.

There was an organization in Faringdon run by a solicitor's daughter who had a list of respectable girls willing to go to the dances. The Entertainments Officer would get in touch with her and say 'Look, we're holding a dance on such and such a day, could you bring twenty girls if we sent the transport?', and then she would ring up all her gang and we would all meet in the Market Square in Faringdon. Sometimes our transport would be an army truck, sometimes they would hire a coach. We went to all sorts of dances ranging from one marvellous affair where they had hired a whole riverside pub, The Rose Revived at Kingston Bagpuize, for the entire evening . . . to a dance run by the Pioneer Corps where the wooden hut was decorated with boughs of trees and we drank 'Coke' and coffee out of cut-down cans and ate doughnuts served in [clean] dustbins.

Rarely was there any shortage of girls willing to accept such invitations, but one eighteen-year-old working in an aircraft engine factory in Leicester, mentioned in the previous chapter, does recall such an occasion.

Sometimes the Eighth Air Force at Cottesmore would hold a dance and would send trucks to wait outside the LMS station. . . . I remember one very cold winter's night when there were only ten girls on the truck. We battled our way through the snow and the journey took four hours. When we arrived at the camp we were the only girls there and about 300 GIs stood in the dance hall and cheered us. I think I danced for two minutes with almost a hundred of them. Then one group decided to take us back to their hut for a meal. . . . Although this was strictly against the rules . . . the GI I was with opened a tin of 'bacon and egg roll' in my honour. I had never heard of this delicacy and when he sliced it and fried it on a makeshift stove I nearly swooned from the smell. We sat around singing 'Off We Go Into The Wide Blue Yonder' and other songs and then it was time to go back to the trucks. Dec (my escort) and Marge's friend decided to come back with us, so they bribed the driver and hid under the seat. After about ten miles the MPs stopped us and poor Dec and the other GI slunk out in the light of the MPs' torch and were arrested on the spot.

Another party we went to was given by the 82nd Airborne in the De Montfort Hall in Leicester. They had slung a parachute from the ceiling and the 'jump boys' vied with each other at swinging from one balcony across to the other, while we girls screamed our heads off.

Transport to American dances was provided as generously as everything else. Bedford was one of many towns where partners were often literally 'picked up'. A Wren stationed at Woburn Abbey, not far away, remembers that on Saturday night 'trucks used to go through Bedford High Street slowly and any girls who wanted to could jump aboard'. She and her friends ignored such opportunities, and when, as one of a thirty-strong party carefully chaperoned by an equally nervous Wren officer, she finally went to an American dance she was, she confesses, 'terrified', having been assured on all sides that 'they always get you drunk and take you to bed'. It was also prudent, she was advised, 'to ask to see their pay books' to confirm that self-styled bachelors were not married. The reality proved strikingly different and unspeakably respectable, and soon the girls were going to two dances a week, the maximum their officers would allow.

How the Americans behaved at the dances they gave themselves was, within limits at least, their own affair. What few people had foreseen was the way in which they would also transform the British dances they attended. One woman who was then a teenager near Prestwick Airport remembers a local dance when 'there was suddenly a great commotion as perhaps six Americans entered the hall, "Hi-ya, fellers! Hi-ya, dames," followed by great wolf whistles. I was invited to "cut the rug" but just stood and stared at the writhing contortions of my partner, and once was enough.'

These 'contortions' were soon notorious as 'jitterbugging', a name which itself had a faintly indecent sound to English ears and consisted, as the newspapers explained, of vigorously performing a few basic dance steps, often in the same spot, and some distance from one's partner who was liable to find herself lifted right off the floor or swung round with skirts flying. 'The dances on the ship were a riot', remembers a then twenty-one-year-old Wren stationed at Portland. ' "Cut a rug, baby?" and we were up. If we couldn't do the dances when we started we could at the end.' A former helper at the Great Ashfield Red Cross club, then seventeen, is proud of the skill she acquired in those hectic evenings: 'We all soon learned to jitterbug and chew gum whilst doing so – no mean feat!' It was not, however, one appreciated by the proprietors of British dance halls. 'No jitterbugging', notices began to appear in many of the more staid establishments although they were usually ignored.

A highly respectable 'Ranger' in Oundle who, at sixteen, was at last allowed to attend dances at the 'Vic' – then officially known as the Victoria Hall – discovered that this was 'not the correct ballroom dancing we had learned at school. It was an exciting jitterbug or slow, cheek-to-cheek shuffle.' For this 'dancing on a dime' the records of Tommy Dorsey and Artie Shaw were especially favoured and the tune 'Nightmare' recalls to one Hereford woman such an occasion, when she was nineteen and attended an informal dance held on the upper floor of an old barn. 'It was a bit creeky because one could see through the gaps in the floorboards. It was a beautiful hot summer evening and we went out to walk in the fields when we became hot and sat in the hay. It was very romantic.' But the NAAFI girls at Tidworth did not appreciate either style of dancing, as one then aged seventeen remembers. 'It was more like an all-in wrestling match than a dance, so in the end we all stopped going.'

As always, the Americans were generous hosts. A Norwich woman remembers 'the most wonderful night' at an air force dance 'with a corsage of violets presented to me at the cloakroom on arrival'. At the end of the evening 'I was given a paper bag and told to please take some food home. . . . I staggered the long mile home laden with bags full of chicken giblets and liver, peanut butter sandwiches, angel cake and, for Mother, a bag of about forty corsages . . . . Mother gave all the ladies in the street a much treasured buttonhole the next morning'. The enthusiasm with which British girls tackled the buffet always delighted their hosts. 'It was quite a sight to see the gals with pineapple rings on their fingers and the juice dripping from their elbows,' remembers one wartime airman, from Aurora, Nebraska.

But for all but the hungriest teenager the music was the greatest attraction. The pre-war period had been a golden age for British dance bands, popularized by the radio, but the call-up had taken its toll here as elsewhere. One twenty-year-old man, serving in the Army Air Corps, speedily decided that British 'bands were quite poor. . . . The players were mostly rather older men, playing was pretty much a mechanical process,' there was 'a lack of well arranged music' and – worst of all in his eyes – 'violins were often used'. All this was to be changed by the coming of the GIs since the USO offered to young people living in the remotest corners of the country the wholly unexpected chance of hearing in the flesh a whole succession of internationally famous bands. The otherwise grim winters of 1943 and 1944 were enlivened for one sixteen-year-old in the small Oxfordshire town of Witney, where their arrival in normal times would have been inconceivable, by the visits of Cab Callaway and his orchestra. A secretary in Falmouth, then in her early twenties, was equally enthralled by the sight of 'top bands, such as Artie Shaw's. The GIs would nearly always drawl "Play 'Stardust' " and . . . would stop dancing, cluster near the stage and just listen.' But *the* dance band of the war without question was Glenn Miller's with its classic 'big band sound'. If the film subsequently made about his life, *The Glenn Miller Story*, is to be believed, Miller himself was far from enthusiastic about having to abandon his civilian career to join up, but the air force speedily re-created his orchestra, and sent it on a series of morale-boosting tours that are still affectionately remembered by those who attended them. 'Moonlight Serenade', 'Little Brown Jug', 'Tuxedo Junction' – nothing is more evocative than such tunes in recapturing for thousands of British women the happy excitement of a wartime concert. Typical is the reaction of a Suffolk teenager then working in the canteen at Great Ashfield, where 'Glenn Miller's band played in one of the hangars non-stop for four hours. . . . I have only got to hear one of his records on the radio and I'm right back in that hangar amid all the smells of men, oil, petrol etc.' 'What a night that was,' remarks a wartime telephonist of a similar occasion in Leicester. 'I remember the decorations of red, white and blue parachute silks, the immaculate uniforms of the boys and the excitement.'

Competition for seats at a Glenn Miller concert was always intense and of all the misplaced protective gestures made towards British women during the war none was more resented than that of an American Sergeant who refused to disclose the addresses of two Plymouth girls to two GIs with tickets for one. 'They're a coupla nice girls and they're not going out with you,' he told the would-be escorts, an act of misplaced gallantry still recalled by one of the victims whenever she hears 'At Last' or 'I Know Why'.

The coming of Glenn Miller to Newbury caused far more excitement than previous visits by the King, for the band was due to play in the main public meeting hall, the Corn Exchange, and some tickets were available for civilians. One woman then working in the local post office remembers how her brother, arriving at the hall, found it 'entirely surrounded by armed Americans on sentry duty. A GI stopped him from mounting the steps. My brother saw red. "I am a British citizen with important business with a British official." The GI looked sad. "Please, sir," he pleaded, "we are having a concert for the boys today. We have very kindly been lent your Town Hall. You see, sir, Glenn Miller is coming over to play for us all." My brother delivered the really cruel British cut: "Who is he when he's at home?" ' which produced such a 'look of intense pain' in the sentry's eyes that the would-be visitor retreated. It was perhaps an awareness that they might never again 'board a "Chattanooga-Choo-Choo" ' which made so many of Glenn Miller's audiences at such concerts respond so enthusiastically to every tune and his music came to epitomize the transitoriness of wartime pleasure.

If all those who claimed to have met Glenn Miller were to be believed his travels must have been almost as extensive as those of the ubiquitous Kilroy, who 'was here' wherever GIs found a blank wall to chalk on, or Yehudi, the imaginary author of every unacknowledged misdeed, whose peacetime job was 'to turn on the light in the ice-box'. A Wren stationed locally remembers how 'a little back room behind a small tea-shop in Stony Stratford' became a place of pilgrimage, because the grand band-leader had enjoyed 'brown bread and butter, cake, jam and tea' there. The licensee of a

Norwich pub recalls an unknown American saying to her, 'You know, you are playing that tune all wrong,' and when, annoyed, she suggested, 'Perhaps you would like to play if you think you can do it better,' he sat down and did so brilliantly. It was, of course, the master himself. A Manchester housewife treasures the memory of Miller telling her young daughter, who sang in front of him during a concert at Warrington, to get in touch with him after the war, so he could help to make her a star.

Alas, for Miller there was to be no after. On 15 December 1944 his light aircraft, on a flight from Twinwood near Bedford, to Paris vanished without trace. Although rumours later circulated that Miller had led a double life as a secret agent – or that his plane had been shot down by mistake by British fighters – no evidence to support them has ever been produced. About the effect of Miller's death, however, there can be no doubt, especially coming as it did close to Christmas during a period of miserable weather and just as the Ardennes offensive was beginning. 'His records were put away and gloom settled over the flat,' remembers the housekeeper for four Americans previously quoted. 'We all wept when he was killed,' agrees a woman who was then a storekeeper at the Ordnance Depot at Chilwell, and unquestionably many thousands of other women shed similar tears on that bleak December day when Miller passed from fame into legend.[1]

About the outstanding male vocalist of the war there can be no real dispute. One GI recalls learning in letters from home that 'all the girls were going wild over this new idol' and by 1944 the *Stars and Stripes* was humorously reporting that back in the States the favourite tune was now 'Moonlight Sinatra'. One woman, then a schoolgirl in the Cotswold village of Sherston, recalls 'a teenage GI going into rhapsodies over a "swell singer" of whom I had not then heard. All his friends agreed he was "Sure going places." ' Another girl, working in the Land Army in Dorset, recalls going to see an American musical in 1943 and being 'really smitten with the band vocalist. I had no idea who he was, just knew he was good. Found out later in a movie magazine that he was a new singer by the name of Frank Sinatra.' 'We listened nightly to the American Forces Network,' remembers one woman then in her late teens and living near Polebrook. Frank Sinatra was in his heyday, singing 'Nancy,' 'This is a Lovely Way to Spend an Evening' and 'I Couldn't Sleep a Wink Last Night'.

One twenty-one-year-old Wren stationed at HMS *Attack* on Portland Bill spent many evenings at the cinema of the American 'ship' watching 'a Frankie, young and boyish and very frail.... The girls were entranced with him. All we got from the back was "Oh, Frankie" and the Yanks pretending to swoon. We never did hear a word Frankie said.'

Many GIs in Britain were emphatically not members of the Sinatra Fan

1. In July 1974 an aircraft believed to be Miller's was found in mid-Channel. It was reported that attempts might be made to recover it.

Club. Why, the GIs wanted to know, should this good-looking guy be
following his well-paid normal occupation, getting all the headlines, while
they were stuck in the ETC fighting a war? When, in July 1945, Sinatra was
reported to have made critical remarks about USO camp shows in Europe
his popularity was affected. The *Stars and Stripes* gleefully reported how one
man had thrown an egg at the singer and three GIs in the United Kingdom
promptly started a fund to buy a chicken farm 'to insure a sufficient supply of
hen fruits' to keep up the good work with future singers, donations for the
present being passed on to the paper's orphans' fund. The name of the hero
who had thrown the original egg, 'let it not be forgotten', urged the paper,
'is Edward J. Dorogokleepetz', which to British readers was a joke in itself.

The ever-increasing availability of American music and records had a
marked effect upon popular taste. One nineteen-year-old girl employed in
running a record request programme in a Norwich battery-making factory
found that requests for 'American bands and singers' rapidly ousted the
previous pleas for British performers like Anne Shelton and Vera Lynn.
She herself remembers best 'Round Her Neck She Wears a Yellow Ribbon'
and 'I've Been Working on the Railroad'. A landgirl stationed near Evesham
is still whisked back to the early 1940s whenever she hears 'Over There', and
'Mom, I Miss Your Apple Pie'. 'The song that always raised the roof at any
gathering of American servicemen,' found one woman working in Grosvenor
Square, was 'The Caissons Go Rolling Along', a semi-official march rarely
heard by civilians. A Leamington woman remembers best a very different
tune because it 'fitted in with gum-chewing', 'Mairzy Doats and Doazy
Doats', one of the 'nonsense' songs popular at the time. (The words are a
corruption of 'mares eat oats and does eat oats', though British humorists
found that 'Mersey Docks and Harbour Board' fitted them equally well.)

Britain in the 1940s was well-equipped with dance halls – more so than
most parts of the United States – and many are still recalled with affection
by GIs, like the Dorothy in Oxford, and the Tower Ballroom in Blackpool.
Most famous of all was the Hammersmith Palais in West London. One then
war worker from Barking, farther east, who was a constant visitor there,
remembers one near-romance that began while dancing with one 'backwoods boy who had seen little of city life before being drafted' and believed
himself to be 'in a real den of iniquity, performing a daring deed by his mere
presence. He thought that I was far too nice a girl to be in such a place.' One
Detroit man, now married to an Englishwoman, was deeply impressed by
'Covent Garden Opera House converted into . . . the most sumptuous dance
hall in existence'. Equally attractive to an airman from Plymouth, Massachusetts, was a 'fantastic dance hall in Cricklewood', discovered by chance
by a group of his friends serving at Debden in Essex. 'Usual attendance,'
he remembers, 'about 200 of England's prettiest girls, maybe fifty English
male civilians, twenty-five English servicemen and at most a dozen GIs.

From a poor dancer like I was could do well. When they had a "Ladies Excuse-me" dance it was chaos. You hardly had time to introduce yourself to the girl before you were tagged by someone as lovely or lovelier.' On leave in Edinburgh he rapidly explored the local dance halls, discovering one that like most others in Britain was firmly 'dry'. 'No booze [was] allowed in the dance hall and they had uniformed ladies at the door frisking the Yanks. I'd like to have a dollar for every GI who claimed to have a pint taped to his crotch. The ladies always investigated such claims.'

Although the girls were usually rigorously chaperoned, attending a dance at an American camp always contained an element of hazard. One Wren driver, stationed in Bath, found that after a time volunteers for such functions became few, since 'the GIs preferred girl friends who liked to be fondled. . . . The Americans on their part found the Wrens in Bath too stuck-up and . . . called . . . them "The high-class Navy dames".' One Admiralty worker in the same town, who at twenty-one was assumed to be more responsible than her younger colleagues, found herself appointed their unofficial watchdog with strict instructions to return with 'at least as many girls as on the outward journey'. This was difficult enough, but what was far harder was deterring stowaways. One eighteen-year-old's first dance at a Norwich air base was also her last, for several amorous GIs were smuggled aboard and the journey home was enlivened by the sight of 'three couples . . . having sexual intercourse on the floor'.

Of all the dances attended by a girl working at Erricsons Telephone Factory at Beeston near Nottingham, after the 508th Paratroops moved in to Wollaton Park, the one she remembers best was an informal affair in the clubroom 'above the milk bar on the High Road where all the dates were made', given by her particular boy friend, 'Lucky' to celebrate his birthday. He was, she learned later, only seventeen that day, having falsified his age to enlist. She arrived soaking wet, from a sudden summer thunderstorm, but her ' "stepping-out dress" a green crêpe silk thing . . . flared at the bottom hem' dried rapidly 'while we all sat around wishing "Lucky" a happy birthday, with several bottles of beer'.

Then Lucky asked me to dance. We were a right clever pair with the 'jitterbug' . . . we were clapped on to the floor by his pals and off we went spinning, turning, leaping, then suddenly, to our amazement, the gramophone was ruthlessly stopped, right in the middle of our performance and . . . the manager of the joint walked up to me shouting, 'Get out of my clubroom!' There was an awful lot of stamping and booing from the other guys. Lucky asked the manager what . . . we had done. . . . He said, '*You* can stay, and so can the rest of you, but *she* goes! You must be blind, the lot of you, if you can't see she's under age.' I argued that I was nearly nineteen years of age, but he called me a liar, so four of the GIs lifted me up, making a sort of chair-lift with their arms, and carried me the whole length of the room, collecting as we went, like the Pied Piper, all the rest of the GIs and their friends. Like a queen I was carried down the stairs to the exit . . . and the manager was left with an empty club-room. . . . Lucky and I . . . had barely got away from the clubroom, when a policeman stopped us . . . and asked us how old I was. I told him but had to report to the police station next day with my identity card, to prove it, because he didn't believe it either. . . . Only when I got home . . . did I realize what a child I looked, for my crêpe dress had shrunk . . . revealing my pants, and with being so tiny and having such big baby blue eyes I could have been taken for no more than ten. Lucky having had his birthday broken up . . . after seeing me home . . . decided to celebrate on his own . . . started back to camp in the wrong direction and was picked up in the early hours of the morning at Chilwell shouting 'Where's my Rosie?' . . . . He was placed in the 'glasshouse' until the next scheduled jump in a few weeks.

25

THE ONLY VIRGINS IN TIDWORTH

'Heard about the new utility knickers? One Yank and they're off.'

— *Popular wartime joke, c. 1943.*

'GIRLS were either officers' girls or other ranks' girls. They were sub-divided into those who did and those who didn't.' This recollection of one who didn't, then a single woman in Chippenham and today a divorcee in New Jersey, would probably be echoed by many people from both countries, now in middle age. 'A new aspect of sex opened before us,' recalls one highly respectable, unmarried English woman, then living near Tidworth. 'It was not wrong to indulge and . . . right and proper if you were in love. We pooh-poohed these arguments at first but we were all worn down in the end. I stuck to my principles for ages, even refusing an invitation to a cottage which someone had lent to Larry' – her tall and handsome West Point beau from the 2nd Armoured Division – 'for a week. I spent a weekend in Bournemouth with him without anything untoward happening. Then his room-mate at Tidworth went off for a weekend and I madly and irresponsibly joined him there and that was it. Fortunately his boast that American contraceptives were the best in the world turned out to be a fact. Larry, by the way, whimsically kept his in a small cocoa tin.'

The myths that all Yanks were either near-rapists or irresistibly skilled seducers die hard, even though they are mutually contradictory. The truth seems to be that in their approach to sex – as distinct from mere female companionship – American servicemen were as varied as British women were in their response. At one end of the scale were the GIs, recently returned from 'a long fighting spell' whom one woman, then a child in Beaminster in a house next door to their camp, remembers literally 'climbing up the drain-pipes to get into the windows when they heard there were young ladies living there' – her sisters aged nineteen and twenty-one. So persistent were the intruders that her father, a Regimental Sergeant-Major in the Dorset Regiment, was actually granted compassionate leave to protect his family, who 'eventually had to stay for safety's sake, with an aunt'. At the other extreme was the easily discouraged Romeo of a Cheshire teenager. 'One night I remember saying,' she recalls, 'I wanted to keep my self-respect and be clean when I married after the war.' He said, "So you shall, honey." I sent him back to camp with a present from my mother – a large coconut cake. I don't think I ever saw him again.'

But many girls were more accommodating. 'The girls were pretty and friendly,' fondly remembers a B–17 crew-member from Connecticut. 'Once on the night train up from Bury I was able to have intercourse in a crowded compartment with a girl whose name I didn't know and who didn't know mine.' On another occasion having met a girl in a dance at Cambridge, he discovered, on her leading him to a quiet corner of the local cemetery that though 'not much for talking, she was very passionate'. He soon established, too, a most satisfactory understanding with the daughter of a Newmarket publican, who 'would invite me to spend the night. As soon as Papa and Mama went to sleep the daughter would knock on the wall of my room to let me know all was OK and I would go to her room.'

Where there was no convenient bedroom, love still managed to find a way. 'There were several haystacks near our hospital,' one army nurse from Jackson Heights, New York, remembers of her time at the 121st General Hospital near Yeovil and 'the GIs gave me reports on their experiences in a haystack. It was warm, dry and private . . . I noticed bicycles parked by them. One time a little canvas tarpaulin was attached, like a porch. One saw lots of hay on the uniform after a date in the country. One always thought about the British being prim and proper – and now it wasn't true.'

Some English women were meanwhile revising all they had heard about Americans, for though all agree that almost any GI would ask for sex – certainly three out of four in the opinion of one Oxfordshire policewoman – it came as an agreeable surprise to find that the vast majority took a rebuff in good part. 'A girl could do what she liked,' sums up one woman journalist, who spent three years surrounded by US Navy men of all ranks in the Public Relations Office in Grosvenor Square.

I was young and reasonably attractive. I could have gone to bed with one every night . . . but once you put up the respectability sign you had no more trouble with the Americans than with the British . . . I still had a perfectly wonderful social life. 'Yes' or 'No', you were still good for a dinner and a movie and they always took you home afterwards. Ironically, it was with the British I had the most difficulty . . . because they thought if I worked with the Americans I probably slept with them too and if with them why not with the British? This is not to say I remained unsullied throughout, but any sullying was done with co-operation on both sides.

If, as one woman from Anglesey believes, the GIs 'were no different from any local or foreign boys where sex was concerned', where they did differ, as many other informants would also agree, was that 'they were more candid and open about sex than we were'. 'At least they asked plainly,

33. Slapton Sands. The area of South Devon known as the South Hams was totally cleared of its occupants to provide a battle-training area resembling Normandy. These soldiers have just 'hit the beach'.

34. Beachhead Devon. These troops, landed on the beach, are now 'advancing' into 'hostile' territory in Southern England.

35. Embarkation: Tor Bay, 3 June 1944. Assembling the invading armies for their cross-Channel journey was an immensely complicated process.

36. Embarkation: Portland Harbour, 30 May 1944. For weeks before D-Day the roads of Dorset and Devon were choked with military traffic, including the unwieldy amphibious 'Dukws'.

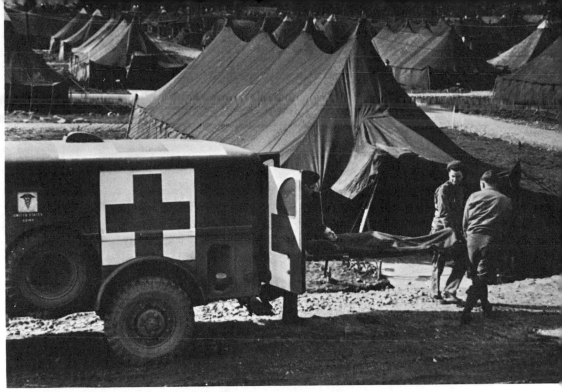

37. Casualty. To accommodate the expected flood of wounded tented hospitals had to be used to supplement the hutted ones already built. This man was arriving during a pre-D-Day exercise, in May 1944.

38. Departure for the wars. Owing to the secrecy surrounding the preparations for D-Day, and the constant rehearsals, many GIs left with no chance to say goodbye.

39. The Price of Victory. Men killed during training, or by enemy action prior to 1944, were often buried in specially built local cemeteries, like this one. The number of graves is a reminder of the losses suffered before the main fighting began.

40. The Price of Victory. In 1944 a permanent American military cemetery was opened in Cambridge, to which the bodies of all US war dead in the British Isles were transferred, though most have since been removed to the United States. After the war the buildings shown here were constructed, including a Memorial Wall, listing the names of those with no known grave.

41. Memorial. After the war a simple monument was unveiled on Slapton Sands to all the GIs who had trained in the area, for which many still retain a warm affection.

42. Going home. Local residents are here seen waving goodbye to a Liberator. The Liberator was used extensively for coastal and sea patrol work, but most heavy bomber wings were equipped with B—17s.

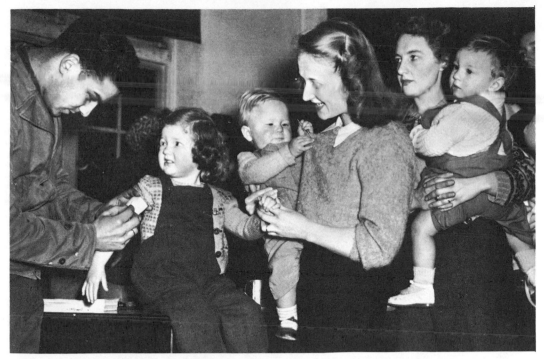

43. Goodbye, England. GIs embarking on the *Queen Elizabeth* in 1945. Many were convinced that, being so large and modern, it must be an American ship.

44. Hello America. This photograph was taken from a helicopter as the *Queen Elizabeth*, loaded with 14 000 returning GIs, entered New York Bay.

45. 'It won't hurt.' Like their mothers the children of GIs had to be inoculated at the processing camp at Tidworth before setting sail. Here two-year-old Sandra from Lambourne, Berkshire, is being prepared for her journey to Nashville, Arkansas, on 23 January 1946.

46. 'Don't forget to write.' GI brides taking their last look at their relations, when embarking on the liner *Argentina* 26 January 1946.

47. 'So this is America.' On 10 February 1946 the *Queen Mary* delivered 1707 GI brides and 640 small children to New York. Among them was ten-month-old Susan, destined for Fresno, California, here being carried by a Red Cross nurse and her mother.

openly and hopefully,' remembers a former Wren, without rancour, of many such requests while serving near Lyme Regis. 'Usually they pleaded on the lines that it would be good for them, or benefit their health.' 'More than one, in answer to my "No",' remembers a woman who was then surrounded by GIs as a helper in a Red Cross club in Exeter, 'has said "Why not? You're clean, I'm clean".' A softer 'sell' in favour of permissiveness was encountered by a Plymouth teenager, who asked the friend of one 'sad-eyed Italian American why Joe always looked so sad. "Because," he said with complete solemnity, "he's twenty-three and still a virgin." ' But she failed to take the hint. A woman who worked at an American research establishment near Princes Risborough found her suspicions that one escort's behaviour was 'too good to be true' vindicated when 'one night he got carried away . . . and when I resisted said, "Gee, honey, I bin walking round the minefield, now when do I expect to get the Purple Heart?" ' The girl from Barking, quoted in an earlier chapter, who soon realized that the softest 'endearments were simply the preliminaries for the final "assault course" ' took to replying unfeelingly to such complaints, 'Well, you backed a loser, Buster.' But many GIs genuinely found such an attitude puzzling. A wartime Admiralty clerk then in her twenties remembers being approached in the street in Bath by a GI with a simple business proposition: ' "How would you like a parachute? Pure silk. Yards and yards. I've booked a room in a hotel. All you have to do is spend the night with me." He didn't seem to understand that he had made a mistake.' The memory of an army electrician from Philadelphia was that 'nylon stockings got you a weekend in bed, candy bars and cigarettes at least the evening. I personally found a few beers and a gentle way most rewarding.' At US Army Headquarters in Grosvenor Square one British employee discovered the most-prized items from the PX, such as 'nylons, nail varnish . . . and perfume' were known as 'shack-up' material and reserved for girls with whom the donors hoped to 'make it'.

The prize for the approach least likely to succeed with any British woman must go to the argument that she owed the GIs her favours 'because we've come over to win the war for you'. To this suggestion, remembers one ex-ATS girl, who had, as it happened, been a volunteer, 'My reply was unprintable.'

A then WAAF, waiting for the 'Liberty bus' back to camp outside a Northampton cinema with a girl friend, also proved able to hold her own in the battle of the sexes:

Out of the black-out came two Yanks. They never stood on ceremony . . . they walked up to us and asked us straight out if we would go to bed with them! My friend sensed what was coming and pleaded for me not to cause any trouble – when I shot my fist into the Yank's face and he sprawled unconscious into the gutter. From nowhere a jeep complete with two 'Snowdrops' tore round the corner, picked up the unconscious Yank and slung him into the jeep. They came back to us and asked if these men were annoying us! I said, 'Not now and I doubt if they ever will again!' The other one of the pair had meantime climbed into the jeep with his mate, very subdued. The airmen around were cheering and shouting, 'Good old Corp,' as they were never very friendly with the Yanks. From then on I was a hero on camp.[1]

Another WAAF, a teleprinter operator stationed at Leighton Buzzard, remembers achieving a quieter but, in its way, equally resounding victory over an American Lieutenant, who, having asked her to dance several times, 'informed me he'd told his Sergeant he'd "Have my pants off" before the end of the evening. The stunned reply he got was "You and who else's army?" Needless to say, he did not accompany me home. However, I was so amazed at his audacity and his insistence on seeing me again ... I felt this to be a challenge.' So began a long struggle, all through the early months of 1943, at first in the pub where her visitor was billeted, where he 'never failed to try seducing me when the coast was clear', and finally in London, where 'I went on our next thirty-six-hour pass on the understanding there would be "no strings" attached'. After a tea-dance at the Piccadilly Hotel, dinner out and finally a visit to a night-club – with gin at £5 a bottle – she returned to her hotel room at around 3.30 a.m. to find already there 'a tray with a bottle of Scotch and two glasses. . . . Then the seduction scene started again. After a long struggle he left and I retired somewhat exhausted to bed. About half an hour later the phone rang and he apologized profusely for his behaviour. . . . After breakfast he informed me he'd take me out and buy me anything my heart desired . . . because I had stuck to my principles, something he had never encountered in all his experiences with British girls.'

Girls who did call for help on such occasions rarely got much sympathy, as one in a Cambridge hotel discovered. Having summoned the manager after an American officer had forced his way into her room and refused to leave, 'they were *both*', a friend remembers, 'thrown out'. Hotels must indeed have witnessed many a GI disappointment. One London woman now looks back with amusement on the evening when she fully intended to lose her 'old-world virginity' to a 'tall, handsome, intelligent and fascinating American' in the highly respectable Cumberland at Marble Arch. 'We'd got as far as his bed . . . still fully dressed, when he spoke of his wife.' It was a fatal mistake. 'I exclaimed, "Oh, you're married!" and acted virtuously.' It is hard not to sympathize, too, with the Texan who became 'a trifle over-friendly' while escorting home a young Oxford girl along a well-known 'lovers' lane', the towpath by the River Isis:

It was a rainy night and I had an umbrella in my hand. I brought this up sharply

1. This informant adds, 'I must in fairness say that whenever we were invited to American air force bases . . . they treated us like queens.'

from behind my back and gave him what was intended to be a good-natured warning tap on the head. To my horror he crumpled at the knees and collapsed and for a moment I honestly thought I might have killed him. However, he came round and I helped him indoors where my landlady gave him some of her precious hoard of whisky. He soon recovered except for a nasty bump which came up on his head. He was well over six foot and a PT instructor so I expect he came in for some leg-pulling. He was really very nice about the whole thing, although he never did ask me out again.

An umbrella, a large old-fashioned gent's model, was regularly carried to work by a 'tall . . . elegant . . . clergyman's widow' in her seventies who regularly arrived to help at the Red Cross club in Cheltenham, pushing 'an old heavy bicycle. We were all intrigued' as to the reason, admits a colleague, who finally learned it: 'One very dark night . . . she was stopped by a GI, who was drunk. . . . She told him she was old enough to be his mother and he said, "Gee, honey, who cares? All cats are grey at night!" ' The bicycle and umbrella were her defensive armament against similar 'admirers'.

Amid all the refusals there were many who said 'Yes', though the experience of one Sergeant in Norfolk seems to have been unique. According to his account, having taken a girl 'for a walk into one of the local parks she lay down and invited him to have sexual intercourse', explaining that 'the local Mayor had called a public meeting and asked all the townsfolk to give the GIs a good welcome when they came and she thought this was the way she could help'. Many Britons who worked alongside GIs soon discovered, however, from the conversations they overheard, that reports of GI success among British women were by no means exaggerated. One woman journalist at US Headquarters in Grosvenor Square found it revealing that the Roman Catholics in her office constantly attached themselves to new churches in order to 'confess at different ones each week'. A young clerk-telephonist, working at an American hostel near Stafford, soon found herself being 'asked to ring up famous hotels in London and book a double room for one of the officers and English girl friend to spend the weekend'. As 'personal calls were not really allowed', she silenced her scruples by imposing a private tax on sin, asking 'before I put their calls through . . . what it was worth. This was usually a box of chocolates or cigarettes'. One 'very strictly brought-up' Edinburgh girl, was shocked when a girl friend, a fellow physiotherapist, became involved in 'a full-blown love affair' with a GI which could hardly have begun under less romantic circumstances; the two had met in the 'Path Lab' of her hospital, where 'they were testing about 700 slides a day for VD'.

What British women thought of the sexual performance of the Americans is not on record, but one former B–17 crew member from Connecticut, who admits that 'the English girls were very generous with sex', after extensive research, reached his own conclusion. 'In plain language, they were a lousy lay. They would lay just like a board and not move at all.' What other GIs remember best of their sexual experience in Britain, however, is that, strictly speaking, it was often not a 'lay' at all. 'The English,' remembers one infantryman from New Hampshire, of his time near Swindon, 'had a curious custom of fucking on foot, fully clothed.' One hospital commander near Belfast soon discovered why his men were anxious to leave punctually at the end of the working day: 'all the best doorways', they explained to him, were taken up by the earliest couples to arrive. A Jewish chaplain from Iowa remembers being puzzled, while 'driving around Birmingham at about 9 p.m. in mid-June, to see all his countrymen carrying their overcoats, until he learned they were 'wrapped around themselves and their girls as they copulated standing up'. An airman from Connecticut, serving on B–17s, felt himself a true sophisticate when he learned this was the meaning of the mysterious whispered offers from Piccadilly whores: 'Hey, Yank, quick, Marble Arch style.' Even before leaving the United States, remembers one infantryman from Troy, New York, 'we heard the usual stories of "Wall Jobs", because the girls [believed they] couldn't get pregnant that way.'

Even those Britons who tolerantly accepted that 'boys will be boys' (though less willing to admit the corollary that 'girls will be girls') tended to express disapproval of GIs' liaisons with married women, especially those whose husbands were away in the forces, and many were the tales told of GIs rudely dragged out of the marital bed and pitched into the street through the bedroom window by husbands who returned unexpectedly.

How satisfactory such a relationship could be to all parties involved was discovered by one B–17 gunner at Bassingbourn who had arrived in England – his home was in Detroit – in 1943. 'At first,' he remembers, 'we had a fine choice of girls,' but – as more squadrons arrived – 'the boy–girl ratio finally changed and the girls had their choice of thousands of GIs'. However, he admits, he 'was lucky', for after seeing home several times a woman he had met in a pub 'she asked me in for a cup of tea', and explained that 'her husband was stationed in a remote part of England'.

This went on for a while until one evening, while at the house, it started to rain like mad, and me with no raincoat. I waited for a while but . . . finally she said I had better get in bed and get some sleep as the rain probably wouldn't let up till morning. I slept with her that night and the next and she thought something was wrong with me as I hadn't put a hand on her. I told her I had to really like a girl before I made love to her. About the third night human nature proved I did and I took over as the man of the house until after VJ-Day when I was shipped back home. . . . The only exceptions were the times that her husband was home. He and I got along fine from the beginning, although his third leave home he must have suspected something when an old Biddy . . . was making remarks about the shameful way the local girls were carrying on with the Yanks while their husbands were away. . . . When he asked me to hang behind with him while the rest walked on home from the pub I thought for a moment I was in for a good beating (he was all muscle and tough). . . . When they were out of earshot, he told me that he rated me tops and since he was the head of his house, I was welcome to his home at any time and for as long as I wished. . . . He even asked me to build some cupboards, etc., when I had my next leave. . . . When coming home on leave he always had a lay-over in London, so he would wire when he arrived in London, spend the night at his mother's place and proceed out to the country the next morning, arriving about noon. This gave me time to move my clothes into an unused closet in another part of the house. This he knew, of course, but, as he said, 'It was better to know that I was there watching out for his wife and child, than who knows who or how many others.'

Another airman, from Hamilton Field, California, who reported to his wife that he had found an English girl to take her place while he was away, found she was 'broad-minded' about it and that she not merely wrote in friendly terms to her stand-in but 'sent packages of food' to her family.

Such tolerance, at least among British husbands, was probably more common than was generally realized. 'The lack of jealousy from English males never ceased to amaze me,' recalls a former US Engineer officer of his months in Cornwall. 'On several occasions I saw British men look around the partition separating the "public" and "private" bar areas and exclaim that there was their wife with a Yank . . . without any sign of anger.' A landgirl stationed at Rodwell in Essex found that her landlady regularly went out to dances at the Willingdale air base while her husband looked after their children, and she returned home escorted by GIs, who hung around the house all weekend, with no protest from him. But not every husband was equally complaisant. One airman remembers that the first casualty on his base in Norfolk was 'at the hands of the British', in the shape of a soldier who arrived back from North Africa, 'found one of our men in bed with his wife . . . threw the GI out of a second-storey window and killed him. He was sent to prison.'

Even if they usually received full co-operation in doing so, the ability of the GIs to 'fix themselves up' with a girl friend in almost any circumstances soon became famous. Few environments could have seemed less promising than an English boys' boarding school, but when a party of a dozen GIs were invited to stay at Charterhouse it was their hosts who learned most. 'One thing the Americans proved to us in no time,' one remembers, 'was that all the . . . stories about their liking for women were more than true . . . without exception all had organized themselves in this respect, usually with housemaids, or other house staff, within forty-eight hours of arrival.'

By British standards, the GIs seemed remarkably uninhibited about making love in public. Another schoolboy, at Witney in Oxfordshire, fifteen when the GIs arrived, recalls how 'the bolder young men of the town engaged in the game of "pyking", i.e., following and watching the Americans and their girl friends, but it was a hazardous venture and . . . ceased altogether when someone was alleged to have been fired on by an irate lover'. A then British airman recalls an incident he witnessed with a special constable friend in broad daylight in the middle of Reading:

Whilst we were talking we became aware of . . . an erotic sound and lo and behold by the side of the Law Courts were a Yank and a girl. The girl was very young even to me – I was about nineteen – her knickers were around her ankles and his trousers were open and by the time we had finished gasping this couple had completed the act. What staggered me was that he was smoking a fat cigar whilst this was going on.

It came as a disappointment to many GIs, to whom all Europe was one equally sinful spot, to discover that the United Kingdom lacked one useful amenity. Only two weeks after the arrival of the first American in Chippenham, one woman who was then a teenager remembers, one officer entered her father's jewellery shop, 'bought something, then confidentially asked, "Say, sir, is there a brothel in this town?" Father replied, "Oh no . . . we don't have brothels in England, you'll have to wait until you get to France." '

In a village in Northamptonshire one family living close to the village green became hardened to Americans knocking on their door and asking for 'Fanny', a local landworker with a husband in the forces, who supplemented her meagre income by entertaining Americans at five shillings (about $1) a visit. ' "Kind" friends informed her husband what was going on, which resulted in her being turned out into the streets and . . . she had to spend the night in the open with her two small boys.' Rumour even had it that the GIs 'were not averse to the oldest lady in the village, aged eighty-three, but this was probably spiteful gossip as she had been rather a gay spark in her time'.

Unused as they were to being away from home, some younger GIs failed to identify members of the oldest profession, occasionally with embarrassing results. One Technical Sergeant from Manhattan, Kansas, already an experienced twenty-two when drafted from his architecture course at Kansas State College, remembers 'a real innocent boy from camp' near Eighth Air Force headquarters applying to him for help in obtaining his first ever date in Britain.

Since I had time on my hands I took him out in the afternoon and told him to pick the girl and I would get him the date. . . . There was a pair of them, one tall, a stunning beauty, and a shorter one, who still didn't look too bad. He wanted the tall one. So I just crossed the street, stopped them and asked if they would be busy that evening. It was that easy. The tall one was Barbara and the short one was Drene. We made a date to meet them at the Red Lion for drinks. . . . Later he had to be back on duty, so I went over to a bowling green to watch the old men bowl ... I also found a thin and not too attractive woman there. It didn't take long to find out that she was a professional prostitute and considered herself a notch above the streetwalkers. She told me she was also off-duty and she only went out with some of the officers. I needled her and asked if she went out with the Colonel and she told me he was her next conquest. She was charming and good company and also told me that the tall Barbara had given a dose of the clap to an officer on the base. I thanked her for the information. That evening I told that innocent boy to be sure to go to a pro station after we left them, and, you know, that was the first he knew what they were. He just took off his clean shirt and refused to go out of the camp with me at all. Seemed to feel it was my fault. Some time later I saw the high-class dame with that fat old Colonel and she smiled at me and gave me the thumbs-up signal behind his back.

The American authorities here took a tolerant – and it must be felt – a sensible attitude to this ancient problem of their men's sexual needs. 'The commander got tired of finding his officers shacked up with some woman in the grass along the Wye river,' remembers the same informant, 'so he built a "cat-house". Inside the main gate a short distance was a barracks cut up into little rooms for officers and their women. At midnight an MP would knock on the door and tell them to send the women home. All the girls would walk off together and the officers would go back to their barracks.'

Far more troublesome to the authorities than its resident prostitutes were the women who invaded American-occupied areas. The nuisance had first made itself felt in Northern Ireland. One infantry Lieutenant, from Baltimore, assigned to administrative duties with the 79th General Hospital at Lurgan in County Armagh, found that the 500 enlisted men, the 100 female nurses and sixty officers, mainly doctors, in his charge, presented him with far fewer problems than the predatory women clustered round its gates and thronging the local towns:

I was more or less a country boy, having lived in the country all my life and while not a complete innocent ... had never had contact with loose women ... finally met my wife and we married and there was never anyone [else] for either of us before or since. ... Consequently I was more or less unprepared for my first visit to Belfast. I wasn't two blocks from the stations, walking down the street, taking in the sights, when a very attractive girl steps from a doorway and in a low, sexy voice asks, 'Would you like to lay me, big boy?' I was too surprised to talk ... I just kept walking. ... After talking with the local people, listening to the men of my unit extol their conquests, I became fully assured in my own mind that the people here felt sex was something necessary in life and it was not subdued and more or less frowned on as it was in the States. I found it to be taken as a life requirement, as food might be, partly for pleasure, and in all too many cases a livelihood.

One eighteen-year-old at Great Ashfield observed that the airmen 'having found that we were not easy meat or there on the base just to hop into bed with them', began 'importing trainloads of tarts from London, all fares paid'. Women who actually took up residence in US camps, proved a particular nuisance. One Peterborough woman, sixteen in 1941, has never 'seen anyone so disgusted and revolted' as a GI friend who described how, returning from late duty, 'as he sat on his bed to take his shoes off something had moved, and, on switching the lights on, he found a girl in his bed. He promptly tipped the bed up and the girl with it, and told the others in the billet to get her out of there.'

But those who tried to keep the camps clear of women were fighting a losing battle. The daughter of the village shopkeeper at Appleshaw near Andover remembers an incident when, looking for the door of the Motor Pool office at Tidworth House to arrange about transport home after a dance, she 'opened the wrong door. . . . In there was a girl who promptly scampered under a bed and out through a hole cut in the plywood partition. One GI called out: "Leave her alone. She's only a shack rat." ' On another occasion in the camp, that most respectable-sounding of amusements, a Sunday afternoon tea-dance, included an unusual 'floor-show' provided by the efforts of 'the MPs . . . to catch a couple of "camp-followers" ':

The Provost Marshal briefed us to get the two girls in our truck and keep them there should they thumb a lift when we were returning home. This they did and we blocked the back of the truck to stop them jumping out. The truck doubled back and the MPs dragged into the Provost Marshal's office two rather smelly prostitutes. Within seconds of being taken to the guard room one girl jumped through the glass window.

The problem existed equally, if not more, in coloured camps. A Cornish newspaper reported in September 1944 a typical case where a married woman from Bude admitted 'having spent three days in a camp', occupied by coloured troops, 'sleeping in huts with soldiers during the night and removing to a wood during the day'. She was sentenced to two months in jail and a younger girl with her was placed on probation for twelve months. An American officer revealed in court that 'at least fifteen men had been court-martialled for absence from duty caused by the presence of defendant and other women at the camp'.

Tidworth, of course, was a magnet for such women as one engine driver on the base remembers. 'In the summer there were GIs and their women laying up everywhere.' Following complaints, the 'Military Police rounded all the women up in the barracks and locked them in, waiting for the civil police. . . . Some of our Pioneer Corps troops . . . working for the GIs . . . busted the doors in and let the women go. . . . From then onwards the police didn't interfere. . . . We used to let them lay up in the railway box vans during the day when the GIs were training.' His two locomotives called ' "Molly" and "Betty" soon became known all over Canada, Australia and America as the only two virgins in Tidworth '

Women who tried to cheat GIs rarely did so twice, as one resident of Hitchin in Hertfordshire remembers:

A female of easy virtue contacted a GI one night in the saloon bar of a local public house and after many drinks took her escort to the air-raid shelter in the churchyard at the back of . . . St Mary's . . . induced the GI to remove his pants and promised on her part to do likewise. She thereupon ran out of the shelter with his trousers and, of course, his well-packed wallet. For obvious reasons he could not follow, but his shouts attracted the MPs, who after a search found the trousers minus the wallet.

Two nights after, the GI plus his friends came looking for the woman who was foolish enough to be in the same bar. They seized her and carried her screaming to the old market-place and threw her into the static water tank, which was deep enough to drown her. Fortunately the local police were following and rescued the very frightened female – and there the matter rested.

British mothers feared, with some reason, that their daughters, on taking up war work away from home, might, in every sense, fall among Americans. One woman then aged nineteen and living in Essex, who decided that 'it was time I broke the strings' and volunteered for the Land Army, remembers her striking introduction to this new danger. Her mother, protective to the last, insisted on travelling with her on the first stage of her journey, by train to Chelmsford, where she had then to catch a bus to a village they had never heard of, called Roxwell:

I felt half afraid and conspicuous in the brand new, clean uniform. My mother was lecturing me on the sins of all men in uniform. I sat silent, listening or half listening to her tales of venereal disease, blindness and all the things that happen to young girls who are promiscuous. . . . The bus depot was swarming with GIs. One came over and put his arms around me and kissed me on the cheek. He smelt strongly of beer. My mother beat him off, and said to me, 'I don't like it. I don't like all these Americans, they all have venereal disease, promise me you won't have anything to do with them. . . .'
The bus pulled up and with goodbyes I left my mother and got a seat near the window so I could wave. An American sat beside me, and I could see the worrying frown on my mother's face. I . . . couldn't hear but I could guess what she was saying.

For this mother's warnings there soon proved to be a good deal of reason, as her daughter rapidly discovered. The house where she lodged was constantly full of GIs brought home by her landlady, and she found herself sharing a room with the wife of a British officer serving overseas.

One day I caught her crying and she let me read the letter from her husband. In it he said he was having a good time with the opposite sex and *she* should do likewise. I think he forgot he had a brand-new son and one doesn't shove it under the bed and go out for the evening. Anyway I volunteered to look after the baby while she went out to the American base dance. She came back from the dance absolutely charmed by her American escort. 'Perfect gentleman,' she said. 'He brought me straight home and we just had a kiss and a cuddle.' She was full of it and I was pleased for her, but that was to be short-lived. She complained of a sore mouth after a couple of days and visited her local doctor. When she came back from the doctor she was very indignant: 'How dare he, how dare he suggest such terrible things?' . . . the poor woman was broken and her mother and brother came to take her home to Ilford.[1]

This unfortunate woman was almost certainly suffering from gingivitis, a condition misleadingly described by the medical dictionary hastily consulted by another victim, a sixteen-year-old typist with the US Army in Cavendish Square, as 'a form of venereal disease of the gums'. 'I must have looked terrified on my next trip to the dental hospital,' she remembers. ' "Don't worry," the dentist assured me, "most of the girls we have here with it have been with the Americans at some time or another." I sat glued to the chair. They did not know where I worked, and although my conscience was clear, I could hardly expect them or anyone to believe me. They must have seen my expression and quickly explained to me that . . . in my case it was due to overcrowded teeth.'

The arrival of the GIs also gave a sharp upward twist to the already rising curve of cases of ordinary venereal disease. One GI from Roxbury, Massachusetts, remembers that his unit had only been in Belfast for two months when their commanding officer assembled them for a stern warning: 'The infirmary had advised him that a large number of men were reporting with VD. . . . If this continued they would be confined to quarters and . . . not be permitted to leave. As a result of this tongue-lashing the VD rate dropped markedly.' But such effects tended to be temporary and in the hospital at Lurgan, previously mentioned, one whole ward, and part of another, were soon set aside for cases of venereal disease and the administrative Lieutenant quoted earlier found himself approached by a British Sergeant who 'was both mad and upset' because 'his wife, a registered nurse, was becoming seriously and intimately involved with a GI, a patient in our hospital'. The unwilling Lieutenant, in his thirties, found himself pressed by the husband to give a fatherly talk to the delinquent wife on 'a subject that was taboo for discussion in mixed company through my life time'.

I talked all round it and offered suggestions and finally, in desperation, I broke military medical rules and simply asked the lady if she was aware of the fact that the GI with whom she was so infatuated was a syphilitic patient. I don't know who turned the whiter, the lady or her husband. Silence reigned for several seconds and

1. The ironic end of the landgirl's own story is best told in this extract from a letter home to her mother a year later: 'Dear Mum, I need your signature so that I can marry my sailor. I am pregnant, so I can leave the WLA and come home. . . . Hope you will forgive me, but I did keep my promise about not going with Yankees.'

the lady made a wild dash from the house. I learned later she immediately went to the local civilian hospital and had herself examined and preventive treatment administered. She never visited our hospital again.

Warned by what had happened in Northern Ireland the authorities did their best to prepare women in England for the perils to come. A WAAF stationed at Uxbridge remembers that two days before the first Americans arrived they were all 'compulsorily ordered to attend a film in the camp cinema about the treatment and symptoms of VD'. On the whole, however, such warnings proved ineffective and by December 1942 the number of cases in the United Kingdom had already risen by 70 per cent since the start of the war. By March 1943, when a conference was called in London to discuss remedial measures, two full-length feature films warning of the dangers were being distributed to army camps, while in May the *Stars and Stripes* cartoonist was pressed into the battle: a drawing showed a soldier embracing a girl in front of a wall on which the chalked 'V' sign had been altered to read 'VD'. That month the army announced that VD had already

put more than 2000 GIs out of action in the UK so far that year, of whom 1806 men had contracted gonorrhoea, 166 syphilis and twenty-eight other diseases, giving a rate of infection 50 per cent higher than among American troops in the United States. Propaganda against running risks was intensified. Warned one American Colonel: 'Any woman who can be "picked up" or "made" by an American soldier can be, almost certainly has been, "picked up" or "made" by countless others.'

In case exhortation proved ineffective, the Americans also distributed free prophylactics to all applicants. A Southport girl remembers that it was the duty of her US naval officer friend to 'stand at the top of the gang-plank', as the young sailors under his command went ashore, 'warn them about the danger of picking up the women who hung around the dockside cafés and hand out to each boy a packet of rubber condoms'. A Wren stationed at Rosneath on the Clyde remembers that the familiar little square paper packets were openly carried by US sailors in their hats. A housewife living at Poynton near Stockport in Cheshire recalls how 'the churchyard used to be littered with contraceptives. It was the only dark place in the village and by the bus stop.' For those who failed to use a 'rubber', fifty prophylactic or 'Blue Cross' stations had been set up throughout the United Kingdom by mid 1943 – that at Rainbow Corner was probably the busiest – but the VD figures went on rising. The biggest increase of all – 50 per cent in six weeks – occurred just after VE-Day. The widely held belief that it was combat troops, having a last fling before action, who were most promiscuous was wrong. It was always among supporting units, and when danger was least, that the VD rate was highest, with the ground elements of the air force and Services of Supply men in the lead.

More lasting and tragic in its consequences than VD was the other all-too-common consequence of sexual indulgence, of whose dangers most women in the 1940s were only too well aware, though few can have been so safety-conscious as the seventeen-year-old Cornish girl who agreed to sleep with an engineer officer from New York City. When, he remembers, 'I had sneaked a condom on . . . she made me add a second . . . which probably made me the most heavily insulated male in history.'

'They certainly left no debris behind in the form of rubbish or litter,' recalls a then Cornish teenager rather sourly, 'but we had another mark of their presence . . . a minor population explosion nine months later.' The full number of such offspring is unknown, because the children's parentage was often concealed, but must have run into many tens of thousands. Almost everyone can recall cases among their acquaintance. One wartime factory worker, then aged eighteen and living in a community of young girls near High Wycombe, decided that 'they must have put our hostel there on purpose. Out of the fifty girls I started with, only eighteen of us were still there' at the end of the war. 'All the others got pregnant.'

This was the end to many such relationships. One GI in Salisbury, a local resident remembers, 'paid all confinement expenses' for his child's mother, 'proudly went to see her in hospital armed with chocolates and flowers and went to the parish church and arranged with the vicar for his son's christening', but still 'went back to his wife after the war'. But even this degree of interest was unusual. A Nottingham woman remembers the outrageous but effective response of one GI father in Nottingham. He announced that he could not get married because he was suffering from VD, 'an absolute lie, as events proved, but causing tremendous anguish to the girl and her family, all respectable'. A commoner excuse, often true, was that the offender was married already. A Norwich woman remembers how her nineteen-year-old cousin learned too late that her boy friend had a wife already and 'brought her baby up and later married an English boy'.

This was by far the commonest fate of such children. One former British airman from Bedford knows personally of three such cases. 'I am quite certain that none of these now adult people know of their origin, as it was decided by the three families never to tell them, so that they could feel integrated with other children, which in each case came along later.' Some women, half-hoping perhaps to bring back their errant partner, gave their children American names, and there must be many Earls and Peggy-Lous now in their thirties who have long since guessed the reason for this un-British choice. Usually, however, everyone concerned, especially the girl's parents, wished to live down the whole episode as quickly as possible, though one man then living in Abertillery, South Wales, recalls a couple who 'despite the shocked scandal going around . . . after the baby was born . . . hung a huge American flag from the bedroom window'.

Although it was clearly no joke for the people most directly concerned, the GI baby boom prompted many witticisms. 'Next time,' ran one popular gibe, 'just send the uniforms. We've got the bastards here already.' 'Those horrible Yanks,' ran another gibe, 'making up for drinking the pubs dry by filling up the nurseries.' It was said that in Burtonwood – and no doubt in other heavily GI populated areas – a notice appeared by the roadside: 'To all GIs: Please drive carefully, that child may be yours.' One American Sergeant in a map-making unit became nationally famous after fathering quadruplets on a British woman. His wife refused to divorce him, but the army, it was said, assigned him to 'reproduction duties'.

Generous in so much, both the US Army and individual GIs were usually as unhelpful as they could be once a baby was on the way. A Beeston girl remembers occasions when his 'pals . . . found people in the States who would adopt' a married GI's illegitimate child, while some girls 'had played so loose with different Americans that they had no idea who the father was', but even when a hitherto virtuous, and often very young, girl had 'given in' to a single persistent GI, the army usually 'didn't want to know'. The then manageress of a NAAFI at Wattisham airfield in Suffolk recalls her disgust at what happened after one of her staff confessed she was 'in trouble' by a GI, who immediately, with the army's full co-operation, got himself assigned elsewhere. 'As we were waving them off in the trucks, he had a most awful smirk on his face, while two big tears rolled down her cheeks. If I'd had a gun I would have shot him.'

Collecting a paternity allowance from an unwilling GI was virtually impossible. One Boston man, in charge of soldiers' allotments in a unit in Belfast, remembers the chaplain coming to see him about 'a young lass of twenty-three who was in the family way and . . . accusing a GI of being responsible. My chaplain was a sad man when I informed him that there was no way to have the United States Army pass the lass a subsidy unless the culprit acknowledged fatherhood.'

A then sixteen-year-old recalls what happened when, with two other members of the 'Children of Mary', a Roman Catholic young people's society, she called at the local GI barracks in Plymouth:

> We arrived at the gate and asked the guard to direct us to Father S. . . . He said: 'Go away.' Thinking he had not heard aright, we said, again, 'Please can you direct us to Father S.'s office?' 'No,' he said, and called another guard, both complete with bayonets, and said, 'Beat it girls.' . . . Nell told them we had been invited to supper. 'That's a new one,' they said. 'Look, girls, we know what you're after. Clear off.' We tried to protest but they jeered at us, walking away and carrying on their patrol. I for one was nearly in tears so we went to the nearest telephone box. In a voice full of indignation I told Father S. what had happened. 'Oh dear,' he said, 'we get so many girls in trouble demanding to see me that the guards have orders not to let them in. Come back to the gate and I'll be there.' As I went to put the phone down I . . . heard him roaring with laughter.

If the fate of a white illegitimate child was unenviable, that of a coloured one, born into a white household, was far worse, and what should have been a happy event became a heart-breaking one. A woman then living in Plymouth recalls the tragic case of a 'devout, elderly Roman Catholic widow hurt and shocked' to discover that her strictly brought-up daughter was pregnant who then faced two further blows when the daughter died in childbirth, leaving behind a black baby whose sad lot it was to begin life in an orphanage. One Cambridge woman recalls becoming speechless on peering into one young girl's pram in the street to find looking back at her two handsome identical twins, both very black indeed. A then eighteen-year-old Oxford girl knew of one 'none too bright' husband who duly took his wife's 'dusky baby' into his home when assured that it was 'the result of having been startled by a black soldier when out walking one night during her pregnancy'.

If the social climate of the time was critical of illegitimacy it was even more hostile to abortion, which for all practical purposes was at that time illegal in Britain. There were nevertheless many 'back-street' abortions. Among British girls working at the US Headquarters at Bushy Park, the number, one British secretary discovered, was 'tremendous'; one girl had no fewer than five self-induced miscarriages. Many GIs claimed to know a simple and infallible method of getting a girl 'out of trouble' which was sometimes applied with fatal results. A British airman recalls a court-martial following one such tragedy where the accused GI was acquitted on the grounds that no one without medical knowledge could have practised this technique, although many servicemen knew better. Sometimes an American did what was quaintly called 'the decent thing' and paid for a woman to go to a qualified abortionist. One woman then in her twenties and living in Belfast – she later married, and divorced another GI – describes the experience:

I was overdue. A friend on the base said he would help. Meet him at the GC Hotel. Put £20 in an envelope. We done that, he went off and returned with another envelope with an address on it. 'Go there and she will see you OK.' When we got home we steamed open the envelope. There was £5 and a short note saying that I was a friend of his and to please see to me. Anyway there was nothing we could do and we needed the contact so I went to the address, but I felt much older and wiser.

While they would certainly not have approved of such behaviour most British people, understanding what it was like to be a long way from home with only the prospect of action ahead, adopted a surprisingly tolerant attitude to the GIs' more minor peccadilloes. One woman who was then a switchboard operator at the huge Woodlands hostel at Chorley in Lancashire, which accommodated nearly 2000 war workers, recalls a typical incident there:

A girl woke up to find an American entering her room through the window. She gave one scream, and the American lost his cap in making a quick exit through the window. . . . The American authorities said this was a serious offence and the young officer would be demoted. Our warden was very upset . . . made extensive investigation into the affair [and found] that the American was innocently involved with some irresponsible girls and had got the wrong room in the black-out. . . . He was allowed to keep his rank and let off with light punishment.

A few people, however, felt that sterner measures were needed, among them William Kendall, MP, representing Grantham in the heart of Eighth Air Force country, whose campaign on this subject was taken seriously enough to be considered by the War Cabinet. Kendall had, on 25 May 1944, complained in Parliament, under the traditional guise of asking a question, that there were towns where 'It is unfit for a women to walk unescorted at night due to the ineffectiveness of the American military forces to . . . prevent unconcealed immorality and to give proper protection to women.' The Government spokesman, armed with formal denials by the

Lord Lieutenant of the County, the Mayor and the Watch Committee –
official guardians of public morals – denounced the suggestion as 'mis-
conceived and rather mischievous' and declared that 'the innuendo is quite
unjustified'. Kendall, undeterred, then announced his intention, as the War
Cabinet were told, to invite 'twenty or thirty leading citizens to attend
luncheon to hear certain statements regarding the conduct of American
troops. . . . It was clear that no action could be taken to prohibit the meeting
under Defence Regulation 39E.' The Cabinet finally 'decided that . . . the
best course was that all possible action should be taken to prevent publicity
being given to Mr Kendall's allegations' and 'the Minister of Information
was asked to approach the Press in this sense'. This unofficial censorship
proved effective. Little more was heard of the subject and ten days later,
with the landings in Normandy, the Press had something more important
than sex in Grantham to occupy its front pages.

BEACHHEAD IN DEVON

'On weekends we used to sneak away to Seaton to visit our "adopted" families.'
— GI from 4th US Division recalling pre D-Day training, 1944.

FROM the moment the first American soldiers arrived in the British Isles they knew that their way back to the United States lay across the beaches of France. Instead of, however, as they had expected, invading Europe, those early contingents went instead to North Africa, in October 1942, then in July 1943 into Sicily, only reaching the mainland of Europe, at the tip of Southern Italy, in September 1943. For the American Generals, as for the British and American public, all these operations were only a substitute for the real, decisive action which alone could win the war. 'It was correctly believed', wrote General Eisenhower later, 'that only on the historic battle-fields of France and the Low Countries could Germany's armies in the West be decisively engaged and defeated', but it was not until April 1943 that planning began in earnest for what everyone insisted on calling the Second Front. The target date was then fixed at 1 May 1944, a time, incidentally, we now know, when it would have enjoyed ideal weather conditions. The main outlines of the operation were agreed at the Quebec Conference in August 1943, but on 1 February the starting date, or D-Day, for the assault now named OPERATION OVERLORD, was pushed back to 'not later than 31 May', mainly to secure more landing craft. On 17 May, wrote the Supreme Commander later, 'I set 5 June as the "final" date for the assault, subject, of course, to last-minute revision if the weather should prove unfavourable.'

From October 1943 events moved steadily towards their climax, creating new problems for the British Cabinet. The urgent need now was for more training areas, especially for the five US armoured divisions and on 4 October the Secretary of State for War warned his colleagues that these would require 'about 141 000 acres' of fertile land in the 'agricultural' belt of Oxfordshire, Wiltshire and Hampshire, since other areas were either in use by the British forces or did not provide the necessary 'firm subsoil and natural features essential to realistic training'.

It was in vain that the Minister of Agriculture protested that this demand was on top of the 16 500 acres already requisitioned for their use and would affect nearly 500 farms, 90000 acres of prime arable land, nearly 26000 cattle, 'many of the dairy herds being attested', i.e., of exceptional quality, and 56000 sheep, among them 'many ram-breeding flocks of Hampshire Down. If the American proposals are approved,' warned the Minister, 'it will mean that my efforts to maintain, and even increase . . . the 1943 level of home food production will be seriously affected.' But with little hesitation the Cabinet agreed that the British public would simply have to tighten its belt one more notch; the Americans got their land.

The new training areas – and others, acquired later, for infantry and airborne troops – required few extra buildings, though many damaged barns and shattered gateposts soon needed replacing, but the hard-pressed Office of Works and Royal Engineers now faced a new demand, for embarkation 'hards' for the troops and vehicle approach roads to them and to the ports. By the late autumn of 1943, the location of the seventy-four new hards had been agreed and work was being passed ahead, not merely on building them but on constructing seventeen miles of brand new road and widening 230 miles of existing highway, to a 'minimum carriage-way on two-way routes' of 'twenty-two feet and on one way sixteen feet, with laybys', of which nearly 750 were needed, 'at quarter-mile intervals'. Five new bridges were built and fifty-six more had to be widened and strengthened. For a nation now in its fifth year of war all this involved a prodigious effort, but by the scheduled date every new hard stood ready for the feet of the departing soldiers and every new 'turning circle' awaited the ungainly bulldozers, tanks and field guns swivelling round on their way to the beaches of France.

While in the far west, which in England was mild rather than wild, the surveyors and sappers plied their trades with theodolite and pickaxe, in London the planners were studying very different maps. On 14 January 1944 General Eisenhower had arrived back from Algiers, via the United States, 'to undertake', as he wrote, 'the organization of the mightiest fighting force that the two Western Allies could muster'. His presence was soon felt. 'As on my first arrival in London in June 1942 I found headquarters staffs concentrated in the heart of the city, but this time I determined I would not be defeated in my plan to find a suitable site somewhere in the countryside. I found one, and there were protests and gloomy predictions. Once concentrated in the Bushy Park area, however, we quickly developed a relationship that far more than made up for minor inconveniences.'

The happy spirit which prevailed at SHAEF is well illustrated by a mock paper prepared by some army staff officers to satirize naval objections to giving the army more authority over the invasion beaches. It was entitled OPERATION OVERBOARD and on the front, replacing the usual inscription 'American SECRET = British MOST SECRET', was the legend: 'American STUPID = British MOST STUPID'.[1]

The essence of OVERLORD, as finally agreed, was for a seaborne assault by five divisions on a fifty-mile front, from about three miles short of Quineville, on the Cotentin Peninsula, some twenty miles from Cherbourg, to just short of Cabourg, near the mouth of the River Dives, about fifteen miles from Caen. It was to be supported by three airborne divisions, to protect the exits from the beaches, to hold off German reinforcements and – considered vital by General Eisenhower – to facilitate the capture of the deep-water port of Cherbourg, through which reinforcements and supplies for the American forces could then be poured in direct from the United States. The British lines of communication would meanwhile run from the Channel ports, such as Calais and Dieppe, and later Ostend and Antwerp, back to Southampton, Dover and Newhaven.

The basic strategic decision that the American forces were to attack on the right flank was to have a profound effect upon both the ordinary GI and the civilian population of South-West England, for it meant that the jumping-off base for these armies would not be the areas where they were already stationed but the coastline fronting the English Channel from the Eastern border of Dorset to the far tip of Cornwall. The Eighth Air Force largely stayed where it was, while the newly formed Ninth Air Force, with its headquarters at Sunninghill, near Ascot, was already in the heart of GI territory. Hospitals and major supply depots also stayed in their existing sites, but with these exceptions most combat units and the services linked directly to them were uprooted and moved westward, while formations arriving from North Africa or Italy were sent straight there. Increasingly as the months passed American sailors took over ports like Falmouth and Plymouth, Dartmouth and Weymouth, and, almost overnight it seemed, small towns and villages in Dorset, Devon, Somerset and Cornwall, which had so far rarely seen a GI, now felt the full impact of American occupation.

The west in peacetime had been the great holiday area of England, a tranquil countryside of thatched cottages and little towns of honey-coloured stone, earning its living from agriculture and tourism. Now in its small fishing harbours and historic deep-water ports the US Navy mustered an array of vessels larger than any they had seen since the little ships of Drake and his captains stood out from Plymouth to challenge the Armada. On its splendid sandy beaches the landing craft, time after time, were run aground to disgorge their cargo of assault troops. (One American who sketched the

1. A copy of this document reached America and narrowly escaped publication in the West Point magazine *The Pointer*. The highest security classification for both countries later became TOP SECRET, while people who knew the date of D-Day were described as BIGOTED.

scene humorously captioned his drawing: 'GIs disembark on the most likely stretch of beach and rush madly for the best picnic spots.')

There had long been Americans in Plymouth but now they seemed to be everywhere in its ancient streets and in the smaller south-west ports like Weymouth and Dartmouth, famous as the home of HMS *Britannia*, the Royal Navy College for training future officers. At a civic welcome, presided over by the Mayor, 'The CO's speech in reply,' remembers a local bank manager, 'was short and to the point. They were over here to fight a war and the sooner they got on with this, the better for all concerned.' One young man from Enterprise, Alabama, steering landing craft up and down the River Dart with a harbour craft company, still remembers with delight the summer of 1944 in this ancient town. 'The land rising from the Dart river is lovely, divided by hedgerows, green and beautiful. The river [was] so much cleaner than streams in America I've seen. We swam in it joyfully, admiring the birds perching on the buoys and learned to feel the river's channels were like our auto highways at home.'

Dorchester, one of the smallest and most unspoiled of English county towns and still recognizable as the 'Casterbridge' of Thomas Hardy's novels, also decided to give the first American units a ceremonial welcome. They belonged to the 1st US Division and arrived, a local councillor observed, 'rather chastened after their experiences in Tunisia', but made a lively entrance into the town, headed by a 'jingle johnny', a soldier festooned with bells. The official speech of welcome by the Mayor in the largest cinema was well received and even more effective in breaking the ice was the punch served at the subsequent cocktail party given by the Council. This looked like innocuous fruit juice, but, due to the shortage of alcohol, had been laced with surgical spirit and, 'served in tumblers', the same councillor recalls, 'took a respected teetotal alderman by surprise'.

The same councillor, a director of the local brewery, remembers an unexpected request his company received. Could the division use the brewery's steam plant to clean out their anti-tank guns, which were thick with protective grease after their recent sea voyage? The men arrived less well protected, appearing, another Dorchester resident remembers, 'in tropical kit, though the bitter east wind was blowing'. A week later the troops' warm clothing caught up with them and 'the streets seemed full of hundreds of GIs each carrying a coathanger. They must have bought up the entire stock of all the drapers' shops to carry their discarded garments.' Behind the scenes there were other, less obvious, preparations. One corner of their camp at Dorchester contained some discreetly covered objects whose purpose was betrayed by its nickname: Coffin Corner.

In the little village of Lytton Cheney, a few miles from Dorchester, the GIs easily outnumbered the villagers and made a long-remembered début at the local pub. 'At opening time,' recorded a resident, 'they were all lined up outside the White Horse and to the landlady's amazement the first man in handed up a bucket saying, "Eighteen pints please," for the cooks who could not come down to the inn.' At Lyme Regis, a little farther west, even this request was surpassed. The Americans collected their 'rough' cider from one pub in a full-size zinc bath.

Before long few places in the West Country remained unaffected by the great move westward. A woman then living at Launceston in Cornwall remembers how suddenly an obscure railway halt ten miles away, Halwill, became 'an important railhead and all along the main Launceston–Bude road the coloured troops started erecting open-ended Nissen-hut type structures to store boxes of ammunition'. That November these men, from the 64th Ordnance Battalion, staged 'a revue called *Dixieland* in Launceston Town Hall. . . . It was a great show, the audience gave the lads a standing ovation afterwards.' On the other side of the peninsula, in the little fishing village of Newlyn, 'all the girls', observed one landgirl, 'were delighted at the sudden influx of partners and greatly impressed by the compliments which the GIs gave so naturally . . . . We were all greatly flattered and it was a new experience for the girls in that far end of England.'

From January 1944 onwards the flow of American men and supplies into Britain accelerated. It had already, by July 1943, reached a rate of 750 000 tons a month; now it climbed towards its pre-D-Day peak of 2 000 000 tons. To handle this vast flood, the supply organization expanded steadily until 'Com Z' – short for Communications Zone – employed 31 500 officers and 350 000 enlisted men, nearly a quarter of the 1 526 965 American troops (excluding sailors) in the United Kingdom, at their maximum strength just before D-Day.

A high proportion of the new arrivals were combat troops. Among them was a twenty-three-year-old radio operator from Bridgeport, Connecticut, in peacetime an electrician, who arrived with the 2nd Battalion of the 8th Regiment of the 4th Infantry Division at Liverpool in January, and soon afterwards found himself in Devon. Fourth Division Headquarters were at Tiverton, but its regiments were distributed all over the county and this man found himself assigned to Seaton, a small resort on the coast which had had its share of British troops – who had now moved out – but had not so far seen a single GI. Now Claridge House, a popular pre-war hotel, sheltered headquarters company, the chalets of a holiday camp accommodated 'F' Company and provided the whole battalion with its mess hall, and this man's company, 'G', was scattered in other empty buildings in the town. 'When not out of town on manoeuvres our troops manned gun emplacements along the beach,' he remembers, firing enthusiastically on any German bombers that flew overhead, pleasurable, and not too dangerous, excitement being provided by the bombs unloaded by fleeing aircraft. On one red-letter night, perhaps to the gunners' own surprise, the barrage brought down a

Junkers 88 'in a small field between Seaton and Beer' and the battalion was turned out to search for the crew. This brought them their first sight of the face of the enemy, 'a real young Lieutenant, of nineteen years' found hiding in some woods until carried off in triumph to the Seaton 'lock-up'.

During weekend leaves this soldier visited bomb-devastated Coventry and Manchester and it gave him, he admits, 'much satisfaction in later months to see the score evened, and then some, in Germany'. But mostly the men tried, off-duty, to forget the grim task ahead of them, entering cheerfully into the life of the little town. His own hours off-duty were brightened by bicycle excursions into the countryside and picnics on deserted stretches of beach. Other recreations were visits to the local tearooms, 'a steak dinner each month on pay-day', 'a public dance each Wednesday and Saturday evening, which we never missed', and evenings out at the Blue Dolphin 'a favourite pub in the village of Beer, over some hills along the coast, which took about one half-hour to walk each way; it being blacked out at first we had several casualties every night, from GIs who ran into courtyard walls, trees and most everything one could bump into in the dark.'

But as winter gave way to spring – nowhere in England lovelier than in Devon and never more appreciated than in 1944 when every man knew it might be the last he ever saw – more and more time was spent in the serious business of training. This soldier recalls 'a couple of weeks across England, on the Bristol Channel', near Barnstaple, one of the main rehearsal areas, and though in theory confined to camp 'on weekends we used to sneak away and return to Seaton to visit our "adopted families" '. For reasons of security the men never knew whether they 'were going on a manoeuvre or to a ship to . . . France', so each time they said 'final' goodbyes to their hosts. Private possessions could, for the same reason, not be sold or given away but had to be left in a store-room and this Sergeant still mourns the loss of his faithful bicycle, 'a real beauty, with coaster brake on the rear and caliper brakes both front and rear', and 'a barracks bag full of clothes, personal belongings, etc., which I never did see again.'

While the vast majority of Americans in Britain could only train – and wait – a small number were already in France, helping the Resistance on behalf of the Office of Strategic Services, American equivalent of the British Special Operations Executive. Early in 1943 the first of 375 French-speaking Americans were dropped in enemy territory and they were followed from the end of the year by 'Jedburgh' teams, named after their training area in Scotland and consisting of a Frenchman, an American and a Briton, who wore uniforms and served in areas already under the control of the Maquis. Later they were reinforced by eleven Special Operation Groups, totalling nearly 400 officers and men, whose very existence was a secret.

With the spring the great exodus from London began. Lieutenant William Bostick, US Navy, who had been working in the West End on maps of the invasion beaches, now witnessed what he called the 'retreat from Eisenhower Plate'. Bootick himself, like many other naval officers, ended up in Plymouth where 'bombed buildings', he wrote, 'were known to have waited days before toppling over because of the thick fog which supported their walls'.

But in spite of the occasional light relief which invariably accompanies military exercises the large-scale manoeuvres in which these months were spent were a grim and weary business. One helper at the Red Cross club in Exeter remembers how at this time 'men would arrive on the Saturday night, with no bookings ... muddy, tired and glad of a rest. As soon as eleven o'clock came and the dance was over mattresses would be laid on the floor in the main rooms, even in the cloakroom, and along the wide passages, so that there was somewhere for them to sleep.'

Although there was also a training area on the north coast of Devon, overlooking the Bristol Channel, around Barnstaple, the main invasion rehearsals took place at Slapton Sands, the northern section of a seven-mile stretch of coarse sand and shingle, with a steeply shelving beach, near Start Point in Devon, in the thinly populated area known as the South Hams. Conditions here were as close as could be found in Britain to those of the French beaches selected for use on D-Day, with most of the terrain only fifty feet above sea-level, but with one 350-foot-high cliff. The villages affected have never achieved the fame of those on the actual battlefield, but their names surely deserve to be recorded: Blackawton and Strete, Torcross and Stokenham, Chillington, East Allington and Slapton. Late in 1943, to enable the troops to practise undisturbed using live ammunition, the whole district was evacuated, a major upheaval affecting 3000 civilians over an area of twenty-six square miles. Soon columns of GIs dressed for combat were moving through ghost-like streets, where one could find shops and post offices, pubs and churches, schools and cottages, but not a single occupant, animal or human, to be seen. 'The sight bothered me,' the Sergeant previously quoted admits. 'As we used to follow tanks through fields and fields of turnips and beets which were planted and just left in the ground ... we thought what a shame when foodstuffs were so badly needed in Great Britain.'

It was not until mid-August that the local population was allowed to return. They found every window shattered, and although historic buildings had been marked with white tape to prevent troops 'attacking' them, Slapton church roof had received a direct hit and the fields and beaches were littered with mines and shells, rapidly cleared by Negro engineers, to whom the inhabitants still feel a debt of gratitude. Later a local schoolmaster was to write a play recording these turbulent months, *The Red Earth*.

Exercises under combat conditions inevitably brought casualties, most of them during the final 'dress rehearsal' when each of the five assault forces carried out a mock attack on a beach resembling its final objective. On this occasion, in the early hours of 27 April, German E-boats penetrated the convoy carrying Force 'U' from Plymouth, torpedoed two landing craft and damaged a third, leaving 700 men – two-thirds of them soldiers – to drown. (On D-Day itself, so strange are the fortunes of war, Force 'U' got ashore almost unscathed.)

Only one major formation taking part in the first wave of the assault, the 82nd Airborne Division, was not, by May 1944, situated in the West Country, being based around Leicester. One former Infantry Reserve Captain, who joined it in April via Algiers, Glasgow and Bristol, can still recall 'the thrill of seeing the British Isles after a year in the sand and heat of North Africa'. His first pre-invasion duty was unexciting, if not untypical, taking 'about 3000 jackets to a nearby town to be dyed a greenish, camouflage colour. . . . The girls working in the factory giggled and whispered as they stared at us.'

Even the GI inmates of the Disciplinary Training Centre, or military prison, at Langport in Somerset, knew that something was in the air, one of the Centre's medical officers, from Oakdale, California, remembers. 'Our prisoners were put to work making wooden pallets for shipping supplies. We began working day and night shifts. The pressure was on to get them out – and fast.'

If adult civilians were mainly conscious of the sadness of separation from GI friends and the dangers to which these would soon be exposed, for children the months before D-Day were the most fascinating time of the whole American occupation. A fourteen-year-old schoolgirl at Tavistock enjoyed standing in the market square while the band of the 29th Division 'roused the rustics' with its Sousa marches, the population being thrilled to see General Eisenhower on one of his many visits of inspection. For her, too, this period ended abruptly. 'A couple of months before D-Day things went very subdued and there was a great air of secrecy and solemnity where before there had been fun and lightheartedness. Everyone I knew seemed to disappear and I felt that a phase of my life was over.' Tidworth, however, still retained many of its GIs, and a schoolboy living in the district remembers the fields adjoining his school being 'stacked with crates and boxes' while – far more intriguing – 'the American forces brought a mobile laboratory to our village used in analysing samples of water from the local river. As the river runs through several farms and public sanitation had not arrived, and the sample was always taken by the outflow from the local pub, the results must have been interesting.'

In April a ten-mile-wide coastal strip stretching from the Thames Estuary to Land's End, as well as along parts of the east coast and the Clyde, was banned to visitors, those who arrived without a permit being put on a train back by the police. As D-Day drew nearer, movement even for those already resident within the restricted area became increasingly difficult as more and more districts were sealed off and one-way systems were imposed in the towns and along many miles of narrow West Country lanes. One woman was then a seventeen-year-old commercial college student, living in the little village of Nanpean in Cornwall, remembers how 'as the American army took over all vital routes to the east for convoys, local traffic came almost to a halt; our parish [St Stephen-in-Brannel] became entangled in a web of military movement. It became increasingly difficult to go to work or school or pursue normal activities, as at every major crossroads there was a barricade and only people with passes could go through.'

The full effect of the restrictions became apparent as the date her sister's wedding approached, for the family had chosen Thursday, 1 June:

When the great day came it was evident that a marriage in that particular church was going to be impossible as that end of the parish was completely cut off from our end. So last minute panic saw very involved plans to transfer the wedding service to another church, further away, but easier of access. On enquiry from the one barricade between home and the church the authorities said they would allow only three wedding cars through at a stipulated time, so the usual programme planned for the arrival of guests, ending up with the last car bringing the bride and her father had to be scrapped. We were all bundled into three cars and the bridesmaids and bride's mother actually travelled with the bride and her father. When we got to the barrier we all had to show identity cards and passes and we were quickly sped on our way by the friendly guards. We hardly knew who would turn up at the service because friends and relations from all parts of the country had been invited; but it appeared that it was easier to travel on the main line railway from towns many miles away than it was to cross our county for five miles.

May, an unusually fine month, was everywhere a time for goodbyes, as the troops began their journey towards their embarkation areas. A young woman working on a farm near Chippenham, close to an American camp, became accustomed to 'their girl friends coming at all hours through the back ways of the farm' to say goodbye. Finally: 'At seven on a Sunday morning they moved off. I was on my way to work and . . . got off my bike and stood and waved for a while. Now I'm older I should probably cry with realization, but then I just accepted that they had not come to Chippenham to sit the whole war out. I had never failed to see an American in the town each time I went to school or work. Now it was to seem peculiarly empty.' She also spared a thought that morning for the least threatening invader then on his way to France, a baby squirrel picked up by a GI friend during manoeuvres on Salisbury Plain 'which he kept as a pet . . . let loose in our garden or snuggled in his pocket to the movies or on walks'. Also *en route* for the Continent was Dagwood, the canine mascot of the regiment billeted in Lytton Cheney and a great favourite of the villagers. He had, they later learned with pride, 'jumped ashore from his usual perch on the bonnet of the leading officer's jeep so tiny Lytton was well to the fore on that great day'.

For those who had befriended individual GIs this was a sad time, with barely a moment to regret the loss of one familiar face before others, too, were gone. A Pfc from Bridgeport, Connecticut, remembers his departure from his 'second family' near Bristol:

Mr F. and his son-in-law had to go to work and said their goodbyes to me early in the morning. Mrs F. made tea and we sat and talked until the trucks started to arrive. We stood out on the sidewalk, hugged and kissed and had our spell of tears. . . . It was quite a sight to see everyone out on the sidewalk saying their goodbyes to each family. I can still see Mrs F. standing there waving goodbye to me as we drove off. . . . I never saw her again.

A regimental dental surgeon from Portsmouth, Virginia, has not forgotten his very different departure from Bodmin. An English friend gave him a treasured possession, 'a little medicine bottle of Scotch', the recipient promising to do the contents justice and then to 'throw the bottle at the Germans for good luck'. A Winchester housewife recalls how, when, late in May, the two GIs they had so often entertained left, her husband, suddenly silent, set off to dig furiously on his allotment, while, equally distressed, she busied herself in the routine of wartime shopping.

Sometimes there could be no formal goodbye. A housewife living in the Sussex village of Singleton, on the road between Midhurst and Chichester, remembers how the men of the 4th Cavalry Regiment stationed there would never say 'Goodbye', regarding it as 'too final', only 'So long'. For weeks, she remembers, they had filled in time painting names on their tanks and encouraging the local children to climb all over the vehicles 'whilst fed with candy and told about the glories of the USA'. Several soldiers had become regular visitors to her home, where they played chess with her husband or 'enjoyed a quiet snooze on the sofa', until, one morning early in June, 'on pulling my cottage curtains I noticed odd packages on the window sill'. They proved to be 'wallets with mothers' and girls' pictures and suchlike treasures, asking me to care for them until they could call again'.

Least painful, perhaps, were partings where there was only time for a hurried exchange of good luck wishes, like those of a Bridlington family, woken at 4 a.m. by a Sergeant from Hull, who 'dashed upstairs to kiss us all goodbye, as they were moving south . . . "Gee," he exclaimed, "I've stopped the whole convoy to say goodbye to you!" ' A retired nurse living near Newquay was astonished by the sudden arrival of two GIs, 'sent to a camp fourteen miles away to be isolated in secrecy . . . in preparation for D-Day [who] broke out and hired a taxi to come and say goodbye'. A Henley-on-Thames woman had become hardened to the loss of one set of friends after another, as each unit occupying a camp in a park opposite her house moved on, but the departure of one artillery regiment, shortly before D-Day, was, she realized, different. One 'warm, quiet and peaceful evening my children were tucked up in bed and I leaned for a few moments out of the window, thinking about how far away war seemed when, very quietly at first, I heard the sound of "Eternal Father Strong To Save" coming from the camp. It became louder as more voices joined the singing. It was so moving my eyes filled with tears. . . . That night we heard the rumble of midnight traffic. The next day . . . nothing.'

From the village of Mountfield, in Northern Ireland, remembers one man who was then a schoolboy, 'The Yanks left as suddenly and as quickly as they arrived. One day they were there, the next they were gone. We watched them leave. They waved wildly and cheered happily from their trucks. We all waved back somewhat sadly, waved goodbye to our Yanks and our daily candy ration. Some local girls received one or two letters, then silence' – explained by the rumour, probably well founded, 'that they suffered heavily on the beaches' of Normandy, a far cry from the lush green pastures of County Tyrone.

No one mourned the GIs' going more than the children. A Tidworth schoolboy, who had been 'adopted' by one GI, remembers how his friend 'arrived at the village school one morning asking for me. I went out to the cloakroom where the smell of his cigar directed me and found him with his driver . . . on the road outside. He gave me a slip of paper with his full field postal address, together with a large cardboard carton full of sweets, sugar, soap and other luxury or unobtainable items. I wrote twice, but never received a reply.' Considerate to the last, the GIs stationed in the Cotswold village of Sherston arranged for their young friends a kind of treasure hunt. 'Before one particular unit left,' remembers a woman who was then aged nine, 'we were told to visit a certain spot on their camp site after their departure. We . . . found a box of tinned foods, butter, fruit, etc., and a note saying, "Goodbye and thanks; it was great meeting you." ' In the Dorset village of Langton Maltravers there was such a wholesale distribution of 'candy' that, the village history records, 'the day they left schooltime was one protracted chew'.

Only occasionally was the GIs' departure marred by any untoward incident. One family who regularly left a pound note hidden in their hedge, in return for a ham which would mysteriously appear in their garden from the local American cookhouse, got up one morning to find the money gone – and no ham. A civilian at Tidworth who regularly collected up the GIs' watches for repair, leaving the camp with them strapped halfway up each arm, failed, when one unit was due to leave, to return with the last consignment and was never seen again.

Some civilians had reason to regard the approach of D-Day with special poignancy, like a landgirl working at Uplyme, on the Dorset/Devon border, who, as will be described in a later chapter, had just married a jeep driver of the 1st US Division:

As the tanks rumbled through the village streets, shaking the walls and windows, convoy upon convoy, we knew the invasion day was drawing nearer. We had about three weeks together. Bob's final overnight pass came and he walked down the street that morning after our goodbye and out of sight into the morning mist that was coming in from the sea. From then on they were confined to barracks and one morning a friend and myself walked up the hill to Green Acres [his billet] and they were gone.

The departure of the coloured contingent from Dorchester, whose arrival has been described in an earlier chapter, was preceded by a very different kind of celebration, witnessed by a local woman, who was then a schoolgirl. Officially the party was in honour of her sister's tenth birthday. The date was Saturday, 3 June:

All us children went ahead loaded with picnic stuff and the mums came by road, pushing the prams with the little ones – I suppose about three families, as not being able to go to the seaside, this was a treat. Teapots at the ready, our darkie friends arrived with extra things cook had managed to rustle up. Mum managed a chocolate cake and her dark cake with a bit of icing on. This was quite a talking point as they hadn't tasted a cake dark inside and white outside before and cook wanted the recipe. It was a strange concoction by today's standards, consisting of dried egg, no fat, prunes cut up, bits of apple and carrot, mixed spices, black treacle and flour. How the icing stayed on with no marzipan, I'll never know. We must have made a strange picture, a group of darkie soldiers around a fire, a dozen children, mums and friends, babies in push-chairs. The picnic was laid out and we shared their rations, meat, biscuits, coffee, tea, chocolate and gum, soda bread, marg., and butter mixed, JAM, a real treat. . . .

I remember planks of wood, tin trays were found and we slid down the hillsides like toboggans, rode in jeeps, bumping up and down. We walked around the top in groups. We played card games. We told them the history of Maiden Castle. Around the fire we exchanged songs from our countries, voices from the Deep South against the children's voices from Dorset. We pointed out the way to the sea, little knowing soon they would be sailing to the Normandy beaches.

But not all the troops in Dorchester prepared for their coming trial in such an innocent fashion. One middle-aged woman, arriving back at Dorchester at 11 p.m. one night – she had been allowed out of the 'prohibited area' to attend her father's funeral in Bristol – long remembered the 'ghastly sight' which greeted her outside the station. 'American GIs were strewn across the pavement, some lying flat, others in the gutter. . . . The men who were not quite drunk lurched forward and held out their hands.' As her husband had met her, she got home unharmed, though she sympathized thereafter with the parents who 'stopped their daughters coming for lessons' in the evenings at her commercial college. Like others who witnessed such scenes she was tolerant about their cause. 'One couldn't altogether blame the men,' she recognized, 'for trying to drown the thought of the ordeal they knew they had to face.'

Many men, even if they made the fact less obvious, also felt they deserved a final fling. One Plymouth teenager attended many 'farewell dances' at this time at which the boys would ask ' "How's about a souvenir, honey?" But their "souvenir" meant only one thing, and we didn't intend to have any "souvenirs" left behind, only happy memories.' Not all women in embarkation areas were equally unbending. One young war widow whose naval officer husband had been fatally wounded in the invasion of Sicily, and who spent Easter 1944 with his parents near Salcombe in Devon, remembers how 'after dark it was difficult to find space between the couples on the beach'. She herself 'had a brief affair with a young naval officer . . . a pleasant lad, from Boston . . . who wished to taste a little life before D-Day'.[1] One sailor from a strict Baptist home in Alabama confesses to a similar desire. The day before he was due to cross the Channel, as one of the crew of a landing craft, he picked up a girl outside a cinema in Dartmouth and 'we made love in two or three different shelters, and I gave her all the money I had, which wasn't much'.

The wildest farewell of all seems to have been the 'grand barbecue' given by the paratroopers stationed at Tollerton, just outside Nottingham, on Saturday, 22 May. One guest was a nineteen-year-old girl who, having been carefully 'vetted' by the Red Cross, had previously attended many camp dances there and found them highly decorous and strictly chaperoned.

We girls had been to the usual Tuesday dance and were invited to the barbecue, with buses laid on to take us, but not (this time) with Red Cross escorts. Off we went on the Saturday afternoon. It was fine but cloudy; this turned to heavy rain. There was food laid on, BUT also unlimited alcohol. Most of the troops were drunk when we arrived. I remember my own escort turned up partly drunk. Then we found that the camp was full of all the local prostitutes and after a time the whole thing degenerated into a free-for-all with each man trying to get a girl, any girl, into his tent. . . . The buses had been sent away by the troops and the whole camp had girls of a decent standard trying to stick together to get out. . . . We were well into the country, several miles from town – while taxi-loads of tarts poured in. I literally fought my way out of that camp with a girl friend and we were fortunate enough to be seen by a paratrooper who had known us on happier occasions. He grabbed a taxi and paid for it to take us home. I remember lying in bed safe at home and shaking with terror all that summer night. Even now it seems like a scene from some bizarre film.

Many men, all observers agree, faced their coming ordeal with sober resolution. The often-used description of the liberation of Europe as a crusade was no mere form of words. One Roman Catholic priest then living in St Ives, Cornwall, remembers a record congregation at Mothers' Day services two weeks beforehand, drawn from the men of 'A' 'B' and 'C'

1. It is pleasant to record that this informant has now happily remarried and has celebrated her silver wedding.

companies of the 175th Infantry Regiment of the 29th Division, from Baltimore, some of whom had got to know him well since their arrival in the previous September. As they left the church he found himself given 'a lot of names and addresses . . . jotted down on scraps of paper, with the words "Please, Father, write to my mom" '. A few days afterwards he visited the hotels which his flock were now preparing to leave and 'heard their confessions in corners of rooms or under staircases as their buddies bustled around carrying all sorts of things to the lorries. And so they pulled out and a strange, sad silence fell over St Ives, so accustomed to hear the sound of marching feet early each morning.'

In Nelson's navy men had dressed for action by putting on clean linen, which was less likely to cause wounds to become infected, and the Americans, impressed British observers remarked, also prepared for combat as if for a parade. One Wren stationed in Newhaven noticed how the American ships in the harbour 'caused amusement by the amount of washing the crews did. They were always hauling up their "smalls" between the masts, even travelling up the harbour with their lines of washing waving, which was not the kind of thing the Royal Navy would do.' The visitor to Salcombe, previously quoted, where in late May 'every empty house was filled with American sailors', recalls being equally intrigued at the sight of 'an apple tree in a garden festooned with their white hats, washed and hung up to dry, looking like some strange fruits'.

On 1 June, surely a little late in the day for training in elementary tactics and fieldcraft, the *Stars and Stripes* began publishing hints on how to 'Stay Alive in Battle: Keep to the high ground. . . . Watch out for "dead" Germans. They may shoot you in the back.' On the following day it was able to reassure its readers that, even in the front line they would not lack for entertainment. 'Soldiers of the ETC's Special Service companies,' it reported, 'trained to the hilt for combat, are preparing for the war's biggest job of under-fire entertaining. . . . In mess tents and field hospitals, perhaps in a clearing under shell-torn trees . . . their orders call for them to set up their movie projectors, PA [Public Address] system–radios, bring forth their musical instruments and baseball bats.'

27

THE FAR SHORE

'You will enter the continent of Europe and . . . undertake operations aimed at the heart of Germany and the destruction of her armed forces.'

— *Directive to the Supreme Commander, Allied Expeditionary Force, 12 February 1944.*

By early June 1944, the signs that D-Day was almost here were everywhere unmistakable. One woman working in the post office at Newbury remembers the strange quiet as the troop carriers which had for months been flying day and night on exercises from Greenham Common, overlooking the town, were grounded, waiting to set off in earnest, and the base was ringed by armed sentries. Briefly one night the peace was broken by a solitary shot, when a Texan sentry, waking from an illicit doze to see a rabbit nearby, had, without thinking, lifted his rifle and fired. Hastily he had hidden the dead rabbit and 'pulled through' his rifle, but not before the base had been subjected to 'an all night full security search', which yielded nothing.

Tidworth had been full of GIs as long as most people could now remember, but that spring, one seventeen-year-old from Appleshaw observed, 'Perham and Tidworth Hill were so crammed with tanks you could scarcely walk between them'. Then suddenly they were gone, leaving only a lingering smell of American coffee beneath the beech trees. A mile or two away one school boy observed an even plainer clue to coming events when 'the large convoys passing through the village on a summer evening', watched by 'us villagers from the village green and cottage doorways', instead of 'as usual turning towards Tidworth continued on towards Southampton'.

Nearer the coast the signs were even easier to read. One woman working in a canteen on the Isle of Wight remembers looking across the Solent and barely accepting the evidence of her own eyes. 'It was alive with craft. Packed tight.' A secretary at Falmouth found the pavements near the docks had sprouted tents overnight, full of GIs waiting to go on board ship. A Plymouth girl, arriving at the barracks at Crownhill to say goodbye, found the gates locked; the men were confined to quarters, awaiting embarkation, but eagerly shook hands, like prisoners, through the bars.

Although the secret of where and when the landings were to be made was

astonishingly well kept, the men who were to form the first wave of the
assault were in little doubt as they finally left the camps where they had
lived and trained for several months that their destination was the French
coast. The journey was, however, a slow and protracted one. The seaborne
assault troops went first to 'concentration areas', where men not taking part
in the initial landings were left behind, then from 26 May to 'marshalling
areas' nearer the coast, consisting of closely guarded barbed-wire enclosures,
patrolled by unwontedly uncommunicative sentries. A Dorchester woman
remembers seeing troop transporters whose sides were draped with barbed-
wire, to prevent 'careless talk' during the frequent halts, and notices near
small encampments reading: 'Please do not talk to the troops'. Now at last
the men were briefed on their missions, though maps and models still bore
false names, and were divided into individual shiploads. At last on Tuesday,
30 May, those facing the longest journey began to file aboard their transport and tank landing craft, both a far cry, except for the seasickness and
overcrowding, from the great liners on which they had arrived.

Helping to man one small ship on which 200 men of the 29th Division
were to sail to the landing area known as OMAHA was a naval officer from
Iowa, now president of a bank. Looking back, he recalls the 'old inns' and
'quaint villages' of 'Totnes, the Dart river, Dartington', but, most of all,
'Fowey, where we stayed for the week preceding D-Day', while the men
played poker for high stakes and he cooked them much-appreciated doughnuts. Time in those last few days was slow to pass. 'The day before we
sailed for France,' he remembers, 'our main and only entertainment was
watching a couple make love on the shore. We only had a few sets of bino-
culars, and it was rewarding to have a pair but also frustrating to share
them.'

Destined for UTAH, the other American landing area, was the Sergeant
from Connecticut whose stay at Seaton, with the 4th Division, has previously been described:

> We went by truck to the outskirts of Torquay, to a tent city on the side of a hill,
> and we knew for sure that this was to be no manoeuvre but for the record. . . . At
> this time we were getting briefings each day. Many GIs had nerves . . . which were
> getting closer to the surface, everyone was on edge and eager to go.

These men belonged to Force 'U', intended for beaches TARE and
UNCLE in the UTAH sector, on the extreme right of the attack, their
destination being the area to the west of the Vire Estuary, at the base of
the Cotentin Peninsula. They came from VII Corps, whose 4th Division was scheduled to touch down first, to be followed by the 90th and
9th Divisions. Besides Torquay, Force 'U' embarked at Dartmouth, a
small, old town clinging to steep hillsides above the Dart estuary, at
Brixham, a small seaside resort with a picturesque harbour and at Salcombe,

an even smaller place with a peacetime population of only 2000, hitherto famous only as the inspiration for Tennyson's poem 'Crossing the Bar', the strip of sand and rock protecting the harbour entrance.

While Force 'U', which faced the longest journey of all the Allied armies, was already at sea, Force 'O', drawn from V Corps, was filing aboard a second armada of troop-carrying vessels, some forty-odd miles to the east, at the other tip of Lyme Bay, where four years before Hitler had planned to land the follow-up forces for *his* invasion. The Americans embarked from Poole, in peacetime a large if undistinguished holiday resort, from Portland, a much-bombed peninsula of solid rock, containing a prison, a famous naval base and little else; and Weymouth, a large, somewhat unattractive town with fine sandy beaches and a normal peacetime population approaching 40 000. In 1944 its amenities found themselves in demand for unexpected purposes. In the pleasure park known as the Alexandra Gardens the waiting GIs, as one humorist wrote, had to 'line up for their last chance of Brussels sprouts', while the small theatre, used by pre-war concert parties, now sheltered the production of its life, with huge maps of the French beaches providing the back drop for briefing sessions, before the men embarked, most inappropriately, from the Pleasure Pier. The vehicles meanwhile were mainly loaded at Portland, adjoining Weymouth, but separated from the mainland by a long causeway and bridge.

Force 'O' was destined to make its next contact with dry land on four beaches, stretching for about five miles along the shores of Normandy, part of the OMAHA sector which covered about twenty miles of coastline from the right flank of the British sector at Colleville-sur-Mer to the left flank of Force 'U' (for UTAH) near the mouth of the River Vire. In the lead were to be the 116th Infantry, of the 29th Division, landing on the two right-hand beaches labelled CHARLIE and DOG, and the 16th Infantry, of the 1st Division, storming EASY and FOX. In the second wave, also landing on D-Day, were the 18th, 27th and 115th infantry regiments, of the 1st Division, with, waiting offshore, the 9th Division, reinforcing UTAH, and the 90th Division, securing OMAHA. On the left of the main OMAHA sector the 2nd Ranger Battalion was to carry out, it was hoped, a classic assault operation, scaling a cliff to capture a key gun emplacement.

Leaving England last but arriving in France first were the paratroopers and glider troops of the 82nd Airborne Division. Their journey to the war, recalled by the Staff Captain previously quoted, began in Leicester, by train. The date was 28 May 1944:

After several hours' ride we left the train at a small country village. I . . . remember the name Honiton.[1] We marched, perhaps an hour, through a picturesque

1. Honiton is in fact a small town in Devon, not far from Exeter, and famous in the past for its lacemaking. It had ealier in 1944 been occupied by the 4th Division, which had just before D-Day moved on to embarkation areas near Torquay.

countryside and finally entered a very wooded area which was completely en-
circled with an impregnable wire fence. Pyramidal tents were already set up for us
and I remember the next several days being spent visiting a large tent daily to study
the sandbox model of what would supposedly be the exact area in which our unit
would land in France. . . . The rest of the time was spent in writing last letters home
to loved ones and checking and re-checking weapons and personal equipment. . . .

I remember meeting a Sioux Indian from South Dakota, a World War I veteran,
who was in the intelligence section of one of the parachute units and who was
expected to communicate 'in clear' in his native tongue after landing in France,
since it was highly unlikely a German monitor could decipher whatever he transmitted.

Late in May, General Eisenhower had moved from near Kingston to
Southwick House behind Portsmouth, and it was here, in the early hours of
Sunday, 4 June, that he decided, because of the bad weather, that D-Day
must be postponed for twenty-four hours. The unexpected, additional,
delay was 'agonizing', remembers the naval officer previously quoted,
waiting to set off from Fowey for OMAHA; to the Sergeant who had
sailed from Torquay as one of a boatload assured that 'we would hit the
UTAH beaches in eighteen hours', it was even worse, for they faced another
day of close-packed misery tossing on the grey and choppy waters of the
Channel. But their ordeal was almost over. At 4.15 a.m. on the morning of
Monday 5 June, with the familiar English rain so detested by all GIs lashing
the windows, after a 'mile-long trip through muddy roads' from a 'little
camp . . . shaking and shuddering under a wind of almost hurricane pro-
portions', General Eisenhower made his famous decision 'to go ahead with
the attack' on the following morning. Unknown to those around him, he
had already drafted a communiqué to be issued in case of catastrophe,
personally accepting all the blame. Knowing that he could do no more and
that all now depended on the gods of war and the ordinary fighting man,
the Supreme Commander spent the latter part of D–1 visiting some of the
far-flung headquarters of his vast command. A WAAF officer – who like
all who worked closely with him considered him 'a wonderful commander'
and a 'delightful personality, full of humour' – was given the place of honour
next to him at the air force station in Oxfordshire where he dined that night.
'We talked about general things,' she remembers. 'He told me how pleased
he was I got on well with "his boys", asked me did I like their food? . . .
We talked about America . . . the difficulty the GIs had in evaluating our
money and those awful bicycles some of the British naughtily flogged them.
. . . After grace at the end of the meal he shook my hand and said, "Good
luck," and I said, "And to you, sir, and your boys." ' On leaving, Eisenhower drove to Greenham Common, near Newbury, an airfield which
three years before had been an unfenced expanse of grass and heather, and
was now laden with gliders assembled on the nearby racecourse. By the

time 'Ike' left, the noise of the last slow-moving Dakota, heading for the Normandy coast laden with one of the first Airborne Division, had died away. It was half an hour after midnight and D-Day had begun.

Among the first to learn that the great decision had finally been made were the men, or, in the British forces, more commonly, women, manning the signal and radar stations ashore. The Wren Petty Officer at Lyme Regis, previously quoted, was on duty that night as, by her own choice, she had been every night for the past month, being unwilling to entrust the lives of 'her' GIs to anyone else. Also on duty was a young male cryptographer of the Ninth Air Force from Braddock Heights, Maryland, training at an RAF Group Headquarters at Hill House, near Box in Wiltshire:

At Hill House, the plotting room was built many many hundreds of feet under the ground. You had to go down by elevator. The day before the invasion, I was on the eleven to seven shift at night. When I got down to the Ops' Room . . . we were told that the invasion would begin on the morrow. We were not allowed to go up again, and in fact, we were able to watch the fascinating groupings for the Normandy invasion right on the Ops' map which was painted in front of us on a huge board. We traced the ships as they began their journey across the board. We watched with utter disbelief as the hundreds of planes left the English coast heading for the French. Finally, seven o'clock came around, and we were allowed up. I can recall clearly coming up out of the elevator and walking out into the sunlight and listening. You could hear the distant sounds and I kept thinking to myself about all the men who must be dying on such a beautiful day.

One Eighth Air Force Flight Engineer, whose airman's eye-view of the assembled armada a few days earlier has already been quoted, had a restless night, listening to the incessant sound of RAF night bombers passing over Suffolk towards the coast and then returning. Now it was the American Air Force's turn:

As dawn approached our planes began their droning. Actually thousands of them in their familiar tight V formations, ever circling to gain altitude and finally heading towards the east. The sky looked like we were being invaded by locusts. Some of the early birds were returning to load up again and make another trip. Having been one of the early Americans to cross the Channel when fifty to a hundred planes was an enormous flight, it put a lump in my throat and a tear in my eye. The Luftwaffe had had its day and now we were having ours. I had the feeling that our lost buddies were flying with them to spur them on.

By now the landing was well under way. The first British gliders, of the 6th Airborne Division, had touched down twenty minutes after midnight; the first American parachutists, of the 82nd Airborne Division, dropped to earth on French soil about an hour and a half later. Dawn, or 'first light', as the soldiers liked to call it, was at 5.55 a.m. Thirty-five minutes later, the landing craft of the 4th US Division grounded on UTAH, followed around

7.30 a.m. away to the east by the 1st Battalions of the Hampshire Regiment and the Dorset Regiment leading the British airborne assault.

And so the long years of preparation and training reached fulfilment. What happened to the American armies on the Far Shore, as they always called the Continent, is outside the scope of this book, but two men's experiences that day may typify those of the million others for whom Britain had briefly been home. This was the short but painful experience of combat of the Sergeant from Connecticut who had lived at Seaton and had last stormed ashore on Slapton Sands:

As we got behind UTAH beach I was wounded in the left heel and thigh by a shell from a German 88[1] . . . . A US Navy Non-Com with a big .45 automatic pistol in his waving hand headed two German soldiers my way. They picked me up, at his bidding, and carried me to an aid station beside one of the German pill-boxes. The next morning, before dawn, I was put on a ship and evacuated to Portland, England, but not before I was wounded again, while in this first-aid area, against the bunker. This time I got it in the right lung. . . . After being hit for the second time I . . . didn't know too much, but I knew I had been put on a ship for evacuation back to England. It was a so-called LST and we were placed along a narrow deck, right under the muzzles of some of the ship's guns, which were always firing, whenever I came to. After about a week and a half, of which time I have no recollection, as I had been through an operation to remove shrapnel from my right lung . . . I learned we had docked at Portland and I was in a US station hospital . . . near the town of Blandford not far from Bournemouth . . . I wrote to friends in Seaton and used to get visitors from my adopted English town. I was flown back to a hospital in Staten Island, New York, in October.[2]

Another man who went into action that day was a Staff Captain of the 82nd Airborne Division, whose arrival at Honiton a few days earlier has already been described:

Finally on the night of 5 June I remember getting word that tomorrow would be our departure date. There was no sleep that night and I remember our column marching out of our area about 2 a.m. . . . walking about an hour and finally arriving at a large airfield at the top of a long hill. We were directed to our gliders and sat around for an hour or so before entering the aircraft. . . . About 5 a.m. we departed by serial and each glider was towed by a C-47 airplane. In the early daylight I recall seeing the air literally filled with aircraft converging from all directions and from many airfields in Southern England as we headed across the Channel for our rendezvous before heading for our drop zone. I remember seeing people in every street and on every doorstep waving at us as we passed overhead. A Staff Sergeant . . . a Pfc who was my jeep driver, and myself, flew in that particular glider . . . together with some minor assorted equipment. I remember sitting in the

1. The German 88 mm cannon was the most effective, and feared, of all field artillery pieces.

2. This GI recovered from his wounds and is now an electrical contractor in Connecticut.

jeep with the driver behind the wheel and how sick he became and, although this is hard to believe, I actually dozed much of the way across the Channel . . . The Channel was filled with ships of all descriptions and it made me feel very confident to know that all that support would soon be right with us. It almost seemed to me that one could have walked across the Channel that morning without getting one's feet wet because of the continuous line of ships.

They 'landed in a field near St Mère Église in somewhat of a crash landing', for 'the pilot had misjudged the height of the hedgerow surrounding the field and knocked the wheels off the glider', but happily no one was hurt and this officer survived to fight his way through the notorious 'hedgerow country of Normandy' until late July, when his division 'returned to England for rest and recreation'.

As the first troops were landing in Normandy reinforcements were still passing into the British Isles. That morning the members of one Harbour Craft Company, responsible for operating tugboats and inshore salvage work, arrived in Glasgow aboard the *Queen Elizabeth*. As their train, on an elevated track, drew level with the upper windows of buildings alongside the track, 'women leaned out of their windows and yelled, "It's D-Day. They're landing in Normandy." ' By nightfall the men were, one remembers, themselves far nearer the war, in 'a city park covered with tents' in Plymouth, followed soon after by a move to the former Royal Naval College at Dartmouth.

The first civilians to hear that the invasion had begun were the Germans and the reports of the landings already broadcast by German radio were quoted, without comment, in the BBC news at 8 a.m. At about the same time, at the Ministry of Information Headquarters in the Senate House of London University, the news was released to correspondents, but the doors were locked while they wrote their stories, until at 9.30 the presiding officer dropped his arm as a signal that the rush to the telephones could begin. 'In the next fifteen seconds,' he announced, 'the invasion flash will go out to the world.' At 9.32 the BBC ushered in a broadcast by General Eisenhower with the simple announcement 'D-Day has come'. In the United States the long-awaited communiqué flashed along the West Coast at 12.33 a.m. local time, while many people were still up. Excited listeners telephoned their friends and in some places the church bells roused the sleeping people, as though victory had already been won. In many a darkened town lights began to come on, shining through windows where hung the paper stars proudly revealing an absent member of the family, away in the forces. In New York it was 3.30 a.m., but many people were still about and learned the news from the message spelled out in lights on the newscasting machines on the front of the newspaper offices, or from taxi drivers, who, having heard it on their cab radios, pulled in to the kerbs and hailed passers-by, while in factories working on the night shift it was announced over the public address system.

Many people in Southern England had already guessed the news. Since before dawn the skies of Southern England had been filled with the drone of aircraft, many with the yellow-and-black-striped gliders, like giant wasps, swooping silently behind them. One girl living at Whitchurch, whose social life had for two years revolved round the 2nd Armoured Division at Tidworth, alerted by the gliders passing over, phoned an officer friend on the administrative staff. 'If we come to the dance on Saturday will we see our boy friends?' she asked. ' "No, Jean," he said, "I'm afraid not." ' The girls' dashing partners of many a mess party now had a sterner date to keep. A Plymouth girl, arriving for work in the Home Guard office at the docks at 9 a.m., looked down at 'hundreds of GIs boarding boats . . . and . . . knew they were bound for France. . . . My heart ached. I could hardly see for tears.' Other girls hurried to the Hoe, the great open space close to the centre of the city which commands a fine view of its sea approaches, to find that the vast armada of craft recently assembled there had vanished in the night.

Everyone's thoughts were now fixed on Normandy, where by mid-morning it was clear that on UTAH the landing had gone better than anyone had dared to hope. Casualties had been almost unbelievably light; by far the least in any of the five sectors. On OMAHA it was very different. The opposition there was the worst encountered anywhere on D-Day, the losses being at a level which General Eisenhower had feared might be suffered everywhere. At 11 a.m. the German commander of the division behind the beach was confident enough to divert his reserves to attack the British on his right flank. But by midday the first GIs from OMAHA, though as yet in small, disorganized parties, were off the beach and beginning to make their way inland, as those from UTAH had been doing since dawn. Just before 5 p.m. the Chief of Staff of the German Seventh Army received a signal reporting 'the desire of OKW' – the German High Command – 'that the enemy in the bridgehead be destroyed by the evening of June 6th as there is a danger of fresh landings by sea and air'. But like many German desires this was to remain unfulfilled. The build-up continued through the remaining hours of daylight and long after dark, until by midnight 57500 Americans had been brought ashore, plus another 15500 who had dropped from the skies by parachute or glider. Some units, especially the Rangers, and the engineers and infantry first ashore on OMAHA, had suffered appallingly, but overall American casualties on D-Day amounted to about 6000, of whom 700 were airborne troops. Thus about one man in eleven who landed that day was killed, wounded or missing.

Although this was above all the ordinary doughboy's day – and he paid by far the heaviest price for the ground captured – it would have been im-possible without the sailors and the airmen. On D-Day the full extent of the American presence in the British Isles was revealed and Anglo-American co-operation attained its peak. British paratroopers flew to battle in American troop-carriers and gliders; American infantry were carried to the beaches in British troopships and ferried ashore in British landing craft. Of the 10 000 first-line combat aircraft available on D-Day, just over half were flown by Americans, and the United States IX Troop Carrier Command operated nearly 1700 aircraft and 500 gliders on D-Day, compared with 700 and 350 respectively flown by the RAF. At sea the reverse was true. Although 53 000 US sailors contributed to OPERATION NEPTUNE, as the assault phase of OVERLORD was called, they formed little more than a quarter of the naval personnel involved and of the 1200 warships of all types which escorted the invading armada (totalling all told some 7000 vessels) or bombarded the enemy positions only 200 were American, although they included such famous names as the battleships *Texas* and *Arkansas*, the cruiser *Tuscaloosa*, and nineteen destroyers. Both the airmen and the sailors escaped with relatively minor losses. Only 127 Allied aircraft failed to return from 14 000 sorties, and though many landing craft were lost, few seamen were drowned, although the USS *Osprey*, a small minesweeper, earned the sad distinction of being the first casualty of the whole operation when it hit a mine off the Normandy coast late on 5 June and sank with the loss of six sailors.

By the time civilians in Britain were going home from work that Tuesday, the first cautious headlines in the evening newspapers were proclaiming, 'Our troops are ashore and moving inland', and that evening the leaders of both nations broadcast to their peoples. At 8 p.m. British time King George VI called on his subjects to join in prayer 'as the great crusade sets forth', while two hours later, East Coast time, President Roosevelt read a special prayer he had composed for the occasion. At no time since Pearl Harbour had the two nations been so close.

The initial landings were, of course, only the beginning. While the first waves of assault troops had for security reasons been kept apart from the local population, follow-up units, their destination no longer a secret, found themselves, whenever they stopped, surrounded by Britons eager to wish them luck. One Lieutenant from Rhode Island, a Fire Control Officer in an artillery battalion, remembers D-Day in Arundel, five miles from the Sussex coast. Here, all through the night, the sentries had 'watched the planes and gliders of the airborne troops' heading for the coast. Now it was their own unit's turn.

At 0900, we received orders to load up and prepare to move to a marshalling area prior to our movement to Normandy. We were . . . ready . . . shortly after noon, but it was to be more than eight hours before we would leave Arundel.

While we waited, many of the Arundel people put aside their own problems and visited with us. Some of them even brought out food and tea to share with us. There were many tearful farewells when the trucks finally started to move. . . . If there was a special girl as far as I was concerned it was the elder daughter of a local police sergeant. . . . We had a number of dates [but] she had a friend in the RAF and I had at least a tentative arrangement with an American nurse who was stationed in the South Pacific. Hence . . . our relationship was . . . most frequently a friendly bantering of a boy versus girl type. We were sober and serious only the last afternoon and evening in Arundel as we waited for the convoy to move out to the marshalling areas. At the last moment, she kissed me and hugged me tightly for just a few seconds as we said goodbye.

In many towns, as each formation moved out, others moved in, and convoy followed convoy through the streets, or pulled up in the residential roads to wait its turn to embark. A Southampton woman remembers how delighted the hot and sweating crews of the tanks parked outside her family's house were to be invited in to wash and shave. Her mother readily agreed to press the 'pants' of one man, which he hastily slipped off for the purpose, while other GIs enjoyed the lemonade offered to them or slept on the family's front lawn beneath a heavily laden peach tree, a peaceful interlude before battle. A resident of Dorchester remembers seeing a priest standing on the corner of one street 'all day long while he made the sign of the cross as each vehicle went by, and the men bowed their heads'. The consolation she and her neighbours offered was less spiritual: jugs of tea, 'a wash and brush-up', and on one occasion, 'late one Saturday night . . . three pieces of apple tart', which the men enjoyed after 'sitting on the top of their tank opening a tiny tin of meat with a huge knife'. An hour later they called to press cigarettes upon their benefactors, although the visit was not wholly appreciated, for 'one man had a hand grenade in his cap, which he evidently thought I would like to see. I was scared stiff . . . and pressed him to take the beastly thing outside.'

The convoys pouring through Dorchester, directed by the 'Snowdrops' on duty at every street corner, were making for Weymouth, which, as the weather improved late in June and early July, presented a strangely incongruous picture. One local woman remembers how as she and her husband 'sat in a shelter and enjoyed the sun shining on the promenade, trucks . . . were unloading troops for embarkation. . . . An American Red Cross van was pouring out music and Red Cross girls were dispensing coffee and doughnuts to the waiting crowds.' The men, this eyewitness found, were far less worried about the dangers ahead of them than about 'the sea crossing. They had had a rough one coming to this country and didn't fancy another one like that.'

28

GOODBYE, ENGLAND

'I raise you twenty demob. points.'

> – Gambling GI in Stars and Stripes *cartoon, 12 June 1945.*

'AFTER D-Day there was a strong feeling for the Americans from the locals. The ones that were still in the area were held in high regard and were treated in pubs.' This memory of a Reading man would undoubtedly be echoed by other civilians elsewhere. Far more remarkable was the softening of traditional enmities. British and American troops, one member of the ATS observed, 'mixed more freely than ever before. They were comrades in arms and had been through the same kind of hell.' In Hull, noticed one Englishman in astonishment, even 'the coloureds were accepted' by white GIs at public dances; 'they had been in action'. A Wymondham woman also remembers seeing the two races mix for the first time without trouble in the wards of the 231st Station Hospital, now receiving its first battle casualties.

It was indeed the flow of American wounded from Normandy which finally brought home to the British public the reality of life just across the Channel. A Weymouth schoolmaster who a few days earlier had watched his boys cheer the departing convoys heading for Portland spent a Sunday morning soon afterwards watching 'a constant stream of stretcher parties' unloading men from 'three large tank landing craft' on to one of the newly built 'hards'. As a skilled first-aider he was struck by the 'good work already done on the other side of the Channel' in the shape of 'limbs already splinted or in plaster'. The effect on troops embarking for the same beach, OMAHA, was different. One naval officer from Iowa remembers the almost visible drop in morale among the reinforcements filing aboard his ship as they caught sight of the bandaged and blood-stained figures being discharged alongside them. A Wren Petty Officer at Lyme Regis remembers walking on the morning after D-Day – D+1 in military jargon – to 'where the main road from Weymouth to Bridport passed underneath in a tunnel. The American ambulances were coming along in a constant stream the whole half-hour I stood there.'

The arrangements made for coping with the wounded were as humane and efficient as everything else about the American army's preparations for D-Day. Five hospital trains had been made ready in the southern counties, two based at Bournemouth and others at Exeter, Temple Combe, and Westbury. A British fireman (i.e. driver's mate) who served on one of them recalls that they were excellently equipped with 'hammocks, hot and cold water, kitchen, surgical ward and even a padded room, which fortunately was never used on our train'. Apart from the British driver and fireman, who 'ate, lived and slept' on board, the trains were manned by five US officers, mainly doctors, and about forty nurses and NCOs, all of whom worked well together. Their high morale was very necessary, for the work was extremely hard. This train usually loaded up at Netley, near Southampton, before carrying its passengers to destinations as far apart as Henley, Leominster ['Lemster'], Malvern and Abergavenny. Its official complement of 385 passengers was regularly raised to 'as many as they could fit in'. For the fireman this meant 'hard work on the shovel. . . . I lost about two stone superfluous fat the first month.' But 'owing to the exceptionally good food I was able to keep up with miles of heavy slogging', and he looks back on the men he worked with as 'a grand crowd'.

The nearness of the battlefield meant that a few GIs were soon being seen again in their old haunts. A Tavistock woman remembers being astounded to meet in a local café two GI friends whom she thought had left the town for ever only two weeks before. They were convalescing after being wounded, and were able to give her news of other friends. Gradually in such ways many families learned of the fate of men they had befriended and as postal services to Normandy began, only a week or two later, more news filtered back across the Channel. One Paisley housewife's experiences were typical of many, for her letter to an 'adopted GI was returned with the word "Deceased" rubber-stamped on it. . . . The British Red Cross were very helpful and found out for me that he had been wounded in the landing in France and had died four days later in hospital.'

Some men were visibly scarred by their recent experiences. A British airman serving with an American air transport unit near Northampton, from which 'Dakotas, aircrews and paratroopers' had suddenly vanished 'in the early dawn of D-Day' remembers 'meeting a paratrooper while patrolling a day or two later. He still had blacking on his face, was obviously severely shocked and incoherent.' A Solihull woman was equally horrified at the change in the infantryman who returned from France to see her family. 'Joe came in and collapsed. His nerves were completely shattered. He could not even cross the road alone. He had gone out a happy laughing boy and came back a complete wreck.'

On 9 June Allied aircraft began to use landing strips on French soil and by the end of the month more than thirty squadrons were flying from bases inside the beachhead, which on 10 June had become a continuous

front. Each American soldier or airman who landed in France meant one
fewer in Britain and on 12 June one Londoner noted wryly in his diary that
an Englishman could now again secure a taxi. Week by week the number of
GIs in Britain visibly dwindled. One large contingent formed 'Follow-up
Force "B" ', which sailed from the ancient deep-water port of Falmouth,
in the far west of Cornwall, and from Plymouth many GIs embarked via the
same Mayflower Steps in the Barbican down which the Pilgrim Fathers had
set off on their quest for liberty. The main departure points, however,
remained Portland and Weymouth, where on the Esplanade a monument
presented by the 14th Major Port Detachment still stands, commemorating
the passage through the twin ports between D-Day and the end of the war
of nearly 518000 men and 114000 vehicles.

At first the British troops in Normandy outnumbered the American, for
although between 10 and 16 June 278000 GIs were landed this was still
1000 fewer than those from British and Canadian regiments. But by the end
of July the balance had decisively tilted in the Americans' favour and they
now numbered 900000 compared to the 660000 British. Thereafter the
American army became increasingly the major partner in the alliance until
by VE-day there were 3000000 GIs on the Continent in sixty-one divisions,
though many had reached the battlefield via the Mediterranean or direct from
the United States and had not passed through the British Isles.

After D-Day the two operations involving American troops which most
closely concerned British civilians were the Allied landings at Arnhem in
September – an honourable defeat, which ended all hope of winning the war
in 1944 – and the Battle of the Ardennes, fought out in nightmare conditions
of snow, fog and confusion around Christmas, 'when the American armies
finally halted the totally unexpected last German offensive of the war. One
woman who worked at the ARC Club in Watford remembers the sad day
when she learned that many of the 200 GIs recently stationed there had been
killed in the Arnhem battles. 'It is their faces I always remember when I
think of the GIs,' she confesses. 'I have often thought how proud their
mothers would have been of them had they seen them at a dance the evening
before they had their orders.' The Ardennes battle, in which the 101st
Airborne Division, fighting as ordinary infantry, managed though surrounded to hold Bastogne, the key to the whole front, took an even heavier toll
of American lives. One Henley woman remembers the Colonel of one artillery regiment replying sadly to her request for news of other old friends,
Please don't ask me who has gone.'

Although the airborne units tended to suffer the heaviest casualties, they
also enjoyed periods of 'rest and recreation' back in England, and one officer
remembers as the most agreeable period of his war the months he spent after
returning from France in July 1944 at Pheasy Farms, a large requisitioned
housing estate near Birmingham. From here he made almost daily visits to

the Perry Barr dog track, to the Princess Hotel, where 'Allen Rook and his three-piece string ensemble played delightfully at tea-time', and to the Repertory Theatre, where old playbills featuring Greer Garson, who had begun her career there, still decorated the walls. Other evenings passed agreeably 'standing in line for fish-and-chips' or attending the Cattle Market Hotel for the ceremonial opening of the solitary nightly bottle of Scotch 'with forty or more people clamouring for a drink', until in late September he returned to the war.[1]

But inevitably most American thoughts were now concentrated on the other side of the Channel. The *Stars and Stripes*, which over the past two years had laboured so indefatigably to interpret to its readers the bizarre customs of the British, was by mid June advising the GIs in its familiar man-to-man way on how to conduct themselves among an even more alien race:

> Don't be surprised if a Frenchman steps up to you and kisses you. That doesn't mean he's queer. It just means he's emotional, French and darn glad to see you. . . .
>
> You'll see a lot of funny little iron cages on French street corners. They're called *pissoirs* or tin tabernacles. They're simple public comfort stations and serve the same functions as the underground affairs you find in British towns.

Strangely enough, the *Stars and Stripes* also felt its readers needed advice on coping with the opposite sex:

> It is not true that all French women are 'easy'. . . . Any guy who has the idea that the way to make friends and influence Frenchmen is to slip up alongside of the first good-looking gal he sees and slip her a quick pat on the fanny is going to be in for trouble. . . . It's easy to tell the difference between 'good' and 'bad' girls in France. The nice ones don't smoke on the street, nor do they drink too much in public. The whores smoke as they walk, give you plenty of the old come-hither look, wiggle their shanks, use too much make-up and otherwise look just like the commandos around Piccadilly or the City Hall in Belfast.

But there was not as yet much time to enjoy the delights of French social life; the war was still very far from over. In mid June the flying-bomb attack on London began, reaching its peak in July and August and prompting a wry joke in the *Stars and Stripes*: 'All GIs who volunteer for service in France will be considered cowards.' In September, as the V–1 bombardment tailed off, the V–2 rockets began to arrive, and both missiles continued to be fired until almost the end of the war.

Then in mid December came the Ardennes offensive. I can well remember with what consternation and near disbelief the news of von Rundstedt's major attack was received even in my own branch of SHAEF remote from the fighting in South Kensington. In headquarters nearer the front it came as a devastating surprise, although General Eisenhower appreciated the

1. This informant survived, to return years later a Lieutenant-Colonel.

seriousness of the new threat far sooner than his subordinate commanders. By early January the danger was over, after the famous 'Battle of the Bulge', which had involved more American troops, and heavier American casualties, than any previous action in history. By February victory was again in the air. The first American troops had already crossed the German frontier; on 8 February a major advance began. On the night of 22 March came the most important milestone since D-Day, the crossing of the Rhine by the 5th US Infantry Division, followed a day later by the main Allied assault.

And then, on 12 April, the whole Allied world suffered another totally unexpected blow, the sudden death of President Roosevelt. Many people remarked that one saw suddenly a very different side to the usually carefree GIs, who were in their turn impressed at how the English seemed to share their own grief. One army postal clerk, from Connecticut, stationed near Warrington, remembers 'being stopped on the street by at least a dozen people who expressed their sympathy to me as if he had been one of my own family'. The Stars and Stripes flew everywhere at half-mast and all Red Cross clubs in the United Kingdom were closed until after the funeral. At Rainbow Corner that melancholy afternoon a large board in the entrance proclaimed the sad news, and 'within a few minutes', observed a reporter, 'the Piccadilly area was as quiet as a small back street'. It is a night still remembered by one Norwich girl because her boy friend, with whom she had been 'going steady' for two years, 'came into the city' on one of the dance trucks 'with the news that dances were cancelled. . . . He was sent home before our next date.' A British member of the staff, arriving at the military hospital at Taunton found 'one tough Sergeant with tears in his eyes. "Ma'am, to me it feels like a personal loss. I've never known any other President." '

Despite the shock of the President's death, April was a month of victories. The German army was clearly beaten at last; the Shermans and Grants rolled forward almost unchallenged; the B–17s and P–47s roamed at will through skies empty of enemy aircraft. The month came to a joyous conclusion when on the 30th the Führer killed himself, thus cheating of his legitimate prey one Pfc from Sulphur Springs, Hopkins County, Texas, who before leaving home had been officially appointed a deputy sheriff and given a warrant authorizing him 'to arrest one Adolf Hitler for murder and high crimes' and to bring him back 'to answer a charge by the state of Texas'.

On 7 May General Jodl formally surrendered the surviving German armies in the West to General Eisenhower's Chief of Staff in a schoolroom at Rheims.[1] When at 9.30 the next morning the news reached New York,

1. A singularly ill-judged attempt was made to hold up the release of the news, to please the Russians. It merely created irritation and confusion in both Britain and the United States.

couples danced in Times Square, servicemen found themselves being
kissed by passing girls, and a deluge of paper descended in celebration into
the streets of Manhattan.

That day, Tuesday, 8 May 1945, the *Stars and Stripes* brought out its
largest type for the jubilant headline: 'Germany Quits'. All men on pass, it
was announced, need not report back for forty-eight hours. By now there
were in fact few GIs left in London, and, though I spent that evening – after
a day spent packing up for the long-delayed move to the Continent next
day – in the West End, I noticed few Americans, though some could be
seen singing and dancing on the Tube and joining in the ritual shouts of
'We want the King' outside Buckingham Palace. Already a GI in a British
city was becoming conspicuous and a Cardiff woman remembers two she
saw that night:

> Outside the City Hall, thousands and thousands of people gathered, completely
> covering the gardens and lawns. . . . Among the crowd were two dark Americans,
> boy and girl, in service uniform. They danced with an abandon of joy the new
> dance which was then becoming the vogue, 'jive', which we had never seen before.
> The crowd with one accord formed a circle round them, and professional dancers
> could never have achieved such a unison of movement in pure joy as those two
> young people.

One Preston woman, then a teenager, remembers taking a young American Lieutenant on a tour of the town: 'Everyone was dancing in the streets,
and I walked him miles! We went to the town hall to join in the celebrations
[and] I took him around the back streets to see the ordinary people who had
collected wood, furniture, old tea-chests, etc., and were having terrific
bonfires. It was two in the morning when I finally got home.' At Chorley in
Lancashire the switchboard operator at one hostel remembers, 'The Americans were confined to barracks, because there was a shortage of beer,' and
some well-meaning officer had 'felt the British were more entitled to it'.
But it needed more than an order to keep Americans indoors that night.
When 'we all went into town we met an array of Americans all carrying the
remains of the blankets which they had used to scramble over the barbed-
wire boundary to get out of camp'.

This was VE night in Salisbury as witnessed by a twenty-five-year-old
widow, who after working until midnight was escorted home by a GI
Sergeant through milling crowds of cheerful GIs:

> The pubs had been drunk dry. 'Funny things', blown up like balloons, being
> waved about, milk bottles rolling down the streets. 'Give me your arm,' said the
> Sergeant . . . 'I'll change places with you, Mac,' was yelled out a dozen times. The
> auctioneers' stand which stood in the Market Square, something like an upright
> piano, with an open front on four iron wheels [was] crammed full of GIs [and]

others were dragging it around. As we walked up Castle Road they came tearing round a corner with the thing, turned it right over . . . 'Guess we're the only two not celebrating,' said the Sergeant. 'Everything is closed, there's nothing to do,' I replied. 'We could go in the Park, over there,' said GI Joe. 'Is that what you had in mind, when you offered to walk me home?' 'Oh, no, Honey, forget it, just a hope. Just to show you I mean it, meet me tomorrow.' Next evening Sergeant and I went to a movie. I can't remember the name, but during the story a girl accused the young man of taking her for a loose person, and he obviously has this in mind all the time. . . . It was so similar to the night before . . . we both started laughing. 'Come on,' he said, 'Lets' git outa here, get a drink some place.'

Many people had equally private celebrations. One Dorset woman, working on late duty in a Red Cross club, recalls seeing 'VE-Day in with two Red Cross girls from the deep South and a Colonel who had toted a bottle of pink and a bottle of ordinary champagne all over Europe so that he could drink to the end of the war. . . . We four just sat and quietly drank and talked very little. It seemed it couldn't be true after so long.' In the 'cheese' village of Stilton, a local woman remembers, the GIs 'went wild at the Bell celebrating the good news. Next day we found the piano outside on a stone ledge above the archway over the gate.' That night the officers in the Dorchester Club at Liverpool offered to wash the dishes when the news of victory came through so that the British staff could get away early. In fact the usual transport proved to be elsewhere, so one local woman remembers 'we had records on and did barn dancing and it must have been nearly five o'clock before we got home'. On VE-Day a High Wycombe grandmother achieved a long-standing ambition and rode in a jeep, while, more traditionally, the people of Appleshaw, one of them remembers, 'danced around on the village green. My father produced a little whisky and some bottles of home plum and blackberry wine. One "pie-eyed" Yank was so elated he tried swimming in a dry ditch shouting, "Pa, I'm on my way home!" '

With victory almost every GI had the same thought: to get back home as quickly as possible. Knowing its readers, the *Stars and Stripes* on VE-Day itself prominently featured a story: 'WD [War Department] to announce points on discharge priority' and three days later it published the details of this draft in reverse. To qualify for immediate release a man needed eighty-five points, those being awarded on a complicated scale with one for each month of service since September 1940, another for each month spent overseas, twelve points for each child aged under eighteen, up to a maximum of three, and a bonus of five points for each combat medal. To attain, or approach, the magic figure, which was lowered as the months passed, became the overriding ambition of every soldier, presenting the cartoonists with an endless round of new jokes. 'Sir, I have a problem. Exactly forty-three points,' one GI, preparing to hang himself, explains to his chaplain.

'And I raise you twenty demob. points,' declares a reckless gambler in the middle of a hard-fought poker game.

The first combat division arrived back in New York in mid June and, the *Stars and Stripes* assured its impatient readers, 370 ships were being used to ferry them home, against the 270 that had brought them to Europe. All but fifty were British, including the *Aquitania* and both Queens, which alone could carry 50 000 men a month, so that for the next twelve months an average of 3000 men a day would be arriving in New York, with 1500 disembarking in Boston and at Hampton Roads. Several thousand more were to go by air.

Competition for every aircraft seat or place on a ship – 'berth' it could hardly be called – was keen, as one woman then working for the main transportation office in London discovered:

I would be given a list of ships or planes departing on such and such a date and had to prepare rosters of the soldiers according to the number of their points. . . . What joy could be seen in their faces when they were given a definite sailing date for home. . . . One incident stands out in my memory. . . . A Jewish boy working for the Special Services . . . asked me if I would like a radio . . . and . . . said if I could get him a quick passage home he would bring me one. Somewhat con-science-stricken I accepted the radio. . . . It so happened that a week or so later we had a request for four GIs to accompany the records of the first United Nations meeting held in London back to the States aboard the *Queen Mary*. Major C. gave the first two places to a Sergeant and a Corporal working in our office, and then asked me if I had any suggestions for the other two, with more or less requisite points. Needless to say, Sol M. came to mind, and within seconds I was phoning him up . . . with the glad news I'd got him a passage.

The system as a whole was, she discovered, 'fair and methodical' and it is hard to see how demobilization could have taken place much faster. Certainly it was far swifter than in the British Army. Eight hundred and fifty thousand Americans were scheduled to leave within three months of VE-Day, 1 185 000 within six months, 2 837 000 in nine and 3 100 000 – all those not remaining for the occupation forces – within a year.

Already by VE-Day the United Kingdom had been drained of most of its GIs, the vast majority of whom sailed for home from the Continent. Priority in passages from the United Kingdom was given to the wounded, who at their peak had numbered 120 000 in British hospitals; by the end of June only a tenth of these remained. There were still some 245 000 GIs in the British Isles, but the total was dropping daily as one man after another received his orders to report to one of the three staging camps, at Tidworth, Barton Stacey or Southampton, the usual port of departure.

Farewell parties were few, for there was usually little warning of a unit's final departure, and men went one by one as their points entitlement –

lowered to eighty in early September and later to sixty – was reached, until all men with two years' service were promised their discharge within a year. A telegraphist at the Gloucester Post Office remembers a whole series of celebrations. 'The final one would be, say, on Tuesday, then a phone call to my office would inform me that their departure had been delayed, so we had another "final" party on Thursday, and so on.' A then nineteen-year-old girl in Herefordshire, invited to another farewell party, remembers having 'to creep out after everyone had retired to bed. . . . It was a lovely party, but rather sad. I knew we would never meet again.' A Ramsbury, Wiltshire, housewife recalls the 'evening full of nostalgia' when the American Red Cross Club closed down. 'The GIs took candles and wrote all our names on the walls in candlesmoke.' And sometimes, though rarely, it was the civilians who left first, like a Croydon housewife, who with her small son had taken refuge from the bombing of London on a houseboat on the River Tamar at Saltash. 'My small son and I were given a right royal send-off, first a party at the houseboat, then the journey in an American jeep to the station, about two miles away, accompanied by eight jolly sailor boys. They had wrapped Michael in one of their soft fluffy blankets . . . their parting gift to him. He used it for many years as a bedspread.'

"I don't care if the war is nearly over—I'm not selling my cab for a fiver for a souvenir."

The GIs' mementoes were rarely so substantial. 'They took home most odd souvenirs, pipes, small kettles, teapots,' remembers a Suffolk woman who had worked in the airfield club at Great Ashfield. 'Daddy lost a cap to one called Joe. He had always wanted it and as it was so awful Mummy had promised him he could have it.' A literary-minded WAC from Vacaville, California, carried in her luggage a piece of slate from the roof of Words-worth's cottage in the Lake District. Most typical of all are the items still pasted in the scrapbook of one Eighth Air Force Dental Corps officer, now retired to Virginia: a list of exhibits at Madame Tussaud's; ticket-stubs for the London Coliseum, the Piccadilly Theatre, and the Palace Theatre, Reading; a book of British stamps; the visiting card of a West End tailors; lodging passes at various Red Cross clubs; a leaflet about forthcoming attractions at the Regal Cinema, Cheltenham: and, most evocative of all, perhaps, a twopenny ticket of the Cheltenham and District Bus Company.

It was Cheltenham which in July 1945 the *Stars and Stripes* selected to illustrate the effects of the GIs' departure: 'Ben Hill Farms, General Lee's headquarters', discovered the reporter, 'has been taken over by the British Ministry of Pensions and you can get into the local cinema without queuing up. You'd hardly think there had been a Yank in the place . . . until a couple of the young set spot you a couple of hundred yards off on main street. Then up the avenue waft childish voices: "Got any gum, chum?"' But, he decided, 'this quaint, tree-shaded English town where elderly British came to sleep, perchance to die', was finding it hard 'to settle back into the posture of repose', from which it had been roused in July 1942. 'Cheltenham misses its GIs – and frankly admits it.'

Not all memories of the Americans' departure are so affectionate, for many units indulged on leaving in a senseless orgy of destruction which still rankles a generation later. A Bury St Edmunds woman witnessed what happened at Great Ashfield:

The Americans left in a blaze of ill-feeling. When they were packing up to go *all* food, canned as well as fresh, the entire PX stores, everything there was, was taken in lorryloads and dumped in the middle of the airfield and burnt. All the cans were punctured and armed guards put on it day and night. . . . A lot of people tried to get some of this and were fired on. It went on every day for three weeks. There must have been tons of food destroyed. You could smell it burning in the village two miles away; there was a near riot over that. When it came to the canteen's turn to be cleared out, we were searched at the guardroom each time we left the camp. We never once heard any of them express regret at all this. Their attitude was, 'We don't want it any more, so why the hell should anyone else have it?' The same happened to hundreds of bikes, they were piled into a tremendous heap and tracked vehicles ran over them to smash them up. . . . They even boasted about it all in the local pubs. . . . After a few incidents like these the general feeling was that it was high time that they all went.

Protests at such scenes, repeated all over the country, led to the issuing of an order formally forbidding the destruction of unwanted items, but since the Brigadier-General concerned also announced that he was 'pledged that the United States will not take a loss or give anything away in any shape, form or manner' this made little difference. A woman at Newcastle, County Down, remembers, for example, how the departing troops 'had to burn everything: watches, radios, blankets, sheets', all items strictly rationed, or wholly unobtainable, in Britain, as they were to be for several years to come.

Officially at least, the policy was prompted by a desire not to undercut British tradesmen, but where the British forces were concerned malice clearly played some part. A Wren who belonged to a small unit near Glasgow learned that 'when the navy had originally handed the base over to the Americans it had been done in a none-too-friendly manner and the RN took away everything they could. . . . To retaliate, the Yanks were determined to leave nothing for the British. They gave us as much as we could cope with in sweets and meat . . . and . . . then proceeded to throw crate upon crate of food into the Clyde.'

Sometimes, despite the GIs' efforts, sufficient was left behind to make a former American camp a treasure-trove for later visitors, as one woman who worked on a Wiltshire farm remembers:

The day after the soldiers left their camp the farmer sent me down to the field to clear up the left-overs. The men had discarded an assortment of articles. I picked up three cartloads of wood, makeshift chairs and tables, shower partition and stands, for instance. There was even food. I remember finding a fifty pound bag of white flour . . . a partial crate of tomatoes . . . hundreds of coat hangers, some . . . with dry cleaners' names and addresses in the States on them. There were armed forces pocket books; I collected fifty of them. Kids from a nearby school discovered this paradise later on in the day. They also discovered boxes of prophylactics. Not knowing what they were, they used them as balloons and left them lying all over the place. The farm labourers laughing at them were in a dilemma. If they were to stop the children playing with them they would have to give a reason why. And that might cause questions at home. So they said nothing. Eventually the supply of 'balloons' ran out, but they were durable and the evidence was around for weeks later.

On 10 August 1945 the BBC announced that the Japanese had asked for an armistice. While the British awaited news of a final surrender the Yanks, the *Stars and Stripes* reported, 'blew their top'.

From Rainbow Corner the news swept over the West End. Yank met Yank and asked, 'Did you hear the news?' The news swept down to Aldwych, where . . . American soldiers stationed at Inveresk House began heaving basketfuls of torn paper, torn UK telephone directories, newspapers, through the windows. Aldwych looked after a while as white as if a snowstorm had hit it. The fun really began at

Piccadilly Circus. Hundreds of Yanks converged on the pedestal of Eros, still boarded up, and impromptu parades were started. One conga line, led by two Air Corps Lieutenants . . . and an army nurse, congaed round the base, up Shaftesbury Avenue and down to Leicester Square. . . . The GIs were so happy they even hoisted one embarrassed MP to shoulder-level and carried him for several blocks.

The official news that the Japanese war was over only came four days later, at midnight on Tuesday, 14 August, and VJ-Day, the 15th, was for the GIs an anticlimax, made worse by 'the dripping weather, which some called typically British. London's GI-ville', reported the *Stars and Stripes*, 'was deader than a Philadelphia Sunday.' Although there was inevitably some feel of a repeat performance about VJ-Day, to many GIs, dreading assignment to the Pacific, it came as even more joyful news. 'Nothing could compare with the declaration of peace with the Far East,' remembers one woman then working for the American army in Gloucestershire. 'When VJ-Day was declared the GIs broke camp and came into Tewkesbury during the small hours of the morning, knocked doors and rang bells and generally roused all the girls whose home addresses they knew.' A teenager who worked in a telephone factory at Beeston was roused in the same way. 'A jeep full of Yanks knocked us up . . . to tell us the war was over and we lit a big bonfire in the street and danced around it till daybreak in our nighties and pyjamas. Everyone was too excited to care.' A fourteen-year-old girl in Liverpool watched the celebrations in Aintree, on whose racecourse so many homesick GIs had spent the first few nights in England. The district 'was alive with trucks and jeeps driving through the streets laden with soldiers and civilians, and children. Sirens and horns blowing, singing and shouting. I didn't go to bed that night. I could play the piano a little and we had an old one in the street banging away on it while a few GIs were strumming banjos.' For a Norfolk schoolboy, one year older, the day was fixed in his mind by his first grown-up, American-style, meal out as guest of a Lieutenant: 'My first glass of wine, steak, chips, peas – and jam on the steak.'

The liveliest rejoicing of all seems to have been at Burtonwood, vividly observed by a British WAAF:

At midnight we were all awakened by the most awful noise of fireworks and shouts and a distant band. We all got up and put on various articles of clothing, some only had dressing gowns over their pyjamas, and went off to the main gate to find out the trouble and there a sight met our eyes never to be seen before. Down the lane came hundreds and hundreds of men following a band, and throwing fireworks around like snowballs. They forced open the gates of our compound, and grabbed each one of us, and off we all went, marching behind the band, round the quiet country lanes of Lancashire, between St Helens and Warrington. We marched for what seemed hours, singing our heads off. Had our mothers seen us in our bizarre clothes, they would have had heart attacks on the spot. On the return journey we all stopped at the WAAF gates and an American in a grass skirt did a snake dance on the roof of one of the huts with two searchlights trained on him. One of the WAAF officers then came through the gates sitting on the bonnet of a 15 cwt van. She jumped off and declared the dance hall open, and everyone who wanted went in and danced until the dawn came up. How we enjoyed ourselves, but I'm afraid the local inhabitants thought it scandalous. . . . This I think was typical of how the Americans could enjoy life, and, on this occasion, had every right to do so. It was such a difference from VE-night, a few months earlier, when I had been stationed in Suffolk on an RAF 'drome. We just had a quiet dance in the NAAFI and all went to bed at 11 p.m. as if a war was won every other week.

A week after VJ-Day the doors of the Eagle Club shut for the last time and on Monday 15 October 1945 the final London edition of the *Stars and Stripes* appeared, sadly headlined 'Goodbye, England'. Henceforward the few Americans left in the British Isles would be served by the edition printed in Paris. As counterpoint to the message of welcome from Winston Churchill which had greeted the GIs on their arrival, they were sped on their way by a valediction from his successor, Clement Attlee:

Today, when, after three years of publication, the *Stars and Stripes* issues its last British edition, I am glad to have an opportunity of saying to its readers how much we in Britain have enjoyed the contacts made with them while they have been here. . . . Now, when the immense tasks of war have been brought to a glorious conclusion we look forward to continue an ever-growing friendship with the United States in the achievements of peace. We believe that the friendships made between so many British and American men and women during the war will provide one of the durable strands in the companionship. Through you I wish our wartime guests from America God-speed and happiness in the manifold activities of peace as they return home.

29

BUT YOU DON'T MARRY THEM

'I asked if the moon ... shone that bright in Virginia and he told me to come over and find out for myself.'

– British woman, recalling 1944.

INVADING armies had traditionally carried off with them the young women of the land they had occupied. The Americans, doing things as usual on the grand scale, removed whole shiploads, the largest, and certainly the most willing, such contingent ever to leave the shores of Britain. They came from every corner of the British Isles, including those which had barely seen an American soldier. One Belfast woman, a GI bride herself, recalls the heartfelt comment of the Major she met who was organizing the brides' passages from the province: 'Boy, did our chaps get around!'

It did not take the Americans long to begin their marital forays into the ranks of British spinsters. By December 1942 applications to marry had already become so frequent that the US Army authorities issued a reminder to intending bridegrooms that their commanding officer's permission must be sought at least two months in advance. Intending wives were warned at the same time that marriage to an American did not make one an American citizen, though it did exempt one from the normal immigration 'quota' and entitle one to priority, if naturalization were sought later. British women were not discouraged. In the Land Army hostel at Appleshaw, near Andover, weddings to GIs soon became a common event, while many girls working for the evacuated Bank of England at Whitchurch, close to Tidworth, were, a colleague remembers, soon sporting 'veritable search-lights' on their engagement fingers in place of 'the modest gems' that indicated one's betrothal to an Englishman.

Some GIs hinted at matrimony at only a first or second meeting, though it was generally felt it was not the marriage-bed they had in mind. 'After a few times of dating' her boy friends, remembers a woman who was then an eighteen-year-old civil servant, 'would want to get engaged, but this was only the war talking.' But a considerable number were in earnest. 'Many Americans,' observed one wartime ATS girl, stationed at Burton-on-Trent, 'were hell-bent on taking home a British wife.' No doubt availability had something to do with it, but many GIs did believe that British girls had many other attributes to offer, especially a softness and femininity not always observable among their countrywomen, combined with a capacity for hard work and – particularly marked in wartime – a readiness to make the best of things. It is noteworthy that very few GI brides were drawn from the privileged 'upper crust'; the largest groups were munition workers, secretaries, servicewomen and, best represented of all, those most visibly long-suffering and industrious of all war-workers, members of the Women's Land Army.

One would-be husband, a Sergeant, was remarkably candid about his reasons, remembers a then Peterborough teenager to whom he proposed in a pub at their sixth meeting.

He asked me if I'd marry him and put a wad of money on the table saying it was for my wedding clothes and that he'd arranged for me to meet his CO also! I was amazed, and naturally asked why on earth did he want to marry me? He then told me that after the war, he and his parents were hoping to have a hotel and he thought I'd be just fine because he figured out I was a good worker (by the amount of time I had to work overtime on my war job) and that his parents could work a twelve-hour shift and then he and I work twelve-hour shifts in the hotel.

This suitor was turned down. Sometimes, however, it was a British woman who was disappointed in her hopes to marry a GI. One who was then a young factory worker in Gravesend has equally vivid memories of saying goodbye to 'Bill' on his departure for Belgium in November 1944; he had only confessed that he was already married when she was 'head over heels in love'.

When we said goodbye at the station I thought my heart would break. 'Goodbye, honey, stay as sweet as you are, you'll be happy with some nice Englishman some-day.'[1] The words still go round in my head and the way he called through the train window, 'Rusty! Thanks for the memory.' I never saw him again. . . . Later I thought about his wife back in Springfield, Massachusetts . . . how happy she must be to have him back, and I was glad nothing too bad had happened between us.

The engagement of a civil servant working for the Admiralty in Bath also came to nothing. 'When eventually hostilities were over, he came to say goodbye as he was flying back, and was then to buy my wedding clothes over there and come back here to England. I heard nothing more from him, but from a relative. . . . I . . . heard that he had been killed in an air crash and that he had a wife . . . I felt truly nothing but relief.' Such discoveries were not uncommon. One Technical Sergeant stationed at Wendling remembers how, 'searching the effects of a little air gunner from Brooklyn . . . killed in combat . . . they found he was married in Brooklyn, also in London,

1. This prediction proved correct, though this informant wrote to me care of a friend, as her husband 'would not approve' of her having befriended a GI.

also in King's Lynn. He had babies in at least two of the places and girl friends in a few other places who didn't know he was married at all.'

Other proposals were turned down, or engagements broken off, for a variety of reasons. Religious differences were a frequent cause. One GI, who fell in love with a Newbury girl he met while in hospital after the 'Battle of the Bulge' in the Ardennes, found the fact that 'I was a Catholic and she Church of England an unsurmountable barrier'. For months after returning home 'I continued to pursue her, even with phone calls from the States, but it never did jell.' One Norwich office worker, aged twenty in 1944, already troubled by her fiancé's violent colour prejudice, finally decided not to marry him for similar reasons:

He was of Irish Catholic descent and mentioned a girl 'back home' who married into his family and was made unwelcome because she was not Catholic. I thought this dreadful . . . I went a few times to the Catholic Church with him . . . it was all in Latin and just mumbo-jumbo to me. . . . He wrote after he returned to the States, and offered to send the fare over, said how much he longed for me and sent cuttings of the GI brides embracing their husbands, but . . . I never went.

The intended marriage of a WAAF stationed at Swanage was disrupted by her future mother-in-law. 'She wrote to me several times making it clear that she expected him to come home and settle down with a certain girl there and seemed slightly anti-British. I felt I couldn't cope with mother-in-law trouble in a strange country, so broke it off.' One girl from South Wales who fell in love with a GI was literally discouraged by the thought of having to change her name; she felt, she confesses, 'a sense of shock' at the idea of becoming Mrs Infantino.

Yet, despite all the obstacles, by April 1944 the number of marriages was already large enough to justify monthly classes for GI brides at Rainbow Corner, in which such lecturers as a female journalist from the *Chicago Daily News* warned that 'the corner drugstore may not look as beautiful to them as their nostalgic husbands painted it' and that though 'American men are very protective . . . they expect a lot of their wives'.

Marriages to GIs began in a variety of situations. This is how one airman from Plymouth, Massachusetts, then aged nineteen and serving in an anti-gas detachment at Debden, became, in his own words, 'a Limey lover'.

I met her while I was on duty watering the golf greens of Saffron Walden, Essex, County Club. We would drive our 'decon' [i.e. decontamination] trucks to a nearby stream, fill up the 400 gallon tanks with water and then . . . sprinkle the greens . . . in preparation for the Officers'–Enlisted Men's Golf Tournament. On the way to the stream we had to drive past a sugar-beet field which was being harvested by twenty-eight Women's Land Army girls. Needless to say, we stopped. We made dates with four of these girls. They accepted, thinking we would never show up. It was eleven miles from our base to their hostel.

What did I find attractive in my partner? Everything. Face, figure, smile, manner of speech, size and personality. To pick her out of twenty-eight she had to be pretty special. We were finally married on 4 August 1945 . . . two years to the day after I left the States.[1]

Another landgirl, then aged nineteen, first noticed her future husband when he appeared 'grimy and dirty' with an equally dishevelled 'buddy' in a services club in Lyme Regis. Noticing the enquiring looks from this girl and her friend, the GIs moved to their table and explained they had come from fighting a fire; their 'outfit', billeted in a thatched house, had stoked the grate too well and set the roof ablaze. The two fire-fighters, this woman remarks, 'ended up our husbands, as the other guy dated and married my girl friend'. Her own courtship was carried on largely in Uplyme, where she worked, and especially in the village pub, where the lovers made the acquaintance of an elderly couple who invited them to their home. Here the 1st Division found its third Uplyme wife, for billeted in the house was another girl, from Dagenham in Essex, who duly became 'engaged to one of the boys in Bob's company'.

As for Bob himself, his proposal was all that the most romantic nineteen-year-old could have desired:

He had been telling me about the mountains of Virginia, where he was from. We were sitting on a bench on the sea-front on a beautiful, clear, moonlight, starlight night. I asked if the moon and stars shone that bright in Virginia and he told me to come over and find out for myself. When I asked him how, he said by marrying him. I had a week's leave coming up, so we went home. Bob and his friend Jack from Georgia also had a three-day pass, so they came on later. Mother and I met them at the railroad station. They liked the family and family liked them. Mother couldn't get over how each morning they would meticulously press their pants before going out.

Another marriage began at adjoining tables in a Belfast restaurant when a waiter delivered a note to one woman diner from a neighbouring American: 'I think you are the prettiest girl I have ever seen. Please write to me. Sergeant Harold T.' – the gallant Sergeant being undeterred by the fact that he was in the company of another girl and the recipient of his letter was in a mixed group of six. They were soon visiting restaurants and clubs together until 'we were sitting in a lounge bar one evening when the MPs came in to say, "Return to the base at once, bud,"' and, with no time for a further goodbye, 'bud' was on his way to North Africa, not to be reunited with his wife-to-be for several years.

One of the youngest GI brides was just sixteen and a chambermaid in a local hotel when the man with whom she was to spend the rest of her life sat down beside her in a Clacton café and politely asked her to settle the

1. He adds: 'We are still married, having had five children.'

argument he had been having with his friends: 'Was she a real blonde or a "bottle" one?' Later that evening, sitting with him in a sea-front shelter, she discovered that 'Matt', a master baker in an airforce cookhouse was really 'very shy'. Next day she met him by chance in the street while with her mother, whose response to his cheerful 'Hello' was a suspicious 'How do you know my daughter?' But 'he was so nice to her, she invited him home to tea the next time he was in Clacton.' A few months later, on Christmas afternoon, mother and daughter having given their guest up and eaten their Christmas dinner without him, 'at 5 p.m. the doorbell rang and there was one dead-beat GI, who just said, "Hi, merry Christmas," and sat down on the sofa and fell asleep.' Finding no transport, he had heroically walked the twenty-five miles from his camp at Sudbury. His devotion was well rewarded. Four weeks later they were married.

It was shorthand which in January 1944 brought together one eighteen-year-old secretary, living at New Malden, Surrey, while working in a solicitors' office in the City, and *her* future husband, then stationed at Bushy Park, for on the journey home she was intrigued to see a GI opposite reading shorthand notes in the relatively uncommon Gregg system she used herself. Although, she admits, 'rather nervous . . . of Americans' she was reassured to learn that he was the author of some of the articles she had read in the Gregg magazine, so that 'when he asked for my telephone number before I left the train . . . to my astonishment, I gave it to him'.

A half-smoked cigarette was the initial cause of one young Glasgow woman meeting the Eighth Air Force Staff Sergeant whom she later married. Her brother, a seventeen-year-old student, doing a vacation job at the docks, mentioned how he had picked up an almost unsmoked cigarette thrown away by one GI who had then given him 'a fatherly lecture', followed by a present of several new packets. 'My sisterly reaction,' she remembers, was '"He must have been nice. Could you understand his accent?" My brother answered that I would be able to judge for myself as he had invited the Sergeant to come to our house for supper.'

It was, by contrast, her thirteen-year-old sister who 'arranged' the match between one Leicester shorthand-typist, then aged twenty, and a Master Sergeant in the Quartermaster Corps, from Wilkes Barre, Pennsylvania, for, chatting with the GI on guard at the gate of 'the old county cricket ground along the Aylestone Road', where part of the 82nd Airborne Division was stationed, she generously offered him a date with her older sister. 'Curiosity,' the latter admits, 'made me turn up that Sunday night in 1943 and we went to see Judy Garland in . . . *Me and My Gal*. He whistled and sang the title song all the way home . . . I thought his voice was atrocious, but . . . his manners just perfect.'

Despite the GIs' reputation for fickleness, one young B–24 bomb-loader from Pittsburgh, stationed in East Anglia, 'never went to dances or dance halls . . . and never went out with any girl other than the one who subsequently became my wife.'

I met her on the railroad station in Norwich on the way to London on my first leave. By the time the train got to London we had conversed quite a bit and I found her very pretty and friendly. . . . As a lark I asked her, when I found out she was working in a show, to let me know where she would be when I got my next leave. She did so and I found myself spending my leaves where she was. I saw so many performances of the revue my girl was in I think I could have understudied almost anyone in the cast. We were married on the 4 July 1944.

The love affair of one Nottingham woman began, unusually, with an expression of moral disapproval by a GI, whom she had met in a pub and who criticized her for being there when 'on the way home I told him I was already writing to a GI. I said to him,' she remembers, '"Well, you can't expect me to stay at home all the time waiting for Mr Right to come along," but he had different ideas.' In fact Mr Right *had* come along, for 'On the Sunday a little boy came to our house with a note and it was from Don asking to meet me in town, so I went and romance really got on the way.'

The first meeting with her future fiancé of a girl from Portsmouth, living in a hostel away from home while working in an aircraft factory, also began with a disagreement. Hurrying one evening out of the Falcon, in High Wycombe, after finding herself the odd girl out in a party of six girls and five GIs, she went flying down the steps and twisted her ankle. While she was sitting 'on the step to try to bind up my foot with a hankie' a GI came by, asked 'What's the trouble, honey?', and then took her to the station in a taxi. Naturally she agreed to meet her rescuer again, when he sadly marred his earlier reputation by 'trying to get fresh' in the movies. She immediately walked out, to be followed by her unrepentant escort, who explained frankly that, knowing the reputation of the hostel where she lived, and imagining that when they first met she had just been thrown out of a pub, he 'thought I was OK. "Oh, did you?" I said. "Well, thanks for telling me. Goodbye!" and caught a bus back to the hostel.' But a determined GI was hard to shake off. 'He came up to the hostel four times to apologize,' she remembers, 'sent flowers, did everything but kneel, so I said, "OK. Let's start again."'

One woman then living in Norwich remembers joking to her family on hearing the news of the first GIs arriving in Britain 'I wonder if my cowboy is among them?' and, so strange is fate, two years later she *did* marry a cowboy from a ranch in Wyoming. He was, however, very different from the Hollywood variety and first impressed her during a dance at the Samson and Hercules Club in Norwich 'by his courtesy and quiet reserved manners and interesting conversation'.

Another young American literally 'cut in' on the life of a WAAF radio operator stationed at RAF Headquarters, Belfast, after some newly arrived Americans had set up their camp in a requisitioned country mansion, known as the Palace Barracks, and invited the local WAAFs to a dance. 'We were all curious,' she admits, and as 'our watch came off duty at 7 p.m. and returned to duty at midnight,' the girls decided to accept. 'The music seemed very loud and unusual. . . . Cutting in was quite new to us. . . . I was dancing with a Private when a Corporal tapped him on the shoulder the Corporal in turn was replaced by a Sergeant. The Sergeant was tapped on the shoulder by a young Lieutenant. The young Lieutenant was Jim . . . Jim was very good-looking, had perfect manners and was an idealist. We stayed together that evening and when it was time for us to return to our hostel he walked me almost home.' 'Almost' because she remembered, too late, the strict rule 'that no escorts were allowed inside the hostel grounds' and 'grabbing Jim by the arm I pulled him into the woods bordering the drive', on hearing a WAAF Sergeant approaching. He was 'sent back to the gate' with strict instructions 'to stay out of sight' – a conspiratorial beginning to a friendship which soon became something more.

The arrival in November 1943 of the 45th Evacuation Hospital in the little Gloucestershire town of Wotton-under-Edge, hitherto as sleepy as its name, had an equally lasting effect upon the marital future of one 'woodchopper' of the Women's Timber Corps, a branch of the Women's Land Army, formerly a shop assistant in Worksop. She talked to her first GIs at a Sunday-afternoon concert and tea party arranged by the WVS at the Town Hall to enable the locals 'to meet the boys', an aim so successfully realized that soon her 'special American . . . from Brooklyn', who resembled 'a young Raymond Massey', but was 'quiet [and] didn't smile much', was giving me 'dancing lessons in the kitchen where I lived. We took long walks around the Cotswolds, talked a lot about everything but marriage. He was very concerned about not getting involved with any girl before the war was over; in fact he told me he was divorced just to set me back a bit,' but as will be mentioned later, she refused to be 'set back'.

For a twenty-two-year-old girl clerk in the Great Western Railway goods office at Droitwich Spa – another name hardly evoking thoughts of a gay and riotous time – wartime life was, she admits, 'pretty dull' until in the spring of 1943 the GIs moved into a nobleman's mansion near the city and she was invited to a party given by the local Mayor to welcome them. As they left, her girl friend, who had engineered her invitation, was shocked to learn that she had not arranged to meet any of her partners again, 'flew off the truck, dashed back into the hall and had a date fixed for the four of us. After that . . . Bob', a Lieutenant from Illinois in General Patton's Third Army, 'made his own dates with me. Within three weeks we knew some day we would be married.' Bob was soon providing an unofficial guard of honour for his future bride from his men, marching them into town and 'halting them right outside our house just when I had to be leaving for the office'. The end of the war brought a telegram: 'Coming home to marry', and so in September 1945 they did.[1]

Few GIs remember as vividly as their wives the details of their first meeting but an exception is a former Eighth Air Force Technical Sergeant from Illinois, who was introduced to his wife – also a WAAF radio operator – while employed at a Bomber Command Headquarters near Bedford. 'I was,' he recalls, 'on temporary assignment to try to cross-index our supply catalogues', and 'the personnel had a party for their girl friends, wives, etc., and had invited a group of WAAFs from a nearby camp. When they arrived, I noticed that none of the regular people on the camp were making any effort to welcome them, so I introduced myself, showed them the cloakroom, rest room, and then took them to the refreshment counters, trying to make them feel at home.' His efforts so impressed one of the party that when, she remembers, 'we in turn had a fancy dress dance at camp and invited a group from the American base, one . . . was the GI who had met us before.'

Other courtships followed a less traditional pattern. One Belfast man, summoned to the docks in 1942 to sing welcoming songs to the first GIs, made a second visit four years later to see his cousin off to America, to marry 'a very shy soldier who would come to our house and sit for hours without saying a word. He suddenly disappeared after courting my cousin for a year and she did not see or hear from him for two years. One day he arrived at her door, said that he had been in France and could not remember her address, but knew where she lived. . . . He was flying home to the States that same day for demob . . . gave my aunt £100 in notes and said that he would marry my cousin if she cared to come over to America. Although we all thought she was mad,' go she did – and lived happily ever after.

Nor were older women impervious to the GIs' insidious charms. One Cricklewood, North-West London, divorcée, working as an inspector in a war factory and already in her thirties, wrote off the first GIs she encountered as 'loud-mouthed show-offs, slovenly soldiers and sex-crazy' and her first date with one 'ended before it had begun', for she had no sooner got into a taxi with him than 'he got hold of me, grabbed my blouse, and almost ripped it off', to which she responded 'by getting out of the cab and running like hell'. But eventually, through a friend, she met another American working in the air transport office in Central London, who though still 'a loud-mouth' was also 'kind and soft-hearted', an assessment confirmed by his behaviour when, on returning from a walk with him in the cold and wet,

1. When twenty years later their 'completely happy, full life' together was ended by Bob's death 'we were', remembers his widow, 'as much in love then as we were in Droitwich'.

'he took off my shoes and stockings, opened his shirt and put my feet, which were like ice, on his chest until they were warm'. He was to have many more opportunities for such gallantry, becoming her second husband.

Apart from the parties chiefly concerned, very few people at the time were in the least anxious to see British girls married to American males. Even in circles where prestige attached to having a Yank of one's own, this extended only to boy friends; to have an American fiancé or husband carried no social cachet whatever. One WAAF who had met many GIs from the time she danced with some of the earliest arrivals at the Tower Ballroom, while on a course in Blackpool, remembers how 'We didn't take any of them seriously; they would be "here today and gone tomorrow" without trace; and we had heard many warnings . . . about the tall tales they gave of their life in the States. . . . Many married English girls [it was said] neglecting to mention that they already had a wife at home.' When, two years later, she herself became engaged to a Technical Sergeant from Illinois, many 'friends I had made in the WAAF simply stopped writing' and 'people told me: "But you don't *marry* them."' Another WAAF remembers the equally unsympathetic response she encountered when, after breaking out in a nervous rash, following her brand-new fiancé's departure for North Africa, 'I went to the MO for help. . . . Before I ever saw him I heard a medical orderly say in a loud voice, "God knows what she's got, she goes with an American!"'

To wish to marry an American was widely regarded as not merely foolish, but unpatriotic. The GIs, public opinion held, were all very well as escorts while 'our lads' were away fighting, but to regard them as husband material was carrying a good joke too far. British servicemen were particularly bitter at the slight which such alliances seemed to imply on British males. One WAAF, then stationed near Bedford and now living in Illinois, was upset that her brother, who 'had formed a very poor opinion of the American troops' serving with him in Italy, completely ignored 'my mentioning in letters our plans for the wedding'. Another WAAF, working in Belfast, could only imagine the reaction of the British naval officer whose last words to her before he left to join a Malta-bound convoy had been 'Stay away from the Americans', when she wrote to break similar news to him, for he immediately stopped writing. An Essex girl wryly recalls the horrified reaction of her brother, then serving in the RAF in Burma, who 'wrote me a long letter begging me to reconsider and choose an Englishmen'; the advice proved unnecessary, for the man she loved soon afterwards turned out to be married already.

If not nearly as frequent as rumour suggested, such disillusionments were far from uncommon. One British girl who announced her engagement in her husband's home-town newspaper to give him a surprise, received one herself, a letter from his wife. Rumours of such experiences reached an assistant in a grocery warehouse in Nottingham who 'fell for' a GI she met in a pub soon after D-Day: 'I asked him for his home address so I could write to his mam' not, as he thought, out of mere friendship but to confirm that he was not married. 'His mam wrote back and told me he wasn't . . . and we got engaged about October time. . . . One day he said he didn't want to leave anyone behind, so I said, "Well, I could be killed in a raid, just the same as you," so after a lot of considering we decided to get married on 27 December 1944.' Then, after a three-day honeymoon in a farmhouse close to his base at Chalgrove, near Oxford, and a few nights together in a 'bed-and-breakfast' boarding house in Oxford, the new husband left for France.

So damaging to morale in the British forces were engagements between British girls and GIs felt to be that in the summer of 1944 a speaker described as 'a British Army civilian lecturer' actually addressed a public meeting in the Pump Room, Bath, on 'The disadvantages of Anglo-American marriages'. GIs, he warned his fifty-strong all-female audience, presided over by an ATS officer, 'get engaged to an English girl "to keep her quiet"', while even if in earnest to start with 'The time limit imposed on applications snuffed out two-thirds of them.' The surviving fiancées would also be lucky to see the shores of the United States, for returning troops 'will not go via Britain and will not be able to take their wives along with them'. But those abandoned in Britain would be the lucky ones.

Mr Page pointed out that these men will meet other attractive girls in other countries, or they may wish to marry their own girls at home. The men get an easy divorce. The English girls will probably know nothing about it. They will get no alimony, no child maintenance, and will have lost their British nationality, and will not be granted American nationality. I am sure that hardly one in ten of Anglo-American wartime marriages will outlive the war.

Sadly no GIs were present to hear this stirring attack, to which the local newspaper devoted a sole column, but its sentiments would have been echoed by many parents, particularly fathers, who were always less susceptible than their wives to American charm. The WAAF from Belfast previously quoted remembers how breaking the news of her engagement to her family began with a misunderstanding. Her mother responded with delight as her daughter proudly displayed her engagement ring on coming home on leave, 'Ah, the naval Lieutenant!', to which she had, rather deflatingly, to reply, 'No, the American one.' Her mother, however, 'was happy because I was happy but my father and I were to spar over the engagement until he met Jim three years later'. When her sister, also in the forces, came home on leave, her father commented pointedly, 'Thank God the Chinese haven't sent an army over here yet!' When there were the inevitable wartime difficulties over finding rations for the reception he launched 'a final attack: couldn't I see how much trouble I was causing my mother? I said: "Daddy, when Jim gets leave, we don't have to have a wedding but we are going to have a honeymoon." He never said another word against the wedding.'

Another young woman, then working as an engraver at Stone in Staffordshire, faced an even tougher battle when she planned to marry Ed, who was 'nineteen years old, over six feet tall, fair-skinned, blond and came from Kansas'. She had been forbidden to meet GIs at all and Ed was eventually introduced to the house only by a ruse, pretending to call, as a casual acquaintance, to enquire after her health after missing her at a recent dance. The moment when her brother, rather tactlessly, announced, 'There's a Yank at the door to see Sis,' was nevertheless a traumatic one in the household and, though Ed was, reluctantly, allowed to call again, the courtship proceeded under a stern parental eye.

We were never allowed to show affection, we could not sit together on the sofa, or hold hands. When he left at 10 p.m. if I was more than a minute at the door my dad would call, 'That's enough, come in!' After a time we asked if we could become engaged but every time he ignored us, so one Saturday we went to Hanley and got the ring. I wore it at the tea-table and my dad said, 'What's that on your finger?' I held out my hand and he slipped the ring off and threw it in the fire. What a row followed, Ed trying to get the ring out of the fire with the poker, Mom shouting we'd asked him often enough, and me howling. After it had calmed down, he agreed.[1]

A pained, reproachful display of disappointment at one's choice was perhaps even harder to bear than outright opposition, as one shorthand typist, aged nineteen in 1943 when the 82nd Airborne Division arrived in Leicester, remembers. She had begun, in secret, to go out with one of its members, a Master Sergeant, and was soon deeply in love with him.

I never dared tell my parents though. The usual gossipers did that, for I was born in the house in which we were then living and . . . my father, who had never said a cross word to me in his life was very hurt and upset. My grandmother, who was a very Victorian type of lady and who I thought I would have the most trouble with, was the one who eventually won my mother and father over. For grandma thought my American was wonderful, she said he showed her so much courtesy. . . . From then on it was plain sailing. We were engaged in the spring of 1944, prior to him going to Normandy.

Sometimes a father who objected to all Americans in principle rapidly succumbed as soon as he met one in the flesh, often justifying his change of front with the face-saving formula, 'He doesn't really seem like a Yank.' The experience of a South Harrow girl, whose mother had encouraged her to keep a date with her first GI, met at a local dance, while warning her not to tell her father was typical:

1. Dad – and the Bath lecturer – were, alas, proved right about this GI. The marriage never took place.

When Jimmy brought me home that evening he said he would like to meet my folks. I thought this would be a good way to get rid of him. So in we went and my poor mother's face was a sight to see. Jimmy and Dad looked at one another, liked what they saw and settled down for a nice talk on World War I (my dad) and World War II (Jimmy). From then on every night here came Jimmy.

The departure of the Americans from an area was often cause for rejoicing by the fathers of marriageable daughters. One young Cornish landgirl, eighteen when the first GIs reached her native Newlyn in late 1943, recalls how her father the following June uttered 'heartfelt expressions of relief when the 29th Division moved out without capturing any of us', but he had celebrated too soon. Much later, another GI, employed at Southampton on dispatching GI brides back to the United States, on a visit to relatives in Cornwall carried off one of her two sisters to Porchester, New York.

Even the end of the war did not guarantee immunity from such dangers. A young Chippenham girl, touring the Wiltshire countryside as a milk tester for the Ministry of Agriculture, first saw her future husband on VJ night leading the conga line of celebrating citizens round the market-place, where 'he stood out as the one . . . most at ease with the local people.' Meeting him at a dance three months later she discovered he was stationed at Tidworth after being wounded in Normandy, and, as she had expected, 'made friends easily, was tolerant, always cheerful'. Their friendship flourished on long walks 'through dripping trees and mushy fields' on 'damp, dull, December, West Country days' and on weekly illicit jaunts to Bournemouth in a truck laden with his company's dry-cleaning, where 'depending on the weather, we would go to the beach, shop or walk in the parks. On one of these trips he bought me my first long evening dress . . . and he never failed to bring me a corsage each time I wore it,' while after the return journey to Tidworth 'I would be escorted home, usually in a jeep, which I sometimes drove on the remoter parts of the journey.'

As the months went by, Father thawed considerably. At first he wasn't sure Johnnie was genuine. Would Johnnie like to come fishing on Sunday afternoons and help with the weeding? Johnnie would. In Father's waders he cut blanket weed in the stream, I raked it on to the banks and Father planned further sorties down-stream. Would Johnnie like a change of clothes, perhaps he'd feel more comfortable in an old pair of flannels and tweed jacket? Johnnie would. Then petrol rationing came in again. If Johnnie would like to drive the car he might if he got an English licence. Johnnie did. He asked me to marry him in March [1946]. I refused to think about such a serious matter. He asked me again when he knew he was leaving. I decided I couldn't bear life without Johnnie (or was it Chippenham without John-nie?) so we married. He went to the States in June and I followed in July.

But marrying an American was far from being the straightforward matter this account suggests, for American 'moms' were highly suspicious of seeing their innocent boys lured into a disastrous match by some alien adventuresses. In August 1945 the *Stars and Stripes* recorded under the headline 'Judge OKs nuptials nixed by parents' how a British magistrate had helped true love to find a way. A twenty-year-old boatswain's mate from Detroit, refused by his family permission to marry a London girl of the same age, had appealed to a British court – and won.[1]

Obtaining parental consent was, however, only the first of a long series of obstacles to be overcome, as the Hanley girl previously mentioned, whose engagement led to a family row, soon discovered:

Then it really began. I was Roman Catholic, Ed Episcopalian. My priest said mixed marriages never worked, but we got over that. Then the base padré saw my mom and said RCs were not very popular in the mid-west. We survived that. Next his CO had my morals, background, etc., all looked into. We filled in what appeared millions of forms, his parents had to send affidavits to say they would take responsibility for me in the States. It was all set, the banns were called, my dress was ready, Mom made the cake (she had to use soya flour for the marzipan, as we could not get almonds, but it looked lovely) and then he was moved. No warning – half the permanent staff went. The next I heard he was at Bushey Park. A couple of weeks later I was at a church garden fête when he appeared. He'd got a pass to London and sneaked down to Stone. We left the fête and he said he wouldn't be seeing me for some time as something was coming up and I stood on that funny little railway station waving him goodbye and not realizing it really was. A few days later the Normandy landings began, and weeks later I got mail from France. I watched the icing on my cake discolour from the soya flour and at Christmas we ate it.

An intimidating ordeal still remembered by many women is the official interview with an American officer, usually a chaplain, required before an application to marry was approved. A sixteen-year-old Clacton girl was, she admits, 'scared stiff' when summoned for the customary interrogation by 'Father Red', as the GIs called their Roman Catholic padre, and the veteran cleric soon made clear that he had no illusions about his flock, his first question being 'Was I having a baby? I wasn't.' A Manchester woman, who had met her future husband, an infantry Captain, while teaching French at an international club, found her interview difficult for a different reason. The officer concerned had to be at least two ranks higher than the applicant and 'The only Lieutenant-Colonel who could be found in the vicinity was an Engineer Officer about the same age as I.' He was most embarrassed, as he had to ask me personal questions as to my religion and whether I was really single. He had anticipated an innocent eighteen-year-old. I was running a successful photographic studio at the time and was twenty-seven and a company director.'

1. Such cases were common in Britain at this time, when one was legally a child until the age of twenty-one. The comparable age today is eighteen.

The interview once survived – and both these candidates sailed through theirs – the paper chaos began. The amount of documentation required of a GI bride was formidable enough to daunt even the most starry-eyed. She was warned in an official *Bride's Guide to the USA* that to obtain a visa for admission to the United States she would require her husband's 'sworn affidavit of support', indicating his salary, bank deposits, insurance and other financial resources – a very necessary protection, since she was only allowed to take with her £10 in British money – a 'statement from her husband's commanding officer, confirming the information contained in the affidavit' and, if she were going ahead of her husband, 'documentary evidence . . . from the relatives indicating their willingness and ability' to receive her into their home. But this was only the start. Before she could leave she also needed to produce a British passport, two copies of her birth certificate, two copies of her 'police record', if she possessed one, her original marriage certificate, her discharge papers, if she had served in the forces, three photographs 'on thin paper with light background', evidence showing that on arrival in the United States she would have 'a railroad ticket or enough money to buy one' and finally £2 or $10 to cover her visa fee. After all this, and assuming her ship were not torpedoed on the way, 'If your papers are in order and if you have not come down with a contagious disease on the ship, you may expect to be allowed to proceed without being detained on Ellis Island.'[1]

Many women still remember the flood of forms with horror. One Portsmouth girl remembers spending weary hours answering questionnaires which demanded: 'If we had anyone of the family who has been in gaol or were communists' and she recalls 'wasting a whole day trying to find a Notary Public, which I found out was an American name for our Commissioner of Oaths'. A Norwich woman, married to an airman from Wyoming based at Shipdham, remembers how for fifteen months after her wedding on New Year's Day 1944, she 'endeavoured to obtain a passport. The British Passport Office personnel would say, "We'll be glad to give you a passport if the Americans will give you a visa", whereupon I would scurry over to Grosvenor Square, only to be told by the Americans, "As soon as the British give you your passport we'll supply the visa". In the meantime Frank was returned to the United States for rest and recuperation and I was temporarily a woman without a country. When my passport was at last issued it was stamped,' reproachfully she felt, '"British by birth, wife of an American serviceman."'

Although some commanding officers were not above moving a man away without warning if he had formed an unsuitable attachment or was in danger of becoming the victim of a 'shotgun wedding' when a marriage was quietly

1. A woman engaged to a GI required the same documents, less the marriage certificate.

prevented it was often in the bride's own interests. 'On the whole,' decided one British woman who worked at the headquarters of US Naval forces in Europe, 'the navy was pretty good about investigating characters before they were permitted to marry,' and she recalls only one thoroughly disreputable character who 'slipped through the net' to become the husband of 'a most respectable and nicely brought-up greengrocer's daughter. . . . When the bride's father said [at the reception] that it didn't matter a bit that the groom was Lithuanian so long as he was a good boy, we writhed.'

The two peak periods for marriages were the spring of 1944, just before D-Day, and the summer of 1945, between the end of the war in Europe and the departure of most units for the United States. During these months the churches and registrars' offices of Southern England, where most Americans were now concentrated, constantly resounded to American voices promising 'I will', and most brides seem to look back on their wedding day arrangements – whatever the subsequent course of their marriage – with pleasure and satisfaction. One Suffolk girl, working in the Red Cross canteen at Great Ashfield, remembers how for the wedding of one of the girls there the 'GIs really rallied round. Some got hold of a parachute and we all made clothes like mad. The cooks made a beautiful three-tiered cake with icing, even sending home for the decorations. Bottles of drinks appeared, presents galore, "bobbypins" for her hair, nylons, etc. – they joined in as if it was one of their own family.'

A Leicester girl, marrying in September 1944 in her local church, found as she came up the aisle that 'though big it was packed to overflowing', and she was touched when the vicar, who had years before married her parents and later baptized and confirmed herself:

. . . said during his address to the congregation that he thought it was a good thing for girls of this country to marry Americans as this would surely strengthen the ties which existed between our countries. A lorry-load of American servicemen came to the reception. They had collected for us and handed me a considerable sum of money with a paper with all their names on it. . . . My parents had done all the catering and it was super. . . . There was tongue, home-boiled, and ham. To cap it all, one of the servicemen in the camp was an Italian and made ice-cream in the States. He made us a gallon with fruit in it and most of the children present had, of course, never seen or tasted ice-cream. My parents distributed it all over the street.

One WAAF from Kent, serving near Bedford, remembers that special permission from the Archbishop of Canterbury was needed to marry in the village church, which she was eager to do, since both she and her husband were living elsewhere, and she then 'managed to make a wedding dress from a paper-based material which looked like cut velvet and was coupon free. . . . The bridesmaids were in dresses made from damaged parachute nylon, provided by my husband,' courtesy of the Eighth Air Force.

The honeymoon was traditionally a romantic, even idyllic, time, but in wartime it was often neither. One woman who worked in the canteen at the RAF base at Goxhill near the bleak and windswept Lincolnshire coast remembers what happened to a colleague who married a GI in nearby Grimsby one cold March Saturday in 1944.

They planned to have a short honeymoon at a resort on the Yorkshire coast, but owing to wartime restrictions there was no ferry over the Humber till twelve o'clock on Sunday. Arriving in Hull about one o'clock, they found there wasn't a train till four o'clock. They went for coffee – had a walk; more coffee, more walk. It was bitterly cold, bomb sites all around – and on a hoarding opposite the station was a poster announcing Ralph Lynn in *Is Your Honeymoon Really Necessary?* 'No, it bloody well isn't', said R. – and they took the ferry back to Grimsby.

Although many girls managed to achieve something approaching a peacetime wedding, this was usually impossible, and the bride might find herself having to take on duties that normally fell to the bride's father and the groom, like the landgirl previously mentioned, who had met her fire-fighting Pfc in Lyme Regis and whose wedding, with D-Day approaching, was set for the spring of 1944:

Our wedding day in April proved very hectic for me. Bob just had an overnight pass and didn't get off until noon and the wedding was at four o'clock. I had to take the train to Exeter that morning, get the licence and myself a corsage. I also got myself a new hat – I was out of clothing coupons so couldn't get a new dress. . . . We were married in the village church at Uplyme. . . . The elderly couple mentioned earlier fixed us a wedding supper with the help of a few extras from Bob's Mess Sergeant. We called my mother and father and told them we were married, for although my father had signed forms (in triplicate) and had been investigated by an American chaplain, the one-night pass was suddenly given with no time for my folks to get there from Brighton. We went that night in a jeep with some of Bob's friends a little farther along the coast than we usually went, to a pub, to celebrate. We almost ended up in gaol . . . as we were further away from our own area than we were supposed to be without permission . . . [and] the local police thought we might be spies.

This evening out was to be their honeymoon, though the new husband managed to get away most evenings until three weeks later his 'final over-night pass came' and he set off for the war, driving the jeep, named, in honour of his bride, *Darling*, the letter assigned to his company being 'D'.[1] Back home in Brighton with her family she heard the news of D-Day and went to see *Gone With The Wind* to take her mind off it, while, she later learned, Bob and *Darling* were landing on OMAHA. Before long his

1. *Darling* suffered an honourable end, being blown to pieces while carrying ammunition up to the front line.

letters began to arrive. 'I remember one especially, where he said he was in a foxhole with a radio and it was playing 'It Had To Be You' and [he wrote] "It had to be you, too!"'

But this was not – at first at least – to be a story-book romance:

Our baby was born that winter, a little girl named Wanda Marie, and about three weeks later one night, while we were sitting around the fire listening to the radio a knock came at the door . . . a telegram for me. I guess I knew it was news of Bob. . . . It said he'd been seriously wounded in action. The next few days I was on 'pins and needles' for further news, then instead of a letter from the army there was one from Bob himself. . . . He had been flown to an American Field Hospital in Devizes, Wiltshire, and he was wanting me to come to him. He still didn't tell me how much he was hurt, just to come and bring his dress shoes that he had left with me. . . . Not knowing where we could stay, I left the baby with my mother and on a cold dreary New Year's Eve, 1944, my father and I boarded the train. . . . After travelling all day and several changes and a couple of long waits on cold, foggy, country platforms we finally got to Devizes about 9 p.m. We went to the MP station and enquired where the hospital was, two of the MPs were heading that way and they gave my father and I a lift in their open jeep. It sure was cold. Although it was after visiting hours the MPs got us in and there was Bob sitting in a wheelchair. I was so relieved at seeing him sitting up, I really didn't notice what was wrong at first, then I noticed one leg was missing. It had been amputated just below the knee.

He had in fact been wounded during the advance near Aachen near the German border when his jeep had been attacked by aircraft, probably Allied, after he had volunteered to fetch extra rations for the men in the front line. For his new young wife, aged barely twenty, it was a tragic reunion and, after a long search for somewhere to stay, 'I finally went to bed in a strange room, in a strange town to the sound of the bells ringing the old year out and the New Year in' – the year, everyone expected, of victory. For three months, after fetching the baby and moving into lodgings in the town, she visited the hospital twice every day, once wheeling the baby the two miles each way, once by herself.

Finally hope began to revive. Winter started into spring, the wild geese were flying back and the snowdrops were blooming in the woods. They let Bob have an overnight pass before going back to the States . . . but you could tell his leg was bothering him too much for him to really enjoy himself. He went back to the States the end of March 1945, to Walter Reed Hospital in DC, for further surgery and rehabilitation. I went back to Brighton. . . . The baby developed a mastoid, she was operated on, but died at the age of four and a half months. I was quite despondent after that, but finally snapped out of it.

Very different was the next stage in the love-story of the WAAF stationed in Belfast, previously mentioned, whose father had fought a bitter battle against her marriage. The problem of what to eat at the reception had finally been solved, 'a small fruit cake', with, for canapés, colourful if not exactly luxurious, 'peas on toast fingers'. The determined bride had made other plans, too:

Visiting with a friend . . . I learned of the perfect place for a honeymoon, the Bell Inn at Hurley, west of London. . . . They had a vacancy for a week beginning March 5th. I reserved it. . . . With everything under control I returned to camp. The month of February passed without anything definite. On the evening of Friday, March 2nd [1945], I was on duty watching the radar tube. Around 10.30 p.m. the phone rang in the Ops Room. It was for me. . . . A voice said 'Hi'. I might have been the Air Chief Marshal, the co-operation I received in getting me on the first train for London the next morning. . . . My mother, father and Jim met me in London . . . Jim [had] guessed the size of my wedding ring . . . by buying one to fit his little finger . . . . The vicar had been contacted and the wedding set for 10 a.m. Monday . . . Jim and I picked up our special licence in Westminster, had lunch at the Trocadero before returning to Chislehurst.

To her great relief her father's opposition had, at the eleventh hour, miraculously melted away, and he insisted on meeting his future son-in-law at the station.

As my mother said, she knew everything was all right because when they came up the drive they were talking. In fact Jim was so acceptable that soon after they arrived home Dad had produced his last precious bottle of port from pre-war days and . . . my mother served a rare real egg in an eggcup, which he unfortunately had no idea how to eat.

Monday morning finally came and at breakfast I realized I didn't have a hat. My mother had given me some of her precious coupons and I had bought a corduroy suit at Wetheralls . . . . That and a pre-war wool suit and one dress made up my trousseau. I didn't have any flowers either. My sister and I grabbed a couple of bicycles and pedalled into Bromley for hat and flowers. I don't remember a word of my marriage vows. As I started down the aisle on my father's arm I felt a sharp pang of disappointment that there was no music. I remember Jim trying to put the ring on two different fingers before he hit the right one and later, as we were signing the register, the not too distant boom of a V–2.

Jim had brought four bottles of French champagne in a specially built crate. We still use the crate as a stand for our Christmas tree. We served the champagne at the reception along with my mother's fruit cake. The peas on toast fingers were good for a laugh, every time you bit one the peas rolled on to the floor. At last it became a respectable time to catch the train for London and on to Hurley. The Bell Inn is eleventh-century, modernized for comfort and completely unspoiled. It was a bit embarrassing asking for our room with double bed, reserved by a Miss. . . . The receptionist said breakfast was served in bed if we liked . . . and then she added with great pride that an egg was on the menu. We had a beautiful room, fully carpeted, fireplace, our own bath. . . . Drinks in front of the fire in the evening. During the day we would take long walks along the Thames. Once we went into town and bought a dozen tulips at an outrageous price. . . . One day as we walked along the Thames the sky overhead became black with planes, troop carriers and gliders . . . but for us the war had stopped for a week.

The aircraft they had seen were setting off in support of the crossing of the Rhine. Eight weeks later the war in Europe had stopped for everyone.

30

DEMURE AND MODEST BRITISH BRIDES

'And over to the States they'll travel
(Congress guarantees free rides).
Domestic tangles to unravel;
demure and modest British Brides.'

— *Verse in GI Brides' Magazine, 1946.*

THE cynics who had predicted that when the Americans set sail from Europe they would leave their womenfolk behind were proved right, though not for the reason they had predicted. Everyone agreed that priority should be given to getting 'the boys' home and as a result most GI brides faced a wait of from a few months to more than a year, the most frustrating and lonely period of their whole marriage, made worse because girl friends married or engaged to British servicemen were now welcoming them home for good.

Defining a GI bride as someone who married an American serviceman who had been stationed in the British Isles at some time before mid August 1945 – though the actual wedding might not have taken place until later – the number of women needing transport totalled about 70 000, many with one or more small children. By January 1946 some 27 000 wives and children had already been sent across the Atlantic or were 'in the pipeline'; most travelled during that year – the peak was around March and April, nearly a year after the fighting had ceased – but brides were still arriving in large numbers well into 1947, and at least one marriage, of a Glasgow woman, resulting from an initial meeting during the war, occurred eight years later.

Apart from those who made private arrangements, only those brides who had already been married for some time managed to reach America before the end of the war, though, with the great troopships returning empty, passages then were easier to find than they later became. A Harrow girl, an only child, who had married her husband in June 1943, remembers that 'my mother and father were very upset' when in October 1944 she was finally warned to be ready to leave from Liverpool while, having 'no idea how long it would be before my husband got back', she did not enjoy the eight-day crossing on the *Mauretania* with her small son and ninety other brides and children . . . seasick and scared stiff of U-boats'. Suddenly, however, 'we looked out and could see the huge buildings of New York and right in the middle the Statue of Liberty'.

Women whose husbands had already been sent back to the United States because of wounds or sickness were also at an advantage in gaining passages. One of them, whose husband had formerly been stationed at Shipdham, remembers arriving home from a thanksgiving service at Norwich Cathedral for the end of the war in Europe to find an American MP on the doorstep who 'handed me a sealed envelope and I was sworn to secrecy. In this furtive way I had to say goodbye to all those I held dear and four days later I loaded my very limited amount of luggage into a taxi and set out alone for Thorpe railway station. . . . Another MP handed me more sealed instructions and admonished me not to open them until I had boarded the London train.' All this secrecy, she soon discovered, was quite unnecessary and merely meant that at Waterloo station a crowd of relatives were 'gathered to bid their fond farewells' to her fellow passengers while she had no one to see her off.

Air travel to the United States in 1945 was still an expensive rarity: the single flight, via Lisbon, cost £141, compared to £40 to £65 for a sea passage, but even aircraft seats were at a premium. One WAAF, whose idyllic honeymoon with her Lieutenant has been described in an earlier chapter, was given in deep secrecy (the original source was a friend of her husband's sister) the name of someone in the Pan American agency in London who 'might help' and who did indeed offer her a seat – but only on Christmas Day 1945. This was not the season to be leaving one's homeland, but the airline did their best to create a festive mood. 'At Shannon they gave us a bottle of Irish whiskey. At Gander they gave us a bottle of port. At New York someone swiped my whiskey.'

These women were the lucky ones. Most GI brides were still stranded in Britain, often fearing that, if they were separated too long, their brand-new husbands would lay all memories of them aside along with their uniforms and discharge papers. By October the 'GIs' Wallflowers', as they had been nicknamed, often visibly pregnant or with babies in their arms, were wandering hopefully from one shipping office to the next. One even threatened to kill herself there and then in the offices of the Cunard White Star Company if refused a berth.

That month Lieutenant-Commander Herbert Agar, US Navy, bravely confronted the stormiest scene of his career in Caxton Hall, Westminster, where 200 angry women, many pregnant or with small children, staged a demonstration of protest at the delay, waving banners proclaiming them 'Forgotten GI Wives' and chanting their already well-known slogan: 'We want a boat!' The proceedings nearly ended in uproar when one four-month-old baby, eager to be reunited with 'Pop', already back home in Reading, Pennsylvania, 'let out a howl and could not be quieted', but eventually, the reporter recorded, baby Anita was promoted to sitting on the platform and was 'rock-a-byed behind Mr Agar's chair'. The meeting did not achieve much – the ships were simply not there to send – but did reveal a common anxiety: many of the women were expecting a baby and afraid that they would be unable to travel if their turn did not come soon.

"Well, Yank, I suppose you'll forget all about England when you get back to America!"

Although nothing like as often as had been predicted, some GIs did indeed change their minds once back in their native country. Still living in one Norfolk village is a woman whose husband, a local resident remembers, 'went back to America after the war and has never been heard of since', an incident recalled because, perhaps already betraying some inner doubt, he appeared in church for his wedding wearing one black shoe and one brown, and, his first-name being Gabriel, he was nicknamed 'Angel'. The sixteen-year-old Clacton bride quoted earlier remembers that when her new husband left 'Mum was so upset she took me into the pub', unheard of behaviour for a strict Salvationist, and 'we both had a drink and a smoke that night'. That summer 'I thought Matt had forgotten me' and when she lost her baby 'I didn't care if I lived or died'. Next day thirty-five letters for her arrived, one for each day since her husband's departure, and in May 1946 they were reunited in New York, 'Matt six feet four inches and wearing cowboy boots,' towering over his bride, a whole foot shorter – the start of 'a wonderful happy marriage' to 'a very gentle, lovable guy and a wonderful father and husband'.

The uncertainty of a Staffordshire girl, living in Stone, was ended a good deal less happily. After her fiancé's departure just before D-Day she had prepared herself for marriage by corresponding with his family, until at last 'our army was moving into Germany and suddenly the war was over. The next I heard Ed was in the States and out of the army. Then came a letter to say he'd got a girl pregnant, gone to a Justice of the Peace and was married. I thought the end of the world had come.' Two years later came the curious sequel – a letter from the faithless Ed announcing that he had divorced his wife and inviting her to become wife number two. She declined, being now married herself, but did eventually visit his family, most successfully, and finding the man who had jilted her unchanged 'shed a few tears for what might have been'.

Far more tragic was the experience of a Nottingham girl, who having, as mentioned earlier, carefully checked with her boy friend's mother that he was free to marry, was, by July 1945, in hospital expecting her first baby when her husband, on furlough from France, arrived with a present of 'two marvellous nightdresses from France'. He learned by telephone that he had a son and 'later on in the day I had a lovely bunch of roses from him', but this was to prove their final contact, for 'I never heard from Don again', and after weeks of heartbreaking uncertainty she learned his aircraft had crashed in France, killing all the crew. Bravely she decided to go to America as already planned, but six months after crossing on the *Queen Mary*, in February 1946, she was back in England, the victim of homesickness.[1]

Although much was heard of GIs who had conveniently forgotten their marriage vows, or promises to marry, less was heard of British women who failed to arrive as promised. 'In the end I refused to join him in the States,' remembers one former WAAF who was 'very much in love' with a Sergeant pilot from San Francisco, previously stationed at Bassingbourn. 'When it

---

1. Curiously enough, as a result of her subsequent visits to her in-laws her son became intensely American-minded, followed his dead father into the United States Air Force, and married an American girl.

came to it I could not bear the thought of leaving my home and family and was terrified of going to a strange country.'

'It was the fact that he went back two months before me that did it,' confesses another victim of last-minute cold feet, a girl from Portsmouth, who until then even survived the news, broken to her by an air force doctor, that her husband-to-be, a widower with a small daughter, could have no more children, and had resigned herself to frequent separation from him since he was an oil-driller from Oklahoma whose usual home was a caravan. At the very last minute she realized she could not bear to leave her own happy, close-knit family. 'At 10 o'clock on the night before I was going to leave at 8 a.m. the next morning I wrote him a letter, tore up my sailing tickets on the *Queen Mary* and all my papers and passport and that was that.'[1]

But the vast majority of brides were eager to be gone, and in some places even formed their own clubs to help the weary months pass till their turn came to set off. The 48 Club in Oxford, named after the number of waiting wives, not the date when they expected to sail, had regular meetings in a local café, duly described by one member in its own magazine, *State Express*, launched in Febuary 1946:

> Giggle, giggle, chatter, chatter,
> Laughter, lots of girlish fun.
> They're all quite mad, but does it matter?
> The party, boys, will soon be done.
>
> And over to the States they'll travel
> (Congress guarantees free rides),
> Domestic tangles to unravel,
> Demure and modest British brides.

Other contributions included a lesson in American history, and an account of a Christmas party in a church hall, where the 'olde English frolic known as "Winking" ' was considered acceptable 'but "Postman's Knock", which one gentleman put forward as being his idea of the most warming game of all, was rejected by Madame la Présidente . . . as being a shade too compromising'. Most GI brides would still recognize, too, this account of 'A Day in the Life of a GI Bride'.

Another grey day at the office. Three people drift in to say 'Haven't you gone yet?' You could break their necks. . . . Lunch with bosom friend, Barbara. . . . Being a nice girl she doesn't ask you when you expect to leave. . . . Round to the bank, and praise-be, the Board of Trade permit has at last been authorized by the Bank of England so you can finally send off that parcel of wedding presents. . . . Home again and there's a letter from the Transportation Office enclosing a fresh

1. Here too the story had a final twist. She later married a British sailor who had broken off his engagement to a girl from Cleveland, Ohio.

set of all the forms you've already sent in, just to see if they can fool you. You begin to feel like you're crawling through a great jungle of red tape with only your love to guide you, but there are also four lovely letters from Joe, so the temperature rises several degrees. . . . Then you get to thinking how big a thing it is that you two ever met and got yourselves married, with him coming from the other side of the world and all. . . . You cut out the deep thinking and sit down to write a long letter to your husband – the nicest part of the day.

While she waited the impatient wife could also console herself with *A Bride's Guide to the USA*, a booklet remarkably like the serviceman's *Guide to Great Britain* in reverse, and equally sensible and practical:

Don't mind if at first you feel left out of some of the jokes that go by you in conversation. No one expects a newcomer to get them. . . . Kidding is perhaps harder to get used to, but you have to learn. It may consist of mimicking, to see if you 'can take it'. . . . Later you may learn to kid back, but don't try it till you know how.

The American ideal is often higher than common American practice. . . . There is some unfriendliness between people of different ancestry when they are settled in large groups still recognizable as 'foreign'. There is prejudice in some areas against Negroes, in some areas against Jews, in some against Catholics, and in some against Orientals, especially Japanese.

The stern advice which followed – 'Don't just sit around and die of homesickness' – seemed barely to be needed for clearly Mrs GI Bride was unlikely to have much time to feel sorry for herself:

Americans . . . by 'settling down' . . . mean finding . . . a line of work with prospects of higher pay and a 'future' rather than security. Love of home . . . is not necessarily connected with love of a house . . . Americans move often and may attach their home feeling almost entirely to their furniture and car. . . . You may as well like it, for this is the way of life that has built the British Commonwealth of Nations as well as the United States. This is how your people have made history and now it is your turn.

By early 1946 the movement of GI brides across the Atlantic was well under way, the operation bearing, as was often pointed out, a remarkable resemblance to the way in which their husbands had arrived three or four years earlier. Tidworth, known to so many GIs, was the assembly point, Southampton the usual port of departure, the ships involved – the *Queen Mary* reinforced by smaller troopships as they became available – the same as those which had brought so many troops to the war. There were, however, some visible – and audible – differences. A BBC woman reporter, approaching in February 1946 the brides' transit camp at Perham Down, near Tidworth, which the brides reached by special train from Waterloo, found herself driving through serried ranks of girls chanting their customary battle-cry 'We want ships', and a noise from the surrounding huts, of 'the clanking of spoons on plates and baby howls'. The girls were waited on at meals by German PoWs, who, deprived of their own families, seemed to enjoy looking after those of their late enemies, and scattered over the camp, sleeping four to a room, were 640 women, with an average age of twenty-three, the youngest, being a fifteen-year-old (a fact not broadcast) travelling from Surbiton to North Carolina, the oldest, whose age was also discreetly omitted, from Dorking destined for Manhattan Beach, California, having a seventeen-year-old daughter by a previous marriage. With them were 176 babies, who 'slept in the deep steel drawers taken from the filing cabinets ... fine draught-proof cradles'. The organization, this reporter discovered, was excellent, with a theatre and PX to occupy the women while they waited. 'Processing' occupied most of a day, and involved filling in a form over two feet long, which demanded 'every imaginable detail, including whether the bride had ever been in prison or an almshouse' and 'whether she intended to try and overthrow by "force or violence" the Government of the United States'.

Most who made the journey agreed about the excellence of the arrangements. One local woman who constantly visited the camps at Tidworth and Ludgershall at this time, as her GI boy friend – later to become her husband – was among the administrative staff was impressed by the profusion of 'everything the girls could possibly need ... baby bottle nipples to notepaper, lipsticks to deodorants'. She was less taken however, with some of the women themselves:

The brides were a mixed bunch of every shape, size, age (sixteen to sixty-six), class and means. I met hundreds [but] I could never categorize them except for two things. None were from the 'top drawer' and seldom did one see a shy or retiring girl. . . . At the camp I saw girls breaking loose from their quarters at night to go with the GIs. Some went with the German PoWs, but those found out never got to the States, so Johnnie said. Some girls neglected their children shamefully, others didn't know how to take care of them. Here the Red Cross girls did a valiant job, they took the children while their mothers were being processed, dried the tears of the homesick and bolstered the courage of girls who were having doubts about their journey.

Such last-minute fears were common; leaving one's homeland *was* an emotional wrench and tears were rarely far away in these last days on British soil. One woman living at Appleshaw who attended a farewell concert with her friend, a GI bride, around this time remembers that when 'the band started up with "If You Were The Only Girl In The World" the rest of the song was drowned by sobbing'. A young Irishman who saw his cousin off to America from Belfast remembers that as the ship cast off the crowd broke even more movingly into '"When Irish Eyes Are Smiling", which they certainly weren't.'

Unlike their husbands, most GI brides look back on their transatlantic journey with pleasure. These were the experiences of the woman from Norwich, previously mentioned, who received her sailing orders on VE-Day:

At 5 p.m. we were aboard the *Thomas H. Barry* and by 11 p.m. we had anchored off Land's End. What a motley passenger list! Sixty war-brides, twenty babies, and 2500 United States repatriated prisoners and wounded GIs. Early the next day we set sail in . . . the last convoy to cross the Atlantic after World War II. As the last jagged tip of English soil receded into the distance my heart sank to rock bottom. Despite being desperately seasick for the first three days the ten-day journey was pleasant and stimulating. Black-out restrictions were lifted when we were midway across the Atlantic and a wild cheer went up from all decks as siren answered siren in recognition of this momentous occasion. Each afternoon the war-brides visited the wounded. . . . They gave us tips on what to do and what not to do . . . and assured me that I'd be scalped by Indians when I reached Wyoming. We dined with the officers. The food was lavish and very rich – hard to take after years of rationing. . . . On the tenth afternoon we sailed past the Statue of Liberty, the GIs glad to see her, the war-brides with mixed feelings. There was a tremendous welcome – for the GIs we found out later. Bands were playing the latest pop-tunes like 'Accentuate the Positive', chorus girls danced aboard passing ferries and each bit of river traffic whistled a salute. We all crowded to the rails, the wounded beating time to the music with their crutches. By midnight we had been processed and were at a hotel in New York.

The chief memory of those who crossed during stormy periods in spring or autumn is like that of so many GIs before them – of being almost permanently ill. A Droitwich woman, one of 1000 who left England on the *Alexander*, on a 'gloomy foggy day' in March 1946 remembers her less happy memories of the crossing. 'It took nine days . . . I was seasick all the way, what with all new kinds of food and the smell of paint on the boat [which] was enough to turn anyone green.' The other aspect of the voyage which bulks largest in most women's recollection is the food. 'There was a lot of overeating at first,' remembers one abstemious observer. Passengers used to wartime rations stared in amazement at unlimited eggs, meat, and sugar and one at least pleaded, unsuccessfully, with the steward to take back her 'large pat of butter, about one ounce, as it had not been touched. . . . We told him that that pat of butter was half one week's ration in England but it didn't seem to make much impression.'

If they fed much better than the GIs, however, the brides probably suffered even more from a shortage which also features large in their husbands' memories, lack of water, a recurring theme in many women's reminiscences. Typical are those of a young woman from New Malden, whose meeting with her husband in a train due to a common interest in shorthand has been described in an earlier chapter. The detailed diary which she kept in shorthand of her experiences – she and her husband later set up a secretarial agency in New York – is probably the fullest account which exists of what it was like to be a GI bride.

The great adventure began for her, rather dispiritingly, in the early hours of Saturday, 20 April 1946:

5 a.m. I rose very hurriedly and dressed and washed. After this we went to a queue for breakfast. . . . Porridge, bacon, bread, pancake and coffee (so-called). After this we went and tidied up a little then . . . piled onto buses and were driven to Tidworth station. Here we were helped very eagerly into the train by GIs. After about two hours' delay – it was about 8.30 by then – we pushed out of the station, waving to the GIs, and so we started – very cold and a little hungry.

About 8.45 we arrived in Southampton. We piled off the train and . . . piled onto the ship. It looked pretty good and is very clean. The cabins have twenty-two bunks, two-tiered, are somewhat cramped. There is not much room to hang or even *put* anything. We were all just about starving by this time and lunch (first sitting) was at 12.45. . . . We sailed at 3.30 . . . as planned. We watched the shores of England gradually disappear without the least unhappiness as we were so glad to be on the ship at last and actually on our way. . . . We went down to supper about 5.30, had fried steak . . . peaches and chocolate and vanilla ice-cream (!) Then after a few turns around the deck we went to bed.

Next morning found her 'upon deck being pretty ill', unable to face anything except some dry biscuts (which like a good American she already called 'crackers') brought her by a fellow sufferer but by the afternoon had moved away from 'the state where death seemed preferable to life', which other sufferers from seasickness will readily recognize, and had decided 'If the sea doesn't get rough I shall be able to stand up to this okay and enjoy the voyage.' By Saturday, seven days out, however, 'the sea was rather rough and . . . they placed ropes all over the ship for those brave spirits who dared venture from their cabins and the bunks just rocked. It was pretty awful and I just lay and prayed (almost).' Even when, as they did eventually, the high seas abated, another problem remained.

No baths, and showers are locked. I can see I shall arrive in New York looking like a tramp. . . . It is really a terrible job here trying to keep clean. We wash in seawater, of course, and it feels so sticky afterwards. We have some special soap . . . and it has an awful smell. You can guess washing is not a popular diversion here. . . . We were lying on our bunks – too lazy to go up on deck – and a Negro stewardess came by, saying 'Anyone want a bath?' Of course we just flew for our towels and stuff and rushed along the corridor after her. We went up to the cabins of the mothers with babies who have separate bathrooms and were assigned two to each room. Joan Minnesota[1] and I were together and had beautiful hot baths – the first time we felt clean after leaving Tidworth.

Fifth Day. In the mornings we usually sit on the deck . . . and read, talk etc.

---

1. The women knew each by their first names, plus the name of the state to which they were going.

Two days back I went to a lecture on the City of New York . . . the transportation system and the educational system. Yesterday Jean Maine and I went to an informal lecture on the Deep South. A lanky Lieutenant from Florida gave it in his Southern drawl, which he said was hardly a drawl at all. . . . This morning Jean and I went to an informal talk by a WAC from New Hampshire on the New England States, New Hampshire, Vermont, Maine, Rhode Island, Connecticut and Massachusetts. 'The New England States,' she declared, 'are the backbone of America.' She told us about corn roasts, the New England shore dinner (made up entirely of sea food – about ten courses) and the hay rides.

In the afternoon we usually sit on deck and read our library books or magazines, eat our candy, smoke etc. We have a very nice library . . . up to date and interesting books. We have been to two movies, one new one with Fred Astaire and the other the usual type of detective film. Eighth Day. This morning we were issued with landing tags. . . . We were also given a souvenir passenger list . . . [which] . . . we had signed by our particular friends and acquaintances. Joan California and I had a bath this afternoon and feel pretty well set up for the departure tomorrow. Most of us spent the afternoon in our cabin beautifying ourselves, plucking eyebrows, manicuring nails, setting hair, etc. We shall all look so glamorous tomorrow that our husbands won't know us. The Red Cross girl said that half the girls last time went right past their husbands and didn't know them on the dock. No chance of that where I am concerned. If Al's not there to meet me the war will start all over again. It is amazing how much happier everyone has been looking today even though some of them, like Joan California, have four or five days' journey to go.

And so, on 29 April, came 'the great day at last'.

I was up at 6.30 as we had a medical inspection at 7 o'clock. I walked around the deck for a while. It was freezing cold so . . . I went down and watched the other girls making frantic efforts to get all their belongings into their suit cases . . . until the colonel announced, about 12.30, that we had sighted land. We all made a dash for the stairs and looked out from the deck. If you followed the sky-line along very carefully you could just see two little bumps of cloud. That was land.

About 1 o'clock we reached the lightship in the harbour. . . . Another small craft came to meet us with a GI band on board, all playing 'Roll Out The Barrel' very lustily. The Terry Sisters sang for us and there was also a Negro singer. They came along beside us for quite a long way and it made us all very excited to think that they were welcoming us so happily. . . . The decks were crammed with girls. . . .

First we sighted Coney Island, the wheel and the parachute jump on the starboard side, then we saw the Atlantic highlands of New Jersey on the port side. . . . The ships in the harbour gave us two big hoots on their sirens to welcome us and we had to give them two hoots back, saying 'Thank you'. The sirens gave us all the jitters after the comparative silence of the sea voyage. They made the babies cry, so after about half-an-hour the colonel said we would not return the hoots. . . . We saw the *Washington* just coming out from New York . . . on her way to Germany with occupation troops and their wives. We cheered each other and some of our girls shouted out 'You're going the wrong way!'

And now, at last, came the long-awaited moment of reunion.

As we came into the dock they started to call out names on the loud-speaker. These girls were to report to the immigration officers in the lounge and have their landing cards stamped and then to the library for their luggage tags . . . I went up there with a girl from our cabin and we stood in line . . . I said goodbye to the two Joans, promising to write, of course, then . . . dashed for the gang plank. An official took my landing card and I found my luggage for a porter to carry to the gate. . . . When I got to the gate I told a chap with a microphone my name and this he called out, so that Al, somewhere in a bunch of men at the other end of the dock, could come and sign for me. . . . He came rushing through the gate and – well, you can guess the rest.

This meeting was all that the most sentimental young bride could have looked for:

As we went down the steps, Al told me that Emily, Gladys, and Tom [his sisters and a GI friend] were there to meet me also. . . . We managed to get a cab to the Lincoln Hotel where Al had arranged for us to stay that night, as he felt I would be . . . tired. . . . We went up to our room to clean up a bit and I put on the heavenly flowers Al had brought me – two white gardenias, with a heavenly perfume. Also he had bought me a most wonderful 'Hello' gift – a dear little wrist watch . . . and this I also put on immediately. We went down to the foyer where the other three were waiting. We walked through Times Square – very bright, but I was hungry and didn't appreciate it. We went to a Chinese restaurant, where they had menus about two feet by one foot. I had American dishes as it was my first dinner in America. . . . We talked and talked about all kinds of things. It was so unreal to be with Al again and his two sisters and I kept feeling I would wake up and find myself still in my bunk on that wretched ship, rocking about and not feeling too well. But everything was quite real and everyone was very happy. After dinner we walked up to Radio City, where they are having an Easter show. All round the buildings there, and around the ice rink, they had Easter lilies planted, it was really lovely to see those beautiful flowers among the skyscrapers of a big city. . . . Then we . . . went back to the hotel. It was a very nice room on the 14th floor with a bathroom attached. Oh, the joy of a hot bath in fresh water again. I have never known such a noisy place as New York by night – cars tooting horns, whistles blowing, buildings being knocked down, and police sirens (just like the movies) kicking up such a din that after the life at sea it seemed just shattering. . . . We had breakfast in bed at 7 o'clock. The usual two fried eggs, coffee, tomato juice etc. The rest of the day was the start of my new life . . . I feel that this is the beginning of a very happy adventure.

And so, indeed it proved, at least at first.

His parents were dead, the sister who lived at home (where we stayed for the first year) had entirely refurnished a bedroom for us and bought me pretty undies and trinkets. It was a large frame house in Staten Island, New York, and I was very happy running it and cooking for Al and his sister. . . . Al's sister had a cottage in the mountains of northern New Jersey where we spent our first summer and many weekends in subsequent years. This way of life was completely new to me – paddling a canoe down the lake to get provisions from the little local store and picking up the post from a numbered mailbox.

The warmth of their welcome, both official and private, reassured many brides like one arriving from Wiltshire four months later. 'What other country but the United States,' she wondered, 'would have had a band to greet the umpteenth shipment of war brides arriving at a remote New York pier?', in her case on Staten Island:

Johnnie had bought a 1941 Dodge, which, of course, impressed me with its size, comfort and amount of parking room needed. Carefully installed in the front seat, I was introduced to America, the two family frame houses of Staten Island, the ferry ride across the superb harbour (I tried to think of it as the first explorers had seen it), driving through Wall Street with Trinity Church ringed with sky-scrapers. Our destination was a midtown hotel. It was August, New York was hot and humid. We had cool, salad meals in a little restaurant with a black and white tiled floor. . . . It was run by one of the chefs whom I had met at Tidworth, a familiar face. . . . We bought sandals for my hot feet, encased in clumping English shoes. I saw a beggar in Times Square with a change machine attached to his belt. Johnnie took me to Palisades Amusement Park where I saw a girl with a bra that put her breasts in the region of her chin . . . I admired the *chic* brassiness of the New York girls until I was reminded one of the reasons Johnnie married me was because I didn't look that way.

One Manchester woman's dominant emotion, on arriving on the *Queen Mary* in the same year, in a contingent of 1100 brides, 700 babies and 'fifty unfortunate civilian passengers', was relief at regaining her identity. 'We were tagged back and front throughout the voyage. . . . I insisted to my husband's horror on wearing my tags on arrival at the hotel, since I had had the indignity for the past three weeks.' A woman from Droitwich still remembers 'the thrill' in March 1946 of the three-day drive back to Elgin, Illinois, beside her husband, after a week of seasick misery on board ship, although at the last minute her courage failed her and her husband 'drove me to the local park until I had enough courage to face his family'.

To their great relief many women now discovered that their husbands had understated rather than exaggerated their prosperity and social position. One Belfast girl who, her cousin acknowledges, 'came from a poor family and did not even have a bicycle', found awaiting her in Georgia 'a good second-hand car as her own personal gift', and as her husband 'had five brothers who had no girl friends she was soon being "treated like a queen" . . . and has lived happily ever after'.

Their friendly reception, both public and private, made a lasting impression upon many brides. One of the very first, who had arrived from Harrow in October 1944 while the war was still very far from over, said, 'People all the way down on the train were wonderful to me. The Pullman porters hovered over me like I was royalty. About 200 people met the train at Optima, in the Panhandle of Oklahoma, which was about all the people in the area. Everyone wanted to see this foreign daughter-in-law.' As for her husband's parents 'they also had just the one child and really acted like I was the daughter they had always wanted'.

The Norwich woman who set off just as the war in Europe finished – the flow of brides continued until well into 1947 – was equally delighted with her new country and its people.

My impressions of America and Americans in general were, and always have been, heartwarming and delightful. The first five days I spent in New York with an Italian family, relatives of a GI buddy of my husband. They gave me the 'grand tour' of New York and . . . even offered me a temporary home should I not like Wyoming. Then I headed out west, by train; a three-day journey. I had a self-contained 'roomette' and never did emerge until we reached Chicago eighteen hours later. I did not understand the American menus or the accents of the black porters. What a good thing my friends in New York had packed me a large lunch; I ate the left-overs for breakfast. After a twelve hour stop in Chicago I boarded another train for Casper, Wyoming. This time I slept in an upper berth. The occupants of the lower berth – a jovial lady from Florida and her quite sophisticated teenage daughter – soon befriended me and when we reached Casper took me to their family home there until my bus to Worland, Wyoming, was due. The bus rattled along beside jagged mountain peaks rising steeply on one side of the highway and on the other a tortuous thundering river smashing over rocks in the canyon below. Again a fellow passenger reassured me. When the bus stopped at the Main Street of Worland it was 2 a.m. and not a soul in sight. I began to panic but soon the manager from the hotel close by came over, giving me information about my husband's family. We all met the next morning and spent a lovely day in town together. The bank president, who hailed from Scotland, insisted on taking us out to lunch and people stopped us on the street 'to say "Hi" to the little English girl'. I spent three weeks at the ranch and during that time a Square Dance was held in my honour; the neighbours (who lived over a fifty-mile radius) gave me a belated bridal shower . . . and many relatives attended a pot luck picnic so we could get acquainted. Then I was off again, to Liberal, Kansas, where Frank was now stationed, another two-day train journey. . . .

Her wanderings were still not over. She spent her first Fourth of July *en route* for Denver, Colorado, where her husband was discharged, her wedding anniversary, New Year's Day, in Seattle, Washington, and finally ended up in the 'territory' – soon to become a state – of Alaska, where in the capital, Juneau, like true pioneers, 'we literally built our own home in a lovely little valley surrounded by mountains and a glacier'. The ex-WAAF from Surrey who descended – minus her whiskey – on New York at Christmas 1945, soon found herself escorted to 'a sleeper on the first train heading for South Bend, Indiana', where 'Jim's family welcomed me with open arms'. She was, however, like many others, surprised by the foreignness of some of her newly acquired relations. Her husband's aunt and uncle, she discovered, still spoke with a strong German accent, recalling the land of their birth. 'Now I was meeting the melting pot,' this Englishwoman reflected. Her other surprise came when she attended 'a women's softball game in South Bend. . . . The players argued with the referee and the spectators made noises to distract the pitchers and batters. Frankly, I didn't think it was very sporting.'

The Chippenham milk-tester, previously quoted, although conscious her husband's name was Italian, had not really understood the implications on her 'leisurely' journey from New York 'to Buffalo via the Finger Lakes', though enjoying its contrasts. 'One night we slept in a very crude cabin with an earth closet . . . the next two nights in the bridal suite at a motel. The proprietor had given it to us for the price of a room when he found I was a war bride.'

Finally we reached home, Lackawanna, New York [State]. It is a steel town, populated originally by immigrants hired by Bethlehem Steel in the first decade of the century. . . . In 1946 all the men in Johnnie's family, except his brother . . . worked in the plant and the economy of the town revolved around it. Nationalities were voluntarily segregated, name a country in Europe and I could tell you the streets in Lackawanna where people of that nationality and their children lived.

Johnnie's family lived in the newer area of the Italian section . . . Ma and Dick (Johnnie's stepfather . . . his father, a grocer, had died during the depression) lived in a house at a corner of a rectangular block of land. Three other brothers and sisters lived in houses on the same block of land and they all shared the area between the houses. Also sharing it was Ma's chicken run, Charlie's house-painting paraphernalia, George's concrete block-making machine, a few beds of struggling tomatoes, and hot peppers, and last, but certainly not least, Dick's pride and joy, his 1928 model A Ford, the rumble seat full of the necessary tools for his work as an odd-job man.

We got out of the car and I felt what I was to the grandchildren watching, a complete unknown. It was out of context for [anyone from his family] to marry a non-Italian, let alone a non-American. . . . Ma came bustling forward, a little Neapolitan peasant woman whom life had treated harshly but had not been able to destroy her natural dignity and pride and sunny nature. . . . I was taken into the house and seated at the kitchen table with a cup of black (oh how black, it could be spooned from the pot) coffee. The kids came in to stare and stay, then their parents, then the sisters and brothers from farther away. Momentarily I felt quite lost, not even in America, as Ma didn't speak English so all the talk was in rapid, excited Neapolitan dialect. Then Johnnie's eldest brother and his wife came in and I had met my first American friends.

When she had time to look round the house this woman realized how different it was from her own former home.

By American standards, it was poor, by my standards it was crowded but materially better off than my home in England. My mother-in-law, 'Ma', had an antiseptic-white kitchen with a huge refrigerator, a bathroom with all civilized facilities, the house had hot air central heating, storm windows and so on. I thought the linoleum on the floor not much . . . compared to carpets, but it turned out to be very practical to clean up after a family party.

And parties soon proved to be a frequent occurrence, the very first being held that day to welcome the new daughter-in-law:

> They gave me a marvellous welcome. Our arrival became an excuse to have a family party. All the seven sisters and brothers and the twenty-seven grandchildren came. There was spaghetti and meat sauce, huge bowls of salad, long loaves of crusty bread, wine from the barrels in the cellar and more of that black coffee. All the adults and older children sat round three tables put together to form one long one, and the younger children were fed picnic style in the kitchen and chased outside. After, Dick played Neapolitan songs on his accordion. . . . Ma spent six months teaching me Neapolitan cooking. I learnt to make their special tomato sauce, home-made 'spaghets', Easter pie, hot pepper relish, and how to bottle fruits and vegetables on a large scale. I watched Dick making wine in September. First the five barrels were washed by pumping water through them with a hose and rolling them around the cellar with chains in them. On a prearranged Sunday his brother from the wine-grape-growing area of New York State would arrive with a truckload of grapes. These were pounded in tubs, the resulting juice was put into the barrels and fermentation began. . . . The first tasting took place around February. . . . Most of the wine would be drunk much too soon. . . . But the ritual gave a pattern and coherence to the family. After a few jugs of wine came up from the cellar no one noticed how it tasted anyway.

The chief impression left on many brides by those first few strange weeks in a new country was of the vast size of America. One woman from Kent, a densely populated county of small and ancient villages, by the time she reached Alton, Illinois, after two overnight journeys and the usual wait in Chicago, 'was quite ready to take the first ship back to England. I had only a vague impression of vast empty spaces and tiny neat towns, with little white houses.'

I found the people for the most part singularly uninterested in other States, much less other parts of the world . . . they would enquire politely about conditions in Britain, say 'It must have been terrible' and proceed to tell me what a bad time they had here, [although] as far as I could see . . . the area was very little affected by the war. . . . I arrived in March and there was still snow on the ground, but, being dressed in woollies and tweeds, I found the central heating unbearable. The temperature was kept at about eighty and windows were never opened. It also took me a long time to be able to eat the meals provided by people trying to be kind to me after rationing. The violence bothered me, both of weather and people. . . . A year after I arrived a tornado almost wiped out two small towns nearby; also it seemed accepted that everyone should have guns and use them, there seemed very little respect for the law or policemen.

The 'language barrier' of which the official guides to both Britain and the United States tended to make a good deal proved the most easily surmounted of all. One Surrey woman, settled in Indiana, was 'helped enormously' by 'an ex-WAAF from Warwickshire who had been here a year who soon had me knitting with yarn and pins instead of wool and knitting needles'. A Glasgow woman, settling in Pennsylvania, has still not lived down her efforts to buy an 'aluminium girdle' to cook her husband's breakfast pancakes; the Americans called it an 'aluminum griddle'.

Some marriages did not take place until long after the end of the war. The experience of a Worksop woman, who while working as a 'wood-chopper' in Gloucestershire had fallen deeply in love with a man from Brooklyn, was far from unique:

When he went to Europe I kept writing and I did get a few letters back . . . and so when the war was finally over and I knew he had survived and was home with his family . . . I was sure that my wartime romance was just that. So when the job in Wotton was finished I went home . . . to a similar shop job. One Saturday afternoon my mother came into the shop and said, 'Here is a letter from America. I don't know that I should let you read it after all this time.' It was May 1946 and my American was asking me to please write to him. . . . And so the letters flew back and forth across the Atlantic. . . . When he proposed I said if he would come to Worksop to meet my parents and they approved I would say 'Yes'. So in the summer of 1947 we were married in the church where my parents were wed and by the same minister.

The two-day honeymoon was spent – a pleasant touch – in Wotton. 'How quiet it was', this young bride felt, without an American in sight or earshot – except, of course, hers, as after 'an interesting twenty-five years, most of it good,' he still is.

A London woman, now happily settled in California, remembers having had only two dates with her future husband before he was sent home in 1946. 'We thought it was goodbye to a short but happy friendship,' she remembers, 'but fate had other plans in store for us. In 1947, one day after coming over to marry me, we were indeed wed. . . . My instincts told me he was right for me.' Even more romantic, or reckless, according to how one looked at it, was the story of the girl working in a Hendon bank, whose sister had fallen in love with a GI but refused to marry him as she already had a husband, serving overseas. Once back in America, however, the disappointed lover decided that 'he could not live without having an English girl as his wife, and wrote and asked whether, as he could never marry her, she had a sister whom he could marry'. As it happened she did and this girl duly set off, solely on her sister's recommendation, to marry a man she had never met. On a later visit to England, a colleague remembers, 'she came into the bank to see us. . . . She was very happy with her husband and loved America.'

Any GI bride who crossed to America after the first contingents had left did so in the face of a flood of discouraging rumours, some of them true. One was that, divorce being so easy in the United States, she might arrive to find herself already an 'ex-wife'. One woman who arrived in August 1946 remembers some such cases among her own shipload, who returned 'heartbroken' to England on the same boat. Less well substantiated was the story of the girl who arrived in Oklahoma or Colorada to find that the promised ranch had shrunk to a wigwam, or of the woman who had expected to live comfortably on the income from a 'chain of gasoline stations' only to find herself dispensing petrol from her husband's single pump. One Watford man recalls a story of a local girl who 'as she walked down the gangplank saw her husband standing beside a barrow loaded with flowers'. To her delighted response, 'Joe, how lovely of you to bring all these flowers!', he was said to have replied: 'That's OK, honey. As soon as you've put your things away you can come out and help me sell them.' But not all such stories were inventions. A Newquay woman, herself happily married to an American Captain, 'met several brides who were so disillusioned. Expecting wonderful homes, they found shacks with ant-eaten floors and corrugated toilets at the end of a field.' One helper at the Red Cross club in Cheltenham recalls a GI boasting to his fiancée of his family's 'racing stable'. Later his friends 'let the cat out of the bag: His "racing stable" was a pigeon loft and he and his father had six racing pigeons, which had never even won a race.' Another Cheltenham girl, 'a solicitor's daughter, married a Greek American who said his father had a string of posh restaurants in New York. She came home after she found the "restaurants" were peanut stands outside the baseball grounds and she was expected to serve in one.'

Such experiences, though nothing like as common as legend suggested, were not wholly imaginary. One London woman who had met her husband while working in the Red Cross club in the former Clarendon Hotel at Oxford remembers that her reaction to the 'farm on the prairies of South Dakota', to which her husband took her, was 'that I'd moved back a generation in time. Kerosene lamps, no bathroom, one had to go outside to the "little house", cooking done on a coal and wood-burning range, no electric iron, just the irons heated on the stove. Neighbours, however, when I was introduced would ask: "Don't you like it here? Isn't it a fine place to live?"' Tactfully she used to reply, with truth, that 'people are so friendly and it's wonderful to eat eggs and fruit again'.

When I wrote home I only told of the good things; I'd been told by so many people that 'You'll regret going over there, my girl, you'll be back, he's probably got a wife and kids, just wait and see, we told you so.' I decided that even if it had all turned out as predicted I'd not go back. So, naturally, I wrote of the friendly folk, the wedding 'shower' given at the little country church for us [which] seemed

like a combination birthday and Christmas Day. . . . My father-in-law was quite
proud of me and sometimes would say Ann is like Naomi in the Bible. She said to
her husband: 'Whither thou goest, I will go, thy people will be my people,' and I
thought it was very sweet of him.[1]

An unexpectedly low standard of living and the general unfamiliarity of
life in America does not seem to have been a major cause of the failure of
such marriages. Those break-ups which did occur seem to have been
largely due to personal factors which would have applied anywhere and
they were not nearly as numerous as the cynics had predicted. Of the
twenty-three marriages on which I received detailed information, either
from one or both partners, or from a close relation, only five had ended in
divorce. The remaining eighteen are still flourishing or were ended – in
five cases – only by the death of a much-loved and still-mourned husband
or wife. As so often, however, it was the unhappy exceptions which gained
the publicity and whose story was heard in Britain: the contented wives,
happily making a success of their new marriages, remained unseen in the
United States.

" But, honey—where did you get the idea that all Americans live in skyscrapers ? "
(Acknowledgments to Paul Webb)

1. Her early endurance was rewarded. The couple now have 'a nice, modern farm and
two fine sons'.

The returning brides were in the early days also newsworthy in a way the happy marriages were not. One Manchester woman, arriving on the *Queen Mary* in 1947, saw for herself the premature end of some brides' marriages: 'No husband turned up to claim them, so they were turned back home with the ship.' One mother, returning from visiting her own happily married daughter in 1948, found that British women, already deserted by, or in flight from, their husbands, made up a sizeable portion of the passenger list. One Belfast woman, supporting herself after her own marriage had broken up by working in a hotel in New York, found it full of other disillusioned brides, 'some French, some German, but all a long way from home'. A Beeston, Nottinghamshire, woman remembers how, of four GI brides she knew, 'two came back within months, disillusioned'. Such women were not necessarily the worse for the experience, at least financially. 'They went to America', ran the cynical saying of the time, 'came back, and lived happily ever after on the alimony.'

Why did a considerable number of Anglo-American marriages end in divorce? One bride's mother, visiting the United States in 1947, heard an ingenious theory: 'Many of the men were homesick for "Mom" and saw in their English sweetheart a substitute. On returning home this was no longer necessary.' A woman from the little Cotswold town of Winchcombe, married in 1944, who left her husband for good in December 1946 after ten unhappy months at Baton Rouge and Harding Field, Louisiana, has another explanation why her marriage failed.

I met my future husband at a dance in October 1942 when I was eighteen and there were no English boys around. I was attracted to him physically and being immature did not look further than his physical appearance. . . . It didn't work out for two reasons. First I developed asthma very badly and the cause of it . . . I have since realized . . . was just plain homesickness. . . . I can trace my family back to 1611 living in Winchcombe all that time and . . . have come to the conclusion that my roots go down too deep to be uprooted. . . . The other reason was that he was the biggest liar I have ever met – he even lied about things it isn't worth lying about – and the combination of these two things plus having a small child was too much for me. . . . My husband got heavily into debt buying the small amount of furniture we did have and quite frankly I was not mature enough to cope with the situation.

But she looks back without rancour on what now seems a strange and distant interlude in her life. 'I found most of the Americans I met extremely friendly and helpful. The doctor who treated me for asthma never sent me a bill: my neighbours at Harding Field' – her husband had rejoined the air force when he lost his civilian job – 'were very good to me.' And for her first husband she has, in the tranquillity of middle age, and after a happy second marriage to an Englishman, no hard feelings: 'It was all experience and he *was* very good-looking.'

What was clearly fatal to any marriage was to be disappointed both in one's new husband and in his country, like a Belfast woman who arrived in August 1946.

Nothing I had heard or read had prepared me for the size and speed of the States. New York in August was so hot. We went by train to Chicago, we had a couple of hours between trains and had a walk around. . . . We got lost and found ourselves in Skid Row. I was shocked. Drunks lying about. This was not the land of plenty I had expected. From Chicago we went to Omaha, Nebraska. We were married there. . . . We had to have blood tests and queue for the licence. The couple in front of us were very young and the girl did not even know the chap's surname. Everything was so strange to me. The people had to have their money first before they would even listen to you. In the evening I could hear a funny noise – crickets all over the place about four inches long. When I went into the garden they landed on me. I nearly went mad. . . . Perhaps too much water had passed under the bridges; the magic was gone . . . Harold had lost all his swagger. . . . He counted his change over there. He compared prices when we went shopping. This was not my GI Joe at all. We parted. Eventually I got a divorce and got on the train for New York. . . . There was a dock strike on. I had to wait a few days for my boat. Everything was so expensive. I was so worried in case I ran out of money. When I got on board the *Queen Mary* again at last I could have kissed the deck.[1]

The former wife of an RAF test pilot from Ramsbury, who crossed the Atlantic after her divorce to marry a GI whom she had found 'kind and considerate and fatherly towards my son', also discovered that in Sacramento, California, he was no longer the man she had known back in Wiltshire. 'He had returned to a world which did not understand what he had been through. No Americans that I met did, except veterans. He was drinking heavily and did not want to marry me.' A year later, still single, she decided to come home again.

If one lesson can be deduced from the wartime marriages of British women to Americans it is that generalization about what makes for an enduring relationship is impossible. Some marriages where the partners were in their teens and had only met two or three times before becoming engaged have proved a great success; so, too, have others where at first everything, including a shared house and primitive living conditions, seemed against them. Yet some relationships cautiously entered into after a long period of acquaintance have long since failed. The Chippenham milk-tester, for example, who had seen her future husband almost every day, and whose father had carefully 'vetted' the young man's suitability, found, despite the heart-warming welcome, already described, from her Italian in-laws, that her marriage was soon heading for the rocks: 'The winters in New York State are long and cold. After Johnnie and I had moved

1. This informant adds, however: 'Everything seemed so quiet and slow when I got back home . . . I thought I had made an awful mistake in coming back.'

to our new home I soon found time to think about my new life and my marriage' and especially 'of my husband's Italian temperament which I had never seen . . . in England. He was quick to lose his temper and quick to make up. I could not react fast enough.' Two years later she went back to work and eventually divorced her husband.

The diary-keeping secretary from New Malden, whose happy first months on Staten Island have already been described, soon had sadder events to record. 'We drifted apart,' she sums up, and by 1955 they were divorced. The Cricklewood divorcée, who had been agreeably surprised at the comfortable home provided by her husband in Connecticut, later reluctantly abandoned her marriage on medical advice, for he became incurably paranoiac and was for ever 'in and out of mental hospitals'.

But there were many happier stories. A woman who worked for the Bank of England during its wartime stay in Whitchurch, and who saw many colleagues marry men from Tidworth, testified that 'all our girls fell on their feet and, when on holiday in England, visit the bank looking madly expensive and with strong American accents'.

A Sidmouth woman who herself could look back in 1966, when her husband died suddenly, on twenty happy years in Elgin, Illinois, and Denver, Colorado, 'knew about sixteen English girls over in the States, all extremely happy, despite all the rumours. I feel, though I was married to Bob only twenty years, we led such a completely happy full life we lived a lifetime.'

Finally what of the Brighton girl quoted earlier, who accepted her husband's invitation in the Dorset moonlight to join him in Richlands, Virginia, and whose marriage began under the twin shadows of the death of her baby and her husband's loss of a leg in action? She had not wanted to leave England, but the couple were happily reunited in Virginia, where she found 'the mountains and rivers of the South-West portion . . . beautiful' though strange 'to someone raised among the rolling Sussex downs'. Apart from acquiring a splendid family of four children, 'nothing spectacular' she claims, 'has happened since' – surely a splendid tribute to the success o any marriage.

31
FOREVER STATESIDE

'The barbarians from America unloosened the English character.'
— *Former Technical Sergeant, from Osawatomie, Kansas, 1973.*

THE skies are silent now. Occasionally a solitary far-off jet screams upwards, but the massed squadrons of Fortresses and Liberators no longer drown all other sounds as they claw their heavily laden way into the air and the Lightnings and Mustangs no longer roar down the newly built runways which have now vanished beneath the encroaching grass and clover. Apart from a few still surviving American bases – self-contained communities whose occupants venture out little and then usually in civilian clothes – the wide horizons of East Anglia enclose only the sounds of peace.

In ancient Cambridge the only American accents one hears belong to the camera-draped tourist; not even a ghost remains of the jostling, horse-playing, pleasure-bent GIs who once filled its ancient streets. And nowhere is more peaceful than the American Military Cemetery just outside the city. This thirty-acre site was dedicated on Memorial Day, 30 May 1944 – American equivalent of the then British Armistice Day – not merely, it was said, as a resting place for the fallen, but 'as a lasting memorial to the United States' dead of this war'. After a simple service conducted by a British Bishop, wreaths were laid by a British General and by Lieutenant-General Karl Spaatz and General John C. Lee, representing General Eisenhower. Although after the war most families asked to have their sons' remains repatriated to the United States, 3811 are still buried there, among them twenty-four who were never identified and whose headstones are inscribed: 'Here rests in honoured glory a comrade-in-arms known but to God.' Listed on a memorial wall, too, are the names of 5125 soldiers, sailors and airmen whose bodies were never found. Apart from one solitary grave in the parish churchyard of Morton, near Blackpool, all the American war dead of World War II buried in Britain lie here. Standing in this peaceful spot, amid the immaculately kept paths and neatly trimmed grass, beside the long, open pool whose waters now reflect only the empty sky, it is hard to associate it with the gay young men whose story has been described in this book.

> They shall not grow old
> As we who are left grow old

a British poet has written of the Flanders dead of World War I.[1] It is no less true of the Americans who died in World War II. Here is one small corner of England that will always be American and whose occupants will be in spirit forever Stateside.

There are other places, too, where these now-vanished 'Yanks' still seem particularly close. Scattered about the British Isles are a variety of commemorative stones and plaques to the units stationed there, or to their dead. Often one comes upon them unexpectedly, especially in little village churches in East Anglia or the Midlands, where a commemorative tablet on a wall records the thanks of some locally stationed squadron, or, oddly incongruous amid the surrounding saints and prophets, the American eagle or even giant Fortresses fly across a stained-glass window. In the War Memorial garden at Saffron Walden dedicated to the town's own dead, one finds a tribute to those lost by the 52nd Fighter Wing; in the 'lovely garden of Sawston Hall, near Cambridge,' one officer who served there remembers, 'is a stone commemorating the only member of the Headquarters staff of the 66th Fighter Wing to lose his life'. In the parish church at Wrexham hangs a US flag alongside a bronze plaque recording that it was 'Presented to the town of Wrexham with gratitude for its hospitality' by 'the 129th General Hospital US Army, 1945.' In the village of Appleshaw, near Tidworth in Hampshire, one may still find traces of a less formal memorial, the names of 'Joe', and 'Harry', 'Poloch' and 'Leroy' still carved in the trees by GIs with an idle hour to fill. But for the most part the GIs have vanished without trace. One woman who worked on the domestic staff of the 130th Station Hospital, near Swindon, describes how 'the huts are gone now, and the foundations are ploughed in. The peewits are calling and the mists rising on the bare downland. You would never guess what had been there once, in the Second World War.'

This has been the common experience of the many men who have come back, as they vowed they would, to see Britain in peacetime. There was 'not a clue or sign that we had ever been there', decided a visitor from Alton, Illinois, who returned, during a trip to mark his twenty-fifth wedding anniversary, to the corner of Bushy Park that had once housed SHAEF. 'The park had been completely restored. . . . Smooth grass where the buildings had stood, only a few faint signs in the walls that the bricks had been replaced.' A Colorado man who paid a nostalgic visit to the base at Horham, near Wickham Market, that was home to him and the 95th Bombardment Group for two years, found that it had slipped back into its rural past and that here the sword had almost literally become a ploughshare.

---

1. US war dead of World War I are buried at Brookwood, near Guildford.

'A huge mound of tarmac indicates where the runway was; what was once the hospital is now a farmer's granary, and cows now find shelter where once endless cups of beer were dispensed to thirsty GIs.'

Occasionally time and chance have partly spared such memorials to the past. Another airman from Pittsburgh, who visited 'former Army Air Force Station 134', near Eye in Suffolk, in 1970, 'found one runway still intact. I walked out on the runway and could almost see and hear the Libs and Forts rolling off the hardstands in the chilly dawn.' The greatest transformation of all was discovered by a doctor from Oakdale, California, who visited the site of the former military prison at Langport, Somerset, where he had once been Medical Officer: 'The whole unit now served as a poultry and egg distribution centre. . . . Our guard unit buildings were now chicken houses . . . there were several thousand chickens there. The caretakers of the chickens were using "my" office and quarters as their home.'

Paradoxically, the people their occupants knew have often proved more lasting − or at least more recognizable − than the buildings. Another visitor to Bushy Park, from Biloxi, Mississippi, disappointed that 'Widewing' had vanished without trace, felt amply compensated to discover that 'all the local pubs were still going strong' and was delighted 'when one of the old boys we played darts with called me by name. I didn't recognize him, but he remembered me.' A Manchester woman witnessed the delight of the Colonel who returned to see her and to visit 'the former Red Cross building now a warehouse', when he was recognized by a barmaid in 'the pub where the officers used to go' and again 'by one of the waitresses in the Midland Hotel. He said . . . when he had an Army reunion and told his story the other fellows would be coming over in droves, as they were so nostalgic about their ETO days.' More difficult to identify were those who, back in the 1940s, had not finished growing. A man from Pennsylvania, visiting his 'second home' in Suffolk twenty-five years after leaving it, found the whole experience 'like a movie where suddenly all the characters got older. Mrs H. changed the least. The children, all grown now, were harder to recognize', especially the young schoolboy son, 'now a married man with a young son' of his own.

Familiar faces made up for any changes in the surroundings, but, inevitably, some visitors have been disappointed that Britain is no longer quite the same country they remembered. 'The things I knew aren't quite the same,' complains one former member of the Corps of Engineers from Grosse Point, Michigan, who has several times brought his family with him 'to visit and enjoy the things I knew. . . . The high-rise buildings in London keep it from being the London that I knew. . . . Somehow I feel that it is sacrilegious to alter the skyline − it isn't London any more.' The passage of time has sharpened such disappointments. One former airman from Westport, Connecticut, who served in Yorkshire and Rackheath, recalls the contrast between two post-war visits, in August 1964 and June 1971, to the place where he had inspected the ruins of a building demolished by a V–1 near Liverpool Street Station in 1944 while he was waiting to board a train for Norwich. 'In August 1964 . . . it was easy to find it, as it was the only "new" building on the street. In June 1971 . . . only this new building remained; all the buildings surrounding it had been torn down for re-development.' 'We notice a difference each time we get over there,' remarks a man from Tulsa, Oklahoma, who often takes his wife back to see her family in South Harrow, 'the biggest difference being that the pubs seem to be run by the teenagers. The older people who used to go for a pint and a chat seem afraid to now. The pub that the wife and I met in has so much trouble now that the bus won't even stop there on the nights they have dances.' The verdict of a former army officer from Sarasota, Florida, has a sting in its tail. 'London has become quite the swinging town and has changed markedly. Outside London, however, does not seem to have changed so much. You can still find an old inn here and there where you can freeze to death in solid comfort.'

For many returning veterans all roads still lead to France, like the path travelled by a former US Navy man, now president of an Iowa Bank. 'The five-hour boat trip across the English Channel that I had crossed seventy-two times in 1944–5 was extremely pleasant', he noted in a letter home in 1973. 'What a contrast – the screaming schoolchildren on this trip compared to the seasick soldiers on the other trips. How much nicer a 600-foot ship compared to my 120-foot LCI.' To the area where he had waited for D-Day his reactions were mixed. 'Fowey had not changed' – nor, less surprisingly, had Salisbury Cathedral and Stonehenge, which he also revisited – but 'Lymington was my first disappointment. I had remembered it as a charming little village. . . . Now it was a harbour loaded with expensive yachts.' The high spot of this man's tour was sailing up the Dart River where he had waited for D-Day and revisiting a house at Weymouth where, back in 1944, his host would invariably 'go down to his cellar and try to find me a beer that had not been destroyed by the twice bombing of his house. When I left in 1945 he saved a bottle for our reunion. He had died in December 1972 but his children presented this to me.'

Thousands of others have made similar, solitary pilgrimages, but most such visitors have come in organized parties, for the Americans are great 'joiners' and veterans' associations flourish, like one attended by a GI stationed in Warwickshire, whose members meet annually to reminisce about 'the happy days and the good people they met whilst in Nuneaton'. The great aim of most such organizations, however, is to revisit their old haunts and every spring and summer, as the chartered aircraft disgorge their plane-loads of veterans, the hotels of Plymouth, London and Norwich resound once again to the same voices that used to call in vain for Scotch on the rocks and cold beer. The speakers are a good deal more subdued now. There is a tight timetable to be kept to, with no time allowed for SNAFU, no chance even, with wives in tow, and hairline receding and waist filling out, to stop and chat to the girls. It is pleasing to find, however, despite the notorious dangers of trying to re-create the past, how successful such visits usually prove. The experiences of one member of the New England Chapter of the self-styled 'Fighting Fourth Division', who trained around Seaton (as described in an earlier chapter) and was wounded on UTAH, are probably typical. In his 'twenty-fifth reunion' party, in May 1969, were 395 men, an impressive turn-out after so long an interval, and it soon became clear that they were far from forgotten:

After three wonderful days and nights in London we went south by motor coach to Devon. Our first stop was for a reception at Tiverton, sponsored by the townspeople. I actually saw elderly ladies crying because they could find no one among us they had known who was stationed at Tiverton with the 4th Division headquarters. From Tiverton we, in hut No. 3, went on to Honiton, where we visited a modern-day British army camp which had been our 8th Regiment head-quarters. . . . It was here, on the parade ground in 1944, that Montgomery and Eisenhower looked us over. From Honiton we went on to Torquay . . . and stayed the night in the hotel overlooking Torbay. . . . From my window I could look out on to the dock on which we marched out to our invasion ship.

The following day myself and three others who had been stationed at Seaton rented a cab and went to Seaton, Beer and Exmouth. . . . Upon arriving at Seaton, it was like coming home. . . . In one corner of the fenced-in area were the buildings which housed my own 'G' company. Here an Englishman had a small shop in which he constructed furniture for children's rooms. He was as thrilled as we were that the Yanks had returned to Seaton. . . . This man left his shop and walked about town with us telling everyone the 'Yanks are back'. I met a lady on the beach whom I had known in 1944. She went out with a friend of mine from 'F' Company. . . . She looked exactly as she did twenty-five years before, only older. There was no pub or business in Seaton this day who would take our money. Everything was 'on the house'.

Even those GIs who have not managed to make the trip back to the ETO have often kept up their wartime contacts by letter, and invitations to weddings and christenings, graduation ceremonies and silver weddings still flow across the Atlantic to now ageing British couples who became 'second moms' and substitute 'pops' to some homesick GI. Typical is the food parcel which one former radio intelligence officer with the 29th Signal Company, from Charleston, South Carolina, dispatches every Christmas to former friends in England, 'although I know they do not need that . . . in remembrance of the times they had me to dinner . . . and I often got the only egg in the house'. Nor has the old GI respect for anniversaries and family parties waned. One Norfolk couple casually mentioning in a letter to one man to whom they had waved goodbye twenty-five years before that they were about to celebrate their 'ruby' wedding – they had been married for forty years – were astonished to receive a reply asking if he could come 3000 miles to the party, which he duly did, complete with his wife and son.

The trouble taken by many ex-GIs to renew old friendships also testifies to how deep their roots went. This was how a Liverpool couple who had invited a newly arrived and homesick GI at Christmas 1943 were reunited with him in 1971:

On arriving home from holiday . . . we received a message from my mother-in-law to say that Larry had called the previous day and would expect us for dinner at the Adelphi Hotel that evening. As we walked into the foyer, an older, heavier and more prosperous-looking Larry came forward to meet us. (He had always been so thin and pathetic-looking in his strictly too large uniform.) He told us that he had flown over on a business trip for five days in London, his first visit since the war, and had come up the previous day to look us up. . . . He went straight from the station to the Adelphi Hotel . . . because during the war he wanted to go in and was told 'Sorry, officers only'. He dumped his bags and called a taxi and it was only when he came to tell the driver the address that he realized he had forgotten it. He did, however, remember that the name of the road had 'green' in it. . . . The cab driver did a tour of all roads, streets, avenues, etc., that he could think of which were 'green' before arriving at Broadgreen Road, which Larry recognized. On finding the house he was told that the present occupiers had been there for fifteen years and did not know anyone of our name. Larry then knocked on every door in the vicinity until he found someone who remembered us and had a vague idea of the area to which we had moved. . . . Eventually my mother-in-law was contacted and all was well.

Many Britons have discovered on visiting the United States the legacy of goodwill left by wartime contacts. A Carlisle woman, *en route* to see her GI bride daughter shortly after the war, remembers an incident unthinkable on an English aircraft:

I was . . . on a stopping plane from New York to the Deep South . . . and was the only passenger until the first stop where many more joined me. When we got going the air hostess, to my great embarrassment, announced, 'Ladies and gentlemen, we have a VIP on board, a lady from England from away near the Lake District, on her first visit to the USA.'

Immediately about a dozen young men left their seats and all of them shook my hands and fired questions at me. 'Proud to meet you, ma'am', 'How was good ol' London looking?', 'Are the lakes as beautiful as ever?', 'Is Bonnie Scotland just as Bonnie?', 'We loved little old England and her people' etc., . . . I felt like a queen, it was heart-warming. They really meant it and said they had many happy memories of Britain and her lovely people. I will never forget my welcome to the USA from those really wonderful, one-time GIs.

In Boston, despite its reputation for a standoffish 'correctness', a former teenager from Swinton in Lancashire had a similarly 'wonderful experience.

I arrived with no knowledge of hotels or anything and not much money. A taxi driver told me it was "Welcome to the English" week and took me on a one-hour drive round Boston for free because of the kind hospitality he had received from the people of Liverpool during the war.' Another wartime teenager had equally striking proof of the enduring nature of American gratitude. An ex-GI lawyer came to her rescue when she was in trouble over a parking offence shortly after arriving in Chicago, in memory of his happy times in distant Devon.

The opening up of transatlantic air travel to people of modest means since the war has made a reality of many of the invitations, or promises, to visit the United States, which when offered or given in 1945 seemed little more than a dream. A Dereham woman, who, as mentioned in an earlier chapter, was 'mother' to a Sergeant from Wendling on Mother's Day 1944, found herself in 1969 spending a month in Iowa with his family, where he is now a prosperous accountant. 'I have never before met such friendly and generous people,' she remembers. Another woman, from Southgate in North London, who visited a GI from Cleveland, Ohio, found herself treated 'like a queen' by his relations, and 'everybody made such a fuss of me I felt bewildered', while by special request, she cooked him once again 'an English breakfast and made him an apple pie'.

Other couples who befriended GIs found they had acquired unknowingly a whole network of willing hosts, like a woman from Northwood, Middlesex, who had often entertained airmen and WACS from US Fighter Command Headquarters at Bushey Hall. Once news of her first visit, to one couple in 1956, had spread, 'they got busy telephoning and airmailing their army friends spreading the news. I found myself inundated with invitations . . . and returned four months later, having travelled over 24 000 miles. . . . Every home I visited gave me the same delightful feeling, as if I was returning home after years of absence.' One man she encountered was in fact altogether too kind, a taxi driver in New York 'who paid me some lovely compliments . . . kept turning round . . . and remarking about my hat, saying, "It was that hat that did it" . . . and concluded that he was divorcing his wife and would like to take me on. . . . After I had returned home the telephone rang, my taxi driver of NY now in London. He made a note of my name from my luggage labels. I had quite a job putting him off.'

And now, a whole generation later, with the first romantic bloom long since rubbed off by the long haul of marriage, have the GI brides settled in their adopted country? The mixed feelings of one woman from a small village in Kent, who has lived since 1946 in Alton, Illinois, are probably typical:

I miss the quiet Kent spring. Here the temperature jumps overnight and all of the spring flowers bloom at once . . . no woods with primroses, no cherry blossom or lambs. I miss walking; no one walks here, both because it doesn't appeal to them and because it is not safe; most of all I miss the sea, never seeing it unless I am going back to England. I have never been naturalized as I could never swear in court to give up allegiance to Britain and still feel that I will never belong to this country.

The problem of citizenship has troubled many GI brides, representing as it does an emotional, as well as a legal, commitment to the United States. 'I became a citizen in 1955 because it seemed the logical thing to do,' confesses a Norwich woman, now living in Alaska. 'I had never been able to vote before. . . . Yet I hated to give up my British citizenship; it was a very, very traumatic experience. . . . The thing that bothered me most was when I was expecting my first baby and the thought struck me that he would not be an English child. However, America has been very good to me and mine and I shall always stand by her. It's rather like having a father *and* a mother.' One woman from Chippenham reached her decision during her first visit home, from Lackawanna, New York State, in 1949. 'My personal criterion was that I would fight on the American side if she ever went to war with England. This used to horrify some of my English friends but I have met many German- and Italian-born US citizens who had to chose and later to fight.' Twenty-five years later, despite a broken marriage, she has not regretted the decision. 'I have never wanted to live in England permanently. Life for a woman of my age is much freer in the States. I dislike English weather, the food, the reliance on the traditions to solve problems and the class system.' But the ties of blood remain strong. 'I go to my family almost every year and I feel I will always be a woman of Wiltshire soil.'

An ex-WAAF from Chislehurst whose father's opposition to her marriage has been described in an earlier chapter found that although she was married to a lawyer in Param, Idaho, becoming naturalized was no mere formality:

I nearly failed my citizenship over the fourth of July. I knew the year of independence, 1776, but when the friendly interrogator asked the day the Americans celebrate my mind was a blank. The helpful hint of 'fireworks' only brought 5 November to mind [and] our son's artwork at school: a naval battle in full force and every ship not sinking proudly flying the Union Jack.

But she passed and has settled down contentedly in her new country.

I enjoy the casualness of the American way of life. I enjoy the American people. Of course we do live in the last refuge from the rat race, Idaho. We have mountains, rivers, lakes and if you water it, practically everything will grow. We have a lovely 'old-world' type English garden that is only twelve years old. . . . Our house is full of English books. Jim's favourite recording artist is still Vera Lynn. . . . We drive an MG. Jim is 100 per cent American and I am as English as the day I was born. Our children are 100 per cent American but they have a soft spot for England and I feel I have the best of two worlds, England and America.

A couple from Leicester, and Wilkes Barres, Pennsylvania, faced the citizenship question in reverse. After ten homesick months in the United States the wife returned to England, with her husband, who was able to attend a local technical college under the 'GI Bill of Rights', which paid his fees and maintenance, and 'is quite settled and has talked of becoming a British subject', although his wife is 'against this as I've always had at the back of my mind that his American citizenship might come in useful some day'. And some brides still cherish the thought of returning to England eventually when their husbands stop work. 'The thought of retiring to an English village is an attractive one,' to a former platoon Sergeant with the 5th Armoured Division, from Washington, DC, who married a British WAAF. 'The slower pace of life in the smaller communities appeals to us very much.'

Looking back, from the perspective of a whole generation later, it is clear that most GIs remember their years in Britain with pleasure. 'I loved every day I was there,' declares a former air force Technical Sergeant from Osawatomie, Kansas. 'It must have been difficult for the English to cope with many of the Americans who were loud, boisterous and selfish at times, but the English seemed to understand and forgive. They were far more civilized than we were, yet they made room for us in their rigid way of doing things. Then, too, I think we had some influence on the English. We did things that they would not do and did not die from it. The barbarians from America unloosened the English character.' 'I developed a great love for England after having lived there for over a year,' agrees an airman from Illinois of his time in Norfolk. 'It can be considered a sort of second home, even after thirty years.' A B–17 crew member, from Bridgeport, Connecticut, often quoted in earlier chapters, returned, more peacefully, in 1965 and 'fell in love all over again with the country. My wife says I'm a frustrated Englishman.' A citizen of Denver, Colorado, then in his early twenties, who served with the 95th Bomb Group in East Anglia, pays his wartime hosts an equally heartfelt tribute: 'In spite of the reason for which I was there, the two years I spent in England were the happiest years of my life and I shall carry many fond memories of it for the rest of my days.' So, too, will a coloured GI from Wyoming, stationed near Westbury. 'The green countryside, the friendly people, the polite "Bobbies" – Boy, what a contrast! My experiences in the British Isles were truly a highlight in this lowly ordinary man's life and, Lord, how I pray I could return and visit that beautiful country again!'

It is clear that those Britons who, thirty years ago, apologized for the shortages and shabbiness of their country in wartime might have saved their breath. Many former GIs would echo the conclusion of a former soldier from Coral Gables, Florida, who admits that he often used to grumble about being sent to this damp and dismal island, but 'I now realize how fortunate I was to see the English people in their most difficult hours, with their hair down, fighting for their lives and their country and still being kind and thoughtful.'

What effects – apart from its obvious military importance – did the American 'occupation' have on Britain? First, and most important, is the pleasure the Yanks' coming brought to so many millions of war-weary citizens. 'I wouldn't swop my past with anyone else's,' remarks one woman from Prestwick who grew up during that GI-dominated period. 'I can almost feel slightly grateful to Hitler.' To a woman who then worked in a country hotel near Shrewsbury those three years 'seem like a slice of life sandwiched in the middle of before and after'. 'The war took my best years, from seventeen to twenty-three,' recalls a Norwich factory-worker, 'but despite the bombing, I enjoyed the last three years . . . thanks to the Americans.' 'It was the end of an era of colour and laughter when they went for good,' feels another girl of the same age, who had worked in a munitions factory in Stafford. 'I don't think any Liverpool girl really regrets the coming of the Yanks to our shores,' believes one of them. 'It was sweet while it lasted.'

Few Englishmen had as much to do with the GIs as their female contemporaries, but those who did – mainly the middle-aged and the very young – also look back on them with admiration. 'There was never a dull moment with the GIs,' concedes a railway man who worked for them at Tidworth. And a former inmate of an appalling Lancashire orphanage, transformed when the GIs 'adopted' it, pays its 'liberators' the final compliment: 'I would have been proud to become an American citizen.'

Apart from the much-needed light relief they brought into British life at a time when it was sorely needed, has the close, if enforced, contact between 2 000 000 Americans and 50 000 000 Britons, on the latter's home ground, left any lasting legacy? A woman then living at Upton-on-Severn in Worcestershire attributes to the GIs' 'jitterbugging at the village hall, drinking at the local pubs and lack of inhibitions – the broadening of our yokel minds'. 'The Americans changed England more than the English like to . . . admit,' believes a then landgirl from equally rural Chippenham. 'They challenged the British way of life, shook basic concepts, such as the Empire, changed food habits . . . but made people aware we really did live in England's "green and pleasant land".' 'Their coming was an education and gave me a broader outlook on life,' believes a Liverpool woman. 'They gave me an insight into democracy . . . the free-and-easy way with their officers, yet the job was done.' And even deeper taboos crumbled when exposed to the healthy blast of American enthusiasm. 'The coming of the GIs had a tremendous impact upon me,' acknowledges a woman from South Wales. 'I was utterly inhibited sexually, almost regarding joy and pleasure as sinful. The Americans I met helped me to laugh and enjoy life. They liberated me from the narrow outlook on life in which I had been brought up.' The reaction of a woman who was a sixteen-year-old, living in Newlyn, at the time of Pearl Harbour, a place outside the mainstream even of British life, are probably typical. 'I fluctuate between sympathy and impatience, the same emotions I felt as a young girl during the GI "invasion" of the extreme South-West.' The conclusion of another woman, who, in her early twenties, worked for three years in the all American ambience of the Navy Public Relations Office in Grosvenor Square is that 'I confess I believed them capable of a greatness that has evaded them. I knew then, and used to tell them . . . that they needed to know more about the world before they could lead it.'

Three years – even three years as crowded as those from 1942 to 1945 – is not long in the life of a nation. Already ten times that period has passed since the last wartime GI climbed the gangplank leading homewards and today half the citizens of both countries are people not even born when the war ended. The number of survivors of the great encounter dwindles year by year, though it will be well into the twenty-first century before the last veteran dies who once, as a young and raw recruit, enquired in Bristol or Bognor for the nearest drugstore, or the final Englishman who, as a small child, clamoured for gum or cookies outside an American camp. What still remains of this epic meeting of two different nations? Two of those involved, now in middle age, despite their different backgrounds share a remarkably similar conclusion. The first was a schoolboy in Birmingham, when he met his first American in 1942:

Whatever happens to the 'special relationship' at national level we worked out our own special relationships all those years ago. . . . They were never merely 'them' and they rapidly became 'us'. I for one will never lose the sense of good comradeship, generosity and basic solidarity we developed then. I have always been sympathetic to the Americans and their problems since the war.

And in Schenectady, New York, an American sailor a few years older who had never been out of the United States until he landed at Plymouth, Devon, also looks back benevolently:

On review of this whole story, I think I understand the people of the UK as well as I do the people of the US. In other words, I could hang my hat on either side of the Atlantic and say 'I'm home again'.

Appendix

THE RATES OF PAY OF THE BRITISH AND AMERICAN FORCES

COMPARISON of the respective rates of pay of the British and American forces is very difficult – so difficult that the British Ministry of Defence was unwilling to provide figures on the grounds that the whole subject was too complicated to be understood by the layman. Fortunately I was able to obtain them from other sources and the Department of Defence in Washington, DC, proved more helpful.

It is true, however, that it is almost impossible to find a 'typical' British soldier and a 'typical' American serviceman owing to the many variable factors involved. For example, British soldiers with specialist qualifications received 'trade pay' on top of their normal scales, while in the American army 'technicians' of various grades formed a separate category and many senior officers received 'command pay'. 'Flying pay', for members of aircrew, special payments to parachute troops, allowances to officers in quarters lacking certain basic amenities, and – most important – the differing deductions made from a man's pay for an allowance to his family, are additional complications. In the American army, too, NCOs tended to be more plentiful than in the British, while all Americans in the British Isles, but no British soldiers, whether serving at home or in Europe, recieved 'overseas pay'. The system of long-service pay in the American army, which automatically increased a man's earnings after a certain number of years, also favoured the GI, and, even more, senior officers in the highest ranks which tended to be filled by professional soldiers.

For all these reasons the figures which follow should be regarded as an approximate guide only. They are based on the rates of pay prevailing after 1 June 1942 for a man who had recently entered his existing rank and received no additional allowance of any kind, except 'overseas pay'. I have not attempted to quote separate figures for Royal Navy, US Navy and RAF, but these are roughly comparable on a 'rank for rank' basis. For ease of comparison I have 'translated' all figures into weekly rates for 'other ranks' and EM, and monthly rates for officers, and have given them both in the 'pounds, shillings and pence' then used in Great Britain and in the decimal currency now in use.

RATES OF PAY IN THE BRITISH ARMY

as at 1 June 1942

	$ c.	£ s. d.	£ p.
Officers		*Per month*	
Field Marshal	1109.26	275. 5. 0	275.25
General	998.01	247.12.11	247.65
Lieutenant-General	832.52	206.11. 7	206.58
Major-General	554.65	137.12. 8	137.63
Brigadier	357.50	88.14. 3	88.71
Colonel	305.42	75.15. 9	75.79
Lieutenant-Colonel	263.54	65. 7.11	65.40
Major	174.67	43. 6.10	43.34
Captain	101.15	25. 1.11	25.10
Lieutenant	79.68	19.15. 5	19.77
Second-Lieutenant	67.42	16.14. 7	16.73
Warrant Officers			
Warrant Officers, Class I	73.55	18. 5. 0	18.25
Warrant Officers, Class II	52.09	12.18. 6	12.93
Other Ranks		*Per week*	
Staff-Sergeant or Colour-Sergeant	11.28	2.16. 0	2.80
Sergeant	8.46	2. 2. 0	2.10
Corporal or Bombardier	5.64	1. 8. 0	1.40
Lance-Corporal or Lance-Bombardier	4.58	1. 2. 9	1.14
Private	2.82	14. 0	70

RATES OF PAY IN THE US ARMY

as at 1 June 1942

	$ c.	£ s. d.	£ p.
Officers		*Per month*	
General of the Army	1135.42	281.14.10	281.74
General	722.22	179. 4. 3	179.21
Lieutenant-General	722.22	179. 4. 3	179.21
Major-General	722.22	179. 4. 3	179.21
Brigadier-General	722.22	179. 4. 3	179.21
Colonel	375.00	93. 1. 0	93.05
Lieutenant-Colonel	315.97	78. 8. 1	78.40
Major	270.83	67. 4. 1	67.20
Captain	216.67	53.15. 3	53.76
First-Lieutenant	180.56	44.16. 0	44.80
Second-Lieutenant	162.50	40. 6. 6	40.32

Warrant Officers		*Per month*	
	$ c.	£. s. d.	£. p.
Chief Warrant Officers	175.00	43. 8. 6	43.42
Warrant Officers Junior Grade	150.00	37. 4. 4	37.22

Enlisted Men		*Per week*	
Master Sergeant	38.21	9. 9. 8	9.48
Technical Sergeant	31.57	7.16. 8	7.83
Staff Sergeant (or Technician third grade)	26.58	6.11.11	6.60
Sergeant (or Technician fourth grade)	21.60	5. 7. 2	5.36
Corporal (or Technician fifth grade)	18.28	4.10. 8	4.53
Private first class	14.95	3.14. 2	3.71
Private	13.85	3. 8. 9	3.44

A NOTE ON SOURCES

M Y principal source was the material specially written for me by informants on both sides of the Atlantic, many of whom also sent me contemporary documents. My main printed source was the London edition of the *Stars and Stripes*, supplemented by *Yank* magazine. I also used extensively the excellent account by a former army NCO, Robert Arbib, *Here We Are Together* (Longman, London, 1946; extracts reproduced by permission of Curtis Brown Ltd), and the more lightweight commentary by an ex-naval Lieutenant, William Bostick, *England under GI's Reign* (Congress House, Detriot, 1946). On conditions in wartime Britain generally I used my own *How we Lived Then, A History of Everyday Life During the Second World War* (Hutchinson London, 1971, and Arrow Books, London, 1973), which American readers may find useful in providing background information including details of rationing.

I consulted a number of regimental histories, but they proved disappointing, consisting either of a list of operations on the Continent or, more commonly, of little more than a list of names linked by a heavily facetious commentary. Similarly the biographies and autobiographies of leading American commanders, like General Arnold or General Mark Clark, tend to deal very cursorily with their experiences in the British Isles. The official histories are more helpful, though sometimes contradictory in details; for example, the number of Americans recorded as landing each month by a naval historian is different from the figures of arrivals compiled by the army. The practice of the American authorities of regarding the whole of Europe as one theatre of war has also presented me with some problems over statistics, especially after D-Day, and where these proved insoluble I have made the best estimates I can. The American works I consulted most were the long series published by the Chief of Military History for the Department of the Army *The United States Army in World War II* (Government Printing Office, Washington DC, various dates), especially Roland G. Ruppenthal, *Logistical Support of the Armies* (two volumes, 1953). I also consulted G. A. Harrison, *Cross Channel Attack* (1951) and the official *Pictorial Record* (three volumes, 1951). A separate publication containing some useful figures is Jacob L. Devers (General, US Army Command), *Report of Activities, Army Group Forces, World War II*

(Addressed to the Chief of Staff, 10 January 1946). On the British side the factual material I used most is unpublished but readily available to historians in the War Office and Foreign Office archives and in the Cabinet Minutes and Papers available in the Public Record Office.

As this book is primarily intended for the general reader I have not attempted to give a detailed reference for every statement in the text where the item concerned cannot be consulted outside a specialist library. I have, however, indicated the general source and date. To save space, full details of each book, and the place of publication, are given only the first time it is mentioned, with a cross-reference under later chapters where necessary.

CHAPTER 1

The arrival of the first US troops in Northern Ireland is described in *The Times*, London, for 27 January 1942, the *Stars and Stripes*, 9 May 1942, Ruppenthal (see above), and John W. Blake, *Northern Ireland in the Second World War* (Her Majesty's Stationery Office, Belfast, 1956). Blake also describes the military construction programme in Ulster. Mr Leonard Miall, formerly BBC correspondent in Washington, told me the story of the GI interviewed by the BBC. Eire's reactions to the US presence are recorded in the Cabinet Papers for January 1942. The royal visit to Washington is described by John W. Wheeler-Bennett, *King George VI, His Life and Reign* (Macmillan, London, 1958) and American opinion in London in James Leutze (editor), *The Observer, The Journal of General Raymond E. Lee 1940–1941* (Hutchinson, 1972). The weakness of the US forces is described by (General) Dwight D. Eisenhower, *Crusade in Europe* (Heinemann, London, 1948). The Wall Street banker who joined the Royal Navy was (Commander) A. H. Cherry (RNVR), *Yankee RN* (Jarrolds, London, 1951). The American LDV unit's history can be found in 'Our Debt to the USA' in *Our Empire*, Volume XXI, No. 3, 1945. The *New Yorker* correspondent quoted was Mollie Panter-Downes, *London War Notes, 1939–1945* (Longman, London, 1972). Churchill's reactions to Lend-Lease can be found in Winston S. Churchill, *The Second World War* (Volume II, Cassell, London, 1949). The Eagle Squadron's exploits were recorded by (Colonel) James Saxon Childers, *War Eagles* (Heinemann, London, 1943). Walter Lord, *Day of Infamy* (Holt, New York, 1957) described how America learned of Pearl Harbour, as does Churchill, Volume III, and a retrospective article in the *Stars and Stripes* for 7 December 1942.

CHAPTER 2

The 'shortsnorter' club is described by (Major) John M. Redding and (Major) Harold I. Leyshon, *Skyways to Berlin* (Hutchinson, n.d., c. 1943).

The various pamphlets quoted are: *A Short Guide to Great Britain* (published by the Departments of the Army and Navy, Washington DC, various editions from 1942); W. J. Hinton, *Meet the Americans* (No. 22 in the series *Current Affairs*, Army Bureau of Current Affairs, London, 18 July 1942); Louis MacNeice, *Meet the US Army* (HMSO, 1942); Margaret Mead, *The American Troops and the British Community* (Hutchinson, 1944), also issued under the title 'The Yank in Britain' in *Current Affairs*, No. 64 (ABCA, 11 March 1944).

CHAPTER 3

Churchill's experiences in Washington are in his *History*, Volume III, and Eisenhower's in his *Crusade*, while his life in London was witnessed by Kay Summersby, *Eisenhower was my Boss* (Laurie, London, 1949). Ruppenthal describes the start of ETOUSA and Ralph Ingersoll, *Top Secret* (Partridge Publications, London, 1946) its later existence, and the trials of 'Com Z' in Paris. The work of the BOLERO Committee is explained by C. H. Kohan, *Works and Buildings* (HMSO, 1952), in the official *History of the Second World War*, United Kingdom Civil Series. Apart from the War Cabinet Papers referred to, details of the accommodation required by the US forces in various army commands in Britain can be found in the War Office Papers under the general heading of *Joint BOLERO Key Plan*, with associated maps.

CHAPTER 4

The Atlantic convoys are described by (Captain, RN), S. W. Roskill, *The Navy at War 1939–1945* (Colins, London, 1960) The subject is also discussed by Churchill, Volume III, and in the Cabinet Papers for 16 June 1942. Shipboard contacts with the WACs are described in the *Stars and Stripes* for 15 July 1943 and I also used *DZ Europe, The Story of the 440th Troop Carrier Group* (publisher and date unknown), whose authors crossed on the *Louis Pasteur*. The jaundiced view of the ladies of Prestwick was recalled by a private informant, like most of the reminiscences in the chapter.

CHAPTER 5

The 'local historian' mentioned, and main source, is Blake (see Chapter 1). 'The Yanks in Ireland' song appears in the *Stars and Stripes* for 4 July 1942, the GIs' 'settling in' is described in numerous entries in *The Times* for January to June 1942, and Cherry (see Chapter 1) was involved in the Londonderry bar encounter.

CHAPTER 6

My sources were private informants, plus Arbib (see Chapter 1).

CHAPTER 7

The Nissen hut definition comes from *Meet the Boys, The History of the 332nd Service Squadron USAAF* (no publisher, n.d., but *c.* 1945) and living conditions generally are described in *452nd Bombardment Group, A Pictorial History* (printed Jarrolds, Norwich, n.d., *c.* 1945). The miseries of life on a bomber station and the 'mistress' story appear in *Target: Germany, The U.S. Army Air Forces' Official Story of the VIII Bomber Command's First Year over Europe* (HMSO, 1944). The 'Ode to a WC' was recorded by Bostick (see Chapter 1).

CHAPTER 8

The details about American depots and the work of the Services of Supply are mainly taken from the *Stars and Stripes* for 13 October 1945, supplemented by War Office BOLERO papers.

CHAPTER 9

This chapter is based on private information from contributors.

CHAPTER 10

The unfavourable impression of the British Army is quoted by Lee (see Chapter 1) and British reaction to US discipline by the *Stars and Stripes* (6 May 1944), which also carried on 2 June 1944 details of US pay sent home. The WACs' arrival was recorded on 13 May 1943, but my main source on the whole subject was Mattie E. Treadwell, *The Women's Army Corps* (1954) in the *United States Army in World War II* series. On army nurses I consulted Blanche B. Armfield, *The Medical Department, U.S. Army* (1963) in the same series. Kay Summersby's later history was mentioned in *The Times* on 26 November 1973 and the *Daily Telegraph*, London, on 11 February 1974. Bostick was the naval Lieutenant mentioned and the British journalist who commented on British troops' inferior position was James L. Hodson, *The Home Front* (Gollancz, London, 1944). Details of the decorations won by the various services appear in the *Stars and Stripes*, 10 March 1944.

CHAPTER 11

The army historian who referred to the use of black troops in combat is Charles B. MacDonald, *The Mighty Endeavour, American Armed Forces in the European Theatre in World War II* (Oxford University Press, London, 1969). The Marble Arch incident is described in the Foreign Office Papers for 3 April 1942, the liberal-minded publican was quoted in the *Stars and Stripes* for 25 July 1942, and Eisenhower described his policy in *Crusade*. Charles Graves, *Great Days* (Hutchinson, n.d., *c.* 1943), recorded the 'Colonel Cohen' joke and the Cabinet Papers for 3 October 1943 official reaction to the activities of the wife of the Somerset vicar. I also used an article in the *Sunday Times Magazine* (London) for 6 December 1973. The Home Office letter dated 4 September appears as an appendix to a Paper dated 10 October 1942. The visiting black officer was quoted by the *Stars and Stripes* on 3 October 1942. Churchill's tasteless witticism was preserved in the *Diaries of Sir Alexander Cadogan, 1938–1945* (Cassell, London, 1971). Roger Parkinson, *Blood, Toil, Tears and Sweat* (Hart-Davis, London, 1973) contains a number of quotations from the Cabinet Minutes on the colour question, though no real substitute for the originals. The *Notes on Relations with Coloured Troops* are quoted in the Cabinet Paper submitted by the Secretary of State for War on 3 October 1942, the rival views of other ministers in Papers circulated between 2 and 12 October, and the Cabinet's decisions in its Minutes for 13 and 20 October. The intercepted correspondence is from the Foreign Office files, for February and March 1944. The song 'Choc'late Soldier from the USA' was published by the Dash Music Co. of London, to whom kind acknowledgement is due for its use. 'Negro Week' was described in the *Stars and Stripes* on 19 February 1944. Foreign Office file FO 371/38624, June 1944, recorded the story of the black soldier convicted of rape near Bath. 'The Colour Problem as the Americans See It' appeared in *Current Affairs*, No. 32, 5 December 1942.

CHAPTER 12

For background I used *Target: Germany* (see Chapter 7) and for information about individual wings, and even aircraft (including their names), I consulted Roger A. Freeman, *The Mighty Eighth, A History of the US 8th Army Air Force* (Macdonald, London, 1970). Colonel Galland's admiration for the B–17 is quoted by David Irving, *The Rise and Fall of the Luftwaffe* (Weidenfeld, London, 1973) and the RAF's dislike of it by (General of the Air Force) H. H. Arnold, *Global Mission* (Hutchinson, 1951), which includes (on page 198) General Eaker's speech quoted as an epigraph to the chapter. 'The best aircrew material in the world' quotation and other information can be found in General Arnold, *Report of the Commanding General of the*

Army Air Forces to the Secretary of War (no publisher, 4 January 1944), supplemented by his *Second Report* (Government Printing Office, Washington, January 1944, reprinted HMSO, London, 1945), and his *Third Report* (November 1945, HMSO, 1946). For a German view of the Eighth Air Force I consulted Hans Rumpf, *The Bombing of Germany* (Muller, London, 1961) and Werner Baumback, *Broken Swastika, The Defeat of the Luftwaffe* (Hale, London, 1960). A balanced assessment of the whole campaign, with a useful map of Eighth Air Force bases, can be found in Anthony Verrier, *The Bomber Offensive* (Batsford, London, 1968) while Alastair Revie, *The Lost Command* (David Bruce and Watson, London, 1971) is informative about Schweinfurt. Edward H. Sims, *American Aces of World War II* (Macdonald, 1948), quotes the references to 'Debden gangsters' and the 'seven ton milk bottle'.

CHAPTER 13

The reactions of 'First Wing' to the Midlands are given by Redding and Leyshon (see Chapter 2). The *Stars and Stripes* covered the Walthamstow crash on 18 January 1945, the rest home for aircrews on 21 June 1943 and air force dogs on 5 April 1943. I made much use of the Anglia Television transcript and private information.

CHAPTER 14

The arguments over the legal status of US troops can be found in Home Office Papers 45/19314 of 6 November 1941 and a Cabinet paper of 8 April 1942. The decision on claims is in the Cabinet Minutes for 23 February 1944. *Let's Get Acquainted* was broadcast by the BBC Home Service on 26 June 1942. The *Stars and Stripes* criticized the British telephone system on 25 July 1942, the BBC on 28 November, and the Hays Office (on *In Which We Serve*) on 9 December.

CHAPTER 15

Apart from *Here We Are Together*, I relied on unpublished information.

CHAPTER 16

Apart from the Norfolk licensee (who appeared on Anglia Television), my contributors supplied my material.

CHAPTER 17

The regimental history quoted is *Meet the Boys* (see Chapter 7). The *Stars and Stripes* described British trains on 11 December 1942 and British Rail the history of first and second class. The civil servant who 'had no addresses' was 'Timoleon', *King's Cross to Waverley*, (William Hodge and Co., London, 1944).

CHAPTER 18

The 'land among sprouts' story appears in Redding and Leyshon, as does the information on aircrew diet and the high quality of food on bomber stations. *Target: Germany* contains statistics about imported food and the 'she gave me a real egg' story and Bostick dedicated his book to the Brussels sprout and was critical of 'K' rations and 'Boston-cream pie'. Home-made ice-cream was mentioned by the *Stars and Stripes* on 9 August 1943 and the interview with Mr Horner appeared on 6 April 1944, with other Spam references on 17 March 1943, 10 May 1944 and 21 November 1944 .'K' rations were described on 18 July 1942 and 10 May 1944 and British coffee abused on 4 December 1942.

CHAPTER 19

Meet the Boys (see Chapter 7) warned of drinking bicycles and Redding and Leyshon mentioned the crews who ate a pub lunch to obtain whisky. The 'village bobby at Wymondham' appeared on Anglia Television. The history of The GI public house appears in *The House of Whitbread* magazine, Volume VIII, No. 1, 1946, and in information supplied by the company.

CHAPTER 20

The 'fishing net' anecdote appears in J. H. Leakey, *School Errant* (Dulwich College Preparatory School, London, 1951). The setting up of the War Orphans' Fund was described on 26 September 1942, its progress on 5 November and 7 December 1942 and 20 March 1944. 'Sweet Pea's' airfield visit was described on 4 January 1843 and by Redding and Leyshon.

CHAPTER 21

The facts about US premises in London are taken from Ruppenthal. Details of PX entitlement appeared on 26 January 1943, the report on GIs' tips to taxi drivers on 24 March, the warning against 'females of questionable

character' on 2 April and the cartoon about ATS girls on 26 August. The
joke about pigeons with rubber eggs appeared on 26 May 1944, those who
chirped 'Any crumbs, chum?' were immortalized on 15 July and the cartoon
of the fog-bound taxi on 27 December 1944. Harold Nicolson's sad
experience of GIs is described in his *Diaries and Letters 1939–45* (Collins,
London, 1967). The woman author living in Shepherd Market who is
quoted is Mrs Robert Henrey, *The Incredible City* (Dent, London, 1944),
and *The Siege of London* (Dent, 1946), which includes the 'commando'
anecdote and the parade in Green Park. Lieutenant Bostick observed the
'naval task force' on patrol in Piccadilly, MacDonald described 'Willow
Run' and Ruppenthal commented on its chef. Geoffrey Williamson, *Star-
Spangled Square* (Bles, London, 1956) and John G. Winant, *A Letter from
Grosvenor Square* (Hodder, London, 1947) described respectively its early
and later history. Mollie Panter-Downes (see Chapter 1) referred to sheep
who slept in Piccadilly, details of Rainbow Corner were printed in the
Stars and Stripes on 2 December 1942 and the list of other clubs appeared
in *London, For US Armed Forces in UK* (printed by Spottiswoode, Ballan-
tyne and Co., London n.d., but *c.* 1943).

CHAPTER 22

The main source, from which the doughnut quotation is also drawn, was
George Korson, *At his Side, The Story of the American Red Cross Overseas
in World War II* (Coward-McCann, New York, 1945). I also consulted
MacDonald (see Chapter 11), and the *Stars and Stripes*, which listed the
dates at which various clubs opened. It also described the 'aeroclubs', on
22 February 1943, and the most popular camp shows on 29 July.

CHAPTER 23

The 'Lament of a Limey Lass' is taken from Bostick, with some amendments
based on versions supplied by other contributors.

CHAPTER 24

The footnote about Glenn Miller's aircraft is based on a report in the London
Daily Telegraph for 13 July 1974. The 'Moonlight Sinatra' pun appeared
on 21 November 1944 in the *Stars and Stripes*, the singer's criticism of
USO camp shows on 9 July 1945 and Edward J. Dorogokleepetz's memorable feat on 24 October 1944.

CHAPTER 25

This chapter is based on exceptionally private information, apart from material appearing in the *Stars and Stripes* on the following dates: 10 December 1942, 1 March, 15 May and 29 May 1943 and 22 June 1945.

CHAPTER 26

The main account I consulted on the strategy behind D-Day was *Report by the Supreme Commander to the Combined Chiefs of Staff on the Operations in Europe of the Allied Expeditionary Force, 6 June 1944 to 8 May 1945* (HMSO, 1946). On the detailed planning I used (Sir) Frederick Morgan, *Overture to Overlord* (Hodder, 1950) and, on the events of the day itself, Cornelius Ryan, *The Longest Day* (Gollancz, 1960). The US forces' need for land for training is examined in War Cabinet Papers WP (43) 429 of 4 October 1943 and the subsequent building programme is described by Kohan (see Chapter 5). Eisenhower describes his wish to move from London in *Crusade* (see Chapter 1) and details of the JEDBURGH teams, and the MOST STUPID story, appear in MacDonald (see Chapter 11). Lieutenant Bostick (see general note) observed the 'rush for the best picnic spots', while the dog Dagwood, the thirsty GIs of Lytton Cheney and the 'protracted chew' at Langton Maltravers are recorded in the manuscript 'War Record' of the Dorset Federation of Women's Institutes. Local topography is described in Reginald J. W. Hammond (editor), *Torbay and South Devon* (Ward Lock, London, 1969) and the disaster to Force 'U' in (Major) L. F. Ellis, *Victory in the West, Volume I, The Battle of Normandy* (*History of the Second World War*, United Kingdom Military Series, HMSO, 1962). The evacuation of the South Hams area is described in the *Stars and Stripes* for 19 August 1944 and the last-minute advice to troops and the reference to Special Service Companies appeared on 1 and 2 June.

CHAPTER 27

On military events I used Ellis (see above), Eisenhower, the *Report* (see above), Ryan, MacDonald, who also described reactions in the United States, and Chester Wilmot, *The Struggle for Europe* (Collins, 1952). Bostick joked about Brussels sprouts at Weymouth; the *Stars and Stripes*, 8 June 1944, described the scene at the Ministry of Information.

CHAPTER 28

The availability of taxis after D-Day was noted by Charles Graves, *Pride of the Morning* (Hutchinson, n.d., *c.* 1945) The *Stars and Stripes* carried

advice on behaviour in France on 8 June 1944, commented on V–1s on
1 September and described reactions to President Roosevelt's death on
13 and 14 April 1945. The Texan warrant for Hitler's arrest appeared on
14 May 1943, reactions to the 'demob points' scheme and transportation
plans on 11 May, 18 May, 12 June, 18 June, 28 June, 5 July and 25 July 1945.
VJ-Day was reported on 16 August 1945 and Attlee's farewell message on
15 October.

CHAPTER 29

The 'reminder to bridegrooms' appeared in the *Stars and Stripes* on 29
December 1942, the Rainbow Corner classes were mentioned on 6 April
1944 and the obliging judge on 8 August 1945. The Bath lecture was
reported in an undated cutting from an unidentified local newspaper lent
to me. The documentation required by GI brides was set out in *A Bride's
Guide to the U.S.A.* (*Good Housekeeping* magazine, London, in conjunction
with the US Office of War Information, n.d., but probably 1945).

CHAPTER 30

The introductory verse and the account of the brides' club at Oxford are
from *State Express* (Oxonian Press, Oxford, 1946). The *Stars and Stripes*
referred to the brides' problems on 1 August 1945 and 10 and 12 October
1945, when it described Commander Agar's ordeal. Former brides contributed all the remaining material.

CHAPTER 31

The dedication of the cemetery at Cambridge was recorded in the *Stars and
Stripes* on 30 and 31 May 1944 and my description of it is based on a personal
visit. Other details were supplied by the US Battle Monuments Commission.
The English poet I quoted was Laurence Binyon, 'For the Fallen', in his
Collected Poems (Macmillan, 1931).

APPENDIX

The British rates of pay are taken from the *Royal Warrant on Pay* of
March 1940 and the American from *Rates of Pay allowed by Law to Officers
of the Army* authorized under an Act of 16 June 1942 and *Monthly Rates of
Active Pay of Enlisted Men*, as amended by Act, 2 December 1942, both
effective from 1 June 1942.

LIST OF CONTRIBUTORS

A. E. Amond, Hingham, Norwich; Mrs N. G. Abbey, Shipdham, Thetford, Norfolk; Mrs E. Adams, Weymouth, Dorset; D. G. F. Acutt, Weymouth, Dorset; R. D. Ackland, London EC2; Mrs Anne Ambrose, Norris Green, Liverpool; Lieutenant-Commander Howard Ashenfelter, Budleigh Salterton, Devon; Mrs Beatrice M. Abrams, Manchester; Mrs E. L. Appleyard, South Oxhey, Watford; Mrs Phyllis Adams, London NW6, Mrs J. M. Ashford, London W6.; Miss Elsie Inglis Alexander, Fulwood, Preston; Mrs M. Aitken, Glasgow; Mrs B. M. Anderson, Trowbridge, Wiltshire; Mrs L. Amies, North Lopham, Diss, Norfolk; Mrs E. Austin, Hamworthy, Poole, Dorset; Mrs M. H. Addison, Edinburgh; Mrs K. Anderson, Ontario, Canada; E. F. Brady, London W11; A. Baynes, Hull; C. Barber, Tidworth, Hampshire; Mrs R. Breverton, London SE11; Inspector J. Briggs, Bangor, Co. Down; D. M. Brown, High Wycombe, Buckinghamshire; Mrs M. Burleigh, Dereham, Norfolk; Mrs A. W. Booth, Leigh-on-Sea, Essex; F. Barker, Hackford, Wymondham, Norfolk; Mrs V. I. Burford, Abbotsworthy, Winchester, Hampshire; Mr and Mrs G. Barrett, Dorchester, Dorset; Mrs E. F. Barrett, Weymouth, Dorset; John Bee, Worcester; Mrs Doreen Bailey, Kempsey, Worcester; Mrs B. M. Ballsdon, Headington, Oxford; Brian Bond, Peterborough; J. L. Brown, Bromborough, Wirral, Cheshire; Sir Herbert Barber, Southport, Lancashire; Miss J. Blankley, Nottingham; Mrs O. D. Bates, Birkdale, Southport, Lancashire; Mrs D. Bates, Dagenham, Essex; R. J. Bennett, Melksham Forest, Wiltshire; Mrs M. Brooker, Ryde, Isle of Wight; Mrs Joyce Broomfield, Layer-de-la-Haye, Colchester, Essex; Mrs R. Burley, Remenham Hill, Henley-on-Thames; Mrs Betty Bans, Hereford; Mrs M. P. Brown, Flitton, Bedfordshire; J. P. Bovingdon, Birchington, Kent; E. E. Babington, Gainsborough, Lincolnshire; A. E. Bowyer, Warblington, Havant, Hampshire; Mrs Beryl Barker, Hereford; Miss Alice Bacchus, Hove, Sussex; Mrs S. M. Brooks, Bleasby, Nottinghamshire; Mrs S. Ball, Parkstone, Poole, Dorset; Mrs S. Butler, Tunbridge Wells, Kent; Mrs M. Bartlett, Caversham, Reading, Berkshire; Mrs M. Blogg, Norwich; Mrs A. C. Bailey, Whippingham, Isle of Wight; Miss L. L. Burton, Moredon, Swindon, Wiltshire; Mrs J. M. Berntzen, Maenporth, Falmouth, Cornwall; Mrs E. Bongerino, Bedford; Mrs R. M. Baber, Plymouth; Mrs J. Blyth, Hornchurch, Essex; Mrs P. M. Barwick,

Rye, Sussex; John Barnet, Leith, Edinburgh; Mrs J. I. Brooks, Orpington, Kent; Mrs I. Barnes, Londonderry; Mrs I. Brewer, Upper Dicker, Hailsham, Sussex; Mrs M. A. Booton, Highfields, Leicester; Miss A. Brindley, North Lopham, Diss, Norfolk; Miss L. Brindley, Bungay, Suffolk; Miss N. Bull, Westbury, Wiltshire; Mrs Edith Barham, London N14; Mrs E. Baughen, Thrapston, Kettering, Northamptonshire; H. Banham, Nairn, Scotland; E. H. Beesley, Mansfield, Nottinghamshire; Miss Carole Baker, Plymouth; Miss R. W. Carr, Felixstowe, Suffolk; Miss D. E. Cushion, Fundenhall, Norwich; Mrs M. Cain, Woodbridge, Suffolk; E. Caesley, Winchester; Mrs A. K. Chapman, Thetford, Norfolk; Mrs E. M. Catt, Winchester, Hampshire; Neill Crone, Dewsbury, Yorkshire; Mrs K. Crawford, Edinburgh; Mrs T. Caldwell, Edinburgh; Mrs V. E. Castledine, Sleaford, Lincolnshire; Miss R. D. Carver, Whitby, Yorkshire; Mrs M. Callaghan, Peterborough; J. T. Colpitts, Beeston, Nottinghamshire; Ian Cross, Liverpool; J. Carroll, Liverpool; Mrs J. Cassidy, Darlington, Co. Durham; Mrs J. M. Carley, Falkenham, Ipswich, Suffolk; Miss Betty Crewes, Bitterne, Southampton, Hampshire; Mrs V. R. Cooke, Tankerton, Whitstable, Kent; Mrs Muriel E. Cope, Histon, Cambridge; Mrs S. Carmichael, Hove, Sussex; Mrs Betty Cook, Skipsea, Yorkshire; Mrs Joy Cullinan, London NW1; Mrs C. M. Coast, Helenburgh, Dunbartonshire; Mrs E. B. Cozens, Northam, Bideford, Devon; Miss D. M. Coles, Ryde, Isle of Wight; Mrs V. Casley, Lympstone, Exmouth, Devon; Mrs Eve Charlton, Whitchurch, Cardiff; Sir Leonard Costello, Uffculme, Cullompton, Devon; W. F. Corfield, Potters Bar, Hertfordshire; Mrs P. D. Carter, Stratford-upon-Avon, Warwickshire; Miss S. Campagnolo, Clifton, York; Mrs F. E. Clark, London SW16; Mrs E. Cockerton, Sidcup, Kent; Mrs Gladys Charlton, London SW16; Mrs A. Creed, Hastings, Sussex; Mrs M. E. Clithero, Hull; Mrs E. M. Cross, Hornchurch, Essex; Mrs B. M. Cotes, Dorridge, Solihull, Warwickshire; Miss P. K. Crimmin, Englefield Green, Surrey; Mrs N. F. Carnon, Worthing, Sussex; Miss B. Cooksley, Dunkeswell Abbey, Honiton, Devon; Mrs M. E. Copperwaite, London SE24; Mrs I. Cooper, Limbe, Malawi; Mrs S. Crothall, Andover, Hampshire; Miss Lesley Clay, Nairobi. Kenya; Mrs M. W. Caesar, Canterbury, Kent; P. M. Cave, Devizes, Wiltshire; Mrs G. Critoph, Wymondham, Norfolk; Mrs D. E. Cox, East Wittering, Chichester, Sussex; Mr and Mrs K. Dormer, Thorpe, Norwich; The Rev. A. W. Delaney, St Ives, Cornwall; B. G. Dye, Ipswich, Suffolk; Sidney S. T. Davis, Weymouth, Dorset; Miss Sylvia Davies, Clehonger, Hereford; Mrs M. Dunn, Todmorden, Lancashire; S. P. Derek, Tilehurst, Reading, Berkshire; Mrs G. Dickinson, Little Sutton, Wirral, Cheshire; Mrs E. Deaville, Stoke on Trent; Mrs K. G. Devereux, Kings Heath, Birmingham; Mrs R. Darby, New Barnet, Hertfordshire; Mrs D. Duro, Nottingham; Miss Marion Dobson, Brinscall, Chorley, Lancashire; Mrs J. Daniels-Little, Woodford Bridge, Essex; Mrs P. Dixon, London W13;

Miss Suzanne Dumesnil, Basing, Basingstoke, Hampshire; Mr and Mrs H. Douglas, Whittlesford, Cambridge; Mrs K. G. Dooltray, Lichfield, Staffordshire; Mrs J. Douglas, Four Oaks, Sutton Coldfield, Warwickshire; Mrs D. Dunkley, Prestwich, Ayrshire; G. S. Davis, Carmarthen; Mrs G. L. Daniel, Lyme Regis, Dorset; J. W. Dossett-Davies, Witney, Oxfordshire; Ed Donnelly, London W1; Mrs W. Elsden, Holt, Norfolk; Mrs M. Emerson, Finaghy, Belfast; B. H. Ellis, Upper Sheringham, Norfolk; Mrs C. A. Eastwood, Hurstbourne Tarrant, Andover, Hampshire; Mrs M. Edwardes, Leigh-on-Sea, Essex; Mrs F. Evans, Chichester, Sussex; Mrs D. Elliott, Salisbury, Wiltshire; The Rev. Nigel Eva, London SE9; Major E. J. Edwards, Buxted, Sussex; Miss Sally Elliott, Leeds; Mrs M. Edwards, Haywards Heath, Sussex; Mrs D. Finlow, Old Coulsdon, Surrey; Mrs J. Francis-Pope, Weston, Bath, Somerset; Mrs J. M. Fillingham, Lincoln; Miss M. P. Frost, Hunstanton, Norfolk; Mrs Emma Fisher, Treorchy, Rhondda, S. Wales; E. France, Didsbury, Manchester; Mrs M. G. Forster, St Albans, Hertfordshire; Mrs M. Farmer, Northampton; Mrs Joyce Farquharson, Cheam, Surrey; Mrs I. C. Foster, Dinas Powis, Glamorgan; Mrs T. G. Freke, Slimbridge, Gloucester; Mrs E. Fernbank, Gosport, Hampshire; Mrs R. Finch, Banstead, Surrey; Mrs M. Free, Abingdon, Berkshire; Mrs J. Fidler, Higher Poynton, Stockport, Cheshire; Mrs G. Frost, Poynton, Stockport, Cheshire; Mrs S. Forbes, Sutton Coldfield, Warwickshire; Mrs E. Fuller, Felpham, Sussex; Mrs M. Fairbrother, Long Eaton, Nottinghamshire; Mrs M. Frost, Colchester, Essex; Mrs I. Fox, Bear Cross, Bournemouth, Hampshire; W. S. George, Aldeburgh, Suffolk; Mrs B. Gilbert, St Cross, Winchester; James W. Goss, Portsmouth; Mrs H. R. Green, Andover, Hampshire; J. Gardner, London NW6; Fred Gray, Cregagh, Belfast; Mrs M. E. Gray, Rednal, Birmingham; Miss D. Galley, Norwich; Mrs Nellie Griffiths, Bushbury, Wolverhampton, Staffordshire; Mrs J. Gillman, Bexley, Kent; Mrs Norma Golden, London N2; Mrs M. P. Goodhew, Slough, Buckinghamshire; Mrs L. Gillett, Brightwell, Wallingford, Berkshire; Mrs N. A. Gudgeon, Boscombe, Bournemouth; Mrs Monica Godfrey, Stanmore, Middlesex; Mrs S. Gaskell, Thornton Hough, Wirral, Cheshire; Mrs M. L. Grose, Leicester; Mrs M. Gardner, Glasgow; Mrs W. M. Godfrey, Littlehampton, Sussex; Mrs E. Curd, Southampton; Mrs H. George, Henley-on-Thames, Oxfordshire; Thomas Glenny, Craigavon, Co. Armagh; Mrs G. Gaudry, Eastbourne; Mrs K. Hurrell, King's Lynn, Norfolk; J. A. Hill, Dagenham, Essex; Mrs W. Heath, Harrogate, Yorkshire; Miss K. Hearns, Appleton, Warrington, Lancashire; F. T. Hartlett, Wollaton, Nottingham; Mrs Marion Hale, Heaton Moor, Stockport; S. Hughes, Northampton; R. Hartley, Watford, Hertfordshire; Mrs Olive Hudson, Grimsby, Lincolnshire; Mrs R. Hilton, Rayleigh, Essex; Mrs Mary Howell, South Harrow, Middlesex; Mrs F. Heginbotham, Cheadle, Cheshire; Miss J. Hall, Worthing, Sussex; Mrs

Betty Hawkes, Combe Down, Bath; Mrs H. R. Hall, Seend, Melksham, Wiltshire; Mrs F. J. Hixson, Ponterdulais, Swansea, Glamorgan; Mrs C. Hoare, Exeter; Miss Vicky Henton, Langwith, Mansfield, Nottinghamshire; Mrs P. V. Howard, Leeds; A. J. Heraty, Clayton, Newcastle, Staffordshire; R. R. Hudson, London NW1; Mrs J. C. Hey, Solihull, Warwickshire; B. P. Hanley, Hollym, Yorkshire; V. Hudson, Eastbourne, Sussex; Mrs Florence Hine, Tiverton, Bath; Mrs Nora Hall, London, SE5; Mrs Y. G. Hunter, Galashiels, Selkirkshire; Mrs A. L. Halsey, Berkhamsted, Hertfordshire; Mrs P. D. Harrop, Dunham Massey, Altrincham, Cheshire; Mrs Irene Hinkley, Gravesend, Kent; Miss E. Harrington, Renfrew, Scotland; A. L. Howard, Nottingham; Mrs F. A. Hunwicks, London SE2; Mrs F. V. Hackett, Great Barr, Birmingham; Mrs H. W. Hill, Chichester, Sussex; Mrs E. C. Houghton, Pontesbury, Shrewsbury; Mrs M. R. Hemmings, Christchurch, Hampshire; Miss Hartley, Cheltenham, Gloucestershire; M. J. Harlow, Roath, Cardiff; Miss T. D. Hall, Alwoodley, Leeds; Mr and Mrs E. C. Hadley, Pleck, Walsall, Staffordshire; Mrs V. F. Hunt, Enfield, Middlesex; Mrs S. J. Hedges, Malvern, Worcestershire; S. Hudson, March, Cambridgeshire; Mrs Jean Helsdon, Lakenham, Norwich; Mrs M. H. Hugo, Stoke, Plymouth; D. G. E. Hurd, Wokingham, Berkshire; Miss Joan Ierston, Birmingham; Mrs Enid Ingram, London SW15; Mrs I. D. Jacobs, Portsea, Portsmouth; Miss M. E. Jelley, Chute, Andover, Hampshire; R. Jones, Winchester, Hampshire; Mrs F. Jones, Clayton, Newcastle, Staffordshire; R. W. Jackson, Watford, Hertfordshire; Derrick A. Jones, Cheadle, Cheshire, Mrs L. W. Johnson, Kettering; Northampton; Mrs V. W. E. Jones, Goldthorpe, Rotherham, Yorkshire; Mrs Rosemary Jones, Wrexham, Denbighshire; Thomas Jackson, Ettrick, Selkirk, Scotland; Mrs Pam Jarvis, Wellingborough, Northamptonshire; Miss Christine Jennings, Penarth, Glamorganshire; Mrs M. J. James, Kenley, Surrey; Mrs Ivy Jones, Ramsgate, Kent; Mrs Betty Jenkins, Warminster, Wiltshire; Mrs S. Keay, Cotes Heath, Stafford; Mrs A. M. Kelly, Liverpool; Mrs M. H. Keene, Leamington Spa, Warwickshire; Mrs E. Keeping, Poole, Bournemouth; Mrs D. Kilby, London NW7; Mrs V. E. King, South Ockendon, Essex; Miss J. E. Kayler, Bristol; Miss Finola Keogh, London SW1; Mrs Rosemary Kearton, Lyme Regis, Dorset; Mrs A. Last, Woodbridge, Suffolk; O. F. Laffineur, West Chinnock, Crewkerne, Somerset; Mrs D. Lea, Hull, Yorkshire; Mrs B. Lewis, Sheringham, Norfolk; Harold Lord, Stockton-on-Tees; Mrs V. Lasbrey, Belfast; Mrs W. Y. Lawson, Enniskillen, Co. Fermanagh; Mrs M. F. Lucas, Dorchester, Dorset; L. W. R. Lee, London NW11; Dame Mary Lioba, Worcester; R. Lowde, Manchester; T. Lester, Betley, Crewe, Cheshire; Miss D. E. Lusty, Chiseldon, Swindon, Wiltshire; Mrs Joan Lewis, Addlestone, Surrey; F. Leigh, Horton, Leek, Staffordshire; Mrs Doreen Lloyd, Sefton, Liverpool; Mrs M. Lande, London NW2; P. A. Lapworth, Walsall, Staffordshire; Mrs P. Lardlaw, Inverness; Mrs

V. Lacey, West Coker, Yeovil, Somerset; Miss A. E. F. Fraser Lloyd, Bournemouth, Mrs M. J. Longstall, Cyncoed, Cardiff; Mrs I. L. Langmead, Plymouth; Mrs V. Luckham, Chandler's Ford, Hampshire; Mrs E. J. Lea, Luton, Bedfordshire; Mrs M. Law, Cobham, Surrey; Mrs E. M. Leggat, Edinburgh; Mrs J. Ludlow, Basingstoke, Hampshire; Mrs P. Larrad, Long Eaton, Nottingham; Mrs A. M. Legg, Bawthorne Hill, Bracknell, Berkshire; Mrs L. R. Lane, Horsham, Sussex; J. Lush, Cross In Hand, Heathfield, Sussex; Miss M. J. Leslie and Mrs G. Leslie, Cheltenham, Gloucestershire; Miss Mary Larkin, Liverpool; Mrs J. MacFarlane, Ipswich, Suffolk; Capt. D. J. Marshall, Blandford Camp, Dorset; G. J. Mills, Diss, Norfolk (deceased); S. J. Meggitt, North Ferriby, Yorkshire; Mrs G. Mason, Ipswich, Suffolk; W. Malcomson, Belfast; Mrs N. McLaughlen, Auchenback, Barrhead, Glasgow; William McKnight, Marlow, Buckinghamshire; Mrs Joyce Mann, Prestwich, Manchester; Mrs Elsie Millin, Charlbury, Oxfordshire; Mrs E. Morris, Salford; W. P. Murphy, Salford; Mrs B. McDonald, London E17; Mrs Doreen Mayers, Upminster, Essex; Mrs M. Mould, Knowle, Solihull, Warwickshire; Mrs E. M. Macleod, Dibden Purlieu, Southampton; Mrs W. Morton, Warton, Preston, Lancashire; Miss Muriel Moss, Knutsford, Cheshire; Mrs Louise Mackie, Broadstairs, Kent; Mrs J. Makin, Anne Port, Gorey, Jersey, Channel Islands; Miss S. McGough, Blaydon, Co. Durham; A. Minall, Leatherhead, Surrey; Mrs Olive L. Meen, Bunwell, Norwich; Mrs G. E. Moore, Headington, Oxford; Mrs M. Maxwell, Knowle, Bristol; Mrs B. J. Mitchell, Yeovil, Somerset; Mrs Nancy Mitchell, Newport, Monmouthshire; Mrs B. Morgan, Bulwark, Chepstow, Monmouth; Mrs M. R. Mason, Hall Green, Birmingham; Mr and Mrs W. F. Mayoss, Loughborough, Leicestershire; Mrs P. J. Martin, Hounslow, Middlesex; Mrs M. I. Swann Mortin, Woodley, Cheshire; David Manderson, Sarisbury Green, Hampshire; Mrs J. McConnell, Marlow, Buckinghamshire; Miss Doreene Moorcroft, Lymm, Warrington, Cheshire; A. MacRae, Lochearnhead, Perthshire; Mrs B. Morrish, Brighton; L. McCorry, Lurgan, Co. Armagh; Mrs L. Maguire, Biggleswade, Bedfordshire; Grace Murphy, Newcastle, Co. Down; Mrs S. J. Marcus, London W5; Miss Isobel Maclean, Edinburgh; Mrs Macrow, Redbourn, Hertfordshire; Miss Daphne Miles, London E11; Mrs E. Murray, Bury, Lancashire; R. F. McIlvenny, Belfast; Mrs Judy Miles, Teddington, Middlesex; Mrs M. E. Newcombe, Meysey Hampton, Gloucestershire; Mrs B. R. Neilson, Haworth, York; Miss Jean Newell, London SE6; Mrs M. I. Nott, London SW3; Miss D. M. Newell, London SW1; V. H. Neat, Westbury, Wiltshire; Mrs E. Nuttall, Fovant, Salisbury, Wiltshire; Alec Newman, London N2; Mrs V. O'Connell, Potters Bar, Hertfordshire; Mrs M. Oliver, Liverpool; Mrs Olive Ornstein, Stretford, Manchester; Mrs Sheila Peal, Cringleford, Norwich; Mrs Phyllis Peters, Croydon, Surrey; Mrs B. Pardington, Bear Flat, Bath, Somerset; Mrs Vera Pennefather, Knotty Green, Beaconsfield, Buckinghamshire;

Mrs Helen Porter, Londonderry; A. C. R. Pope, Dorchester, Dorset; Mrs N. Plowman, Minster Lovell, Oxfordshire; Mrs Anne Peters, Prestwich, Lancashire; Mrs Peggy Parish, Watford Heath, Hertfordshire; Mrs Jean Pocock, Burpham, Guildford, Surrey; Mrs Jane Pethybridge, Hurdsfield, Macclesfield, Cheshire; George Pulley, Southmoor, Abingdon, Berkshire; Mrs Margery Price, Westerhope, Newcastle on Tyne; Mrs Doreen Palmer, London E17; Mrs B. Peacock, Liverpool; Mrs Nancy Peart, Stocksfield, Northumberland; Miss J. H. Pinnington, Beckenham, Kent; Mrs J. M. Pickering, Bishopthorpe, Yorkshire; Mrs K. M. Parsons, Woodley, Berkshire; Mrs Frances Parker, Warrington, Peterborough; Mrs Audrey Potts, St Helens, Lancashire; Miss I. Page, Kingston-on-Thames, Surrey; Miss V. B. Pridmore, Pulborough, Sussex; Miss Anne Peare, Upminster, Essex; Mrs J. P. Powell, Brighton, Sussex; Mrs Winifred Penwarden, Brighton, Sussex; Mrs M. D. Pegler, Elstree, Hertfordshire; Mrs J. H. Price, Mytholmroyd, Halifax, Yorkshire; Mrs Mercy Pepper, Perivale, Greenford, Middlesex; Mrs Margaret Phayre, Little Sutton, Wirral, Cheshire; Ivan E. Phillips, Summerland, British Columbia, Canada; Mrs B. M. Porter, Walton-on-Thames, Surrey; Robin Page, Belfast; Miss R. M. Phillips, Goldsithney, Penzance, Cornwall; R. W. Quinton, Hitchin, Hertfordshire; Mrs Joan Roberts, Gillingham, Kent; Mrs J. Reid, Dalkeith, Midlothian; Miss Joan Rendell, Launceston, Cornwall; M. Robertson, Cardonald, Glasgow; T. R. Rogers, Ipswich, Suffolk; Mrs Margot Towell, Newquay, Cornwall; Mrs W. Rowlandson, Manchester; Mrs J. Rodwell, Hollins, Bury, Lancashire; Mrs Reynolds, Spratton, Northampton; R. B. Rowell, Hemelstead, Hertfordshire; Mrs L. M. Russ, Dagenham, Essex; Mrs P. Reynolds, Carpenders Park, Watford, Hertfordshire; Mrs I. B. Rowe, Riseley, Reading, Berkshire; F. Routley, Heytesbury, Warminster, Wiltshire; Mrs M. Innes-Robinson, Boscombe, Bournemouth, Hampshire; Thomas Riordan, Reading, Berkshire; Miss Ethel Rogers, Margate, Kent; Mrs J. Rogers, Worcester; Mrs Margaret Riedinger, Sturry, Canterbury, Kent; Mrs M. Rogers, London SW16; Mrs M. Richmond, Dartmouth, Devon; Miss F. B. Rickter, Sutton, Surrey; Mrs D. K. Rennison, Sidcup, Kent; Mrs Jean Ross, Hailsham, Sussex; Mrs G. M. Stocker, Felixstowe, Suffolk; Mrs Anne Solomons, London NW6; Miss Kathleen Sellers, Hull, Yorkshire; Mrs P. G. Smith, Cheam, Surrey; Mrs Rosalind Smissen, Winchester, Hampshire; Mrs E. S. Saunders, Westcliff-on-Sea, Essex; Mrs Ann Scammell, Bristol; Miss Pamela Standley, Wymondham, Norfolk; T. M. Slight, Edinburgh; G. R. Swindells, Duckinfield, Cheshire; Mrs E. C. Somerville, Didsbury, Manchester; Mrs B. Steven, Chiddingfold, Surrey; R. F. Salmon, Birkenhead, Cheshire; V. R. Sismey, Weldon, Corby, Northamptonshire; Mrs V. B. Smith, Frodsham, Cheshire; Mrs I. A. Shepherd, Hampton Hill, Middlesex; Mrs Ann Stockhamer, London SW1; Mrs D. M. Seaton, Leesthorpe, Melton Mowbray, Leicestershire; Mrs F. G. Spencer, London SE10;

Arthur Strange, Tuffley, Gloucester; J. L. Stevenson, Hillsborough, Co. Down; Mrs Betty Spridgeon, Thorney, Peterborough; Miss E. Smith, Preston; Miss Phyllis Stanbra, Farrington Gurney, Bristol; Miss Muriel Searle, St Budeaux, Plymouth; Mrs M. Shay, Luton, Bedfordshire; Mrs R. Shaw, London E8; Mrs A. Saville, London SE6; Mrs E. A. Sutton, Harwich, Essex; Mrs Mary Smart, Whinmoor, Leeds; Mrs Ann Salter, Brading, Isle of Wight; Mrs Sheila Sipthorp, Stretton on Fosse, Moreton-in-Marsh, Gloucestershire; Miss M. Salter, Bramshaw, Hampshire; Mrs Ruth Speyer, London N12; Miss V. Smith, Glasgow; Mrs Rhoda Shilleto, Stamford Bridge, Yorkshire; Mrs F. J. Smith, Taunton, Somerset; Mrs Ethel Smith, Macclesfield, Cheshire; L. P. Thompson, Aldham, Ipswich, Suffolk; Miss A. M. Thompson, Hull; H. E. Twitchen, Kingskerswell, Newton Abbot, Devon; J. A. Taylor, Gomersal, Cleckheaton, Yorkshire; Miss P. E. and Mr J. C. Tait, Bridlington, Yorkshire; Mrs J. Trehane, Truro, Cornwall; C. H. Thompson, Sittingbourne, Kent; P. C. Thomas, Usk, Monmouthshire; Mrs R. Thorp, Woodthorpe, Nottingham; Mrs C. G. Tomrley, Guildford, Surrey, Mrs A. J. Turner, Wollaton Park, Nottingham; Mrs K. Thomas, Gravesend, Kent; Mrs Eileen Turner, Aston, Birmingham; Mrs E. M. Taylor, Wotton-under-Edge, Gloucestershire; Mrs F. Tyler, Sarratt, Rickmansworth, Hertfordshire; Mrs J. Thomas, Fawley, Southampton; Miss C. M. Thompson, Harlow, Essex; Mrs Irene Talbot, Devizes, Wiltshire; Mrs N. F. Thorne, Lynton, Devon; Mrs I. G. Trotter, Carlisle; Mrs P. V. Thompson, Hasketon, Woodbridge, Suffolk; Mrs B. A. Tyler, Thurso, Caithness; Mrs E. M. Tevendale, Holtspur, Beaconsfield, Buckinghamshire; Mrs A. M. Tigwell, Albrighton, Wolverhampton, Staffordshire; Mrs I. A. Ulyat, Nottingham; B. Upshall, Bath, Somerset; Mrs M. Underwood, Newick, Lewes, Sussex; Mrs Joan Underwood, Harrow, Middlesex; Mrs Valerie Uren, Penzance, Cornwall; Mrs Pamela Usher, Enfield, Middlesex; Mrs M. White, Ipswich, Suffolk; F. P. Williams, Fakenham, Norfolk; Mrs M. A. White, Wherwell, Andover, Hampshire; Mrs J. B. Walker, Edinburgh; Miss J. M. Williamson, Beverley, Yorkshire; D. M. Wood, Edinburgh; Miss J. Y. Walsh, Winchester, Hampshire; H. Wilkins, Dorchester, Dorset; S. J. Wood, New Bradwell, Wolverton, Buckinghamshire; John Warburton, Heald Green, Cheadle, Cheshire; Mrs M. P. Wheeler, Fallowfield, Manchester; Mrs E. White, Liverpool; J. A. Whittemore, Liverpool; James Wilson, St Helens, Lancashire; Mrs L. A. West, Goring-by-Sea, Sussex; Mrs Deana Whine, London E11; Mrs E. Wright, Yeovil, Somerset; Mrs E. Wickert, London E11; Miss Elizabeth Wood, Southampton; Mrs E. P. Wright, Northwood, Middlesex; Mrs J. Wheway, Nuneaton, Warwickshire; Miss I. Whittier, London WC2; G. Wilton, Newquay, Cornwall; Mrs K. M. Webber, Bangor, Co. Down; Mrs E. E. Winter, Greenham Common South, Newbury, Berkshire; Mrs D. Wells, London SW2; G. R. Watson, Tettenhall, Wolverhampton; Mrs H. White, Lower

Dicker, Hailsham, Sussex; Mrs Sheila Walton, Sizergh, Kendal, Westmorland; Mrs B. P. Williams, Leominster, Herefordshire; C. G. T. Withers, Grateley, Andover, Hampshire; Mrs Jean Wacey, Vancouver Island, British Columbia, Canada; Mrs E. Wheeler, Penn, Buckinghamshire; Mrs G. R. Ward, Hoxne, Diss, Norfolk; Martin Woolley, Isleworth, Middlesex; Mrs S. E. Yeates, Windsor, Berkshire.

M. H. Affleck, Groton, Massachusetts; Rollie Angier, Minneapolis, Minnesota; Jackson M. Abbott, Alexandria, Virginia; Colonel Lee B. Brownfield, Kettering, Ohio; Dr E. L. Bayton Jr, Portsmouth, Virginia; Stanley Biernacki, Providence, Rhode Island; Howard E. Brihn, Denver, Colorado; Cornelius W. Barton, Staten Island, New York City; Irving A. Bradbury, Fairfield, Connecticut; W. M. Breckinridge, Sarasota, Florida; Lawrence Bernardy, Wabasso, Minnesota; Calvin W. Bailey, South Orange, New Jersey; Phil Blau, New York City; James E. Bevill, Tulsa, Oklahoma; J. J. Barry, Long Island, New York City; General L. P. Collins, Powhattan, Virginia; Mrs Marlyn S. Carlson, York, Nebraska; Mrs Helen R. Contessa, Arvada, Colorado; Robert L. Chandler, Longmont, Colorado; James C. Cunningham, Pittsburg, Pennsylvania; Dr Robert L. Coombs, Newport News, Virginia; Mr and Mrs Robert H. Cadorette, Brockton, Massachusetts; John Chopelas, Killeen, Texas; Captain J. Ferrell Colton, Sonora, Mexico; Mrs Dudley Chambers, Troy, Ohio; C. Owen Davis, Grand Haven, Michigan; W. M. Dalechite, Jackson, Mississippi; Manfred G. Davidson, Minneapolis, Minnesota; John Diekman, Clear Lake, South Dakota; Marion Enderle, Aurora, Nebraska; Joe Eastman, Troy, New Hampshire; Mrs Lucy D. Elliott, Vacaville, California; William Engel, Pittsburg, Pennsylvania; Kenneth W. Engelbrecht, Granville, Illinois; Mr and Mrs E. Forbes, Alton, Illinois; I. A. Ficarotta, Omaha, Nebraska; Neil Farneti, Oglesby, Illinois; Mr and Mrs Joseph T. Falcone, Morwood, Massachusetts; Alfred H. Fenton, Brunswick, Maine; Prof. Leroy H. Fischer, Stillwater, Oklahoma; Joseph J. Garje; Dominic M. Guisto, Brooksville, Florida; Allen L. Gregory, Youngtown, Arizona; Dominico M. George, Brooklyn, New York City; Dr Albert S. Goldstein, Brookline, Massachusetts; Stephen W. Gibson; David M. Grodsky, Newton, Massachusetts; Colonel Jean M. Gray, Newport News, Virginia; Joseph G. Gratton, Silver Spring, Maryland; George H. Hill, Grand Rapids, Michigan; Stuart E. Halwig, Portsmouth, Rhode Island; W. A. Harrison, Utica, Mississippi; John Hines Jr, Hopkins, Minnesota; Kenneth J. Haraldsen, Englewood, Colorado; Mrs Harry B. Hawkins, Englewood, Colorado; George Heris, Greenwich, Connecticut; Edwin E. Hebb, Dearborn, Michigan; Robert F. Hunter, Tulsa, Oklahoma; Robert E. Hunter, Tulsa, Oklahoma; Clifford C. Hart; Clark Houghton, Iowa City, Iowa; Donald R. Judge, Saverna Park, Maryland; Robert L. Kashiwagi, Sacramento, California; Joseph W.

Kelley, Rockland, Massachusetts; Colonel Reid W. Kennedy, Fort Bragg, North Carolina; Francis W. Kendall, Sterling, Massachusetts; Robert M. Kennedy, Troy, New York; B. James Koehler Jr, Parma, Idaho; L. H. A. Klein, Tucson, Arizona; Mike Levva, Wilmington, California; Mr and Mrs Chester Liedtke, Wessington, South Dakota; F. Levandoski, Dunkirk, New York; Richard T. Lebherz, Braddock Hts, Maryland; Earl La Clair, Tampa, Florida; A. J. Lindblad Jr, Norfolk, Virginia; Walter J. Laughlin, Westport, Connecticut; Mrs D. J. McCormick, Seattle, Washington; Mrs Kathleen McEvoy, Omaha, Nebraska; Mr Donald McNew, Grosse Pointe, Michigan; Mrs Charlotte R. Murphy, Tulsa, Oklahoma; Cornelius C. Morelli, Springfield, Virginia; Maureen J. Martin, Lake Park, Florida; Sarsfield E. Mcnulty, Columbia, South Carolina; Raymond P. Miller, Arivace, Arizona; Dorothy M. Mitchum, Jackson Heights, New York; Mrs F. Nilsen, Brooklyn, New York City; George F. Oberlies, Norfolk, Virginia; Wm. Otwell, Traverse City, Michigan; Mrs Edith Pyser, Brooklyn, New York City; Mrs Agnes Roper, Allentown, Pennsylvania; Charles E. Rippe, Everett, Washington; Cooper B. Rhodes, Hudson Falls, New York; Wm. E. Rowe, Columbus, Georgia; Raymond E. Robertson, Hurricane, West Virginia; Robert P. Rogers, Wickatunk, New Jersey; John F. Robuck, Moncks, South Carolina; James W. Richardson Jr, West Baths, Maine; Mrs Kathleen Stoots, Richlands, Virginia; Mrs Margery Schutz, Carteret, New Jersey; Paul S. Seybolt Jr, Manchester, Connecticut; Arthur J. Sullivan, Glen, New Hampshire; Mrs Inez Carmon Schaffer; Mr and Mrs Mario Saccomari, Torrington, Connecticut; Alton G. Shahan, Morgantown, West Virginia; Thomas P. Spada, Stratford, Connecticut; Mrs Franklin B. Shepard, Denver, Colorado; Leo B. Smith, Starkville, Mississippi; Courtney Smith, Yreka, California; Edward W. Sakacs, Schenectady, New York; E. F. Snyder, Greenwich, New York; Alice O. Swenson, Columbus, Ohio; L. J. Schalow, California; Jack Sylvester, South Pasadena, California; Frank Toth, Louisville, Kentucky; Hugh E. Thompson, Manhattan, Kansas; William P. Valerie, Detroit, Michigan; Mrs A. R. Wilson, New Brunswick, New Jersey; Paul Wright, Sedelia, Missouri; F. J. Wittlinger, Blair, Nebraska; Mrs Henry R. Wilson, Lubbock, Texas; Dr M. Waller, Potomac, Maryland.

GENERAL INDEX

Compiled by Gordon Robinson

Note: All place names, except where they relate to events such as the Ardennes crisis, are listed in a separate index.

INDEX OF PLACE NAMES

Compiled by Gordon Robinson